California For Dummies, 2nd Edition

Cheat Sheet

San Diego Trolley System

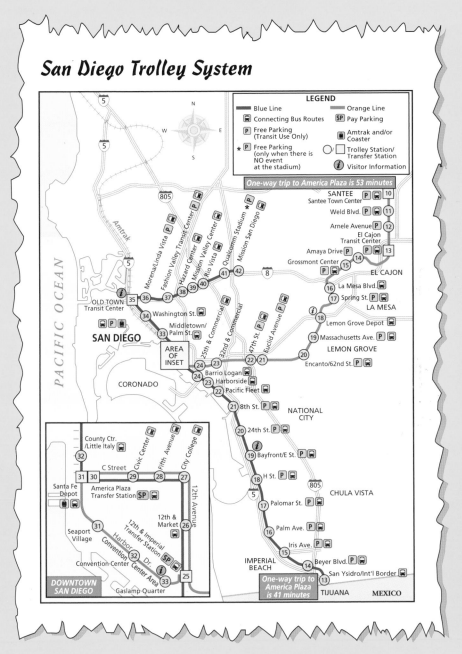

Copyright © 2002 Wiley Publishing, Inc.
All rights reserved.

Item 5449-2.

For more information about Wiley Publishing,
call 1-800-762-2974.

W9-CTR-742

For Dummies: Bestselling Book Series for Beginners

California For Dummies, 2nd Edition

Cheat Sheet

San Francisco Mass Transit

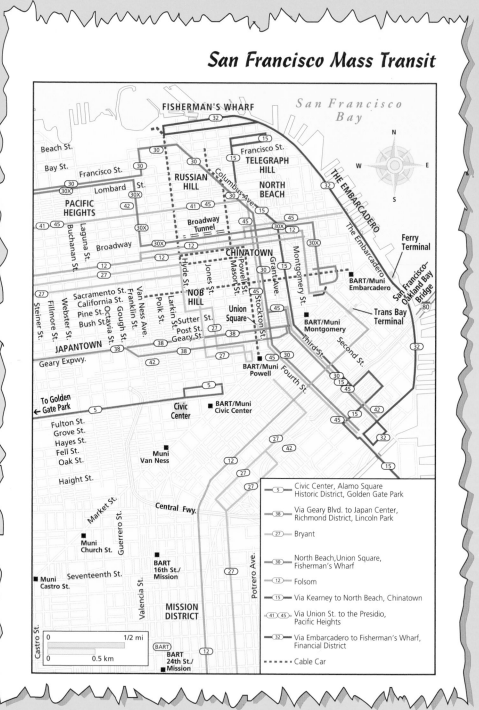

Route	Description
5	Civic Center, Alamo Square Historic District, Golden Gate Park
38	Via Geary Blvd. to Japan Center, Richmond District, Lincoln Park
27	Bryant
30	North Beach, Union Square, Fisherman's Wharf
12	Folsom
15	Via Kearney to North Beach, Chinatown
41 45	Via Union St. to the Presidio, Pacific Heights
32	Via Embarcadero to Fisherman's Wharf, Financial District
- - - -	Cable Car

California

FOR

DUMMIES®

2ND EDITION

by Mary Herczog and Paula Tevis

Wiley Publishing, Inc.

California For Dummies, 2nd Edition

Published by
Wiley Publishing, Inc.
909 Third Avenue
New York, NY 10022
www.wiley.com

For general information on our other products and services or to obtain technical support, please contact our Customer Care Department within the U.S. at 800-762-2974, outside the U.S. at 317-572-3993, or fax 317-572-4002.

Wiley also publishes its books in a variety of electronic formats. Some content that appears in print may not be available in electronic books.

Library of Congress Cataloging-in-Publication Data:
Library of Congress Control Number: 2002110303
ISBN: 0-7645-5449-2
ISSN: 1528-2139

Manufactured in the United States of America
10 9 8 7 6 5 4 3 2

Wiley Publishing, Inc. is a trademark of Wiley Publishing, Inc.

About the Authors

Mary Herczog is a second-generation California native and is married to Paula Tevis's prom date. She writes for Frommer's and Wiley whenever she can, which is quite a bit (*Frommer's New Orleans, Frommer's Las Vegas, Las Vegas For Dummies, Los Angeles For Dummies,* and more!), and she is so happy she can do it in the California sunshine. The rest of the time, Mary works for the film industry, which is a very California thing to do.

Paula Tevis, also a second-generation Californian, was born and raised in Santa Barbara, attended college in Los Angeles, and then moved to her favorite city, where she could cheer for the San Francisco Giants in peace. After an eclectic but blessedly brief career that included stints in the computer and nonprofit sectors, she and her California-bred husband produced a couple of lovely children, and Paula happily relinquished the 9-to-5 world for the 24/7 one that parenting brings. Upon regaining consciousness, she metamorphosed into a freelance writer, and over the years has contributed articles and essays to *Parenting* and *Family Fun* magazines, the *San Francisco Chronicle,* Cityseach.com, *Frommer's Las Vegas* and *Frommer's New Orleans.* She is the author of *San Francisco For Dummies,* the *Berlitz Vancouver Pocketguide,* and the upcoming *Frommer's San Francisco with Kids.* Paula is currently living the expat life with her husband and their daughters in London, but reads the *Chronicle* online daily.

Authors' Acknowledgments

Great thanks to Alexis Lipsitz Flippin and Frommer's for it all. Thanks to Paula Tevis for letting me rope her into this project. Blessings are heaped upon Caroline Kallas, Lisa Derrick, and Sims Brannon for their wisdom, wit, and research. Steve Hochman makes living in California even more fun, if such a thing were possible.

— *Mary Herczog*

Many thanks to my co-author, Mary Herczog, our editor, Alexis Lipsitz Flippin, and the folks who assisted me in one way or another as I researched this update: Vicki Pate, Bev Chin, Patience Tevis, Nick Cann and Peggy Blair, Andrea and Jeff Tobias, Brenda Hughes and Teatro Zinzanni, Karen Hales and Yosemite National Park, Marty and Barb Cohen, Ruth Powning, Irene Levin Dietz, Ina Levin Gyemant, and Cynde Ahart Woods. As always, love and thanks to Mark, Madeleine, and Lili.

— *Paula Tevis*

Mary and Paula especially wish to thank Cheryl Farr Leas, the author of *California For Dummies,* 1st Edition, whose excellent and thorough work made our update infinitely easier to accomplish.

Publisher's Acknowledgments

We're proud of this book; please send us your comments through our Dummies online registration form located at www.dummies.com/register/.

Some of the people who helped bring this book to market include the following:

Editorial

Editors: Tere Drenth,
Alexis Lipsitz Flippin
(Previous Edition: Kathleen M. Cox)

Cartographer: Roberta Stockwell

Editorial Supervisor: Michelle Hacker

Editorial Assistant: Carol Strickland

Senior Photo Editor: Richard Fox

Assistant Photo Editor: Michael Ross

Front Cover Photo: Bob Barbour/
Getty Images

Back Cover Photo: Wolfgang Kaehler
Photography

Cartoons: Rich Tennant,
www.the5thwave.com

Production

Project Coordinator: Ryan Steffen

Layout and Graphics: Melanie DesJardins,
Carrie Foster, Jackie Nicholas,
Julie Trippetti

Proofreaders: Laura Albert, David Faust,
Andy Hollandbeck, Carl Pierce,
Dwight Ramsey, Charles Spencer,
TECHBOOKS Production Services

Indexer: TECHBOOKS Production
Services

Publishing and Editorial for Consumer Dummies

Diane Graves Steele, Vice President and Publisher, Consumer Dummies

Joyce Pepple, Acquisitions Director, Consumer Dummies

Kristin A. Cocks, Product Development Director, Consumer Dummies

Michael Spring, Vice President and Publisher, Travel

Brice Gosnell, Publishing Director, Travel

Suzanne Jannetta, Editorial Director, Travel

Publishing for Technology Dummies

Andy Cummings, Vice President and Publisher, Dummies Technology/General User

Composition Services

Gerry Fahey, Vice President of Production Services

Debbie Stailey, Director of Composition Services

Contents at a Glance

Maps at a Glance

Table of Contents

Introduction

· ·

*I*f you reached for *California For Dummies,* 2nd Edition, because it stood out from the overwhelming pack of California guidebooks or because it just seemed different, pat yourself on the back — you have good instincts.

This book walks you through the whole process of putting together your perfect trip, from the ins and outs of laying out a manageable itinerary to choosing the right places to stay to how much time to allot for which attractions and activities. Not that one right answer exists for anybody, of course. This book gives you the tools you need — and only what you need, not too much — to really help you discover what works for you and what doesn't. We know your time is valuable, so we strive to get right to the point, to give you the clearest picture of what you need to know, what choices you have to make, and what your options are so that you can make informed decisions easily and efficiently.

Think of building your vacation less as a step-by-step process and more as a jigsaw puzzle. This book helps you choose the right puzzle pieces and assemble them so that a) they interlock smoothly, and b) the finished product reflects the picture *you* want, not someone else's image of what your vacation should be.

About This Book

Some parts of California deserve your valuable time and hard-earned money, and others don't. For this reason, we've focused not on covering California comprehensively, but on covering the best that California offers. This book is a reference tool that answers all of your questions about the state's most terrific destinations — places like the Napa Valley and Disneyland.

The resulting guidebook directs you to all the worthiest locales and doesn't bother you with the secondary stuff. You don't have to wade through a big chapter on Sacramento, say, to find the Yosemite National Park recommendations you really want. Capital, schmapital — suggesting Sacramento as a vacation destination is the equivalent of recommending that you cut a New York City vacation short so that you can spend a few days hanging out in Albany. Now, we have nothing against your average state capitol, and Albany and Sacramento are perfectly nice cities, but c'mon — California offers many more interesting and enjoyable places to have a good time.

Conventions Used in This Book

We recently tried to extract some information from a guidebook and found so many symbols that we considered training in hieroglyphics to interpret them all. We are happy to report that the user-friendly *California For Dummies,* 2nd Edition, travel guide isn't like that. The use of symbols and abbreviations is kept to a minimum, as follows:

- ✔ The credit card abbreviations are AE (American Express), DC (Diners Club), DISC (Discover), MC (MasterCard), and V (Visa).

- ✔ We list the hotels, restaurants, and top attractions in A-to-Z order, for the most part, so that moving among the maps, worksheets, and descriptions is easier.

We include some general pricing information to help you as you decide where to unpack your bags or dine on the local cuisine. We use a system of dollar signs to show a range of costs for one night in a hotel or a meal at a restaurant. Check out the following table to decipher the dollar signs:

Cost	Hotel	Restaurant
$	$75 and under	$15 or under
$$	$75 to $150	$15 to $25
$$$	$150 to $225	$25 to $40
$$$$	225 to $300	$40 to $70
$$$$$	$300 and up	$70 and up

Foolish Assumptions

We assume that this is your first California vacation — or maybe you haven't been to California since you were a child, or you haven't visited a particular region within the state. Or maybe you don't want to dedicate your life to trip planning, wading through hundreds of dense pages only to feel more confused than confident about your choices. Maybe you don't like the way that so many conventional guidebooks require you to figure out which hotels, destinations, restaurants, and so on the authors actually like and which they're including because they think quantity outweighs quality.

On the other hand, you may be an experienced traveler, but you don't have a lot of time to devote to trip planning or you don't have a lot of time to spend in California after you get there. You want expert advice on how to maximize your time and enjoy a hassle-free trip.

Rather than just throwing out reams of information for you to sift through until you're too tired to tell Bakersfield from Big Sur, *California For Dummies,* 2nd Edition, cuts to the good stuff. We've done the legwork for you, and we want you to benefit from our expertise. We know that you work hard to set aside a few precious weeks of vacation time and that money doesn't grow on palm fronds. But no matter how much money you have, you don't want to waste it. Consequently, we're willing to take a stand so that you can know what to include in your California vacation — and, even more important, what to pass by. After all, you want to figure this stuff out now, in the planning stage — not after you get there, when it's too late.

How This Book Is Organized

California For Dummies, 2nd Edition, is divided into six parts. The chapters within each part cover specific travel topics or regions in detail. You can read each chapter or part without reading the one that came before it — no need to read about San Francisco if you're heading to Southern California, after all — but we may refer you to other chapters of the book for more information on certain subjects.

Part 1: Getting Started

This first part introduces you to the best of California and touches on everything you'll want to consider before actually getting down to the nitty-gritty of trip planning, including:

- When to go (and when you may want to stay home)

- Tips on planning your itinerary, plus actual time-tested itineraries that you can use as a proven blueprint for your own vacation

- How much you can expect your trip to cost, with tips on how to save if money is a concern

- Special considerations for families, seniors, travelers with disabilities, and gay and lesbian travelers

Part 11: Ironing Out the Details

This is where we get down to the nuts and bolts of travel planning, including:

- Planes, trains, and automobiles: how to get to California and how to get around California after you arrive

- The pros and cons of working with a travel agent versus planning your own trip

✔ The advantages of all-inclusive travel packages

✔ Getting ready to go, from the pluses and minuses of buying travel insurance to making advance dinner reservations to what to pack

Parts III, IV, and V: The Destinations

If you think of this book as a meal, these parts constitute the main course. They form the bulk of the book and cover the destinations you'll visit. Each chapter offers all of the specific details and recommendations you need for a given destination, including:

✔ When to go

✔ How much time you'll need

✔ How to get there

✔ Where to stay

✔ Where to eat

✔ What to do after you arrive

Part III covers Northern California: the San Francisco Bay Area; the Wine Country; the wild North Coast and tall-tree Redwood Country; and the Sierra Nevada mountains, where you'll find spectacular Lake Tahoe and Yosemite National Park.

Part IV covers California's Central Coast, which includes Santa Cruz and such marvelous destinations as the Monterey Peninsula, Big Sur, Hearst Castle, the Santa Ynez Valley, and that gem of the coast, Santa Barbara.

Part V focuses on Southern California, namely Los Angeles, San Diego, the Disneyland Resort, and parts in between. And, if you're the type who never thinks the weather is too hot or too dry, we cover the desert, including Palm Springs.

For a more thorough destination overview, flip to Chapter 1.

Part VI: The Part of Tens

Every *For Dummies* book contains a Part of Tens. If Parts III, IV, and V are the main course of your meal, think of these fun chapters, each their own top-ten list, as dessert. If you feel like doing homework to get you in the proper California mood, check out Chapter 26. Or maybe you want to catch a whiff of genuine Left Coast zaniness while you're on the road? Read Chapter 27 to find out where you can get down and wacky the way actual Californians do (when we're not writing travel guides).

Appendix and worksheets

The Appendix lists the details for easy reference, putting the facts about California at your fingertips, from locating local American Express offices to finding the most accurate online weather forecasts, and everything in between. We've also included a bunch of worksheets to make your travel planning easier — among other things, you can determine your budget, create specific itineraries, and keep a log of your favorite restaurants so you can hit them again next time you're in town. You can find these worksheets easily because they're printed on yellow paper.

Icons Used in This Book

You'll notice the following icons sprinkled throughout the text. Think of them as signposts; we use them to highlight special tips, draw your attention to must-see destinations, and give you a heads-up on a variety of topics.

This icon points out useful advice on things to do, ways to schedule your time, and other tips you won't want to miss.

This icon helps you spot tourist traps, rip-offs, time-wasters, and other details to beware.

These attractions, hotels, restaurants, or activities are especially family-friendly.

Check out this icon for money-saving tips or particularly great values.

This icon points out bits of well-guarded insider advice that give you an edge over those who don't know better.

This icon alerts you to any advance plans that you should schedule before you leave home.

Where to Go from Here

As you read through this book and start to formulate your California vacation, remember this: Planning really is half the fun. Don't think of choosing your destinations and solidifying the details as a chore. Make the homebound part of the process a voyage of discovery, and you'll end up with an entire vacation experience that is much more rewarding and enriching — really. Let your vacation begin right now.

Part I
Getting Started

The 5th Wave   By Rich Tennant

"I think we should arrange to be there for Garlic-Anchovy-Chili Bean Week, and then shoot over to the Breathmint-Antacid Festival."

In this part . . .

This part introduces you to the best of California and touches on everything you want to consider before you travel, so that your California vacation is as spectacular as the state. This part helps you decide when to go, plan your itinerary, and budget for your trip. We also include extra tips for people with kids, seniors, travelers with disabilities, and members of the gay community.

Chapter 1

Discovering the Best of California

● ●

In This Chapter

▶ Introducing the Golden State's highlights

▶ Exploring San Francisco and the natural wonders of Northern California

▶ Journeying along the gorgeous Central Coast

▶ Reveling in the fun and sun of Southern California

● ●

California isn't like any state in the Union. In fact, it's hardly like a state at all. Even national politicians tend to refer to the 31st state as "the nation of California" — a sovereign country all its own, an immense and diverse dominion to be conquered above and beyond the other 49 states.

Their outsize view isn't far from the truth. With nearly 159,000 square miles of land and a 1,264-mile coastline, California is the third largest state in the United States. Sure, both Alaska and Texas are bigger — but California's uniqueness stems from much more than size. California is like the high school homecoming queen whose natural beauty and innate poise make the rest of the student body sneer at her while wanting to bask in her glow at the very same time. They don't call this the Golden State for nothing, after all.

California is really an awesome place, in the truest sense (not the surfer-dude sense) of the word. Its jaw-dropping diversity is what continues to amaze us (and we're from the state), more than anything else. With two of the nation's largest megalopolises — the San Francisco Bay Area, which has grown beyond speculators' wildest dreams with the rise of Silicon Valley, and metropolitan Los Angeles, whose urban sprawl has a glamorous heart called Hollywood — California has the largest, wealthiest, and most urbanized population of any state in the nation. Yet it's also an agricultural wonderland whose bounty runs the gamut from artichokes, raisins, garlic, and asparagus to some of the finest wine-making grapes in the world. And it still manages to be home to some of the country's most striking and varied wilderness — from purple mountains' majesty to arid, marvelously barren desert to coastlines of unsurpassed beauty.

Within the natural landscape alone, the contrast is unparalleled. Take Mount Whitney and Death Valley as a case in point: At 14,494 feet above and 282 feet below sea level, respectively, they are the highest and lowest points in the continental United States — and just 85 miles separates them. Wow.

Unless you have a couple of months to spare for vacation (lucky you!), you're not going to see everything this marvelous, multifaceted state has to offer. You know what? Don't even waste time trying. Frankly, some parts of California are much worthier of your valuable time and hard-earned money than others.

The destinations in this chapter comprise the best of California. You'll discover more about them as you read through this book and begin to plan your trip.

The San Francisco Bay Area

The San Francisco Bay metropolitan area grew by leaps and bounds with the Silicon Valley revolution — and even with the dot-com bust, the city and environs have remained coveted real estate. The prime draw, however, is still the loveliest and most beguiling city in America, **San Francisco** (see Chapter 9). "The city" (as locals call it — never "Frisco") is smaller than you may expect, loaded with personality in all corners, and pleasant to visit year-round. It's also the one destination in the Driving State where you can easily get around without a car.

If San Francisco is the ultimate urban destination, then the gorgeous **California Wine Country** (see Chapter 10) — Napa and Sonoma counties, America's premier wine-growing region — is the embodiment of pastoral escape. These super-fertile valleys brim with world-class wine-tasting rooms and some of the country's finest restaurants and inns.

The North Coast

The wild and woolly coastal region north of the San Francisco Bay Area (see Part III) offers some of California's most breathtaking scenery. It's quiet, remote, and ruggedly handsome, with spectacular nature broken only by the occasional picturesque village. Of those villages, none is more lovely than romantic **Mendocino** (see Chapter 11), a postage stamp of a town situated on a majestic headland. Rife with elegant bed and breakfasts (B&Bs), upscale restaurants, and pricey boutiques and galleries, it's definitely built for two — but families with kids will find

The Regions of California

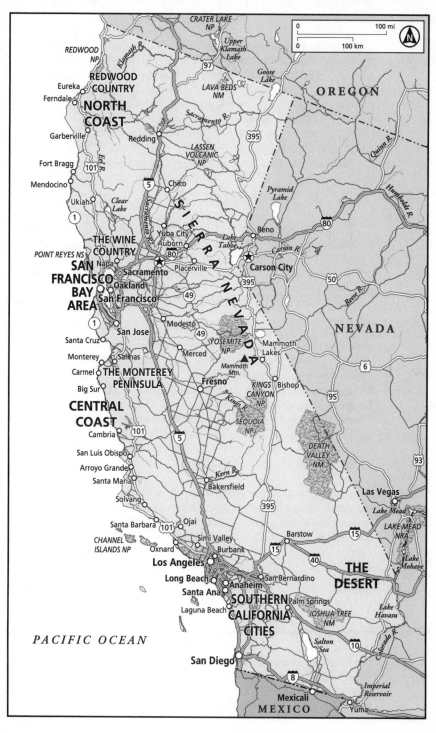

plenty of outdoor activities to occupy them in the surrounding area. Beware the weather, though, which can be cold and misty at any time of the year — all part of the dreamy Mendocino vibe, aficionados say.

Mendocino also serves as a good jumping-off point for exploring the regal **Redwood Country** (see Chapter 12), which starts just inland and north of Mendocino. The towering coast redwoods — the tallest trees on the planet — extend all the way to the Oregon border, but you won't need to travel that far to get your fill of their majesty. You can follow the scenic 32-mile **Avenue of the Giants** to the midpoint as a day trip from Mendocino or dedicate a couple of days to the drive, depending on your sightseeing goals.

The Sierra Nevada

Travel inland from the Bay Area or North Coast and you'll soon reach the **Sierra Nevada,** the magnificently rugged, granite-peaked mountain range that defines northeast and east-central California. This high-altitude region is so uniquely stunning that such geniuses as Mark Twain and Ansel Adams considered it one of their greatest inspirations. The Sierra Nevada stirred John Muir to do no less than found the U.S. National Park system.

Possibly the greatest of the national parks is spectacular **Yosemite National Park** (see Chapter 14), whose natural wonders include such record-setters as **Yosemite Falls** (North America's tallest waterfall) and **El Capitan** (the world's largest granite monolith). Beware, though, because Yosemite is the superstar of California's natural attractions, drawing theme-park-worthy crowds in summer — but we tell you how to do your best to lose them. Just to the south of Yosemite is the year-round recreational playground resort of **Mammoth Mountain,** where you can ski from November to July.

Also in the High Sierra rests the United States' biggest and most beautiful alpine lake, sparkling **Lake Tahoe** (see Chapter 13) — California's finest outdoor playground. Come in the winter to ski, in the summer to hike, bike, kayak, sail . . . you name it. If you're a history buff, consider taking a day to visit the **Gold Country** (see Chapter 13), the epicenter of California's 19th-century gold rush hysteria, on your way to or from Tahoe.

The Central Coast

If you ask us (and you did), the central coast — that stretch between San Francisco and Los Angeles — represents California at its very best (see Part IV). The drive along Highway 1 — the world-famous Pacific Coast Highway — is one of the most scenic in the world. Keep in mind, however, that the drive is slow going and quite curvy — real Dramamine territory, so stock up if you're queasy.

Where the San Francisco Bay Area meets the Monterey Peninsula sits **Santa Cruz** (see Chapter 15), California's quintessential, and kinda wacky, surf town. Kids (and kids at heart) will love Santa Cruz — especially the genuine old-fashioned boardwalk, the West Coast's only beachfront amusement park. Santa Cruz is at its best in summer and early fall, when the beach party is going strong.

Pristine nature meets unbridled commercialism on the **Monterey Peninsula** (see Chapter 16) — and fortunately, nature wins out. This stunning knob of land jutting out to sea cradles Monterey Bay, one of the richest and most diverse marine habitats on earth. On land you'll find the **Monterey Bay Aquarium,** one of California's all-time top attractions, plus a collection of delightful communities, from family-friendly Monterey itself to golf mecca **Pebble Beach** to ultraromantic **Carmel-by-the-Sea.** The marriage of natural beauty and man-made diversions doesn't get any better than this.

In **Big Sur** (see Chapter 17), on the other hand, the spectacular wilderness and breathtaking views are unhindered by all but the most minimal development. Dedicate a full day to the natural splendor of Big Sur even if you don't want to stay in one of the region's funky hotels; you won't regret a minute of it.

Hearst Castle (see Chapter 18), one of the most outrageous private homes ever built and a real hoot to tour, lies on the other end of the man-versus-nature continuum. Even if this monument to excess isn't your style, you'll enjoy the surrounding countryside — neither Northern California nor Southern, it has a distinct, golden-hued beauty all its own — and the amiable village of **Cambria,** a great place to soak up some small-town charm.

Driving farther down the coast puts you squarely in Southern California. If you have little ones in tow or a strong affinity for good pastry, head inland to Danish **Solvang** (see Chapter 19), a storybook town straight out of Scandinavia. Or visit **Santa Barbara** (see Chapter 20), a seaside jewel that embodies the Southern California dream — perfect for clocking in some top-quality relaxation time — and then take a break in the restful surrounds of California's own Shangri-La, the **Ojai Valley**.

The Southern California Cities

Southern California is where things get crazy, in a good way. Certainly, **Los Angeles** (L.A.) (see Chapter 21), the poster child for urban sprawl, isn't for everybody. But think twice before you reject it out of hand. L.A.'s charms may be subtle (and after all, it's easy to be popular when all your goods are in your shop windows, so to speak), but they do exist. In addition to being celeb-rich and gloriously silly, it also happens to be the state's finest museum town. Really.

Do you really need us to tell you to go to **Disneyland** (covered in Chapter 22)? Oh, all right. Just south of L.A. (behind the Orange Curtain, as Angelenos are fond of saying) in Anaheim (Orange County) it is the Happiest Place on Earth and the original theme park, and it's an unadulterated blast for kids of all ages (even grown-up ones with jobs and mortgages). Consider visiting again even if you've been before, because you'll find plenty of new things to see and do — including the latest Disney park, called California Adventure.

Almost midway between L.A. and San Diego are two spots to catch your breath after a hectic urban odyssey. Beach lovers can park themselves in the sand in quaint and calm **Laguna Beach,** perhaps occasionally getting up long enough to browse the goods created by one of the area's many artists. Then follow the swallows to the hauntingly lovely adobe ruins of **San Juan Capistrano**'s fabled mission (see Chapter 23).

In **San Diego** (see Chapter 25), you'll find a wonderfully mellow vibe, golden beaches galore, and plenty of memory-making diversions, most notably three terrific animal parks: the **San Diego Zoo, SeaWorld,** and the **Wild Animal Park.** If that's not enough to keep you and the kids happy and busy, also consider the multifaceted joys of **Balboa Park** (the second-largest city park in the country, after the Big Apple's Central Park) and the metro area's newest theme-park addition, **LEGOLAND.**

The Desert

Unlike the other destinations in this book — which are generally most popular in summer and largely pleasant to visit year-round — California's desert is most fun to visit in any season but summer, when the scorching heat can be a bit much to bear. Still, some people enjoy summer in the desert, when prices are low and crowds are minimal (just pack your sunscreen — number 30 or higher, preferably).

The **Palm Springs** area (see Chapter 24) is the place to go for desert cool. This is the manicured side of the desert, where streets bear names like Frank Sinatra Drive, and golf greens, swimming pools, spa treatments, and martinis rule the day. What's more, easy access to unspoiled nature makes Palm Springs appealing even to those who couldn't care less about the prefabricated glamour or retro-groovy stuff.

Chapter 2

Deciding When to Go

● ●

In This Chapter

▶ Getting to know California's weather

▶ Visiting from season to season — and getting advice for avoiding the crowds

▶ Exploring a year of celebrations, California style

● ●

W.C. Fields once said, "California is the only state in the union where you can fall asleep under a rosebush in full bloom and freeze to death." Surely a gross exaggeration, right? Actually, no.

This chapter helps you uncover a few facts about California's weather patterns before you plan your trip. In addition, this chapter reveals the times when everybody else visits California so that you can a) join the party, or b) avoid it like the plague.

Understanding California's Climate

Don't be fooled by what you think you know about California's weather. "Really," you say, "I've seen *Baywatch* and *90210*. What's there to understand? California is all buffed bikini-clad bods and perpetual sun." Well, yes and no. Sometimes the reality lives up to the myth, and sometimes it doesn't. Frankly, the weather isn't all that predictable.

Microclimates are small areas of uniform climate that generally differ from the surrounding climate — and California has lots of them. A perfectly plausible scenario sees you skiing in Tahoe in the morning, cruising around the Napa Valley in shorts and T-shirts in the afternoon, and bundling up against the damp, cold ocean breezes in Mendocino by evening.

The most important weather predictor is your location: coast or inland, north or south.

As a general rule, the weather will likely be cool and windy along the coastline — even in July and August — and warmer and perpetually sunnier as you move inland. The climate will always be warmer and sunnier in inland Sacramento than in famously foggy San Francisco.

(The temperature drops again as you climb into the mountains to high-elevation places like Lake Tahoe.) Believe it or not, the rule even holds true in the same city: Downtown Los Angeles is more often than not 10 to 20°F warmer than L.A.'s oceanside beach community, Santa Monica, which benefits from cooling ocean breezes. Latitude matters, too, of course; in general, the southern coast — Santa Barbara and points south — sees better beach weather than its northern counterparts.

The one thing you can say for sure about California weather is how darn changeable it is. The temperature may drop at night more than you're used to, no matter where you're located. In many places, both along the coast and inland, daytime temperatures of 80°F and above may routinely drop down into the low 40s in the evening. Cool fog will cover much of the coastline in the mornings, but if the sun breaks through, temperatures will soar by noon or so. The bottom line: Be prepared for dramatic daily changes, even in summer. Layering your clothes is always a good idea.

Knowing the Secret of the Seasons

California is seasonless to a certain degree — anytime is a good time to visit. The state benefits from glorious conditions year-round, with the weather being generally warmer than most other mainland U.S. spots in winter, and cooler and drier than most in summer.

One of the most surprising ticks in California's weather pattern is that summer generally starts late. As the temperature charts in Table 2-1 show, both San Francisco and Los Angeles (and virtually all points in between) don't really start warming up until July. Even blessedly sunny L.A. is notorious for *June gloom:* Morning gray rolls in and stays until afternoon. (The biggest exception is the desert, where high temperatures and bright sun move in early and unpack to stay awhile.)

Table 2-1   Average Temperatures from Sample Cities and Regions (°F)

Lake Tahoe

	Jan July	Feb Aug	Mar Sept	Apr Oct	May Nov	June Dec
High	40 77	42 77	44 69	51 59	60 47	69 41
Low	20 45	21 45	23 39	27 32	33 26	39 21

San Francisco

High	58	60	60	61	62	63
	64	65	67	67	63	58
Low	43	46	46	47	49	51
	53	54	54	52	48	44

Napa Valley

High	57	62	65	69	75	80
	82	82	81	77	65	57
Low	37	41	42	43	48	52
	54	54	52	48	42	38

Monterey

High	60	62	62	63	64	67
	68	69	72	70	65	60
Low	43	45	45	46	48	50
	52	53	53	51	47	43

Santa Barbara

High	65	66	66	69	69	72
	75	77	76	74	69	66
Low	43	45	47	49	52	55
	58	59	58	54	49	44

Los Angeles (downtown)

High	68	69	70	72	73	78
	84	85	83	79	72	68
Low	49	50	52	54	58	61
	65	66	65	60	54	49

Palm Springs

High	70	76	80	87	95	104
	109	107	101	92	79	70
Low	43	46	49	54	61	68
	75	75	69	60	49	42

On the up side, when the warm weather comes, it almost always stays through September and usually well into October. (Unfortunately, in L.A., "warm" often means several days of really stinkin' hot.) Indian summer is common, and fall is universally the best season weatherwise. In September and October, the fog even lifts from perpetually misty spots along the coast like Monterey and Mendocino. In places where the weather starts to crisp in the fall, like Tahoe, clear air and beautiful colors make for gorgeous conditions.

If you're coming to California to hit the beach in your bikini in January, don't count on it — this ain't Hawaii. Still, the weather will likely be milder here than where you're from (especially if you're from the Northeast or the Midwest) — swimming may not happen, but strolling the sands under cloudless brilliant blue skies probably will. No wonder so many people love visiting in winter — 50°F in San Francisco is way better than Chicago's, or even New York's, parka weather. Tahoe is a prime spot for skiing, and snow-blanketed Yosemite is crowd-free and gorgeous. And we've often found the coastal destinations — particularly Monterey, Big Sur, and the like — to be more pleasant, with clearer skies, in December or January than they are in June or July. If you get lucky, you may even end up with a beach day in L.A. or San Diego in those months, when the occasional 80°F day takes a bow.

Examining a California Calendar of Events

Here's a brief rundown of the Golden State's top annual events:

✔ **December–March:** This is **whale-watching season** all along the California coast, from Mendocino down to Mexico. Mammoth gray whales migrate from the cold Alaskan waters to warmer climes for their birthing season and then transport their new pups back home. Just look carefully out to sea for a blow, the puff of steam that can rise 12 feet from the whale's blowhole.

The best place to watch for whales is **Monterey,** which celebrates the annual migration with a two-week party in January called Whalefest. For information, call ☎ **831-649-1770** or point your Web browser to www.monterey.com and search for **Whalefest** for a calendar of this year's events.

Mendocino holds its own celebration, the Mendocino Whale Festival, usually in early March (☎ **707-961-6300;** www.mendocino coast.com).

✔ **January 1:** New Year's Day sees the **Tournament of Roses Parade,** the mother of all college bowl parades, descend upon Pasadena (near Los Angeles) almost at the crack of dawn. Outrageous floats constructed entirely of fresh roses and other flora compete for the spotlight with high-volume marching bands and high-wattage celebs making appearances. Although the festivities happen on New Year's Day, expect to arrive the night before (bring supplies for sleeping on the sidewalk, and remember, it will get quite nippy) if you want to get a spot that lets you see anything. Call ☎ **626-449-4100** or visit www.tournamentofroses.com for grandstand tickets, official tour packages, and other information.

✔ **January–February:** The **Chinese New Year Festival and Parade** in San Francisco, the largest Chinese New Year's celebration in the United States, encompasses two weeks of excitement, the highlight of which is a magnificent parade featuring the legendary Golden Dragon. Events range from the Miss Chinatown USA pageant to street and flower fairs. Chinese New Year begins in late January or February. Call ☎ **415-982-3000** for exact details and 2003 dates, or go to www.sfvisitor.org.

✔ **Late January–March:** The **Napa Valley Mustard Festival,** a celebration of the petite yellow-petaled mustard flowers that bloom in late winter (and everyone's favorite gourmet condiment), has grown into the Wine Country's biggest event. Two full months of high-end hoopla runs the gamut from wine auctions to gallery shows to gourmet food competitions. The festival runs from the end of January through the end of March. Call ☎ **707-226-7459** or check www.mustardfestival.org for the full calendar and/or 2003 dates.

✔ **Late February–early March: Snowfest** in Tahoe City, a weeklong celebration of the ski season, is the largest of its kind in the world. Features include snow and ice sculpture contests, a polar bear swim in Lake Tahoe, the Incredible Dog Snow Challenge (in which man's best friend competes in freestyle frisbee, search-and-rescue, and sledding competitions), and more. It's the most fun you'll ever have in Polartec. Call ☎ **775-832-7625** or visit the Web site at www.snowfest.org.

✔ **Early May:** Celebrate **Cinco de Mayo,** Mexico's favorite holiday, in San Diego's historic Old Town, the original Spanish birthplace of California, or in the Mexican heart of Los Angeles, El Pueblo de Los Angeles State Historic Monument. Expect festive mariachi music, folk dancing, and lots of yummy eats. Events usually take place over the weekend closest to May 5. Call ☎ **213-625-5045** for L.A. information, ☎ **619-296-3161** or 619-220-5422 for San Diego information.

✔ **Mid-May:** The **San Francisco Bay to Breakers,** the world's largest and zaniest footrace, is actually more fun than run. More than 70,000 runners race across the park in their costumed best. For information call ☎ **415-808-5000,** ext. 2222, or point your Web browser to www.baytobreakers.com.

✔ **Memorial Day Weekend:** How could you skip the **Great Monterey Squid Festival,** a scientific and culinary ode to calamari. Lots of yummy, squid-friendly fun! Dial ☎ **831-649-6544** for details.

- ✔ **Late June:** San Francisco hosts the **Lesbian, Gay, Bisexual, and Transgender Pride Parade,** the world's largest and most outrageous gay pride parade. For information call ☎ **415-864-3733.** Though L.A.'s own **Gay and Lesbian Pride Day parade**, also in late June, comes in a close second. It's in West Hollywood. Call ☎ **323-969-8302** or go online to www.lapride.org.

- ✔ **Fourth of July:** Virtually all of California's communities hold their own style of Independence Day celebrations, from San Francisco's fireworks to Monterey's Living History Festival to the Redwood Country's old-fashioned parade and picnic in Victorian-era Ferndale. Contact local visitors bureaus to find out what's on in the town you plan to visit (see the "Gathering More Information" section at the end of each destination chapter).

- ✔ **Early or mid-September:** The **San Diego Street Scene** is a three-day festival of food, music, and fun. Call ☎ **619-557-8490** or visit the Web site at www.gaslamp.org.

- ✔ **Mid-September:** Solvang's Scandinavian glory reaches its tacky-genuine zenith with **Danish Days,** a historic three-day extravaganza celebrating Solvang's heritage. For details call ☎ **800-468-6765** or 805-688-6144.

- ✔ **Third weekend in September:** The **Monterey Jazz Festival,** the world's longest-running jazz festival (44 years and counting), hosts the biggest names in traditional and contemporary jazz. If you want more information, call ☎ **831-373-3366** or point your Web browser to www.montereyjazzfest.com.

- ✔ **Early October: Gold Rush Days** in Marshall Gold Discovery State Historic Park, Coloma, tells the gold rush story in living color through demonstrations, story-telling, and entertainment. Call ☎ **530-622-3470** or 530-622-0390 for information.

- ✔ **October 31: Halloween in San Francisco** is a wild and wacky fete, complete with over-the-edge costumes, entertainment, and behavior. Call ☎ **415-826-1401.** Or join the 400,000 costumed revelers in **Los Angeles** who flood the streets of West Hollywood for some mighty creative merriment. Call ☎ **310-289-2525.**

- ✔ **Late November:** The stars brighten Hollywood Boulevard the Sunday after Thanksgiving in the **Hollywood Christmas Parade** in Los Angeles, a classic celebrity-studded parade that launches the holiday season in glittering Tinseltown style. For details call ☎ **323-469-8311** or visit www.hollywoodcofc.org.

Considering all that goes on every year in California, this brief list is merely a microdrop in the bucket. For a complete rundown of events, call the **California Division of Tourism** (☎ **800-462-2543**) and request a copy of *California Celebrations* or point your Web browser to www.gocalif.com and click on Special Events.

Chapter 3

Great Itineraries

- -

In This Chapter

▶ Planning an itinerary

▶ Exploring Northern California in ten days

▶ Seeing Southern California in ten days

▶ Taking a romantic trip for two

▶ Bringing the kids along

▶ Discovering the natural side of California

- -

*U*nderstand this right now: You will not see all of California. We know actual native Californians (remember that not everyone moved here from someplace else) who've lived here all of their lives and who continue to stumble on new discoveries as they putter around.

Still, it's easy to see quite a bit of the Golden State, even if your vacation time is short. In this chapter, we provide you with a few specific itineraries — ten-day jaunts through Northern and Southern California, romantic idylls for two, kid-friendly road trips, and forays into the wilds of the Golden State — to help you plan your own California dream of a trip.

Using Time-Tested Itinerary Planning Tips

The itineraries we suggest in this chapter give you an idea of what you can see and do comfortably in the time you have. But remember that no one ideal vacation plan exists. Use the itineraries that appear later in this chapter as you see fit — either as proven, hard-and-fast plans, or simply as starting blueprints that you can then customize to your own needs.

Following are some tips that will help you when determining your own itineraries:

✔ **Embrace the hugeness of California — don't deny it.** You'll do a lot of driving as you move from one destination to another, so factor that in when determining your itinerary. If you're the road-trip type and moving around sounds exciting to you, planning an ambitious itinerary is fine. But if getting to really know a place is important to you, you'll want to make plans to settle in for a few days. Or, if spending too much time in the car with the kids is going to feel more like a chore than a vacation, recognize this fact now so you can plan accordingly.

✔ **Know your travel goals.** If golf is on your agenda, shorten your visit to L.A. for extra time in Palm Springs. If you're more the city type than the nature lover, forgo stops on your drive between San Francisco and L.A. so that you have more time for urban dwelling. If you're planning a family vacation, Disneyland may be a better choice than Napa. You get the idea.

✔ **If you have only one week, limit yourself to two destinations or a maximum of three.** If you don't limit yourself, you're going to suffer from the "If it's Tuesday, it must be Big Sur" syndrome. If, for example, you're touring Southern California, start with two days in San Diego, then two days in Disneyland, and wrap it up with three days in Los Angeles. (San Francisco and Yosemite National Park alone can tie up a week.) If you're ultra ambitious, you can add Tahoe to the mix and fly out of Reno, Nevada, but you'll end up with lots of behind-the-wheel time and not really more than two days per destination.

✔ **Seriously consider flying in to one California airport and leaving from another.** The time saved by flying into Los Angeles and leaving from San Francisco, say, or flying into San Jose and departing from Palm Springs, may be worth the extra airline charges and/or rental-car drop-off charges. What's more, depending on your points of arrival and departure, you may not even incur extra fees. Your best bet is to consider a couple of options and price them out with the airlines and car companies (or put your travel agent to work) before you decide.

✔ **Consider your drive part of the adventure.** The choice is yours: You can either drive straight through without stopping or take a leisurely meander off the beaten path — it all depends on how adventurous you are and how much unassigned time you have. California is a gorgeous state, with lots to admire along just about any route you take. You'll want to make time for unplanned stops and serendipitous side trips.

✔ **Don't be overly ambitious and try to cram too many activities into a day when you'll be making a long drive.** Driving long distances can really sap your energy. Keep in mind that estimated drive times in this book don't include rest stops, unforeseen traffic or detours, and so on. If you do have time and energy to do more than simply drive and check in to your new hotel on big drive days, consider it a gimme; use the time to relax. (After all, this is a vacation, remember?)

✔ **Avoid ending up at a super-popular weekend destination on the weekends.** Restful destinations like the Napa Valley, Mendocino, Carmel, Hearst Castle, Solvang, and Santa Barbara become human zoos when urban dwellers escape the city for the weekend. Many also require two-night minimums over the weekend, which can throw a monkey wrench in your plans. See if you can schedule your city visits over the weekends, instead.

You gain no particular advantage by starting at one end of the state over the other, so don't worry about it. Just head north or south based on what's most convenient, appealing, and/or cost-efficient for you.

Northern California in Ten Days

On **Day 1,** fly in to **San Francisco.** Spend **Day 2** and **Day 3** enjoying the City by the Bay (see Chapter 9 for a detailed sightseeing plan for San Francisco).

Itinerary #1

After spending **Day 4** in San Francisco, head to the **Wine Country** (see Chapter 10) early on **Day 5** and spend **Day 5** and **Day 6** getting to know the area. For the ideal introduction, plan on a late-morning or early-afternoon winery tour, perhaps one of the reservation-only tours at Schramsberg or Niebaum Coppola, or one of the terrific first-come, first-served tours offered by Robert Mondavi or St. Supéry. See two more wineries after lunch, and mix it up with a little sightseeing or shopping before resting up for a gourmet feast at one of the valley's stellar restaurants. Book way ahead if you want to eat at **French Laundry,** often named the best restaurant in the United States. On the morning of **Day 6,** stop at one of the valley's gourmet markets to assemble a lunchtime picnic. Plan some additional activities to mix in with your winery-going, such as a hot-air balloon ride, a bit of bicycling, and/or a mud bath and massage.

On **Day 7,** head north from the Wine Country in the afternoon for **Redwood Country** (see Chapter 12). Follow Highway 128 north to U.S. 101, and spend the night along the Redwood Highway, perhaps in charming, Victorian **Ferndale.** On **Day 8,** meander down the Redwood Highway, reaching Mendocino in time for dinner. Spend **Day 9** exploring **Mendocino** (see Chapter 11), hiking the headlands, shopping, or just enjoying the wild beauty of the misty North Coast.

On **Day 10,** drive back to **San Francisco** for your flight home.

You can easily trim this itinerary to eight days by cutting a day off your time in San Francisco and limiting your Redwood Country exploring to a day trip.

Itinerary #2

Depart San Francisco on **Day 4** for the **Monterey Peninsula.** Leave in the morning and spend the day playing on the boardwalk and the beach in **Santa Cruz,** arriving in Monterey in time for dinner. If there's just the two of you and you're looking for romance, consider **Carmel** as a base. If your budget is generous, go all out and spend your nights on some of the most spectacular real estate in the nation, **Pebble Beach** (the California destination for golfers).

The Monterey Peninsula (see Chapter 16) deserves a good chunk of time, so spend the evening of **Day 4** and the following two nights here. Start **Day 5** at the **Monterey Aquarium.** (Don't forget to buy your aquarium tickets in advance to save aggravating time in line.) In the afternoon, rent bikes and follow Monterey's gorgeous bayfront bike path (suitable for all riders) for some spectacular views.

Spend **Day 6** exploring the rest of the peninsula by car, including the justifiably famous **17-Mile Drive** (viewable from that rented bike if you have the energy). Spend the afternoon strolling through charming Carmel; even if the weather is chilly, bundle up for a walk along cypress-lined Carmel Beach, one of the world's most beautiful stretches of sand.

On **Day 7,** drive through gorgeous **Big Sur** (see Chapter 17) to **San Simeon** and **Hearst Castle,** which we discuss in Chapter 18. Resist the urge to stop much along the way (you'll have time for that later). Arrive at your base in nearby **Cambria** in time to see the elephant seals basking in the sun just north of San Simeon and do a little exploring in Cambria before a leisurely dinner.

Dedicate **Day 8** to **Hearst Castle.** Book yourself a morning tour and an afternoon tour, with time for a flick in the five-story-high iWERKS format at the castle visitor center in between (this makes for good resting-your-tootsies time).

Day 9 is for exploring awesome **Big Sur.** In fact, spend the night along the Big Sur Coast so that you'll have plenty of hiking and/or contemplation time.

Fly home on **Day 10.** Consider flying out of **San Jose** to avoid the drive back to the San Francisco airport (SFO).

Southern California in Ten Days

On **Day 1,** fly into Los Angeles. Spend **Day 2** and **Day 3** enjoying Tinseltown. Check out Chapter 21 for a detailed sightseeing plan for Los Angeles.

Itinerary #1

On **Day 4,** go to **Disneyland** (see Chapter 22). In fact, consider making the hour's drive south on the evening of **Day 3** so that you can be first in the park in the morning. (You may even be able to get a jump-start on the masses with an early entrance, a perk currently enjoyed by Disneyland Resort hotel guests, though that may be dropped by the time you read this.) Spend the evening of **Day 4** in Anaheim so that you'll have an entire day in the park. In fact, you may want to consider spending the better part of **Day 5** at Disneyland as well, especially if you want to see the new California Adventure park. You may also want to split up your park time if you have little kids who'll tire out easily, if your own theme-park stamina is low, or if you're visiting at a peak time with long lines and wait times for rides. If you've had your fill of Disneyland by **Day 5,** spend that day relaxing by the pool, soaking up some of those California rays.

In any case, head south to **San Diego** (see Chapter 25) in time for dinner on **Day 5,** so that you can start your animal park adventures early on **Day 6.** Whether you have the kids with you or not, don't miss the **San Diego Zoo;** hyped though it may be, there is a reason it's a major attraction. On **Day 7,** choose between spending the day at **Sea World,** taking your littlest ones on an excursion to **LEGOLAND,** or treating your older kids to the **Wild Animal Park.** Or, if you've had enough theme-park fun for one trip, split your day between San Diego's culture-rich **Balboa Park** and the beach.

After all this running around, you deserve some rest and relaxation time. So, on **Day 8,** head to **Palm Springs** and spend **Day 9** relaxing under the desert sun. This is the place to get in some quality time on the fairway or some pampering at the spa (or some of both, if you're so inclined). If the desert isn't your bag, try the small seaside town of **Laguna Beach** or check out the fabled mission of **San Juan Capistrano** (see Chapter 23).

If you'd rather avoid a lot of running around, simply stay put in **San Diego** on **Day 8** and **Day 9** — it's another terrific place to kick back — and fly out from there on **Day 10.** Either way, you'll be relaxed and contented enough to head home on **Day 10,** whether you leave from Palm Springs International or San Diego's airport (if you've stayed put) or take the easy two-hour drive back to Los Angeles.

Itinerary #2

If theme parks aren't your style, head to **Palm Springs** (see Chapter 24) in the late afternoon of **Day 4,** arriving in time for an alfresco dinner. On **Day 5,** take a desert excursion with Desert Adventures Jeep Eco-Tours. Spend **Day 6** golfing, spa-ing, or just sitting by the pool sipping fruity drinks garnished with umbrellas.

On **Day 7,** head west again, skirting L.A. as you head northwest to lovely **Santa Barbara** (see Chapter 20), arriving in time for dinner.

If you're driving on a weekday, be sure to pass through L.A. before 3 p.m. to avoid getting stuck in rush-hour traffic.

Spend **Day 8** and **Day 9** hanging out in **Santa Barbara,** Southern California's loveliest beach town. If you're not the beach type (or if the weather's just not beachy), and you feel as if you've seen and done it all by midday on **Day 9,** explore Santa Barbara's wine country or take a ride over to **Solvang** (see Chapter 19) for a slice of Scandinavia, Southern California style. Or consider spending a night in the small town of **Ojai** (about half an hour southeast of Santa Barbara — see Chapter 20), where artists congregate and the setting sun turns the bluffs pink every night.

The drive is an easy 100 miles back to L.A. on **Day 10,** your day to fly home.

California in Two Weeks — for Romance-Seeking Couples

Fly in to **San Francisco** on **Day 1.** Spend **Day 2** and **Day 3** enjoying the most romantic city in the United States (see Chapter 9 for a recommended sightseeing plan of San Francisco).

Itinerary #1

Head north on **Day 4.** If you don't mind a long drive, consider the coastal route on your way up, which winds through lovely, artsy seaside towns. Stop at misty **Mendocino** (see Chapter 11), where picnicking, bike riding, strolling the charming seaside village, and snuggling up in front of a roaring fire in the evening are the primary orders of business. Frankly, towns don't get any more romantic — so spend **Day 5** here, too.

On the afternoon of **Day 6,** pick up curvaceous Highway 128 just south of Mendocino and follow it into the **Wine Country** (see Chapter 10). Set up camp at one of the valleys' romantic B&Bs (the Milliken Creek Inn is a great choice) and wine and dine each other on **Day 7** and **Day 8.**

On **Day 9,** cut south, back toward the coast, and make magical **Carmel-by-the-Sea** your love nest from which to explore the **Monterey Peninsula** over **Day 10** and **Day 11.** If the weather's good, work in an afternoon kayaking among the elephant seals and sea otters on **Monterey Bay** (see Chapter 16). And don't forget to take a romantic stroll along jaw-droppingly beautiful **Carmel Beach.**

Leave the Monterey area early on **Day 12** to give you the entire day to meander through **Big Sur** (see Chapter 17) on your way to **Hearst Castle** (see Chapter 18). Make **Cambria** your area base and dedicate **Day 13** to touring Xanadu.

On **Day 14,** drive back to San Francisco (or the **San Jose** or the **Monterey** airport, both a tad closer) to catch a late-day flight home.

Itinerary #2

Spend **Day 4** in San Francisco, and on **Day 5** head directly to the **Wine Country,** and dedicate **Day 5** and **Day 6** to touring the romantic, adult-oriented region (see Chapter 10).

On **Day 7,** drive to **Carmel** (or to the brand-new **Casa Palermo** in **Pebble Beach,** if you have the bucks) and settle in for **Monterey Peninsula** sightseeing on **Day 8** and **Day 9** (see Chapter 16).

On **Day 10,** meander through **Big Sur** country (see "Northern California in Ten Days," earlier in this chapter), arriving in **Cambria** (see Chapter 18) in time for a candlelit dinner (the **Sow's Ear** makes a good choice). Make **Day 11** your castle day — and because you're in the romantic mood, ask your guide for tales of Clark Gable and Carole Lombard's visits to "the ranch."

Take **Day 12** to drive south along the Central Coast to **Santa Barbara** (see Chapter 20), a great place to spend **Day 13** at the beach.

On **Day 14,** drive the easy two hours south to the Los Angeles airport (LAX) to catch a flight home.

California in Two Weeks — with Kids

Kids love California as much as adults do — it's sort of like a giant playground with all the latest toys. Anyone traveling with kids won't have a problem finding things to do; the trick is how to fit it all in.

Itinerary #1

On **Day 1,** fly the brood in to **San Diego.** Spend **Day 2** and **Day 3** enjoying the local animal parks.

Check out of your San Diego hotel on the morning of **Day 4** and head north to either

- ✔ **LEGOLAND** in nearby Carlsbad with the little ones
- ✔ The **San Diego Wild Animal Park,** in Escondido, with the older kids.

Both parks make easy stops along the way to **Anaheim,** where you should check in to your hotel, have an early dinner, and rest up for your big day tomorrow at **Disneyland.** Spread your park time over two days, **Day 5** and **Day 6,** to avoid burnout — your own and the kids'.

On the morning of **Day 7,** head north to **L.A.** Base yourself at the beach for maximum fun. Visit **Universal Studios** on **Day 8.**

On **Day 9,** make the short (two-hour) drive north to cutesy, Danish-themed **Solvang,** which your younger kids are bound to enjoy.

On **Day 10,** head north to **Monterey,** stopping in **San Luis Obispo** for a pleasant lunch break (it's just about exactly at the midpoint of the four-hour drive). The peninsula features plenty to entertain you and the kids on **Day 11** and **Day 12;** the **aquarium,** of course, is a must.

Spend **Day 13** on the beach and boardwalk at **Santa Cruz,** California's historic seaside amusement park (see Chapter 15). It's a real joy, and a must-do for families. You can see the boardwalk in a few ways: You can make it a day trip from your base in Monterey or enjoy it on your way to **San Francisco** (where you're presumably flying out on **Day 14**). However, we recommend spending the night at Santa Cruz so that you can enjoy the neon-lit rides and lively arcades after dark, which is especially fun in summer.

Only a half-hour or so from Santa Cruz, **San Jose** makes the perfect departure point for your homebound flight on **Day 14.**

Itinerary #2

Fly into **San Francisco** on **Day 1.** The City by the Bay has plenty of kid appeal — in fact, more than enough to occupy **Day 2** and **Day 3.** Chapter 9 can help you formulate a sightseeing plan.

On **Day 4,** drive to **Yosemite National Park.** It's an ideal place for kids to learn about and enjoy the natural world on **Day 5** and **Day 6.** (If the weather's warm, consider staying in the tent cabins, which offer both creature comforts and a kid-friendly resemblance to camping.)

On **Day 7,** head back to the coast, basing yourself in **Monterey** or **Santa Cruz** on **Day 8** and **Day 9** for area exploring.

Drive south on **Day 10,** spending the night in **Solvang.** If you choose to spend the day at L.A.'s **Universal Studios,** leave this mini-Denmark early on **Day 11.**

The distance from Monterey all the way to L.A. is one heckuva drive, so if you'd like to wake up in L.A. on the morning of **Day 11,** we recommend departing **Monterey** or **Santa Cruz** on the afternoon of **Day 9** and basing yourself in the **Hearst Castle** area before heading south on **Day 10.** In fact, you'll even have time to catch a castle tour in the morning before you set out, if you wish.

Head to **Anaheim** on the evening of **Day 11** to spend **Day 12** at **Disneyland** (see Chapter 22).

Depart Anaheim early in the day on **Day 13** to make the hour's drive south to **San Diego** with plenty of time to enjoy **LEGOLAND,** the **San Diego Zoo,** the **Wild Animal Park,** or **Sea World** — pick one for your pleasure. Schedule a late flight out on **Day 14** to finish up at another park — and the kids will sleep on the way home like the angels they are.

If you'd like to spend more time in San Diego without adding another day to your trip, consider cutting back a day in San Francisco; leave the city on the afternoon of **Day 3,** arriving at **Yosemite** in time for dinner.

California in Two Weeks — for Nature Lovers

The first two nature-loving itineraries start from Los Angeles. The third uses San Francisco as its take-off point.

Itinerary #1

Fly into **Los Angeles** on **Day 1** — and leave immediately. Drive two hours east to discover the desert beauty of **Palm Springs** (see Chapter 24). (Or avoid the couple hours' drive by flying directly into Palm Springs.) Spend **Day 2** exploring wild, fascinating, untrammeled **Joshua Tree National Park** (see Chapter 24), an excursion that should take the entire day.

Spend the morning of **Day 3** lazing by the pool. After lunch, head out of Palm Springs, skirting L.A. again as you head northwest to **Santa Barbara** (see Chapter 20).

If you're traveling on a weekday, make sure you pass through L.A. before 3 p.m. to avoid getting stuck in rush-hour traffic.

Spend **Day 4** relaxing in the lovely beach town of Santa Barbara, then head to **Big Sur** (see Chapter 17) on **Day 5.** We highly recommend spending at least one night here among the trees, so that you can enjoy this spectacular coast on **Day 6,** too.

On **Day 7,** head to the **Monterey Peninsula** (see Chapter 16), where you should park yourself in **Pacific Grove** for the best outdoors experience today and on **Day 8.**

On **Day 9,** make the drive to **Yosemite National Park** (see Chapter 14), and spend **Day 10** and **Day 11** exploring the park; head for the High Country if you want to avoid crowds, but be sure to dedicate a half-day to seeing the icons of Yosemite Valley first.

On **Day 12,** head north to **Lake Tahoe** (see Chapter 13). Spend **Day 13** admiring this magnificent lake. Schedule a late-day flight out of **Reno** so that you have most of **Day 14** to play, too. (Because you're coming to Tahoe to enjoy its natural beauty, the north shore is probably the better base for you.)

Itinerary #2

Fly in to **Los Angeles** on **Day 1** and get a good night's rest for the mammoth 300-mile drive to **Death Valley National Park** (see Chapter 24) on **Day 2.** Expect it to be a *looooong* driving day.

Spend **Day 3** and **Day 4** exploring the vast expanses of the park. (Consider renting a four-wheel-drive if you want to explore some of the primitive park's backcountry roads.)

On **Day 5,** drive out of Death Valley on the western side and take the I-395 route north to the east (Tioga Pass) entrance of **Yosemite National Park** (see Chapter 14). Again, plan on another very full day of driving. Spend **Day 6** and **Day 7** exploring the park.

You can enter Yosemite only through the Tioga Pass entrance between mid- or late June and the first snowfall, which usually occurs in November. Call ahead at ☎ 209-372-0200 to check road conditions if you're traveling near the beginning or end of this time frame.

On **Day 8,** drive out of the park's south entrance and head to the **Monterey Peninsula** (see Chapter 16). Make forested **Pacific Grove** your base here on **Day 8** and **Day 9** for the best outdoors experience.

On **Day 10,** head to **Big Sur** (see Chapter 17), staying to enjoy this wonderful wilderness on **Day 11** as well.

On **Day 12,** meander south along the view-endowed Pacific Coast Highway to **Santa Barbara** (see Chapter 20), one of the most naturally blessed towns in America; it's a good place to rest up on **Day 13** for the flight home from Los Angeles's LAX airport on **Day 14.**

Chapter 4

Planning Your Budget

● ●

In This Chapter

▶ Adding up the elements: transportation, lodging, dining, and sightseeing

▶ Using AAA membership to your advantage

▶ Getting cost-cutting tips for wallet-watchers

● ●

"So — how much is this trip going to cost me, anyway?"

The question is a reasonable one, no matter where your budget sits on the spending ladder. A vacation is a considerable endeavor, with costs that can add up before you know it — especially if you're traveling with kids, when expensive admission tickets and pricier-than-you-thought meals can multiply the damage in the blink of an eye. Therefore, knowing what to expect before you go makes sense.

Adding Up the Elements of Your Trip

The good news is that structuring a California trip to suit any budget is relatively easy. Sure, you can rub elbows with high-profile celebs or dot-com millionaires by choosing to stay at ultra-luxurious resorts and dine at elegant restaurants, but you don't have to; plenty of affordable choices exist in every destination for those of you with less to spend. Sure, you can spend tons of money at many excellent high-ticket attractions, from the **Monterey Bay Aquarium** to **Disneyland** — but pursuing such pleasures as a stroll on the beach or a mountain hike carries no admission price whatsoever. The budget worksheets at the back of this book will help you figure out where your money's going to go and what you can afford to do.

Totaling transportation costs

Most visitors to California fly in and rent a car to get around this mammoth state. The following sections will help you budget enough for comfortable transportation wherever you want to go.

What things cost in San Francisco

An average latte in North Beach	$2.50
Shuttle from SFO to any hotel	$12–$15 (plus tip)
Taxi from SFO to city center	$35 (plus tip)
One-way Muni/bus fare to any destination within the city (adult)	$1
Ferry ride and admission to Alcatraz	$13
Admission to Exploratorium	$10
A stroll across the Golden Gate Bridge	free!
Luxury room for two at the Huntington	$310–$455
Romantic room for two at Petite Auberge	$150–$245
Budget room for two at the Marina Inn	$65–$135
Dinner for two at Boulevard (with wine)	$150
Dinner for two at Grand Cafe (with wine)	$70
Dinner for two at Chow	$36
A 12 oz. microbrew at The Blue Lamp	$3.50
A tall martini at Top of the Mark	$9.50
Theater ticket for Beach Blanket Babylon	$25–$62

Airfare

Airfare is going to be one of your two big-ticket items (the other is lodging). Predicting airfares is almost impossible, because they can fall to new lows or go through the roof at the drop of a hat. We can tell you, however, that California's main airports — San Francisco, Los Angeles, and San Diego — tend to get so much air traffic (and therefore generate so much competition) that airfares are usually lower than if you're flying into less competitive markets.

Don't quote us on this because prices can always vary, but expect to pay in the neighborhood of $400 to $600 per person for a coast-to-coast flight. You'll pay less if you plan well in advance, stay over on a Saturday night, or get lucky and catch a fare sale; see Chapter 6 for tips on getting the best airfare.

Thanks to Southwest Airlines, prices on air routes within California are usually quite reasonable. At press time, the advance-purchase fare between Oakland and San Diego was just $73 one-way.

Car rentals

Rental cars are relatively cheap in the Driving State. You can often get a compact car for between $100 and $200 a week, depending on your dates and where you pick up your car (Southern California rentals are usually cheaper). If you want a vehicle meant to haul your family, expect to pay more like $200 to $300 a week — frankly, still quite reasonable.

Do yourself a favor and book a rental car with unlimited mileage. You'll be doing a lot of driving as you travel within California, and you don't want to end up paying for your rental on a per-mile basis — you'll end up on the short end of this stick. Luckily, most of the major car-rental companies rent on an unlimited-miles basis, but be sure to confirm this policy when you book.

And because you'll probably cover a good deal of ground, don't forget to factor in gas, which at press time was hovering around $1.69 a gallon (in California prices vary hugely in different parts of the state!). Parking is another cost factor, especially in the cities; play it safe and budget $10 a day, more if you're spending lots of time in the cities. Also remember to account for any additional insurance costs.

For further details on renting a car in California, see Chapter 7.

Paying for lodging

California has a wealth of luxury hotels and resorts, but it also offers plenty of affordable choices. The cities specialize in business- and tourist-oriented hotels, while the smaller destinations feature standard hotels, bed-and-breakfast inns, and motels, plus destination resorts in some locales. We've recommended a range of choices in each of the destinations covered in this book so that everyone has suitable options, no matter what your needs or budget.

In the destination chapters in this book, you see that a number of dollar signs, ranging from one ($) to five ($$$$$), follows each hotel name. These dollar signs represent the median price for a double room per night, as follows:

Symbol	Meaning
$	Super-cheap — less than $75 per night
$$	Still affordable — $75 to $150
$$$	Moderate — $150 to $225
$$$$	Expensive but not ridiculous — $225 to $300
$$$$$	Ultra-luxurious — more than $300 per night

In general, you'll find that if you budget between $100 and $175 to spend per night, you'll be able to balance your costs. Make economical choices in the more affordable locations so that you can comfortably handle any pricier destinations down the road, like Carmel. Staying cheap when possible will make digging a little deeper into your pockets later on easier to bear.

So that you don't encounter any unwanted surprises at payment time, be sure to account for the taxes that will be added to your final bill. The base hotel tax is 10%, but some municipalities add an additional surcharge, bringing taxes as high as 17% in some cities. We note the taxes you can expect to pay in the hotel section of each destination chapter.

Dining with dollars

California prides itself on its culinary prowess — but prepare yourself, because dining out tends to be rather expensive, especially in tourist-targeted destinations like the Wine Country. Main courses can run from $12 to $22 on the average dinner menu. Throughout the destination chapters of this book, however, we make an effort to recommend a range of choices in every destination so that you have options, no matter what your needs or budget.

In the destination chapters, a number of dollar signs, ranging from one ($) to five ($$$$$), follows each restaurant name. The dollar signs are meant to give you an idea of what a complete dinner for one person — including appetizer, main course, one drink, tax, and tip — will likely set you back. The price categories go like this:

Symbol	Meaning
$	Cheap eats — less than $15 per person
$$	Still inexpensive — $15 to $25
$$$	Moderate — $25 to $40
$$$$	Pricey — $40 to $70
$$$$$	Ultra-expensive — more than $70 per person

Of course, just about any menu has a range of prices, and the final tally depends on how you order. The wine or bar tab is more likely to jack up the bill quicker than anything else; desserts also add to the total.

Saving on sightseeing and activities

Sightseeing admission charges and other activity fees can add up quickly, especially if you're traveling with kids. Of course, how much you spend depends on what you want to do. If you're traveling to California largely to discover its scenic towns and natural wonders, you won't have to budget much for sightseeing. Admission to national and state parks is minimal, and activities like hiking, picnicking, and beachcombing are absolutely free (except for the cost of refreshments). Even bike and kayak rentals are inexpensive.

But if you're planning to visit the big-name sightseeing attractions — especially the theme parks — know what your budget can handle. These destinations can be expensive: Expect to pay about $41 per person just to get in the door at **Disneyland,** the same at **Universal Studios,** $39 at **Sea World,** $18 at the **San Diego Zoo,** and $18 at the **Monterey Bay Aquarium.** (Needless to say, the Southern California theme park loop mentioned in Chapter 3 won't be cheap.) Admission is slightly cheaper for kids — but don't worry, they'll find plenty of ways to spend the difference and then some.

Beware, golfers — tee times at California's top courses don't come cheap, either.

In the destination chapters in this book, we tell you how much you can expect to pay for admission fees and activities so that you can budget your sightseeing money realistically.

What things cost in Santa Barbara

An average cup of coffee	$1.25
A ride aboard the Downtown-Waterfront Shuttle	25¢
Surrey for two, 2-hour rental	$15
Guided Tour aboard Old Town Trolley	$10
Admission to Santa Barbara Museum of Art	$5
A day at the beach	free!
Strolling State Street	free! (plus shopping budget, of course)
Luxury room for two at the Four Seasons	$280–$550
Romantic room for two at the Bath Street Inn	$110–$170
Budget room for two at first-ever Motel 6	$61–$91
Dinner for two at the Wine Cask (with wine)	$125
Dinner for two at Brophy Bros. (with beer)	$50
Dinner for two at La Super-Rica (with tacos)	$12–$15
Ticket for summer-stock theater production in nearby Solvang	$18–$20

Allotting funds for shopping and entertainment

Shopping is a huge temptation in California. Many of the state's finest small towns are rich in unique boutiques and other shopping opportunities. We dare you to escape the Napa Valley (see Chapter 10) without spending money on wine or other goodies. But places like Mendocino (see Chapter 11) and Carmel (see Chapter 16) are so pleasant just to stroll through that, if your budget's tight, you won't suffer if you limit yourself to window-shopping while you're there.

Don't blow a wad at the theme-park souvenir stands. Anything you buy at **Disneyland** is available at your local mall's Disney Store. And your teenager doesn't need another **Hard Rock Cafe** T-shirt. Save your dough for something special — a one-of-a-kind souvenir that will recall vivid memories of happy vacation times. Or a really good pair of shoes, at least.

The cities are loaded with nightlife and entertainment options. You can spend a hundred bucks on a pair of theater tickets or nurse a couple of $3 beers in a friendly bar all night — the choice is entirely up to you and your wallet. Outside of the cities, California tends to be quiet after dark, although college towns like Santa Barbara and resort destinations like Palm Springs are exceptions.

Keeping a Lid on Expenses

We don't care how much money you have, but we do know that you don't want to spend more than you have to. In this section, we help you rein in your expenses before they get out of control.

Getting the best airfare

This is such a huge topic that we've dedicated the better part of a chapter to it. Before you even start scanning for fares, see Chapter 6 (also see Chapter 7 if you're interested in traveling *within* California by plane).

Booking accommodations — and avoiding the rack-rate scam

The *rack rate* is the equivalent of the suggested retail price for your hotel room. Don't be unduly alarmed by the prices listed for some of the hotels — many a $300 hotel never charges $300 a night for a room. The best way to avoid paying the full rack rate when booking your hotels is stunningly simple: *Just ask for a cheaper or discounted rate.* You may be pleasantly surprised. But you have to take the initiative and ask, because no one is going to volunteer to save you money.

Here are some other potentially money-saving tips:

- ✔ **Always mention membership in AAA, AARP, or frequent flier/ traveler programs.** You may also qualify for corporate, student, military, or senior discounts.

- ✔ **Call the hotel directly and also call the central reservations 800-number.** We've found that it's worth the extra pennies to make both calls and see which one gives you the better deal. Sometimes the local reservationist knows about special deals or packages, but the hotel may neglect to tell the central booking line. We think it's especially important to phone the hotel directly if you have questions about room configurations and amenities. The nice folks manning the phones at central reservations don't actually know anything more about the individual hotels than what they may have read on a brochure. For the most accurate information, talk to the reservations manager at the hotel.

- ✔ **Consult a reliable travel agent.** Even if you've already booked your own airfare, you may find that a travel agent can negotiate a better price with certain hotels than you can get on your own. For more advice on the pros and cons of using an agent, see Chapter 6.

- ✔ **Bed-and-breakfast inns are generally nonnegotiable on price.** However, always ask if a price break is available midweek or during the off-season; in fact, you'll find that many B&Bs publish discounted midweek and off-season rates.

Keep your eyes posted for the Bargain Alert icon as you read this book. This icon highlights money-saving opportunities and especially good values throughout the Golden State.

- ✔ **Travel midweek to popular weekending destinations.** Rates to destinations like the Wine Country, Carmel, the Hearst Castle area, Solvang, and Santa Barbara are at their highest on the weekends. Schedule your visits to the cities on weekends, when business travelers abandon San Francisco, L.A., and San Diego hotels, leaving them open to bargain-hunting vacationers.

- ✔ **Check the hotel listings in this book.** In the destination chapters, we note the types of discounts that each hotel, inn, or motel tends to offer. We can't guarantee what discounts may apply when you reserve, of course, but these tips should give you a heads up on the kinds of special deals or discounted rates to ask for when you book.

- ✔ **Remember that summer, from June through mid-September, is the busy season.** If you haven't decided on a travel time yet, *consider the off-seasons,* which are not only cheaper and less crowded but often more pleasant, weather-wise. See Chapter 2 for lots of helpful guidance.

Taking the AAA advantage

If you aren't already a member, consider taking a few minutes to join the **American Automobile Association (AAA)** before you launch your California vacation. Unfamiliar roads, unpredictable drivers, unforeseen circumstances (a flat that needs fixing, a battery that needs jump-starting), and unexplainable moments of stupidity (hello, lockout!) are just a few of the reasons for hooking into the club's roadside-assistance network before you leave home.

But AAA membership offers much more than the occasional roadside rescue. Membership can save you money on hotel rates and admission to attractions throughout California (and other locations). Also included in the annual dues are a mind-boggling array of travel-related and general lifestyle services, as well as comprehensive maps. The *AAA Travel Agency* can help you book air, hotel, and car arrangements as well as all-inclusive tour packages — and the staff will always let you know when a AAA member discount is available. American Express traveler's checks are available to members at no charge (see Chapter 8 for more information on traveler's checks).

To find the AAA office nearest you, log on to www.aaa.com, where you'll be linked to your regional club's home page after you enter your home zip code. You can get instant membership by calling the national 24-hour emergency roadside service number (☎ **800-AAA-HELP**), which can connect you to any regional membership department during expanded business hours (only roadside assistance operates 24 hours a day). If you live in Canada, the **Canadian Automobile Association** (www.caa.com) offers similar services (plus reciprocal benefits with AAA).

Bargains from American Express

American Express offers its cardholders a surprisingly good array of discounts at local and national vendors via its Online Zone program (previously called Online Extras). By registering your Amex card with this free program, you can receive discounts — often 20% — from airlines, hotel chains, rental car companies, restaurants, and shops throughout California and the country (even in your hometown), as well as with a good number of online merchants.

Participants change constantly, but the list is usually extensive. American Express is good about keeping these offers current, but be sure to check the expiration dates as well as the terms and conditions carefully. Note that some offers require you to register your American Express card with the Offer Zone program to qualify. Sign up at www.americanexpress.com; click on Offer Zone on the home page.

Chapter 5

Planning Ahead for Special Travel Needs

. . . .

In This Chapter

▶ Taking the kids along

▶ Going to the Golden State in your golden years

▶ Dealing with disabilities

▶ Traveling tips for gays and lesbians

▶ Finding help when you're traveling from abroad

. . . .

G enerally speaking, California is a forward-thinking state, and plenty accommodating if you have special requirements. But you may want to know more, specifically: How welcoming will California be to you and . . . (pick one or more)

   ✔ Your kids

   ✔ Your senior status

   ✔ Your disability

   ✔ Your same-sex partner

If you need answers, you've come to the right chapter.

Vacationing with Kids

With its wealth of parks — both the theme kind, à la Disneyland, and the natural kind, à la Yosemite — California is the ultimate family-vacation state. Knowing on which side its bread is buttered, the Golden State offers a wealth of family-friendly hotels — from luxury resorts to budget motels — restaurants, and other activities. We note the best kid-friendly spots throughout this book.

Some destinations suit families better than do others. Skip romantic Carmel, for example, and head for kid-friendly Monterey. Your kids will probably prefer San Diego over Palm Springs, if you have to choose. Still, families are as individual as snowflakes, and no single blueprint exists for the ultimate family vacation.

Your vacation will go well if you remember to tailor your trip around the things you and your kids like to do. Check out the itineraries in Chapter 3, a number of which take family travel into consideration.

Following are a few tips to help you with your family travel plans:

- **Don't be too ambitious.** We can't say this too strongly: Too much time spent in the car moving from one place to another will result in a trip from hell — for both you and the kids.

- **Take it slow at the start.** Give the entire family time to adjust to a new time zone or to just being on the road. The best way to do this is to budget a couple/few days in your initial destination that don't require strict itineraries or lots of moving around.

- **Look for the Kid Friendly icon as you flip through this book.** We use it to highlight hotels, restaurants, and attractions that your family will find particularly welcoming. Zeroing in on these listings helps you plan your trip more efficiently.

- **Bring plenty of road-trip supplies.** Bring healthy snacks, car-friendly books and games, and a pillow and blanket for naptime. Books on tape are great for entertaining the entire family.

- **Book some private time for mom and dad.** Most hotels can hook you up with a reliable babysitter who will entertain the kids while you enjoy a romantic dinner or another adults-only activity. Ask about babysitting services when you make your reservations.

The following are excellent resources for advice on family travel:

- **BabyCenter** (www.babycenter.com/travel) has good advice for planning baby's first trip and for traveling while pregnant.

- **Family.com** (www.family.com) features a travel page with both general and destination-specific advice (albeit with a Disney slant, because Family.com is part of the ABC/Disney Go network).

- **Family Travel Files** (www.familytravelfiles.com) is a comprehensive Web site dedicated to the subject of family travel featuring both general and destination-specific advice.

- **Family Travel Times** is an excellent Web site, covering all aspects of family travel. The site is updated twice a month with free information and articles; archived articles can only be accessed by subscribers. Subscriptions are $39 a year. You can subscribe online at www.familytraveltimes.com, or by calling ☎ **888-822-4388** or 212-477-5524.

Touring California as a Senior

One of the benefits of age is that travel often costs less. Many hotels and airlines give discounted rates to senior travelers, although the minimum age requirement can vary between 55 and 65. Ditto for Amtrak, many public transit systems, museums, attractions, and even theater performances. Always bring an ID card, especially if you've kept your youthful glow, and don't be shy about asking.

If you're not a member of **AARP** (formerly the American Association of Retired Persons), 601 E St. NW, Washington, DC 20049 (☎ **800-424-3410,** 800-303-4222, or 202-434-AARP; www.aarp.org), do yourself a favor and join. Members qualify for discounts of up to 25% on airfares, hotels, car rentals, and vacation packages. Membership also includes a monthly magazine and newsletter and special rates on insurance, prescriptions, and more. For just $8 a year, with all the associated benefits, you can't afford not to sign up.

A variety of intriguing and entertaining senior study trips are offered by the **Center for Studies of the Future,** a local affiliate of **Elderhostel** (☎ **877-426-8056;** www.elderhostel.org), the well-known nonprofit organization that arranges study programs for those aged 55 and over (and a spouse or companion of any age) in the United States and in more than 80 countries around the world. Most courses last five to seven days and may include airfare, accommodations in hotels or university dormitories (during the summer), meals, and tuition.

Grand Circle Travel (☎ **800-221-2610** or 617-350-7500; www.gct.com) offers package deals for the 50-plus market, mostly of the tour-bus variety, with free trips thrown in if you organize a group of ten or more.

Traveling with a Disability

These days, a disability shouldn't stop anyone from traveling. The Americans with Disabilities Act (ADA) requires that all public buildings be wheelchair accessible and have accessible restrooms. Most hotels and sightseeing attractions (except those grandfathered by landmark status) are outfitted with wheelchair ramps and extra-wide doorways and halls. Many city sidewalk corners have dropped curbs, and some public transit systems are equipped with lifts. Your best bet is to contact local visitor bureaus, because they can provide you with all the specifics on accessibility in their locale; see "Gathering More Information" at the end of each destination chapter.

Because so many of California's hotels are on the newer side, a good number feature rooms dedicated to the needs of disabled travelers, outfitted with everything from extra-large bathrooms with low-set fixtures to fire-alarm systems adapted for deaf travelers. Still, before you book a hotel room, ask lots of questions based on your needs. After you arrive, always call restaurants, attractions, and theaters before you go to make sure they are fully accessible.

These resources provide excellent information on accessible travel:

✔ Disabled travelers can get more general information from the **Society for Accessible Travel and Hospitality** (☎ 212-447-7284; Fax 212-725-8253; www.sath.org), which offers a wealth of travel resources for all types of disabilities and informed recommendations on destinations, access guides, travel agents, tour operators, vehicle rentals, and companion services. Annual membership costs $45 for adults; $30 for seniors and students.

✔ **The American Foundation for the Blind** (☎ 800-232-5463; www.afb.org) provides information on traveling with a Seeing Eye dog.

✔ **The Moss Rehab Hospital** (☎ 215-456-9603; www.mossresource net.org) provides friendly, helpful phone assistance to all disabled travelers through its **Travel Information Service.**

✔ For customized tours, **Flying Wheels Travel** (☎ 800-535-6790; www.flyingwheelstravel.com) offers escorted tours and cruises that emphasize sports and private tours in minivans with lifts.

✔ **Mobility International USA** (☎ 541-343-1284; www.miusa.org) publishes *A World of Options,* a 658-page book of resources, covering everything from biking trips to scuba outfitters, plus a biannual newsletter, *Over the Rainbow.* Annual membership is $35.

✔ **Accessible San Diego** (☎ 858-279-0704; www.accessandiego.com), the nation's first not-for-profit information center for travelers with disabilities, offers complete information on accessibility issues in San Diego, as well as an *Access in San Diego* travel guide that you can order for $5.

✔ If you'd like to drive yourself around, keep in mind that many of the big car-rental companies — including **Avis** (☎ 800-230-4898; www.avis.com), **Hertz** (☎ 800-654-3131; www.hertz.com), and **National** (☎ 800-227-7368; www.nationalcar.com) — rent *hand-controlled cars* for disabled drivers at major airport locations throughout California.

Getting Advice as a Gay or Lesbian Traveler

In the Golden State, homosexuality is squarely in the mainstream, especially in the cities. San Francisco is a mecca for gays, with Los Angeles running neck-and-neck with New York for a close second as gay-friendliest city in the United States. Even relatively conservative San Diego has a huge gay contingent (the Hillcrest neighborhood is the base). Palm Springs is hugely popular with gay travelers, but, by and large, the entire state is welcoming to gays and lesbians.

If you want help planning your trip, **IGLTA,** the **International Gay & Lesbian Travel Association** (☎ **800-448-8550** or 954-776-2626; www. iglta.org), is your best source. IGLTA can link you up with the appropriate gay-friendly service organization or agent. Members are kept informed of gay and gay-friendly hoteliers, tour operators, and airline representatives. The IGLTA site will link you to other useful sites that can also help you plan your California vacation.

Out and About (☎ **800-929-2268** or 212-645-6922; www.outandabout. com) offers a monthly newsletter packed with good information on the global gay and lesbian scene. You can find *Out and About* guidebooks at most major bookstores, but the Web site alone is a first-rate resource.

Exploring California as a Foreigner

The U.S. State Department has a **Visa Waiver Program** allowing citizens of about 30 countries — including Australia, New Zealand, and the United Kingdom — to enter the United States without a visa for stays of up to 90 days. If you're a citizen of one of these countries, you need only a valid passport and a round-trip air ticket upon arrival.

If you're a citizen of a country not included in the Waiver Program, you must have both a *valid passport* that expires at least six months later than the scheduled end of your visit to the United States and a tourist visa, which you can get without charge from any U.S. consulate.

For a quick and easy update on current passport and visa issues, plug into the U.S. State Department's Internet site at www.state.gov. You can get more information from any U.S. embassy or consulate. Always check for the latest before you leave home.

You're not allowed to bring foodstuffs and plants into the United States. You may bring in or take out up to $10,000 in U.S. or foreign currency with no formalities; larger sums must be declared to U.S. Customs upon entering or leaving. For more information regarding U.S. Customs, call your nearest U.S. embassy or consulate, or contact the U.S. Customs at ☎ 202-927-1770 or www.customs.ustreas.gov.

The United States recognizes most foreign driver's licenses, but you may want to get an international driver's license if your home license isn't written in English.

Part II
Ironing Out the Details

Just for the record, it was your idea to book the Yoga/Meditation package tour to California.

In this part . . .

In this part, we discuss all of your travel options: choosing a method of transportation, working with a travel agent, and deciding whether to go the package-tour route or not. This part also helps you finalize those little last-minute details, like making dinner reservations at hot local restaurants, packing the right clothes, and weighing your travel-insurance options. No glamour here — but all necessary.

Chapter 6

Getting to California

• •

In This Chapter

▶ Making your own travel plans versus using a travel agent

▶ Taking advantage of a package deal or going on a guided tour

▶ Arriving in California by plane, train, or automobile

• •

*G*etting there may not *really* be half the fun, but it's a necessary step and a big part of the planning process. Should you use a travel agent or go the independent route? Should you book a package deal or book the elements of your vacation separately?

In this chapter, we give you the information you need to decide what's right for you.

Deciding Whether to Use a Travel Agent

The best way to find a good travel agent is the same way you locate a good plumber or mechanic or doctor — through word of mouth.

Any travel agent can help you find a bargain airfare, hotel, or rental car. A good travel agent will stop you from ruining your vacation by trying to save a few dollars. The best travel agents can tell you how much time you should budget for a destination, find you a cheap flight that doesn't require changing planes in Atlanta and Chicago, get you a better hotel room than you can find on your own for about the same price, arrange for a competitively priced rental car, and even give recommendations on restaurants.

To get the most out of your travel agent, first do a little homework:

> ✔ Read up on your destination (you've already made a sound decision by buying this book) and pick out some accommodations and attractions you think you'd like.

✔ If you want even more recommendations, check out *Frommer's California* (also published by Wiley Publishing, Inc.), a comprehensive guidebook that goes beyond the best sites to include just about every place you can think of to go.

✔ If you have access to the Internet, check prices on the Web in advance (see "Finding the Best Airfare," later in this chapter, for ideas on getting a ballpark sense of costs).

Then take your guidebook and Web information to a travel agent and ask him or her to make the arrangements for you. Because travel agents can access more resources than even the most complete Web travel site, yours should be able to get you a better price than you can get yourself. They can also issue your tickets and vouchers right on the spot. If they can't get you into the hotel of your choice, your agent can recommend an alternative, and you can look for an objective review in your guidebook.

In the past few years, some airlines and resorts have begun limiting or eliminating travel agent commissions altogether. The immediate result has been that travel agents don't bother booking these services unless the customer specifically requests them. But some travel industry analysts predict that if other airlines and accommodations follow suit, travel agents will have to start charging customers for their services.

Finding a travel agent you can trust

Here are a few hints for tracking down the travel agent of your dreams.

✔ **Ask friends.** Your best bet, of course, is a personal referral. If you have friends or relatives who have a travel agent they're happy with, start there. Not only is this agent a relatively proven commodity already, but she's extra-likely to treat you well, knowing she'll lose two customers — not just one — if she screws up your vacation.

✔ **Go with what you know.** If you're pleased with the service you get from the agency that books business travel at your workplace, ask if it also books personal travel. Again, here's another relatively proven commodity — one that has a vested interest in not screwing up. Also, because business travel tends to be booked in volume, a lot of the agencies that specialize in this kind of business act as consolidators for certain airlines or have access to other discounts that they can extend to you for your personal travel.

✔ **Go to the travel agent source.** If you can't get a good personal or business referral, contact the **American Society of Travel Agents** (www.astanet.com), the world's largest association of travel professionals, which can refer you to one of its local member agents.

ASTA asks that all its member agents uphold a code of ethics and has its own consumer affairs department to handle complaints and help travelers mediate disputes with ASTA member agencies. This doesn't guarantee that you'll get an agent you're thrilled with, but it's a giant step in the right direction and offers you a measure of consumer protection in case something goes wrong.

Choosing a travel agent

✔ Look for an agent who specializes in planning vacations to your destination.

✔ Choose an agent who has been in business a while and has an established client base.

✔ Consider everything about the agent, from the appearance of his or her office to the agent's willingness to listen and answer questions.

Remember that the best agents want to establish a long-term relationship with a client, not just make one sale.

Choosing a Package Tour

Package tours aren't the same thing as escorted tours. They're a way to buy your airfare, accommodations, and other elements of your trip, including car rentals, airport transfers, and even some activities, at the same time — kind of like one-stop shopping.

Package tours do have their advantages — someone else does most of the arranging for you, and you almost always save money. But among the disadvantages are limited choices, such as where you stay (the hotels will be fine but unremarkable and are usually located more for the tour company's convenience than yours), or a fixed itinerary that doesn't allow for an extra day of shopping. Some packages offer a better class of hotels than others. Some even offer the same hotels for lower prices than their competitors.

Some tour companies offer flights on scheduled airlines, while others book charters. In some packages, your choices of travel days may be limited. Some packages let you choose between escorted vacations and independent vacations; others allow you to add on a few guided excursions or escorted day trips (also at prices lower than if you booked them yourself) without booking an entirely escorted tour.

Which package is right for you depends entirely on what you want; the time you spend shopping around will be well rewarded.

Separating the deals from the duds

Once you start looking at packages, you're going to find that the sheer number of choices may overwhelm you — but don't let them. Use these tips to help you distinguish one from the other and figure out the right package for you.

✔ **Read this guide.** Do a little homework. Decide what cities, towns, and attractions you want to visit and pick the type of accommodations you think you'll like. Compare the rack rates we list in the destination chapters against the discounted rates being offered by the packagers to see whether you're actually being given a substantial savings or they've just gussied up the rack rates to make the full-fare offer sound like a deal. And remember: Don't just compare packagers; compare the prices that packagers are offering on similar itineraries. The amount you save depends on the deal; most tour packagers can offer bigger savings on some packages than others.

✔ **Read the fine print.** When you're comparing packages, you don't want to be comparing apples and oranges. Make sure you know exactly what's included in the price you're being quoted — and what's not. Don't assume anything: Some packagers include everything but the kitchen sink — including lots of extra discounts on restaurants and activities — while others don't even include airfare. (Tour packagers know better than anybody how fares can fluctuate, and some don't want to get locked into a yearlong airfare promise.)

✔ **Know what you're getting yourself into — and whether you can get yourself out of it.** Before you commit to a package, make sure you know how much flexibility you have. Some packagers require ironclad commitments, while others go with the flow, perhaps charging minimal fees for changes or cancellations. Ask the right questions: What's the cancellation policy if my kid gets sick at the last minute and we can't go? What if the office calls me home three days into my vacation? What if we have to adjust our vacation schedule — can we do that?

✔ **Use your best judgment.** Keep your antennae up for fly-by-nights and shady packagers. If a package appears to be too good to be true, it probably is. *Go with a reputable firm with a proven track record.* This is where your travel agent can come in handy; he or she should be knowledgeable about different packagers, the deals they offer, and the general rate of satisfaction among their customers. If the agent doesn't seem savvy, take your business elsewhere.

Find the packager for you

The best place to start looking is the **travel section of your local Sunday newspaper.** Also check the ads in the back of national travel magazines like *Travel & Leisure, National Geographic Traveler,* and *Condé Nast Traveler.* Call a few package tour companies and ask them to send you their brochures. One of the largest packagers in the east is Liberty Travel (☎ 888-271-1584; www.libertytravel.com), which generally offers good-value packages, with or without air, to the most popular California destinations, including L.A., Disneyland, Palm Springs, San Diego, San Francisco, and Lake Tahoe. The company's agents are willing to help you construct a multi-destination trip.

The biggest **hotel chains** also offer packages. If you already know where you want to stay, call the hotel and ask if it offers land/air packages.

Airlines also often package flights together with accommodations. Although you can book most airline packages directly with the airline itself, your local travel agent can also do it for you. Prices are usually comparable to what you'll get from other packagers.

When you pick an airline, choose one on which you accumulate frequent-flier miles. Most airline packages reward you with miles based not only on the flight, but on all the dollars you're spending — which can really add up and earn you credit toward your next vacation.

The major airlines that offer travel packages to California include these big names:

- ✔ **Air Canada Vacations** (☎ 800-662-3221; www.aircanada vacations.com).

- ✔ **Alaska Airlines Vacations** (☎ 800-468-2248; www.alaskaair.com).

- ✔ **American Airlines Vacations** (☎ 800-321-2121; http://aav1. aavacations.com) features one of the more extensive lists of California destinations.

- ✔ **Continental Airlines Vacations** (☎ 800-634-5555; www.cool vacations.com).

- ✔ **Delta Vacations** (☎ 800-872-7786; www.deltavacations.com) just came out as the price-comparison leader among airline pack- agers in an informal poll conducted by *Condè Nast Traveler.*

- ✔ **Northwest World Vacations** (☎ 800-800-1504; www.nwaworld vacations.com).

- ✔ **Southwest Airlines Vacations** (☎ 800-423-5683; www.swa vacations.com) also offers hotel-only reservations — worth noting if your home airports isn't served by the king of the bargain airlines.

- ✔ **United Vacations** (☎ 800-328-6877; www.unitedvacations.com).

- ✔ **US Airways Vacations** (☎ 800-472-2577; www.usairways vacations.com).

If you're considering either arriving in California by train or traveling around the state by train — or both — check into the all-inclusive travel packages offered by **Amtrak Vacations** (☎ 800-654-5748; www.amtrakvacations.com).

If you're an Amex customer, consider going through **American Express Travel** (☎ 800-AXP-6898 or 800-346-3607; www.americanexpress.com/travel), which can book packages through various vendors, including Continental and Delta.

If you're heading to Disneyland, you may want to contact the official Disney travel agency, **Walt Disney Travel Co.** (☎ 800-225-2024 or 714-520-5050; www.disneyland.com). The company offers Disney-focused packages that can also include a wide range of Southern California extras, depending on your wants and needs. For more on this, see Chapter 22.

Universal Studios Vacations offers similar all-inclusive L.A. vacation deals; call ☎ 800-711-0080 or go online to www.universalstudios.com, click on Theme Parks, and then click on Plan a Trip.

The well-conceived escorted tours of California offered by **Tauck Tours** (☎ 800-788-7885; www.tauck.com) are more luxurious and less structured than your average escorted tour. They're pricey but worth the cost if you'd rather let someone else do the driving.

If you're an information junky, you may want to search www.vacation packager.com, an excruciatingly extensive Web-search engine that can link you up with an exhausting list of package-tour operators that offer California vacations. You'll have to wade through a lot of excess at this site, but doing so is the most thorough way to discover all your options.

Be advised that most travel packagers don't offer comprehensive California vacations. They tend to focus on the large-volume destinations — San Francisco, Los Angeles, San Diego, Disneyland, and sometimes Lake Tahoe and Palm Springs. If you want to hit other destinations, you'll likely have to (or have your travel agent) book those legs of your trip directly.

Still, don't give up on the package route; with a little planning, you (or your travel agent) may manage to link a few smaller packages into the good-value vacation of your dreams.

Finding the Best Airfare

If you need the flexibility to purchase your tickets at the last minute, change your itinerary at a moment's notice, or get home before the weekend, you'll pay the premium rate, known as the full fare — many business travelers fall into this category. If, on the other hand, you can book your tickets far in advance, don't mind staying over Saturday night, or are willing to travel on a Tuesday, Wednesday, or Thursday, you'll pay the least, usually a fraction of the full fare. On most flights to California, even the shortest hops, the full fare is more than $1,000, but a 7-day or 14-day advance purchase ticket is often half that, and even less. Obviously, we can't guess what the fares will be when you book, but you can almost always save big by planning ahead.

The airlines also periodically hold sales, in which they lower the prices on their most popular routes. These fares carry advance-purchase requirements and date-of-travel restrictions, but you usually can't beat the price: sometimes no more than $400 for a cross-country flight (less on some discount airlines). Keep your eyes open for these sales, which are advertised in the newspapers, on the Internet, and sometimes on TV, as you're planning your vacation. The sales tend to take place in seasons of low travel volume. You'll almost never see a sale around the peak summer vacation months of July and August, or around Thanksgiving or Christmas.

All of the following airlines fly to all major California airports:

- **Air Canada:** ☎ 888-247-2262; www.aircanada.ca
- **Alaska Airlines:** ☎ 800-252-7522; www.alaskaair.com
- **America West:** ☎ 800-235-9292; www.americawest.com
- **American:** ☎ 800-433-7300; www.aa.com
- **Continental:** ☎ 800-525-0280; www.continental.com
- **Delta:** ☎ 800-221-1212; www.delta.com
- **Northwest:** ☎ 800-225-2525; www.nwa.com
- **Southwest:** ☎ 800-435-9792; www.southwest.com
- **TWA:** ☎ 800-221-2000; www.twa.com
- **United:** ☎ 800-241-6522; www.united.com
- **US Airways:** ☎ 800-428-4322; www.usairways.com

Using consolidators

Consolidators, also known as bucket shops, are a good place to check for the lowest fares. Their prices are much better than the fares you can get yourself and are often even lower than what your travel agent can get you. You can see consolidators ads in the small boxes at the bottom of the page in your Sunday travel section. Some of the most reliable consolidators include:

- **The TravelHub** (☎ 888-AIR-FARE; www.travelhub.com)
- **1-800-FLY-CHEAP** (☎ 800-359-2432; www.1800flycheap.com)
- **TFI Tours International** (☎ 800-745-8000; www.lowestprice.com)

Another good choice, **Council Travel** (☎ 800-226-8624; www.council travel.com), caters to young travelers, but their bargain-basement prices are available to people of all ages.

Booking your ticket online

The benefits of researching your trip online can be well worth the effort. Often airlines will offer discounts on fares or incentives like extra frequent-flier miles just for booking online. **Last-minute specials,** such as weekend deals or Internet-only fares, are also offered by airlines to fill empty seats. Most of these are announced on Tuesday or Wednesday and must be purchased online. They are only valid for travel that weekend, but some can be booked weeks or months in advance. Sign up for weekly e-mail alerts at airline Web sites or check mega-sites that compile comprehensive lists of last-minute specials, such as **Smarter Living** (http://smarterliving.com) or **WebFlyer** (www.webflyer.com).

Some sites send you **e-mail notification** when a cheap fare becomes available to your favorite destination. Some also tell you when fares to a particular destination are lowest. **Travelocity** (www.travelocity.com or www.frommers.travelocity.com) and **Expedia** (www.expedia.com) are among the most popular sites, each offering an excellent range of options. Travelers search by destination, dates, and cost. **Orbitz** (www.orbitz.com) is a popular site launched by United, Delta, Northwest, American, and Continental airlines. **Priceline** (www.priceline.com) lets you name your price for airline tickets, hotel rooms, and rental cars. For airline tickets, you can't say what time you want to fly — you have to accept any flight between 6 a.m. and 10 p.m. on the dates you've selected, and you may have to make one or more stopovers. Tickets are nonrefundable, and no frequent-flier miles are awarded.

Landing an airport

The major California airports include:

- ✔ **San Francisco International Airport (SFO),** 14 miles south of downtown San Francisco via U.S. 101 (☎ **650-875-8575;** www.flysfo.com)

- ✔ **Sacramento International Airport,** north of downtown Sacramento on Interstate 5, just past the junction with Highway 99 (☎ **916-929-5411;** airports.co.sacramento.ca.us/index.htm)

- ✔ **San Jose International Airport,** gateway to the Silicon Valley, just north of the U.S. 101/I-880/Highway 17 junction, at the intersection of U.S. 101 and Highway 87 (☎ **408-501-7600;** www.sjc.org)

- ✔ **Los Angeles International Airport (LAX),** at the intersection of the 405 and 105 freeways, 9½ miles south of Santa Monica and 16 miles southwest of Hollywood (☎ **310-646-5252;** www.lawa.org)

> ✔ **San Diego International Airport,** locally known as Lindbergh Field, on Interstate 5 right in the heart of San Diego (☎ **619-231-7361;** www.portofsandiego.org)

Chances are good that one of the five major airports listed will serve as your gateway. In addition, major carriers also serve good-size or smaller airports in Oakland, just across the bay from San Francisco (see Chapter 9); in the middle of the state in Fresno, close to the southern gateway to Yosemite (see Chapter 14); in Reno, Nevada, less than an hour's drive from Lake Tahoe (see Chapter 13); on the northern Central Coast in Monterey (see Chapter 16); in Orange County, just a stone's throw from Disneyland (see Chapter 22); and in Palm Springs (see Chapter 24).

Because the Golden State is so darn big and has so many major airports, you'll need to work out a basic itinerary for yourself before you book your airline tickets. The destination chapters in this book will help you do that, as will the itineraries in Chapter 3. For more information on travel distances between airports and destinations, see Parts III, IV, and V, as well as Chapter 7.

Seriously consider flying into one California airport and leaving from another. The time you save by flying into San Diego and leaving from San Francisco, say, or flying into San Jose and departing from Palm Springs, may justify the extra airline charges and/or rental-car drop-off charges. What's more, depending on your points of arrival and departure, you may happily discover that no extra charges apply. Your best bet is to have a couple of options and price them out with the airlines and car companies (or put your travel agent to work) before you make a final decision.

Driving to California

Driving yourself to California can be a smart move, especially if you live relatively close and you'd prefer to tour the state in your own car.

The major interstates that lead into the state are:

> ✔ **I-5,** which enters California from Oregon at the northern border and runs south through the middle of the state all the way to San Diego.

> ✔ **I-80,** which arrives from the east via Reno, Nevada, and runs west through Sacramento to San Francisco.

> ✔ **I-15,** which connects Las Vegas, Nevada, with I-10 just east of Los Angeles.

> ✔ **I-40,** which runs across the northern half of the southern states, cutting through the Texas panhandle, Albuquerque, New Mexico, and Flagstaff, Arizona, before entering California in Needles, California (where Snoopy's cousin Spike is from, if you're a *Peanuts* fan) — otherwise known as the middle of nowhere — and heading west until it connects to I-15 northeast of Los Angeles.

✓ **I-10,** the most popular route into Southern California, which runs from New Orleans, Louisiana, to Los Angeles, passing through Houston, Texas, Phoenix, Arizona, and Palm Springs along the way.

✓ **I-8,** which links Tucson and Yuma, Arizona, with San Diego.

Here are some handy drive times for your road trip:

To San Francisco from:

✓ Portland, Oregon: 636 miles, 10¼ hours

✓ Reno, Nevada: 220 miles, 3¾ hours

✓ Boise, Idaho: 641 miles, 11½ hours

✓ Salt Lake City, Utah: 737 miles, 11¾ hours

✓ Las Vegas, Nevada: 574 miles, 9½ hours

To Los Angeles from:

✓ Salt Lake City, Utah: 690 miles, 11 hours

✓ Las Vegas, Nevada: 270 miles, 4½ hours

✓ Albuquerque, New Mexico: 789 miles, 12½ hours

✓ Phoenix, Arizona: 373 miles, 6¼ hours

To San Diego from:

✓ Las Vegas, Nevada: 332 miles, 5½ hours

✓ El Paso, Texas: 725 miles, 11½ hours

✓ Tucson, Arizona: 407 miles, 6½ hours

Taking the train

Amtrak (☎ **800-USA-RAIL;** www.amtrak.com) serves multiple California cities, including San Francisco, San Jose, Santa Barbara, L.A., and San Diego.

Arriving by train from another state is much slower and not significantly cheaper than traveling by plane. Therefore, explore this option only if you hate flying, saving a little money means more to you than speed of travel, or you're drawn to the romanticism of a train journey. You'll still need to rent a car to do any significant sightseeing, unless you'd prefer to travel around California by train, too; for details, see Chapter 7.

Chapter 7

Getting Around California

• •

In This Chapter

▶ Traveling around California by car (a rental or your own)

▶ Following the rules of the road

▶ Touring the Golden State by plane or train

• •

*F*orget the Golden State moniker — California is really the Driving
State. You'll need a car to get yourself around, no two ways about it.
Even if you choose to move from destination to destination using
planes and trains, you'll likely need an automobile after you get to your
destination. The only California destinations that you can both easily
reach and navigate via other means of transportation are San Francisco,
San Diego (some attractions, not all), and Santa Barbara.

Getting Around by Car

If you don't bring your own car to California, you'll probably need to
rent one. The following companies rent cars at locations throughout
California, including at all the major airports and in the cities:

- ✔ **Alamo:** ☎ **800-GO-ALAMO** (800-462-5266); www.goalamo.com

- ✔ **Avis:** ☎ **800-230-4898;** www.avis.com

- ✔ **Budget:** ☎ **800-527-0700;** https://rent.drivebudget.com

- ✔ **Dollar:** ☎ **800-800-4000;** www.dollar.com

- ✔ **Enterprise:** ☎ **800-325-8007;** www.enterprise.com

- ✔ **Hertz:** ☎ **800-654-3131;** www.hertz.com

- ✔ **National:** ☎ **800-227-7368;** www.nationalcar.com

- ✔ **Thrifty:** ☎ **800-THRIFTY** (800-847-4389); www.thrifty.com

Rental cars are relatively cheap in the Driving State. Of course, we can't
guarantee what you'll pay when you book, but you can often get a compact car for between $100 and $200 a week, depending on your dates
and where you pick up your car (Southern California rentals are usually

cheaper). If you want a car large enough for an entire family, expect to pay more like $200 to $300 a week, which is still quite reasonable.

We advocate flying into one airport and leaving from another so you can see as much of California as possible. And depending on your pickup and drop-off points, you may find that you won't have to pay extra for your one-way car rental. No promises, but we've found that more often than not you won't pay more than if you had picked up and dropped off at the same location.

Price car rentals at the same time you price airfares to make sure that flying into one city and out of another is cost-effective on both counts. Check with a few companies before you make a final decision. If you get a rate quote you like and decide that this is the way you want to go, make your reservation (which will lock in your rate) immediately. This will save you from getting taken to the cleaners after the fact — because policies and prices can change at any time.

For tips on renting hand-controlled cars or vans equipped with wheelchair lifts, see Chapter 5.

Getting the best deal on a rental car

Car-rental rates vary even more than airline fares. The price depends on the size of the car, the length of time you keep it, where and when you pick it up and drop it off, where you take it, and a host of other factors. Asking a few key questions can save you hundreds of dollars:

- ✔ **Weekend rates may be lower than weekday rates.** Ask if the rate is the same for pickup Friday morning as it is Thursday night. If you're keeping the car five or more days, a weekly rate may be cheaper than the daily rate.

- ✔ **Some companies assess a drop-off charge if you don't return the car to the same renting location; others do not.** Ask when you book. Also ask if the rate is cheaper if you pick up the car at the airport or at a location in town.

- ✔ **Ask for the special rate.** If you see an advertised special, be sure to ask for that specific rate; otherwise you may be charged the standard (higher) rate.

Don't forget to mention membership in AAA, AARP, frequent-flier programs, and trade unions. These usually entitle you to discounts ranging from 5 to 30%. Ask your travel agent to check any and all of these rates. And, don't forget: Most car rentals are worth at least 500 miles on your frequent-flyer account!

Using the Internet can make comparison shopping much easier. All the major booking sites — Travelocity (www.travelocity.com), Expedia (www.expedia.com), Yahoo! Travel (www.travel.yahoo.com), and Cheap Tickets (www.cheaptickets.com), for example — feature search engines that can book car rentals for you.

On top of the standard rental price, optional charges can apply to car rentals. You may opt to pay for a **collision damage waiver,** which covers damage in the case of an accident. Many credit card companies (or your existing car insurance) offer this coverage automatically, so check the terms of your credit card before you shell out money for this hefty charge (as much as $15/day).

The car-rental companies also offer **additional liability insurance** (if you harm others in an accident), **personal accident insurance** (if you harm yourself or your passengers), and **personal effects insurance** (if someone steals your luggage from your car). If you have insurance on your car at home, that insurance probably covers you for most of these scenarios. If your own insurance doesn't cover you for rentals or if you don't have auto insurance, consider the additional coverage (as much as $20/day combined).

Some companies also offer **refueling packages,** in which you pay for an entire tank of gas up front. The price is usually fairly competitive with local gas prices, but you don't get credit for any gas remaining in the tank. If you reject this option, you pay only for the gas you use, but you have to return it with a full tank or else you face charges of $3 to $4 a gallon for any shortfall. If a stop at a gas station on the way to the airport will make you miss your plane, then by all means take advantage of the fuel purchase option. Otherwise, skip it.

Following the rules of the road

Know these rules of the road before you drive around California:

- ✓ **All passengers must wear seatbelts at all times.** No cheating in the back seat. You must harness children under four years old or 40 pounds into an approved safety seat (some car-rental agencies now rent these seats; ask when you reserve your car).

- ✓ **Motorcyclists must wear helmets.**

- ✓ **You can turn right on red** as long as a posted sign doesn't say otherwise. Make sure you make a full stop first — no rolling.

- ✓ **The maximum speed limit on most California freeways is 65 mph,** although some freeways carry a posted limit of 70 mph. For two-lane undivided highways, the maximum speed limit is 55 mph, unless otherwise posted. Speed limits vary in populated areas; defaulting to 25 mph is smart if you're not sure. California law states that you must never drive faster than is safe for the present conditions, regardless of the posted speed limit.

✔ **You can pass on the right** on the freeway as long as you act safely and use a properly marked lane.

✔ **Pedestrians always have the right of way** both on crosswalks and at uncontrolled intersections.

✔ **Those kids you brought with you can come in handy.** Some freeways, especially those in Southern California, have a High Occupancy Vehicle (HOV) — a carpool — lane, which lets you speed past some of the congestion if three people are in the car (sometimes two; read the signs). Don't flout the rules; if you do, expect to shell out close to $300 for the ticket.

✔ **Always read street-parking signs and keep plenty of quarters on hand for meters.** Popular destinations and smaller towns with parking crunches often have some of the most stringent rules and gung-ho meter readers. Be extra-vigilant in metropolitan areas.

Save yourself some hassle and just buy a roll of dedicated parking quarters at your bank before you leave home.

✔ **Check the Web for a complete rundown of California state driving guidelines.** The complete *California Driver Handbook* is available online; go to www.dmv.ca.gov and click on Publications, where you can also find rules of the road for motorcycles, RVs, and trailers.

In addition to following the rules of the road, include the following tips among your driving practices:

✔ **Always have a good statewide map on hand.** You can get good maps from AAA or the California Division of Tourism (you can even download the official state map from the CDT Web site at www.visitcalifornia.com).

✔ **Know more about the direction you're heading than simply "north" or "south."** California's freeway and highway signs indicate direction, more often than not, by naming a town rather than a point on the compass: If you were heading east on I-10 to Palm Springs, say, you'd follow the signs that say "Ontario" as you drove out of L.A., not the ones that say "Santa Monica." Review your map carefully so that you know which way to go before you hit the road.

✔ **Know how far you have to go.** See Table 7-1 for some sample distances between California destinations.

Table 7-1   Sample Mileage Between California Destinations

From San Francisco to	From Los Angeles to	From San Diego to
Eureka: 261 miles	Mendocino: 527½ miles	San Francisco: 504 miles
Yosemite National Park: 202 miles	Lake Tahoe: 189 miles	Yosemite National Park: 344½ miles
Napa Valley: 47½ miles	Monterey: 323 miles	Death Valley: 324 miles
Monterey: 119 miles	Hearst Castle: 231 miles	Los Angeles: 122 miles
Hearst Castle: 211 miles	Death Valley: 262 miles	Disneyland: 98 miles
Santa Barbara: 328 miles	Santa Barbara: 97 miles	Palm Springs: 141 miles
Los Angeles: 382 miles	Disneyland: 26½ miles	Tijuana: 16 miles
Disneyland: 408 miles	San Diego: 122 miles	Palm Springs: 108 miles
Palm Springs: 488 miles		
San Diego: 504 miles		

✔ **Prepare your vehicle for the weather.** If you're heading to Yosemite or Tahoe in winter, top off on antifreeze and bring snow chains. If renting a car, ask the agency if chains are provided. Also, check road conditions before you set out. Call the California Department of Transportation (CALTRANS) at ☎ **916-445-1534,** which can fill you in on conditions throughout the state at any time of year. You can also check road and traffic conditions online at www.dot.ca.gov.

✔ **Take along your cellphone or rent one.** A cellphone can be an invaluable lifeline as you drive throughout California. If you're renting a car, you are often able to rent a cellphone along with your vehicle; ask when you call. Cellphones can also be rented at airport kiosks. Or, you can rent a phone before you leave home by calling **InTouchUSA** (☎ **800-872-7626;** www.intouchusa.com), which rents wireless products and even evaluates your own phone's calling capabilities for free before you leave home (call ☎ **703-222-7161** between 9 a.m. and 4 p.m.).

Winging Your Way Around

If time is short and you want to cover great distances without the long drive, consider flying between California locations. After all, an hour-long flight can save you the entire travel day that driving between San Francisco and Los Angeles or San Diego would consume. Even shorter distances — L.A. to Monterey, say — can save you a good chunk of valuable vacation time. Airfares are generally reasonable, too, often between $60 and $100 per leg.

The following airlines are well-versed in shuttling passengers between multiple California destinations:

- ✔ **Alaska Airlines:** ☎ 800-252-7522; www.alaskaair.com
- ✔ **American/American Eagle:** ☎ 800-433-7300; www.im.aa.com
- ✔ **America West:** ☎ 800-235-9292; www.americawest.com
- ✔ **Delta/Skywest:** ☎ 800-221-1212; www.delta.com
- ✔ **Southwest:** ☎ 800-435-9792; www.southwest.com
- ✔ **United/United Express/Skywest:** ☎ 800-241-6522; www.united.com
- ✔ **US Airways:** ☎ 800-428-4322; www.usairways.com

For a rundown of California airports, see Chapter 6.

We can't promise who'll be offering the best deals when you're booking, but we've found that Southwest Airlines is often the cheapest and most convenient airline for traveling within California. Why? Three reasons:

- ✔ Tickets are sold by segments, which makes it cheap and easy to buy one-way fares.
- ✔ Full fares are comparatively low, so you have the freedom to change your itinerary without paying a ridiculous markup or penalty.
- ✔ Internet specials often make the airlines' already low fares even lower.

Keep in mind that the airline saves money by skipping certain frills, including seat assignments. You get a seat by using a boarding card, and passengers are boarded in groups. If you have special seat preferences, or simply want to avoid the infamous Southwest backward-facing rows, be sure to be at your ticketing gate at least one to two hours in advance, so that you can be among the first in line and the first to board.

Going the Amtrak Way

Amtrak (☎ 800-USA-RAIL; www.amtrak.com) runs trains throughout California, including up and down the coast, serving destinations like Sacramento, San Francisco, San Jose, Santa Barbara, Los Angeles, and San Diego, and numerous points in between. Using Amtrak won't save you any time over driving (all too often, we've been the victim of delayed trains, adding hours to our journey), and may not even save you money over flying; still, it's an option if you'd rather not drive yourself and don't like to fly, or if you're just enamored with the nostalgia of train travel.

If you'd like to travel the Amtrak way, consider booking one of the inclusive travel packages offered by **Amtrak Vacations** (☎ 800-654-5748; www.amtrakvacations.com). See Chapter 6 for more information.

Chapter 8

Tying Up Loose Ends

● ●

In This Chapter

▶ Using credit cards, traveler's checks, and ATMs on the road

▶ Dealing with losing your wallet and other money emergencies

▶ Buying insurance and making reservations before you leave home

▶ Packing what you really need

● ●

*T*his chapter helps you shore up the final details — from getting traveler's checks and travel insurance to advance reservations for dining and attractions to packing comfortable walking shoes.

Deciding among Traveler's Checks, Credit Cards, and Cash

Most travelers these days use a combination of traveler's checks, credit cards, and cash to cover all their travel expenses in California. Certainly, having a credit card makes sense if you plan to reserve a hotel room or rent a car. And with the prevalence of ATMs throughout the state, cash is easy to access on the spot. Here is a quick look at all the options at your disposal to pay for your California vacation.

ATMs and cash

These days, most cities and towns have 24-hour ATMs (automated-teller machines) linked to a national network that almost always includes your bank at home. **Cirrus** (☎ 800-424-7787; www.mastercard.com/atm/) and **Plus** (☎ 800-843-7587; www.visa.com/atms) are the two most popular networks; check the back of your ATM card to see which network your bank belongs to. The 800-numbers and Web sites give you specific locations of ATMs where you can withdraw money while on vacation. The easy accessibility of these ATMS means you can withdraw only as much cash as you need every couple of days, which eliminates the insecurity (and the pickpocketing threat) of carrying around a wad of cash.

One important reminder: Many banks now charge a fee ranging from 50¢ to $3 whenever a non-account-holder uses their ATMs. Your own bank may also assess a fee for using an ATM that's not one of their branch locations. This means that in some cases, you'll get charged twice just for using your bank card when you're on vacation. An ATM card can be an amazing convenience when you're traveling in another country (put your card in the machine, and out comes foreign currency, at an extremely advantageous exchange rate). However, banks are also likely to slap you with a *foreign currency transaction fee* just for making them do the local currency-to-dollars conversion math. Given these sneaky tactics, reverting to the traveler's check policy may be cheaper (though certainly less convenient).

Traveler's checks

Traveler's checks are something of an anachronism from the days before the ATM made cash accessible at any time. Traveler's checks used to be the only sound alternative to traveling with dangerously large amounts of cash. They are as reliable as currency, but, unlike cash, can be replaced if lost or stolen.

These days, traveler's checks seem less necessary because most cities have 24-hour ATMs that allow you to withdraw small amounts of cash as needed. However, you're likely to be charged an ATM withdrawal fee if the bank is not your own, so if you're withdrawing money every day, you may be better off with traveler's checks — provided that you don't mind showing identification every time you want to cash one.

You can get traveler's checks at almost any bank. **American Express** offers denominations of $20, $50, $100, $500, and (for cardholders only) $1,000. You'll pay a service charge ranging from 1% to 4%. You can also get American Express traveler's checks over the phone by calling ☎ **800-221-7282;** Amex gold and platinum cardholders who use this number are exempt from the 1% fee. AAA members can obtain checks without a fee at most AAA offices.

Visa offers traveler's checks at Citibank locations nationwide, as well as at several other banks. The service charge ranges between 1.5 and 2%; checks come in denominations of $20, $50, $100, $500, and $1,000. Call ☎ **800-732-1322** for information. **MasterCard** also offers traveler's checks. Call ☎ **800-223-9920** for a location near you.

Credit cards

Credit cards are invaluable when traveling. They are a safe way to carry money and provide a convenient record of all your expenses. You can also withdraw cash advances from your credit cards at any bank (though you'll start paying hefty interest on the advance the moment you receive the cash). At most banks, you don't even need to go to a teller; you can get a cash advance at the ATM if you know your PIN access number. If you've forgotten yours or didn't even know you had one, call the number on the back of your credit card and ask the bank to send it to you. It usually takes five to seven business days, although some banks provide the number over the phone if you tell them your mother's maiden name or pass some other security clearance.

Knowing What to Do if Your Wallet Is Stolen

Almost every credit card company has an emergency 800-number you can call if your wallet or purse is stolen. The company may be able to wire you a cash advance off your credit card immediately; in many places, you can get an emergency credit card within a day or two. The issuing bank's 800-number is usually on the back of the credit card, but that won't help you much if the card was stolen. Copy the number on the back of your card onto another piece of paper before you leave, and keep it in a safe place just in case. **Citicorp Visa's** U.S. emergency number is ☎ **800-645-6556. American Express** cardholders and traveler's check holders should call ☎ **800-221-7282** for all money emergencies. **MasterCard** holders should call ☎ **800-307-7309.** Be sure to block charges against your account the minute you realize your card has been lost or stolen. Then be sure to file a police report.

If you opt to carry **traveler's checks,** be sure to keep a record of their serial numbers so you can handle just such an emergency. You should always keep a list of the traveler's checks numbers in a safe and separate place, so that you're ensured a refund if checks are lost or stolen. Also, dual checks are available for traveling couples, and either person can sign for them.

Odds are that if your wallet is gone, the police won't be able to recover it for you. However, it's still worth informing the authorities. Your credit card company or insurer may require a police report number or record of the theft.

If you need emergency cash over the weekend when all banks and American Express offices are closed, you can have money wired to you from **Western Union** (☎ **800-325-6000;** www.westernunion.com/). You must present a valid ID to pick up the cash at the Western Union office.

Considering Travel Insurance

Before you buy travel insurance to cover trip cancellation, lost luggage, or medical expenses, check your existing insurance policies. You're likely to have partial or complete coverage. But if you need some, ask your travel agent about a comprehensive package. The cost of travel insurance varies widely, depending on the cost and length of your trip, your age and overall health, and the type of trip you're taking. Insurance for extreme sports or adventure travel, for example, costs more than coverage for a cruise. Some insurers provide packages for specialty vacations, such as skiing or backpacking. More dangerous activities may be excluded from basic policies.

Keep in mind that in the aftermath of the 2001 terrorist attacks, a number of airlines, cruise lines, and tour operators are no longer covered by insurers. The bottom line: Always check the fine print before you sign on; more and more policies have built-in exclusions and restrictions that may leave you out in the cold if something does go awry.

For information, contact one of the following popular insurers:

- ✔ **Access America:** (☎ 800-284-8300); www.accessamerica.com)
- ✔ **Travelex Insurance Services:** (☎ 800-228-9792; www.travelex-insurance.com)
- ✔ **Travel Guard International:** (☎ 800-826-1300; www.travelguard.com)
- ✔ **Travel Insured International:** (☎ 800-243-3174; www.travelinsured.com)

Trip-cancellation insurance (TCI)

There are three major types of trip-cancellation insurance:

- ✔ You pre-pay a cruise or tour that gets cancelled, and the tour company doesn't give you your money back.
- ✔ You become ill or someone in your family gets sick or passes away, and you can't travel. (Beware that you may not be covered for a preexisting condition.)
- ✔ Bad weather makes travel impossible.

Some insurers provide coverage for events like jury duty; natural disasters close to home, like floods or fire; even the loss of a job. A few have added provisions for cancellations due to terrorist activities. Always check the fine print before signing on, and don't buy trip-cancellation insurance from the tour operator that may be responsible for the cancellation; buy it only from a reputable travel insurance agency. Don't overbuy. You won't be reimbursed for more than the cost of your trip.

Medical insurance

Most health insurance policies cover you if you get sick away from home — but check, particularly if you're insured by an HMO. Members of **Blue Cross/Blue Shield** can now use their cards at select hospitals in most major cities worldwide (☎ **800-810-BLUE** or www.blue cares.com).

Some credit cards (American Express, certain gold and platinum Visa and MasterCards, and some types of Discover cards, for example) offer automatic flight insurance against death or dismemberment in case of an airplane crash if you charged the cost of your ticket.

If you require additional insurance, try one of the following companies:

- ✔ **MEDEX International,** 9515 Deereco Rd., Timonium, MD 21093-5375 (☎ **888-MEDEX-00** or 410-453-6300; Fax 410-453-6301; www.medexassist.com).

- ✔ **Travel Assistance International** (☎ **800-821-2828;** www.travel assistance.com), 9200 Keystone Crossing, Suite 300, Indianapolis, IN 46240. (For general information on services, call the company's Worldwide Assistance Services, Inc., at ☎ **800-777-8710.**)

The cost of travel medical insurance varies widely. Check your existing policies before you buy additional coverage. Also, check to see whether your medical insurance covers you for emergency medical evacuation: If you have to buy a one-way same-day ticket home and forfeit your nonrefundable round-trip ticket, you may be out big bucks.

Lost-luggage insurance

On domestic flights, checked baggage is covered up to $2,500 per ticketed passenger. On international flights (including U.S. portions of international trips), baggage is limited to approximately $9.07 per pound, up to approximately $635 per checked bag. If you plan to check items more valuable than the standard liability, you may purchase **excess valuation coverage** from the airline, up to $5,000. Be sure to take any valuables or irreplaceable items with you in your carry-on luggage. If you file a lost luggage claim, be prepared to answer detailed questions about the contents of your baggage, and be sure to file a claim immediately, because most airlines enforce a 21-day deadline. Before you leave home, compile an inventory of all packed items and a rough estimate of the total value to ensure you're properly compensated if your luggage is lost. You will be reimbursed for only what you lost — no more. After you've filed a complaint, persist in securing your reimbursement; there are no laws governing the length of time it takes for a carrier to reimburse you. If you arrive at a destination without your bags, ask the airline to forward them to your hotel or to your next destination; they will usually comply. If your bag is delayed or lost, the airline may reimburse you for reasonable expenses, such as a toothbrush or a set of clothes, but the airline is under no legal obligation to do so.

Lost luggage may also be covered by your homeowner's or renter's policy. Many platinum and gold credit cards cover you, as well. If you choose to purchase additional lost-luggage insurance, be sure not to buy more than you need. Buy in advance from your insurer or a trusted agent (prices will be much higher at the airport).

Making Reservations and Getting Advance Tickets

In addition to buying your airfare, booking your accommodations, and reserving a rental car, you may want to take care of a few other items before you leave home.

Consider making reservations or buying tickets for the following five types of activities before you leave home:

- ✔ **Attractions that have long ticket-buying lines** for people who don't plan ahead (such as the **Monterey Bay Aquarium**) or that have restricted daily admission (like the **Getty Center** in L.A.).

- ✔ **Activities that require advance reservations**, like a guided hike of **Yosemite** or an extra-special Napa Valley winery tour.

- ✔ Special events and high-profile exhibitions at museums like the **Los Angeles County Museum of Art,** or parking at the Getty, which calls for advance reservations.

- ✔ **Live theater or musical performances,** which often sell out well before show time.

- ✔ Any **special-occasion dinners** at high-profile restaurants that you don't want to miss out on — especially in San Francisco, Los Angeles, and any other popular weekend destination where you'll want to celebrate on a Friday or Saturday night. (Don't leave home without a dinner reservation at the Napa Valley's French Laundry if you have any hope of eating there.)

As you thumb through this book, look for the Plan Ahead icon. It highlights activities and attractions for which you need to make advance arrangements; otherwise, you may miss out.

We also indicate reservations policies in all restaurant reviews. Be sure to peruse the restaurant listings for those destinations where you may be interested in booking a special meal, and look for red-flag phrases such as "reservations highly recommended," "reservations required," and "reservations a must."

How do you find out what special events and live performances will be available when you're in town? That's easy — just check out the

"Gathering More Information" section at the end of each destination chapter, where you find a comprehensive list of destination-specific resources. You'll have the greatest access to information via the Web — especially in San Francisco, Los Angeles, and San Diego, all of which boast many useful sites with copious arts-and-entertainment listings. Remember, however, that you can always call the local visitors bureau if you want to gather information and recommendations from a real, live person.

And don't forget to check with the museums, attractions, and performance venues directly. They'll give you the most up-to-date and comprehensive schedule and ticket information. Their numbers are included where appropriate in the listings.

Packing the Right Stuff

Start packing by taking everything you think you'll need and laying it out on the bed. Then get rid of half of it.

Not that the airlines won't let you take it all — they will, with some limits — but you'll soon discover that carting loads of stuff around California is a big drag. Believe us, you really can do without that sixth pair of shoes. You can always buy shoes. We encourage that.

Start by packing the essentials, the stuff you want to be sure to bring along, such as

- ✔ **Sunglasses:** Because the sun can be quite strong in California, you won't be able to do without them if you're driving. And how else are you going to look cool in Hollywood?

- ✔ **A bathing suit:** Bring one even if you don't expect to encounter beach weather. Finding an enticing Jacuzzi at your hotel and not being able to use it isn't fun. And even January can bring the surprise beach day to Southern California.

- ✔ **Casual clothes that layer well:** California's weather is frustratingly changeable year-round. You can easily encounter a 20-degree rise in temperature just by moving a few miles inland away from the coast, or a 30-degree drop between 3 and 8 p.m. Be sure to bring a light jacket — yes, even in summer. For more weather guidelines, see Chapter 2 — then prepare yourself for everything.

  In general, keep your clothes casual. Even the fanciest restaurants are relatively informal; only a few require a sports jacket or tie, and men can get by with a nice pair of khakis and a button-down shirt at most. Women will probably do well with a couple of dresses or pants/top combos that are comfy for day wear and dress up well with accessories for evening.

✔ **Good, comfortable walking shoes:** Bring hiking boots, or at least sturdy sneakers, if you plan to hike.

✔ **Sunscreen.** Apply it early and often. Even if there is a layer of cloud/fog in the sky. Your skin will thank us, and you.

✔ **Binoculars:** These come in handy during whale-watching season or to spot dolphins or seals offshore at any time of year.

✔ **Dramamine or nausea-prevention wristbands:** Be sure to include these if you have a tendency towards carsickness.

✔ **An extra pair of eyeglasses or contact lenses:** Bringing a spare is always a good idea to prevent an inconvenient "Ack — I can't see!" emergency.

✔ **An umbrella:** Including an umbrella will probably prevent it from raining, of course.

✔ **Prescription medication:** Of course you'll want to bring all your prescription meds, but don't bother hauling a half-dozen bottles of saline solution, a couple cans of bug spray, or 16 rolls of film from home. California has a fine collection of drugstores throughout the state, and because every community you'll be visiting supports a local population, you won't find an excess of tourist-targeted or prohibitive pricing.

Part III

Northern California: Redwoods, Wine, and Wonder

The 5th Wave   By Rich Tennant

©RICHTENNANT

SAN FRANCISCO'S AMAZING CABLE CARS

Travelers can ride from Market Street to the Financial District, through the Rocky Mountains and on to Denver all for the price of one Muni Passport.

In this part . . .

This part covers Northern California: the San Francisco Bay Area, the wild North Coast and tall-tree Redwood Country, and the Sierra Nevada mountains, where you'll find spectacular Lake Tahoe and Yosemite National Park. San Francisco is the ultimate urban destination, while the gorgeous Wine Country makes for a wonderfully pastoral getaway. The wild and woolly coastal region north of the San Francisco Bay Area offers some of California's most breathtaking scenery. It's quiet, remote, and ruggedly handsome, with spectacular nature broken only by the occasional picturesque village. Travel inland from the Bay Area or North Coast, and you'll soon reach the Sierra Nevada, the magnificently rugged, granite-peaked mountain range that inspired the U.S. National Park system, of which Yosemite National Park is a grand example. Also awe inspiring is sparkling Lake Tahoe, host to California's finest outdoor-recreation center.

Chapter 9

San Francisco

● ●

In This Chapter

▶ Knowing when to go and how to get there

▶ Getting to know the neighborhoods — and how to get around

▶ Choosing the best places to stay and dine

▶ Seeing the sights, shopping, and good times in the night

● ●

San Francisco remains one of America's most enticing destinations. This former gold-rush rowdy may not always bask in the sunny weather of its Southern California sisters, but where else can you sample a touch of Asia, a bit of Parisian *joie de vivre,* a taste of Central America, a hint of Italy, and a good dollop of West Coast style and eccentricity in a single day? San Francisco's secret weapon is its winning combination of big-city sophistication and small-town accessibility. You can always discover something new in the unique neighborhoods of this walking town, from restored Victorian homes to amusing shops to some of the greatest restaurants in the country.

Despite the dot.com implosion and the general economic malaise that followed, the city carries on like a grand dowager. Although office space currently goes begging and sections of Market Street continue to impersonate skid row, there are long-awaited civic improvements nearing completion. The new **Asian Art Museum** is soon to open near City Hall; **Union Square,** in the heart of downtown, is reopening after a much-needed nip and tuck; and the exquisite glass **Conservatory of Flowers** in Golden Gate Park is finally being rebuilt after a violent storm nearly destroyed it in 1995. San Francisco's impressive brick-and-concrete **baseball park,** the "miracle on Third Street," has changed the face of a once-neglected corner of the bay, and the **waterfront,** lined with palm trees, awash in views, and traversed by vintage trolley cars, is a picture of urban glory.

What never fails to beguile visitors and locals alike are the much-loved symbols that are synonymous with the city. The **Golden Gate Bridge, Golden Gate Park,** the **Palace of Fine Arts,** the **cable cars,** and **Chinatown** have changed little over the decades, thank goodness. And despite grumbling from the natives regarding the "good old days," the city of San Francisco has never looked so vibrant.

Timing Your Visit

San Francisco is a year-round city, usually draped in mild to cool temperatures and fog-bound mornings, especially during the summer. If weather is important to you — warm weather, that is — come in September or early October when the city traditionally experiences a hot spell. These, naturally, are the busiest months in the hotel trade, right up there with summer vacation. Be sure to book lodgings ahead of time to ensure a decent place to stay. Winter tends to be cold and drizzly (although we've enjoyed fair skies and mild temperatures in January), but you can often get fantastic deals on hotel rooms after the holidays. In early spring, the flowering plum trees are in bloom and, while the skies may pour, you may find drought conditions. Ya' just never know.

It's always an excellent idea to check dates with the San Francisco Convention and Visitors Bureau to avoid scheduling your vacation during MacWeek or any other large convention when the hotels and restaurants are jammed (☎ **800-220-5747** or 415-391-2000; www. sfvisitor.org.).

Getting There

The Bay Area has two convenient airports:

- **San Francisco International** (SFO) (☎ **650-875-8575**; www.flysfo.com), 14 miles south of downtown
- **Oakland International Airport** (☎ **510-577-4000**; www. flyoakland.com), across the Bay Bridge off Interstate 880

More airlines fly into the considerably larger SFO, but navigating the less crowded, two-terminal Oakland airport is easier. Plus, getting to Oakland International from downtown San Francisco can take just a half-hour, traffic permitting, and it's accessible by Bay Area Rapid Transit (BART) (see the "From Oakland International" section). You'll find tourist information desks on the first floor (baggage level) of both airports as well as ATMs located in every terminal on the upper levels.

From SFO

Travel time from San Francisco International to downtown San Francisco is dependent on the traffic; during rush hours, the trip can take 40 minutes or more, and at other times can run from 20 to 30 minutes. **Super Shuttle** (☎ **415-558-8500**; www.supershuttle.com) and other similar companies offer door-to-door service into the city from the airport. The services are located at center islands outside the upper level, and a guide will direct you to the right area. Fares are around $17; advance reservations are not necessary.

Taxis line up at well-marked yellow columns on the center island out-side the lower level of the airport. The fare is about $35 to downtown, plus tip.

All of the major car-rental firms have SFO locations. If you're **renting a car,** the airport's new automated light rail system will ferry you to the building where all the major companies have counters and cars. Find the light rail cars outside the terminals on the upper level.

From Oakland International

The routine is similar from Oakland International, except that all ground transportation is on one level. **Bayporter Express shuttles** (☎ **800-287-6783**) pick up passengers from Terminal 1 at the center island, and from Terminal 2 around the corner from baggage claim. The fare for the 30- to 40-minute ride to San Francisco is $26 for one person, $36 for two people in the same party, and $5 for kids under 12. Make reservations for the 45- to 90-minute ride.

A 30- to 40-minute **taxi** ride into the city will run you about $40.

BART (Bay Area Rapid Transit; ☎ 510-464-6000; www.bart.org) also runs from Oakland into the city. Take the **AirBART shuttle** (☎ **510-430-9440**) in front of Terminal 1 or 2, which runs every 15 minutes. The fare is $2 for the 15-minute ride to the Oakland Coliseum BART station. From there, transfer to a BART train into San Francisco; the fare is about $2.45. Purchase your ticket from well-marked kiosks inside the airport or at the BART station. If you're staying around Union Square, the city's com-mercial hub, exit BART on Powell Street.

By car

Two major highways can bring you into San Francisco: **Interstate 5 (I-5)** cuts through the center of the state. Drivers traveling along this route are deposited onto **Interstate 80 (I-80),** which leads over the Bay Bridge into the city. The drive to San Francisco from Los Angeles along I-5 takes six to eight hours.

The other major route is **U.S. 101,** which heads up from Los Angeles through the city to Marin County, Napa and Sonoma valleys, and other points north. A prettier, more scenic coastal route, **Highway 1,** takes travelers heading north closer to Monterey and Santa Cruz, but the driving time up from L.A. is approximately eight to ten hours.

By train

Amtrak (☎ **800-872-7245;** www.amtrak.com) trains arrive in Emeryville, just north of Oakland. Buses then drop passengers off at one of six stops in San Francisco, including the Ferry Building (approximately a 30-minute ride), at the foot of Market Street on the Embarcadero, or the CalTrain station (approximately a 40-minute ride), at 4th and King streets.

Orienting Yourself and Finding Transportation

San Francisco covers just seven square miles. The streets are laid out in a traditional grid pattern, except for two major diagonal arteries, Market Street and Columbus Avenue. Market cuts a swath through town from the Embarcadero up to the bottom of Twin Peaks. Columbus runs at an angle through North Beach, starting at the Transamerica Pyramid in the Financial District and ending near the Hyde Street Pier.

Numbered *streets* are downtown; numbered *avenues* are found in the Richmond and Sunset districts southwest of downtown.

Other important thoroughfares include Van Ness Avenue, which begins in the Mission District as South Van Ness and terminates at Aquatic Park; and Geary Street, which begins at Market and winds through the city to Ocean Beach.

San Francisco's neighborhoods

Along with the lovely natural setting, it's the neighborhoods — each with its own quirky personality — that invest San Francisco with so much charm. This isn't a big city, size-wise, so you'll be no more than 20 minutes or so by taxi from all the major sites, shopping areas, and restaurants no matter where you stay.

Union Square

The center of tourist activity, Union Square is tucked inside Sutter, Grant, Market, and Mason streets. Big department stores, expensive boutiques, theaters, many exceptional restaurants, and the greatest concentration of hotels in the city surround the actual square. If you stay here, Chinatown, Nob Hill, the Financial District, and SoMa are all within walking distance.

A few blocks west is the Tenderloin neighborhood, a gritty patch of poverty bounded by Sutter and Mason streets and Van Ness and Golden Gate avenues. The only reason to linger in the 'loin is to visit **Glide Memorial Church,** 330 Ellis St. (☎ **415-771-6300**), for rousing Sunday services. The multicultural choir sings soulful hymns that bring the congregation to their collective feet. Come early to secure a seat.

Chinatown

This densely packed area roughly between Broadway, Taylor, Bush, and Montgomery streets is as colorful and exotic as advertised. The Dragon Gate entrance on Grant Avenue leads to touristy shops, but wander up and around Stockton Street; you'll feel as if you're in another country. See "The top attractions," later in this chapter, for Chinatown's sight-seeing and shopping highlights.

Nob Hill

Posh Nob Hill is a rather rarefied residential district, crowned by **Grace Cathedral,** the magnificent Episcopal Church at the top of California Street. A string of pricey hotels cascades down the hill toward the Financial District, along with the **California Street cable car line.** If you're prepared for the challenge of walking up and down steep grades, Nob Hill is just a short stroll from Union Square.

The Financial District

The Financial District encompasses prime bay real estate roughly between Montgomery Street and the Embarcadero, on either side of Market Street. Major corporations call this area home, and the **Transamerica Pyramid,** at Montgomery and Clay streets, is a skyline landmark. Seek out **Belden Place,** an alley between Kearny, Bush, and Pine streets, which is full of outdoor dining opportunities.

The Embarcadero

Liberated from the pylons and cement of the Embarcadero Freeway, which was damaged by the 1989 Loma Prieta earthquake and subsequently torn down, this area runs along the bay from the eastern edge of Fisherman's Wharf to the beginning of China Basin. **Embarcadero Center,** a collection of five multi-use buildings connected by bridges and walkways at the end of Market Street from Drumm to Sansome, houses upscale chain stores, restaurants, and movie theaters. Take the F streetcar from Union Square.

SoMa (South of Market Street)

Although the dot.com bust tempered the frenzy, South of Market Street (SoMa for short) has exploded in the past ten years, particularly along Mission Street between Second and Fifth streets. Attractions include the **San Francisco Museum of Modern Art,** the **Cartoon Art Museum, Yerba Buena Gardens,** and the kid-magnet **Sony Metreon** (see "The top attractions," later in this chapter).

North Beach

North Beach isn't an actual beach; it's the former Italian enclave that Chinatown is encroaching upon. This is the place to hop from one cafe to another, to browse for books and Italian pottery, and to examine the

San Francisco's Neighborhoods

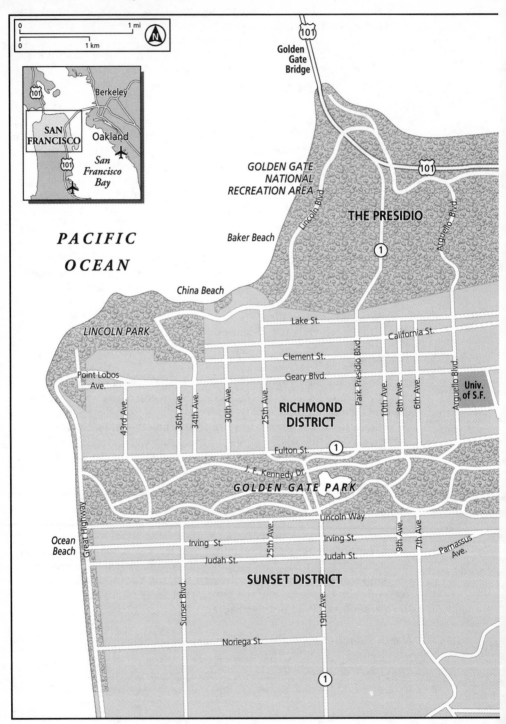

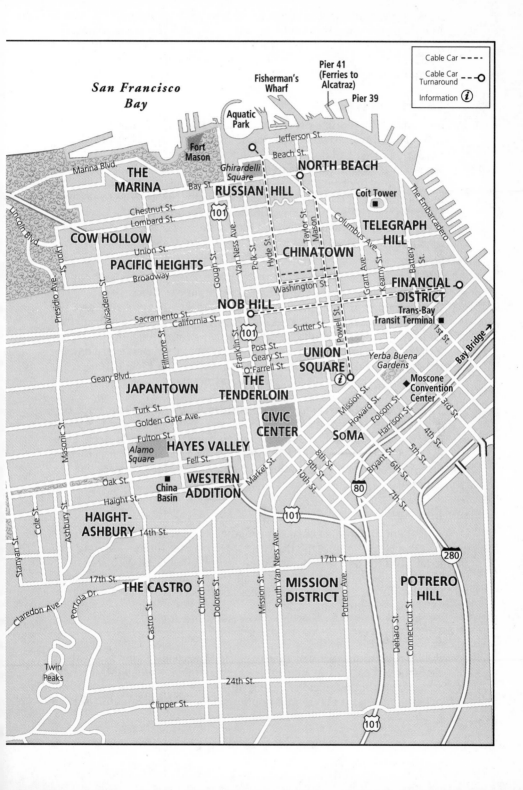

San Francisco
Bay

Cable Car - - - -
Cable Car - - -o
Turnaround
Information ⓘ

Pier 41
(Ferries to
Alcatraz)
Fisherman's
Wharf
Pier 39

Aquatic
Park

Jefferson St.
Beach St.

Fort
Mason

Ghirardelli
Square

Marina Blvd.

THE
MARINA

Bay St.

RUSSIAN HILL

NORTH BEACH

Coit Tower

The Embarcadero

Chestnut St.
Lombard St.

101

COW HOLLOW

Union St.

TELEGRAPH
HILL

Columbus Ave.

Taylor St.
Mason

PACIFIC HEIGHTS

Broadway

Van Ness Ave.

Gough St.

Polk St.

Hyde St.

CHINATOWN

Grant Ave.

Kearny St.

Battery St.

FINANCIAL
DISTRICT

Lincoln Blvd

Presidio Ave.

Arguello

Divisadero St.

Washington St.

NOB HILL

Trans-Bay
Transit Terminal

1st St.

Sacramento St.
California St.

101

Franklin St.

Fillmore St.

Sutter St.

Post St.

Powell St.

Geary St.
O'Farrell St.

UNION
SQUARE
ⓘ

Yerba Buena
Gardens

Bay Bridge →

Geary Blvd.

JAPANTOWN

THE
TENDERLOIN

Moscone
Convention
Center

Masonic St.

Turk St.

Golden Gate Ave.

Fulton St.

CIVIC
CENTER

SoMa

3rd St.

Mission St.

Howard St.

Folsom St.

Harrison St.

4th St.

Alamo
Square

HAYES VALLEY

Fell St.

Bryant St.

5th St.

6th St.

Oak St.

China
Basin

WESTERN
ADDITION

Market St.

8th St.

9th St.

10th St.

80

7th St.

Haight St.

HAIGHT-
ASHBURY

Cole St.

Ashbury St.

14th St.

101

280

Stanyan St.

17th St.

17th St.

South Van Ness Ave.

MISSION
DISTRICT

Potrero Ave.

POTRERO
HILL

THE CASTRO

Castro St.

Church St.

Dolores St.

Mission St.

Deharo St.

Connecticut St.

Claredon Ave.

Portola Dr.

Twin
Peaks

24th St.

Clipper St.

101

delectables at the various Italian delis and pastry shops. **Columbus Avenue** is the main thoroughfare, but family-style restaurants and crowded bars dot the streets from Washington to Grant, while the XXX-rated clubs stick together on Broadway. Use the Powell-Mason cable car to get here from Union Square.

Fisherman's Wharf

Sixteen million tourists per year can't all be wrong, but this most commercial section of town is a matter of taste. Located on Bay Street between Powell and Polk streets, the former working piers have been turned into an embarrassment of commercialism — although you have to come here in order to get to **Alcatraz** (see "The top attractions," later in this chapter). Step gingerly past Pier 39 and the plethora of schlock shops to the **Hyde Street Pier, Ghirardelli Square,** and the **Cannery,** other legitimate reasons to spend time near the docks. Parking is dreadful and/or expensive, so take the F streetcar from Union Square.

The Marina

Many glorious sites are within walking distance of this high-priced district, including the excellent science museum, the **Exploratorium.** The Marina's commercial blocks along Chestnut Street, between Franklin and Lyon streets, are full of coffeehouses, restaurants, and shops. Take a walk to the **Golden Gate Bridge** by way of Marina Boulevard and the redeveloped Crissy Fields. Get to the Marina by the 30-Stockton, 22-Fillmore, 41-Union, or 45-Union/Stockton bus.

The Marina is the gateway to the **Presidio,** 1,500 partly wild acres on the westernmost point of the city that once belonged to the U.S. Army. They're now part of the **Golden Gate National Recreation Area.** Stop in the visitor center, in the Main Post at Fort Mason on Montgomery Street, for maps and suggestions for hikes. Take the 29-Sunset bus to get here.

Cow Hollow

A residential paradise between Broadway, Lyon, and Lombard streets and Van Ness Avenue, the district's main claim to fame — among locals and tourists alike — is **Union Street,** a fashionable haven of shops, restaurants, and those young, urban professionals we all love to hate. To get here, take the 30-Stockton, 22-Fillmore, 41-Union, or 45-Union/Stockton bus.

Russian Hill

Polk Street from Broadway up to around Greenwich Street has suddenly become a chic avenue with a French flair. It's a delightful area for relaxed shopping and snacking with some terrific little restaurants, bakeries, antiques shops, and boutiques. From Union Square, take the California or Hyde Street cable car.

Civic Center

Bordered by Van Ness and Golden Gate avenues and Franklin, Hyde, and Market streets, Civic Center is home to local politicians, city offices, and cultural centers including the **San Francisco Ballet,** the **San Francisco Symphony,** and the **San Francisco Opera. City Hall,** on Van Ness Avenue between McAllister and Grove streets, underwent a spectacular renovation a few years ago, and its glittering black-and-gold dome makes a splendid landmark. It is soon to become neighbors with the **Asian Art Museum** opening in early 2003 in the city's former Main Library on Larkin Street. You can reach this area via the F streetcar. Note that Civic Center also attracts a sizable homeless contingent.

The Castro

The Castro is famous for its ties to an activist gay community, and a walk through the neighborhood will show off beautifully restored Victorian homes and shops catering to buff guys. Shopping and people-watching take place mainly on Castro Street between Market and 18th streets. Take the F streetcar from Union Square.

Haight-Ashbury

Commonly known as the Haight, and bounded by **Golden Gate Park** and Divisadero, Fulton, and Waller streets, Haight-Ashbury hasn't fully recovered from what must have been a real bummer to some — the demise of the '60s. Haight (rhymes with "fate") Street — where the action is — continues to hold a magical spell over scruffy groups of youngsters campaigning for handouts.

Should you be curious enough to drop by, you'll stumble upon a multitude of used clothing stores competing for space with all kinds of commercial endeavors, most of which are perfectly legal. The stretch from Masonic to Stanyon is particularly good for vintage wearables. The N-Judah Muni Metro line will take you to Haight Street.

Japantown

Japantown consists of some downright unattractive indoor shopping centers off Geary Street between Webster and Laguna streets. It's a shame that this area isn't more visually appealing, because the dismal gray buildings attached by a pedestrian walkway house some good, inexpensive noodle restaurants and interesting shops. **Kabuki Hot Springs** is a great place to have a massage and a soak. Across Sutter Street, between Fillmore and Webster streets, look for **Cottage Row,** all that's left of the real Japantown before redevelopment gutted the neighborhood. Catch the 38-Geary or 22-Fillmore bus to get here.

The Mission District

This busy, largely Hispanic community spans the area from Cesar Chavez (formerly Army) Street to Market Street between Dolores and Potrero avenues. The oldest building in the city (1776), **Mission**

Dolores (on Dolores and 16th streets), attracts visitors, as do a wealth of inexpensive restaurants and murals that burst out from the landscape. Valencia Street between 16th and 23rd streets has become a serious destination for foodies. Take BART to the 24th Street exit.

Telegraph Hill

This residential neighborhood lies just to the east of North Beach, behind **Coit Tower** and the **Filbert Steps. Russian Hill** (see "Russian Hill," earlier in this section) is just to the northwest, where you'll find the wiggly part of **Lombard Street** and Macondry Lane, fictionalized in Armistead Maupin's *Tales of the City*. You can reach Telegraph Hill via the Powell-Mason cable car.

Pacific Heights

Pacific Heights, bordered by Broadway, Pine, Divisadero, and Franklin streets, is where the city's wealthy elite lounge in lavish, beautifully landscaped mansions. The 22-Fillmore, 12-Folsom, 27-Bryant, 47-Van Ness, 49-Van Ness/Mission, and 83-Pacific all motor through here.

The Richmond District

Largely residential, the Richmond District is partially framed by **Golden Gate Park** at one edge — *aah*-inspiring, and a great place to walk — and by the Pacific Ocean on another. The N-Judah Muni Metro line provides the easiest way to get here.

Getting around

San Francisco is relatively compact and offers acceptable public transportation, so don't plan on driving around the city. Traffic is heavy downtown, and one-way streets confuse drivers unfamiliar with the territory. That, combined with the lack of parking and the heavy-handed meter maids, makes leaving your car in a parking garage the sensible thing to do.

If you're starting your California trip with a few days in San Francisco and then setting out to explore, arriving carless in the city and picking up your rental just before you leave town is a sound idea. Renting a car downtown is simple and smart.

From Union Square, where most hotels are located, it's an easy walk to Chinatown, North Beach, SoMa, and the Financial District. Buses, Muni streetcars, and cable cars are both convenient and inexpensive ways to reach outlying neighborhoods, but taxis usually require a phone call.

Hoofing it

Walking is the preferred method of travel in San Francisco and the only way to catch the nuances of the neighborhoods. Be careful, however, because vehicle/pedestrian accidents occur with alarming regularity. Although pedestrians have the right-of-way, watch for drivers running red lights or turning right on a red light. Make sure bus drivers see you entering crosswalks.

Catching cabs

Taxis are easy to hail downtown, especially in front of hotels, but you have to call a cab to come get you almost anywhere else. Reaching the taxi companies by phone can take a while, so keep this in mind, and have these numbers handy:

- Yellow Cab (☎ 415-626-2345)
- Veteran's Cab (☎ 415-552-1300)
- Desoto Cab (☎ 415-970-1300)
- Luxor Cabs (☎ 415-282-4141)
- Pacific (☎ 415-986-7220)

Rates are about $2 for the first mile and $1.80 for each additional mile.

Taking the Muni Metro streetcars

The San Francisco Municipal Railway, known as **Muni** (call ☎ 415-673-6864 for gracious directions on how to get where you want to go; www.sfmuni.com), is much maligned by locals for inefficiency, but tens of thousands of commuters rely daily on its buses and electric streetcars for a lift. For information on getting an official Muni map, see "Transit tips," later in this section.

Muni Metro streetcars run underground downtown and aboveground in the outlying neighborhoods. The five streetcar lines, the J, K, L, M, and N, make the same stops as BART (see the "Going underground with BART" section) along Market Street, including Embarcadero Station, Montgomery and Powell streets (both near Union Square), and the Civic Center. Past the Civic Center, the routes branch off in different directions. The **N-Judah** line services the Haight-Ashbury and parallels Golden Gate Park on its way down Judah Street to the ocean. The **J-Church** line passes near Mission Dolores and the Castro. My personal favorite is the **F-Market,** whose antique streetcars run from the Castro Street station down Market Street, over to Mission Street, then down the Embarcadero to Fisherman's Wharf. Muni cars marked "Mission Bay" end their journey at the CalTrain Station on King Street just past the glorious San Francisco Giants baseball park.

The **fare** to ride a bus or streetcar anywhere in the system is $1 for adults and 35¢ for seniors and children, and includes a transfer good for two hours; exact change is required. For information on multiday passes, see "Transit tips," later in this section.

Riding the bus

A fleet of buses chugs throughout the city from 6 a.m. to midnight. Street-corner signs and painted yellow bands on utility poles and on curbs mark bus stops, and buses are clearly numbered on the front. Depending on your destination and the time of day, buses arrive every 5 to 20 minutes. They aren't the quickest means of transportation, but with 80 transit lines, they are the most complete. During rush hours (7 to 9 a.m. and 4 to 6 p.m.), buses are often sardine-can crowded.

Going underground with BART

Bay Area Rapid Transit (☎ 415-989-2278; www.bart.gov) is different from Muni, although visitors often get the two systems mixed up because they share the same underground stations (but different platforms) downtown. Within the city limits, that's not a problem. BART, however, runs all over the Bay Area, and more than one unsuspecting traveler has ended up in Oakland when he intended to exit at the Embarcadero.

Purchase BART tickets from machines at the station. **Fares** to and from any point in the city are $1.10 each way; outside the city, fares vary depending on how far down the line you go.

Hopping aboard the cable cars

No trip to San Francisco would be complete without a ride on a cable car. Three lines traverse the downtown area. The **Powell-Hyde line,** the most scenic and exciting run, begins at Powell Street and ends at the turnaround across from Ghirardelli Square. The **Powell-Mason line** goes through North Beach and ends near Fisherman's Wharf. The **California Street line,** the tamest and least scenic, crests at Nob Hill and ends at Van Ness Avenue. Rides are $2 one way. You may only board a cable car at specific, clearly marked stops. Cable cars operate from 6:30 a.m. to 12:30 a.m.

Transit tips

Here are a few transit tips and information on multiday passes that will make your life much easier and can even save you money in the process:

- ✔ Buy a copy of the **official Muni map.** It costs $2 and is invaluable for public transportation users. It shows all the bus, streetcar, cable car, and BART routes and stations. Maps are available at the Convention and Visitors Bureau Information Center and cable car ticket booths. You can also phone ☎ 415-673-MUNI for route information.

- ✔ The one-stop-shopping number to call for **local traffic** or **public transit information** is ☎ 415-817-1717. This number connects you to whatever information line you need, be it BART or Muni routes, or the latest on traffic conditions. You can also find public transit schedules on the Web at www.sfmuni.com.

✔ **Muni Passports,** which are accepted on buses, streetcars, and even cable cars, but not BART, are a bargain for visitors. A one-day passport is $6, a three-day pass is $10, and a seven-day pass is $15. You can purchase them at the Convention and Visitors Bureau Information Center at Hallidie Plaza, at the Powell and Market or Beach and Hyde streets Cable Car Turnaround Police booth, or online at www.sfmuni.com. You may also purchase single-day passes on board the cable cars.

✔ You can also save money by buying a **CityPass,** which gives you admission to five major city attractions for nine days as well as seven days consecutive travel on all Muni transportation, including cable cars. Buy the CityPass at the first attraction you visit or online at **www.citypass.net**. For more information, see "Exploring San Francisco," later in this chapter.

Where to Stay

The following listings reflect our preferences for the city's best choices in various price categories. You won't find the biggest hotels in town mentioned, though — we're leaving them for the conventioneers.

Hotel room rates fluctuate hugely depending on supply and demand. Historically, in San Francisco, demand is high almost all year, but after September 11, 2001, even the poshest piles are wheeling and dealing. We have to assume that life in the travel business will return to normal, perhaps by the time you leaf through this book. If that's the case, and you're seeking a break on your accommodations, vacation in the winter months or ask about weekend packages at hotels that cater to business travelers. Be advised that lots of hotels in older buildings, especially around Union Square, have surprisingly tiny rooms and baths. If you plan to keep a car, prepare yourself for hefty parking fees.

Count on an extra 14% in taxes being tacked on to your hotel bill.

Best Western Tuscan Inn
$$$$ North Beach/Fisherman's Wharf

Compared with the rest of the chain hotels on Fisherman's Wharf, the Tuscan Inn exudes some personality. The location is appealing to kids, and the rooms are fairly large by local standards. The concierge is friendly and enthusiastic, and all the expected amenities are available including complimentary beverages served in the morning in the lobby. This is a pet-friendly hotel as well.

425 North Point (between Mason and Taylor sts.). ☎ *800-648-4626 or 415-561-1100. Fax: 415-561-1199. Internet: www.tuscaninn.com. Valet parking: $20. Rack rates: $249–$359 double. Deals: Packages available; also ask about AAA, corporate, and senior discounts. AE, DC, DISC, MC, V.*

San Francisco Accommodations

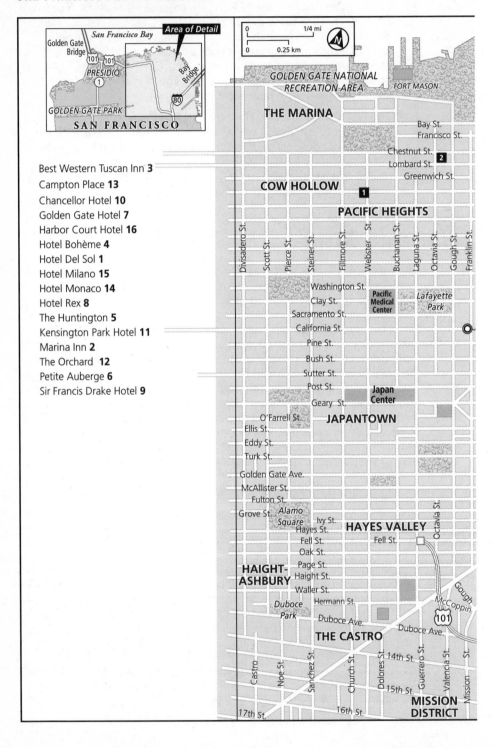

Best Western Tuscan Inn **3**
Campton Place **13**
Chancellor Hotel **10**
Golden Gate Hotel **7**
Harbor Court Hotel **16**
Hotel Bohème **4**
Hotel Del Sol **1**
Hotel Milano **15**
Hotel Monaco **14**
Hotel Rex **8**
The Huntington **5**
Kensington Park Hotel **11**
Marina Inn **2**
The Orchard **12**
Petite Auberge **6**
Sir Francis Drake Hotel **9**

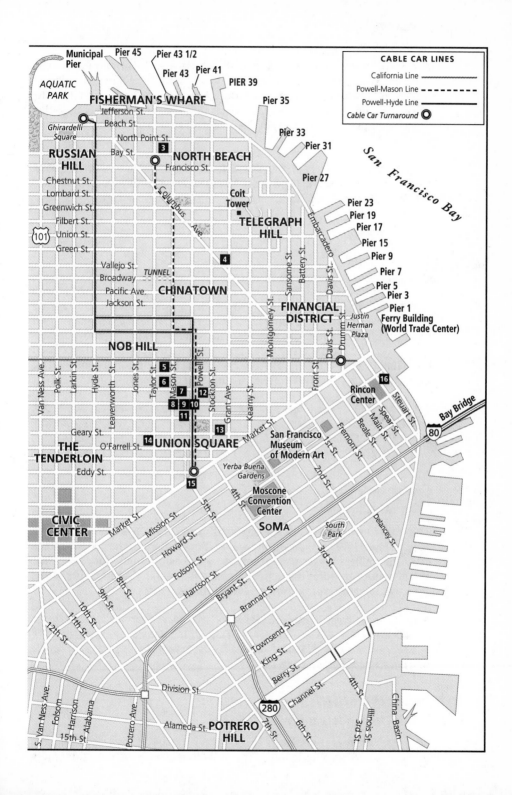

CABLE CAR LINES
California Line
Powell-Mason Line
Powell-Hyde Line
Cable Car Turnaround

Municipal Pier
Pier 45
Pier 43 1/2
Pier 43
Pier 41
PIER 39
Pier 35

AQUATIC PARK

FISHERMAN'S WHARF
Jefferson St.
Beach St.
Ghirardelli Square
North Point St.
Bay St.
Pier 33
Pier 31

RUSSIAN HILL
Chestnut St.
Lombard St.
Greenwich St.
Filbert St.
Union St.
Green St.

NORTH BEACH
Francisco St.
Pier 27

Coit Tower

TELEGRAPH HILL

Pier 23
Pier 19
Pier 17
Pier 15
Pier 9
Pier 7
Pier 5
Pier 3
Pier 1
Ferry Building
(World Trade Center)

Columbus Ave.

Vallejo St.
Broadway *TUNNEL*
Pacific Ave.
Jackson St.

CHINATOWN

FINANCIAL DISTRICT
Justin Herman Plaza

NOB HILL

Van Ness Ave.
Polk St.
Larkin St.
Hyde St.
Leavenworth St.
Jones St.
Taylor St.
Mason St.
Powell St.
Stockton St.
Grant Ave.
Kearny St.
Montgomery St.
Sansome St.
Battery St.
Davis St.
Front St.
Davis St.
Drumm St.

Rincon Center

Steuart St.
Spear St.
Main St.
Beale St.
Fremont St.
1st St.

Bay Bridge

San Francisco Museum of Modern Art

Geary St.
O'Farrell St.
UNION SQUARE
Market St.

THE TENDERLOIN
Eddy St.

Yerba Buena Gardens

Moscone Convention Center

SoMa

2nd St.

CIVIC CENTER

Market St.
Mission St.
Howard St.
Folsom St.
Harrison St.
Bryant St.
Brannan St.

South Park

3rd St.

Delancey St.

8th St.
9th St.
10th St.
11th St.
12th St.

Townsend St.
King St.
Berry St.
Channel St.

S. Van Ness Ave.
Folsom
Harrison
Alabama
15th St.

Division St.

Potrero Ave.

Alameda St.
POTRERO HILL

7th St.
6th St.
4th St.

Illinois St.
3rd St.
China Basin

San Francisco Bay

Campton Place
$$$$$ **Union Square**

The harpsichord music piped in to the classically decorated lobby tells you right away that this is one genteel hotel. Intimate, clubby, reserved — you'll want to use your company manners even as the valet unpacks your bags, fluffs up the bathrobes, and shows off the many luxury amenities (Bose sound system, for one) in the recently renovated and mighty classy rooms.

340 Stockton St. (at Post St.). ☎ *800-235-4300 or 415-781-5555. Fax: 415-955-5536. Internet:* www.camptonplace.com. *Valet parking: $28. Rack rates: $335–$460 double. AE, DC, DISC, MC, V.*

Chancellor Hotel
$$$ **Union Square**

This 137-room family-owned hotel offers a level of intimacy and value you just won't find in many other comparable inns. It's also right on the Powell Street cable car line, a stone's throw from Saks Fifth Avenue. The little bathrooms are well-stocked, the bedrooms are brightly decorated and comfortably furnished, and management recently added a "pillow menu," wherein guests have their choice of pillows. Kids are considered too: Each room has a Nintendo Game System. For views, request front rooms ending in 00 to 05. The hotel has ceiling fans instead of air conditioning.

433 Powell St. (between Post and Sutter sts.). ☎ *800-428-4748 or 415-362-2004. Fax: 415-362-1403. Internet:* www.chancellorhotel.com. *Valet parking: $25. Rack rates: $163 double. Deals: Inquire about discounts and packages. AE, DC, DISC, MC, V.*

Golden Gate Hotel
$$ **Union Square**

The 23 rooms at this charming, small hotel have few amenities, but they're cheerful and light on the wallet. Some share baths. The locale is great for walkers and cable-car lovers, and the complimentary breakfast and afternoon goodies make the bargain even better. Children and adults alike will take to Captain Nemo, the big house cat.

775 Bush St. (between Powell and Mason sts., two blocks from the Chinatown gate). ☎ *800-835-1118 or 415-392-3702. Fax: 415-392-6202. Internet:* www.goldengate hotel.com. *Parking: $15. Rack rates: $85 double with shared bath, $130 double with private bath. Rates include continental breakfast and afternoon tea. DC, MC, V.*

Harbor Court Hotel
$$$$ **The Embarcadero**

Located just footsteps from the bay, the Harbor Court is especially romantic and sophisticated. The spacious rooms are handsomely designed and feature half-canopy beds, and many have bay views. Guests have free access to the state-of-the-art Embarcadero YMCA pool and health club next door. The hotel has an entrance to **Ozumo** (see the "Where to Dine" section of this chapter), a trendy new Japanese restaurant.

165 Steuart St. (between Mission and Howard sts.). ☎ *800-346-0555 or 415-882-1300. Fax: 415-882-1313. Valet parking: $24. Rack rates: $210–$265 double. Deals: Check for specials and packages. AE, DC, DISC, MC, V.*

Hotel Bohème
$$$ North Beach

North Beach is the most European-like neighborhood in the city and is our personal favorite. If you fancy stepping out of your hotel into an Italian-style cafe for your morning latte, the Bohème is for you. The 15 rooms, with pretty iron beds and vivid wall colors, are small; bathrooms are showers only, but in-room amenities are generous. The accommodating staff will assist with restaurant reservations, tours, and rental cars, but you'll have to schlep your own luggage up a flight of narrow stairs. There's no air conditioning, but the windows open.

444 Columbus Ave. (between Vallejo and Green sts.). ☎ *415-433-9111. Fax: 415-362-6292. Internet:* www.hotelboheme.com. *Parking: $25 in a garage a few blocks away. Rack rates: $164–$184 double. Deals: Ask about specials. AE, DC, DISC, MC, V.*

Hotel Del Sol
$$–$$$ The Marina

Paint, mosaic tiles, and a lively imagination can do a lot to reinvent a motel, and you won't find a better example of how well this works than the Del Sol. You'll think you're in Southern California (after the fog lifts, anyway), but here pedestrians can walk around without getting startled looks from drivers. A heated pool and a hammock suspended between palm trees complete the hallucination. Multicolor guest rooms and suites contain quality amenities such as designer soap. Kids are treated to free kites and beach balls and can even check out a teddy bear from the Pillow Library. Some rooms include kitchenettes.

3100 Webster St. (at Filbert St.). ☎ *877-433-5765 or 415-921-5520. Fax: 415-931-4137. Internet:* www.thehoteldelsol.com. *Parking: Free! Rack rates: $145–$165 double. AE, DC, DISC, MC, V.*

Hotel Milano
$$$–$$$$ SoMa

This well-designed and well-maintained modern Italian-themed boutique hotel is neither flashy nor hip, but you won't find a better value in SoMa. It features one of the more spacious on-site fitness rooms in town, plus a concierge, restaurant, and all the expected amenities, including mini-bars. The multistory San Francisco Shopping Centre is a few feet away, and Yerba Buena Gardens is just around the corner, so you won't lack for things to do close by.

55 Fifth St. (between Market and Mission sts.). ☎ *800-398-7555 or 415-543-8555. Fax: 415-543-5885. Internet:* www.hotelmilano.citysearch.com. *Valet parking: $24. Rack rates: $199–$299 double. Deals: Ask about weekend packages. AE, DC, MC, V.*

Hotel Monaco
$$$$ Union Square

Scare up a vintage Vuitton steamer trunk and a foxtail-trimmed scarf, and sashay into the Art Deco–inspired Monaco. The medium-size rooms are replete with canopied beds, floral prints, and modern furniture. All the amenities — a fitness center, room service, robes, and so on — are available, along with the appropriately named Grand Cafe restaurant. The hotel can be slightly overwhelming to some, but quite impressive overall. It's also close to theaters.

501 Geary St. (at Taylor St.). ☎ *800-214-4220 or 415-292-0100. Fax: 415-292-0111. Internet:* www.hotelmonaco.com. *Valet parking: $30. Rack rates: $219–$309 double, from $399 suite. Deals: Ask about packages and specials. AE, DC, DISC, MC, V.*

Hotel Rex
$$$–$$$$ Union Square

At this attractive, sophisticated 94-room gem, room sizes vary from small-ish doubles on up, so if you need space, be sure to request it. All accommodations are colorfully decorated and smartly designed. This is a full-service hotel, with a concierge and such thoughtful amenities as CD players.

562 Sutter St. (between Powell and Mason sts.). ☎ *800-433-4434 or 415-433-4434. Fax: 415-433-3695. Internet:* www.thehotelrex.com. *Valet parking: $30 Rack rates: $215–$245 double. Rates include evening wine. AE, DC, DISC, MC, V.*

The Huntington
$$$$$ Nob Hill

The Boston Brahmin in you will adore this quiet, refined oasis with its subtle elegance, impeccable service, and the most gorgeous spa we've seen in this town. The 1924 building originally housed apartments, so guest rooms (most are suites) and baths are larger than average; six still have kitchettes. Rooms above the 8th floor offer views; the ones listed in this section are extra-spacious. Children are welcome, and the staff, concierge included, will anticipate your every need. Manicured Huntington Park, complete with playground, is across the street.

1075 California St. (at Taylor St.). ☎ ***800-227-4683*** *or 415-474-5400. Fax: 415-474-6227. Internet:* www.huntingtonhotel.com. *Valet parking: $30. Rack rates: $310–$455 double. Deals: Inquire about packages. AE, DC, DISC, MC, V.*

Kensington Park Hotel
$$$ Union Square

This 88-room property, with a theater on the second floor and a well-known (and snobby) restaurant next door, is a find among Union Square hotels in any price range. Larger-than-average rooms were renovated in 1998; the bathrooms were already among the handsomest in the area. The porter/concierge couldn't be friendlier or more willing to assist guests. Request a room above the 7th floor, Nob Hill side or on a corner, if you like views. The hotel includes workout facilities.

450 Post St. (between Mason and Powell sts.). ☎ ***800-553-1900*** *or 415-788-6400. Fax: 415-399-9484. Internet:* www.kensingtonparkhotel.com. *Valet parking: $22. Rack rates: $185–$249 double. Rates include continental breakfast and evening sherry or tea. AE, DC, DISC, MC, V.*

Marina Inn
$–$$ The Marina

This budget 40-room Victorian inn is furnished with simple pine beds, armoires, and small tables. Streetside rooms are bright but noisy; inside rooms are quieter and darker, but natural light comes from a light well. The staff will make tour, restaurant, and airport shuttle reservations, but no room service is available. All in all, this is a very good deal in a fine location convenient to Chestnut Street shopping and Fort Mason.

3110 Octavia St. (at Lombard St.). ☎ ***800-274-1420*** *or 415-928-1000. Fax: 415-928-5909. Internet:* www.marinainn.com. *Self-parking: $12 at the nearest public garage. Rack rates: $65–$135 double. Rates include continental breakfast. AE, MC, V.*

The Orchard
$$$$ Union Square

Opened in 2001, the 105-room Orchard boasts some of the largest bedrooms and most luxurious baths in the area. Conservatively decorated rooms will satisfy you as a business traveler or as a vacationer, because the rooms include CD/DVD players, high-speed Internet access, and top amenities, including room service. Cable cars stop just around the corner.

665 Bush St. (between Stockton and Powell sts.). ☎ ***888-717-2881*** *or 415-362-8878. Fax: 415-362-8088. Internet:* www.theorchardhotel.com. *Valet parking: $30. Rack rates: $229–$299 double. Rates include continental breakfast. Deals: Packages and weekend specials. AE, DC, MC, V.*

Petite Auberge
$$$–$$$$ **Union Square**

Romantics will find true love here among the florals and French-country effects. The high-end rooms are enormous; the less expensive are cozy and have showers only, but are equally comfortable. Along with a full breakfast served downstairs in the homey dining room, the hotel offers complimentary tea, wine, and hors d'oeuvres in the afternoon. It's exceedingly popular, so if you want to experience the charms of a Provençal-style inn, book way ahead.

863 Bush St. (between Mason and Taylor sts.). ☎ *800-365-3004 or 415-928-6000. Fax: 415-775-5717. Internet:* www.foursisters.com. *Valet parking: $30. Rack rates: $150–$245 double. Rates include full breakfast and afternoon snacks. AE, DC, MC, V.*

Sir Francis Drake Hotel
$$$–$$$$$ **Union Square**

Uniformed valets open the doors into the grandly elegant lobby of this historic building. The medium-size, up-to-date rooms won't take your breath away, but if you can secure a corner room above the 10th floor, the view will. A small workout room, cafe, excellent restaurant, and busy nightclub are on-site. Services, including concierge, are superlative. The hotel's close proximity to many of the city's top museums and attractions make this a good place to bring the kids.

450 Powell St. (at Sutter St.). ☎ *800-227-5480 or 415-392-7755. Fax: 415-391-8719. Internet:* www.sirfrancisdrake.com. *Valet parking: $30. Rack rates: $179–$349 double. Deals: Packages available. AE, DC, DISC, MC, V.*

Where to Dine

Eating is not beside the point when you visit San Francisco. The number of restaurants in the city (around 3,300) is astonishing, and the quality of the food in many of them is equally so.

So much food and so little time . . . but there is plenty of competition for seats. Call for reservations before arriving at any but the most casual of restaurants.

Want to eat at the most sought-after tables in town? Try calling the day you'd like to go, right after the reservation line opens. The most popular restaurants often require that guests confirm their intentions by noon, so you may luck out and get in on a cancellation.

Boulevard
$$$$ **The Embarcadero** **CALIFORNIA**

An elegant turn-of-the-century setting and generous plates of seasonal California-French cuisine combine to ensure a rousing good time at this deservedly popular restaurant. Guests without reservations can take a seat at the counter, but you should phone three or four weeks in advance to get a prime-time table.

1 Mission St. (at Steuart St.). ☎ *415-543-6084. Reservations a must. To get there: Muni Metro to the Embarcadero Station; walk one block east to Mission St. Main courses: $18–$28. AE, DC, DISC, MC, V. Open: Thurs–Sat 5:30–10:30 p.m., Sun–Wed 5:30–10 p.m.; lunch Mon–Fri 11:30 a.m.–2 p.m.; bistro menu Mon–Fri 2:30–5:15 p.m.*

Chow
$–$$ The Castro   AMERICAN

Pasta dishes, crispy brick-oven roasted chicken, and thin-crusted pizzas make this great price performer ideal for kids and grown-ups alike. The wood-paneled room is casual and comfortable, the service is kind, and patrons are happy. **Park Chow** (1240 9th Ave.; ☎ **415-665-9912**) by Golden Gate Park, is also terrific.

215 Church St. (at Market St.). ☎ *415-552-2469. Reservations not taken. To get there: Take Muni Metro J-Church or F-Market to Church St. Main courses: $6.50–$13. MC, V. Open: Sun–Thurs 11 a.m.–11 p.m., Fri and Sat 11 a.m. to midnight.*

Delfina
$$$ Mission District   TUSCAN ITALIAN

This casual but energetic bistro defines what's incredible about the city's neighborhood restaurants. Dishes such as Chianti-braised beef ravioli, quail with spring onion-chanterelle bread salad, and roasted beets with local goat's cheese are full of flavor and concocted from only the freshest ingredients, a smattering of herbs, and brilliant preparation. A devoted following makes reservations necessary, but a few tables are reserved for walk-ins.

3621 18th St. (between Dolores and Guerrero sts.). ☎ *415-552-4055. Reservations a must. To get there: Muni J-Church to 18th; walk one block east. Main courses: $15–$20. MC, V. Open: Sun–Thurs 5:30–10 p.m., Fri and Sat 5:30–11 p.m.*

Enrico's Sidewalk Cafe
$$$ North Beach   CAL-ITALIAN

Dining on a patio with a view of the bawdy section of Broadway would liven up any evening, but this friendly, cosmopolitan bar and restaurant also offers jazz and a menu of knockout seasonal fish and meat dishes.

504 Broadway (at Kearny St.). ☎ *415-982-6223. Reservations recommended. To get there: 30-Stockton bus to Broadway; walk two blocks east. Main courses: $10–$22. AE, MC, V. Open: Sun–Thurs 11:30 a.m.–11 p.m., Fri and Sat 11:30 a.m.–12 a.m.*

San Francisco Dining

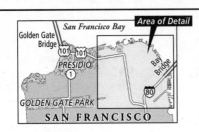

Boulevard **8**

Chow **18**

Clift **11**

Delfina **17**

Enrico's Sidewalk Cafe **5**

Foreign Cinema **15**

Grand Cafe **12**

Greens **1**

Jardiniere **13**

Kokkari **6**

Lichee Garden **4**

Merenda **2**

Plouf **9**

R&G Lounge **7**

Scala's Bistro **10**

Slanted Door **16**

Spoon **3**

Zuni Cafe **14**

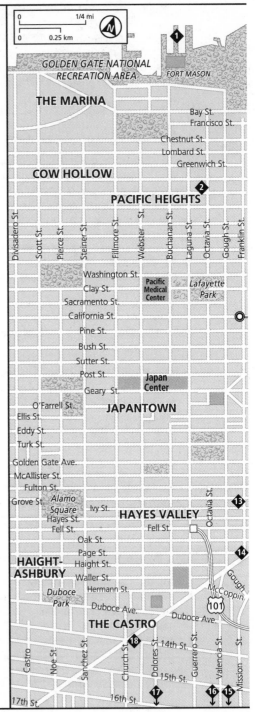

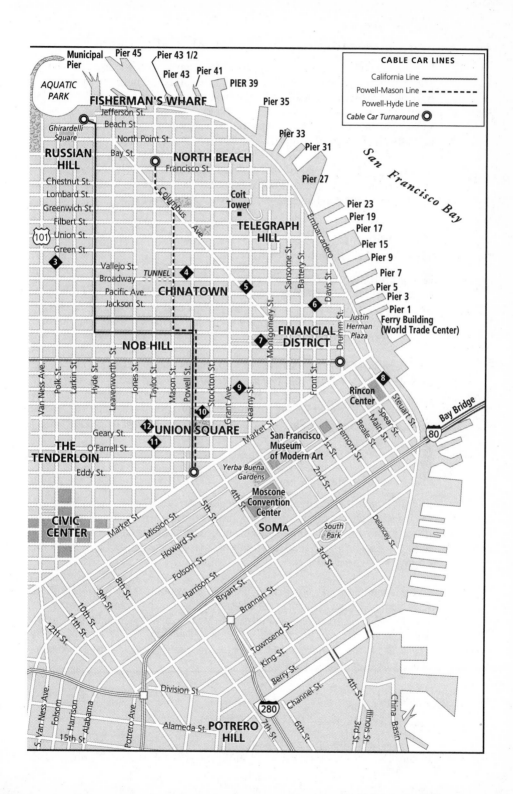

Foreign Cinema
$$$$ **Mission District** **CALIFORNIA-MEDITERRANEAN**

Mission District regulars nearly lost their empanadas when the shiny, chic Foreign Cinema opened in 1999. The expansive dining room — plus outdoor patio where foreign films are screened on a concrete wall — would throw anyone at first, but an elegant plate of escargots or some oysters from the raw bar helps to lower resistance to the inevitable changes in the neighborhood.

2534 Mission St. (between 21st and 22nd sts.). ☎ 415-648-7600. Reservations highly recommended. To get there: BART to 24th St. Main courses: $17–$22. AE, MC, V. Open: Tues–Thurs and Sun 5:30–10 p.m., Fri and Sat 5:30–11 p.m.

Grand Cafe
$$$–$$$$ **Union Square** **FRENCH**

Living up to its name in every aspect, this vast, high-ceilinged, muraled bistro is abuzz with activity and energy. People gravitate to the Petit Cafe pre- and post-theater for brick-oven pizzas, sandwiches, and desserts; and they head to the larger dining room for a rib-eye steak or a lovely, fragrant bouillabaisse.

501 Geary St. (at Taylor St.). ☎ 415-292-0101. Reservations accepted. To get there: Muni Metro to Powell St.; walk two blocks to Geary and two blocks south to Taylor. Main courses: $14–$25; Petit Café $7–$12. AE, DC, DISC, MC, V. Open: Mon–Thurs 5:30–10 p.m., Fri and Sat 5:30–11 p.m., Sun 5–10 p.m; lunch Mon–Thurs 11:30 a.m.–2:30 p.m.; breakfast Mon–Sat 7–10:30 a.m.; Sun brunch 9:30 a.m.–2:30 p.m.

Greens
$$$ **The Marina/Cow Hollow** **VEGETARIAN**

If you've never eaten in a gourmet vegetarian restaurant, or if your past encounters with vegetarian dining have been less than inspired, you're in for a marvelous culinary experience. The Saturday evening prix-fixe menu is enticing, especially when you see the gorgeous bay view that comes with the meal.

Fort Mason, Bldg. A (off Marina Blvd. at Buchanan St.). ☎ 415-771-6222. Reservations highly recommended at least two weeks in advance. To get there: Take the 30-Stockton to Laguna and transfer to the 28-19th Ave. into Fort Mason. Main courses: $15–$19; prix-fixe menu (Sat only) $46. DISC, MC, V. Open: Mon–Sat 5:30–9:30 p.m.; lunch Tues–Sat 11:30 a.m.–2 p.m.; Sun brunch 10 a.m.–2 p.m.; late-evening dessert Mon–Sat 9:30–11 p.m.

Jardiniere
$$$$ **Civic Center** **CALIFORNIA**

This is where the upscale crowd sups before the opera, ballet, or symphony. Expect sophisticated surroundings, a lively bar, and highly touted high-priced food. The risotto is heaven-sent. A jazz combo plays upstairs Sunday through Tuesday.

300 Grove St. (at Franklin St.). ☎ *415-861-5555. Reservations a must. To get there: Muni Metro to Civic Center; walk four blocks north on Franklin. Main courses: $23–$35. AE, DC, MC, V. Open: Sun–Wed 5–10:30 p.m., Thurs–Sat 5–11:30 p.m.*

Kokkari Estiatorio
$$$$ Financial District   GREEK

Your average Mediterranean shipping tycoon would feel perfectly comfortable seated beneath the beamed ceilings of this richly appointed tavern. The California-meets-Greek menu takes familiar dishes to Mount Olympus-style heights. Order the *Yiaourti Graniti* (yogurt sorbet with tangerine ice) for dessert even if you're full.

200 Jackson St. (at Front St.). ☎ *415-981-0983. Reservations a must. To get there: Catch a 2, 3, or 4 bus; transfer to 42 Downtown loop exit at Sansome and Jackson sts. and walk two blocks west to Front. Main courses: $18–$33. AE, DC, MC, V. Open: Mon–Thurs 5:30–10:30 p.m., Fri and Sat 5–11 p.m.; lunch Mon–Fri 11:30 a.m.–2:30 p.m.*

Lichee Garden
$$ Chinatown   CHINESE

This is a particularly great family-style Cantonese restaurant, in a quieter part of Chinatown, with a huge menu filled with familiar dishes (like egg foo yung), lots of seafood, and every Chinese dish you remember from childhood (unless you were raised in China). They also serve a good dim sum lunch. Prices are inexpensive (Peking duck being the biggest extravagance), service is fine, and the room is bright and lively as this place is popular with the locals — and kids, too.

1416 Powell St. (near Broadway). ☎ *415-397-2290. Reservations accepted. To get there: Cable car: Powell-Mason. Main courses: $6.50–$25. MC, V. Open: Daily 7 a.m.–9:15 p.m.*

Merenda
$$$ Marina District   CALIFORNIA-FRENCH

This is the kind of neighborhood restaurant that inspires you to fantasize about moving to the city. A nearly bargain-priced prix-fixe menu allows you to order any combination of courses from the seasonal picks, and you really can't go wrong. There is always a fresh fish and vegetarian selection plus delicate soups, housemade pastas, and delectable starters such as frisée and chicken liver salad. The room is intimate and cozy. Plus, you get a big, delicious cookie along with the bill. We love this place.

1809 Union St. (at Octavia St.). ☎ *415-346-7373. Reservations a must. To get there: Bus 30 Stockton. Prix-fixe meals: $25–$42. AE, DC, MC, V. Open: Wed–Mon 5:30–9 p.m; takeout counter Wed–Mon 11 a.m.–9 p.m.*

Plouf
$$$ Financial District   FRENCH

One in a row of terrific restaurants on Belden Place, Plouf has a menu of fresh fish and mussels prepared with a French twist and served by waiters who look as if they were extras in the movie *Gigi*. The leek tart also elicits raves. Eat outside on the street in good weather and pretend you're in Paris.

40 Belden Place (an alley between Pine, Kearney, and Bush sts.). ☎ *415-986-6491. Reservations advised. To get there: Walk on Stockton St. north from Union Square to Bush St. and turn east for two blocks. Main courses: $15–$24. MC, V. Open: Mon–Wed 11:30 a.m.–3 p.m. and 5:30–10 p.m., Thurs–Sat 11 a.m. to midnight.*

R&G Lounge
$$ Chinatown   CHINESE

You'll find superb Hong Kong Chinese dishes here, downstairs in a setting reminiscent of an airport lounge, or upstairs in a more attractive dining room, so talk your way to a table there. Make room for salt and pepper crab and fresh, crisp vegetables such as Chinese broccoli and *yin choy* (a leafy green vegetable with a red root that's often boiled, then braised with garlic). Bring the family and order a few dishes for all to share. Kids love it.

631 Kearny St. (between Sacramento and Clay sts.). ☎ *415-982-7877. Reservations accepted. To get there: Bus 15-Third. Main courses: $6.50–$8.50. AE, MC, V. Open: Daily 11 a.m.–9:30 p.m.*

Scala's Bistro
$$$ Union Square   ITALIAN

The seductively masculine dining room, with mahogany paneling and warm lighting, complements a well-rounded menu of Italian favorites, including an excellent Caesar salad and flavorful local bass in season. This is a downtown restaurant that's not strictly hype.

432 Powell St. (between Post and Sutter sts., next to the Sir Francis Drake Hotel). ☎ *415-395-8555. Internet:* www.scalasbistro.com. *Reservations recommended. To get there: Powell-Hyde-line cable car. Main courses: $12–$21. AE, DC, DISC, MC, V. Open: Daily 5:15 to midnight; lunch daily 11:30 a.m.–4 p.m.; breakfast Mon–Fri 7–10:30 a.m, Sat and Sun 8–10:30 a.m.; bistro menu served daily 4–5:15 p.m.*

The Slanted Door
$$–$$$ Mission District   VIETNAMESE

Savvy travelers and locals of every stripe swoon over the buttery steamed sea bass, caramelized chicken, and plates of "shaking" beef. If dinner reservations seem impossible to come by, show up around 6 p.m.

and you may get lucky (they hold a few tables for walk-ins). The whimsical ambience is very kid friendly, and you'll see lots of happy toddlers slurping up noodles.

584 Valencia St. (at 17th St.). ☎ 415-861-8032. Reservations a must. To get there: BART to 16th and Mission; walk west one block to Valencia. Main courses: $13–$27. MC, V. Open: Tues–Sun 11:30 a.m.–3 p.m and 5:30–10 p.m. Note: The restaurant has moved temporarily to 100 Brannan St. (Embarcadero) until spring 2003.

Spoon
$$$ Russian Hill   AMERICAN

We fondly remember the duck confit salad with goat cheese–filled cherries, and the double pork chop served with an apple-raisin compote, every scrape eaten gratefully at the bar one night when we arrived without reservations. The food is so delicious at this small, sleek, and terribly popular new restaurant that we'd grovel any day for a seat.

2209 Polk St. (at Vallejo St.). ☎ 415-268-0140. Reservations recommended. To get there: Powell-Hyde cable car to Vallejo, walk two blocks to Polk. Main courses: $15–$20. AE, MC, V. Open: Dinner Tues–Sat 5:30–11 p.m.

Zuni Cafe
$$$ Civic Center   CALIFORNIA

You can always detect a palpable buzz from the smartly dressed crowd hanging around Zuni's copper bar drinking vodka and scarfing up oysters. Everything from the brick oven is great, but the roast chicken and bread salad for two is simply divine. Don't opt for an outside table, because the view on this section of Market Street isn't all that pleasant.

1658 Market St. (between Franklin and Gough sts.). ☎ 415-552-2522. Reservations recommended. To get there: Muni Metro F-Market to Van Ness; walk two blocks southwest. Main courses: $11–$26. AE, MC, V. Open: Tues– Sat 11:30 a.m. to midnight, Sun 11 a.m.–11 p.m.

Exploring San Francisco

You can save money on entrance fees to five major attractions by purchasing the **CityPass** for $34.75 adults, $26.75 seniors over 65, and $25.75 children 5 through 17. It's good for admission to the **Museum of Modern Art, Palace of the Legion of Honor, California Academy of Sciences, the Exploratorium,** a **Blue & Gold Bay cruise,** or **Alcatraz,** and includes a **seven-day muni/cable car passport.** You can get your CityPass at the aforementioned attractions, or order it in advance online at www.citypass.net or by contacting Blue and Gold Fleet Cruise at ☎ 415-705-5555.

San Francisco's Top Attractions

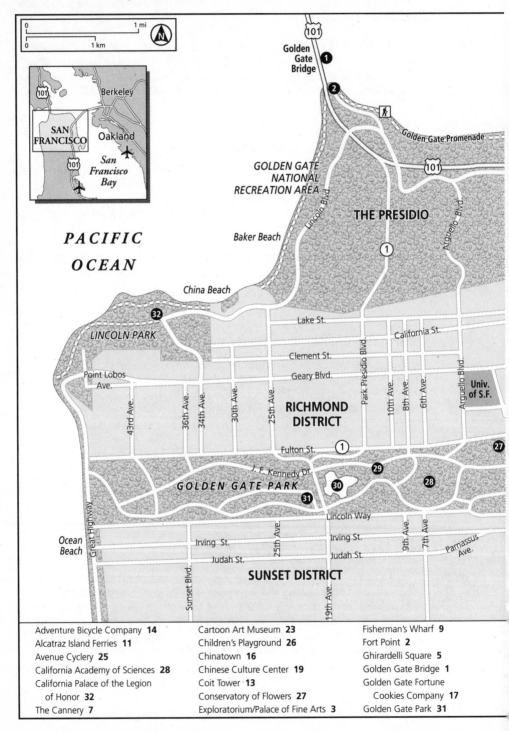

Adventure Bicycle Company **14**	Cartoon Art Museum **23**	Fisherman's Wharf **9**
Alcatraz Island Ferries **11**	Children's Playground **26**	Fort Point **2**
Avenue Cyclery **25**	Chinatown **16**	Ghirardelli Square **5**
California Academy of Sciences **28**	Chinese Culture Center **19**	Golden Gate Bridge **1**
California Palace of the Legion	Coit Tower **13**	Golden Gate Fortune
of Honor **32**	Conservatory of Flowers **27**	Cookies Company **17**
The Cannery **7**	Exploratorium/Palace of Fine Arts **3**	Golden Gate Park **31**

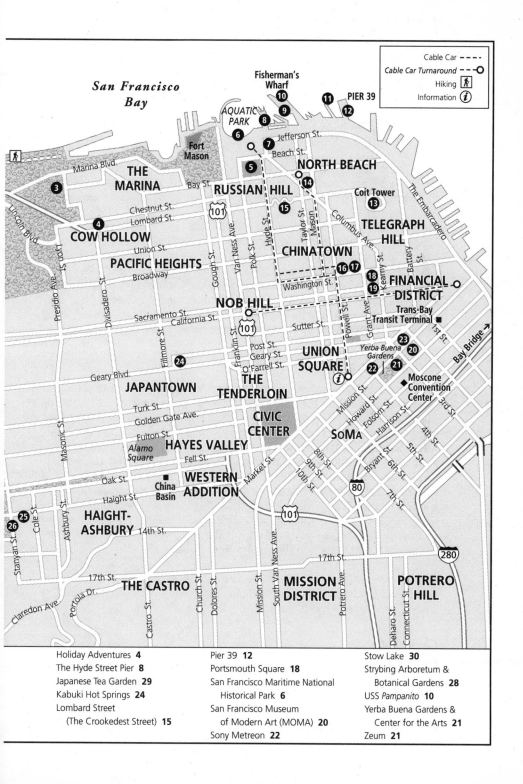

Map Legend:
- Cable Car - - - -
- Cable Car Turnaround - - -O
- Hiking
- Information (i)

San Francisco
Bay

Fisherman's
Wharf

AQUATIC
PARK

PIER 39

Jefferson St.

Beach St.

Fort
Mason

NORTH BEACH

THE
MARINA

Marina Blvd.

Bay St.

RUSSIAN HILL

Coit Tower

Chestnut St.

Lombard St.

COW HOLLOW

Union St.

PACIFIC HEIGHTS

Broadway

CHINATOWN

TELEGRAPH
HILL

Columbus Ave.

Washington St.

FINANCIAL
DISTRICT

NOB HILL

Sacramento St.

California St.

Trans-Bay
Transit Terminal

Sutter St.

Post St.

Geary St.

O'Farrell St.

UNION
SQUARE

Yerba Buena
Gardens

Moscone
Convention
Center

Bay Bridge

Geary Blvd.

JAPANTOWN

THE
TENDERLOIN

Turk St.

Golden Gate Ave.

Fulton St.

Alamo
Square

CIVIC
CENTER

SoMa

Mission St.

Howard St.

Folsom St.

Harrison St.

Bryant St.

HAYES VALLEY

Fell St.

Oak St.

China
Basin

WESTERN
ADDITION

Market St.

Haight St.

HAIGHT-
ASHBURY

14th St.

17th St.

THE CASTRO

MISSION
DISTRICT

POTRERO
HILL

17th St.

The top attractions

Alcatraz Island

If not for the movies, Alcatraz Island (a.k.a. "The Rock") would never have morphed from a rundown, deserted maximum-security prison into a must-see tourist attraction. Self-guided 2½-hour audio tours and talks facilitated by National Park rangers are full of interesting anecdotes. The walk uphill to the Cell House is steep, so wear comfortable shoes, and don't forget to bring a jacket because the island gets windy. Another path up to the prison is now wheelchair-accessible. In the summer, order tickets far in advance for the ferry ride to the island. Plan on a minimum of three hours for the entire excursion.

Pier 41, near Fisherman's Wharf. ☎ *415-773-1188 for information only.* ☎ *415-705-5555 to purchase tickets over the phone with a $2.25-per-ticket service charge. Internet:* www.blueandgoldfleet.com *or* www.telesails.com. *To get there: F Market streetcar; Powell-Mason cable car (the line ends a few blocks away); or bus 30-Stockton, which stops one block south. Admission (includes ferry and audio tour): $13.25 adults, $11.50 seniors 62 and older, $8 children 5–11. Open: Winter, daily 9:15 a.m.–2:30 p.m.; summer, daily 9:15 a.m.–4:15 p.m. Ferries run approximately every half-hour from Pier 41. Arrive at least 20 minutes before sailing time.*

The Cable Cars

These cherished wooden cars creak and squeal up and around hills as unwitting passengers lean out into the wind, running the risk of getting their heads removed by passing buses. San Francisco's three existing lines comprise the world's only surviving system of cable cars. (Brown signs with a white cable car on them indicate stops.) All three routes are worth your time — and kids will demand at least one ride — but the Powell-Mason line conveniently wends its way from the corner of Powell and Market streets through North Beach and ends near Fisherman's Wharf, and the Powell-Hyde line, which starts at the same intersection, and ends up near the Maritime Museum and Ghirardelli Square. The less-thrilling California line begins at the foot of Market Street and travels along California Street over Nob Hill to Van Ness Avenue.

Cars run from 6:30 a.m. to 12:30 a.m. The fare is $2 per person one-way, payable on board; Muni passports are accepted. For more information, see the "Getting around" section, earlier in this chapter.

Chinatown

Crowded with pedestrians and crammed with exotic-looking shops and vegetable markets whose wares spill onto the sidewalks, Chinatown is genuinely fascinating. If you want an authentic experience, veer off Grant Avenue and explore the side streets and alleys. On weekends, Chinatown is extra-jammed with shoppers examining fruits and vegetables piled on outdoor tables. Just walking down the street is an experience.

The **Golden Gate Fortune Cookies Company,** 956 Ross Alley (between Jackson and Washington streets near Grant Avenue), is a working factory where you can purchase inexpensive fresh almonds and delicious fortune cookies (terrific gifts for the folks back home!). It's very tight quarters, but you can stand for a few minutes watching rounds of dough be transformed into cookies. Open daily from 10 a.m. to 7 p.m.

Portsmouth Square, a park above the Portsmouth Square parking garage on Kearny Street (between Washington and Clay streets), is the site of the first California public school, which opened in 1848, and marks the spot where San Francisco was originally settled. A compact but complete playground attracts all the neighborhood preschoolers and, in the morning, elderly Chinese who come to practice tai chi exercises. The landscape includes comfortable benches, attractive lampposts, and young trees. The distinctly San Francisco view includes the Transamerica Pyramid looming above the skyline.

The pedestrian bridge over Kearny Street leads directly into the third floor of the Chinatown Holiday Inn, where you'll find the **Chinese Culture Center.** A gift shop leads to the sole gallery, where changing exhibits may feature, for example, photographs from pre-earthquake Chinatown, Chinese brush painting, or exquisitely embroidered antique clothing and household items. Admission is free, and the center is open Monday through Saturday from 10 a.m. to 4 p.m.

Location: 750 Kearny St., Portsmouth Square. ☎ *415-986-1822. To get there: Take Muni bus 1 California, 9AX San Bruno "A" Express, 9BX Xan Bruno "B" Express, or 15 Third. Admission: Free. Open: Tues–Sun 10 a.m.–4 p.m.*

Coit Tower

You can see this 210-foot concrete landmark from much of the city, but everyone should see it up close. The walls inside are painted with dramatic, not-to-be-missed murals commissioned during the Great Depression. Take an elevator to the top for panoramic views of the city and the bay. This visit will take about 30 minutes from start to finish.

Atop Telegraph Hill (near North Beach). ☎ *415-362-0808. To get there: Take the 39-Coit bus or walk from Lombard St. where it meets Telegraph Hill Blvd. (two blocks east of Stockton St.). Parking: The drive up and the parking lot are always a mass of cars. Admission: $3.75 adults, $2.50 seniors, $1.50 kids 6–12. Open: Daily 10 a.m.–6 p.m.*

Exploratorium/Palace of Fine Arts

One of the finest hands-on science museums anywhere, this attraction makes an interesting stop for all ages. The changing exhibits explore technology, human perception, and natural phenomena with well-written text. Visiting with kids can be humbling if you're science-impaired, but a staff of alert volunteers is on hand to help with the tough questions. When you need to decompress, stroll the lovely grounds surrounding the Palace of Fine Arts. If the weather's balmy, bring a picnic and stay awhile.

3601 Lyon St. (at Marina Blvd.), the Marina. ☎ *415-561-0360. Internet:* www. exploratorium.edu. *To get there: 30-Stockton bus to Marina Stop. Parking: Free and easy. Admission: $10 adults, $7.50 seniors and students over 18, $6 kids 5–17, free kids under 4. Free to all first Wed of the month. Open: Memorial Day–Labor Day, Thurs–Tues 10 a.m.–6 p.m., Wed 10 a.m.–9 p.m.; Labor Day– Memorial Day, Tues and Thurs–Sun 10 a.m.–5 p.m., Wed 10 a.m.–9 p.m.*

Fisherman's Wharf

Don't be disappointed when you arrive at Fisherman's Wharf and see lots of people wandering around, none of whom seem to be fishing for a living. This was once a working set of piers, but today it's a seemingly endless outdoor shopping mall masquerading as a bona-fide destination. Some people really enjoy examining the refrigerator magnets and cable car bookends stocked in one olde shoppe after another; others, dazed in the presence of so much kitsch, hastily plan their escape. Still, because most folks make their way to the wharf for one reason or another, here's a rundown of what's there.

Even when the weather is cold and gray, tourists pack **Pier 39,** a multi-level Disneyesque shopper's dream (or nightmare, depending on your point of view). Arcade halls lined with deafening video games anchor the pier on each end, with T-shirt shops and fried food filling the void. The only plausible reasons to join the mob are for the golden view of Alcatraz from the end of the pier, and to watch the sea lions loitering on the west side of the pier (follow the barking). If you're arriving by car, park on adjacent streets or on the wharf between Taylor and Jones streets. (Be advised — the parking garage charges $5.50 per hour! Do your best to avoid these price-gougers or just don't bring a car here.)

The San Francisco Maritime National Historical Park (☎ 415-556-3002) is a small, two-story museum displaying exhibits and photos marking the city's maritime heritage. Examining the museum's schooners, figure-heads, and photographs only takes about 15 minutes, although children may lose interest after the first five minutes. Still, the museum is very sweet, and admission is free. Open daily from 10 a.m. to 5 p.m.

If you have little kids in tow (or anyone interested in history), you won't want to miss touring the *USS Pampanito,* Pier 45 (☎ **415-775-1943**). This submarine saw active duty during WWII and helped save 73 British and Australian prisoners-of-war. The $27 family pass (for two adults and up to four children) also gets you into the Hyde Street Pier (see the following listing). Otherwise, submarine-only admission is $7 for adults, $4 for seniors, students, and children 6 to 12 (kids under 6 are free). Open daily from 9 a.m. to 6 p.m. in winter, and until 8 p.m. in summer.

The Hyde Street Pier, at the foot of Hyde Street (at Beach St., two blocks east of the Maritime Museum), houses seven refurbished historic ships (six are national landmarks), on which you can roam around. Of particular note is the 112-year-old *Balclutha,* a square-rigger with a past. You'll probably want to spend at least an hour or so touring the vessels. In summer, admission is $4 adults, $2 for kids 12 to 17, free for kids 11 and under; winter admission is half price. Open daily from 9:30 a.m. to 5 p.m.

Ghirardelli Square, the former chocolate factory across the street from the Maritime Park at 900 North Point (between Polk and Larkin Sts.; ☎ 415-775-5500), is one of the more pleasant shopping malls in the area. Granted landmark status in 1982, the series of brick buildings hosts a roster of special events, including an annual chocolate-tasting benefit in September. Street performers entertain regularly in the West Plaza. Open daily from 10 a.m. to 6 p.m., to 9 p.m. in summer.

One block east in what was once peach-canning facilities is the **Cannery,** 2801 Leavenworth St., at Beach Street (☎ 415-771-3112), with yet more shops, jugglers, musicians, and food. Open daily from 10 a.m. to 6 p.m., until 9 p.m. summer.

At the foot of Polk St., on the western edge of the Embarcadero. To get there: Take the Powell-Hyde cable car line to the last stop; the F-Market streetcar; or the 19-Polk, 30-Stockton, 32-Embarcadero, 42-Downtown Loop, or 47-Van Ness bus. Parking: Pricey lots and garages; street parking is difficult.

Golden Gate Bridge

It's the quintessential San Francisco landmark. A walk across the windy, 1.7-mile-long span, hundreds of feet above the water, underscores the point that San Francisco really is like no other city. Bundle up, then set out from the historic Roundhouse visitor center/gift shop on the south end of the bridge. The stroll is noisy and chilly, but exhilarating. The only way to return from the other side is on foot, so assess your fatigue in the middle of the span before continuing on toward Marin. After your stroll, climb below the bridge to walk through the five-acre garden.

No phone, but you can check the Web site: www.goldengate.org. *To get there: The 28-19th Ave. or the 29-Sunset bus will deposit you across from the viewing area, right by a parking lot. Open: to pedestrians daily 6 a.m.–6 p.m.*

Lombard Street

The part of Lombard with the moniker "crookedest street in the world" begins at Hyde Street below Russian Hill. The whimsical, flower-lined block attracts thousands of visitors each year. If you intend to drive this redbrick street (it's one-way, downhill, so take the curves slowly), go early in the morning before everyone else revs up their Chevys. Better yet, walk down the stairs to fully admire the flowers, the houses with their long-suffering tenants, and the stellar view.

Lombard St. between Hyde and Leavenworth sts. To get there: Powell-Hyde cable car line.

San Francisco Museum of Modern Art (MOMA)

It was a big deal when the city finally built a handsome, grown-up museum to house its collection of modern paintings, sculptures, and photographs. The interior is especially beautiful and exudes a warmth that makes viewing the exhibits — including works by Henri Matisse, Jackson Pollock, and Ansel Adams — even more enjoyable.

151 Third St. (two blocks south of Market St., near Howard St.). ☎ *415-357-4000. Internet:* www.sfmoma.org. *To get there: Take any Muni Metro to the Montgomery St. Station and walk one block south to Third St. then two blocks east; or take the 15-Third, 30-Stockton, or 45-Union/Stockton bus. Admission: $10 adults, $7 seniors, and $6 students with ID; half-price Thurs 6–9 p.m.; free for kids under 12. Free to all first Tues of the month. Open: Thurs 11 a.m.–8:45 p.m., Fri–Tues 11 a.m.–5:45 p.m.; from 10 a.m. in summer.*

Golden Gate Park and its attractions

The 1,017 rectangular acres of greenery and cultural attractions that comprise **Golden Gate Park** contain something for everyone. Locals use the park for everything from soccer practice to wedding receptions to fly-casting lessons. On Sundays, when John F. Kennedy Drive is closed to street traffic, bicyclists ride with impunity and in-line skaters converge for dance parties.

A grand park entrance on Stanyan and Waller streets will lead you to the massive **Children's Playground** and its beautifully restored carousel. The imaginative structures and swings will occupy kids for as long as you allow. Remodeling this entrance cut down on the rather large numbers of street people who used to hang out there, but you never know if that will change. In any case, don't let it keep you from enjoying the park; the street folks can look a little scary to the uninitiated, but they are generally harmless. Another entrance at 9th Avenue on Lincoln Way brings you to the **Strybing Arboretum,** the **Japanese Tea Garden,** and the **Academy of Sciences.** The de Young museum is closed for renovations for the next few years, but the **Conservatory of Flowers,** a Victorian glass greenhouse located northeast of the Academy of Sciences off John F. Kennedy Drive, is scheduled to reopen in spring 2003. Modeled after the conservatory in London's Kew Gardens, it was nearly destroyed in 1995 after a horrific storm all but tore it apart; since then, $25 million has been raised to repair and reinvent this San Francisco landmark.

Joggers and parents pushing baby strollers make regular use of the path around manmade **Stow Lake.** The boathouse (☎ **415-752-0347**) rents paddleboats, bikes, and in-line skates by the hour, half-day, and full day. If you aren't driving, walking to the boathouse is a bit of a hike. The boathouse is west of the Japanese Tea Garden on Martin Luther King Drive; it's open daily from 9 a.m. to 4 p.m.

The N-Judah Muni Metro streetcar drops you off on 9th Avenue and Judah Street; walk three blocks to the park from there. Numerous bus lines drive close to or into the park, including the 44-O'Shaughnessy, which you can catch on 9th Ave.; the 21-Hayes; and the 5-Fulton.

Golden Gate Park houses the following museums and attractions.

California Academy of Sciences

Traveling exhibits on everything from dinosaurs to spiders complement permanent natural-history exhibits that put to shame the dusty moose dioramas you may remember from grammar-school field trips. The Earth and Space exhibit includes a popular earthquake simulation — it's as close as you'll want to get to the real thing. Also inside you'll find the **Morrison Planetarium** and the **Steinhart Aquarium;** kids love the hands-on tide pool, where they get to poke (gently) at starfish and sea urchins. Staff members feed the seals and dolphins every two hours, beginning at 10:30 a.m., and the penguins at 11:30 a.m. and 4 p.m. Plan on spending an hour or two here, longer if you attend a planetarium show.

On the Music Concourse. ☎ 415-750-7145, or 415-750-7127 for planetarium show schedules. Internet: www.calacademy.org. *Admission: $8.50 adults, $5.50 seniors and students 12–17, $2 children 4–11; free for all the first Wed of the month. Discount for public transit users (bring your bus transfer). Planetarium show, $2.50 adults, $1.25 seniors and children under 18. Open: Memorial Day–Labor Day, daily 9 a.m.–6 p.m.; Labor Day–Memorial Day, daily 10 a.m.–5 p.m.*

Strybing Arboretum and Botanical Gardens

This splendid oasis contains more than 6,000 species of well-tended plants. It's exceptionally lovely in late winter, when the rhododendrons blossom and wild iris poke up in corners, and no more peaceful a place exists when the skies are drizzling. We recommend the guided tours, offered daily at 1:30 p.m., for anyone who finds identifying any but the most basic of flowers and trees difficult. Plan to spend at minimum a half-hour just wandering around.

9th Ave. at Lincoln Way (turn left of the tour bus parking lot by the Music Concourse). ☎ 415-661-1316, ext. 314 for guided tour information. Internet: www.strybing.org. *Admission: Free! Free guided walks daily at 1:30 p.m. Open: Mon–Fri 8 a.m.–4:30 p.m., Sat–Sun 10 a.m.–5 p.m.*

Japanese Tea Garden

This tranquil spot includes colorful pagodas, koi ponds, bridges, and a giant bronze Buddha. Young children find this piece of the park particularly memorable because they can climb over a steeply arched wooden bridge. Passengers spill through the entry gate of this major tour bus destination with alarming regularity. To avoid the onslaught, arrive before 10 a.m. or after 4 p.m. in summer. Japanese tea, accompanied by a few paltry snacks, is served in the teahouse for $2.95 per person. While the garden is certainly worth the small admission fee, the food isn't.

To the left of the de Young Museum. ☎ *415-752-4227. Admission: $3.50 adults, $1.25 seniors and children 6–12. Open: Oct–Feb, 8:30 a.m.–dusk; Mar–Sept, 8:30 a.m.– 6:30 p.m.*

Yerba Buena Gardens and Center for the Arts

Yerba Buena Center for the Arts

Where once sat nothing but parking lots and derelicts, this 22-acre complex now stands as a micro-destination. It includes a collection of galleries showing a rotating exhibition of contemporary visual and performance art by local artists, lovely gardens, a stage for dance troupes including ODC/San Francisco and Smuin Ballets/SF, and a film/video theater. Interactive amusements include an ice-skating rink, a bowling alley, a children's garden and carousel, and an arts/technology studio for older kids. An entertainment behemoth in a separate building across the street — the **Sony Metreon** — houses restaurants, retail shops, an IMAX theater, and multiplex movie screens. If you take in all that Yerba Buena Center has to offer, you can easily spend the entire day here. Parking's expensive; use public transportation if possible.

Yerba Buena Center for the Arts is at 701 Mission St. (between 3rd and 4th sts.). ☎ *415-978-2700, or 415-978-ARTS for the box office. Internet:* www.yerbabuena arts.org. *To get there: Muni Metro to Powell St. or Montgomery St. and walk two blocks down Third St.; or 14-Mission or 15-Third bus. Admission to the galleries: $6 adults, $3 seniors and students. Open: Galleries, Tues–Sun 11 a.m.–6 p.m.*

You can find the following attractions in and around Yerba Buena Gardens and the Center for the Arts:

Zeum

This modern art/technology center is probably the only attraction specifically designed for older kids and teens that doesn't rely on video games. The hands-on labs give visitors the opportunity to create animated video shorts with clay figures, learn about graphics, sound, and video in the production studio, and interact with the changing gallery exhibits. Even bored adolescents will find it difficult to resist the Zeum offerings.

☎ *415-777-2800. Internet:* www.zeum.org. *Admission: Adults $7, seniors and students $6, kids 5–18 $5. Open: Sat–Sun 11 a.m.–5 p.m. during the school year and most school holidays, Wed–Sun 11 a.m.–5 p.m. in the summer.*

Sony Metreon

Four stories of glass and brushed metal anchoring one block of Yerba Buena Center, the Sony Metreon is quite the sight. Some people call it the future of entertainment centers, and, for the moment at least, nothing else on the planet is quite like it. Of course, eating, seeing movies, and spending money are the major themes. The third floor houses 15 — count 'em 15 — movie screens and the city's first IMAX theater. You'll also find what Sony refers to as family-friendly attractions, one of which is cleverly based Maurice Sendak's popular children's book, *Where the Wild Things Are.* The second is an interactive game arena, likely to swallow up a generation of video-enhanced teens and young adults. Noisy and lit like a Vegas casino, Metreon is best described as awesome.

Mission St. at 4th St. ☎ *800-METREON. Internet:* www.metreon.com. *Admission: Free! Tickets for all three attractions are $17 adults, $13 seniors and kids 3–12; individual attraction prices $7–$10. Open: Daily 10 a.m.–10 p.m.*

Pursuing the arts and other cool stuff to see and do

The **California Palace of the Legion of Honor,** in Lincoln Park between Clement Street and 34th Avenue in the outer Richmond District (☎ 415-863-3330; www.legionofhonor.org), exhibits an impressive collection of paintings, drawings, sculpture, and decorative arts. The grounds around the palace are a draw as well, and there is a very nice cafe. The museum is open Tuesday through Sunday from 9:30 a.m. to 5 p.m., and admission is $8 adults, $6 seniors, $5 kids 12 to 17, free for kids under 12 (free for everyone on the second Wednesday of the month). Take the 38-Geary bus to 33rd and Geary, then transfer to the 18-46th Avenue bus for a ride to the museum entrance.

The **Cartoon Art Museum,** at 655 Mission St. at 4th Street in SoMa (☎ 415-495-7000; www.cartoonart.org), produces exhibits on all forms of cartoon art and often showcases local cartoonists, such as Bill Griffith and the late *Peanuts* creator Charles Schultz. Open Wednesday through Friday from 11 a.m. to 5 p.m., Saturday from 10 a.m. to 5 p.m., and Sunday from 1 to 5 p.m.; admission is $5 adults, $3 seniors, $2 children 6 to 12.

Museé Mecanique is a fantastic collection of lovingly restored and maintained mechanical marvels that were the forerunners to pinball machines. Among the treasures, you can try your hand at World Series Baseball, have your fortune told, and giggle wildly with Laughing Sal, all for a quarter a pop. From its inception, the museum has been housed below the Cliff House, 1090 Point Lobos Rd., at the Great Highway, but at press time, the Park Service announced that the Cliff House was to close for restoration. The Museé Mecanique is relocating, but you'll need to phone them (☎ 415-386-1170), or check the Web site — www.museemecanique.com — to find out exactly where. Open daily (somewhere). Admission is free.

Taking a hike

Fort Point (☎ 415-556-1373), underneath the Golden Gate Bridge at the tip of the peninsula, dates from 1857. It is an easy 3½-mile stroll to Fort Point from the Hyde Street Pier along the paved **Golden Gate Promenade,** which hugs the coast as it passes through the Marina Green and the newly remodeled Crissy Fields through the Presidio. Alternatively, you can reach Fort Point by taking the 28-19th Avenue or the 29-Sunset bus to the Golden Gate Bridge and climb down from the viewing area to a short trail leading to the fort. Open Wednesday through Sunday from 10 a.m. to 5 p.m.

Riding a bike

If you plan to ride in Golden Gate Park, your best bet is one of the bike stores nearby, such as **Avenue Cyclery,** 756 Stanyan St. (☎ 415-387-3155). **Holiday Adventures Sales and Rentals,** 1937 Lombard St. (☎ 415-567-1192), will pick you up at your hotel and drive you to its store in the Marina, which is convenient for rides around the Presidio or over the Golden Gate Bridge. Both shops charge $5 per hour; per-day rates are $25 and $19, respectively, for bike, helmet, and locks.

Walking the beach

Ocean Beach, at the end of Geary Boulevard on the Great Highway, attracts picnicking families and teenagers looking for a place to swill some beer. It's great for oceanside strolls if the tide is low, and the waves can be magnificent. Swimming is dangerous and not allowed, though. The 38-Geary bus gets you within walking distance of the beach, or you can take the N-Judah Muni Metro streetcar to the end of the line.

Soaking it up

For some pampering with a Japanese twist, take the 38-Geary bus to **Kabuki Hot Springs,** 1750 Geary Blvd. at Webster Street in Japantown (☎ 415-922-6000). This is a most respectable communal bathhouse, where you can soak your feet, have a massage, or take a steam bath. Women may use the facilities on Sundays, Wednesdays, and Fridays; men are accommodated on Mondays, Thursdays, and Saturdays; Tuesdays are coed. Massages are by appointment.

Joining the audience

Kind of the poor man's version of *A Prairie Home Companion,* **West Coast Live** is a homegrown public radio show produced around the Bay Area on Saturday mornings from 10 a.m. to noon (☎ 415-664-9500; www.wcl.org). It's hosted by the honey-voiced Sedge Thomson, and guests include writers, musicians, and comedians. It doesn't have a regular home, so check the Web site for scheduling and ticket information.

Seeing San Francisco by Guided Tour

An introductory tour is always a good bet if you have limited time to explore the city. A variety of bus tours pass by the highlights and can certainly provide an overview of the city, but there's nothing to compare to a few hours devoted to pounding the pavement. We also strongly recommend that you spend an hour or two out on the bay — it's brisk, beautiful, and will put a nice glow on your cheeks.

The old soft shoe (s)

Friends of the Library sponsors **City Guides** walking tours (☎ 415-557-4266; www.sfcityguides.org). These tours trod 26 different paths each week, all for free — that's right, no charge! All you have to do is decide which tour appeals to you and show up at the proper corner on time. You can explore the haunts of the original 49ers on the "Gold Rush City" tour, admire the Painted Ladies (San Francisco's collection of beautifully resorted Victorian homes) on the "Landmark Victorians of Alamo Square" tour, or get an insider's view of Chinatown. Highly recommended!

Local cookbook writer and luminary Shirley Fong-Torres operates Chinatown food tours that will have you classifying noodles like an expert. **Wok Wiz Chinatown Walking Tours and Cooking Center,** 654 Commercial St., between Kearny and Montgomery streets (☎ 415-981-8989 or 650-355-9657; www.wokwiz.com), offers daily tours for $40 for adults and $35 for kids under 11. Tours include a seven-course dim sum lunch.

Everyone's favorite neighborhood reaches new heights of giddiness on Saturdays when food writer GraceAnn Walden leads **Mangia! North Beach** (☎ 415-397-8530; www.sfnorthbeach.com/gawtour.html), a 4½-hour, $50 walking, eating, shopping, and history tour. GraceAnn and her followers traipse in and out of a deli, an Irish pub, a truffle factory, a bakery, a pottery store, and a very fine church before ending with a multi-course, family-style lunch at one of her favorite restaurants. This tour offers lots of samples, lots of tidbits about the Italians, and lots of fun. Reservations are a must.

Trevor Hailey provides an introduction to gay and lesbian history from the Gold Rush to the present on her four-hour **Cruisin' the Castro** walking tour (☎ 415-550-8110; www.webcastro.com/castrotour). The $40 tour price includes brunch; reservations are required. It's fascinating.

Bay cruises

The **Blue & Gold Fleet** (☎ 415-773-1188; www.blueandgoldfleet.com, or www.telesails.com for online tickets) operates ferryboats to and from Marin County embarking from Fisherman's Wharf. Blue and Gold's one-hour bay cruise ($18 for adults, $14 for seniors and kids 12 to 18, $10 for kids 5 to 11; check the Web site for specials) travels under the Golden Gate Bridge, past Sausalito, Angel Island, and Alcatraz, then back to Fisherman's Wharf. If you're not interested in landing on these shores, this tour will provide a satisfying, if brief, encounter with the bay.

Our very own **Golden Gate Transit** (☎ **415-923-2000;** www.golden gate.org) operates ferry cruises from the Ferry Building at the foot of Market Street to Sausalito or Larkspur in Marin. A round-trip cruise to the pretty, but admittedly touristy, town of Sausalito will set adults back $11.20; kids 6 to 12 are $8 but free on weekends and holidays when traveling with an adult. You'll have the thrill of riding the waves past the Golden Gate Bridge, albeit without the onboard commentary provided by Blue & Gold Fleet, listed in the preceding paragraph. If you're in town during the summer, check on the Web site for Friday "Lunch with the Office Bunch" trip dates, featuring live music.

Shopping 'til You Drop

Jump right in; the shopping's fine and dandy in San Francisco.

Union Square

With all big department stores within shouting distance of one another, Union Square gets a body in the mood for retail therapy faster than you can say "Charge it!" Stand in the square and turn around slowly; you'll see **Saks Fifth Avenue** on the corner of Powell and Post streets (☎ **415-986-4300**); **Neiman Marcus** at Stockton and Geary streets (☎ **415-362-3900**); and **Macy's** (☎ **415-397-3333**) everywhere else.

A half-block north of Neiman's on Stockton Street is **Maiden Lane,** which is lined with designer shops. You can also find an entrance here to **Britex Fabrics** (☎ **415-392-2910**), probably the most well-stocked notions and fabric store in the country. **Gump's,** at 135 Post Street (☎ **415-982-1616;** www.gumps.com), sells decorative goods, collectibles, and home furnishings in a 1910 landmark building.

Chinatown

Grubby curio shops line Grant Avenue, selling all manner of cheap trinkets and clothing. If you venture off Grant, you'll find many herbal shops, and jewelry stores full of jade of varying quality. The merchants in the less touristy stores don't always speak English and they may not seem friendly, but don't let that keep you from looking around.

Chong Imports, in the Empress of China building at 838 Grant Ave., between Clay and Washington streets (☎ **415-982-1432**), stocks a little of everything. **Tai Yick Trading Company,** 1400 Powell St., at Broadway (☎ 415-986-0961), sells porcelain and pottery at reasonable prices; locals swear this is the best store of its kind in town, and the owners are helpful and friendly. The **Imperial Tea Court,** 1411 Powell St. near Broadway (☎ 415-788-6080), sells everything you'll need to brew a proper cup of Chinese tea.

North Beach

Completely different from the street of the same name in Chinatown, Grant Avenue from Green to Greenwich streets has a bohemian feel, with many stylish boutiques for clothes and accessories. **Biordi Art Imports,** 412 Columbus Ave., at Vallejo Street (☎ 415-392-8096), stocks the most beautiful hand-painted Majolica dishes and serving pieces — as close as you can get to eating off a work of art. **City Lights Bookstore,** the famous Beat-generation bookstore founded by renowned poet and Ginsberg crony Lawrence Ferlinghetti, sits on Columbus Avenue at Broadway (☎ 415-362-8193), and is still a bastion of left-of-center literature.

Union Street, the Marina

Folks who love wandering in and out of specialty shops will think they've hit pay dirt between Fillmore Street and Van Ness Avenue in the Marina District.

Carol Doda, who shaped a career out of her chest long before implants were considered accessories, runs a lingerie shop, **Carol Doda's Champagne and Lace,** at 1850 Union St. (☎ 415-776-6900). The store carries bras in regular and hard-to-find sizes, plus lots of other fun things. On the outside, adorn yourself in locally designed bangles, bags, and other pretty trinkets at **Gallery of Jewels,** 2101 Union St. (☎ 415-929-0259). **Mudpie,** 1694 Union St. (☎ 415-771-9262), sells expensive children's clothes and gifts; sticker shock is slightly lessened in the downstairs sale room, where everything is discounted.

Enjoying the Nightlife

Still have energy after all that sightseeing? Great. You can hit the town. For up-to-the-minute nightlife listings, pick up a free copy of the *San Francisco Bay Guardian* from sidewalk kiosks or in cafes.

Beach Blanket Babylon, baby

A veritable institution, *Beach Blanket Babylon* is the only-in-San Francisco musical revue famous for outrageous costumes and wildly inventive hats that appear to lead lives of their own. The spectacle is so popular that even after celebrating 28 years of poking fun at stars, politicians, and San

Francisco itself, seats for the constantly updated shows are always sold out. Purchase tickets ($25 to $62) through the TIX in Union Square (☎ 415-433-7827), online (www.beachblanketbabylon.com), by mail, or by fax at the number listed below at least three weeks in advance, especially if you want to attend a weekend performance. If you're under 21, you may only attend Sunday matinees, when liquor isn't sold.

At Club Fugazi, 678 Green St., between Powell St. and Columbus Ave., North Beach. ☎ *415-421-4222. Fax: 415-421-4187. Internet:* www.beachblanketbabylon. com. *To get there: The 15-Third, 30-Stockton, or 45 to Columbus and Union St.; Green St. is one block south of Union.*

Play it loud: Live music

The city has no lack of clubs serving up bone-shaking live music, from jazz to blues to rock. This section gives you some recommended venues.

Biscuits and Blues

This all-ages jazz-and-blues venue is in a basement room near the theater district. The Southern-style food is inexpensive, and the musicians range from local faves to legends.

410 Mason St. (at Geary St.), Union Square. ☎ *415-292-2583. To get there: Take the 38-Geary bus to Mason St.*

Blue Bar/Black Cat

Every night brings someone new to the ultra-cool Blue Bar, downstairs from the Black Cat restaurant in North Beach. Vocalists, jazz combos, and drum and bass duos have played here. It's all good.

501 Broadway Ave. (at Kearny St.), North Beach. ☎ *415-593-1471 or 415-981-2230. To get there: The 15-Third, 30-Stockton, or 45 bus to Columbus and Broadway; walk east to Kearny.*

Boom Boom Room

The Boom Boom Room is open every night for dancing to live music, cocktails, and jiving. Lines often form on the weekends, so arrive on the early side and sip your drink slowly. Cover charge ranges from $3 to $15.

1601 Fillmore St. (at Geary St.), Japantown. ☎ *415-673-8000. Internet:* www. boomboomblues.com. *To get there: Take the 38-Geary bus to Fillmore St.*

The Great American Music Hall

This venue presents big-name acts in an ornate but comfortable setting. Phone for an events calendar. This is another all-ages venue.

859 O'Farrell St. (near Polk St.), the Tenderloin. ☎ *415-885-0750. Internet:* www.musichallsf.com. *To get there: Take a cab to avoid the excitement of the Tenderloin by night.*

Jazz at Pearl's

Pearl's features a Monday Big Band Night and local jazz musicians Tuesday through Saturday. A menu of ribs, burgers, pizza, and other snacky items is available. No cover, but expect a two-drink minimum.

256 Columbus Ave. (at Broadway), North Beach. ☎ *415-291-8255. Interrnet:* www.jazzatpearls.citysearch.com. *To get there: The 15-Third, 30-Stockton, or 45 bus to Columbus and Union sts.; walk south on Columbus three blocks to Broadway.*

The Plush Room

This intimate showroom books local and national cabaret acts for runs lasting from a weekend to a few weeks. Expect torch and standards singers, musical revues, or duos of some repute. Reservations are strongly suggested.

In the York Hotel, 940 Sutter St. (between Hyde and Leavenworth sts., four blocks west of Union Square). ☎ *415-885-2800. Internet:* www.plushroom.citysearch.com.

Come here often? Bars and lounges

You may be so intoxicated by the city's natural beauty that cocktails seem redundant. Nevertheless, here are some of our favorite tippling spots in San Francisco.

Backflip

Backflip serves strong cocktails in an aqua-blue setting designed to give patrons the impression that they are drinking in the deep end. The staff wears vinyl. You get the picture.

At the Phoenix Hotel, 601 Eddy St. (at Larkin St.), the Tenderloin. ☎ *415-771-3547. To get there: Take a cab.*

Blondie's Bar and No Grill

Blondie's is on the sizzling Valencia Street corridor in the Mission District. The young and the restless make good use of the free jazz jukebox.

540 Valencia St. (between 16th and 17th sts.), Mission District. ☎ *415-864-2419. To get there: Take BART to 16th St. and walk one block west to Valencia.*

The Blue Lamp

This place includes a fireplace, a pool table, and a handful of tables for two along with a well-stocked bar. Music starts after 10 p.m.

561 Geary St. (between Jones and Taylor sts.), a short walk south from Union Square. ☎ *415-885-1464. Internet:* www.bluelamp.com.

Harry Denton's Starlight Room

This red-boothed venue is popular for dancing, drinking, and mingling in an upscale way. You can also drop by in the early evening to drink in the gorgeous views.

In the Sir Francis Drake Hotel, 450 Powell St. (at Sutter St.), Union Sq. (three blocks from the Powell St. Muni Station). ☎ *415-395-8595. Internet:* www.harrydenton.com.

Top of the Mark

The Top of the Mark has it all — views, music from 9 p.m., dancing, and a convivial crowd of suits. The hotel serves a "Sunset" three-course prix-fixe dinner on Friday and Saturday nights; with 7:30 p.m. reservations, a night on the town is a done deal.

In the Mark Hopkins Intercontinental Hotel, 1 Nob Hill (at Mason and California sts.). ☎ *415-616-6916. To get there: For fun, take the California St. cable car and exit at the top of Nob Hill.*

Experiencing the finer side of the arts

San Francisco has a thriving cultural scene, offering opera, dance, music, and edgy theater. Sample any of the activities in this section, and you won't go wrong.

Theater

Union Square houses at least ten professional theaters of varying sizes, and experimental theaters are scattered about the SoMa and Mission districts in converted warehouses and gallery spaces. The preeminent company in town is the **American Conservatory Theater (ACT),** which produces a little of everything during its October to June season. The sets and costumes are universally brilliant, and the acting is first-rate. Productions take place in the lovely Geary Theater, 415 Geary St., at Mason Street (☎ **415-749-2228;** Internet: www.act-sfbay.org).

Opera

The **San Francisco Opera** season opens with a gala in September and ends quietly in early January. Performances are produced in the War Memorial Opera House, 301 Van Ness Ave., at Grove Street (☎ **415-864-3330;** Internet: www.sfopera.com), in the Civic Center.

Classical music

The **San Francisco Symphony** performs in the Louise M. Davies Symphony Hall, 201 Van Ness Ave., at Grove Street (☎ **415-864-6000;** Internet: www.sfsymphony.org), in the Civic Center.

Dance

Classical and modern dance groups abound, the most recognized being the **San Francisco Ballet,** whose season runs from February to June. The troupe performs in the War Memorial Opera House, 301 Van Ness Ave., at Grove Street (☎ **415-865-2000;** Internet: www.sfballet.org).

Fast Facts

AAA

The office at 150 Van Ness Ave. in the Civic Center provides maps and other information to members. Call ☎ 415-565-2012 for information.

American Express

This full-service office is located at 455 Market St., at First Street (☎ 415-536-2600).

Baby-Sitters

Call A Bay Area Child Care Agency (☎ 650-991-7474).

Emergencies

For police, fire, or other emergencies, phone **911**. From cell phones, call ☎ **415-553-8090.**

Hospitals

Saint Francis Memorial Hospital, 900 Hyde St., between Bush and Pine streets (☎ 415-353-6000), offers 24-hour emergency-care service. The hospital's physician-referral service number is ☎ 415-353-6566. **San Francisco General Hospital,** 1001 Potrero Ave. (☎ 415-206-8000), accepts uninsured emergency patients, but the wait can be brutally long and uncomfortable. The patient assistance number is ☎ 415-206-5166.**Internet Centers**

Cafe.com is closest to Union Square at 970 Market St., near 5th and 6th streets (☎ 415-922-5322); open Monday through Saturday from 8 a.m. to 10 p.m.

Newspapers and Magazines

The **San Francisco Chronicle** is the major daily newspaper. The Sunday Datebook section lists goings-on about town. The weekly **Bay Guardian,** free at sidewalk kiosks and in bookstores, bars, and coffee-houses, is an excellent source for entertainment listings.

Police

Dial **911** in an emergency. For non-emergencies, call ☎ 415-553-0123.

Post Office

The **Rincon Center** houses a post office at 180 Steaurt St., in the Embarcadero. Call ☎ 800-ASK-USPS or log on to www.usps.gov to find the branch nearest you.

Taxes

Sales tax is 8.5%. Hotel tax is 14%.**Taxis**

Yellow Cab (☎ 415-626-2345); **Veteran's Cab** (☎ 415-552-1300); **Desoto Cab** (☎ 415-970-1300); **Luxor Cabs** (☎ 415-282-4141).

Transit Info

☎ 415-817-1717.

Weather

For forecasts, go online to www.wunderground.com.

Gathering More Information

The **San Francisco Convention and Visitors Bureau Information Center** is on the lower level of Hallidie Plaza, 900 Market St., at Powell Street (☎ **800-220-5747** or 415-391-2000). It's open Monday through Friday from 9 a.m. to 5:30 p.m., Saturday from 9 a.m. to 3 p.m., and Sunday from 10 a.m. to 2 p.m.

You'll find the **city's official Web site** at www.sfvisitor.org. For up-to-date information on the city and surrounding areas, try **Citysearch** at www.bayarea.citysearch.com; the *San Francisco Chronicle* Web site at www.sfgate.com; or the *San Francisco Bay Guardian* Web site at www.sfbg.com.

Chapter 10

Napa and Sonoma Valleys: California's Premier Wine Country

. . . .

In This Chapter

▶ Finding your way to and around America's premier wine-growing regions

▶ Choosing a cozy lodging — and wining and dining, Napa and Sonoma style

▶ Wine-tasting tips, tours, and recommendations

▶ Pursuing other valley pleasures

. . . .

*J*ust an hour's drive north of San Francisco is the gorgeous **Napa Valley,** America's most celebrated wine-growing region. Less than 30 miles from end to end, this super-fertile area brims with world-class wine-tasting rooms, excellent restaurants, and marvelous resorts and country inns.

Visiting the Napa Valley is akin to taking a trip to the south of France, without the jet lag or the language barrier. The stresses and strains of regular life just fade away as you cruise gentle Highway 29, the verdant valley's main thoroughfare, stopping in at wineries, pausing between tastings for a gourmet picnic and a bit of boutique shopping.

Just to the west of Napa Valley along Highway 12 is the peaceful **Sonoma Valley.** Sonoma Valley is quieter and less tourist-oriented — but equal to its neighbor as a wine-growing region. First-time visitors may suspect that there's more to see and do in Napa, and they'll be correct. But travelers looking for a place in which to do nothing but eat, drink, and thank their favorite deity that such a paradise exists will be happy as can be in and around Sonoma.

You certainly don't need to be a wine connoisseur to enjoy this section of the state, but we guarantee that if you tour one or two of the wineries we've mentioned, you'll arrive home knowing a lot more about viti-culture than your average drinker. And if it happens that you don't know much about wine (except you know what you like), don't feel intimated. Sure, some pretentious wine-tasting rooms do lurk among the grape arbors, but the valleys are completely visitor-friendly and down-right welcoming to casual wine drinkers. Another point worth mentioning: Neither Napa nor Sonoma valleys will be the bargain destination of your vacation. If you pick carefully, however, you'll discover that affordable places to stay, eat, and drink can be found.

Timing Your Visit

Summer and autumn are the most popular seasons for touring the Wine Country. The valleys are especially gorgeous in fall, and September and October bustle during the grape harvest, or *crush,* which fills the air with the sweet fragrance of *must* (the pulp and skins of crushed grapes). If you plan to visit during these seasons, make reservations early.

As long as the weather is dry, the area is a treat during the winter and spring, when the roads, restaurants, and tasting rooms are relatively unclogged, and the hotels actually offer lower rates. With the vines stripped of their heavy fruit, the valleys are not quite so beautiful, however, and touring can be a downright drag in the rain.

Weekends are always more crowded than weekdays, and the traffic heading north on the Golden Gate Bridge from San Francisco on Friday afternoons (and south on Sunday afternoons) can be torture. Do what you can to plan your visit midweek, while the weekenders are at work; not only will you avoid the crowds and enjoy your stay more, but you're bound to save a few bucks on accommodations.

Although you can easily entertain yourself for a week here, three days and two nights can provide an ideal introduction to the Wine Country. That gives you plenty of time to start with a winery tour, spread out your winery visits over the next couple of days, and work in some other local pleasures — a hot-air balloon ride, perhaps, or some leisurely bicycling or a spa treatment or two.

A single day simply can't do the area justice and will leave you wanting more. But if you can only spare a day out of your San Francisco time, come to Napa Valley. Start out from San Francisco early, because virtually all of the wine-tasting rooms shut their doors by 5 p.m. Plan to visit no more than three to four wineries (all anyone can really handle in a day, anyway), followed by an early dinner before you head back to the city. Drive immediately to Calistoga, at the north end, and work your way down the valley along Highway 29 to make your return to San Francisco a bit shorter.

Don't make this day trip on a summer weekend, because the bumper-to-bumper traffic on Highway 29 will ruin it.

Napa Valley

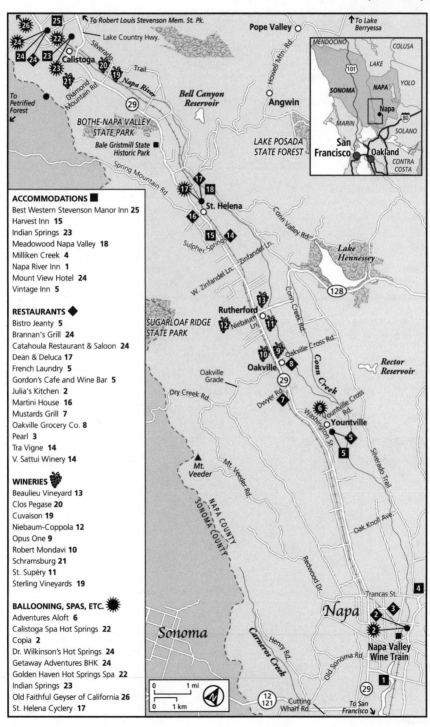

ACCOMMODATIONS ■
Best Western Stevenson Manor Inn **25**
Harvest Inn **15**
Indian Springs **23**
Meadowood Napa Valley **18**
Milliken Creek **4**
Napa River Inn **1**
Mount View Hotel **24**
Vintage Inn **5**

RESTAURANTS ◆
Bistro Jeanty **5**
Brannan's Grill **24**
Catahoula Restaurant & Saloon **24**
Dean & Deluca **17**
French Laundry **5**
Gordon's Cafe and Wine Bar **5**
Julia's Kitchen **2**
Martini House **16**
Mustards Grill **7**
Oakville Grocery Co. **8**
Pearl **3**
Tra Vigne **14**
V. Sattui Winery **14**

WINERIES 🍇
Beaulieu Vineyard **13**
Clos Pegase **20**
Cuvaison **19**
Niebaum-Coppola **12**
Opus One **9**
Robert Mondavi **10**
Schramsburg **21**
St. Supéry **11**
Sterling Vineyards **19**

BALLOONING, SPAS, ETC. ✹
Adventures Aloft **6**
Calistoga Spa Hot Springs **22**
Copia **2**
Dr. Wilkinson's Hot Springs **24**
Getaway Adventures BHK **24**
Golden Haven Hot Springs Spa **22**
Indian Springs **23**
Old Faithful Geyser of California **26**
St. Helena Cyclery **17**

Sonoma Valley

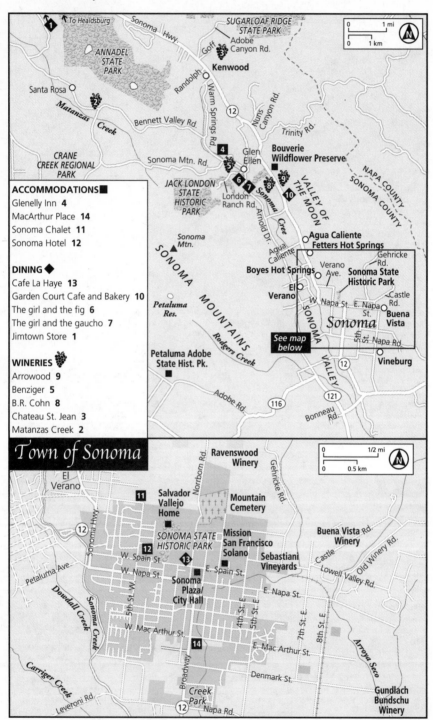

ACCOMMODATIONS ■
Glenelly Inn **4**
MacArthur Place **14**
Sonoma Chalet **11**
Sonoma Hotel **12**

DINING ◆
Cafe La Haye **13**
Garden Court Cafe and Bakery **10**
The girl and the fig **6**
The girl and the gaucho **7**
Jimtown Store **1**

WINERIES 🍇
Arrowood **9**
Benziger **5**
B.R. Cohn **8**
Chateau St. Jean **3**
Matanzas Creek **2**

Town of Sonoma

Getting There

You'll have to drive if you want the best experience. Day-trippers can take a guided tour from San Francisco if need be.

Driving yourself

From San Francisco, two roads take you to the Wine Country:

- ✔ If you decide to take the **San Francisco-Oakland Bay Bridge,** head east from downtown over the bridge (I-80) and north to the Napa/Highway 29 exit near Vallejo; follow Highway 29 north into the heart of the valley. The trip takes about 70 minutes.

- ✔ From the **Golden Gate Bridge,** continue on U.S. 101 north to Novato, where you'll pick up Highway 37 east. Take Highway 121 (the Sonoma Highway) north toward Sonoma and continue north on Highway 12, or stay on 121 east to Napa, if that's your destination, where you'll end up on Highway 29. Make sure to have a map handy. This drive is more scenic but takes about 90 minutes.

If you're coming from the **North Coast,** take Highway 128 out of Mendocino, and follow the road straight into the north end of the valley, which will take a little more than two hours.

From **Lake Tahoe,** pick up I-80 west and take it to Highway 12 for Sonoma. This also will lead you in about six miles to Highway 29 north, Napa's main drag. Expect the drive to take about 3½ hours, whether you're coming from the north or south shore.

Along for the ride: Guided tours

If you don't want to drive yourself to or around the Wine Country, you can join an organized tour. Taking a tour is a good alternative if you need a designated driver; otherwise, we strongly suggest the do-it-yourself option. On a tour, you'll cover a lot of ground in way too short a time, you won't have the freedom to linger in places that catch your fancy, you won't have much of a choice as to where you eat, and you'll miss some great wineries that aren't part of the package.

That being said, the best tour operator is **Great Pacific Tour Company** (☎ 415-626-4499), who will pick you up and deliver you back to your San Francisco hotel after tastings at two Sonoma wineries, a restaurant or picnic lunch, and a tour of **Domaine Chandon,** a sparkling wine producer in Napa. The cost is $72 adults, $70 seniors, and $62 for kids 5 to 11.

Another option is to ride the **Napa Valley Wine Train** (☎ 800-427-4124 or 707-253-2111; www.winetrain.com), basically a gourmet restaurant on wheels that chugs 36 miles through the valley from end to end. Lunch, brunch, and dinner tours range in price from $35 to $110 per person. This is a dining and take-in-the-scenery tour only; only the **Grgich Hills Private Winery Tour and Tasting,** a lunchtime ride ($79 per person), includes a stop. The train sports a wine-tasting car with an attractive bar and knowledgeable host. You can purchase and taste wine without worrying about driving safely back to the station. The three-hour tours depart from 1275 McKinstry St. in downtown Napa, at the south end of the valley. Reservations are essential. If you don't want to drive to Napa to pick up the train, **Grayline** (☎ 800-826-0202; www.graylinesanfrancisco.com) will transfer you by bus from San Francisco to the wine train station for the three-hour lunch excursion; the total cost is $99 per person.

Orienting Yourself

The Napa Valley is compact and very easy to explore. The town of Napa at the south end is just 26 miles from Calistoga at the north end. Take a look at a map of the valley, and you'll see that it resembles a ladder, with two main roads running (roughly) north-south — Highway 29, the main drag, along the west side and the Silverado Trail along the east side — and east-west cross streets at regular intervals, every half-mile or so. The valley is more commercial and developed at the south end, growing increasingly bucolic and spread out as you move north.

The town of **Napa** is the commercial center of the Wine Country and the gateway to Napa Valley. This is where the real people live — hence the fast-food joints and strip malls. Stop by the visitor center (see "Gathering More Information" at the end of this chapter) if you want to pick up a winery map, but don't be in a big hurry to leave — there's lots going on in town, including **Copia,** the new temple to food, wine, and the arts.

Just north of Napa is **Yountville.** Both St. Helena and Calistoga boast more old-fashioned charm, but Yountville wins in the convenience department. Good restaurants abound, and you can't be more centrally located.

Immediately north of Yountville is **Oakville,** then **Rutherford,** two blink-and-you'll-miss-'em towns that really just qualify as map markers. Next is **St. Helena,** about 18 miles north of Napa, an attractive little town with upscale shops tucked away in beautifully restored wooden storefronts.

Around St. Helena, the terrain starts to open up and look like the agri-cultural landscape it is. In another eight miles, you'll reach **Calistoga,** California's version of Saratoga Springs, the east coast's favorite spa town (the name "Calistoga" is a cross of the two: Cali*fornia* and Sara*toga*). This well-preserved, super-charming gold-rush town boasts the natural hot springs that make the Wine Country a first-class spa destination, too. It's our favorite place to stay, although you'll spend a bit more time in the car if you base yourself here. Because the driving is so gorgeous, it's easily worth it — but be aware of the distance, especially if your time is limited.

Be very careful while driving always-busy Highway 29. Even if you're a teetotaler, remember that virtually everybody else has imbibed a bit. This two-lane road serves as the scene of many accidents, especially at night.

Sonoma Valley is smaller and even more rural than Napa Valley, which guarantees that you can see it all in two days. It includes the towns of **Sonoma, Glen Ellen, Kenwood, Santa Rosa,** and **Healdsburg,** two state parks, a few resorts, hotels, and B&Bs scattered among the country roads, and some very fine restaurants.

Where to Stay in the Wine Country

Despite a wealth of choices, high demand keeps room rates on the pricey side. Almost all lodgings have a two-night minimum on weekends and three nights during holidays. Make reservations as far in advance as possible, especially for stays between May and October.

If our recommendations are full, call **Napa Valley Reservations Unlimited** (☎ **800-251-NAPA;** www.napavalleyreservations.com), a free central reservations service. You can find other credible Napa Valley reservations bureaus online at www.napavalleyonline.com.

The **Sonoma Valley Visitors Bureau** is located in Sonoma on the Sonoma Plaza at 453 First Street E., (☎ **707-996-1090;** www.sonoma valley.com). The bureau has an "availability sheet" of rooms in case you forgot to make reservations.

Count on 9 to 12% in taxes being tacked on to your hotel bill.

In Napa Valley

Best Western Stevenson Manor Inn
$$–$$$$ Calistoga

Situated just east of town, this new motel offers great value in an expensive neighborhood. The motel-basic rooms are boosted up a notch by fireplaces or whirlpool tubs, cable TV, fridges, coffeemakers, and hair dryers, as well as on-property extras including a pool, a hot tub, and sauna and steam rooms. Guest rooms with two queen beds won't crowd the family, and kids under 12 stay free.

1830 Lincoln Ave. (west of Silverado Trail), Calistoga. ☎ *707-942-1112. Fax: 707-942-0381. Internet:* www.callodging.com. *Parking: Free! Rack rates: $99–$244 double. Rates include continental breakfast. AE, DC, DISC, MC, V. Guests get 10% off spa services at a nearby spa.*

Harvest Inn
$$$$ St. Helena

This Tudor-inspired complex was renovated in 1999, so all the rooms are light, attractive, comfortable, and roomy enough for a family. Two pools and two Jacuzzis are set in lovely gardens against a dramatic backdrop of mountains and vineyards. Lots of little luxuries help justify the price, including feather beds, CD players, and VCRs. The mid-valley location is central to everything.

1 Main St., St. Helena. ☎ *800-950-8466 or 707-963-9463. Fax: 707-963-4402. Internet:* www.harvestinn.com. *Parking: Free! Rack rates: $240–$319 double, $399–$675 suite. Rates include continental breakfast. AE, DC, DISC, MC, V.*

Indian Springs
$$$ Calistoga

Booking these comfortable, old-fashioned bungalows in summer is not easy; you'll have to edge out the families that come here year after year, drawn by the excellent location and great value. (Hint: Call 48 hours ahead and see if you can get in on a cancellation.) Guests can use the Olympic-size mineral pool until late in the evening (day visitors must leave by 6 p.m.). The wonderful spa offers a full range of treatments, including mud baths.

1712 Lincoln Ave., Calistoga. ☎ *707-942-4913. Fax: 707-942-4919. Internet:* www.indianspringscalistoga.com. *Parking: Free! Rack rates: $185–$245 double studio or 1-bedroom, $265–$295 2-bedroom, $450–$500 3-bedroom. DISC, MC, V.*

Meadowood Napa Valley
$$$$$ St. Helena

Wanna splurge, big time? Stay at this sprawling Relais & Chateaux resort. Each individual accommodation is set among the oaks on 250 wooded acres, which boast a spa, two pools, tennis courts, world-class golf, and more than a few deer. Rooms are supremely luxurious, but in a kick-off-your-shoes way — you'll find no fussiness here. Service is stellar, of course, and the amenities list is as long as your arm. The icing on the cake? The restaurant is one of the finest fine-dining rooms in the valley.

900 Meadowood Lane (off Silverado Trail), St. Helena. ☎ *800-458-8080 or 707-963-3646. Fax: 707-963-3532. Internet:* www.meadowood.com. *Parking: Free! Rack rates: $375–$785 double, $570–$3,560 suite. AE, DC, DISC, MC, V.*

Milliken Creek

$$$$–$$$$$ **Napa**

Cushy, chic, and romantic, the large, airy rooms in this intimate new inn could have come straight out of *Metropolitian Home*. No luxury has been overlooked, from Frette bed linens and L'Occitane bath products to candlelight turndown service. The three-acre creekside gardens are equally stunning and private; you'll find it difficult to tear yourself away, although many excellent small wineries await along the Silverado Trail.

*1815 Silverado Trail, Napa. ☎ **888-622-5775** or 707-255-1197. Fax: 707-942-2653. Internet:* www.millikencreekinn.com. *Parking: Free! Rack rates: $225–$450 double. Rates include breakfast and afternoon wine and cheese. DC, MC, V.*

Mount View Hotel

$$$ **Calistoga**

Ideally situated in the heart of Calistoga, this charming and attractively restored historic hotel is a pleasing place to stay. Done in a cozy California-country style, the rooms are comfortable and well-appointed. The secluded cottages, which have private patios with Jacuzzis, are worth the tariff for romance-seeking couples. A pool and Jacuzzi in the cute courtyard, a well-regarded spa, and one of our favorite restaurants, Catahoula, round out the appeal.

*1457 Lincoln Ave., Calistoga. ☎ **800-816-6877** or 707-942-6877. Fax: 707-942-6904. Internet:* www.mountviewhotel.com. *Parking: Free! Rack rates: $145–$250 double, suite, or cottage. Rates include continental breakfast (delivered to your room). AE, DISC, MC, V.*

Napa River Inn

$$$–$$$$$ **Napa**

The first boutique hotel to reach the city of Napa, the Victorian-influenced Napa River Inn is housed in a converted 1884 warehouse complex that's part of a spiffy redevelopment project along the river. Sixty-six beautifully designed and equipped rooms are situated in three buildings; our favorite is the Embarcadero for its relative privacy. Standard rooms are dark; superior rooms have smallers baths than deluxe, but all include robes, fridges, spa products, and other goodies. Handy location near Copia (see "Immersing yourself in food and wine," later in this chapter) and downtown Napa.

*500 Main St., Napa. ☎ **877-251-8500** or 707-251-8500. Fax: 707-251-8504. Internet:* www.napariverinn.com. *Parking: Free! Rack rates: $159–$400 double, $399–$500 suite. Rates include breakfast and evening cocktail. AE, DISC, MC, V.*

Vintage Inn

$$$–$$$$$ Yountville

This big, attractive French-country inn is conveniently situated near some of the finest restaurants in the valley. Recently refurbished in a French Renaissance decor, rooms are clustered throughout the lovely flowering grounds, and are equipped with fireplaces, fridges, Jacuzzi tubs, coffeemakers, and terry-cloth robes. Tennis courts and a heated pool make this a comfortable mini-resort, good for couples exploring the area.

6541 Washington St., Yountville. ☎ *800-351-1133 or 707-944-1112. Fax: 707-944-1617. Internet:* www.vintageinn.com. *Parking: Free! Rack rates: $210–$420 double. Rates include continental champagne breakfast and afternoon tea. AE, DC, DISC, MC, V.*

In Sonoma Valley

Glenelly Inn

$$$ Glen Ellen

A secluded and peaceful family-run B&B, the modest rooms here are small but quaintly decorated, designed solely for relaxation. Each room has a private entry, terry robes, and down comforters, and most have claw-foot tubs with shower heads — but no phones or TV. A spa in the garden adds to the magic, and you can sit and gaze at the mountains on the verandas.

5131 Warm Springs Rd., Glen Ellen ☎ *707-996-6720. Fax: 707-996-5227. Internet:* www.glenelly.com. *Parking: Free! Rack rates: $150–$175 double. Rates include breakfast. Check on honeymoon, anniversary, and family getaway packages. MC, V.*

MacArthur Place

$$$$ Sonoma

This divine inn is a renovated Victorian that's masterfully connected to newer buildings. The rooms are spacious and comfy, with wonderful four-poster beds that'll make you think twice about getting up. Contented guests relax at the small, well-staffed spa where the practiced hands of a masseuse work out pre-vacation tension. Manicured gardens surround a swimming pool, and there's a steakhouse restaurant in the 100-year-old barn that supplies room service.

29 East MacArthur St., Sonoma. ☎ *800-722-1866 or 707-938-2929. Fax: 707-933-9833. Internet:* www.macarthurplace.com. *Parking: Free! Rack rates: $199–$625 double. Rates include continental breakfast. AE, MC, V.*

Sonoma Chalet

$ Sonoma

Although the views from this private Swiss-inspired farmhouse encompass the mountains and the ranch next door, it's located less than a mile from Sonoma's town square. Antiques and collectibles decorate three big, delightful cottages; inside the house, two pretty upstairs rooms have private facilities while the two downstairs rooms share a bath. A simple and delicious breakfast, including fresh pastries, is included, and you can borrow bikes for your explorations.

18935 Fifth St. West, Sonoma, CA 95476. ☎ *800-938-3129 or 707-938-3129. Internet:* www.sonomachalet.com. *Parking: Free! Rack rates: $110–$210 double with continental breakfast. AE, MC, V.*

Sonoma Hotel

$–$$$ Sonoma

This historic building is located on Sonoma's town square, which makes shopping and dining convenient. The small rooms were recently remodeled with bright bathrooms and stylish furniture that make the lodgings attractive and cozy. The small suites work well for nuclear families, and the kids will have a great time in the park across the street. The excellent restaurant **the girl and the fig** (see the "Where to Dine In the Wine Country" section) is on-site.

110 West Spain St., Sonoma, CA 95476. ☎ *800-468-6016 or 707-996-2996. Fax: 707-996-7014. Internet:* www.sonomahotel.com. *Parking: Free! Rack rates: $95–$245 double with continental breakfast. MC, V.*

Where to Dine in the Wine Country

With excellent restaurants at every turn, the Wine Country is a wonderful place to eat well. However, the best dining rooms often book up ahead, so reserve in advance. If you're visiting on a weekend, calling before you even leave home is a good idea.

In Napa Valley

Bistro Jeanty

$$$ Yountville   FRENCH

This very French bistro is much applauded around the Bay Area for its authenticity, great menu, and vivacious dining room. Eating here satisfies both the appetite and the spirit. The seasonal menu includes rustic dishes like lamb tongue and potato salad or rabbit and sweetbread ragout, plus typical bistro items including coq au vin and steak frites. Adventuresome and timid eaters alike will find something to enjoy and remember here.

6510 Washington St., Yountville. ☎ *707-944-0103. Internet:* www.bistro jeanty.com. *Reservations recommended. Main courses: $15–$25. MC, V. Open: Daily 11:30 a.m.–10 p.m.*

Brannan's Grill
$$$ Calistoga   CALIFORNIA-CONTINENTAL

Brannan's isn't exactly breaking any new culinary ground — and that's precisely why it's so popular. Expect well-prepared grilled Angus hangar steak, braised lamb shank, and a good variety of fish, all served in a lovely, lodge-style dining room with well-spaced tables draped in white linens and stylish arts-and-crafts accents. Brannan's is super-romantic after the sun goes down.

1374 Lincoln Ave., Calistoga. ☎ *707-942-2233. Reservations recommended. Main courses: $10–$19 at lunch, $17–$29 at dinner. AE, MC, V. Open: Lunch: Mon–Fri 11:30 a.m.–3 p.m., Sat–Sun 11:30 a.m.–3:30 p.m; dinner: Sun–Thurs 4:30–9:30 p.m., Fri–Sat 4:30–10 p.m.*

Catahoula Restaurant & Saloon
$$$ Calistoga

You will detect a strong hint of New Orleans in the food and atmosphere of this fun restaurant, both a critical and local favorite. If you didn't make reservations, you can dine at the bar in front of the wood-fired ovens, where busy chefs crank out plate after plate of seasonal Southern-accented dishes, such as an oven-roasted tomato pizza topped with andouille sausage and onion confit; spicy seafood paella with homemade chorizo; and cornmeal-fried catfish with lemon-jalapeño meuniére and Mardi Gras slaw. Excellent!

In the Mount View Hotel, 1457 Lincoln Ave., Calistoga. ☎ *707-942-2275. Internet:* www.catahoularest.com. *Reservations recommended. Main courses: $12–$24. MC, V. Open: Breakfast and lunch: Sat–Sun 10 a.m.–3:30 p.m.; dinner: Sun–Thurs 5:30–10 p.m., Fri–Sat 5:30–10:30 p.m.*

French Laundry
$$$$$ Yountville   FRENCH

Regarded as one of the finest chefs in the United States, Thomas Keller prepares superb multicourse meals for a lucky crowd in his intimate, elegant, universally celebrated restaurant. If you're serious about food, book a table well in advance (it's easier to reserve for lunch), and arrive hungry — you won't want to overlook a crumb. The French Laundry experience is sublime on every front. Keller's butter-poached lobster has entered the pantheon of legendary dishes; if it's on the menu, don't pass it up.

6640 Washington St. (at Creek St.), Yountville. ☎ *707-944-2380. Internet: www.sterba.com/yountville/frenchlaundry. Reservations required. Prix-fixe meals: $80–$105; chef's tasting menu $120. AE, MC, V. Open: Lunch Fri–Sun 11 a.m.–1 p.m.; dinner: daily 5:30–9:30 p.m.*

Gordon's Cafe and Wine Bar
$–$$ Yountville   CREATIVE AMERICAN

Chef-owner Sally Gordon's delicious food is served in a congenial atmosphere reminiscent of a general store. Besides comfort-food favorites at breakfast (perfect for kids) and creative sandwiches at lunch, Gordon's serves a three-course prix-fixe dinner on Friday nights, making the cafe a prime destination for food lovers. The shop is well known for its meticulous selection of fine wines and gourmet condiments, including more kinds of olive oil than you ever imagined existed.

6770 Washington St., Yountville. ☎ *707-944-8246. Reservations essential at dinner. Main courses: $3.50–$8 at breakfast and lunch; $32 prix-fixe dinner. AE, MC, V. Open: Breakfast and lunch: Tues, Wed, Thurs, Sat, and Sun: 7:30 a.m.–6 p.m.; breakfast, lunch, and dinner: Fri 7:30 a.m.–5 p.m. and 6–8:30 p.m.*

Julia's Kitchen
$$$ Napa   CALIFORNIA/FRENCH

Food preferences are entirely personal, but we think this bustling restaurant inside Copia (see "Immersing yourself in food and wine," later in this chapter) served the most delicious meal we ate on our last trip to the valley. Named in honor of Julia Child, the kitchen uses organic produce raised on the grounds, so even a simple green salad shines with bright flavor, and life only gets better from there. The menu changes often, but we loved the seared day-boat scallops and the roasted winter-squash skewer. Portions are moderate, which is kind because desserts must be given their due. You can eat here without paying an entrance fee to Copia.

500 First St. (at Copia), Napa. ☎ *707-265-5700. Reservations advised. Main courses: $17–$26. AE, MC, V. Open: Thurs–Mon 11:30 a.m.–4 p.m. Scheduled to be open for dinner summer 2002; call for hours.*

Martini House
$$$$ St. Helena   AMERICAN

A collaboration between chef Todd Humphries (Campton Place, CIA Greystone) and designer Pat Kuleto (Boulevard and Jardinière, among others), Martini House exudes a sexy, masculine, Old California air that works handsomely with the solid menu. Humphries uses locally grown produce and meats; you'll usually find a steak, grilled pork chop, salmon, a pasta dish — all of which sounds a tad boring but isn't because the kitchen knows what it's doing. A separate entrance or the central staircase takes you to the downstairs bar where you don't need reservations to eat.

1245 Spring St. (off Hwy. 29), St. Helena. ☎ ***707-963-2233.*** *Internet:* www.martini house.com. *Reservations recommended. Main courses: $16–$26 at lunch, $19–$27 at dinner. AE, DC, DISC, MC, V. Open: Daily 11:30 a.m.–10 p.m. Wine bar menu: 3–5 p.m.*

Mustards Grill
$$ Yountville   CALIFORNIA

The California version of a classic pub, this Napa Valley institution is always filled to overflowing with a festive, food-conscious crowd, drawn in by the lengthy menu of delicious American dishes that are always well-prepared but never too challenging. You won't have room for dessert, but loosen your belt and give it a go anyway — you won't be disappointed.

7399 St. Helena Hwy. (Hwy. 29), Yountville. ☎ ***707-944-2424.*** *Reservations recommended. Main courses: $12–$19. DC, DISC, MC, V. Open: Daily 11:30 a.m.–10 p.m.*

Pearl
$–$$ Napa   CALIFORNIA

Probably the most low-key, and certainly the most affordable, good restaurant in the valley, Pearl specializes in oysters (naturally) prepared in four different ways (we can vouch for the barbecued ones). The Napa locals consider this cheerful little place an adjunct to their home kitchens, so you'll see families tucking into healthy portions of linguini and clams, clean soft tacos with two dipping sauces, or a straightforward roasted chicken and mashed potatoes. This is absolutely the place to eat if one more expensive gourmet meal threatens to finish you off. Enjoy patio dining in fine weather.

1339 Pearl St., Napa. ☎ ***707-224-9161.*** *Reservations accepted. Main courses: $9.75–$20. MC, V. Open: Tues–Sat 11:30 a.m.–2 p.m. and 5:30–9:30 p.m.*

Tra Vigne
$$$ St. Helena   ITALIAN

This is an elegant, but not stuffy, place for a Northern Italian meal. The homemade mozzarella and house-pressed olive oil alone (celebrated in no less than *Gourmet* magazine) make a visit worthwhile. Come for lunch on the courtyard patio and you'll feel as if you've stepped into Tuscany. The restaurant also features a delicatessen, the **Cantinetta,** with reasonably priced pizza, wine, and prepared foods to eat here or down the road at a winery.

1050 Charter Oak Ave., St. Helena. ☎ ***707-963-4444.*** www.travignerestaurant. com. *Reservations recommended. Main courses: $13–$19. DC, DISC, MC, V. Open: Daily 11:30 a.m.–10:30 p.m.*

In Sonoma Valley

Cafe La Haye
$$ Sonoma CALIFORNIA

This casual little cafe serves some of the best food around, and unlike many other Wine Country restaurants, it makes no attempt to pretend you're in Italy or France. Plain tables and chairs are carefully set about, as if not to disturb the art that fills the walls, making La Haye's single room resemble a gallery. The menu selection, spare but complete, features whatever's seasonal, and offers organic produce.

140 East Napa St., Sonoma. ☎ *707-935-5994. Reservations accepted. Main courses: $12–$18. MC, V. Open: Tues–Sat 5:30–9 p.m.; Sun brunch 9:30 a.m.–2 p.m.*

Garden Court Cafe and Bakery
$ Glen Ellen AMERICAN

Get a modest breakfast and order lunch to go, or a tasty, filling breakfast that keeps you going most of the day. Wineglasses and a tablecloth for added panache can be included in picnic lunches. If you're in town on the second Wednesday of the month, the four-course prix-fixe dinner is the bargain of the valley. A special kids' menu includes such specialties as Goldilocks Porridge (not too hot and not too cold . . .).

13875 Sonoma Hwy. 12, Glen Ellen. ☎ *707-935-1565. No reservations. Main courses: $4.95–$11. MC, V. Open: Daily 7:30 a.m.–2 p.m. Dinner served 2nd Wed of the month.*

the girl and the fig
$$ Sonoma COUNTRY FRENCH

This upscale little Country French bistro moved to the Sonoma Hotel from its Glen Ellen location in 2001, adding outdoor dining to the delight of its many admirers. The seasonal menu meets the needs of seafoodies, vegetarians, and carnivores alike with one or two dishes in each category. The grilled fig salad with arugula and local goat's cheese is a must-order when fresh figs are available. But the three-course *plats du jour* at $25 (Sunday through Thursday) is the only reason you need to visit during the week.

110 West Spain St., Sonoma, CA. ☎ *707-938-3634. Reservations accepted. Main courses: $11–$20. MC, V. Open: Daily 11:30 a.m.–2:30 p.m. and 5:30–9:30 p.m. Late-night menu Fri and Sat to 11 p.m.*

The girl and the gaucho
$$$ Glen Ellen CALIFORNIA

Few other restaurateurs in Sonoma Valley (besides the owners of this restaurant and "the girl and the fig" in the preceding listing) serve a menu of mouth-watering Latin-inspired dishes like those offered in this

A-framed room, filled with art and kitschy doo-dads. You can make it an evening listening to jazz, sampling the international wine list, and ordering small plates of Spanish cheeses, cured meats, ceviche, roasted corn cakes . . . the list goes on.

13690 Arnold Dr., Glen Ellen. ☎ *707-938-3634. Reservations advised. Small and large plates: $5–$22. AE, MC, V. Open: Daily 5:30–9:30 p.m.*

Touring the Wine Country

The Napa Valley is home to more than 220 wineries (Sonoma has just four dozen or so), some owned by corporations, and others the domain of individuals so seduced by the grape that they abandoned successful careers to devote themselves to viticulture. While no correlation exists between the size of a winery and the quality of the product — which has more to do with the talents of the vintners and variables such as weather and soil conditions — the bigger wineries offer more to visitors in terms of education and entertainment.

If you want to learn more about grape growing, and the blending and bottling process, the first winery you visit should be one that offers an in-depth tour. **Robert Mondavi** offers an excellent introductory tour, as does **St. Supéry.** Book the superb tour offered by **Schramsburg** if you're interested in the production of sparkling wine (a.k.a. champagne; only the French winemakers from the Champagne region fundamentally have the right to call it that).

Don't expect a deal on wine purchased directly from the producers. Wineries sell at full retail so as not to undercut their primary market, wine merchants. Only buy and carry what you think you can't get at home. If you're concerned that you won't be able to locate a particular vintage back at the ranch, most wineries will mail order. If you live outside of California, see the "Bureaucracy in a bottle: Shipping your wine purchases home" sidebar, later in this chapter.

How to tell a cab from a zin

The most prominent varieties of grapes produced in the area include cabernet sauvignon, pinot noir, and zinfandel grapes grown for red wines, and chardonnay and sauvignon or fume blanc grapes grown for white wines.

Of course, the best way to really tell a cab from a zin, in laidback California wine-speak, is to read the label on the bottle. The label identifies the type of grape used if the wine contains at least 75% of that particular variety. The appellation of origin indicates where the grapes were grown — either a viticulture area such as the Carneros region of the Napa Valley, a county, or the state itself. The vintage date is important as it explains when at least 95% of the grapes were crushed. Because many wines taste better as they get older, and some years produce better grapes than others, you'll want to make a note of the vintage.

You can greatly enhance your knowledge of wine by tasting correctly — and what better classroom than a French-style chateau smack in the middle of a vineyard? Remember that wine appreciation begins by analyzing color, followed by aroma, then taste. You do this with your eyes first, then your nose, then your mouth. Don't be shy about asking questions of the person pouring — he or she will happily answer your questions because the more you learn about his or her product, the more likely you are to become a steady customer. And that makes everybody happy!

Here are a few wine-tasting do's and don'ts:

- ✔ **Before the pour, sniff your glass.** It should have a clean aroma. If not, ask for a fresh glass.

- ✔ **Never pour the wine yourself.**

- ✔ **Taste wines in the proper order: whites first, reds second, dessert wines last.** This reflects the order in which food is generally served — white wines with a first course, reds with a hearty main course, and dessert wines with dessert.

- ✔ **Swirl the wine to coat the inside of the glass.** This introduces more oxygen and helps open up the wine flavors and aromas.

- ✔ **Smell the wine.** Think about what the different aromas bring to mind — spice, fruit, flowers, and so forth.

- ✔ **Take a sip and coat the back of your tongue with the wine.**

- ✔ **Along with baseball, wine tasting is one of the few sports where spitting is not only allowed, it's encouraged.** Just make sure you hit the target — a bucket or some other container will be available for this purpose. Spitting is a nifty way to sample many wines without becoming fuzzy-headed.

- ✔ **Don't mistake a tasting room for your friendly neighborhood bar — this is not the time to swill with drunken abandon.** And lose the chewing gum.

If you really want to get into this wine thing, pick up a copy of *Wine For Dummies* by Mary Ewing Mulligan and Ed McCarthy, published by Wiley Publishing, Inc.

The best wineries for first-time visitors

The Napa Valley is home to over 200 wineries, so the handful discussed here represent only the tip of the vine. But the valley contains plenty of other worthwhile wineries, so get a winery map (they're easily available throughout the region) and explore those back roads.

Wine-tasting rooms charge no admission fees, and the tours are usually (but not always) free. Be aware, however, that most wineries charge a fee for tasting, usually minimal and deducted from any purchases you make. In the listings in this section, we've noted current wine-tasting fees and touring policies; keep in mind that wineries can — and do — change their minds. In any case, the tasting fee should always be clearly posted at the tasting counter; if you're not sure, ask.

Beaulieu Vineyard

The vintners at this well-regarded establishment, founded in 1900 and Napa's third-oldest winery, aim to set visitors at ease the moment they walk through the door by passing out glasses of chardonnay. After you relax, take the free half-hour tour through the production facility, given daily from 11 a.m. to 4 p.m. Each tasting thereafter is $5, or $18 for five delicious reserve vintages; be ready to shell out if you want to take home one of these special bottles. Don't be frightened away, however: A number of award-winning regular labels sell for less than $20 a pop.

1960 St. Helena Hwy. (Hwy. 29, just north of Rutherford Cross Rd.), Rutherford. ☎ *707-967-5230. Internet:* www.bv-wine.com. *Open: Daily 10 a.m.–5 p.m.*

Clos Pegase

Attention, architecture buffs: Even if you're not interested in the free 30-minute tour (given daily at 11 a.m. and 2 p.m.; no reservations needed), come to see the house. This stunning Michael Graves–designed winery is a temple to modern winemaking. It's plenty easy to while away a happy hour or more here studying the terrific art collection, walking around the sculpture garden, and picnicking on the vast lawn (you must reserve a picnic table). Wine tasting is $2.50 for current releases, and $5 more to taste three reserve wines. Bottles don't come cheap here, but this is a good place to pick up something special.

1060 Dunaweal Lane (west of Silverado Trail), Calistoga. ☎ *707-942-4981. Internet:* www.clospegase.com. *Open: Daily 10:30 a.m.–5 p.m.*

Cuvaison

Headquartered in a wonderful Mission-style house, this intimate, excellent winery is a great place to taste and learn. Winemaker John Thatcher has crafted world-renowned chardonnay — refreshing, not over-oaked — as well as superb merlot, pinot noir, and cab. The tasting room is one of the most hospitable in the valley; tastings are $5, and you even get to keep your logo glass as a souvenir. A free tour will take you into the state-of-the-art wine cave daily at 10:30 a.m. Bring home a bottle of the rich, ruby Eris Pinot Noir if it's in stock — you won't find this memorable vino in your local wine shop. Picnic tables are here for your use.

4550 Silverado Trail (just south of Dunaweal Lane), Calistoga. ☎ *707-942-6266. Internet:* www.cuvaison.com. *Open: 10 a.m.–5 p.m.*

Niebaum-Coppola

This impressive estate's neo-Medieval grandeur is marvelous — straight out of "Falcon Crest." A museum traces the history of the winery, the former Inglenook Vineyards, and its world-famous current owner, film-maker Francis Ford Coppola, while the second floor houses Coppola-related movie memorabilia, including the desk used by Al Pacino in *The Godfather*. The wines are sophisticated, yet most bottles are surprisingly well-priced. Regular tastings are $7.50, and you can keep the glass. This place is merchandised like mad, but with lots of appealing items, so look around for gifts.

 If you want to take the 1½-hour historical tour (at $20 a pop), which ends with a formal sit-down tasting in one of the wine cellars, make reservations two weeks in advance for either a 10:30 a.m. or 2:30 p.m. slot. But do not bring your picnic lunch here — for some reason, picnicking is verboten.

1991 St. Helena Hwy. (Hwy. 29, at Rutherford Cross Rd.), Rutherford. ☎ **707-968-1100** *or 707-968-1161. Internet:* www.niebaum-coppola.com. *Open: Daily 10 a.m.–5 p.m.*

Opus One

Don't expect a warm and fuzzy welcome at pretentious Opus One, the brainchild of Robert Mondavi and Baroness Phillipine de Rothschild. This imposing facility — the Caesar's Palace of the Napa Valley — is dedicated to the production of one, and only one, wine: Opus One, a dry-as-a-bone, mostly cab blend that goes for a whopping $120 a bottle. The $25 tasting fee (for 4 oz.) is well worth it for wine buffs who want to see what all the fuss is about. If the name means little to you or you're in search of real bottles to buy, you can better spend your money elsewhere.

 Free one-hour tours are offered daily at 10:30 a.m. by appointment only (book well in advance).

7900 St. Helena Hwy. (Hwy. 29, at Oakville Cross Rd.), Oakville. ☎ **707-944-9442.** *Internet:* www.opusonewinery.com. *Open: Daily 10:30 a.m.–3:30 p.m.*

Robert Mondavi

You'll recognize this grand Mission-style winery from the labels on Mondavi's popular wines. It's a bit corporate, but excellent for novices. The first to conduct public tastings, Mondavi continues its dedication to wine education.

 A top-notch 1½-hour winery and vineyard tour — the best in the valley for first-timers — is offered daily throughout the day. The fee is $10, and we highly recommend making advance reservations. More in-depth seminars on wine-growing, wine and food, and other subjects are offered for fees ranging from $10 to $65 (reservations required). Call or visit the Web site for a complete schedule of tours and special events.

7801 St. Helena Hwy. (Hwy. 29, just north of Oakville Cross Rd.), Oakville. ☎ *888-RMONDAVI or 707-226-1395. Internet:* www.robertmondavi.com. *Open: Daily 9:30 a.m.–5 p.m.*

Schramsberg

You can't just stop by this elegant and completely unpretentious 200-acre champagne estate — but advance booking one of the by-appointment-only tours, offered daily from 10 a.m. to 2:30 p.m., is well worth the trouble. Schramsberg is the best sparkling-wine producer in the United States, and the free 1½-hour tour (followed by a $7.50 tasting) is the country's best champagne tour. You'll explore caves that were hand-dug a hundred years ago and learn the whole bottling process, which has hardly changed a whit since then. Follow the tour with a walk through the impeccable gardens. Book at least a week in advance on weekends.

1400 Schramsberg Rd. (turn off Hwy. 29 at Peterson Dr.), Calistoga. ☎ *707-942-2414. Internet:* www.schramsberg.com. *Open: Daily 10 a.m.–4 p.m.*

St. Supéry

If you want an excellent introductory tour that's a little more intimate than the one offered by Mondavi, come to this friendly, first-class winery. Everybody makes a big deal about "SmellaVision," which teaches you about aromas common to certain varietals, but the real highlights are in the demonstration vineyard, where you'll learn about growing techniques up close, and get an excellent lesson in tasting at the end of the one-hour tour. Tours are free, but you'll have to buy a $5 lifetime tasting card. Reserve tastings are in the "Divine Wine" room, where $10 will get you half glasses of the really good stuff (the Meritages are well worth the price).

8440 St. Helena Hwy. (between Oakville and Rutherford Cross Roads), Rutherford. ☎ *800-942-0809 or 707-963-4507. Internet:* www.stsupery.com. *Open: Daily 9:30 a.m.–6 p.m. (to 5 p.m. Nov–Apr).*

Sterling Vineyards

An aerial tram transports you to this whitewashed Mediterranean-style hilltop mega-winery, currently owned by the Seagram Company. After you land, a self-guided tour takes you through the entire operation and into the tasting room, where the helpful staff serves up tastings. It's a bit too corporate, but the spectacular views alone are worth the $6 ticket price (which includes the tasting). Plan on spending at least an hour here.

1111 Dunaweal Lane (a half-mile east of Hwy. 29), Calistoga. ☎ *707-942-3344. Internet:* www.sterlingvineyards.com. *Open: Daily 10:30 a.m.–4:30 p.m.*

Wineries in Sonoma Valley

Arrowood

Arrowood is an intimate, high-end, and somewhat exclusive winery with low-volume production but national distribution. You need to make an appointment for the one-hour tour by calling a day or two in advance. If you don't go on the tour, you can sit on the veranda overlooking grapevines and the mountains and try some great wines. There is a $3 tasting fee.

14347 Sonoma Hwy., Glen Ellen, CA 95442. ☎ *707-938-5170. Internet:* www. arrowoodvineyards.com. *Open: Daily 10 a.m.–4:30 p.m.*

Benziger

Tractor-pulled trams take visitors up a flower-lined path at this beautiful 85-acre ranch near Jack London State Park for a 45-minute guided tour. The ranch has belonged to the Benziger family since 1981. The tram operators discuss nearly everything you need to know about viticulture, including insect control, and how the sun and soil together affect the taste of the final product. You can choose from two tasting opportunities, one of which is complimentary; the other costs $5 for the reserve wines.

1883 London Ranch Rd., Glen Ellen, CA 95442. (Take Hwy. 12 to Arnold Dr. and left on London Ranch Rd.). ☎ *707-935-4046. Internet:* www.benziger.com. *Open: Daily 10 a.m.–5 p.m.*

B.R. Cohn

This tiny tasting room, flanked by olive trees, is just down the road from Arrowood. The wines are worth a sip, although the winery itself is not the most lush and beautiful one you'll see. Some vintages are sold only at the winery, and the olive oil produced here is of the highest quality and makes a great gift. Friendly staff who are happy to talk wine and olives preside over the tasting room. Tastings are free.

15140 Sonoma Hwy., Glen Ellen, CA 95442. ☎ *707-938-4064. Internet:* www. brcohn.com. *Open: Daily 10 a.m.–5 p.m.*

Chateau St. Jean

Driving back on Warm Springs Drive toward Kenwood, turn left on Highway 12 to find a Mediterranean-style mansion on a 250-acre estate. With an expansive front lawn and shady groves, this winery is a great place for a picnic. (You can pick up picnic food at **Cafe Citti,** 9049 Sonoma Hwy.) The magnificent magnolia tree here was planted by the famed botanist Luther Burbank. Self-guided tours only; you can climb the observation tower for a view of the valley. Downstairs, wine tasting is complimentary; $5 is charged for three tastes of reserve wines.

8555 Sonoma Hwy., Kenwood, CA. ☎ 707-833-4134. Internet: www.chateau stjean.com. *Open: Daily 10 a.m.–4:30 p.m.*

Matanzas Creek Winery

Your attention may stray from the grape as you stare at the fragrant and expansive gardens cascading down the hill from the tasting room at this scenic winery. Matanzas produces a line of gift items featuring the lavender they grow and dry on the property, as well as high-quality, award-winning wine. A flight of wines for tasting costs $3, refundable with a wine purchase. A 30-minute tour shows you the basics of barrel-making, viticulture, and corks. (Tour times are 10:30 a.m., 1:00 p.m., and 3:00 p.m.)

6097 Bennett Valley Rd. (Hwy. 12 to Arnold Dr. to Warm Springs Rd.), Santa Rosa, CA 95404. ☎ 707-528-6464. Internet: www.matanzascreek.com. *Open: Mon–Sat 10 a.m.–5 p.m., Sun 11 a.m.–5 p.m.*

More Cool Stuff to See and Do

Tasting wine isn't the only thing to keep you occupied on your trip to the Wine Country. Here are the myriad other activities the region has to offer.

Picnicking the valleys

Sure, the restaurant scene is great — but hardly a better place on the planet exists for picnicking than the Wine Country. A number of fabulous gourmet grocers can supply the delicacies, and many friendly wineries provide pastoral picnic grounds.

Our favorite picnic supplier is the **Oakville Grocery Co.,** 7856 St. Helena Hwy. (Hwy. 29), at Oakville Cross Road (☎ **800-736-6602** or 707-944-8802; www.oakvillegrocery.com). Here you can put together your own gourmet picnic from the excellent bread selection, the deli counter (which runs from first-rate cold cuts to top-quality foie gras), and yummy pastries.

A lot less country store-ish is **Dean & Deluca,** 607 St. Helena Hwy. (Hwy. 29, north of Zinfandel Lane), St. Helena (☎ **707-967-9980;** www.deandeluca.com), the Big Apple's favorite gourmet grocer. Everything at this first-class mega-mart is beautifully displayed — and very pricey. Still, you'll get your money's worth.

Just across the street from Dean & Deluca is **V. Sattui Winery,** 1111 White Lane (at Hwy. 29), St. Helena (☎ **707-963-7774;** www.

vsattui.com), whose mammoth tasting room also serves as a bountiful gourmet shop. If you buy here, you can also dine here on the popular picnic grounds.

It may be a bit out of your way (it's north of Santa Rosa in Healdsburg), but a most memorable stop is the **Jimtown Store** (6706 State Hwy. 128, Healdsburg. ☎ **707-433-1212;** www.jimtown.com). This former gas station may appear self-consciously retro, but it oozes charm and country atmosphere and also delivers with delicious food and a fun, eclectic assortment of wares. You can make a dreamy picnic out of the boxed lunches (try the homebaked ham sandwich with Jimtown's sweet red pepper and tomato spread), daily specials like Basque ragout or corn chowder, or the homemade spreads (spicy chipotle, Asian peanut, fig, and olive) and breads. They even have their own Jimtown label wine to add to your picnic basket.

After you put your picnic together, where should you go? In addition to **V. Sattui, Clos Pegase, Cuvaison, Oakville Ranch,** and **St. Supéry** are among the many wineries that offer pleasant picnic spots (remember to reserve a table ahead at Clos Pegase). You can also take your picnic to **Old Faithful,** where you can munch on your lunch while you enjoy the natural show.

It's considered bad form to bring a bottle of wine from one winery to enjoy at another. If you're going to use a winery's picnic grounds, buy a bottle of wine inside first to enjoy during your alfresco meal.

Getting pampered in Calistoga

People have been taking to Calistoga's rejuvenating mud baths — a blend of ancient volcanic ash, imported peat, and naturally boiling mineral water, which simmers at a comfy 104°F — for more than 150 years. Calistoga's spas are generally friendly, rustic, comfortable places borne out of a therapeutic tradition — nothing like the marble-tiled glamfests that are most resort spas.

Treatments are relatively affordable. Expect to pay between $98 and $155 for a mud bath and one-hour massage. You can reserve a tub, followed by a mineral shower and a massage or a facial, at the following locations:

- ✔ **Dr. Wilkinson's Hot Springs,** 1507 Lincoln Ave. (☎ 707-942-4102; www.drwilkinson.com), probably the most well-known of Calistoga's spas.

- ✔ **Indian Springs,** 1712 Lincoln Ave. (☎ 707-942-4913; www.indianspringscalistoga.com), a tad pricier but you get pool privileges.

✔ **Golden Haven Hot Springs Spa,** 1713 Lake St. (☎ 707-942-6793; www.goldenhaven.com), which boasts late hours and private mud-bath rooms for couples.

✔ **Calistoga Spa Hot Springs,** 1006 Washington St. (☎ 707-942-6269; www.calistogaspa.com), whose mud bath/massage packages are a very good buy.

Check for Internet specials. And if mud just sounds icky to you, these spas all offer alternatives, such as salt baths and aromatherapy wraps.

Hot-air ballooning

Soaring over the vineyards under a colorful balloon, with just a few other souls sharing your basket, is an experience. **Bonaventura Balloon Company** (☎ 800-FLY-NAPA or 707-944-2822; www.bonaventura balloons.com) is one of Napa's most trusted hot-air balloon operators, with a range of packages available. Or call **Napa Valley Aloft/Adventures Aloft** (☎ 800-944-4408 or 707-944-4408; www.nvaloft.com), whose early-morning lift-off includes a preflight snack and a postflight brunch with bubbly. At $195 to $250 per person (depending on the number of persons and extras you choose), however, you may want to keep those feet on the ground.

Touring Jack London country

Jack London State Historic Park, 2400 London Ranch Rd., near Glen Ellen in Sonoma County (☎ 707-938-5216), is where the prolific author of *The Call of the Wild* lived before his death in 1916 at age 40. You can walk on trails to the ruins of Wolf House, London Lake, and Bath House. A museum/library with first editions of London's works and personal memorabilia are on the grounds, as well. It's open daily from 9:30 a.m. to dusk. Take a two-hour group trail ride through the park through **Sonoma Cattle Company and Napa Valley Trail Rides** (☎ 707-996-8566), which has stables on the property. The ride costs around $45. You can also rent horses for private rides at $45 per hour.

Watching Old Faithful blow off steam

The **Old Faithful Geyser of California,** off of Hwy. 29 north of Calistoga at 1299 Tubbs Lane (☎ 707-942-6463; www.oldfaithfulgeyser.com), is one of only three "old faithful" geysers in the world. The natural geyser has been blowing off steam at regular intervals for just about as long as anyone can remember. The 350°F water spews out to a height of about 60 feet every 30 to 40 minutes or so (depending on barometric pressure, the moon, tides, and tectonic stresses). The performance lasts about a minute, and you can watch the show as many times as you wish. Bring your picnic lunch; a few redwood tables offer a front-and-center view.

The natural geyser is a wonder, but what's really so great about Old Faithful is its old-time roadside attraction vibe. The stop includes a video show, a small geothermal exhibit hall, a snack bar, and a few odd-ball narcoleptic goats that suddenly fall asleep on occasion.

Admission is $6 for adults, $5 for seniors, $2 for children 6 to 12. Old Faithful is open daily from 9 a.m. to 6 p.m. (to 5 p.m. in winter).

Immersing yourself in food and wine

Copia: The American Center for Wine, Food and the Arts (500 First St., Napa; ☎ **707-259-1600;** www.copia.org) opened in fall 2001 in the city of Napa and has quickly become one of the must-see attractions in the valley. There are obvious reasons for its immediate popularity: Copia celebrates the finer things in life in a modern museum-like setting, although it's neither solemn nor overly reverential. One permanent exhibit, an interactive presentation on the role of food and wine in American society, is both accessible and amusing. In addition, there's a state-of-the-art theater for concerts, lectures, and films; a full roster of wine and food courses are offered year-round; and a 500-seat concert terrace overlooking the Napa River, surrounded by Copia's orchard and organic gardens, provides warm weather amusement. A great restaurant (see "Where to Dine in the Wine Country," earlier in this chapter), a wine bar, and, of course, a gift shop round out the experience. Check the Web site for current activities during your trip, and try to take in an exhibit, a class, a concert, or a meal — all four if time allows! Admission is $12.50 adults, $10 seniors and students, $7.50 children 6 to 12. It's open in fall and winter (Thurs–Mon 10 a.m.–5 p.m.) and spring and summer (Mon, Tues, and Thurs 10 a.m.–5 p.m., Fri–Sun 10 a.m.–9 p.m).

Many olive trees are planted at wineries and in groves around Sonoma Valley. Olives have become an important crop, and olive-oil tastings are a popular activity now. You can debate the merits of various extra virgin olive oils in Glen Ellen at **The Olive Press,** 14301 Arnold Dr., (☎ **707-939-8900**). The press works 24 hours a day between October and March. Watch the process from the tasting room, while sampling the olive oil and checking out the olive-themed merchandise.

If you have an abiding interest in cooking, sign up for a three- to four-hour class at **Ramekins,** 450 West Spain St., Sonoma (☎ **707-933-0450**), a small B&B and culinary school next to the General's Daughter restaurant. During the day, take in the demonstration classes; then in the evening, glean culinary tips from some major Bay Area chefs. Students have lots of opportunity to sample the goods with a few glasses of wine. Call for a catalog. You can register over the phone, in person, or on the Web at www.ramekins.com.

Gathering More Information

Call the **Napa Valley Conference and Visitors Bureau (NVCVB)** at
☎ **707-226-7459,** or go online to www.napavalley.com. After you
arrive, stop by the NVCVB's office at 1310 Napa Town Center in downtown Napa, where you'll find helpful counselors on staff as well as a
wealth of information; exit Hwy. 29 at First Street.

The **Sonoma Valley Visitors Bureau** is located in Sonoma on the
Sonoma Plaza at 453 First Street E., (☎ **707-996-1090;** www.sonoma
valley.com). Stop by for maps, lodging information, and winery tour
information.

Bureaucracy in a bottle: Shipping your wine purchases home

Having a winery ship directly to your home should be no problem, right? Wrong. Due to absurd and constantly fluctuating *reciprocity laws* — designed to prevent you from easily buying direct from the manufacturer in order to protect the nation's wine distributors — varying regulations in each of the 50 states limit wine shipping across state lines.

What that means is this: Currently, California's wineries can ship only to private individuals within the Golden State and to about 20 other states. Wineries used to look the other way, but now that a few have been punished with severe fines, most will not ignore your state's laws. If you live in a nonreciprocal state, shipping's a no-no.

Do your homework before you buy more wine than you can physically carry home. Be skeptical of any winery that tells you it can ship to nonreciprocal states — chances are good that you'll never get your wine. Although boxing your own wine and sending it to a nonreciprocal state is illegal, some shippers will do it for you. Not that we're recommending you do this, of course, but you may want to carry your wine out of the Napa Valley and send it from a post office, UPS, or other shipping company in another area of California where the issue isn't such a hot potato. Feel free to ask for advice at the winery; they're usually very willing to help, because they want you to buy.

If you need to ship your — ahem — socks home from the valley, try **Buffalo's Shipping Post,** 2471 Solano Ave., Napa (exit at Lincoln off Hwy. 29; ☎ **707-226-7942**); **Aero Packing,** 163 Camino Dorado (off N. Kelly Rd.), just south of the town of Napa (☎ **707-255-8025**); or **Wrap-It Transit,** in the Riverpark Shopping Center, 1325 W. Imola Ave., Napa (exit at Imola off Hwy. 29; ☎ **707-252-9367**). Remember that no guarantees exist; companies have every right to change their policies at any time.

This direct-shipping issue is a super-controversial subject that is evolving all the time. If you want to learn what the current regulations are in your state before you leave home, point your Web browser to www.wineinstitute.org/shipwine and click on State Control Authority Directory, or visit www.freethegrapes.org.

Chapter 11

Mendocino

● ●

In This Chapter

▶ Planning your visit to the rugged North Coast's most refined little town

▶ Finding the ideal places to stay and dine

▶ Taking in the town and surrounding area

● ●

*I*f you want a taste of California's wild and wonderful North Coast, Mendocino is the perfect place to get it. This secluded, artsy, and enchanting town is a West Coast version of a New England seashore village (it actually served as Cabot Cove, Maine, in *Murder, She Wrote*). Mendocino is magically situated atop craggy headlands that jut out into the Pacific, giving the town a ruggedly gorgeous coastline on three sides. The spectacular setting — a world apart from the seaside landscape farther south, even near San Francisco — makes it an ideal spot for a bit of nature-inspired relaxation.

Hugely popular as a romantic getaway from the Bay Area, the town is dedicated to the laid-back, weekending life. You won't find a whole lot to do in Mendocino — and that suits weary travelers just fine. Couples come to stroll, shop, bike, hike, and generally take it slow. Families are welcome, though disaffected teens may not be happy campers among the high-falutin' galleries, and budget-minded parents (or anybody watching their expenses, for that matter) may decry the overall high prices.

Mendocino also offers a good starting point for exploration of California's one-of-a-kind redwood country; see Chapter 12.

Timing Your Visit

Summer or early fall is the best time to come. Mendocino is lovely from May through mid-October. Don't expect warmth, though: Average highs run between 59 and 66°F, and lows can dip below 50°F even in August. Mornings are misty and generally give way to afternoon sun; fog prevails in July and August and sometimes early September. Dress warm, and in layers. Leave your bathing suit in your suitcase, because these waters are never warm enough for swimming. If you travel inland, up the Redwood Highway (see Chapter 10), expect temperatures to increase as much as 15 or 20 degrees.

Visit during the week to avoid the maximum-capacity crowds, highest room rates, and mandated two-night minimum stays.

The weather can be a crapshoot in winter (frankly, this far up the coast, it can be a crapshoot at any time of year). Still, it's not much colder on average — about ten degrees across the board — and you'll save a bundle on accommodations. You'll also find yourself in prime whale-watching territory if you visit between mid-December and mid-April. If you happen to be traveling at the end of January, you can enjoy two of our favorite California pastimes — dining on crab and tasting wine — when Mendocino restaurants celebrate **Dungeness Crab season.** Don't be surprised if you run into some rain, though.

How much time do you need? Two nights will do the trick. You may want to stop by just for one night, to sample the vibe on your way up to the Avenue of the Giants (see Chapter 12).

Getting There and Getting Around

Mendocino's seclusion is a big part of its charm — but that also makes reaching it a big fat drag. The town is 155 miles from San Francisco, and 95 miles from the north end of the Napa Valley. The problem is that no major highway runs to the town; you either have to battle the slow-going mountains, or the even slower-going coast, to get there.

- ✔ **From San Francisco:** The fastest route is to take U.S. 101 north to Cloverdale, then take Highway 128 west to Highway 1, then go north along the coast; the drive takes about four hours.

- ✔ **From the Napa Valley:** The valley's main highway, 129, meets up with Highway 128 in Calistoga, at the north end. Follow 128 west all the way to the coast, which takes 2½ to 3 hours.

Highway 128, which crosses the mountains, is a curving Dramamine route all the way from U.S. 101 to the coast, which is the bulk of the trip no matter what your starting point. If you have a sensitive tummy and would prefer to keep your nausea in check, take U.S. 101 to Willits, pick up Highway 20 west to the coast, and head south on Highway 1. This alternative route will add 45 minutes or an hour to your trip — and Highway 20 is no joy, either — but it's an appreciably smoother ride.

The most scenic drive from the Bay Area is to take the coastal route, Highway 1, all the way. The drive is stunning, but expect it to take six long, nausea-inducing hours.

Mendocino and Redwood Country

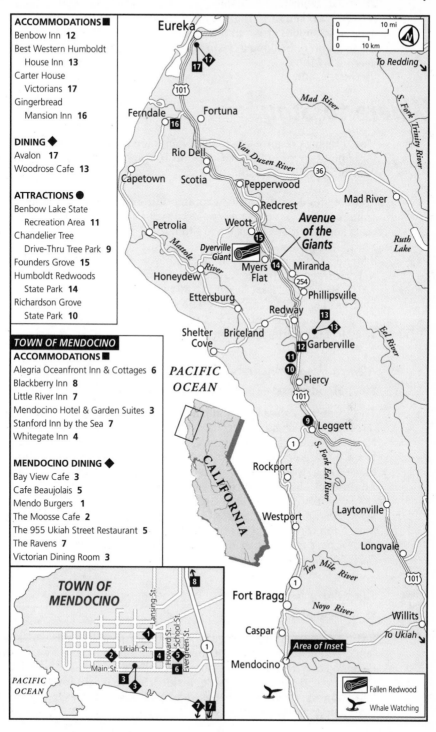

ACCOMMODATIONS ■
Benbow Inn **12**
Best Western Humboldt
House Inn **13**
Carter House
Victorians **17**
Gingerbread
Mansion Inn **16**

DINING ◆
Avalon **17**
Woodrose Cafe **13**

ATTRACTIONS ●
Benbow Lake State
Recreation Area **11**
Chandelier Tree
Drive-Thru Tree Park **9**
Founders Grove **15**
Humboldt Redwoods
State Park **14**
Richardson Grove
State Park **10**

TOWN OF MENDOCINO
ACCOMMODATIONS ■
Alegria Oceanfront Inn & Cottages **6**
Blackberry Inn **8**
Little River Inn **7**
Mendocino Hotel & Garden Suites **3**
Stanford Inn by the Sea **7**
Whitegate Inn **4**

MENDOCINO DINING ◆
Bay View Cafe **3**
Cafe Beaujolais **5**
Mendo Burgers **1**
The Moosse Cafe **2**
The 955 Ukiah Street Restaurant **5**
The Ravens **7**
Victorian Dining Room **3**

0   10 mi
0   10 km

To Redding

Eureka
101
Ferndale 16
Fortuna
Mad River
S. Fork Trinity River
Rio Dell
Van Duzen River
36
Capetown   Scotia   Pepperwood
Mad River
Redcrest
Petrolia   Weott   **Avenue of the Giants**
Ruth Lake
Dyerville Giant   15
Mattole River
Honeydew   Myers Flat   14   Miranda
254
Ettersburg   Phillipsville
Redway   13   13
Shelter Cove   Briceland   Eel River
12   Garberville
11
10
PACIFIC OCEAN   Piercy
101
9   Leggett
CALIFORNIA
1   S. Fork Eel River
Rockport
Laytonville
Westport   Longvale
Ten Mile River   101
1
TOWN OF MENDOCINO
Lansing St.
8
Fort Bragg
Noyo River
Ukiah St.   1   Caspar   Willits
2   4   5   To Ukiah
Main St.   6   Mendocino   **Area of Inset**
PACIFIC OCEAN   3   3
7   7

Fallen Redwood
Whale Watching

After you've arrived in Mendocino, park your car and set out on foot. The town is entirely walkable and easy to get a handle on. Main Street runs perpendicular to Highway 1 along the oceanfront. Lansing is the main north-south street in town, meeting Main at the ocean. The rest of the town unfolds along a basic grid from there, no more than six blocks deep or wide.

Where to Stay

Most lodgings require a two-night minimum stay on weekends and three nights over holidays. Count on 10% in taxes being tacked onto your hotel bill at checkout time.

Contact **Mendocino Coast Accommodations** (☎ 707-937-5033; www. mendocinovacations.com/mcahmpg1.html), a free central reservations service, if our favorites are full.

If Mendo's high rates are too much for you, trek 10 miles up Highway 1 to Fort Bragg and the very nice, value-minded **Harbor Lite Lodge,** 120 N. Harbor Dr., Fort Bragg (☎ **800-643-2700** or 707-964-0221; www. harborlitelodge.com), which boasts rustic appeal, a pleasing maritime vibe, and spacious rooms for $50 to $142 double. Ask for a room away from the bridge to avoid traffic noise.

Alegria Oceanfront Inn & Cottages
$$$ **Mendocino**

This former sea captain's home is the only accommodation in town with direct beach access. Gorgeous ocean views, pretty gardens, and a funky Northern California vibe set a warm, relaxing coastal tone. Each room has a private entrance, a coffeemaker and fridge, TV, and either a fireplace or a woodburning stove. The copious redwood decks with Adirondack chairs offer views galore. Mendo marvelous!

44781 Main St. (west of Evergreen St.). ☎ *800-780-7905 or 707-937-5150. Internet: www.oceanfrontmagic.com. Parking: Free! Rack rates: $189–$249 double. Rates include full breakfast. Deals: Ask about off-season and midweek rates. AE, DISC, MC, V.*

Blackberry Inn
$$ **Mendocino**

If you can get past the hokey Old West theme (and few kids can, so bring 'em), you'll have one of the best values on the coast. The motel is designed as a frontier town — the rooms have names like the Saloon, the Millinery, and the Livery Stable. Inside, they're bright, pretty, spacious, and spotless; even the cheapest has a sitting area, a well-dressed king-size bed, and distant ocean views. Set on a bluff on the opposite side of

Highway 1, it's a long walk or a two-minute drive into town. Resident deer contribute to the storybook ambience.

44951 Larkin Rd. (on the inland side of Hwy. 1). ☎ *800-950-7806 or 707-937-5281. Fax: 707-937-5281. Internet:* www.mendocinomotel.com. *Parking: Free! Rack rates: $95–$160 double, $195 2-bedroom, 2-bath cottage. MC, V.*

Little River Inn
$$–$$$$$ Little River

This is one of our favorite places to stay in Mendocino, although the main buildings are situated off Highway 1, a few minutes drive from the village. Closer in feel to a resort, but completely unpretentious, this family-owned and -operated inn encompasses a nine-hole golf course and pro shop, two lighted tennis courts, a spa, a restaurant, and a most congenial bar. Many rooms have ocean views and range from motel-like simple to outrageously luxe with full-on views, stereos, Jacuzzis, and hot tubs on private decks. Room service is available, which is unique in this part of the woods.

Two miles south of Mendocino on Highway 1, Little River. ☎ *888-INN-LOVE or 707-937-5942. Internet:* www.littleriverinn.com. *Parking: Free! Rack rates: $135–$320. Deals: winter weekday discounts. AE, MC, V.*

Mendocino Hotel & Garden Suites
$$–$$$ Mendocino

This 1878 hotel (a leftover from Mendocino's logging days) is a popular choice in the heart of town, especially if the sometimes stifling intimacy of a B&B isn't your thing. A mix of antiques and reproductions evokes the gold rush spirit, yet all modern comforts are available. Rooms are spread throughout a two-block complex; those in the actual hotel aren't equipped with televisions, but many garden rooms feature fireplaces or woodstoves as well as TVs. Rooms in the back over the kitchen can be noisy early in the morning.

45080 Main St. (between Kasten and Lansing Sts.). ☎ *800-548-0513 or 707-937-0511. Internet:* www.mendocinohotel.com. *Parking: Free! Rack rates: $95 double with shared bath, $120–$215 double, $275 suite. Rates include morning coffee. Deals: Ask about AAA and off-season discounts, and check the Web site for packages. AE, MC, V.*

Stanford Inn by the Sea
$$$$–$$$$$ Mendocino

This rustic-sophisticated lodge sits on extraordinary tiered grounds populated by llamas, horses, and other critters in a woodsy setting near the Big River, a five-minute drive from town. The wood-paneled rooms are done in a supremely comfy California-country style and boast working fireplaces, fridges, and VCRs; the suites are great for families. The grounds feature a gorgeous greenhouse with a lap pool, sauna, and Jacuzzi; a gym; a good vegetarian restaurant; and canoes and mountain bikes for rent. It's one of the pet-friendliest hotels in California, too.

At Hwy. 1 and Comptche-Ukiah Rd. ☎ *800-331-8884 or 707-937-5615. Fax: 707-937-0305. Internet:* www.stanfordinn.com. *Parking: Free! Rack rates: $245–$295 double, $320–$720 1- or 2-bedroom suite. Rates include full breakfast, afternoon tea, and evening hors d'oeuvres. AE, DC, DISC, MC, V.*

Whitegate Inn
$$$–$$$$ Mendocino

For midtown romance, you can't beat this splendid Victorian B&B, whose caring owners show an impeccable eye for detail. The big, luxurious, antiques-filled rooms feature enveloping featherbeds, gorgeous private baths, fireplaces, TVs, and bucketloads of flowery Victorian style. The inn boasts gracious public spaces and lovely gardens, too. This place is classic, elegant, and utterly wonderful.

499 Howard St. (at Ukiah St.). ☎ *800-531-7282 or 707-937-4892. Fax: 707-937-1131. Internet:* www.whitegateinn.com. *Parking: Free driveway and street parking. Rack rates: $149–$289 double. Rates include full breakfast and evening wine and snacks. Deals: Check Web site or ask about winter specials. AE, DC, DISC, MC, V.*

Where to Dine

Far be it for us to encourage hotel dining, but the **Victorian Dining Room** ($$$$) at the Mendocino Hotel is wonderful for lunch and dinner. It's slightly more formal than most in town, with exemplary service and pleasing continental cuisine with a California flair; main courses run $13 to $30.

Stanford Inn by the Sea also has a pretty dining room, **The Ravens** ($$), which serves creative vegetarian cuisine prepared with organic home-grown veggies and lots of Asian slants; entrees cost $10 to $16.

The **Little River Inn** ($$$) is the place to eat during crab season in particular, when crab cakes and local Dungeness — steamed, cracked, and served with two dipping sauces — are available. The Mediterranean-influenced menu is well executed; entrees range from $19 to $27.

Bay View Cafe
$–$$ Mendocino   AMERICAN

This casual, second-story restaurant serves up just-fine food and excellent ocean views. Expect sandwiches, burgers, homestyle breakfasts, and liberal use of the fryer, plus Southwestern-style selections at dinner. This restaurant is hugely popular, especially at breakfast time, so expect a wait on weekends.

45040 Main St. (between Kasten and Lansing sts.). ☎ *707-937-4197. Reservations not taken. Main courses: $5–$8 at breakfast, $6.50–$15 at lunch and dinner. No credit cards. Open: Breakfast, lunch, and dinner daily.*

Cafe Beaujolais
$$$ Mendocino   CAL-FRENCH

Here's Mendocino's best-known restaurant. The room is pretty, dimly lit, almost Victorian, but the attention-getting cuisine — creative Cal-French with a Southwest flair here and there — is thoroughly 21st-century modern. The menu changes regularly, but past successes have included wild sturgeon pan-roasted in truffle emulsion and ahi wrapped in apple-wood-smoked bacon and dressed in a spicy tomatillo salsa. Among the key notes are organic produce, house-baked breads, and inventive wine pairings. The midweek fixed-price meal is a relative bargain.

961 Ukiah St. (at Evergreen St.). ☎ *707-937-5614. Internet:* www.cafebeaujolais. com. *Reservations recommended. Main courses: $21–$28; Tues–Thurs 3-course prix-fixe $25. DISC, MC, V. Open: Dinner nightly.*

Mendo Burgers
$ Mendocino   BURGERS

You want the best burger on the coast? You got it. Six variations are on hand, including fresh ground chuck, turkey, grilled fish (petrale sole), and homemade veggie (falafel, carrots, sweet red peppers). Be sure to ask for a side of the generously cut, finger-lickin'-good fries when you place your order in the luncheonette-style kitchen. If it's a nice day, opt for one of the pleasant courtyard picnic tables over the plain dining room. Look for the sidewalk sandwich board; it's down the path, in back (behind the Mendocino Bakery & Cafe).

10483 Lansing St. (between Ukiah St. and Little Lake Rd.; you can also enter from Ukiah St.). ☎ *707-937-1111. Reservations not needed. Burgers: $5–$10. No credit cards. Open: Daily for lunch and early dinner (Mon–Sat to 7 p.m., Sun to 5 p.m.).*

The Moosse Cafe
$$–$$$ Mendocino   CALIFORNIA

A bit more casual, and less romantic than its compatriots, this charming restaurant is housed in a simple warren of rooms clad with contemporary art. The short but smart regularly changing menu features a yummy pasta de jour, an excellent selection of fresh fish, and perhaps a lavendar-smoked double pork chop. Prices are relatively moderate for Mendo.

In the Blue Heron Inn, 390 Kasten St. (at Albion St.). ☎ *707-937-4323. Internet:* www. theblueheron.com. *Reservations recommended. Main courses: $12–$22. MC, V. Open: Lunch and dinner daily.*

The 955 Ukiah Street Restaurant
$$–$$$ Mendocino CAL-FRENCH

Cafe Beaujolais has a higher profile, but many locals consider this cozy, unpretentious restaurant to be the most consistently excellent in town (and friendlier). The extensive, creative, and reasonably priced menu includes a good number of low-priced pastas and veggie dishes for diners on a budget, as well as heartier steaks, lamb shank, duck, and the like. Ask for a table overlooking the gardens for maximum romance and comfort.

955 Ukiah St. (between Howard and Evergreen sts.). ☎ *707-937-1955. Internet:* www.955restaurant.com. *Reservations recommended. Main courses: $12–$25. MC, V. Open: Dinner Wed–Sun.*

Exploring Around Mendocino

The primary occupation of most visitors to Mendocino is . . . well, nothing. Most people come to stroll through town, enjoy the charming seacoast vibe, soak up the views, and separate themselves from some of their disposable income.

Gallery hoppers should head to the visitor center at the Ford House Museum to pick up the **Mendocino Gallery Guide,** which offers a good gallery map. If local lore interests you, visit the **Ford House Museum,** 735 Main Street at the end of Kasten Road (☎ 707-937-5397), and the **Kelley House Museum,** 45007 Albion St., just a few doors down and across Main (☎ 707-937-5791), both legacies from Mendocino's 19th-century boomtown days as the logging capital of the North Coast.

A great place to start gallery-hopping is the **Mendocino Art Center,** 45200 Little Lake Rd., at Williams Street (one block west of Kasten; ☎ 707-937-5818), Mendocino's unofficial cultural headquarters. Multiple gallery exhibits are always on display; you'll find plenty of art to buy and lovely gardens.

Straightforward shopping highlights include **Mendocino Gift Company,** 321 Kasten St., just off Main St. (☎ 707-937-5298), which features the work of local craftspeople. Also stop in at **Moore Used Books/Main Street Bookshop,** 990A Main St., across from the Presbyterian Church (☎ 707-937-1537), a pleasing shop that used-book hounds should seek out.

Exploring the Headlands

Basically, all the waterfront territory that surrounds town makes up **Mendocino Headlands State Park.** In spring, wildflowers blanket the spectacular area; winter is a great time to watch for California gray whales, who cruise close to shore between mid-December and mid-April.

Three miles of easy trails wind through the park; stop by the visitor center at the Ford House (described in the previous section) for an access map. Easiest access is behind Mendocino Presbyterian Church, on Main Street, where a trail leads to stairs that take you down to a small but picturesque beach.

Drive out to Heeser Drive (via Little Lake Road) to reach more remote areas of the park. A number of parking lots along the route lead to short trails and magnificent views along the wild coast, which reminds us very much of Scotland. (Aye!)

Big River Beach, the park's finest stretch of sand, is accessible from the highway just south of Comptche-Ukiah Road. The beach is good for picnicking, walking, and sunbathing, but don't even think about going in the frigid water.

Big River Beach meets the mouth of the Big River, which you can explore via top-sitting kayak or canoe. Double kayaks rent for $18 per hour ($54 for the full day) from **Catch a Canoe & Bicycles, Too!,** just below the Stanford Inn at Highway 1 and Comptche-Ukiah Road (☎ **707-937-0273;** www.stanfordinn.com). They'll also rent you a top-flight mountain bike for $10 per hour ($30 a day).

Visiting Russian Gulch

Several other state parks dot the rugged coastline around Mendocino. The best of the bunch is **Russian Gulch State Park** (☎ **707-937-5804** or 707-937-4296), located off Highway 1 about two miles north of Mendocino. It's more remote and forested than Mendocino Headlands, and quite spectacular. Picnic Area Drive leads right to the park's main attraction, a churning collapsed sea cave with swirling tides called the **Devil's Punchbowl** that's well worth checking out. The well-marked, three-mile **Falls Loop Trail** is an easy walk through the redwoods to a lovely waterfall. The day-use fee is $5.

Riding the Skunk Train

Riding the Skunk Train is an easy way to see the redwoods without having to drive yourself. Founded in 1885 as a logging railroad, the **Skunk Trains** (☎ **800-77-SKUNK** or 707-964-6371; www.skunktrain. com) are vintage train cars that will take you through gorgeous — and otherwise inaccessible — North Coast redwood territory. (Originally gas powered, the trains emitted a distinctive odor that prompted locals to claim "you can smell 'em before you can see 'em" — hence the name.) The line runs 40 miles between Fort Bragg and Willits to the north. Half-day trips, which take three hours and turn around at the midpoint, Northspur, are $29 for adults and $16 for kids. The full-day loop, which traverses the entire route and takes eight hours (including a lunch stop in Willits), is $45 for adults, $25 for kids. Adult/Child combo tickets provide a discount. You should book summer excursions a month in advance.

Taking in the sweet smell of Fort Bragg

Fort Bragg is the commercial hub of North Coast life (car dealerships, fast-food joints — you get the picture). It's also home to the **Mendocino Coast Botanical Gardens,** 18220 N. Hwy. 1 (☎ 707-964-4352; www. gardenbythesea.org). This lovely public garden blooms year-round and features gentle trails with terrific ocean views — well worth a couple of hours for green thumbs. Admission is $6 for adults, $5 for seniors, $3 for kids 13 to 17, $1 for younger kids. The gardens are open March through October daily from 9 a.m. to 5 p.m., and November through February daily from 9 a.m. to 4 p.m. The main trails are wheelchair accessible.

You can book winter whale-watching excursions and deep-sea fishing charters for tuna, halibut, and salmon at Fort Bragg's Noyo Harbor. Call **North Coast Fishing Adventures** (☎ 877-546-4263; www.fortbragg fishing.com).

Gathering More Information

Before you arrive, call the **Fort Bragg/Mendocino Coast Chamber of Commerce** (☎ 800-726-2780 or 707-961-6300), or point your Web browser to www.mendocinocoast.com. You can visit the chamber's walk-in center in Fort Bragg at 332 N. Main St. (Highway 1), between Laurel and Redwood streets, across from the Guest House Museum. For other online information, the Mendocino County Alliance gives an excellent overview of the area on its Web site at www.gomendo.com.

In Mendocino, stop at the **Ford House Museum,** on the ocean side of Main Street near Kasten (☎ 707-937-5397). Free publications and maps are available at shops and restaurants around town, and your hotel can also supply you with a wealth of information.

For more information on Mendocino's state parks, visit the official California State Parks Web site at www.cal-parks.ca.gov; click on North Coast, and then click on Mendocino County. At the visitor center, ask for a copy of the **Mendocino Coastal Parks Guide,** an informative newspaper that's well worth the 25-cent price tag.

Chapter 12

Redwood Country

● ●

In This Chapter

▶ Deciding on the length of your visit

▶ Separating the trees from the cheese along the Avenue of the Giants

▶ Finding a place to stay and dine among the redwoods

● ●

*Y*ou don't have to drive all the way up to **Redwood National Park,** in the far reaches of Northern California near the Oregon border, to experience the state's giant redwoods. Frankly, by the time you got there, some 300 miles north of San Francisco, you'd have already seen enough of the towering trees to last a long while. A day excursion from Mendocino that takes you partway up the famed Avenue of the Giants — or a trip that incorporates one night in Mendocino with a second night farther north along the route — will provide plenty of exposure to the majestic trees.

The **Avenue of the Giants** is a 32-mile scenic byway that follows a portion of the old two-lane Highway 101, and parallels the modern freeway (as well as the Eel River) from Phillipsville at the south end to Pepperwood at the north. The "giants" are the magnificent coast redwoods, the tallest trees on earth, which often exceed 300 feet in height. These trees are the longer, lankier cousins to the stout giant sequoias of the Sierra Nevada. The Avenue is a relatively easy drive, curvaceous but not too challenging, that passes through some of the most spectacular territory offered by California. If you drive as far as **Humboldt Redwoods State Park** (roughly the midpoint of the route), you'll witness the largest stand of virgin redwoods in the world.

Unfortunately, you won't see just pristine nature. Tacky attractions blight the route, turning the gorgeous highway into a schlocky sideshow. From drive-through trees to a statue of Bigfoot, many of the attractions feel like leftovers from the Eisenhower era — a '50s B-movie that's lost its kitschy kick. The good news is that the sheer majesty of the trees makes stomaching *le grand frommage* easy.

To get your bearings and locate accommodations, dining, and attractions in Redwood Country, see Chapter 11.

Timing Your Visit

Whether you visit the Avenue of the Giants on a day trip or an over-nighter, try to set aside plenty of daylight hours to truly appreciate the mammoth redwoods.

Day tripping from Mendocino

You can make the Avenue of the Giants a day trip from Mendocino, leaving in the morning and returning for dinnertime. (This timetable works best in summer, when you have more daylight hours to enjoy.)

You don't have to follow the entire route to get an eyeful of the tall trees. A number of towns exist along the way where you can stop and eat lunch, and connecting back up with U.S. 101 is easy at about a half-dozen points if you tire of the meandering roadway. If you have good day-trip stamina, you can travel as far as **Humboldt Redwoods State Park** and back in the course of the day, with time to stop for some communing with nature. The drive is about 98 miles, or 2½ hours in each direction (not counting stops).

If that sounds like too much for you, just go as far as **Richardson Grove State Park,** off Highway 101 before the start of the Avenue, about 68 miles (about 1½ to 2 hours) north of Mendocino. This park makes a great place to discover the coast redwoods, which serve as the area's main tourist attraction. Also, the first leg of the drive takes you past some spectacular coastline. Beyond the park lies more of the same, with one-horse logging towns and tacky attractions thrown in. However, you will find some marvelous pristine stretches if you venture farther, with pullouts to hiking trails and day-use areas.

Because pickings are slim along the route, putting together a picnic lunch at Mendocino Market or Tote Fête (see Chapter 11) before you leave Mendocino is a very good idea, especially if you'd like more than a grilled-cheese sandwich from a lunch counter. The drive will present you with plenty of picnic spots from which to choose.

Finding options for overnighters

If you want to spend more time among the trees, you can (see "Where to Stay along the Route," later in this chapter). If you want to take it slow, consider setting aside a full day to meander north from Mendocino and up the Avenue of the Giants; then stay in a Ferndale or Eureka B&B for a night (it's 134 miles to Ferndale, 145 to Eureka). In the morning, hop on U.S. 101 for a speedy return south.

If your goal is the redwoods and you don't care about the coast — or someone in your party forgot her Dramamine and Highway 1 just isn't going to cut it — skip Mendocino altogether. The weather is much warmer and sunnier inland, and you'll save time and energy (not to mention a few bucks on accommodations) by sticking to U.S. 101 for northern destinations. Garberville makes a great southern base (especially the very nice **Benbow Inn**) if you follow this strategy. You can also zip your way to the top, stay in Eureka or Ferndale, and meander down the Avenue the next day. Driving the route northbound presents no particular advantage.

Getting There

From Mendocino, follow Highway 1 north along the shoreline to Leggett, where you'll pick up U.S. 101 (the Redwood Highway) north. The distance to Leggett is about 53 miles, with the first 30 or so winding along the coast; the scenery becomes really spectacular after you pass through Fort Bragg. It's slow going, so be prepared. Pick up U.S. 101, and 15 miles later you'll reach **Richardson Grove State Park.** The Garberville exit is another 8½ miles. Six miles beyond Garberville you can pick up the southern end of the Avenue of the Giants, formally known as Highway 254.

If you're bypassing Mendocino and coming from the south, take speedy U.S. 101 all the way north to the Avenue of the Giants exit at Phillipsville (6 miles north of Garberville). This exit is 211 miles from San Francisco straight up the 101, 158 miles from Calistoga (at the north end of Napa Valley) via Highway 128 to U.S. 101.

Driving the Avenue of the Giants

You can see the following highlights as you proceed north on the Redwood Highway, U.S. 101, picking up the Avenue of the Giants, Highway 254, at its southernmost gateway. You'll also pass much more of both the sublime and the obscure: pristine woodland stretches with pullouts that lead to wonderful hiking trails and day-use areas in the woods, and more silly attractions than you can shake a stick at. Watch for any number of blink-and-you'll-miss-'em towns along the road where you can stop to buy a casual lunch or a kitschy souvenir.

At the junction of Highway 1 and U.S. 101 sits the **Chandelier Tree Drive-Thru Tree Park** in Leggett (☎ 707-925-6363), the first of many such attractions on the Redwood Highway. Other corn-pone variations along the route include the "world famous" treehouse and the one-log house. If you're doing the cheeky Roadside Americana version of this tour, don't worry — you can't miss 'em. Each attraction sports a massive sign (usually a whole set) that's more attention-getting than a ten-foot-tall carnival barker.

Lest you think this drive-thru tree business is anything natural, Chandelier will dispel that notion right quick. Way back whenever, somebody cut a car-size hole in the base of a mammoth redwood, and you pay three bucks for the right to drive your car through. This cheesy activity is not really worth the $3, but if you're curious, this is as good a place as any to get it out of your system. And we defy you to bypass it with a small child in your car. In fact, this stop is better than most, because the picnic area provides a pretty spot for lunch. We spotted deer coming out of the woods for a sip from the pond on our stop. The park also boasts the requisite gift shop.

Here's where things really start to get good. Any itinerary should include a visit to **Richardson Grove State Park,** 15 miles north of Leggett (7 miles south of Garberville) on U.S. 101 (☎ **707-247-3318,** 707-247-3319, or 707-247-3415; www.calparks.ca.gov/DISTRICTS/ncrd/rgsp.html). The park includes a terrific visitor center with a grocery store and a nice shop, where you can pick up maps and pamphlets covering the entire region. A short (ten-minute) interpretive loop offers an excellent intro-duction to the towering trees, complete with explanatory placards. More extensive trails include an easy 1.6-mile woodland loop; stop in at the staffed center for a map. The day-use fee is $2.

Even if you're not staying at the Benbow Inn, the adjacent **Benbow Lake State Recreation Area** (☎ **707-247-3318;** www.calparks.ca. gov/DISTRICTS/ncrd/blsra.htm) makes an excellent stop for pic-nicking, sunning, and lake swimming in summer, and includes nice grassy areas and a rocky beach. The dining room over at the Benbow Inn (see "Where to Stay along the Route" in this chapter) makes a good stop for lunch (served in summer only).

About 14½ miles from Phillipsville, the first access point for the Avenue of the Giants is **Humboldt Redwoods State Park** (☎ **707-946-2409;** www.humboldtredwoods.org). Much larger than Richardson Grove, this 53,000-acre park is the real heart of the Avenue. Humboldt Redwoods features the Redwood Highway's main visitor center, plus 100 miles of hiking trails. You can pick up a trail map in the visitor center. If you plan to spend some serious time here, check out the extensive Web site. The day-use parking fee is $2.

About two miles north of the visitor center, still in Humboldt Redwoods State Park, is **Founders Grove,** one of the most impressive redwood groves in the region. Its name honors the enlightened folks who founded the Save-the-Redwoods League way back in 1917. A gentle, half-mile interpretive loop meanders through the grove. This walk is an enjoyable introduction to coast redwood ecology, and also takes you past the

Dyerville Giant — a 370-foot monster of a tree that was designated the "Champion Coast Redwood" before it fell about a decade ago. Here it remains, lying on the forest floor, its rootball alone measuring three stories long.

Where to Stay along the Route

If you want to spend quality time among the redwoods, here are a few good places to stay. **Garberville,** the unofficial hemp-producing capital of the state, remains a charm-free bend in the road off Highway 101 near the southern gateway of the Avenue of the Giants. The town is perfectly serviceable if you'd like to skip the coastline altogether and head straight for the trees. You can also stop here for a bite of lunch (see "Where to Dine along the Route," later in this chapter).

The tiny but stately burg of **Ferndale** presents a picture-perfect gingerbread slice of authentic Victoriana just past the north end of the drive. A visit to the town is well worth the 5-mile detour off U.S. 101.

Eureka is about 10 miles north of the Avenue's northern gateway. The largest town on the North Coast doesn't look like much at first glance, but if you turn west off U.S. 101 between B and M streets, you'll discover a charming Victorian Old Town along the waterfront.

For more choices, contact the visitors bureau (see "Gathering More Information," later in this chapter), whose Web site offers an excellent rundown of options throughout the area.

Hotel taxes in this neck of the woods vary; count on 7.9% to 10% being tacked onto your bill at checkout time.

Benbow Inn
$$–$$$$ Garberville

This wonderful Tudor-style hotel is tucked away in the woods on swimmable Benbow Lake. The appealing Americana-style rooms vary from petite to grand, but all are homey and comfy with pretty, tiled bathrooms; some have VCRs, pullout sofas, terraces, and/or fireplaces. The hotel has lovely lakefront grounds, a nice terrace restaurant, and attentive service. All in all, it's a great value — and an ideal place to base yourself as you frolic among the redwoods. The dining room specializes in fresh regional cuisine and offers a special children's menu.

445 Lake Benbow Dr. (off Hwy. 101), Garberville. ☎ *800-355-3301 or 707-923-2124. Fax: 707-923-2897. Internet:* www.benbowinn.com. *Parking: Free! Rack rates: $125–$255 double, $325 cottage. Rates include afternoon tea and scones and evening hors d'oeuvres. Closed Jan–Mar. Deals: Ask about off-season deals. AE, DISC, MC, V.*

Best Western Humboldt House Inn
$–$$ Garberville

This good-value chain motel hasn't much in the way of curb appeal, but the clean, spacious rooms are surprisingly well-furnished with new beds, tables, and dressers. All are nicely equipped with TVs, irons, hair dryers, and coffeemakers. Triples give families stretching room. The facilities include a pool, Jacuzzi, and guest laundry facilities. Ask for a room by the pool.

701 Redwood Dr. (off Hwy. 101), Garberville. ☎ *800-528-1234 or 707-923-2771. Fax: 707-923-4259. Internet:* www.bestwestern.com. *Parking: Free! Rack rates: $69–$104 double, $96–$148 family units. Rates include continental breakfast. Deals: Ask about off-season deals as well as AAA, senior, corporate, and government discounts. AE, DC, DISC, MC, V.*

Carter House Victorians
$$–$$$ Eureka

This grand collection of Victorians is well-situated in Eureka's Old Town. Let price and taste dictate your booking, which may be in the magnificent Carter House mansion, which also houses the highly regarded **Restaurant 301;** the full-service Hotel Carter; or one of two quaint cottages. No matter which you choose, you can count on impeccable accommodations, plush bedding, terry robes — the works. Peruse the full range of options online.

301 L St. (at Third St.), Eureka. ☎ *800-404-1390 or 707-445-1390. Fax: 707-444-8067. Internet:* www.carterhouse.com. *Parking: Free! Rack rates: $95–$187 double, $125–$297 suite, $497 cottage. Rates include two-course breakfast and evening wine and hors d'oeuvres. AE, DC, DISC, MC, V.*

Gingerbread Mansion Inn
$$$ Ferndale

In a town of pristinely preserved Victorian homes, the Gingerbread Mansion stands head and shoulders above the rest. It has been exquisitely restored and furnished in high Victorian style. Each of the 11 unique rooms includes a private bathroom (some with clawfoot tub and/or a fireplace; one with two clawfoot tubs!) and luxurious extras like plush bathrobes and turndown service. Honeymooners (or even would-be honeymooners) should consider blowing the budget and booking the Empire Suite, probably the most over-the-top room we've visited. Bring your own laurel crown.

400 Berding St., Ferndale (use the Fernbridge/Ferndale exit off U.S. 101 and go 5 miles). ☎ *800-952-4136 or 707-786-4000. Internet:* www.gingerbread-mansion.com. *Parking: Free! Rack rates: $150–$195 double, $195–$385 suite. Rates include full breakfast and afternoon high tea. Deals: Check the Web site or ask about romance packages and other current specials. AE, MC, V.*

Where to Dine along the Route

This area is not a gourmet ghetto, but you can dine supremely well if you like. The Carter House dining room, **Restaurant 301** (entrees $16–$26), regularly receives *Wine Spectator* awards, as does the restaurant at the Benbow Inn (see information for both in the preceding section). Here are a few more recommended dining choices.

Avalon

$$$ **Eureka   CALIFORNIA/FRENCH**

A refugee from the nerve-racking San Francisco restaurant scene, Avalon's owner, Beverley Wolfe, remodeled a historic building in Eureka's old town and opened a sophisticated bistro. The Avalon showcases the works of local artists on the walls and often local jazz musicians on the CD player, but the delicious food takes a back seat to neither. If it's on the seasonal menu, you can't go wrong with the Chilean sea bass or a rare filet mignon with a generous dollop of hollandaise. The bar area is comfy and inviting; the tables are set far enough apart to allow for intimate conversation.

3rd and G Streets, Eureka. ☎ 707-445-0500. Internet: www.avaloneureka.com. *Reservations recommended on weekends. Main courses $8.50–$23. MC, V. Open for lunch Wed–Fri and dinner Tues–Sat.*

Woodrose Cafe

$ **Garberville   Healthy**

Sure, it's Garberville, but you don't have to go hungry. This small diner is a haven for tasty sandwiches, soups, salads, and, if your timing is right, breakfast. Organic ingredients are used when possible, vegans are catered to, and this is the place to go to get a good look at the locals. It's Humboldt County at its purest.

911 Redwood Dr. (the main street in town), Garberville. ☎ 707-923-3191. No reservations. Main courses $4.95–$6.95. Cash only. Open for lunch Mon–Fri and breakfast daily.

Gathering More Information

Your best bet is to contact the **Eureka! Humboldt County Convention and Visitors Bureau;** call ☎ **800-346-3482** or 707-443-5097, or go online to www.redwoodvisitor.org, where you'll find individual city links in addition to information on the area as a whole.

For more on the region's state parks, including campground information, visit the official California State Parks Web site at www.calparks. ca.gov; click on North Coast, and then click on Mendocino County and/or Humboldt County.

The main visitor center is midway along the route, at **Humboldt Redwoods State Park** (☎ **707-946-2409**), 2 miles south of Weott (near the Burlington Campground) and 20 miles north of Garberville, but you can get all the maps you'll need at **Richardson Grove State Park.**

Chapter 13

Lake Tahoe

● ●

In This Chapter

▶ Deciding when to visit, where to go, and how long to stay

▶ Finding the perfect places to dine and dream

▶ Getting active on shore — and out on the water — in any season

▶ Mixing it up with lady luck at the casinos

▶ Stepping back in time with a side trip to the Gold Country

● ●

*I*f you're looking for the Golden State's biggest and best playground, look no further — you've found it. When we Californians — who have more than our fair share of beautiful places to visit — want to get outside and ski, snowmobile, boat, hike, mountain bike, ride horse-back, fish, kayak, or jet ski (the list goes on), we come to Tahoe.

Lake Tahoe isn't just any ol' hole in the ground; it's one of the more spectacular bodies of water in the world, and definitely one of the most beautiful that we've ever seen. Tahoe is the largest alpine lake in North America — 22 miles long and 12 miles wide, with a surface area of nearly 192 square miles, which means it can hold about a half-dozen Manhattans (the *city*, darling, not the cocktail).

To refer to it as "sparkling" barely does this crystalline lake justice. Science even has an explanation for it: The water is 99.9% pure, about the same purity as distilled water. It's so clear that a white dinner plate resting 75 feet below the surface would be visible to the naked eye. What's more, Lake Tahoe is the eighth-deepest lake in the world; it holds so much water that, if you tipped it on its side, the contents would flood the entire state of California to a depth of 14 inches.

Evergreens and snowy peaks rising from the shoreline make the lake look that much deeper, broader, and majestic. But don't just take our word for it; listen to Mark Twain, who described Lake Tahoe as ". . . the beautiful relic of fairy-land forgotten . . . ." While Tahoe certainly isn't forgotten anymore, Twain's flight of fancy continues to hold true.

Timing Your Visit

When's the best time to visit? Simple: Come in winter if cross-country or alpine skiing is your game. This is also the time, at least during the week, when you'll have Tahoe to yourself. Otherwise, come in summer. Or try autumn, the secret season in Tahoe. The colors are beautiful, the air is crisp, activities abound, and hotel rates are low, low, low. Skip yucky spring altogether. The snowmelt turns the terrain into mud.

Even in summer, prepare yourself for cool weather. In July, average highs don't hit the 80s, and evenings can dip well below 50°F. And because the upper 12 feet of the lake warms only to about 68°F, don't expect to splash around in your floaties. Chances are, it'll be all you can do to dip your toes in.

Tahoe is a favorite weekend getaway among San Franciscans, so you'll always save money — and, even more important, avoid the crowds — by scheduling your stay for Monday through Thursday.

A three-night stay in Tahoe will give you plenty of time to fully explore the area and play. If you cut your stay back to two, you risk spending too much time in the car (getting there and leaving), and not enough time in Tahoe. Budget four nights if you want to experience both shores. For more on this topic, check out the next section.

Choosing between Two Shores

The 30-mile drive between Lake Tahoe's north and south shores can become a two-hour bumper-to-bumper (or snowstorm-y) nightmare in the high seasons, so choose your shore carefully. Both boast first-rate skiing, good restaurants, lake views, and plenty of on-the-water fun — but that's pretty much where the similarities end.

South Lake Tahoe is more developed and generally cheaper; more hotels mean more competition, so you'll get better accommodations for your money. The big Nevada casinos are at hand (in town for all intents and purposes), so this is your shore if you want some nightlife. Getting out on the water is easier from the south shore, too, because it boasts more marinas, more outfitters, plus some excellent shoreline state parks not far from town. At the moment, the downtown is undergoing redevelopment to make the area more user-friendly, with a pedestrian plaza, new timeshare hotels, and the demolition of some of the seedier motels. By the time you arrive, much of this work should be finished, but you can check up on the progress at www.virtualtahoe.com.

If Mark Twain were waxing poetic about today's Tahoe, he'd be writing about the north shore. **North Lake Tahoe** is much, much prettier than its southern shore. It's more remote and country-like, with a diverse selection of ski resorts and first-class accommodations — but you can still find slot machines close by if you feel the urge. **Squaw Valley,** six miles from the lakeshore, is one of the best outdoor recreation centers ever, and, with its newly built alpine-style village, is poised to become a one-stop destination. **Tahoe City,** although not as commercially spoiled as South Lake Tahoe, does get way too crowded for its own good in the high seasons. And if affordability is a concern, you won't get as much value for your dollar here.

While we prefer the north shore, skiers will find either one convenient. Our best advice: Avoid the weekends and *never* drive to Tahoe on a Friday afternoon unless you want to sit in traffic on a two-lane highway with no escape. On weekdays, you'll also have an opportunity to enjoy the wonderful drive along Highway 89 at an easy pace so you can investigate both shores for yourself.

Getting There

Lake Tahoe straddles the California/Nevada border, a four-hour drive east (slightly northeast, actually) from San Francisco.

 ✔ **If you're coming from San Francisco:** Take I-80 east to Sacramento, then U.S. 50 to South Lake Tahoe on the south shore, or stay on I-80 east to Highway 89 south to reach Tahoe City on the north shore.

 ✔ **If you're coming from Yosemite:** Take Highway 120 east out of the park to I-395 north to U.S. 50 east; at the U.S. 50/Highway 28 split, follow U.S. 50 to South Lake Tahoe, Highway 28 to Tahoe City on the north shore.

The 3½-hour drive is doable only between late June and the first snowfall (usually early November), because Yosemite's east gate closes in winter. Otherwise, the drive becomes a five- or six-hour trek north on winding Highway 49 to I-50, which can be slow going in bad weather.

 ✔ **If you're coming from points south:** Take I-5 through central California to Sacramento, then pick up I-80 east to the north shore or U.S. 50 east to the south shore.

Whether you're taking I-80 to the north shore or U.S. 50 to the south shore, you can easily work in a side trip to the Gold Country on your way to Tahoe. All you need is a few hours to spare and the desire to see some small towns; for details, see "Side-Tripping to the Gold Country" at the end of this chapter.

 ✔ **If you're heading to Squaw Valley:** Follow Highway 89 (River Road) at the 89/28 split in Tahoe City. Go five miles and turn left at Squaw Valley Road.

Lake Tahoe

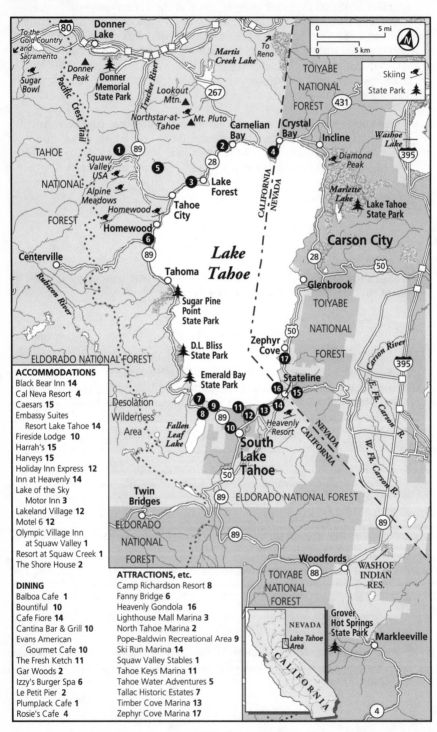

ACCOMMODATIONS
Black Bear Inn **14**
Cal Neva Resort **4**
Caesars **15**
Embassy Suites
 Resort Lake Tahoe **14**
Fireside Lodge **10**
Harrah's **15**
Harveys **15**
Holiday Inn Express **12**
Inn at Heavenly **14**
Lake of the Sky
 Motor Inn **3**
Lakeland Village **12**
Motel 6 **12**
Olympic Village Inn
 at Squaw Valley **1**
Resort at Squaw Creek **1**
The Shore House **2**

DINING
Balboa Cafe **1**
Bountiful **10**
Cafe Fiore **14**
Cantina Bar & Grill **10**
Evans American
 Gourmet Cafe **10**
The Fresh Ketch **11**
Gar Woods **2**
Izzy's Burger Spa **6**
Le Petit Pier **2**
PlumpJack Cafe **1**
Rosie's Cafe **4**

ATTRACTIONS, etc.
Camp Richardson Resort **8**
Fanny Bridge **6**
Heavenly Gondola **16**
Lighthouse Mall Marina **3**
North Tahoe Marina **2**
Pope-Baldwin Recreational Area **9**
Ski Run Marina **14**
Squaw Valley Stables **1**
Tahoe Keys Marina **11**
Tahoe Water Adventures **5**
Tallac Historic Estates **7**
Timber Cove Marina **13**
Zephyr Cove Marina **17**

Reno/Tahoe International Airport is at U.S. 395 just south of I-80 in Reno, NV (☎ 775-328-6400; www.renoairport.com). All the national car-rental companies have airport locations. The drive takes 50 minutes to Tahoe City on the north shore; take U.S. 395 north to I-80 west to Highway 89 south. For South Lake Tahoe, take U.S. 395 south to U.S. 50 west, a 70-minute drive.

These airlines fly into Reno/Tahoe:

- ✔ **Alaska Airlines:** ☎ 800-426-0333; www.alaskaair.com
- ✔ **American Airlines:** ☎ 800-433-7300; www.aa.com
- ✔ **America West:** ☎ 800-235-9292; www.americawest.com
- ✔ **Continental:** ☎ 800-525-0280; www.continental.com
- ✔ **Delta/Skywest:** ☎ 800-221-1212; www.delta.com
- ✔ **Northwest:** ☎ 800-225-2525; www.nwa.com
- ✔ **Southwest:** ☎ 800-435-9792; www.southwest.com
- ✔ **United:** ☎ 800-241-6522; www.united.com

Getting Your Bearings

On the south shore, two main highways meet at a prominent "Y" intersection in South Lake Tahoe: U.S. 50, which continues up the east (Nevada) shore of the lake to midpoint and then shoots off east; and Highway 89, which runs up the west (California) side of the lake to Tahoe City, then turns northwest away from the lake. Highway 28 picks up where 89 leaves off, running along the north shore from Tahoe City to midpoint on the Nevada side, where it meets up with U.S. 50, completing the continuous 72-mile circle around the lake.

Lake Tahoe's biggest town is South Lake Tahoe, which runs along the south shore. Its main drag is U.S. 50, which is called Lake Tahoe Boulevard in town. After you cross the California/Nevada line, you're immediately in Stateline, Nevada. It's easy to tell; the casinos practically trip you after your toes pass over the border.

Follow Highway 89 about 31 miles north along the west shore, past camplike resorts and stunning lakefront homes, and you'll reach Tahoe City, the commercial hub of the north shore. Go six miles northwest on Highway 89 to breathtaking Squaw Valley, whose thriving Olympic Village was built for the 1960 Winter Games.

Along with a few other casino/hotels, another prominent community sits on the northeast shore, Nevada's Incline Village. But we've concentrated on the California side because we're partisans — this *is* a book about California, after all.

Where to Stay

For additional choices throughout the region, contact **Lake Tahoe Central Reservations** (☎ **888-434-1262,** 800-824-6348, or 530-583-3494; or www.mytahoevacation.com). They charge $12 to make your reservations, and you won't get the best room prices, but the staff is knowledgeable. You can also try **Tahoe Reservations.com** (www.tahoe reservations.com), a free, real-time service that specializes in South Tahoe. For ski packages, contact **Ski Tahoe** (☎ **888-982-1088;** www. skitahoe.com).

Expect to see 10 to 12% in taxes added to your hotel bill.

On the south shore

The big-name casinos at Stateline, Nevada, which resemble unattractive office complexes, display none of the outrageousness of Las Vegas, but do offer gaming, entertainment, and amenities, such as indoor pools and spa facilities. They're fairly equivalent in their middle-of-the-road comforts and prices, which can range from $79 to $279 and up depending on the day and season. These places thrive on packages, so always ask.

- ✔ **Harrah's** (☎ **800-427-7247** or 775-588-6611; www.harrahs.com) is attractive and low-key, comparatively speaking, and appeals to a slightly less raucous vacationer.

- ✔ **Harveys** (☎ **800-553-1022** or 775-588-2411; www.harrahs.com/our_casinos/hlt/) is the rock-and-roll casino and draws in a young, sophisticated crowd.

- ✔ **Caesars** (☎ **800-648-3353,** 888-829-7630, or 775-586-7771; www.caesars.com) is the sole themed casino (think grown-up toga party) and attracts the major talent to its showroom.

In addition to the more unique choices below, South Lake Tahoe also has some excellent-value motels:

- ✔ **Holiday Inn Express,** 3961 Lake Tahoe Blvd. (☎ **800-544-5288** or 530-544-5900; www.holidayinnexpresstahoe.com), has high-quality rooms tucked among the trees to ensure quiet. Rooms run $69 to $210, family-size suites $150 to $270, including continental breakfast.

- ✔ **Motel 6,** 2375 Lake Tahoe Blvd. (☎ **800-466-8356** or 530-542-1400; www.motel6.com), is the best motel value in town for penny-pinching travelers. Rooms run $44 to $75.

Black Bear Inn
$$$–$$$$ South Lake Tahoe

Wow! This stunning lodgelike B&B looks like it rambled straight out of a Ralph Lauren advertisement, complete with gleaming knotty-pine woodwork, bearskins, and a two-story riverstone fireplace in the soaring living room. Extraordinary craftsmanship, witty rustic-goes-chic decor, beautifully outfitted rooms (gorgeous bathrooms!), lots of lounging space, and charming hosts add up to the most gracious place to stay on the south shore, period. Geared toward adults and kids over 16.

1202 Ski Run Blvd., South Lake Tahoe. ☎ *877-BEAR-INN (232-7466) or 530-544-4451. Fax: 530-544-7315. Internet:* www.tahoeblackbear.com. *Parking: Free! Rack rates: $205–$245 double, $265–$475 cabin. Rates include full breakfast. MC, V.*

Embassy Suites Resort Lake Tahoe
$$$ South Lake Tahoe

Skip the bland Embassy Suites hotel down the street and book into this lakefront condo resort instead. The sun-filled suites are gorgeously decorated in subdued Southwest colors and high-quality everything. Each one comes with a cute balcony and a fully equipped kitchenette or kitchen. This hotel offers an excellent indoor/outdoor pool, pretty grounds, exercise room, video-game room, coin-op laundry, and far more style and value for your dollar than you'd expect. A winner!

901 Ski Run Blvd., South Lake Tahoe. ☎ *800-362-2779 or 530-541-6122. Fax: 530-541-2028. Internet:* www.embassyvacationresorts.com. *Parking: Free! Rack rates: $125–$350 studios, 1- and 2-bedroom suites (1-bedrooms from $145, 2-bedrooms from $185). Deals: AAA and senior discounts available; ask about packages. AE, DC, DISC, MC, V.*

Fireside Lodge
$$–$$$ South Lake Tahoe

Recently renovated, these nine tidy little country-pine suites are cozy (read small), but fully equipped with kitchenettes, gas fireplaces, and TV/VCRs. It's owned and run by a local family (they also own the Inn at Heavenly), and the location is unbeatable — close to some great restaurants and the marvelous facilities of Camp Richardson, but far enough from the main drag to keep your mind on the mountains. Dogs and kids are most welcome. The staff will even lend you bicycles, float tubes, and videos.

515 Emerald Bay Rd., South Lake Tahoe. ☎ *800-692-2246 or 530-544-5515. Internet:* www.firesidelodge.com. *Parking: Free! Rack rates: $89–$155 double. Rates include continental breakfast. Deals: Check for off-season specials. AE, DISC, MC, V.*

Inn at Heavenly

$$–$$$ South Lake Tahoe

These upscale motel rooms are low-ceilinged and teensy, but they're dec-orated in a dreamy-cute wooden-beam style, each with a gas fireplace, VCR, ceiling fan, and kitchenette with microwave, fridge, and cof-feemaker. Swings and picnic sets dot the lovely grounds. Amenities include steam room and sauna, warm-hearted innkeepers, and a cozy common room with games and videos. It's pet-friendly, so bring Fido.

1261 Ski Run Blvd. (just downhill from Heavenly ski resort), South Lake Tahoe. ☎ 800-MY-CABIN (800-692-2246) or 530-544-4244. Fax: 530-544-5213. Internet: www.inn-at-heavenly.com. Parking: Free! Rack rates: $135–$175 double, $195–$395 cabin (sleeps 8–12). Rates include continental breakfast, snacks. Deals: AAA and senior discounts available. Some kind of discount or package deal almost always exists; off-season rates as low as $69. AE, DISC, MC, V.

On the north shore

Shooting craps actually gives us hives — unless we're winning — but one more casino straddling the north-shore border merits mention. Once owned by Frank Sinatra (until the gaming authorities intervened), the **Cal Neva Resort** (2 Stateline Rd., Crystal Bay, Nevada; ☎ **800-CAL-NEVA** or 775-832-4000; www.calnevaresort.com; doubles $79–$189) is our personal choice for a Tahoe gambling den. While the others are definitely flashier, the Cal Neva offers some history and a little soul, and the spacious guest rooms have glorious lake views.

Lake of the Sky Motor Inn

$–$$ Tahoe City

This '60s motel is a walk from restaurants, but far enough from the tourist fray to offer some measure of peace. Expect only the basics, but rooms have been recently remodeled, beds are firm, housekeeping is neat, and beamed ceilings add a lodgelike touch. The lakeview rooms include fridges. The friendly owners keep the coffeepot on all day. The motel offers a pool and free local calls, too.

955 N. Lake Blvd. (Hwy. 28), Tahoe City. ☎ 530-583-3305. Fax: 530-583-7621. Parking: Free! Rack rates: $59–$149 double. Rates include continental breakfast. AE, DC, DISC, MC, V.

Olympic Village Inn at Squaw Valley

$$–$$$ Squaw Valley

This Swiss chalet–style all-suite hotel is the best value in the gorgeous Olympic Valley. The suites can sleep four, and are attractively done in a country accent and boast fully equipped mini-kitchens, VCRs, and stereos. The lovely grounds are a stone's throw from Squaw Valley USA activities. Timeshare owners get first dibs, so call early (midweek is your best bet).

1909 Chamonix Pl. (off Squaw Valley Rd.), Squaw Valley. ☎ *800-845-5243 or 530-581-6000. Fax: 530-583-4165. Internet:* www.olympicvillageinn.com. *Parking: Free! Rack rates: $115–$315 one-bedroom suite. AE, DISC, MC, V.*

Resort at Squaw Creek
$$$$$ Squaw Valley

This 626-acre destination resort is built to take prime advantage of the valley and forest views. The rooms aren't overly special, however. Come, instead, for the unparalleled facilities, which include a wonderful pool complex, spa, first-rate dining, golf, tennis, biking, cross-country ski center, ice-skating in season, private chairlift at Squaw Valley USA, great kids' program, and more.

400 Squaw Creek Rd., Squaw Valley. ☎ *800-327-3353 or 530-583-6300. Fax: 530-581-6632. Internet:* www.squawcreek.com. *Parking: $15 to valet, free self-parking. Rack rates: $250–$350 double, $420–$525 suite, from $750 penthouse. Rates include continental breakfast. Deals: Ask about golf, ski, spa, valley-view upgrades, and other packages. AE, DC, DISC, MC, V.*

The Shore House
$$$–$$$$ Tahoe Vista

A great choice for lakefront amour, this wonderful B&B sits 15 minutes at most from Tahoe City in gorgeous, upscale Tahoe Vista. The rustic-romantic rooms are built for two and have private entrances, knotty-pine walls, cuddly Scandia down comforters on custom-built log beds, gas fireplaces, and CD players (no TV). The B&B offers a sandy beach next door, lots of restaurants nearby, welcoming and attentive innkeepers, and plenty of lake-facing lounge spaces — including a lakeside hot tub.

7170 North Lake Blvd., Tahoe Vista (8 miles east of Tahoe City). ☎ *800-207-5160 or 530-546-7270. Fax: 530-546-7130. Internet:* www.shorehouselaketahoe.com. *Rack rates: $160–$285 double. Rates include a delicious full breakfast. DISC, MC, V.*

Where to Dine

Tahoe is at full capacity most weekends, so book Friday and Saturday dinners in advance to avoid disappointment.

On the south shore

Bountiful

$ **South Lake Tahoe** CALIFORNIA/HEALTHY

A former hamburger stand (a rootbeer mug signpost marks the spot), Bountiful has been spottily remodeled into a breakfast/lunch cafe much loved by those in the know. Breakfast includes a bit of everything you'd want to eat including eggs, pancakes, and oatmeal (it's good for you), and at lunch we've gratefully tucked in to a bowl of housemade soup and one of the substantial sandwiches on the menu. Vegetarians will love the brown rice and tofu bowls, packed with veggies. Small, funky, and terrific.

717 Emerald Bay Rd., South Lake Tahoe. ☎ *530-542-4060. Main courses: $5–$8. No credit cards. Open: Breakfast and lunch Tues–Sun. Dinner served in summer.*

Cafe Fiore

$$$ **South Lake Tahoe** ITALIAN

Lower profile than neighboring Nepheles, Cafe Fiore is definitely the superior restaurant. The dining room is rustic but lovely, with just seven white linen–dressed tables, plus a handful more on the alfresco terrace in summer. The creative Italian fare is prepared with culinary expertise and care; the garlic bread alone is enough to bring us back, begging for more. A regular winner of the *Wine Spectator* Award of Excellence, this restaurant is ultra-romantic and simply divine.

1169 Ski Run Blvd. (between U.S. 50 and Pioneer Trail), South Lake Tahoe. ☎ *530-541-2908. Internet:* www.cafefiore.com. *Reservations highly recommended. Main courses: $13–$23. AE, MC, V. Open: Dinner nightly.*

Cantina Bar & Grill

$$ **South Lake Tahoe** CAL-MEXICAN

This Southwestern cantina is consistently named best Mex by locals. It's attractive and lively, with first-rate margaritas and 30 different beers free-flowing during the weekday 3 to 6 p.m. happy hour and beyond. The kitchen gets creative with specialties like rock shrimp quesadillas and calamari rellenos, but you won't be disappointed by tried-and-true faves such as top-notch burritos, taco combos, and the like.

765 Emerald Bay Rd. (at Hwy. 89 and 10th St.), South Lake Tahoe. ☎ *530-544-1233. Internet:* www.cantinatahoe.com. *Reservations not taken. Main courses: $8–$15. MC, V. Open: Lunch and dinner daily.*

Evans American Gourmet Cafe

$$$–$$$$ **South Lake Tahoe** CONTEMPORARY AMERICAN

Tucked away in a vintage ski cabin in the woods is Tahoe's best restaurant, on any shore. It's intimate and sophisticated, but completely unpretentious. Ingredients are fresh and top-quality. Preparations are somewhat complex, but Chef Aaron Maffit's hand is so practiced and his touch so light that even the foie gras starter doesn't seem too heavy. Desserts are swell, too. This terrific restaurant could stand on its own in New York or San Francisco.

536 Emerald Bay Rd. (on Hwy. 89, a mile north of U.S. 50), South Lake Tahoe. ☎ 530-542-1990. Internet: www.evanstahoe.com. *Reservations highly recommended. Main courses: $19–$25. DISC, MC, V. Open: Dinner nightly.*

The Fresh Ketch
$$–$$$$ **South Lake Tahoe   SEAFOOD**

The well-worn, casual downstairs bar offers first-rate seafood and good views, while the pretty upstairs dining room maintains a more formal atmosphere. We like the bar for lunch; golden-wood backgammon tables even let you settle in for a game as you nosh on oysters on the half shell, delicately breaded calamari with a zippy dipping sauce, fish-and-chips, and ahi tacos. The New England clam chowder may be the best you'll find west of the Mississippi.

At Tahoe Keys Marina, 2433 Venice Dr. (off U.S. 50 at the end of Tahoe Keys Blvd.), South Lake Tahoe. ☎ 530-541-5683. Internet: www.thefreshketch.com. *Reservations recommended for dining room. Main courses: $9–$11 at downstairs bar, $17–$26 in upstairs dining room. AE, DC, DISC, MC, V. Open: Lunch and dinner daily (dining room dinner only).*

On the north shore

Balboa Cafe
$$$ **Squaw Valley   CALIFORNIA**

The Plumpjack boys got a jump on the competiton at the new Village at Squaw Valley, opening the brasserie-style Balboa Cafe before the paint was even dry in the first of the new condos. They serve the same nearly famous hamburgers here as in the San Francisco haunt of the same name, along with a good steak frites and delicious roast chicken nicely accompanied with potato-mushroom gratin and our personal love, Brussels sprouts. The decor is western eclectic, the bar is fun, and it's sure to be a magnet for ski bums of all persuasions. They serve takeout from a little counter next door.

Directly across from the base lifts in the village, 1985 Squaw Valley Rd., Squaw Valley. ☎ 530-583-5850. Internet: www.plumpjack.com. *Reservations recommended. Main courses: $10–$23. AE, MC, V. Open: Breakfast, lunch, and dinner daily.*

Gar Woods

$$$ Carnelian Bay   AMERICAN

The large lakefront deck is a popular gathering spot in summer, but this friendly restaurant/bar draws the crowds every season. Along with the grand views, patrons suck up creative cocktails, enjoy live music Friday and Saturday nights, and party down with their pals. The menu, while not particularly creative, covers familiar surf/turf/pasta territory and includes such toothsome appetizers as beer-batter coconut prawns. Quite a scene.

5000 North Lake Blvd. (Hwy. 28, between Tahoe City and Tahoe Vista), Carnelian Bay. ☎ 530-546-3366. Internet: www.garwoods.com. *Reservations recommended. Main courses: $9–$17 at lunch, $17–$25 at dinner; bar menu $9–$18. AE, MC, V. Open: Lunch Fri–Sun; dinner nightly; Sun brunch.*

Le Petit Pier

$$$$ Tahoe Vista   FRENCH

For a romantic splurge, this *Wine Spectator*–award-winning restaurant in gorgeous Tahoe Vista is well worth the 15-minute drive east from Tahoe City. Spectacular lake views enhance the pretty dining room and inspire relaxed conversation. The traditional caviar service is always a fine choice to begin with, followed by a lovely asparagus salad in season, and the lobster. This is haute cuisine made to put someone in a most magnanimous mood, indeed.

7238 N. Lake Blvd. (Hwy. 28, about eight miles west of Tahoe City), Tahoe Vista. ☎ 530-546-4464. Reservations recommended. Internet: www.lepetitpier.com. *Main courses: $20–$30. AE, DC, DISC, MC, V. Open: Dinner nightly.*

PlumpJack Cafe

$$$$ Squaw Valley   CONTEMPORARY MEDITERRANEAN

The best restaurant in Squaw Valley is this first-rate resort version of the San Francisco favorite. The Mediterranean-accented modern cuisine revolves around seasonal ingredients, always a good sign (and if the duckling trio is on the menu, order it). The room is one-hundred-percent high-design chic but utterly comfortable nonetheless. Service is impeccable in a not-too-formal way, and the wine list boasts well-chosen labels at reasonable markups. Excellent through and through.

At PlumpJack Squaw Valley Inn, 1920 Squaw Valley Rd., Squaw Valley. ☎ 800-323-7666 or 530-583-1576. Internet: www.plumpjack.com. *Reservations highly recommended for dinner. Main courses: $22–$28. AE, MC, V. Open: Breakfast, lunch, and dinner daily.*

Rosie's Café
$–$$ Tahoe City   AMERICAN

Two floors of tables usually ensure a short wait, if at all, at this shingled, lodge-style family-owned restaurant. It's noisy and casual, perfect for families, and servings are plentiful. A big menu offers breakfasts designed to rev up skiers, as well as hamburgers, grilled chicken sandwiches, and chef-type salads for lunch, and two-course dinners starring meat (the pot roast is hard to resist) and fish. You won't mistake it for gourmet, but you'll like the value and ethos.

571 North Lake Blvd., Tahoe City. ☎ *530-583-8504. Internet:* www.rosiescafe. com. *Reservations accepted for dinner. Main courses: $5–$10 at lunch, $14–$22 at dinner. DISC, MC, V. Open: Breakfast, lunch, and dinner daily.*

Enjoying Lake Tahoe

You have to get out on the water to truly appreciate the grandeur of Lake Tahoe.

The 570-passenger *M.S. Dixie II* (☎ **775-588-3508** or 775-882-0786; www.tahoedixie2.com), an authentic paddle-wheeler, offers lake cruises year-round from Zephyr Cove Marina, on U.S. 50, which is 4 miles east of the CA/NV state line. We like the two-hour Emerald Bay Sightseeing Cruise best; it gives you a general feel for the lake and takes you into the stunning bay where you can see Fanette Island and Vikingsholm up close without having to take the difficult walk (see "Driving along the spectacular west shore," later in this chapter). Fares are $24 adults, $7 for kids under 12; reservations are recommended.

If you'd like a more intimate ride, book with **Woodwind Sailing Cruises** (☎ **888-867-6394;** www.sailwoodwind.com). Trips, which originate from Camp Richardson Resort or Zephyr Cove, start at $24 for adults, $22 for seniors, $10 for kids 12 and under. The sunset champagne cruise is smooch-worthy.

On the north shore, catch a ride aboard the *Tahoe Gal* (☎ **800-218-2464** or 530-583-0141; www.tahoegal.com), which offers tours from the Lighthouse Mall Marina, 850 N. Lake Blvd., in Tahoe City from mid-April through October. Prices start at $19 adults, $9 kids.

Boating for do-it-yourselfers

Expect to pay in the neighborhood of $109 to $139 per hour for a power-boat and between $100 and $140 for a jet ski; the fourth hour is often free. Always reserve ahead.

On the south shore:

- ✔ **Zephyr Cove Resort Marina,** on U.S. 50, 4 miles east of the CA/NV state line (☎ **775-589-4908** or 775-588-3833; www.tahoedixie2. com), rents late-model boats between 16 to 28 feet, plus runabouts, ski boats, pontoons, pedalboats, kayaks, and canoes.

- ✔ **Tahoe Keys Boat Rentals** (☎ **530-544-8888,** 530-541-8405, or 530-541-2155) rents powerboats from Tahoe Keys Marina, conveniently located in South Lake Tahoe off Lake Tahoe Boulevard (U.S. 50) at the end of Tahoe Keys Road.

- ✔ A great place to launch a kayak is **Timber Cove Marina,** on Lake Tahoe Boulevard at the end of Johnson Boulevard, which has the largest public beach on the south shore. Rentals are available from **Kayak Tahoe** (☎ **530-544-2011;** www.kayaktahoe.com). Call ahead to arrange for a guided tour.

- ✔ **Camp Richardson Marina** at Camp Richardson Resort, 2 miles west of the U.S. 50/Highway 89 junction (☎ **530-542-6570;** www. camprichardson.com), rents a full slate of boating equipment similar to that at Zephyr Cove.

On the north shore:

- ✔ **North Tahoe Marina,** 7360 N. Lake Blvd. (Highway 28, 1 mile west of Highway 267), in Tahoe Vista (☎ **800-58-MARINA** or 530-546-8248; www.northtahoemarina.com), rents 19- to 24-foot powerboats, plus skis and tow lines.

- ✔ **Tahoe Water Adventures** is at the Lakehouse Mall, just off North Lake Boulevard at the end of Grove Street, in Tahoe City (☎ **530-583-3225**). They'll rent you powerboats with wakeboards or skis, canoes, kayaks, jet skis, or environmentally friendly inflatable watercraft.

Sportfishing

The most respected charter company around is **Tahoe Sport Fishing,** which operates from two south-shore locations: **Ski Run Marina,** off U.S. 50 at the end of Ski Run Boulevard, a mile west of the state line (☎ **800-696-7797** or 530-541-5448); and **Zephyr Cove,** on U.S. 50, 4 miles east of the state line (☎ **800-696-7797** or 775-586-9338; www. tahoesportfishing.com). Four- to seven-hour trips run $70 to $100 per person, including all gear, tackle, and bait. If you're lucky enough to hook a salmon or a big Mackinaw lake trout, the fee includes cleaning and sacking.

Driving along the spectacular west shore

The entire drive along Highway 89 offers spectacular scenery. It's worth dedicating the better part of a day to explore (be sure to make your exploration day a bright, clear weekday to avoid traffic).

Here are your best stops, from south to north:

✔ The best public-access beaches are part of the **Pope-Baldwin Recreational Area,** which begins just west of the Y intersection with U.S. 50. Expect to pay $3 to park at most public beaches, such as pretty **Pope Beach** and at the beach at **Camp Richardson.** Camp Richardson's **Beacon Bar & Grill** is the ideal place to enjoy a sunset Rum Runner (practically the official Tahoe cocktail) because the patio is right on the sand, just a stone's throw — literally — from the water.

✔ Next up is the **Tallac Historic Estates,** three landmarked 1920s homes open for tours in summer. More interesting is **Visitors Center Beach** (turn right at the USFS Lake Tahoe Visitors Center sign). Follow the **Rainbow Trail,** an easy ten-minute walk along a paved walkway dotted with interpretive placards, to the **Stream Profile Chamber,** which offers an eco-lesson in water clarity and the freshwater food chain through a submerged window onto **Taylor Creek.** The view is like looking into an aquarium, only it's the real thing — very cool. Walk ten minutes in the opposite direction from the visitor center, following the "Beach Access" sign, to a very nice stretch of beach.

Hikers should stop into the visitor center to pick up a copy of the invaluable *Lake of the Sky Journal,* which details a number of great hikes throughout the area.

✔ From the **Visitors Center Beach,** the highway begins to climb northward. Soon you'll see the aptly named **Emerald Bay,** a 3-mile-long finger of sparkling green water jutting off the lake. This bay also has the lake's only island — tiny **Fanette Island** — where you'll find the ruins of an old stone teahouse.

Pull into the lot marked "Emerald Bay State Park/Vikingsholm" for the favorite lake photo op, bar none. The walk down to the lakeshore is 1½ miles long, but at the end you'll find **Vikingsholm,** a Danish-style castle built by the same (kinda wacky) lady behind the teahouse on Fanette Island. Back in 1928, the lake so reminded her of a Scandinavian fjord that she decided to drive the theme home. The castle is a sight to see — but remember, you'll have to walk back up that steep 1½-mile hill. The mansion is open for tours in summer only (☎ 530-525-7277).

✔ A couple of miles farther up the road sits **D. L. Bliss State Park** (☎ **530-525-7277**), a gorgeous spot with one of the lake's finest beaches (come early in summer to ensure a parking space). Attention, hikers: Moderate-level **Rubicon Trail** is a worthy 5-mile hike along Emerald Bay.

✔ Another 7 miles on is **Sugar Pine Point State Park** (☎ **530-525-7982).** This terrific park offers 1¾ miles of shoreline with sandy beaches, more than 2,000 forested acres laced with hiking trails, the historic Ehrman Mansion (open for guided tours in summer), and a nature center. Parking is $5.

✔ After you reach Tahoe City, take note of **Fanny Bridge,** on Highway 89 just south of the Y intersection with Highway 28 (next to **Izzy's Burger Spa,** a great spot for juicy burgers and thick shakes), so named for the view of derrieres as folks bend over the rail to catch sight of the leaping trout below.

Golfing and other warm-weather fun

Hitting the links is a very big deal in North Tahoe. A half-dozen excellent courses lie within easy reach of Tahoe City, including the award-winning Robert Trent Jones, Jr.–designed links-style course at the **Resort at Squaw Creek** (see "Where to Stay" earlier in this chapter), honored by *Golf* magazine as one of the Top 10 resort courses in America. For tee times here or at another course, contact **North Lake Tahoe Central Reservations** (☎ **800-824-6348** or 530-583-3494; www.tahoefun.org). These friendly folks can also direct you south-shore vacationers to great courses, too.

Taking a heavenly ride

When it's not busy shuttling skiers, the **Heavenly Aerial Tram** (☎ **775-586-7000;** www.skiheavenly.com) will take you on a mile-high ascent for some of the most spectacular views ever, here or anywhere. After you're done gawking at the scene during the five-minute ride, you can follow a 2-mile path through a lovely forest, or lunch at the Monument Peak Restaurant, which offers standard American eats. The ride costs $20 for adults, $12 for kids 4 to 12; ask for pricing on dining combo tickets, and make a reservation if you intend to eat. Guided hikes are offered in summer; call for the schedule. Heavenly is off U.S. 50 at the top of Ski Run Boulevard.

Heavenly also operates a brand-new **gondola** a half-block west of Stateline right on U.S. 50. The ride ($20 for adults, $12 for kids 4 to 12) takes you 2.4 miles up the mountain to an observation deck at 9,123 feet. While the views are breathtaking, there's not much to do up there but come back down. You may get more for your money taking the cable car at Squaw (see the listing in this section).

River rafting

Truckee River Rafting (☎ **888-584-7238** or 530-583-7238; www.truckee
riverrafting.com) offers one cool north-shore activity; a leisurely
float along a 5-mile stretch down the Truckee River from Tahoe City to
River Ranch Pond. You'll even hit a couple of baby rapids for a few
thrills. The kids will just love it. The ride is $25 for adults, $20 for kids,
including all equipment and pickup at the end. Reserve ahead, and
allow two to four hours for the adventure.

Playing at Squaw Valley's High Camp

Squaw Valley High Camp (☎ **530-583-6955;** www.squaw.com) is a
wonderful place to play in summer, and a great way to experience the
Olympic Village. After a scenic cable-car ride to 8,200 feet, you can ice-
skate at the mountaintop Olympic Ice Pavilion, or swim and spa in the
Swimming Lagoon. Hikers can pick up a trail map at the base information desk and follow any one of a half-dozen mountain trails, ranging
from easy to difficult. Mountain bikers can rent a front-suspension bike
at the **Squaw Valley Sport Shop,** in the Olympic Village (☎ **530-583-
3356**), take it to the top, and explore the snowless slopes. Expect half-
day rentals around $30, and full-day rentals in the neighborhood of $40,
helmets included; call to book a bike and avoid disappointment.

Hitting the slopes in ski season

Tahoe is more popular as a ski resort than anything else. It's home to
the state's best skiing, and the country's largest concentration of downhill slopes. The ski season usually lasts from November through April
but has been known to extend into the early summer. Most resorts welcome snowboarders, but always check first.

Lift tickets for adults cost between $18 and $57 for a full day, depending on the resort, with convenient Heavenly and Squaw Valley on the
high end. Resorts often issue money-saving multiday tickets, and kids
and seniors always qualify for discounts. Your lodge will probably have
discounted tickets on hand as well.

Contact the local **visitor centers** (see "Gathering More Information,"
later in this chapter) or www.tahoesbest.com/skitahoe for more
information about all the area ski resorts. Also inquire about ski packages, which can usually save you a small fortune, especially if you ski
midweek.

The top south shore slopes

Heavenly (☎ **775-586-7000;** www.skiheavenly.com) is off U.S. 50 at
the top of Ski Run Boulevard (turn left). It features the region's steepest
vertical drop (3,500 feet) and one of its largest ski terrains (4,800 acres),
not to mention one of the world's largest snowmaking systems. A third

of the trails are set aside for envelope-pushers, but the rest are dedicated to beginners and intermediates. Excellent for families, with everything from kiddie ski schools to daycare.

Kirkwood (☎ 877-547-9663; www.skikirkwood.com) is a 30- to 45-minute drive outside of South Lake Tahoe on Highway 88 (from U.S. 50, take Highway 89 south to 88 west). This resort ranks among *Ski* magazine's Top 10 in North America for snow, terrain, and challenge. A terrific choice for spring skiers thanks to high average snowfall. It's now a destination resort, so inquire if you want to stay.

The top north shore slopes

Midsize **Alpine Meadows** (☎ 800-441-4423 or 530-581-8374; www.skialpine.com), 8 miles west of Tahoe City, has the best spring skiing around. In early May 2000, when everybody else was closed for the season (even Kirkwood), Alpine Meadows was still going strong. A local favorite, it maintains a committed following.

Diamond Peak (☎ 775-831-3211 or 775-832-1177; www.diamondpeak.com) is 17 miles east of Tahoe City in Incline Village, Nevada. Diamond Peak has taken great care to target families, and it's the north shore's best resort for kids. It's also smaller and less expensive than most. Kids as young as 3 can learn to ski, and the resort maintains a terrific snowplay area.

If you want spectacular lake views while you ski, take to the slopes at **Homewood** (☎ 530-525-2992; www.skihomewood.com), right on the lake's west shore, 6½ miles south of Tahoe City. It's small, intimate, and a local favorite. Weekday lift tickets are a great value.

Northstar-at-Tahoe (☎ 800-466-6784 or 530-562-1330; www.skinorthstar.com), 11 miles east of Tahoe City, is a terrific choice for families, with 75% of the ski terrain devoted to beginners and intermediates. A well-rounded resort, with lots of good facilities and other activities.

Ever dream of Olympic glory? Live the fantasy at **Squaw Valley USA** (☎ 530-583-6985; www.squaw.com), nine miles from Tahoe City, site of the 1960 Olympic Winter Games. Spanning six Sierra peaks, gorgeous, excellently outfitted Squaw Valley is Tahoe's most state-of-the-art ski area and boasts its most challenging array of runs. A must for serious skiers.

Cross-country skiing and snowmobiling

The north shore offers the most — and best — cross-country options. **Lakeview Cross Country Ski Area** (☎ 530-583-9353) has more than 40 miles of groomed trails, a full-service day lodge, state-of-the-art equipment, and a convenient location, just 2 miles east of Tahoe City off Highway 28 at Dollar Hill (turn at Fabian Way).

Northstar-at-Tahoe (☎ **530-562-2475**) has a terrific cross-country, telemark, and snowshoe center with 40 miles of groomed trails. **Diamond Peak** (☎ **775-832-1177**) lets you bring Bowser along as you explore more than 20 miles of groomed trails and more backcountry area on skis or Atlas snowshoes. See the "Hitting the slopes in ski season," earlier in this chapter, for details on both resorts. The **Resort at Squaw Creek** (☎ **530-583-6300**) is much smaller, with just 11 miles of trails, but the Squaw Valley setting is unparalleled.

On the south shore, head to the **Cross-Country Ski Center** at Camp Richardson Resort, on Highway 89 which is 2½ miles north of the U.S. 50/89 "Y" intersection (☎ **530-542-6584**).

The south shore's **Zephyr Cove Snowmobile Center,** on U.S. 50, 4 miles east of the state line (☎ **775-588-3833**; www.tahoedixie2.com), is the largest snowmobiling center in the United States. You can rent and set out on your own (kids as young as 5 can accompany you on a double machine), or take a guided tour (recommended if you're a newbie). Reservations recommended.

On the north shore, contact **Snowmobiling Unlimited** (☎ **530-583-5858** or 530-583-7192). Tahoe's oldest snowmobile touring company, this company leads two- and three-hour guided tours.

Trying your luck at the casinos

One of the great advantages of a Tahoe vacation is the proximity to the casinos just a skip across the border in either Stateline or Crystal Bay, Nevada. You can throw a snowball and hit any of them from the California side. These are the best of the bunch.

- ✔ **Cal Neva Resort** (☎ **800-225-6382** or 775-832-4000; www.calneva resort.com), once owned by Frank Sinatra, has its diehard fans, including us, who prefer the north-shore location and low-key atmosphere. The showroom, built to the specifications of Ol' Blue Eyes himself, isn't used much anymore and there's only a medium-size gaming room with blackjack, roulette, craps, and slot machines, but photos of Marilyn Monroe, Sinatra, and his cronies line the walls, providing a cool piece of history and a hint of past glamour that's irresistible to some.

- ✔ **Harrah's** (☎ **800-427-7247** or 775-588-6611; www.harrahstahoe.com) draws a generally older crowd. The jam-packed showroom schedule offers a wide array of entertainment, from crowd-pleasing Vegas-style revues starring leggy showgirls to big-name headliners, including many baby-boomer faves (Ringo Starr, Smokey Robinson, the Smothers Brothers, and so forth).

- ✔ **Harveys** (☎ **800-427-8397** or 775-588-2411; www.harrahs.com/our_casinos/hlt) rocks, with video monitors and speakers blasting radio-friendly sounds throughout the largest and most stylish casino in Tahoe. Terrific racing and sports book. Harveys draws in a young, sophisticated crowd. The showroom focuses on cabaret-style shows and sexy revues, while the **Hard Rock Cafe** hosts live music on Friday and Saturday nights.

✔ **Caesars Tahoe** (☎ **800-648-3353** or 775-586-7771; www.caesars tahoe.com), the only real theme casino in Tahoe, is also the most glam. Caesars contains the best of the sports books, although Harveys gives it a run for its money. It offers the best showroom, too, with such heavyweight headliners as Wynonna, David Copperfield, and Tom Jones as well as championship boxing. Attention party animals: Caesars houses **Nero's 2000,** Tahoe's biggest and best dance club.

If you hope to catch a big-name headliner, check the schedule before you leave home and make reservations to avoid disappointment.

The casinos make sure families feel welcome. Harrah's, Harveys, and Caesars all offer sizable video arcades where classics like Pac Man and Donkey Kong buzz and beep alongside the latest virtual-reality games. In addition, the casino showrooms often offer all-ages entertainment, such as magic shows, at earlier family hours.

Gathering More Information

Lake Tahoe offers far more to do beyond what's mentioned here. Contact one of the local visitor organizations for more information, especially if you're interested in an activity we haven't discussed.

The **Lake Tahoe Visitors Authority** (☎ **800-AT-TAHOE,** 530-544-5050, or 530-583-3494; www.virtualtahoe.com) can give you all the information you'll need on South Lake Tahoe and environs. After you arrive, stop by the **South Lake Tahoe Chamber of Commerce,** located at 3066 S. Lake Tahoe Blvd., just east of Altahoe Boulevard (☎ **530-541-5255;** www.tahoeinfo.com), open Monday through Saturday from 8:30 a.m. to 5 p.m.

For information on the north shore, contact the **North Lake Tahoe Resort Association** (☎ **800-824-6348** or 530-583-3494; www.tahoefun. org). After you arrive, stop by their terrific visitor center at 245 North Lake Blvd. (on the north side of Highway 28; the sign says "CHAMBER OF COMMERCE") in Tahoe City, open Monday through Friday from 9 a.m. to 5 p.m., Saturday and Sunday from 9 a.m. to 4 p.m.

If you'd like information on the Nevada side of the north shore, contact the **Incline Village/Crystal Bay Visitors Bureau** (☎ **800-468-2463** or 775-832-1606; www.gotahoe.com).

For Tahoe **road conditions,** call ☎ **800-427-7623;** for **weather,** call
☎ **800-752-1177** or 530-546-5253.

Side-Tripping to the Gold Country

California's gold-rush country is rich in color and history. Dotted with
19th-century-mining-towns-turned-cutesy-B&B havens, the region is a
big weekend destination for Northern Californians. The area has plenty
to see and do, but nothing so major that you should devote the half-
week you'd need to drive the region's main thoroughfare, Highway 49,
from end to end. Leave that for a future visit, after you've covered so
many of California's highlights that you have the time to dedicate to it.

However, a portion of the Gold Country is so easy to reach on the drive
to or from Lake Tahoe that we highly recommend you dedicate half a
day to seeing its main (and most fascinating) attraction, the **Marshall
Gold Discovery State Historic Park,** where the gold rush began. You
can also stop in a gold-rush town or two to see what the Gold Country
is like.

Getting there

The section of Highway 49 — the **Gold Chain Highway** — on which
we suggest you focus, runs roughly north-south between I-80 (the road
to North Tahoe) and U.S. 50 (the road to South Tahoe). I-80 connects
with Highway 49 at **Auburn,** about 35 miles (or 40 minutes) east of
Sacramento, 78 miles (or a gorgeous 1½-hour drive) west of Tahoe City.
U.S. 50 connects with the section of Highway 49 you're concerned with
on the south end, in **Placerville** (originally dubbed Hangtown for its
single-minded justice system), about 43 miles (or 45 minutes) east of
Sacramento, 55 miles (or a little more than an hour's drive) west of
South Lake Tahoe.

The roughly 23-mile drive between Auburn and Placerville along the
Gold Chain Highway takes about an hour thanks to one narrow lane in
each direction and more than a few hairpin turns. **Coloma,** the hairs-
breadth of a town where you'll find the Marshall Gold Discovery Park,
is roughly midway between the two.

If you're heading to South Tahoe: Pick up I-80 (which you may already
be on if you're coming from the Bay Area) in Sacramento, turn south on
Highway 49 to do your exploring, and then head east to South Tahoe
after you meet up with U.S. 50. If you're leaving from South Tahoe,
reverse the process by taking U.S. 50 west, Highway 49 north for
exploring, then I-80 west when you're done.

If you're heading to North Tahoe: Take U.S. 50 east from Sacramento, then take Highway 49 north, then I-80 east to Tahoe City. **From North Tahoe?** You got it — I-80 west, Highway 49 south, U.S. 50 west to your destination.

The Gold Country can be brutally hot in summer, so dress accordingly.

Marshall's gold and Sutter's mill

The **Marshall Gold Discovery State Historic Park** is nestled in the golden Sierra foothills on Highway 49 between Auburn and Placerville at Coloma (☎ **530-622-3470** or 530-622-0390; www.parks.ca.gov or www.windjammer.net/coloma). Actually, about 70% of Coloma *is* the park. This is where James Marshall, a carpenter, discovered two itsy-bitsy gold nuggets on January 24, 1848, at John Sutter's mill on the dusty banks of the American River. This discovery managed to launch gold-rush mania and redirect California history in the process.

A working re-creation of Sutter's mill, a few intact gold-rush-era build-ings, and enlightening exhibits capture the pioneering spirit and excite-ment of that day and the '49ers get-rich-quick craze that followed. This place is very cool, and kids will enjoy it more than you may expect. To take maximum advantage of this historic site, start out at the **Gold Discovery Museum Visitors Center,** just off Highway 49 at Bridge Street. Come early, and ask the rangers about guided discovery tours and sawmill demonstrations (usually Thursday through Sunday at 11 a.m. and 1 p.m. in summer). You may even get a chance to pan for gold yourself! The buildings are open daily from 10 a.m. to 5 p.m. (4:30 in winter), and the fee is $5 per car. Bring a picnic lunch or snack.

By the way: James Marshall, poor soul, never saw a dime of the gold in them thar hills.

Old Town Auburn

In Auburn, the area just off I-80 at Nevada Street (bounded by Court Street, Lincoln Way, Washington Street, and Maple and Commercial streets), is **Old Town Auburn.** This is an ideal example of an Old West gold town transformed into a boutiqued downtown. Nevertheless, it still maintains a strong historic feel with original buildings boasting false storefronts along steep, cobbled streets. Head to the **Bootleggers Old Town Tavern & Grill,** 210 Washington St. (☎ **530-889-2229**), for a lunch stop with an appealing local vibe.

To get some background history on the area, stop at the **Placer County Courthouse,** the notable neoclassical building with a mismatched hat — a Renaissance gold dome — at the top of the hill at 101 Maple St.

(at Court Street and Lincoln Way). Inside is the petite **Placer County Museum** (☎ **530-889-6500**), which tells the story of Auburn's rise as a mother-lode gold-rush town. This is a great place to pick up information on other attractions in the area.

Seeing more of the Gold Country

If you want to spend more time in Gold Country, the following places are good bets for lodging:

- ✔ Located within the bounds of the Marshall Gold Discovery Park, the **Coloma Country Inn Bed & Breakfast** (☎ **530-622-6919;** www.colomacountryinn.com) captures the spirit of the locale in a lovely and well-appointed 1852 farmhouse.

- ✔ In Auburn, your best bet is the **Holiday Inn of Auburn,** on Highway 49 within walking distance of Old Town (☎ **800-814-8787** or 530-887-8787; www.holiday-inn.com).

For more information on the Auburn area, including local B&B recommendations, check out www.auburnweb.com, or contact the **Placer County Visitors Council** (☎ **530-887-2211;** www.placer.ca.gov/visit).

If you're going to spend more time in the region, consider heading south to cute-as-a-button Sutter Creek (whose **Chatterbox Cafe** the *New York Times* noted "may be the finest luncheonette in North America"), and nearby Jackson. The **Amador County Chamber of Commerce** (☎ **209-223-0350;** www.cdepot.net/chamber) can provide more information.

Or head to the far north end of Highway 49 to Nevada City and Grass Valley, which many consider to be the finest tourist towns in the Gold Country. Contact the **Grass Valley/Nevada County Chamber of Commerce** (☎ **800-655-4667** or 530-273-4667) or the **Nevada City Chamber of Commerce** (☎ **800-655-6569** or 530-265-2692), or go online to the very useful site www.ncgold.com.

Certain accommodations near **Yosemite National Park** make ideal bases for exploring the region, especially the **Groveland Hotel** and hotels in Oakhurst, such as the posh **Château du Sureau.** See Chapter 14 for details.

Chapter 14

Yosemite National Park

● ●

In This Chapter

▶ Planning your trip to America's favorite national park

▶ Deciding where to stay and dine within Yosemite

▶ Weighing your options in the nearby gateway towns

▶ Exploring Yosemite — on, and preferably off, the beaten path

▶ Discovering the delights of Mammoth Mountain

● ●

*P*repare to meet one of the most spectacular places in the world. **Yosemite National Park** encompasses nearly 1,200 square miles and a wildly diverse landscape that soars from 2,000 feet to an awesome 13,000 feet above sea level. It's a blue-ribbon destination all the way: home to the world's most impressive glacier-carved canyon (Yosemite Valley); three of the world's 10 tallest waterfalls, including North America's tallest (2,425-foot Yosemite Falls); the world's largest granite monolith (El Capitan); and the world's biggest and oldest trees (the Giant Sequoias). However, those nature-bending records don't even begin to describe the wonder of Yosemite — you must come and see this breathtaking place for yourself.

The mile-wide, seven-mile-long **Yosemite Valley** is the attraction-laden heart of the mammoth park — much of the rest is unreachable wilderness. When you arrive, you see why this valley is called the ultimate example of a glacier-carved canyon: Its flat, open meadows and oak and mixed-conifer woodlands come to an abrupt halt on all sides, where sheer walls suddenly soar to the sky. The towering cliffs, craggy monoliths, rounded domes, and tumbling waterfalls will have you craning your neck in wide-eyed amazement. Between Memorial and Labor days, however, the mammoth crowds may give you a migraine, because 90% of the park's visitors congregate in the valley floor. Think of it as the Waikiki of Yosemite.

You shouldn't miss the valley, but schedule some time to poke around the quieter areas of the park, especially if you're craving a more genuine wilderness experience. Head for the serene, (largely) crowd-free **High Country** in the summer. The entire Sierra Nevada doesn't get any more beautiful than this splendid mix of verdant subalpine meadows and forest, crystal-blue glacial lakes, granite spires, and domes. Or make time for **Mariposa Grove,** the sky-scraping stand of giant sequoias at the lovely, woodsy, civilized south end.

The beauty of Yosemite is that it's a foolproof park. To accommodate all those tourists, the Park Service has become very visitor-friendly, offering lots of available guidance, great facilities, and easy hikes and river access, making Yosemite an ideal place to vacation with children. The summer madness horning in on your communion with nature will seem like the biggest, best summer camp in the world to a kid.

Remember: Even at the height of the summer chaos you can have a genuine wilderness experience in Yosemite if you want one. You don't have to be a survivalist to venture out of the valley and into one of the more remote areas of the park. Whenever you visit, give yourself the space and time (at least two days; more is ideal) to truly appreciate this humbling, awe-inspiring place.

Timing Your Visit

Overwhelmingly, most people visit Yosemite in June, July, and August — which means that if you don't have to come during those months, you shouldn't. The Yosemite Valley becomes so crowded in the summer that it seems more like a theme park than a natural wonderland. But if your vacation falls during these months, don't feel that you have to stay away.

If you're not staying in the park, enter early (the superintendent has been known, on a few occasions, to close the gates when the park reaches maximum capacity), and plan to spend much of your visit in areas other than the Yosemite Valley, where most visitors congregate. On the up side, summer is the best time to visit **Tuolumne** (pronounced too-ALL-oh-mee) **Meadows,** glorious subalpine meadows at an altitude of 8,600 feet, and take the drive to the summit of **Glacier Point,** at 7,214 feet, for spectacular views over the valley.

Mid-September through October is a magical season. Visitorship drops, but the park remains fully accessible; the roads to Tuolumne Meadows and Glacier Point generally don't close until November.

If you really want the park all to yourself, visit in winter. The valley is marvelously peaceful and the snow provides an exquisite contrast to all that granite. (The average annual accumulation on the valley floor is about four feet.) If the weather gods are with you, you'll wonder why anyone bothers to come here in the summer. The **High Country** is under about 20 feet of snow from November through May, however, and pretty much off limits. Another plus: Accommodations are usually discounted.

When you're deciding how much time to spend touring Yosemite, go with more rather than less. One day, even a full one, is simply not enough. Give yourself at least two days; three full days comes closer to the ideal.

Accessing the Park

You can enter the park through any one of four main entrances:

- ✔ The most commonly used entrance (and most traffic-congested in summer) is the **Arch Rock Entrance,** on the west side of the park via Highway 140, through the blink-and-you'll-miss-it town of El Portal. (Note: This entrance closes nightly between 10:30 p.m. and 6:30 a.m.) This gateway offers the most direct access to Yosemite Valley, where your first stop should be the main Valley Visitor Center after you dump your car in a day-use lot (if you're staying outside the park) or at your accommodation. The center is open daily from 8:30 a.m. to 5 p.m.

- ✔ On the west side, north of Arch Rock, is the **Big Oak Flat Entrance,** on Highway 120, which takes you through Groveland first. It's also valley-convenient, but allows you to pass by the congested valley and head straight for the High Country if you so choose. If you're going to bypass the valley, be sure to stop by the **Big Oak Flat Information Station** (☎ 209-379-1899), just inside the park gate, for information and maps; open daily from 9 a.m. to 6 p.m.

- ✔ You can also arrive via the **South Entrance,** on Highway 41, about 35 miles south of Yosemite Valley. It's the most convenient entrance for those coming from points south, and it boasts some of the most wonderful vistas in the park. You'll also use it if you choose to stay at **Tenaya Lodge** (see the listing of places to stay outside the park later in this chapter) or at one of the accommodations options in Oakhurst. The **Wawona Information Station** (☎ 209-375-9501) is open only in summer from 8:30 a.m. to 4:30 p.m. daily. Turn off Highway 41 at Chilnualna Falls Road and take the first right after the stables.

- ✔ The **Tioga Pass Entrance,** the eastern High Country gateway on Highway 120, is open only in summer. You'll use this entrance if you come from Lake Tahoe (see Chapter 13), or from **Death Valley National Park** (see Chapter 23). The **Tuolumne Meadows Visitor Center** (☎ 209-372-0263) is open daily in season from 9 a.m. to 7 p.m.

Getting there by car

From Lake Tahoe, you can take U.S. 50 west out of Tahoe to I-395 south to Highway 120, which will lead you into the park's High Country via the summer-only Tioga Pass Entrance. The 3½-hour drive is doable between late June and the first snowfall (usually early November). Otherwise, you'll have a five- or six-hour drive down winding Highway 49, which can be extra-slow going in bad weather.

Yosemite National Park

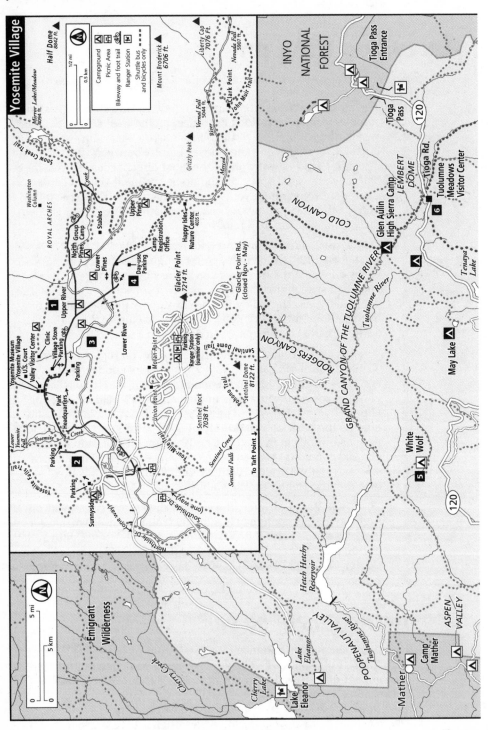

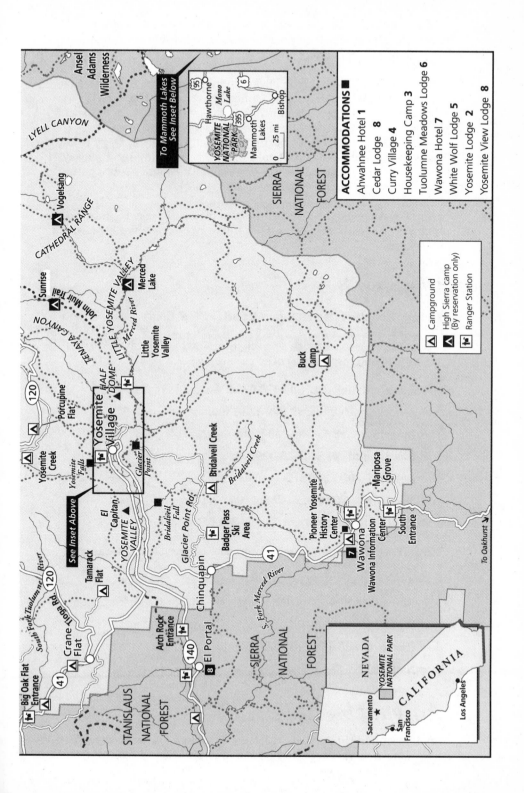

Ansel Adams Wilderness

LYELL CANYON

To Mammoth Lakes
See Inset Below

ACCOMMODATIONS ■

Ahwahnee Hotel **1**
Cedar Lodge **8**
Curry Village **4**
Housekeeping Camp **3**
Tuolumne Meadows Lodge **6**
Wawona Hotel **7**
White Wolf Lodge **5**
Yosemite Lodge **2**
Yosemite View Lodge **8**

95

6

Hawthorne

Mono Lake

Bishop

395

0   25 mi

YOSEMITE NATIONAL PARK

Mammoth Lakes

SIERRA NATIONAL FOREST

Vogelsang

CATHEDRAL RANGE

Sunrise

John Muir Trail

Merced Lake

Merced River

TENAYA CANYON

LITTLE YOSEMITE VALLEY

Little Yosemite Valley

Buck Camp

▲ Campground

◪ High Sierra camp (By reservation only)

🏠 Ranger Station

120

Porcupine Flat

HALF DOME

Yosemite Village

Yosemite Creek

Yosemite Falls

Glacier Point

See Inset Above

El Capitan

Bridalveil Fall

YOSEMITE VALLEY

Tamarack Flat

Tioga Rd

Crane Flat

120

South Fork Tuolumne River

Big Oak Flat Entrance

41

STANISLAUS NATIONAL FOREST

Bridalveil Creek

Bridalveil Creek

Glacier Point Rd.

Badger Pass Ski Area

Chinquapin

41

S. Fork Merced River

Arch Rock Entrance

140

8 El Portal

SIERRA NATIONAL FOREST

Mariposa Grove

Pioneer Yosemite History Center

Wawona

7 Wawona Information Center

South Entrance

To Oakhurst ↘

NEVADA

YOSEMITE NATIONAL PARK

CALIFORNIA

Sacramento ★

San Francisco

Los Angeles

From San Francisco, the drive is about 3½ hours. Take I-580 west to I-205 to Highway 120, then plan the rest of your route along highways 120, 99, or 140, depending on where you're staying.

From the Central Coast, you have a couple of options, depending on your departure point. From the Monterey Peninsula, take U.S. 101 to Highway 152 to Highway 99 north to Highway 140 to the Arch Rock Entrance — roughly a five-hour drive — or Highway 99 south to Highway 145 to Highway 41 north to the South Entrance. If you're starting farther south on the coast, take U.S. 101 or Highway 1 to Highway 41 (near Morro Bay) and follow it all the way to Yosemite's south gate. Expect to spend about 5½ hours on Highway 41.

From Los Angeles, the drive lasts about 6½ hours. Take I-5 north to Highway 99 to either Highway 41 or Highway 140, depending on where you're staying.

Winging it

Fresno Yosemite International Airport, 5175 E. Clinton Ave., Fresno (☎ **559-498-4095;** www.fresno.com/flyfresno), is 90 miles south of Yosemite. From the airport, take Highway 180 to Highway 41 north to the park's South Entrance. These airlines fly in:

- ✔ **Alaska Airlines:** ☎ **800-426-0333;** www.alaskaair.com
- ✔ **American Airlines:** ☎ **800-433-7300;** www.aa.com.
- ✔ **America West:** ☎ **800-235-9292;** www.americawest.com
- ✔ **Continental:** ☎ **800-525-0280;** www.flycontinental.com
- ✔ **Delta:** ☎ **800-221-1212;** www.delta.com
- ✔ **Northwest:** ☎ **800-225-2525;** www.nwa.com
- ✔ **United/United Express:** ☎ **800-241-6522;** www.united.com

The following national car-rental companies have airport locations:

- ✔ **Avis:** ☎ **800-331-1212;** www.avis.com
- ✔ **Budget:** ☎ **800-527-0700;** https://rent.drivebudget.com
- ✔ **Dollar:** ☎ **800-800-4000;** www.dollar.com
- ✔ **Hertz:** ☎ **800-654-3131;** www.hertz.com
- ✔ **National:** ☎ **800-CAR-RENT;** www.nationalcar.com

Arriving by train

Another option is to arrive in Merced, 73 miles southwest of the Arch Rock Entrance, via **Amtrak** (☎ **800-872-7245;** www.amtrak.com). You can then book transportation or a park tour with **VIA Adventures/ Gray Line of Yosemite** (☎ 800-842-5463; www.via-adventures.com), which also offers packages that include accommodations.

Entering and navigating the park

Admission to the park is $20 per car, or $10 per person if you arrive by bus, bike, or on foot. Your ticket is good for seven days, so keep it handy. Reservations are not required and you are free to drive around the park as you please, but these policies can change; call ☎ 209-372-0200 or visit the official site at www.nps.gov/yose to check the latest before you go.

Do everybody a favor while you're in Yosemite Valley: Park your car once (you'll be directed right to a day-use lot if you're not staying within park bounds) and use the shuttle system, bikes, or your own tootsies to move around the valley floor. Free shuttle buses loop the valley daily year-round, and as frequently as every ten minutes in high season. Park management is so eager for you to take advantage of this alternative that they make it a breeze to use. If you'd rather two-wheel it, bike rentals are available for the entire family at **Curry Village** (☎ 209-372-8319) year-round, and from April through November at **Yosemite Lodge** (☎ 209-372-1208). Use your car only to reach other, far-flung areas of the park.

In May 2000, in an effort to alleviate some traffic congestion, the Yosemite Area Regional Transportation System (YARTS) started offering bus service from some of the gateway communities, allowing you to leave your car behind at the motel. This service is particularly useful if you're staying at **Cedar Lodge** and **Yosemite View Lodge** just outside the Arch Rock Entrance, both of which have on-site pickups. You can also meet the bus if you're staying farther west on Highway 140 in Mariposa. If you're staying at the **Wawona Hotel** in the southernmost section of the park, you can use YARTS to reach Yosemite Valley. For exact schedule and fare information, call ☎ 877-989-2787 or 209-372-4487, or visit www.yarts.com.

Preparing for Your Visit

Here are a few tips to help you get your visit off on the right foot:

- ✓ **Wear appropriately sturdy shoes.** Hiking boots are best, but at the least bring sneakers. Platform slides just aren't going to cut it here.

- ✓ **Always bring a jacket.** Even if the valley floor is hot, the air can really cool off after you ascend to the High Country. Rain is most common in the colder months, but thunderstorms can happen at any time.

✔ **In summer, bring a swimsuit.** A hot day may tempt you to take a dip in the Merced River. An excellent swimming hole exists at Stoneman Bridge, near Curry Village in the valley.

✔ **In winter, come with the appropriate snow gear.** Bring snow boots, snow coats — the works. Don't leave home without tire chains in the trunk if you're driving your own car, or inquire about them when you book your rental vehicle.

✔ **In the High Country, opt for an easier hiking trail than you might normally choose.** The thinness of the air at these elevations can really tax your system and sap your energy.

✔ **Heed all warnings about the bear problem.** Terribly spoiled by years of human leftovers, black bears have decided that they prefer Big Macs, Cheetos, and PB&J sandwiches to Mother Nature's eats. As a result, they've become a real menace to personal property (and to themselves — Yosemite's bears are in danger of losing their natural hunting and gathering instincts).

✔ **Don't leave food in your car.** Don't even leave a stray french fry in the trunk. Bears have become experts at ripping open cars as if they were tin cans (most often, they just wiggle their claws into the gap above the door and bend down). Statistics prove that they're particularly fond of white minivans — why, nobody knows. During the month of April 2000 alone, bears broke into 45 cars — and trust us, you do not want to have to explain this to Avis. If you camp or stay in a tent cabin, *diligently use the metal food storage boxes.*

Where to Stay and Dine Inside the Park

If you're not thrilled with your lodging or campground reservation, call back one month before your arrival date to inquire about an upgrade. The majority of cancellations occur either 3 days or 30 days before arrival; in fact, rooms often turn over two and three times.

Mariposa County room tax adds an extra 10% to your bill.

Yosemite Concession Services manages all in-park accommodations. You can make reservations up to one year and a day in advance. Call central reservations at ☎ **559-252-4848** to reserve, ideally 366 days before your intended arrival, especially if you're hoping to stay here between Memorial and Labor days. The phone lines are open Monday through Friday from 7 a.m. to 6 p.m., Saturday and Sunday from 8 a.m. to 5 p.m. (PST), and the service accepts all major credit cards. You also can make real-time online reservations at www.yosemitepark.com. Park hotels book up further in advance than you may expect, so make reservations as early as possible.

All rates are based on double occupancy. Expect to pay between $3 and $11 for each extra person ($20 at the Ahwahnee). Kids can sometimes stay free, so ask. Call the special offer hotline at ☎ 559-454-0555 for discounted prices on winter stays (mid-November through March).

Ahwahnee Hotel
$$$$ Yosemite Valley

The park's most elegant place to sleep is this baronial, ultra-romantic landmark lodge, handsomely decorated in Native American style. Despite the elegance, it's right at home in the valley — it has the same grand scale. Afternoon tea is served in the great lounge, and dinner is a reservations- and jacket (or sweater)-required affair in the stunning dining room. Feel free to come for lunch in your shorts and tennies.

Rack rates: $326–$366 double, $515–$860 suite.

Curry Village
$–$$ Yosemite Valley

Sitting in the shadow of Glacier Point is Curry Village, whose accommodations include a few standard motel rooms, rustic wood-frame cabins (some with private bath, some without), and canvas-covered tent cabins that are halfway to camping but still have wood floors, electricity, and maid service; they share a couple of central bathhouses. The whole place has a summer-camp-gone-to-heck vibe about it, but it's convenient and fun if privacy isn't a big concern. The village includes a cafeteria, a burger shack, a coffee and ice cream counter, and a pizza parlor, plus an activities desk with bike rentals (cross-country skis in winter). Fifty heated tent cabins are available in the winter.

If you book a tent cabin at Curry Village, ask when you arrive if any cancellations have cleared the way for an upgrade. If it's available, chances are good they'll give it away for free. It never hurts to ask, especially outside the summer season.

Rack rates: $49–$112 double.

Housekeeping Camp
$ Yosemite Valley

This arrangement is the closest you can get to roughing it without toting your own tent. The camp basically consists of a collection of semi-furnished concrete-and-canvas lean-tos on the banks of the Merced River. The experience is like camping at a KOA, with shared bathhouse, laundry, and a small grocery store.

Rack rates: $43 double.

Tuolumne Meadows Lodge and White Wolf Lodge
$ **High Country (North Yosemite)**

Both of these lodges have the same metal-frame canvas tent cabins that Curry Village has, but without the chaotic squatters' vibe. They are clean and neat, and most cabins sleep four and have wood-burning stoves. (White Wolf also has four cute wood cabins with private baths.) White Wolf is a bit more out of the way and has fewer facilities; breakfast and dinner are served in the restaurant/general store. Tuolumne Meadows is larger and has a burger stand, a grocery store, stables, a mountaineering school, a gas station, and a dining tent for breakfast and dinner.

Rack rates: $49–$83 double. Open summer only.

Wawona Hotel
$$ **South Yosemite**

The Wawona, whose rooms were recently renovated, isn't as spectacular or luxurious as the Ahwahnee, but this landmark lies in the much quieter southern section of the park (providing great relief from the valley crowds in summer) and boasts great Roaring Twenties charm. The rooms contain no TV or telephones, and only about half offer private baths. Facilities include a nice restaurant that serves three meals; a pool; a tennis court; and nine holes of golf.

Rack rates: $94–$161 double.

Yosemite Lodge
$$ **Yosemite Valley**

Yosemite Lodge is a pleasant motel (sorry, no TV) right in the heart of the valley bustle. The standard rooms are fine, but go for a lodge room if you can, which will get you a bit more space and a view of Yosemite Falls from a patio or balcony. The lodge includes a food court, a lovely restaurant, and a snack shack by the pool.

The dinner menu at Yosemite Lodge's Mountain View restaurant and at the Ahwahnee are nearly identical, as is the quality of the food, but the prices are lower at the lodge.

Rack rates: $92–$115 double.

Yosemite has so many campsites that managing them is its own cottage industry. Still, they book up very quickly, so call as early as possible, especially for stays from May through September. Park services accepts campsite reservations up to five months in advance, starting on the 15th of each month. (In other words, on February 15 you can begin to make reservations for June 15 through July 14.) Calling on the first day is wise if you want your first choice.

More Yosemite eats

In addition to the food choices available in the accommodations listed in the "Where to Stay and Dine Inside the Park" section, **Yosemite Village** boasts a number of casual restaurants, including a deli, a pizza-and-pasta joint, and a burger grill in summer. The choices may not be gourmet, but you won't have to forage either.

You can find a complete rundown of the camping options online, including fee information and locations, at www.nps.gov/yose/camping.htm. You can also get all the information you need by calling the reservations line at ☎ 800-436-PARK (436-7275) or 301-722-1257 daily between 7 a.m. and 7 p.m. (PST). You can make online reservations at reservations. nps.gov. If Yosemite campgrounds are full, the reservations agents will gladly refer you to the National Forest campgrounds just outside the park.

Where to Stay and Dine Outside the Park

Each of the hotels in this section is near one of the park's main gates. In addition to the two motels closest to the park, Cedar and Yosemite View lodges (see the listings in this section), Yosemite Motels (☎ 888-742-4371; www.yosemite-motels.com) also runs the just-fine **Comfort Inn Oakhurst** ($–$$), 15 miles south of the South Entrance, as well as two motels in Mariposa: the **Best Western Yosemite Way Station** ($–$$) and **Comfort Inn Mariposa** ($–$$). The Mariposa motels are fine choices if everything else is booked, but you're better off trying to stay closer to the park first.

If you stay at **Cedar Lodge** or **Yosemite Lodge** (see the individual listings later in this section), or at any of the Mariposa choices discussed previously, you can leave your car behind and use the YARTS shuttle to reach the park if you choose (see "Entering and navigating the park," earlier in this chapter).

The area can get booked up in the busy season, so if our favorites are full, contact the Yosemite Sierra Visitors Bureau (☎ 559-683-4636; www.yosemite-sierra.org) for additional options.

Because the region is so rural, expect to eat at your hotel restaurant. Only if you stay at an Oakhurst or Mariposa base will you have other restaurants to choose from. Even there, pickings are slim — limited largely to pizza and fast food — so don't let dining dictate your choice of base. The exception: **Erna's Elderberry House** at the sumptuous **Château du Sureau** in Oakhurst (see the listing later in this section).

Best Western Yosemite Gateway Inn

$–$$ Oakhurst

This perfectly nice motel, 15 miles due south of the park, offers pleasant rooms that are big enough for families. All rooms have coffeemakers, many have microwaves and fridges, and some have kitchens. Facilities include an indoor pool area with a spa, sauna, and exercise equipment; an outdoor pool and spa; and a coin-op laundry.

40530 Hwy. 41, Oakhurst. ☎ *800-528-1234 or 559-683-2378. Fax: 559-683-3813. Internet:* www.bestwestern.com. *Parking: Free! Rack rates: $44–$99 double, $79–$134 suite. Rates include continental breakfast. Inquire about off-season deals. AE, DC, DISC, MC, V.*

Cedar Lodge

$$ El Portal

Another nice motel, this one is located eight miles outside of the Arch Rock entrance in a hilly setting along the Merced River. Rooms are motel-standard but quite comfortable. On site are two pools (one indoor, one outdoor), a spa, a grocery store, and two restaurants — one a nice dining room and the other a casual pizza parlor.

9966 Hwy. 140, El Portal. ☎ *888-742-4371 or 209-379-2612. Fax: 209-379-2712. Internet:* www.yosemite-motels.com. *Parking: Free! Rack rates: $99–$110 double, $140 suite. AE, MC, V. Off-season rates drop as low as $59 double, $99 suite.*

Château du Sureau

$$$$$ Oakhurst

Finding one of America's finest inns in the rinky-dink town of Oakhurst, just a 20-minute drive from Yosemite's South Entrance, is wild. Staying at this gated Relais & Chateaux villa is like being entertained by European royalty, complete with maids to bring you tea and cookies and butlers to press your dinner clothes. The inn is supremely gorgeous and comfy — and the staff won't bat an eye when you stumble in dusty after a day in the park. Even if you're accustomed to luxury travel, you'll never forget this place. One of California's most celebrated restaurants, **Erna's Elderberry House,** is on the premises. The French provençal–style cuisine is well worth a special-occasion splurge, even if you don't stay here ($82 prix-fixe).

48688 Victoria Lane (just off Hwy. 41, 15 miles south of Yosemite's South Entrance), Oakhurst. ☎ *559-683-6860, or 559-683-6800 for restaurant reservations. Fax: 559-683-0800. Internet:* www.chateaudusureau.com. *Parking: Free! Rack rates: $350–$550 double. Rates include an elegant two-course breakfast. AE, MC, V.*

Groveland Hotel
$$ Groveland

The charm of this sweet historic inn and the Wild West–style one-horse town makes up for the drive (23 miles outside the Big Oak Flat Entrance). The hotel houses the finest restaurant in town, plus a groovy gold-rush-era saloon. Rooms are furnished with antiques and have private baths. A great in-between base if you'd also like to do a bit of Gold Country exploring along Highway 49.

18767 Main St. (Hwy. 120, east of Hwy. 49), Groveland. ☎ ***800-273-3314** or 209-962-4000. Fax: 209-962-6674. Internet:* www.groveland.com. *Rack rates: $135–$155 double, $210 suite. Rates include continental breakfast and evening wine. Ask about midweek winter getaway specials. AE, DISC, MC, V.*

Tenaya Lodge
$$$–$$$$ Fish Camp

This gorgeous destination lodge draws in parkgoers as well as conference groups with its stone's-throw proximity to the park, terrific facilities, on-site activities, and rustic-glamorous wilderness-lodge-goes-modern ambience. The ultra-comfy rooms are done in area-appropriate style and boast all the latest comforts. The facilities include two pools, three restaurants, game room, gym, spa services, and a terrific kids' program.

1122 Hwy. 41, Fish Camp (2 miles south of the South Entrance). ☎ ***888-514-2167** or 559-683-6555. Fax: 559-683-8684. Internet:* www.tenayalodge.com. *Rack rates: $179–$269 double, $209–$389 suite. Check for packages and Internet specials, as low as $149 in season. AE, DC, DISC, MC, V.*

Yosemite View Lodge
$$ El Portal

Just two miles outside the Arch Rock Entrance, this large motel complex is the closest you can get to Yosemite without actually staying within park bounds. Rooms are large and very comfy; all have kitchenettes, and many have Jacuzzi tubs, gas fireplaces, and balconies overlooking the rushing Merced River (we recommend spending a little extra for one of these). On site are three pools (two outdoor, one indoor) and five spas, a just-fine restaurant, a bar, a pizza parlor, and a well-stocked general store.

11136 Hwy. 140, El Portal. ☎ ***888-742-4371** or 209-379-2681. Fax: 209-379-2704. Internet:* www.yosemite-motels.com. *Parking: Free! Rack rates: $125–$155 double, $185–$205 suite. MC, V.*

Exploring Yosemite

We highly recommend launching your visit with the two-hour guided **Valley Floor Tour,** conducted aboard an open-air tram in warm weather, a cozy bus in winter. The tour is an absolute must if your visit is limited to one day, because it's the only way you'll see all the park's major features. You can see the valley highlights by tour in the morning, and then spend your afternoon exploring the High Country or heading south to Wawona. Tours run daily year-round, at regular intervals throughout the day. Tickets are $20, and you can buy them at a booth just outside the Valley Store in Yosemite Village, or at any park accommodations tour desk. For more information, call the **Yosemite Lodge Tour Desk** (☎ 209-372-1240). Also ask about similar seasonal tours of other regions of the park.

If you're driving into Yosemite Valley from the South Entrance along Highway 41, stop at **Tunnel View** for one of the park's most stunning vistas. Pull over along with everybody else after you pass through the Wawona Tunnel on Route 41 for a bird's-eye overview of the valley. You can also catch this view on the drive south from the valley to Glacier Point Road or the Wawona section of the park.

Yosemite Valley highlights

The mile-wide, seven-mile-long **Yosemite Valley** is the attraction-laden heart of the mammoth park. Most park services are located in **Yosemite Village,** which even has a post office and a sizable store.

Make the Valley Visitor Center your first stop in Yosemite Village. You can pick up all the maps and information you need here, watch a short introductory movie, check the schedule of orientation programs and ranger-led activities, and learn enough about glacial geology and the local flora and fauna to give you a basic understanding of the park.

Next to the visitor center sits the **Yosemite Museum,** where you can learn about life in the valley before the Europeans showed up, and the **Ansel Adams Gallery,** which is wonderful for both browsing and buying the works of the master photographer as well as contemporary photographers who have a special talent for training their lens on the natural world. Shuttle service can take you to all corners of the valley from here (see "Entering and navigating the park," earlier in this chapter).

You won't want to miss these Yosemite Valley highlights:

- ✔ Even before you reach the valley, you'll see beautiful **Bridalveil Fall** on your drive in; just look to the right. It's one of the prettiest falls in the park. You can pull into the parking lot and follow an easy, short trail to the base of the falls. (Of course, both Bridalveil and Yosemite falls usually are dry in the summer.)

- ✔ To your left as you drive in, past Bridalveil, is **El Capitan,** the largest piece of solid granite in the world. Pull in to the turnout at El Capitan meadow to scour the immense face of this 3,593-foot-tall monolith for rock climbers. (Climbers are a cinch to spot after dark, when they turn their headlamps on.)

✔ From shuttle stop no. 7, just west of the visitor center, take an easy half-mile round-trip walk to the base of lower **Yosemite Fall.** As you stand on the bridge facing the spray, you'll really feel the impressive force of the continent's tallest waterfall.

✔ From the valley floor, look to the northeast and you can't miss **Half Dome,** Yosemite's most famous feature — 4,733 extraordinary feet of 87-million-year-old brawny rock.

✔ The **Nature Center at Happy Isles,** on the easternmost shuttle loop (stop no. 16), has great hands-on nature exhibits for kids, plus wheelchair-accessible paths that run along the banks of the Merced River. Stop here early in your visit for information on the Valley Junior Ranger Program, which gives kids the opportunity to earn awards for completing special park projects.

Glacier Point

In summer, you can drive the 32 miles from the valley floor to 3,200-foot **Glacier Point,** which offers the park's most stunning panoramic views. Not only will you be able to see all the valley's highlights, but you'll catch views of the High Sierra to the north and west that are beyond breathtaking. From the valley, take Highway 41 to the Chinquapin junction and turn left onto Glacier Point Road (turn right if you're coming up from the South Entrance); allow about an hour each way for the drive. Sunrise from Glacier Point is spectacular.

If you're visiting in winter, bring your cross-country-ski gear (or rent it at Badger Pass). You can drive as far as Badger Pass Ski Area (less than halfway), and ski your way to Glacier Point from there. Call ahead to inquire about overnight cross-country-ski excursions to the point.

Wawona/South Yosemite

Mariposa Grove, at the quieter, woodsy southern section of the park (about 35 miles south of the valley via Highway 41), is the most impressive of the park's three groves of giant sequoias, the world's largest trees. Giant sequoias are shorter but more massive than their lanky cousins, the coast redwoods (see Chapter 12), with distinctive bell-bottom bases as large as 35 feet in diameter. That is one big tree — and you'll find a whole stand of 'em here! Grizzly Giant, the oldest tree in the grove, is one of the largest sequoias in the world.

An easy interpretive trail leads through the grove from the parking area, with placards offering a self-guided tour. The grove also has a small museum. From the valley, follow Highway 41 south and take the signed turnoff; expect the drive to take about 1¼ hours. You can also hop on a shuttle bus to reach the grove, but the far distance from the valley makes driving more efficient for time-challenged visitors. The grove is open year-round, but heavy snow occasionally closes the access road.

The High Country

At 8,600-feet elevation, stunning **Tuolumne Meadows** bursts with wild-flowers in summer (this high up, where the snow sticks around through June, summer seems more like spring). The 55-mile drive from the valley takes 1½ hours along the gorgeous Tioga Road (Highway 120; open in summer only). The magnificent drive alone is half the fun, so allow more time to stop at the myriad overlooks. You'll pass lush meadows, thickly wooded forests, granite domes, and ice-blue glacial lakes — the most notable being **Tenaya Lake,** a popular spot for windsurfing, fishing, and canoeing.

Consider buying a copy of *The Yosemite Road Guide* at the visitor center before you set out. This publication contains a good self-guided driving tour of the route. After you arrive, stop at the Tuolumne Meadows Visitor Center for orientation, trail, and program information.

Walking the walk: Hiking and nature trails

With 860 miles of trails, Yosemite has a hike for you, no matter what your level of stamina and experience. Nature writers dedicate whole volumes to hiking the park, so you're better off referring to a more complete source for the full range of options.

In addition to the walks to **Yosemite Fall** and **Bridalveil Fall** (see "Yosemite Valley highlights" earlier in this chapter), here are some of the best day hikes. Check the *Yosemite Guide* newspaper for additional day-hiking options. A very useful "Yosemite Valley Day Hikes" single-sheet handout is also generally available. Be smart and remember to check conditions at the visitor center before you set out.

✔ The easy mile-long round-trip walk to **Mirror Lake** will reward you with remarkable views. The trailhead leaves from shuttle stop no. 17 (behind the stables). You can then follow the lovely five-mile loop around the lake if you choose.

✔ The **John Muir/Mist Trail** is the park's most popular hike, so set out early or save it for later in the day. The trail leaves from **Happy Isles** (shuttle stop no. 16) and climbs alongside the Merced River (whose rushing whitewater naturalist and park godfather John Muir called "the symphony of the Sierras") to **Vernal Fall.** The initial 7⁄10-mile portion of the trail is moderately difficult and follows a paved but steep trail that leads to a bridge with terrific views of the falls.

The hardiest of you can continue along the strenuous ⁹⁄₁₀-mile "Mist" portion, which sharply ascends 600 more feet (for a total elevation gain of 1,000 feet) directly alongside the fall (expect spray) and includes countless granite steps (that StairMaster experience will really come in handy here, folks) before you reach the pool at the top. Allow two to four hours.

✔ Up at Tuolumne Meadows, try the easy 1½-mile round-trip walk to **Soda Springs.** The trailhead leaves from just east of the visitor center and follows a gurgling river through a peaceful section of meadow to a bubbling carbonated spring.

✔ Hardcore hikers may want to tackle the 17-mile cable-hike ascent to the top of **Half Dome,** a full-day affair that's only for the hardiest. You'll need hiking boots with serious traction and leather gloves. Call the **information line** at ☎ **209-372-0200** for details or consult a ranger before you go.

If you'd like to tour the park with a knowledgeable guide — an excellent idea, especially if you want to venture off the busiest trails — go with **Yosemite Guides** (☎ **877-425-3366;** www.yosemiteguides.com). They'll lead you on natural history walks, birding tours, and even take you fly-fishing. They have a desk at the **Yosemite View Lodge** (see "Where to Stay and Dine Outside the Park," earlier in this chapter), but we highly recommend booking before you arrive.

Talking the talk: Ranger-led programs

In addition to guided tram and bus tours (see "Exploring Yosemite," earlier in this chapter), park rangers offer a phenomenal number of guided walks and interpretive programs. The calendar is chockfull from morning until night with morning-light photo walks, birding walks, bear talks, Discover Yosemite family programs, brown-bag lunch lectures, fireside discussions . . . you get the picture. A number of children's programs are offered, and the Junior Ranger program is excellent. Some activities carry a fee, but many are free. Check the *Yosemite Guide* newspaper or inquire at the visitor center for the complete schedule.

The artist in you may want to check the schedule of free, informal, outdoor art classes offered in various media throughout the summer by the **Art Activity Center,** located in Yosemite Village next to the Village Store. You can find the schedule on the Yosemite Valley Activities page at www.yosemiteparktours.com.

The highly respected **Yosemite Theater** program stages dramatic interpretive programs (actorly portrayals of *John Muir in Yosemite,* for example, or *A 49er's Life with the Yosemite Indians*), as well as occasional concerts in the evenings. Tickets are usually under $10 for adults and under $5 for kids. These events are hugely popular, so buy your tickets early in the day to avoid disappointment.

Finding more cool stuff to do

Fun activities abound year-round, from horseback riding, river rafting, and rock climbing in summer to ice-skating, snowshoeing, and skiing (both downhill and cross-country) in winter. Whatever you want to do, one thing's for sure: It's administered by **Yosemite Concessions Services** (☎ 209-372-1000). Check their easy-to-use Web site at www.yosemiteparktours.com and click on Tours & Activities for a rundown of available activities with all the details — including prices, access, and reservations information.

The Ahwahnee Hotel (see "Where to Stay and Dine Inside the Park," earlier in this chapter) is the scene for extra-special events in the winter, including two- to three-day **Vintners' Holidays** in November and December, and **Chef's Holidays** in January and February. For travelers who love good food and wine, these events include seminars with professional winemakers or cooking demonstrations with well-known chefs and a gala banquet on the final evening. Dates and reservations information is available on the park Web site.

Gathering More Information

Call the park's 24-hour **information line** at ☎ 209-372-0200, or go online to www.yosemitepark.com. You can also use this number to check road conditions (always a good idea). More information is available from **Yosemite Concessions Services** at ☎ 209-372-1000. Request a copy of the official *Yosemite Guide* when you call. You can easily find this seasonal newspaper in the park, but it contains lots of invaluable trip-planning information — including the latest on road construction and policy changes to mitigate traffic congestion — that can come in handy before you go.

The Yosemite Association maintains a useful site at www.yosemite.org, complete with an online bookstore where you can order materials to read up on the park before you go. The association has a helpful **information line** at ☎ 900-454-YOSE (454-9673) that lets you talk to a real person. Be prepared with your questions and talk fast, because the meter will tick at $1.95 for the first minute, 95¢ per minute thereafter (all proceeds go to benefit the park).

For information on the surrounding area, your best source is the **Yosemite Sierra Visitors Bureau,** 40637 Hwy. 41, Oakhurst (☎ 559-683-4636; www.yosemite-sierra.org). In addition to providing general visitor information, they're happy to help with just-outside-the-park lodging reservations. Another good site is www.yosemite.com.

Mammoth Mountain Ski Resort

One thing any true Californian is likely to brag about early on is how the state's diverse terrain and climates make it possible for a person to both surf and ski in the same day. Sure, it can be done, but it's a two-hour drive (okay, three with traffic) from the beach to Snow Summit in Big Bear. We suggest instead that if you want to surf, spend the day at the beach. And if you really want to ski — in prime conditions, mind you, weather permitting — you can drive just a bit farther, five hours in fact (from San Francisco and L.A. both), to **Mammoth Mountain,** on the eastern side of the Sierra Nevada mountains, and in summer the eastern gateway to Yosemite National Park. The resort's top-notch conditions, from facilities to consistency of snowpack to outright beauty, make it well worth the trip. And heck, you could always get some surfing in early in the morning before the drive!

Let's start with some facts. Mammoth Mountain stands 11,053 feet tall at its summit. In winter, that allows for 3,500 acres of skiable terrain on top of the annual average snowfall of 353 inches. There are three large day lodges, two high-speed gondolas, and 30 lifts to service this vast space. In summer, that translates into 70 miles of groomed mountain biking trails and unlimited hiking opportunities.

Just as important: Mammoth is blessed with an exceptionally long ski season because of its height and heavy snow, with opening day in early November and skiing continuing until July most years. Further good news is that the snow tends to come in large dumps, rather than in small sprinklings. The result is that most days are clear and sunny and ideal for skiing. But skiing is just one activity at Mammoth; for more on the many year-round recreational opportunities at Mammoth, see "Outdoor activities," later in this chapter.

Timing your visit

You can visit Mammoth any time of the year. The winter crowds come for ski season and holiday weekends, especially Christmas, New Year's, Martin Luther King Day, and Presidents Day. In summer, August is the busiest month. The best bargains on accommodations are during the week.

Getting there

Until the airport expansion is completed, you will need to drive. Mammoth is accessible year-round from Highway 395, which runs from

Reno down to the Mojave Desert. (From Reno, the drive to Mammoth takes almost three hours.) Hooking up to Highway 395 from the south will vary with your point of origin, but there are numerous options whether you start in Los Angeles, Palm Springs, or San Diego. The drive on Highway 395 presents spectacular views of the eastern Sierra Nevada, including such landmarks as Mount Whitney and Mono Lake. From L.A. the drive should take 5½ hours, and although the distance is the same from San Francisco, it can take longer coming this way during the winter if snow has closed Highway 120. Mammoth is a 45-minute to one-hour drive to the Tioga Pass entrance to Yosemite National Park when the road is open in the summer.

Orienting yourself and getting around

The town of **Mammoth Lakes** is the main hub for lodging, dining, and shopping. After you arrive and check into your hotel or condo, you can pretty much leave the car alone. The **Mammoth Area Shuttle** (☎ 760-934-3030) is a well-run, free shuttle service that connects the ski area, hotels and other accommodations, restaurants, and shopping; it operates both day and night in the winter season only. The Mammoth Mountain trail map (available at the visitors bureau) has complete shuttle information. If you're driving, the town is small enough that you can find your way around quickly using the town map, available at the visitors bureau or at most lodgings.

Where to stay

There are over 8,000 hotel rooms and condominiums available in the Mammoth area, and that number is growing as new developments crop up. Prices vary with time of the stay, holiday weekends being most expensive and weekdays the lowest, and vary again according to proximity to the ski slopes.

For hotel-type accommodations, the choices range from the new luxury all-suite **Juniper Springs Lodge,** with a full complement of amenities and direct access to the ski mountain, to such well-known chain names as **Holiday Inn** and **Motel 6.** Prices vary widely by size, facilities, and time of stay. See the "Gathering More Information" section for more information about the Mammoth Lakes Visitors Bureau and the Mammoth Mountain Ski Area. Be sure to check for packages that include hotel, lift tickets, and equipment rental.

The better value in Mammoth, and the clear choice if you have kids or are with a group, is renting a condo. Condos are plentiful and come in a wide range of sizes and prices. In winter, during the week, a nice condo on a shuttle line can cost as little as $100 per night and handle up to six people. In summer, that price can fall to as little as $50 a night. On the other hand, the sky's the limit on size and price for luxury condos and houses. A number of companies specialize in condo rentals. Among the best is **Mammoth Premiere Reservations** (P.O. Box 7522, Mammoth Lakes, California 93546; ☎ **800-336-6543**; www.mammothpremiere.com). Multi-night discounts and weekly rates are often available.

Where to dine

Mammoth offers a wide variety of dining options. For lunch or snacks during ski time, there are numerous choices at the main base lodges and on the mountain, from simple "grab-and-go" facilities to a full-service sit-down restaurant. Prices are typical of ski resorts (read: a little on the high side).

The town of Mammoth Lakes offers a full complement of fast-food out-lets, local eateries of all shapes and sizes, and two grocery stores. If you have taken the condo option, it's easy to buy stuff to eat at home (especially for breakfast or snacks), or simply get delivery from most restaurants and pizza places.

Outdoor activities

A full range of winter activities is available at Mammoth: downhill skiing, cross-country skiing, snowboarding, dog sledding, mountaineer-ing, snowshoeing, guided and self-guided snowmobile tours, and natu-ralist tours.

In warm-weather seasons, the traditional favored pastime is fishing on the beautiful chain of alpine lakes. Also popular are hiking, horseback riding, golf, tennis, boating, rock climbing, and mountain biking on the 80 miles of singletracks and more-challenging trails. The **Mammoth Mountain Bike Park** is open from June 22 to September 30; bike rentals, Park Pass sales, maintenance and repair, and biking accessories are available at the **Mammoth Adventure Center,** located at Panorama Station at Main Lodge (open daily 7:30 a.m.–6 p.m.). A one-day Park Pass costs $28 adult, $14 kids 12 and under.

Mammoth is kid-friendly and truly a family resort. The ski mountain is a favorite of parents because of its outstanding children's ski school, **Woollywood** (☎ **760-934-2571, ext. 3258**), with an adorable mascot drawn to resemble the ancient woolly mammoths that once lived in the area. Woollywood offers top-notch ski training for kids of all ages and can also fill in as baby-sitter when Mom and Dad want to ski alone. The adult ski school is also world-class.

The McCoy family, who founded the ski operation, recently hooked up with Canadian ski developer and operator Intrawest (owners of Whistler in British Columbia and Mont Tremblant in Quebec). A $700-million expansion and redevelopment plan is in full swing, including an airport expansion to allow for daily scheduled airline service.

Shopping Mammoth

Mammoth Lakes has several large-scale sporting-goods stores, packed with the latest in outdoor equipment and providing rentals for most anything you would need. Most offer free demo ski trials if you're looking to buy. There are also stores specializing in fishing gear for the summer visitor.

Shoppers will appreciate the **Mammoth Factory Stores,** with big discount outlets such as Ralph Lauren, Coach, Bass, and others. The bargains are good, and the merchandise is not limited to ski apparel (although skiwear is available).

Gathering more information

The **Mammoth Lakes Visitors Bureau** publishes the comprehensive "Mammoth Lakes Resort Guide," which is offered for free (☎ **888-GO-MAMMOTH** or 888-466-2666; www.visitmammoth.com). The bureau also jointly operates the Mammoth Lakes Visitor Center and Ranger Station, located on Highway 203 at the entrance to town, which offers comprehensive information on the town and recreational opportunities in the Inyo National Forest.

For complete vacation planning, contact the **Mammoth Mountain Ski Area** (part of the Intrawest network of destination resorts) (☎ **800-MAMMOTH;** www.mammothmountain.com).

Part IV
The Central Coast

By Rich Tennant

"SINCE WE LOST THE DOLPHINS, BUSINESS HASN'T BEEN QUITE THE SAME."

In this part . . .

*T*his part covers California's Central Coast, which
includes such wonderful destinations as the Monterey
Peninsula, Big Sur, Hearst Castle, and our personal favorite
(and home town), Santa Barbara.

Where the San Francisco Bay Area meets the Monterey
Peninsula sits Santa Cruz, California's kinda wacky surf
town. If you ask us (and apparently you did), the Central
Coast — that stretch between San Francisco and L.A. —
represents California at its very best. The drive along
coastal Highway 1 is breathtaking, in more ways than one.
The Monterey Peninsula cradles Monterey Bay, one of the
richest and most diverse marine habitats on earth, plus a
collection of the state's most delightful communities, from
family-friendly Monterey itself to world-class golf mecca
Pebble Beach to cozy Carmel-by-the-Sea. Be sure to dedicate a full day to the natural splendor of Big Sur, even if
you don't want to stay in one of the region's funky hotels;
trust us, you won't regret it. Hearst Castle, Cambria, fairy-
tale Solvang, gorgeous Santa Barbara, and the peaceful Ojai
Valley complete this thoroughly charming part of the state.

Chapter 15

Beach Blanket Babylon: Santa Cruz

*S*anta Cruz, the quintessential college town, beach town, and surf mecca, sits just a stone's throw from the Bay Area at the northwestern end of Monterey Bay. Monterey is the prime destination along the coast (see Chapter 16), but Santa Cruz is within easy reach of San Francisco — perfect for Northern California vacationers who want a taste of genuine Golden State beach life, or anyone who wants to avoid the tourist throngs that can overwhelm Monterey in summer.

Families with kids in tow will especially enjoy the **Santa Cruz Beach Boardwalk,** the West Coast's only seaside amusement park. If you hail from the East Coast, push those visions of the gritty Jersey boardwalk from your mind — Santa Cruz's version is everything a seaside boardwalk was meant to be. It's clean, family-friendly, and filled with amusements, from arcade games ("Getcha stuffed Elmo right he-ah! Three plays for a dol-lah!") to cotton-candy and funnel-cake vendors to thrill rides — even an old-fashioned wooden roller coaster that's rickety good fun. And, in summer, the beach scene out front is straight out of the movie *Gidget*.

Inland from the beach lies a charming downtown whose hippie element has been minimized, but not eliminated, by necessary post-earthquake gentrification. (Santa Cruz was seriously damaged in the 1989 Loma Prieta earthquake.) As a result, you'll find a nice blend of affordable but high-quality restaurants and boutiques, and a genuine and appealing laid-back California coast vibe.

Santa Cruz

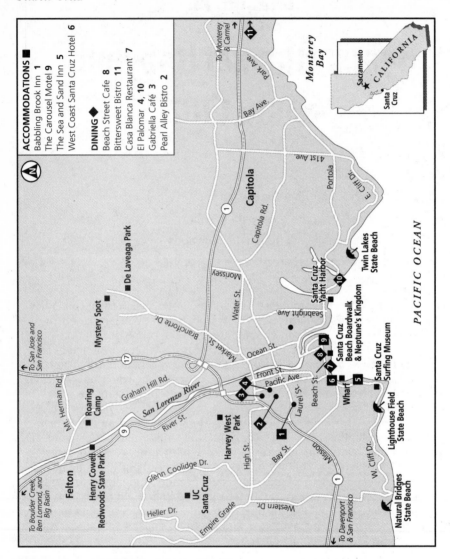

ACCOMMODATIONS ■
Babbling Brook Inn **1**
The Carousel Motel **9**
The Sea and Sand Inn **5**
West Coast Santa Cruz Hotel **6**

DINING ◆
Beach Street Cafe **8**
Bittersweet Bistro **11**
Casa Blanca Restaurant **7**
El Palomar **4, 10**
Gabriella Café **3**
Pearl Alley Bistro **2**

Timing Your Visit

California's middle coastline enjoys mild weather all the time, with highs in the mid-70s in summer and the mid-50s in winter. Late summer — from mid-July through September, and often into October — is usually best for sunny beachgoing and boardwalk fun. Crowds do not present a huge problem; in fact, we like Santa Cruz best on summer weekends, when it's at its liveliest.

Boardwalk operation is limited to weekends in spring and fall and restricted to holidays in winter, so be sure to check the schedule before you head here with the kids in the off-season.

If you want to stay in Santa Cruz, plan on one or two nights and a couple of days to enjoy it all, with maybe a third full day to book a fishing charter or kayak trip. If you're driving between Monterey and the Bay Area, allot at least a few hours to stop and enjoy the boardwalk and downtown a bit before continuing on your journey.

Getting There

Santa Cruz is 76 miles southeast of San Francisco. You can choose the quick route or the scenic route:

- ✔ **For the quick route:** Take I-280 to Highway 85 to Highway 17, which deposits you onto Ocean Street, leading right to the beach.

- ✔ **If you prefer the scenic route:** Take Highway 1 the entire way, which takes about twice as long. One stretch of Highway 1, called Devil's Slide, isn't for the faint of heart — as you may have guessed from the name — but the rest is pretty easy driving.

If you're heading to Santa Cruz on a weekend morning, skip the quick route in favor of Highway 1, because Highway 17 tends to logjam with Bay Area beachgoers.

If you're coming from Monterey, 45 miles away, take Highway 1 north. The drive takes about an hour.

Orienting Yourself and Getting Around

Santa Cruz is small and easy to navigate. Both Highway 17 and Highway 1 take you straight into the heart of town. Exit Highway 1 from River Street and follow it to Front Street to reach the shopping and dining district in the heart of downtown (Front Street is the main drag).

Proceed down Front to oceanfront Beach Street to reach the beach. Head west along Beach until it becomes West Cliff Drive, whose beachfront path offers gorgeous ocean views and an excellent look at the local surfing action (and probably a few clusters of fuzzy sea lions sunning themselves on the rocks below).

Where to Stay in Santa Cruz

Because Santa Cruz is a beach destination, summer rates are significantly higher than winter rates. You'll also pay more for the privilege of visiting over the weekend — and expect a two-night minimum if you include Saturday in your stay.

If you'd like more options, call the Santa Cruz County Accommodations Hotline at ☎ 800-833-3494.

Count on an extra 12% in taxes being tacked on to your hotel bill.

There are lots and lots of inexpensive motels by the beach, none of which sport much in the way of curb appeal, but we do approve of the Carousel Motel (see the listing in this section). The **Best Inn Santa Cruz** at 600 Riverside Ave. (☎ **831-458-9660;** www.bestinnsantacruz.com) is another economical choice; rates go as low as $75; check for special online rates.

Babbling Brook Inn
$$$ **Santa Cruz**

If you're looking for romance, book into this little oasis. It's just a two-minute drive (or a ten-minute walk) west of downtown, but, because it sits among an acre of gorgeous gardens, you'd hardly know it. You can choose from 13 charming rooms, all based on an art theme (the Cezanne, the Monet, the Van Gogh, and so on). Baths have been newly renovated to include whirlpool tubs, and fireplaces have been added to many rooms. Lovely but not too cutesy, thank goodness — a real romantic treat.

1025 Laurel St. (at California St.). ☎ *800-866-1131. Fax: 831-427-2457. Internet:* www. babblingbrookinn.com. *Parking: Free! Rack rates: $165–$250 double. Rates include full breakfast and afternoon wine and hors d'oeuvres. AE, DC, DISC, MC, V.*

The Carousel Motel
$–$$ **Santa Cruz**

This is the budget choice for vacationers destined for the boardwalk and the beach. You enter the main building by way of a room cardkey-accessed gate, a security feature that either strikes you the right way or the wrong way. Rooms are spacious, neat, and plainly furnished with pine pieces, microwaves, refrigerators, and TVs. Views encompass more building than ocean, but the price is right. Vacation packages that include boardwalk tickets make an even better value.

110 Riverside Ave. ☎ *800-214-7400 or 831-425-7090. Internet:* www.santacruz motels.com. *Parking: Free! Rack rates: $59–$149 double, $89–$179 double with spa. Rates include continental breakfast. AE, DISC, MC, V.*

The Sea & Sand Inn
$$–$$$ Santa Cruz

This friendly and fabulously situated oceanfront motel is a true gem. It lies clifftop above the surf, just a short walk from the beach and board-walk. The motel rooms are really nice, all with good-quality furnishings and panoramic ocean views. The lovely garden, with a furnished terrace overlooking the water, is a wonderful place to relax. With a kitchen and a private patio with Jacuzzi, the suite is well worth it if you're looking to splurge or have the kids in tow. A terrific choice. Make reservations three months in advance for summer weekends.

201 W. Cliff Dr. ☎ 831-427-3400. Fax: 831-466-9882. Internet: www.beachboard walk.com/02_sea_and_sand.html. *Parking: Free! Rack rates: $109–$199 double, $139–$279 double with spa, $209–$359 studio or suite. Rates include continental breakfast, plus afternoon refreshments in most seasons. AE, MC, V.*

West Coast Santa Cruz Hotel
$$$ Santa Cruz

This very nice hotel is the only lodging in town with direct beach access. The rooms are unremarkable, but very comfy; in-room extras like Sony Playstations, minifridges, and coffeemakers mean they're family-friendly, too. The beachfront pool area is well-furnished and leads right to Santa Cruz's prime stretch of sand. This pleasing choice is hard to beat if it suits your budget.

175 W. Cliff Dr. (adjacent to the Santa Cruz Wharf). ☎ 800-426-0670 or 831-426-4330. Fax: 831-427-2025. Internet: www.westcoasthotels.com/santacruz. *Parking: Free! Rack rates: $169–$273 double, $225–$450 suite. AE, DISC, MC, V.*

Where to Dine in Santa Cruz

Santa Cruz boasts a thriving restaurant scene, so you can expect to eat well here. The following are our local favorites.

Beach Street Cafe
$ Santa Cruz   AMERICAN

You may be tempted to sup on the wharf, but take a nice walk out on the pier, admire the ocean, then turn around and breakfast at this friendly little cafe where the eggs are fine and the bacon isn't greasy.

399 Beach St. ☎ 831-426-7621. www.beachstreetcafe.com. *No reservations. Main courses: $5–$9. MC, V. Open: Breakfast and lunch daily 8 a.m.–3 p.m.*

Bittersweet Bistro

$$$ Aptos   CALIFORNIA

A meal at this stylish and hugely popular restaurant is well worth the 20-minute trip south of town. Chef Thomas Vinolus uses the freshest produce and a wood-fired oven to craft hearty, not-too-fussy California cuisine with a Mediterranean accent. The large menu offers something for everyone, from excellent seafood preparations and steaks to creative mini-pizzas for more casual tastes. The restaurant regularly receives the *Wine Spectator* Award of Excellence. The desserts are divine, too, named "Best in County" several years in a row.

In the Deer Park Shopping Center, 787 Rio Del Mar Blvd. (off Hwy. 1, about 10 miles SE of Santa Cruz), Aptos. ☎ 831-662-9799. Internet: www.bittersweetbistro. com. *Reservations recommended. Main courses: $19–$27. AE, MC, V. Open: Dinner daily 5:30 p.m. first seating; bistro: Daily 3–6 p.m.*

Casa Blanca Restaurant

$$$$ Santa Cruz   CONTINENTAL/SEAFOOD

This wonderful restaurant is one of the most romantic in town. The white linen–covered tables are terraced so that every diner has ocean views, and twinkling white lights add to the ambience. The old-school, seafood-heavy menu more than lives up to the stellar setting. Look for such winning dishes as ruby-red ahi crowned with fresh mango and roasted green chili sauce, and New York steak in a bourbon-peppercorn demi-glace. Excellent service and a great wine list, too.

In the Casa Blanca Inn, 101 Main St. (at Beach St.). ☎ 831-426-9063. Reservations recommended. Main courses: $17–$26. AE, DC, DISC, MC, V. Open: Daily 5–9:15 p.m.

El Palomar

$$ Santa Cruz   MEXICAN

This airy, cheerful Mexican restaurant in the heart of downtown is a great place to enjoy an affordable meal. It doesn't have the best Mexican grub in California, but the generous plates are well-prepared and quite pleasing. Expect all your favorites, from saucy enchiladas to sizzling fajitas. Seafood lovers shouldn't miss the excellent ceviches, all freshly prepared and perfectly seasoned with lime (the octopus is particularly good). The Santa Cruz Harbor location is cheaper and even more casual.

1336 Pacific Ave., downtown. ☎ 831-425-7575. Cafe El Palomar: At the Santa Cruz Harbor, 2222 E. Cliff Dr. ☎ 831-462-4248. Reservations recommended for dinner. Main courses and combo plates: $7–$19. AE, DISC, MC, V. Open: Mon–Fri 11 a.m.– 3 p.m, 5–10 p.m; Sat 11 a.m.–10:30 p.m.; Sun 11 a.m.–10 p.m.

Gabriella Café

$$ Santa Cruz   CALIFORNIA

This charming and romantic restaurant is a terrific bet if you want a touch of sophistication for a reasonable tariff. Expect fresh, organic veggies; well-poached local sturgeon and pan-seared pork loin; daily-made gnocchi and risotto; and "pan amore" — homemade focaccia with delectable roast garlic, basil pesto, and heirloom tomato spreads. The restaurant also offers alfresco seating in the cute alley garden.

910 Cedar St. (between Locust St. and Walnut Ave., one block over from Pacific Ave.), downtown. ☎ *831-457-1677. Internet:* www.gabriellacafe.com. *Reservations recommended. Main courses: $16–$22. AE, DC, DISC, MC, V. Open: Mon–Fri lunch from 11:30 a.m.; dinner from 5:30 p.m.; Sat and Sun brunch from 10 a.m.*

Pearl Alley Bistro

$$$ Santa Cruz   California French

This attractive, slightly funky bistro is an excellent spot to enjoy an innovative meal. Expect French classics like vichyssoise and bacon-wrapped sweetbreads; but don't be surprised when the chef takes California-style liberties in preparation, offering such dishes as giant sea scallops served on artichoke bottoms and aromatically seasoned with lavender and thyme. An oddity is the do-it-yourself Mongolian barbecue, which you cook at your table on a sizzling rock. The restaurant offers friendly service and a nice wine selection, too.

110 Pearl Alley (between Lincoln and Walnut Aves.), downtown. ☎ *831-429-8070. Internet:* www.pearlalley.com. *Reservations recommended. Main courses: $13–$26. Open: Daily 11:30 a.m.–5 p.m, 5:30–11 p.m.*

Hitting the Boardwalk

All the good-time boardwalk fun detailed in this section faces **Cowell Beach,** a vast stretch of sand that really comes alive in summer. So grab your beach towel and catch some rays alongside the bevy of beachgoers, which range from vacationing Bay Area families to bikini-clad co-eds to volleyball-playing surfer dudes.

The Santa Cruz Beach Boardwalk

This landmark oceanfront boardwalk — the only beach amusement park on the West Coast — is a retro jewel. The well-kept, beautifully maintained wooden boardwalk (here in one form or another since 1907) offers nearly 30 rides, plus dozens of skill games, tacky souvenir shops, and food vendors (hot dogs, cotton candy, funnel cake) — more than enough to entertain kids of all ages well into the evening, when a rainbow of bright lights heightens the appeal. The boardwalk boasts two national landmarks: the wooden **Giant Dipper** roller coaster, a 1924 original and still a marvelous thrill ride; and the 1911 **Looff Carousel,** a work of art with hand-carved wooden horses and a magnificent pipe organ. The boardwalk also includes a good kiddie area with nine rides. You'll pay for rides with tickets you buy at booths strategically placed along the boardwalk; the booths also offer unlimited-ride passes for committed thrill-seekers. The boardwalk is hugely popular, especially in summer, but the crowds are all part of the fun.

Along Beach St., between Pacific and Riverside aves. ☎ *831-426-7433 or 831-423-5590. Internet:* www.beachboardwalk.com. *Admission: Free! Rides $1.80–$3.60. All-day unlimited ride pass $28.95. Open: Memorial Day–Labor Day, daily from 10 a.m.–late; spring and fall, Sat–Sun noon–5 p.m.; limited holiday operation in winter. Hours change regularly, so call for current schedule.*

Buy your unlimited ride passes online and save $5; also check for online coupons.

Neptune's Kingdom and Casino Fun Center/Supercade

Think the boardwalk is limited to nostalgic entertainment? Not hardly! These enormous indoor family fun centers feature loads of millennium-worthy fun, including the **MaxFlight CyberCoaster,** the world's only rider-programmable virtual roller coaster; laser tag; a two-story minia-ture golf course with a pirate theme; and enough classic and cutting-edge arcade games to exhaust the National Mint's supply of quarters.

Adjacent to the boardwalk at 400 Beach St. ☎ *831-426-7433 or 831-423-5590. Internet:* www.beachboardwalk.com. *Admission: Free; charges vary for indi-vidual games and attractions. Adventure Package (includes one bowling game with shoe rental, one round of Laser Tag, one miniature golf game, and $5 in arcade tokens) $10. Open: Daily 11 a.m.–11 p.m.; limited hours in winter.*

Santa Cruz Municipal Wharf

This old-time pier isn't as grimy or commercial as Monterey's; it has a nice maritime vibe, but it's still a shade on the tacky side. Locals cast and crab from the wooden pier, which is lined with cheesy shops, sportfish-ing charters, and a succession of mediocre seafood restaurants, the best of which is **Sea Cloud** (☎ 831-458-9393). **Santa Cruz Boat Rentals** (☎ 831-423-1739) offers equipment rentals as well as bait and tackle. **Stagnaro's Fishing Trips** (☎ 831-427-2334) can take you deep-sea fish-ing as well as on whale- and sea lion-watching cruises. The wharf also offers an excellent photo op of the boardwalk.

You can park here, too, for a minimal charge, but be aware that traffic can really back up; you may be better off putting your wheels in a street lot.

On Beach St. just west of the boardwalk. ☎ *831-420-6025. Admission: Free! Open: Daily 5 a.m.–2 a.m. (most shops open daily 7a.m.–9 p.m.).*

Surfing and Other Cool Stuff to See and Do

Follow Beach Street west from the boardwalk and it quickly turns into West Cliff Drive, a gorgeous clifftop road lined with fine old houses on one side and spectacular ocean views on the other.

At Lighthouse Point (within walking distance of the wharf) sits the petite **Santa Cruz Surfing Museum** (☎ 831-420-6289; www.cruzio.com), which traces surfing history from both local and broader points of view (with a nice accent on oft-neglected female surfers). You can easily see the collection of surfboards and other memorabilia in an hour or less. It's open daily except Tuesday from noon to 4 p.m. The suggested donation is $1.50.

Lighthouse Point also serves as the perfect vantage for **Steamer Lane,** Santa Cruz's infamous surfing spot. If you're lucky and the surf's up, you'll see some daredevil pros riding the waves.

Kayaking the bay

Monterey Bay is a fabulous place to kayak in summer, even for beginners. You'll glide right by sunbathing sea lions and snacking sea otters as shorebirds swoop through the air around you. **Venture Quest Kayaking** rents kayaks to experienced paddlers at their wharf location (☎ 831-425-8445). You can schedule a guided bay adventure ($40 per person) by calling the Beach Street location (☎ 831-427-2267; www.kayaksanta cruz.com). Venture Quest also offers a guided tour of Elkhorn Slough, a calm-as-can-be, wildlife-rich estuary of Monterey Bay ($59).

Browsing Pacific Avenue

One of the best things about Santa Cruz is its charming downtown, which boasts an authentic laid-back California coast vibe — not to mention a fair amount of shopping, most of it unique and affordable. The main drag for browsers is Pacific Avenue, which is chock-a-block with boutiques, bookstores, and record shops from Mission to Laurel streets. You'll find some gems on the side streets just off Pacific, too, such as **Annieglass,** at 109 Cooper St. (☎ 831-427-4260), an outlet store for locally made art-glass jewelry and housewares — a real find if you're looking for gifts.

Marveling at the Mystery Spot

Okay, so you won't exactly marvel at the **Mystery Spot,** 465 Mystery Spot Rd. (☎ 831-423-8897; www.mystery-spot.com), but lovers of kitsch will enjoy this funhouse in the woods. Ads tout it as a natural phenomenon where the accepted rules of gravity, perspective, compass, velocity, and height no longer exist (phooey on you, Newton!). It's a real hoot if you like silly stuff, and it's open daily from 9 a.m. to 5 p.m. The tour lasts only 35 minutes, but expect an hour-long wait in summer. Admission is $5 for adults and $3 for kids. Finding the Mystery Spot alone can be a mystery: From Pacific Avenue, turn right on Water Street and left on Market Street, which turns into Branciforte Drive; follow the signs.

Taking a ride through the redwoods

Want a glimpse of California's majestic redwoods and pioneering past, but don't have time to visit the North Coast or the Gold Country? Catch a ride on the **Roaring Camp & Big Trees Narrow Gauge Railroad** (☎ 831-335-4484; www.roaringcamprr.com), which takes riders aboard the nation's last steam-powered passenger railroad through the Santa Cruz Mountains on a 1¼-hour round trip. Trips leave from Roaring Camp, a half-hour's drive from Santa Cruz, daily year-round (weekends only in December). Rates are $15.50 adults, $10.50 kids 3 to 12. They also offer a beach-to-redwoods round trip for $17 adults, $12 kids.

Adding some drama to the proceedings

The University of California at Santa Cruz has been home to a well-regarded and popular summer **Shakespeare Festival** since 1975. The season begins the second week of July and runs through the end of August with weekend matinees and evening performances. Much of the festival takes place outdoors, and regulars bring blankets or cushions to sit on, plus picnics to enjoy before the show. This isn't a student-run program — actors from all around the country vie for roles, and the direction is often edgy and provocative. For information on the summer season, ticket prices, and dates, check online at www.shakespearesantacruz.org or phone the box office between Tuesday and Saturday afternoons at ☎ 831-459-2159.

Gathering More Information

Call the **Santa Cruz County Conference and Visitors Council** (☎ 800-833-3494 or 831-425-1234), or point your Web browser to www.scccvc.org. After you arrive, stop in at the friendly and helpful staffed visitor center at 1211 Ocean St., at Kennan Street, across from McDonald's and next to the Baker's Square restaurant.

Chapter 16

The Monterey Peninsula

*P*repare yourself for some of the most spectacular real estate you've ever seen when you visit this rocky, cypress-dotted stretch of California coast. A mystical, foggy shoreline rich with natural beauty and steeped in maritime history, it's home to the continental United States' largest marine sanctuary as well as some of the state's most charming communities.

The Monterey Peninsula juts out into the ocean at the south end of Monterey Bay. The bay is the deepest part of the ocean just off the North American coast, twice as deep as the Grand Canyon. As a result, it houses one of the most diverse collections of marine animals on the planet. Sea lions, otters, pelicans, gulls, even whales are a major presence and set the tone for life here. (More than one hotel manager reports that guests in ocean-facing rooms frequently call to complain about the barking dogs that wake them in the predawn hours — to which the manager explains that sea lions don't respond well to requests for quiet.)

The biggest draw on the peninsula is the town of **Monterey,** home to the justifiably world-famous **Monterey Bay Aquarium,** one of the premier attractions in the Golden State, and **Cannery Row,** the sardine-canning center immortalized by John Steinbeck and since transformed into a family-friendly tourist zone. The aquarium actually lies half in Monterey and half in neighboring **Pacific Grove,** which we discuss in conjunction with Monterey because the dividing line is unnecessary for our purposes. From a base in either town, you can easily enjoy the charms and attractions of both.

The Monterey Peninsula

ACCOMMODATIONS ■
Asilomar Conference Grounds **24**
Best Western Victorian Inn **8**
Casa Palermo **20**
Cobblestone Inn **31**
Cypress Inn **30**
Grand View Inn/Seven Gables Inn **1**
The Inn at Spanish Bay **21**
The Lodge at Pebble Beach **19**
Los Laureles Lodge **17**
Mission Ranch **18**
The Monterey Hotel **13**
Monterey Plaza Hotel and Spa **9**
Pacific Gardens Inn **25**
Quail Lodge Resort and Golf Club **17**
Rosedale Inn **25**
Spindrift Inn **7**
Village Inn **27**

DINING ◆
Cafe Fina **10**
Cafe Gringo **29**
Caffé Napoli/Little Napoli **30**
Casanova **26**
The Culinary Center of Monterey **7**
Flying Fish Grill **28**
The Duck Club **9**
The Fishwife at Asilomar Beach **22**
Jack London's Bar & Grill **25**
Montrio **12**
Passionfish **2**
Rosine's **14**
Sea Harvest Fish Market & Restaurant **6**
Stokes Adobe **13**
Turtle Bay Taqueria **15**

ATTRACTIONS ●
Cannery Row **5**
Carmel Mission **18**
Dennis the Menace Playground **16**
Fisherman's Wharf **11**
Garland Regional Park **17**
Maritime Museum of Monterey **11**
Monarch Grove Sanctuary **23**
Monterey Bay Aquarium **4**
Monterey State Historic Park **11**
Pacific Grove Museum of
    Natural History **3**

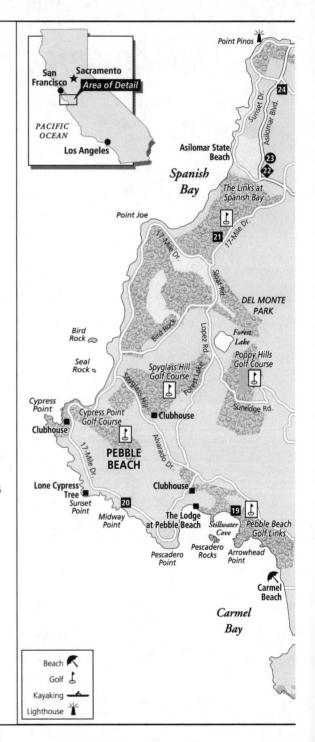

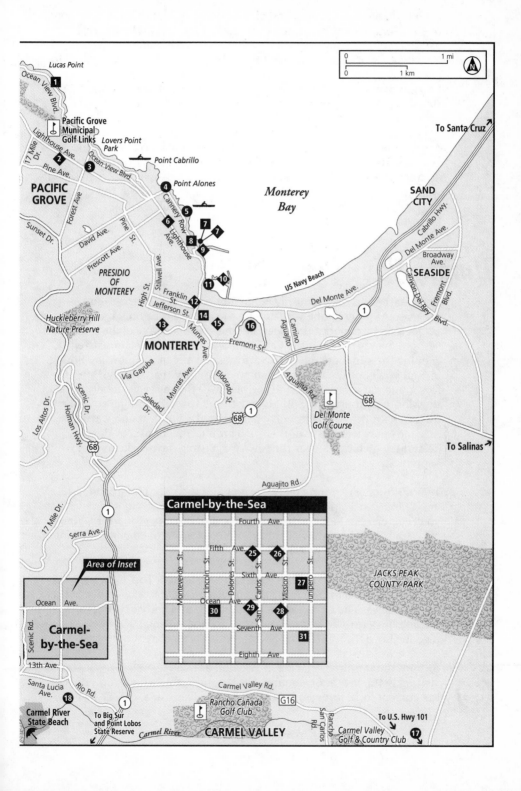

Sculpted out of the midsection of the peninsula is **Pebble Beach,** home to some of the most beautiful woodlands, priciest residential real estate, and best championship golf resorts in the country. If you're looking for world-class greens, this is the place to be — but be sure to pack that platinum card, because it doesn't come cheap. You'll even have to pay to tour this territory — $8, to be exact — along the **17-Mile Drive,** a gorgeous private road that traverses hill and dale along a meandering loop.

At the south end of the peninsula is **Carmel-by-the-Sea,** one of the sweetest little towns around, and home to one of California's most stunning beaches. This upscale haven exists to delight you even if you want nothing more to do than eat, shop, and amble about the village. But don't worry: You can enjoy its charms without blowing a wad in the process.

Timing Your Visit

The weather on the Monterey Peninsula is moderate year-round — the average daily temperature along the coast varies only by about 12 degrees throughout the calendar year, with average highs in the mid 60s and average lows in the low 50s. Fog can be a factor, consistently keeping the summers misty and gray, especially in the morning hours; in fact, you could see more sunshine in January than in July. Don't let fog-bound days keep you away, however — the misty haze only adds to the Monterey mystique. Still, the best time to visit is Indian summer, from August through October, when days are sunniest and warmest. Jazz fans may want to plan their trip around the **Monterey Jazz Festival,** which takes over the town for a three-day weekend every September.

Temperatures are appreciably warmer and days sunnier inland. While most of the area's prime destinations lie along the coast, if it's sun that you're after, consider making Carmel Valley your headquarters. You have to drive inland only 15 minutes or so for temps to climb well into the 80s or 90s in July or August.

Expect spikes in summer and weekend hotel rates. The good news for off-season travelers: You just may end up with the best weather at the lowest prices. The exception is late January and early February during the celebrity pro/am golf tournament in Pebble Beach: Even the pigeons have trouble finding accommodations at that time.

Be sure to take along a jacket, a sweater, and long pants, even if you're visiting in the height of summer. Shorts and T-shirts just won't do. For the current local forecast for the Monterey Peninsula, call ☎ **831-656-1725.**

The distance is less than 5 miles from Monterey on the north end to Carmel on the south end, but this action-packed peninsula boasts lots of attractions. Exploring the entire area can easily occupy you for five or six days. If your time is limited, two days is enough to explore Monterey thoroughly, but set aside at least a half-day for the aquarium. Plan to spend a third day in Carmel (you can enjoy a lovely stretch of the 17-Mile Drive on your way there) lounging by the hotel pool or driving your way around a golf course.

Getting There

The Monterey Peninsula is just off Highway 1, about 46 miles south of Santa Cruz, 122 miles south of San Francisco, and 86 miles north of Hearst Castle. To get there:

- ✔ **From Santa Cruz:** Take Highway 1 south for about an hour; follow the exit signs into Monterey, or proceed another 3 miles south to the Ocean Avenue exit, which leads you to Carmel. (Watch for the Ocean Avenue exit, because it doesn't explicitly say "Carmel.")

- ✔ **From San Francisco:** Follow the route suggested in Chapter 15 to Santa Cruz and pick up Highway 1 as described in the preceding bullet.

- ✔ **If you're heading north from Cambria:** Follow Highway 1 through Big Sur. This spectacular drive is slow going and can easily take a full day with stops; see Chapter 17 for details.

You can fly into Monterey Peninsula Airport, located on Olmsted Road 4 miles east of Monterey off Highway 68 (☎ **831-648-7000;** www. montereyairport.com). Serving the airport are:

- ✔ **American Airlines/American Eagle:** ☎ **800-433-7300;** www.aa.com

- ✔ **America West Express:** ☎ **800-235-9292;** www.americawest.com

- ✔ **United Airlines:** ☎ **800-241-6522;** www.united.com

The national car-rental companies that have airport locations include:

- ✔ **Avis:** ☎ **800-331-1212;** www.avis.com

- ✔ **Budget:** ☎ **800-527-0700;** https://rent.drivebudget.com

- ✔ **Enterprise:** ☎ **800-RENT-A-CAR;** www.erac.com

- ✔ **Hertz:** ☎ **800-654-3131;** www.hertz.com

- ✔ **National:** ☎ **800-CAR-RENT;** www.nationalcar.com

You can also catch a ride with Yellow Cab/Carmel Taxi (☎ **831-624-3885**), which usually has cabs circling the airport; expect the fare into Monterey to cost about $18.

Before you pay for a taxi, check with your hotel to see if they offer a complimentary shuttle service.

Monterey and Pacific Grove

As the capital of California when the state was under Spanish rule, the first capital of the Golden State, and the hub of West Coast nautical life, Monterey has a rich history. The **Monterey State Historic Park** and the nicely preserved downtown boast beautifully restored Spanish adobes. Despite the dissolution of the sardine-canning industry, the town still thrives on its maritime past. Barely a day goes by without someone making a reference to the city's favorite literary light, novelist John Steinbeck.

Don't come expecting some bastion of historic high-mindedness, however — Monterey is quite comfortable maintaining its mass-market appeal, thank you very much. In fact, some feel that the town fathers have gone too far, succumbing to the worst impulses of tourism — witness campy **Cannery Row** and tacky **Fisherman's Wharf,** they say. It's true — you have to wade through some touristy schlock in these areas. But you can't argue with the appeal of the wonderful aquarium and that one-of-a-kind bay (be sure to get out on it if you can). And even Cannery Row and the wharf are good for a brief bit of fun, as long as you take them with the grains of salt they deserve. Beyond the prime tourist zones, you'll discover a genuine ocean community with beautifully preserved architecture, stunning panoramic vistas, top-quality restaurants, and more.

Gorgeous **Pacific Grove** makes a great base if you'd rather revel in the area's natural wonders and don't mind the short drive or bike ride it takes to reach the main attractions. If convenience is more important to you, or you want a more urban feel, book a room in Monterey proper. But even if you stay in Pacific Grove, the distances won't be that much of a factor. The Pacific Grove lodgings may seem out of the way, but the drive into Monterey along Ocean View Boulevard is only around five minutes without traffic.

Orienting yourself and getting around

Monterey is divided into two main sightseeing areas:

- ✔ **Downtown** (centered on Alvarado Street) and adjacent **Fisherman's Wharf,** where you'll also find Monterey State Historic Park.

- ✔ The **Cannery Row** area (sometimes referred to as "New Monterey"), where the aquarium is also located.

Cannery Row is roughly to the west/northwest of downtown and the wharf; beyond Cannery Row is Pacific Grove, which is easily reachable

by bicycle and perfect for exploring on two wheels. The downtown–
Fisherman's Wharf area and Cannery Row are both very pedestrian-
friendly, but you'll most likely need to drive, bike, or take public
transport between the two.

Parking can be somewhat difficult in Monterey's tourist areas, so you
may want to park your car at your hotel when you arrive and leave it
there for the duration of your stay. (All the recommended hotels are
centrally located, making it easy to do just that.) If you do drive
between sites, your best bet is to park in one of the paid lots. If you
choose to rely on metered spots, be sure to have quarters on hand,
and pay attention to time.

If you visit between Memorial Day and Labor Day, you can use the
Waterfront Area Visitor Express (WAVE) shuttle to get around. The
WAVE operates buses between all the major tourist sites and hotel
areas in Monterey and Pacific Grove daily from 9 a.m. to 7:30 p.m. in
season. Rides are absolutely free — a bargain at twice the price, considering what you'll save on parking fees and headaches. For the latest
information, contact Monterey Salinas Transit (☎ **831-899-2555**), or
visit www.mst.org.

For the lowdown on renting bikes — a very popular pastime — see
"More cool stuff to see and do," later in this chapter.

Where to stay

You may want to try booking your room through a free reservations
service such as **Monterey Peninsula Reservations** (☎ **888-655-3424**;
www.monterey-reservations.com) or **Resort II Me** (☎ **800-757-
5646**; www.lodgingreservations.net). Because they have established relationships with local hotels and inns, they may be able to
negotiate a better rate for you than if you call the hotel directly; your
best bet is to compare. They can also refer you to other reliable properties in the area if the choices in the sections that follow are full.

Most hotels require a two-night minimum on summer and holiday
weekends. Count on an extra 10% in taxes added to your final hotel bill.

Always inquire about packages — which may include aquarium tickets
or other incentives — even at the cheapest motel.

Asilomar Conference Grounds
$$ Pacific Grove

Situated on 105 gorgeous oceanfront acres of pines and dunes, this woodland conference center is open to individual bookings, and it's a great
bargain for families on a budget. Rustic but immaculately kept stone-and-
log lodges house basic guest rooms (private baths, but no phones or

TVs), plus a great room for lounging. Facilities include a heated pool, ping-pong, and billiards; a boardwalk leads to the beach and tide-pools. This is a wonderful outdoorsy, summer camp–like retreat, with Monterey's attractions just minutes away. Cafeteria-style dining halls (pay-one-price lunch $8.75, dinner $14) mean you save on meals, too.

800 Asilomar Blvd., Pacific Grove. ☎ 831-642-4242 or 831-372-8016. Fax: 831-372-7227. Internet: www.visitasilomar.com. *Reservations accepted up to 90 days in advance. Parking: Free! Rack rates: $106–$127 double, $160–$215 cottage or suite. Rates include full breakfast. MC, V.*

Best Western Victorian Inn
$$$ Monterey

This nice motel is just two blocks from Cannery Row. Don't let the Victorian theme fool you; the office is housed in a period home, but guest rooms are in a modern annex. Still, they're pleasant and feature nice extras: marble fireplaces, minibars, coffeemakers, and VCRs. Rack rates are *way* too high, but snagging a good rate through Best Western is pretty easy. Book a concierge-level room if you can, which adds cathedral ceilings, featherbeds, whirlpool tub, CD player, and robes to the mix.

487 Foam St., Monterey. ☎ 800-232-4141 or 831-373-8000. Fax: 831-373-4815. Internet: www.victorianinn.com. *Parking: Free! Rack rates: $179–$369 double. Rates include continental breakfast and afternoon wine and cheese. Promotional packages as low as $129; rates as low as $89 (from $81 for seniors and AAA members) through* www.bestwestern.com.

Grand View Inn/Seven Gables Inn
$$$–$$$$$ Pacific Grove

These gorgeous sister inns are two of the most spectacular we've ever seen — and they're ideally located to boot, along the stunning coast road and situated so that just about every room has an ocean view. The Edwardian style of the 1910 Grand View is somewhat subtler than the Seven Gables' more elaborate 1886 Victorian (which you may remember from old American Express commercials), but it's really a matter of taste. Everything is impeccable, from the marble baths to the faultless service. Romance-seeking couples simply can't do better. Book well ahead, especially for weekends.

555–557 Ocean View Blvd., Pacific Grove. ☎ 831-372-4341. Internet: www.pginns.com. *Parking: Free! Rack rates: $175–$385 double. Rates include full breakfast and afternoon tea. MC, V.*

The Monterey Hotel
$$$–$$$$ Monterey

This very charming Victorian hotel is beautifully located in the retail heart of downtown Monterey, an easy walk to Fisherman's Wharf. Opened in

1904, it's been impeccably restored, with beveled-glass details and mahogany polished to a high sheen. The smallish but lovely period rooms are elegantly and comfortably furnished, and have posh marble-tiled baths. If you can, go for a *double-double* (two double beds or two queen beds) or even a junior suite for the most space. The staff is attentive and helpful. *Note:* There is no working elevator, but valet service is available.

406 Alvarado St., downtown Monterey. ☎ **800-727-0960** *or 831-375-3184. Fax: 831-375-2899. Internet:* www.montereyhotel.com. *Valet parking: $15. Rack rates: $139–$189 double, $219–$299 suite. Rates include continental breakfast and afternoon and evening refreshments. Deals: Ask about weekday rates and aquarium packages. AE, DC, DISC, MC, V.*

Monterey Plaza Hotel and Spa
$$$–$$$$$ Monterey

Monterey's finest waterfront hotel is dramatically situated to maximize the lovely bay views, and although it's next door to Cannery Row, it feels worlds away. Elegant teak-paneled public areas lead to spacious, extremely comfy guest rooms with big marble baths and all the little luxuries. Go ocean-view if you can, but even guests in the cheapest inland-view rooms can relax on the bayfront terrace. Service is top-notch, and facilities include a gym, a full-service spa, and a terrific restaurant (see "Where to dine," later in this chapter).

400 Cannery Row, Monterey. ☎ **800-631-1339,** *800-368-2468, or 831-646-1700. Fax: 831-646-5937. Internet:* www.woodsidehotels.com. *Valet parking: $15. Rack rates: $185–$505 double, from $450 suite. Ask about spa, golf, aquarium, breakfast, and romance packages. AE, DC, DISC, MC, V.*

Pacific Gardens Inn
$$ Pacific Grove

This cute, AAA three-diamond choice is a little more motel-like than the Rosedale Inn, but it's pleasing nonetheless. All the simple but clean country-style rooms contain coffeemakers and popcorn poppers, and most have wood-burning fireplaces; suites offer full kitchens and large living rooms (great for families). Two on-site Jacuzzis and a coin-op laundry round out the appeal of this good value.

701 Asilomar Blvd., Pacific Grove. ☎ **800-262-1566** *or 831-646-9414. Fax: 831-647-0555. Internet:* www.pacificgardensinn.com. *Parking: Free! Rack rates: $125–$140 double, $155–$190 suite. Rates include continental breakfast and afternoon wine and cheese. AE, MC, V.*

Rosedale Inn
$$ Pacific Grove

Here's our favorite among Pacific Grove's sweet cottage-style motels. The dreamy lodgelike complex is actually much nicer than a motel. All the large rooms are beautifully done in a comfy country style and feature cathedral ceilings (with ceiling fans), VCRs, fireplaces, kitchenettes with microwaves and minifridges, and whirlpool tubs and hair dryers in the very nice baths. About half are two-room suites, which also have a sleeper sofa in the living room — perfect for families. Management is super-friendly, too. This place is a winner.

775 Asilomar Blvd., Pacific Grove. ☎ 800-822-5606 or 831-655-1000. Fax: 831-655-0691. Internet: www.rosedaleinn.com. *Parking: Free! Rack rates: $135–$155 double, $195–$235 two-room suite. Rates include continental breakfast. AE, DISC, MC, V.*

Spindrift Inn
$$$–$$$$$ Monterey

If the Monterey Plaza Hotel is too swanked-out for your tastes, but you'd like some bay views with your breakfast, this smaller boutique property in the center of Cannery Row should fill the bill. You'll feel completely sheltered inside these charming, well-appointed, and spacious rooms. Fireplaces, hardwood floors, feather beds, marble baths, and stunning ocean vistas are among the treats in store, but pony up for a bayview room — it can be noisy on the street side.

652 Cannery Row, Monterey. ☎ 800-841-1879 or 831-646-8900. Fax: 831-646-5342. Internet: www.spindriftinn.com. *Parking: Free! Rack rates: $159–$499 double. Rates include continental breakfast and afternoon tea. AE, DISC, MC, V.*

Where to dine

Cafe Fina
$$$ Fisherman's Wharf, Monterey   ITALIAN/SEAFOOD

This restaurant stands head-and-shoulders above the mostly mediocre eateries on the wharf. After a friendly greeting, a host will lead you into the attractive bilevel dining room, all clean lines and water views, where an Italian-accented seafood menu lets you dine as casually or elaborately as you like. Expect fresh local and flown-in fish, pizzas-for-one from the wood-burning oven, and mesquite-broiled steaks, plus veal Marsala and other authentic Italian specialties.

47 Fisherman's Wharf, Monterey. ☎ 831-372-5200. Internet: www.cafefina.com. *Reservations recommended. Main courses: $8–$17 at lunch, $10–$24 at dinner. AE, DC, DISC, MC, V. Open: Daily 11:30 a.m.–2 p.m.; 5–9 p.m. (open later on Fri and Sat).*

The Culinary Center of Monterey
$$ Monterey   INTERNATIONAL

Conveniently located within walking distance of the aquarium, this combination cooking school/cafe is a welcome addition to the neighborhood.

On fine days, a beef-tip sandwich on the patio overlooking the water can't be beat, although a close second is a lager accompanied with beer-battered onion rings at the bar before dinner. The atmosphere is California casual, and the bustle from the classroom kitchens adds to the family feel. Highly recommended when you need a break from admiring the sealife.

625 Cannery Row (at Hoffman), Monterey. ☎ *831-333-2133. Internet:* www.culinarycenterofmonterey.com. *Reservations recommended. Main courses: $3.50–$17 at breakfast, $8–$9 at lunch, $13–$22 at dinner. MC, V. Open: Tues–Fri 10 a.m.–9 p.m., Sat 8 a.m.–9 p.m., Sun 8 a.m.–6 p.m. Closed Mon.*

The Duck Club
$$$$ Monterey   CONTEMPORARY AMERICAN

A great over-the-water setting and a skilled kitchen using top-quality seasonal ingredients make this a winner in the special-occasion category. It's a bit more clubby and formal than most local restaurants, but it's still comfortable. Chef James Waller has created a contemporary menu that's strong on wood-grilled and -roasted fish and meats (including an excellent caramelized duck, natch). The hearty dishes are pleasing across the board, and the knowledgeable staff will help you pair your choices with a bottle from the award-winning wine list.

In the Monterey Plaza Hotel & Spa, 400 Cannery Row, Monterey. ☎ *831-646-1706. Internet:* www.woodsidehotels.com. *Reservations recommended. Main courses: $18–$26 at dinner. AE, MC, V. Open: Mon–Fri 6:30 a.m.–11 a.m. (to noon on weekends) and 6–9 p.m.*

The Fishwife at Asilomar Beach
$$ Pacific Grove   SEAFOOD

This hugely (and justifiably) popular fish house serves up affordable, top-quality meals in a pleasing ocean-view room that bustles with a friendly mix of tourists and locals. The always-fresh seafood comes grilled, golden-fried, included in excellent house-made pastas, and as tasty sea/garden salads. The lunch menu features sandwiches, too, as well as steak and non-seafood pastas. Kids get their own color-in menu.

1996½ Sunset Dr. (Hwy. 68), at Asilomar Blvd., Pacific Grove. ☎ *831-375-7107. Internet:* www.fishwife.com. *Reservations recommended. Main courses: $6–$10 at lunch, $9–$15 at dinner. AE, DISC, MC, V. Open: Mon–Thurs 11 a.m.–9 p.m.; Fri and Sat 11 a.m.–9:30 p.m.; closed Sun.*

Montrio
$$$ Downtown Monterey   CALIFORNIA

Considered one of the more stylish restaurants in town, Montrio is actually a blend of sizzle and substance that works for couples as well as for families seeking a good meal in grown-up surroundings. The menu, incorporating organic produce when available, includes a hamburger and a turkey sandwich for casual eaters, and raises the bar with crab cakes, rare steaks, or oven-roasted portabello mushrooms for more serious diners. Our paper-topped table included crayons, always a nice touch for busy hands.

414 Calle Principal (at Franklin St.), downtown Monterey. ☎ *831-648-8880. Reservations recommended for dinner. Main courses: $6.50–$11 at lunch, $9.25–$14 at dinner. MC, V. Open: Mon–Sat 11:30 a.m.–5 p.m.; Sun–Thurs 5–10 p.m.; Fri and Sat 5–11p.m.*

Passionfish
$$$ Pacific Grove   CREATIVE AMERICAN

Easily one of the best restaurants in the area. Dinner here is worth the short drive if you are bunking in Monterey. The daily changing menu is innovative yet accessible; fish lovers should investigate the day's Passionfish stew, which might feature mussels, swordfish, salmon, and bright green spinach gnocchi in a butternut squash broth — beautiful to behold and a joy to eat. The wine list cuts a swath through California and beyond, service is subtle, and the crowd enjoys every bite.

701 Lighthouse Ave., at Congress St., Pacific Grove. ☎ *831-655-3311. Internet:* www.passionfish.net. *Reservations recommended. Main courses: $13–$19 at dinner. AE, DISC, MC, V. Open: Sun–Thurs 5–9 p.m.; Fri and Sat 5–10 p.m.; closed Tues.*

Rosine's
$ Monterey   WHOLESOME AMERICAN

If dessert is your downfall, you can't fall much farther than a slice from the triple-layer cakes in the glass counter near the entrance of this cheery downtown restaurant. Rosine's is the place to satisfy morning and midday cravings, with dishes to keep the entire family chewing happily. Breakfast is straightforward and filling with eggs, bacon, pancakes, and oatmeal; lunch consists of sandwiches and salads and, of course, a slice of cake.

434 Alvarado St., at Bonifacio St., Monterey. ☎ *831-375-1400. Main courses: Breakfast $4–$7, lunch $5.50–$7. AE, DISC, MC, V. Open: Mon–Thurs 7:30 a.m.– 9 p.m.; Fri 7:30 a.m.–10 p.m.; Sat 8 a.m.–10 p.m.; Sun 8 a.m.–9 p.m.*

Sea Harvest Fish Market & Restaurants
$–$$ Monterey   SEAFOOD

This friendly place is a fish market first and a restaurant second — which means that you pick your fillet right out of the case. It's grilled or fried up on the spot, and served along with soup or salad at one of the casual tables. Fish simply doesn't come more off-the-boat fresh. The kitchen pre-pares delicious homemade Louis dressing and stellar chowder, too. Perfect if you'd rather avoid the Cannery Row tourist traps in favor of an authentic local meal.

*598 Foam St. (2 blocks inland from Cannery Row, at Hoffman St.), Monterey.
☎ 831-646-0547. Full meals: $7–$16. MC, V. Open: Daily lunch and early dinner (to
8 p.m. Sun–Thurs, to 9 p.m. Fri and Sat).*

Stokes Adobe

$$$$ Monterey   CALIFORNIA-MEDITERRANEAN

This attractive historic adobe gets major points for its Southwest-style
charm and constant raves for its contemporary fare. The main dining
buzzes with energy and flair, while Chef Brandon Miller makes the most
of the local bounty in his innovative but unfussy cuisine. The *San
Francisco Chronicle* calls it "possibly the best food on the Monterey
Peninsula." The restaurant is simply wonderful in every way.

*500 Hartnell St. (at Madison St., just east of Pacific St.), Monterey. ☎ 831-373-1110.
Internet: www.stokesadobe.com. Reservations recommended. Main courses:
$7–$10 at lunch, $15–$26 at dinner. AE, MC, V. Open: Mon–Sat 11:30 a.m.–10 p.m.;
Sun 5–9 p.m.*

Turtle Bay Taqueria

$ Downtown Monterey   MEXICAN

The people behind the local favorite the Fishwife (see "The Fishwife at
Asilomar Beach" listing in this section) have brought casual coastal
Mexican eats to downtown Monterey. Everything is prepared with fresh
regional produce, fish, and meats. Take out or sit down at this cute, colorful joint, where you can nosh on hearty burritos, Caribbean-inspired rice-
and-black bean bowls, substantial salads topped with char-broiled fish and
meats, and well-prepared Mexican staples. Beer and wine is available.

*431 Tyler St. (at Bonifacio St.), downtown Monterey. ☎ 831-333-1500. Internet:
www.fishwife.com/turtlebay.htm. Main courses: $4–$6.50. AE, DC, DISC,
MC, V. Open: Mon–Thurs 11 a.m.–9 p.m.; Fri and Sat 11 a.m.–9:30 p.m.; closed Sun.*

Monterey's top attractions

Cannery Row

Immortalized on the page by John Steinbeck, this former aromatic row of
working sardine canneries is now a temple to the tourist dollar, rife with
mass-appeal shopping, dining, and nightlife. The fish that fed the local
sardine-canning industry — the largest in the world, processing ¼-million
tons in 1945, the year Steinbeck's *Cannery Row* hit bookshelves —
disappeared in the late 1940s from overfishing of the bay. Complaining
about what replaced the canneries is easy (and believe us, locals do), but
even Steinbeck found it to be an improvement over what was. In the '60s
he wrote, "The beaches are clean where they once festered with fish guts
and flies. The canneries that once put up a sickening stench are gone,
their places filled with restaurants, antique shops, and the like."

Stay away if you're averse to this kind of commercialism. But if you're not, you'll find that the T-shirt shops and theme restaurants haven't entirely quashed the row's maritime character. It's a nice renovation, and recent years have brought in a better quality of merchant to supplant some of the cheesier businesses. Highlights include the **Taste of Monterey** Wine Tasting Center (see "More cool stuff to see and do," later in the chapter), and the **Ghirardelli Chocolate Shop and Soda Fountain,** in Steinbeck Plaza, 660 Cannery Row (☎ 831-373-0997), where you can indulge your sweet tooth San Francisco style.

Just off the Pacific Grove end of the row, on Ocean View Boulevard, is the **American Tin Cannery Premium Outlets** (☎ 831-372-1442), which boasts such big names as Reebok and London Fog among its 40 or so stores. Just off the other (Monterey) end is the **Cannery Row Antique Mall,** 471 Wave St. (☎ 831-655-0264), housing two levels of antiques and collectibles dealers.

What's probably the world's finest walking/biking path parallels the row, connecting up with it at a couple of points; for details, see "More cool stuff to see and do," later in this chapter.

Cannery Row: Bayfront west of downtown Monterey, between David and Reeside aves. (the heart of the action is between David and Drake aves.). ☎ 831-373-1902.

Fisherman's Wharf

Cannery Row not cheesy enough for you? Don't worry — Fisherman's Wharf will be. Larger and more commercial than Santa Cruz's wharf but not quite as touristy as San Francisco's, this wooden pier is packed with T-shirt shops, seafood restaurants, and bay-cruise and sportfishing operations out to snare a tourist buck or two. That said, it's still worth a look, primarily because the bay views are to die for, and this is one of Monterey's best perches for watching the frolicking seals and barking sea lions that populate the bay.

If the weather's good, buy yourself a chowder-filled sourdough-bread bowl and park yourself along the pier to watch the offshore action. If it's not, find a bayfront seat at one of the pier's seafood restaurants; the best of the bunch is Italian-accented **Cafe Fina** (see "Where to dine," earlier in the chapter).

If you're the plan-ahead type who'd like to hit the water for some sportfishing or whale-watching, contact these operators:

Monterey Sportfishing and Cruises, 96 Fisherman's Wharf (☎ 800-200-2203 or 831-372-2203; www.montereybaywhalecruise.com), offers daily year-round whale-watching cruises. Be aware, however, that you'll spot only the big'uns — California gray whales — from December through March. Trips run $25 to $39 for adults and $18 to $33 for children 4 to 12.

Chris' Fishing Trips, 48 Fisherman's Wharf (☎ **831-375-5951;** www.chrissfishing.com), has four large (51 to 70 feet) boats leaving on daily deep-sea hunts; cod and salmon are main catches. Full-day trips run $40 to $50 per person.

If you'd rather watch the pros haul in their daily catches, head over to **wharf no. 2** (just next door to Chris's), which is today's working commercial pier. If you'd like to wiggle your toes in the chilly surf, head a bit farther east to **Monterey Bay Park,** where the big white-sand beach gradually slopes into sandy shallows that are just warm enough.

Fisherman's Wharf: Waterfront at the end of Alvarado St., downtown Monterey. Wharf no. 2: At the end of Figueroa St. www.montereywharf.com. *Admission: Free!*

Monterey Bay Aquarium

One of the best, largest, and most enjoyable aquariums on the planet, the Monterey Bay Aquarium sits on the shore of one of the most spectacular marine habitats in the world. It's terrific for all ages, with gliding bat rays and other sea creatures to touch, instructive shows throughout the day (some featuring friendly, spotlight-savvy sea lions), interactive exhibits, and well-written placards at every display that even younger children can understand and enjoy. Exhibits tie in closely to the immediate surroundings, bringing home the reality of the marine environment and the message of conservation.

Have we mentioned how jaw-droppingly awesome this aquarium is? It displays more than 300,000 sea plants and animals representing 570 different species. At the heart of the loftlike, indoor/outdoor complex is a three-story tank replicating a kelp forest, which you can walk around up a spiral ramp, viewing the leopard sharks and bay fish from all sides.

Better yet is the **Outer Bay** exhibit, featuring inhabitants of the open ocean in a phenomenal million-gallon tank with the *largest window on earth.* Almost cooler than the giant green sea turtles, schools of sharp-toothed barracuda, and threatening-looking sharks are the jellyfish, which move in slo-mo, translucent unison like a modern art exhibit come to life.

The aquarium regularly mounts new exhibits, but, unlike art shows, they stay awhile. Currently running until the end of 2004 is **Jellies: Living Art,** which draws parallels between some unusual and extremely beautiful jelly specimens and modern art, video, poetry, and music. Little kids will be irresistibly drawn into the **Splash Zone,** a permanent hands-on exhibition that combines live-animal displays (including tuxedoed penguins) with staff-led learning programs and good old-fashioned play areas.

Aquarium time-savers

The ticket lines just to get into the Monterey Bay Aquarium can be a nightmare, especially in summer. Even on a Tuesday people may wait 15 to 30 minutes throughout the day. Do yourself a favor: Avoid the lines at the gate by arranging for admission tickets in advance.

Many of Monterey's hotels offer packages that include aquarium tickets. Even if you just book a straight daily rate, call ahead and ask the front desk if they sell advance tickets; most do.

If your hotel doesn't sell aquarium tickets, you can order them directly from the aquarium by calling ☎ 800-756-3737; the flat $3-per-order service charge is well worth the time saved. Don't worry about mailing time; the tickets can be left at will-call, where you'll never encounter a wait.

Here are some tips to help you make the most of your aquarium visit:

- Allow a minimum of three hours to see the aquarium; budget four or five if you want to see everything.

- You're allowed to leave and come back in the same day, as long as you get your hand stamped. We highly suggest leaving for lunch or a rest, which will give you a break from the ever-present crowds and rejuvenate you for more looking.

- Review the "Today at the Aquarium" schedule as soon as you arrive, so that you can budget your touring around any live programs you'd like to see (they usually last 15 to 30 minutes).

- If time is limited, head straight for the Outer Bay, followed by a visit to the two-story Sea Otter exhibit, and then a walk along the Habitats Path to the Touch Pool for maximum satisfaction.

886 Cannery Row, Monterey. ☎ *800-756-3737 or 831-648-4937 for tickets, 831-648-4888 for 24-hour information.* www.mbayaq.org. *Admission: $17.95 adults, $14.95 students (13–17 or with college ID) and seniors 65 and over, $7.95 disabled visitors and children 3–12. Open: Daily 10 a.m.–6 p.m. (from 9:30 a.m. on holidays and in summer); check for extended hours in summer.*

Monterey State Historic Park

At the gateway to Fisherman's Wharf sit a dozen or so beautifully restored historic adobes that served as California's capitol under Spanish, Mexican, and initial U.S. rule. The state now collectively protects these buildings as Monterey State Historic Park. Even if you're not a big history buff, check out this area simply for the beauty of the buildings and the setting. You can tour it in a number of ways.

Do-it-yourselfers who just want to explore a bit can stop into the **Visitor Center** at the Maritime Museum and pick up the free Path of History map.

The center shows a free 20-minute continuous-loop film on the history of Monterey. The map will lead you through the historic park and adjacent Old Monterey (the beautifully restored downtown area), highlighting buildings of note along the way. You won't be able to enter the buildings, but the exteriors alone are worth a look.

If you'd like a little more background, take the **guided-tour** route. A number of tours are offered daily; you pay one price, and your ticket is good for any tours you wish to take. We recommend starting with the introductory walking tour (offered at 10 a.m., 11 a.m., and 2 p.m.), which provides a general exterior overview. Follow that tour with a house tour or two (or a garden tour, if you're visiting between May and September) of the buildings that caught your fancy in the course of your initial tour. Highlights include the **Cooper-Molera Adobe,** which depicts family life in the mid-1800s with living-history demonstrations throughout the three-acre complex, and the **Larkin House,** generally considered to be the finest still-standing example of Monterey Colonial architecture.

You can also explore the **Maritime Museum of Monterey (☎ 831-372-2608;** www.mntmh.org/maritime.htm), which tells the story of Monterey's seafaring past, from the Spanish conquistadors through the sardine fishers (note the separate admission fee).

Visitor Center: At the Maritime Museum of Monterey, Stanton Center, 5 Custom House Plaza (at the end of Alvarado St.). ☎ **831-649-7118.** www.mbay.net/~mshp. *Guided tour fees: $5 adults, $3 teens 13–17, $2 kids 6–12. Maritime Museum admission: $3 adults, $2 seniors and teens 13–18, free for kids 12 and under. Open: Visitor center, museum, and most buildings daily 10 a.m.–5 p.m. Call for tour schedules.*

More cool stuff to see and do

Don't miss the **Monterey Peninsula Recreation Trail,** one of the most scenic walking paths in the country. And the good news is that you don't have to hoof it; bikers and in-line skaters are welcome, too. You can pick up the paved path anywhere along Monterey's coastline and follow it into Pacific Grove all the way to Asilomar Beach.

Past the aquarium, in Pacific Grove, you'll ride along the beach side of Ocean View Boulevard. If you look inland, you can admire the gorgeous ocean-facing homes (including some stunning Victorians); on the bay side, gorgeous purple heather and the occasional gnarled cypress separates you from the frolicking sea lions and colorful kayaks gliding along the water.

Go at least as far as **Lovers Point Park** (where Ocean View meets Pacific Avenue in Pacific Grove), a gorgeous grassy point that juts out to sea. With a sheltered beach and tables for picnickers, it's the perfect place to take a load off and relax. From here, push on around the curve, where the road becomes Sunset Drive, and take it past picturesque **Point Pinos Lighthouse** (the oldest continually operating lighthouse in the West, since 1854) to undeveloped **Asilomar State Beach,** where you can spend a quiet day among the dunes, tidal pools, and barking sea lions. Hardy folks can continue along the **17-Mile Drive;** you'll find a gate on Sunset Drive just past Asilomar Avenue, and bicyclists can enter for free. (For more on the 17-Mile Drive, see the "Cruising the 17-Mile Drive," section, later in this chapter.)

Rent your bike or skates from **Adventures by the Sea** (www.adventures bythesea.com), which has a few convenient locations: 299 Cannery Row, across from the Monterey Plaza Hotel (☎ **831-372-1807**); 201 Alvarado Mall, next to the Maritime Museum (☎ **831-648-7235** or 831-648-7236); and at Lovers Point Park in Pacific Grove (summer only; no phone). Bikes cost $6 an hour or $24 per day ($30 overnight); locks and helmets are provided. Skates are $12 for two hours or $24 for the day, with all safety equipment included. Service is very friendly, and gear is in good condition. Advance reservations are gladly accepted.

Kayaking the bay

Monterey Bay is a great place to kayak in summer, even for beginners. You'll glide right by sunbathing sea lions and snacking sea otters as shorebirds swoop through the air and schools of jellyfish skirt just below the surface of the water. (A kayaking companion of mine once called it "a horror movie in the making," but the gooey creatures are simply mesmerizing.)

Again, contact **Adventures by the Sea** (see the preceding section for locations and contact information). Kayaks cost $30 per person for the day, including waterproof gear and instruction to get you started. The bay is glassy enough for fearless novices to set out on their own in summer, but we highly recommend booking a tour if you're the least bit nervous, or if the surf is kicking up. The cost is $50 per person for a two-hour tour, and you should reserve ahead.

Exploring the underwater world

If you're an experienced scuba diver, pack your certification card — this national marine sanctuary is a dive you shouldn't miss. Contact **Monterey Bay Dive Center,** 225 Cannery Row (☎ **800-60-SCUBA** or 831-656-0454; www.mbdc.to), a PADI dive center that can arrange guided dives with pro divemasters. Call at least 48 hours in advance to schedule your dive, sooner if possible. The office is closed on Wednesdays.

Cooking by the bay

The new **Culinary Center of Monterey** (625 Cannery Row, ☎ **831-333-2133;** www.culinarycenterofmonterey) encompasses nearly everything food lovers could wish for, including hands-on cooking classes, a wine bar, a wine shop, kitchenware and cookbooks, a restaurant (see "Where to dine," earlier in the chapter), and gourmet takeout, all located in a bayfront building with those stunning only-in-Monterey views from the patio. The lengthy roster of classes covers everything from sauces to soufflés and bread-baking. Classes run about four hours and include copious tastings so that you don't faint from exertion. Even if you don't cook on vacation, it's fun to browse the retail area, then sit at the bar with a glass of wine and a snack.

Tasting the local grape

Monterey's wine country has really grown up in recent years, becoming California's third most prominent wine-growing region, behind Napa and Sonoma (even the *New York Times* has called it "The Next Napa"). Go ahead, review the shelves at your local wine store or the next wine list you're handed. The number of Monterey labels there may surprise you, as will the number of Monterey County winery names you know: Morgan, Estancia, Jekel, Talbott, J. Lohr, Smith & Hook, Chalone, and many others. The local vintners tend to specialize in chardonnay, pinot noir, and cabernet sauvignon — all popular grapes that are suited to the region's A-1 soil and growing conditions — and they're making some of the best wines that the California wine country has to offer.

For a free map to the region's wineries, the *Monterey Wine Country Wine-Tasting Guide,* stop by **A Taste of Monterey,** the Monterey County Wine and Produce Visitors Center (upstairs at 700 Cannery Row, next to the Bubba Gump Shrimp Co. ☎ **831-646-5446;** www.tastemonterey.com, open daily 11 a.m.–6 p.m.). This bayfront tasting room is a serious wine-tasting center and a great place to learn about, try, and buy local wines — ideal for one-stop shoppers. If you want to wend your way through the local vineyards and tasting rooms in person, ask the friendly staff for tips on where to go.

The map is also available at local visitor centers (see "Gathering More Information" at the end of this chapter).

You can arrange your wine-country tour in advance by going online to the very useful Web site run by the Monterey County Vintners and Growers Association at www.wines.com/monterey. Here you can preview the wineries you'd like to visit and order a free copy of the aforementioned wine-tasting guide (or order an advance copy at ☎ **831-375-9400**).

Side-tripping to the National Steinbeck Center

The **National Steinbeck Center** is a 20-mile drive northeast from Monterey, at 1 Main St. in the agricultural town of Salinas (☎ **831-775-4720;** www.steinbeck.org). The state-of-the-art museum is well worth a visit if you're a fan of the county's most beloved author John Steinbeck (*Cannery Row, East of Eden, Of Mice and Men*).

Even if you're not a literary buff but are simply interested in the history of the region, you'll find the tour engaging, because many of Steinbeck's works were rooted in the local culture. The tour also appeals to film fans, because the multimedia approach makes prime use of the many first-rate, star-studded films that were crafted from Steinbeck's stories.

The museum is deliberately designed to be multi-sensory, and it largely succeeds. A few of the exhibits fall flat — who wants to scrub rags on a fake washboard, and does that really help anybody to better understand *The Grapes of Wrath?* — but most are well thought out and compelling. You can easily make your way through the museum in an hour or two; the kids will have enough to keep them busy. The center is open daily from 10 a.m. to 5 p.m. Admission is $9.95 for adults, $7.95 students and seniors, $6.95 kids 13 to 17, $5.95 kids 6 to 12. To get there from Monterey, take Highway 68 east, which will lead you right through Old Town Salinas to the center (the biggest, brightest building in town — you can't miss it).

Strolling and shopping Old Monterey

Monterey's charmingly restored downtown, inland from Fisherman's Wharf and centered on Alvarado Street, is well worth exploring. History and architecture fans should pick up the **Path of History Walking Tour** (see the section on the Monterey State Historic Park earlier in this chapter), while shoppers should just hit the streets.

Tuesdays, Alvarado Street is blocked off from about 2 p.m. until 8 p.m. for the weekly farmer's market. The local fruit and vegetables are toothsome, if somewhat impractical to pack, but vendors also hawk tie-dyed T's, handmade soaps, candles, olive oil, and such. There's also delicious-smelling barbecued ribs, chicken, and other snacking opportunities.

Wintering with the monarch butterflies in Pacific Grove

Pacific Grove is also known as "Butterfly Town, USA." Why, you ask? Because monarch butterflies, it seems, know a good thing when they see it. Thousands of brilliant black-and-orange monarch butterflies converge on the town annually in October or early November, and stay until February or March. The best place to see them is in the **Monarch Grove Sanctuary,** between Grove Acre Avenue, Ridge Road, and Lighthouse Avenue (☎ **888-PG-MONARCH** or 831-373-7047), where they alight in the eucalyptus trees. Tour guides are usually on hand on the weekends in season to answer questions about the fluttering beauties.

You can also peruse a detailed display on the winged winter visitors at the **Pacific Grove Museum of Natural History,** 165 Forest Ave., at Central Avenue (☎ **831-648-3116**). It's open Tuesday through Sunday from 10 a.m. to 5 p.m., and admission is free.

Leave your nets at home, collectors — the fine for harassing a butterfly in Pacific Grove is $1,000.

Playing with Dennis the Menace

Families with kids should definitely budget a couple of hours to run and jump at the **Dennis the Menace Playground** (☎ **831-646-3866**), at Camino El Estero and Fremont Street, just east of downtown Monterey. Designed by Dennis creator (and Pacific Grove homeboy) Hank Ketcham, the way-cool playground boasts an old steam train to climb on, more colorful jungle gyms than we could count, rope-and-plank suspension bridges, a giant swing ride, and lots more low-tech, old-fashioned fun. It's open Tuesday through Sunday and Monday holidays from 10 a.m. to dusk; admission is free.

Pebble Beach: Nirvana for Golfers

Carved out of the middle of the peninsula is a whole different kind of world, Pebble Beach, where platinum cards and nine-irons rule the day. Rolling championship fairways, lush woodlands, and magnificent vistas are broken only by million-dollar homes and a few ultra-luxury resorts that cater to a big-money, high-profile crowd. In golf terms, this is the big time — Pebble Beach is home to some of the most famous golf courses in the world. It hosts the star-studded annual **AT&T Pebble Beach National Pro-Am,** which has paired club-swinging celebs with PGA Tour stars annually (late January or early February) since 1937, and has played host to multiple U.S. Open Championships throughout the years (including 2000's).

If you need to chat with your banker before making reservations in Pebble Beach, you probably can't afford to stay here. Even if you can, but you're the jeans-and-T-shirts type, Pebble Beach may not be for you. But you don't have to sleep over — or buy into the big-budget golf life — to enjoy the marvelous scenery. Everybody can — for a nominal fee — tour this spectacular territory along the **17-Mile Drive** (see "Cruising the 17-Mile Drive," later in this chapter), a gorgeous private loop road.

If you don't want to stay but do want to play a round of unparalleled golf, you can do that, too — with a little effort and luck.

Where to stay and play at the resorts

The **Pebble Beach Company** (☎ **800-654-9300;** www.pebblebeach.com) runs all the Pebble Beach resorts, making price-shopping and comparing amenities easy. Always ask about packages that may include greens fees in the price. And always check with a travel agent, who may be able to get a better package price at these super-luxury resorts than you can get on your own.

Guests at any of the Pebble Beach resorts get preferred service at all of Pebble Beach's facilities; facilities are accessible to nonguests on a more limited basis. (Read: The high-paying resort guests get first dibs.) See "Hitting the links," later in this chapter, for details on the world-class golf courses, with information on greens fees and tee-time availability for resort guests and nonguests.

Of course, you'll be needing a nice body scrub after all that golf, and you can now get one at the 22,000-foot Mediterranean-style **Spa,** next to Casa Palermo; call ☎ **888-565-7615** or 831-649-7615.

Book your tee times at the same time that you reserve your room, about a year ahead of schedule.

Casa Palermo
$$$$$ Pebble Beach

Pebble Beach's newest resort is very exclusive — just 24 super-luxurious suites housed in a magnificent Mediterranean villa right on the fairway. It feels like a private estate, complete with fireplace-lit living room, cozy library, and clubby billiards room. You'll want for nothing here — and if you do, your personal concierge will be happy to get it for you in a snap. Shockingly priced, but stunning.

17-Mile Drive, Pebble Beach. ☎ *800-654-9300 or 831-625-8557. Fax: 831-644-7960. Internet:* www.pebblebeach.com. *Parking: Free! (At these prices, it should be.) Rack rates: $625–$1,950 cottage or suite, plus $20 gratuity per night. Rates include continental breakfast. AE, DC, DISC, MC, V.*

The Inn at Spanish Bay
$$$$ Pebble Beach

One of the few resorts to hold Mobil's highly coveted five stars — and named the second-best place to stay in North America in *Travel & Leisure*'s 1999 World's Best poll — Spanish Bay is a wonderful choice if you like big resorts. Rooms are large and done in a super-luxurious contemporary style. We'd choose this one over the Lodge at Pebble Beach (see the following listing) for its winning facilities and its location in the heart of the gorgeous Scottish-style Links at Spanish Bay. Still, it's hard to go wrong at either property.

17-Mile Drive, Pebble Beach. ☎ *800-654-9300 or 831-647-7500. Fax: 831-644-7960. Internet:* www.pebblebeach.com. *Parking: Free! Rack rates: from $450 double to $2,425 for the 2-bedroom Presidential suite, plus $20 gratuity per night. AE, DC, DISC, MC, V.*

The Lodge at Pebble Beach
$$$$$ Pebble Beach

The Lodge is somewhat more stately and formal than its sister resort at Spanish Bay, but it's equally elegant, service-oriented, and satisfying. The amenity-laden, utterly luxurious guest rooms are scattered throughout the glorious oceanfront property — most convenient for golfers set on teeing off on the legendary Pebble Beach Golf Links.

17-Mile Drive, Pebble Beach. ☎ *800-654-9300 or 831-624-3811. Fax: 831-644-7960. Parking: Free! Rack rates: from $500 double, $1,600 suite, plus $15 gratuity per night. AE, DC, DISC, MC, V.*

Cruising the 17-Mile Drive

The only private toll road west of the Mississippi, the stunning 17-Mile Drive is well worth the $8 per auto price of admission.

Bicyclists can enter for free; see "More cool stuff to see and do," earlier in the chapter, for details on renting bikes. The ride is easy — mainly downhill — toward Carmel, but average folks may find it a real chore to make the uphill climb back. If you're not a long-distance biker, either stick to the Pacific Grove portion of the drive, or arrange for a pick-up at the **Lodge at Pebble Beach** or in Carmel.

The spectacular loop wends through the Monterey Peninsula, linking Pacific Grove to the outskirts of Carmel along the coast, then turning inland, hitching up with the main highway for a moment, and then heading back toward Pacific Grove through the **Del Monte Forest.** It takes you along the stunning rocky coastline, past the most beautiful cypress trees on the peninsula, and through unspoiled woodlands. (FYI: The gnarled, windbent cypress trees that lend the peninsula such a distinct beauty are native only to this region; they can live to be 4,000 years old.) You'll see championship golfers and native deer cohabiting on some of the most scenic golf greens in the world, and watch sea lions and harbor seals bark and cavort in the whitecaps just offshore. The only buildings you'll see are massive — and we do mean massive — luxury homes tucked discreetly among the trees, and three world-class resorts, should you wish to seek them out (see the previous section).

You can enter the drive through five different gates, paying your fee in exchange for a handy-dandy full-color map and brochure of the highlights along the route. You're likely to use one of these three:

✔ From Monterey or Pacific Grove, the most convenient gate is the **Pacific Grove Gate.** Follow Ocean View Boulevard from Monterey to Sunset Drive; after the road turns inland, you'll soon see 17-Mile Drive on your right.

✔ From Carmel, enter at the **Carmel Gate;** from downtown, turn right off Ocean Avenue onto San Antonio Avenue (one block before the beach).

✔ If you're just passing by the peninsula and want to take a gander at this remarkable real estate, enter at the **Highway 1 Gate,** just off the main road at the Holman Highway exit.

Leisurely dining along the 17-Mile Drive

If you're not staying in Pebble Beach but you'd like to enjoy an elegant breakfast, lunch, or dinner here (and maybe a glimpse of a luxe resort in the process), book a table at **Roy's Pebble Beach** ($$$$), at the Inn at Spanish Bay (☎ 831-647-7423). Roy's is the best of Hawaii celebrity chef Roy Yamaguchi's mainland restaurants. Expect well-prepared Euro-Asian cuisine with inspired sauces and pleasing California and island twists. Entrees are pricey, averaging in the $20s, but keeping the bill down is easy if you make a meal of Roy's signature wood-fired pizzas or choose from the extensive appetizers list; don't miss those killer short ribs (better than dessert!).

If you'd rather put together a picnic to enjoy along the drive, stop into the **Pebble Beach Market** ($$), a gourmet deli at the Lodge at Pebble Beach, which has a lawn where you can spread out and enjoy your ready-to-eat meats, veggies, cheeses, and other gourmet goodies.

Allot a leisurely afternoon for the drive. If you don't have a few hours to spare, you can see part of the route by using it to travel between Monterey and Carmel (or vice-versa). The disadvantage of this plan is that you'll have to choose between coastal and inland portions; we say go coastal, but it all depends on your aesthetic sensibilities.

The map features about 20 points of interest, and you can use pullouts at scenic points all along the drive. If you'd rather avoid a lot of stop and go, focus on these natural highlights:

- ✔ **Point Joe,** on the northern end of the coast, which offers a gorgeous vantage for spotting migrating whales between December and March.

- ✔ About midway down the coast are **Seal Rock** and **Bird Rock,** where you can spot countless gulls, cormorants, and other offshore birds, plus harbor seals and sea lions, gathering just offshore.

- ✔ **Fanshell Overlook** offers awesome views of Fanshell Beach, where harbor seals gather to birth their pups each spring.

- ✔ **Cypress Point Lookout** offers the drive's most spectacular coastal view and is ideal for sunset collectors.

- ✔ A little farther down the coast is the famous **Lone Cypress,** one of the peninsula's most distinctive and mesmerizing images. The magnificently gnarled, windblown tree looks as if it's growing right out of bare rock, but its insistent roots have actually burrowed deep through the rock's crevices. You're not allowed to get up close, but the view from the deck beside the parking area is magnificent.

You can see the best forest-and-ocean panorama from **Huckleberry Hill,** along the inland curve a little bit north of the Highway 1 Gate, which is the highest point along the drive.

Hitting the links

We won't lie to you — getting a tee time on one of the prime Pebble Beach courses without booking a room at one of the resorts is nearly impossible, even in the off-season (November through March). But try.

Pebble Beach Golf Links, The Links at Spanish Bay, Spyglass Hill Golf Course, all on the 17-Mile Drive, and **Del Monte Golf Course,** in Monterey, are all administered by the Pebble Beach Company (☎ 800-654-9300; www.pebblebeach.com). If you'd like to book a lesson, call the **Pebble Beach Golf Academy** (☎ 831-622-1310), home to two of *Golf Magazine's* Top 100 Teachers in America for 1999–2000, Laird Small and Dan Pasqueriello.

✔ **Pebble Beach Golf Links,** at the Lodge at Pebble Beach, is the Big Kahuna of Pebble Beach golf courses. A links legend since 1919, this par-72, 6,799-yard rolling oceanfront beauty regularly ranks among the top five courses in the world, and many of golf's biggest names have called it the finest course they've ever played. This is a mature course with old-root trees and massive bunkers, at one with the land like few courses on earth.

Unless you're willing to foot the bill for a Pebble Beach hotel room, don't get your heart set on playing here, though — nonguests can book tee times just a day in advance, which means you have to get very lucky and catch a last-minute cancellation (near to impossible). And expect to pay to play, big time: Greens fees are $350 for resort guests and $375 for nonguests.

✔ **Spyglass Hill Golf Course,** at Stevenson Drive and Spyglass Hill Road in Pebble Beach, Robert Trent Jones, Sr.'s par-72, 6,859-yard legend is one of the toughest golf courses in the world. Expect to test your skills — and every club in your bag — if you get to play here. Greens fees are $260 for resort guests and $285 for nonguests. Nonguests can book tee times up to a month in advance for this course — easier to get on than Pebble Beach, but still tough. (Even winter tee times book up a month in advance.)

Your best bets for garnering available tee times are the **Del Monte Golf Course** and **The Links at Spanish Bay,** where nonguests can book up to two months in advance. You should call as early as possible, even marking your calendar to dial at the two-month and one-month mark. If that fails, just call back and try to snag a cancellation.

✔ **Del Monte Golf Course,** at the Hyatt on Sylvan Road and Hwy. 1 in Monterey, is the oldest course west of the Mississippi. This par-72, 6,339-yard inland course has been challenging golfers since 1897, as well as wowing them with its tree-lined charm. And by Pebble Beach terms, greens fees are reasonable: $95 plus $20 for the cart.

✔ Designed by Robert Trent Jones, Jr., Tom Watson, and Frank Tatum, **The Links at Spanish Bay,** at the Inn at Spanish Bay, is the foremost Scottish linksland-style course in the United States; Tom Watson has said "It's so much like Scotland, you can almost hear the bagpipes." Greens fees are $215 for guests, $240 for nonguests.

It's an even playing field for tee times at the public **Poppy Hills Golf Course,** just off 17-Mile Drive on Lopez Road (☎ **831-625-2035;** www. ncga.org/poppy.htm), where everybody has an equal shot. Robert Trent Jones, Jr., designed this par-72, 6,865-yard course, which is a favorite among duffers. The course accepts reservations up to 30 days in advance. Call as early as possible within that time frame for your choice of tee times, but you can usually snare a slot a week in advance. Greens fees are lower, too: $125 Monday through Friday, and $150 Saturday, Sunday, and holidays.

Carmel-by-the-Sea and Carmel Valley

If Monterey sounds too touristy, Pebble Beach too *chi-chi,* and Big Sur's accommodations too woodsy or rustic, Carmel is the place for you. This high-end haven is among the stars of the California coast, and one of the loveliest towns in all of America. It's more like an elite artists' colony than a mass-market tourist town, with galleries and boutiques galore, quaint views or sweeping vistas at every turn, and a relaxed vibe that whispers "away from it all" like sweet nothings in your ear.

Carmel exudes charisma by the bucketload. This village displays its assets like a starlet in Cannes, with picture-perfect, cypress-dotted streets leading gradually downhill to one of the most spectacular beaches on the California coast. And 15 minutes away up Carmel Valley Road, the ocean gives way to mountains, ranches, and resorts.

Not everyone adores Carmel, however. For one, complaints of commercialism abound from those who knew it when, before Saks Fifth Avenue and all those cute inns set up shop. And like its most famous resident, Clint Eastwood (who served a high-profile stint as mayor a few years back), virtually all the residents are seven-figure types. As a result, prices are high across the board, restaurants are more upscale than casual, and an air of elitism prevails.

Also, Carmel isn't really suited for the children; romance-seeking couples rule the day here. If you have the kids in tow, you'll probably be happier basing yourself in the Carmel Valley, Monterey, or Pacific Grove instead. You will find, however, that no one's more welcome in Carmel than the family pet; this is West Coast nirvana for those who travel with Fido.

Carmel is rather quiet and not overloaded with sightseeing "attractions" per se. Visiting is more about slowing down a bit — browsing the boutiques, ambling the back streets to admire the fabulous homes, and strolling that breathtaking beach. If you're looking for relaxation, stay awhile. All you need is a day or so to explore the village itself, but Carmel also makes a good base for tooling around the entire peninsula, and even the stupendous Big Sur Coast (see Chapter 17).

Orienting yourself and getting around

Carmel-by-the-Sea is petite and easy to navigate. The town is laid out on a basic grid pattern, with Ocean Avenue running due west from Highway 1 to Carmel Beach and serving as the village's main drag.

Parallel to Ocean Avenue run numbered avenues: Fourth, Fifth, and Sixth avenues to the north, and Seventh and Eighth avenues to the south. (The town extends farther in each direction, but these streets shape downtown.)

Perpendicular to Ocean and the numbered avenues run a number of name streets: Mission Street, San Carlos, Dolores, Lincoln, and so on. You can get an easy-to-follow, cartoony map of downtown labeling most major businesses almost everywhere about town; for a preview, point your Web browser to www.carmelfun.com. **Carmel Valley** is reached via G16, Carmel Valley Road, just south of Carmel-by-the-Sea on Highway 1.

Note that this quaint village has no need for such big-city affectations as street addresses. Thus, all addresses are given in general terms: San Carlos Street at Seventh, Sixth between Lincoln and Monte Verde, and so on.

Everything in town is within walking distance. Most likely, you'll be able to park your car at your inn or motel and leave it there for the duration of your stay. Parking has strict time limits in the downtown area, but moving a few blocks off Ocean Avenue into more residential territory usually yields less restricted space. A free lot sits at Third Avenue and Torres Street, and another at the beach, plus a paid lot at Eighth Avenue and San Carlos Street.

Where to stay

Carmel is so completely adorable that it's a hugely popular weekend destination. Book well in advance if you're planning a visit over a Friday or Saturday night. And be aware that most places require a two-night minimum stay on weekends. Accommodations upvalley are a little easier to reserve, but you'll still want advance reservations in the summer.

You may want to try booking your room through a free reservations service such as **Monterey Peninsula Reservations** (☎ 888-655-3424; www.monterey-reservations.com); **Resort II Me** (☎ 800-757-5646; www.resort2me.com); or the **Carmel Area Reservation Service** (☎ 888-434-3891 or 831-659-7061; www.carmel-california.com). You can sometimes get a better rate through these services than you can obtain by calling direct, and they'll make alternative suggestions if the suggestions in this section are full.

Count on 10% in taxes being tacked on to your final hotel bill.

Cobblestone Inn
$$–$$$ Carmel-by-the-Sea

This charming B&B offers flowery, romantic accommodations at moderate prices. The 24 rooms encircle a lovely courtyard. Each room features a fireplace, TV (not a given in B&Bs), and minifridge. The staff serves afternoon goodies in a warm and lovely living room. On the down side, the cheapest rooms are very small, and only two of the rooms with private baths have tub/shower combos. But the sacrifices are minimal considering the charms. Bikes are available for exploring.

Junipero St. between Seventh and Eighth aves. ☎ 800-833-8836 or 831-625-5222. Fax: 831-625-0478. Internet: www.foursisters.com. Parking: Free! Rack rates: $125–$255 double. Rates include full breakfast and afternoon wine and hors d'oeuvres. AE, DC, MC, V.

Cypress Inn
$$–$$$ Carmel-by-the-Sea

Carmel's pet-friendliest hotel is famous for being co-owned by screen legend Doris Day, whose movie posters grace the bar. This Moorish-Mediterranean inn is beautifully styled, but the building is old — we were dismayed to see space heaters in the guest rooms. Some of the standard doubles are small and on the spare side as well (and #111 is dark). You can enjoy breakfast in the lovely courtyard on nice days, and the comfy fireplace-lit living room is a guest magnet in the evenings. The service is accommodating.

Lincoln St. and Seventh Ave. ☎ *800-443-7443 or 831-624-3871. Fax: 831-624-8216. Internet:* www.cypress-inn.com. *Parking: Free! Rack rates: $125–$235 double, from $295 suite. Rates include a generous continental breakfast spread. AE, DISC, MC, V.*

Los Laureles Lodge
$$ Carmel Valley

Carmel Valley has a number of expensive resorts, but us regular folk are quite fond of this historic ranch dating from 1830. Courtyard doubles, converted from former stables that once housed the Vanderbilt thoroughbreds, are comfortable and simply decorated around warm knotty-pine walls. Families with young children can cozy up in a Surrey Lane room, large enough for a queen bed and pullout sofa. There's a swimming pool, an outdoor bar so you don't have to supply your own piña coladas, and an extremely good restaurant. If you brought the kids, this is an especially pleasant place to stay.

313 West Carmel Valley Rd., Carmel Valley. ☎ *800-533-4404 or 831-659-2233. Fax: 831-659-0481. Internet:* www.loslaureles.com. *Parking: Free! Rack rates: $90–$155 double, from $175 suite. Ask about golf, horseback riding, bicycling, and fly-fishing packages. AE, MC, V.*

Mission Ranch
$$–$$$ Carmel-by-the-Sea

With the kindly assistance of Dirty Harry himself, Clint Eastwood, this 1850s farmhouse and its outlying buildings have been transformed into an elegant complex worthy of Martha Stewart. The ranch lies on the outskirts of town, a good walk away from the village, but sheep-filled pastures and ocean views make it almost picture-perfect. Rooms vary depending on price and location, but all have an appealingly cozy ranch-land vibe. On-site is an excellent restaurant, plus a fitness room and tennis courts. No pool, however; too cold.

26270 Dolores St. (near the Carmel Mission). ☎ *800-538-8221 or 831-624-6436. Fax: 831-626-4163. Parking: Free! Rack rates: $95–$275 double, $225–$250 1- or 2-bedroom cottage. Rates include continental breakfast. AE, MC, V.*

Quail Lodge Resort and Golf Club
$$$$–$$$$$ Carmel Valley

Owned by the Peninsula Group — one of the world's finest hotel chains — this magical destination resort spreads across 850 pastoral acres with gorgeous gardens, sparkling lakes, wildlife-dotted woodlands, and championship fairways. Luxuries abound in the spacious French-country rooms, and the extensive facilities — tennis courts, pools, hiking paths, and more — will keep you happy for days on end.

8205 Valley Greens Dr., Carmel Valley (4 miles east of Carmel-by-the-Sea). ☎ *888-624-2888 or 831-624-2888. Fax: 831-624-3726. Internet:* www.quaillodge. com. *Parking: Free! Rack rates: Apr–Nov $275–$370 double, $450–$685 suite, plus $15 service charge per night. Ask about golf, romance, and holiday packages. AE, DC, MC, V.*

Village Inn
$$ Carmel-by-the-Sea

This superbly located motel is Carmel's best bet for budget-minded travelers. The cute rooms have a bit more charm than you usually find at such bargain rates, as well as fridges and nice, newish baths. The attractive property is spic-and-span, and management is conscientious and friendly. The double queens are a good bet for families.

Junipero and Ocean aves. ☎ *800-346-3864 or 831-624-3864. Fax: 831-626-6763. Internet:* www.carmelvillageinn.com. *Parking: Free! Rack rates: $69–$200 double, $108–$380 suite. Rates include continental breakfast. AE, MC, V.*

Where to dine

It's really hard to go wrong dining out in Carmel. The locals have loads of discretionary income, so they can afford to demand the best. Of the more than 60 restaurants in this tiny town, most are better than average. This section describes our favorites — but if you pass something else that strikes your fancy, chances are good that it won't disappoint you.

Reservations are a must on weekends.

Cafe Gringo
$$ Carmel-by-the-Sea   MEXICAN

Tucked away in a charming courtyard, Cafe Gringo offers pleasing nouveau-Mexican fare. Chef Zenda Willemstein takes a creative, health-conscious approach to the Tex-Mex style of cooking, using all-fresh ingredients and shunning lard and deep-frying. The food is zesty and flavorful, but not too spicy for uninitiated palates. Choose between the colorful, casual dining room or the heated brick patio.

In the Paseo San Carlos, San Carlos St. between Ocean and Seventh aves. ☎ *831-626-8226. Reservations accepted. Main courses: $8–$14. AE, MC, V. Open: Lunch and dinner Thurs–Tues.*

Caffé Napoli/Little Napoli
$$ Carmel-by-the-Sea   ITALIAN

These mirror-image sister restaurants bring a true slice of Naples to Carmel. Between the charming decor (think red gingham, braids of garlic), the excellent country-style cooking, the extensive all-Italian wine list, and the low prices, it's no wonder that these restaurants inspire such local loyalty. Expect hearty favorites like crispy-crust pizzas, hand-stuffed canneloni, and Neapolitan-style seafood. Everything's fresh from the field or the bay. This restaurant is terrific — and a grade-A value to boot.

Caffé Napoli on Ocean Ave. near Lincoln St. ☎ 831-625-4033. Little Napoli in the El Paseo Building, Dolores St. between Ocean and Seventh aves. ☎ 831-626-6335. Internet: www.littlenapoli.com. *Reservations highly recommended for dinner. Main courses: $9–$15. MC, V. Open: Mon–Thurs 11:30 a.m.–9:30 p.m.; Fri–Sun 11:30 a.m.–10 p.m.*

Casanova
$$$$ Carmel-by-the-Sea FRENCH/ITALIAN

In a town full of dreamy restaurants, this is far and away the most romantic. The Mediterranean-style house (former home of Charlie Chaplin's cook) spills over with candlelit old-world charm. But don't let all this talk of ambience fool you: The French-Italian menu is top-notch, the service is excellent, and the 30,000-bottle wine cellar is an award-winner. Considering that the meals include antipasti and dessert, prices aren't bad, either.

Fifth Ave. between San Carlos and Mission sts. ☎ 831-625-0501. Internet: www.casanovarestaurant.com. *Reservations recommended. Three-course prix-fixe: $22–$40. MC, V. Open: Mon–Sat 11:30 a.m.–3 p.m.; Mon–Sun 5–10 p.m.; Sun brunch 10 a.m.–3 p.m.*

Flying Fish Grill
$$$–$$$$ Carmel-by-the-Sea PACIFIC RIM/SEAFOOD

Chef/owner Kenny Fukumoto's dark and intimate pan-Asian seafood house is one of our favorite restaurants on the Monterey Peninsula. Expect creative, beautifully prepared seafood dishes with Japanese accents — almond sea bass and *yosenabe* (clay-pot seafood) are shining stars on the universally pleasing menu — plus specialties like rib-eye shabu-shabu for nonseafood eaters. Great!

In Carmel Plaza, Mission St. between Ocean and Seventh aves. ☎ 831-625-1962. Reservations highly recommended. Main courses: $16–$25. AE, DISC, MC, V. Open: Daily 5–9:30 p.m. (closed Tues in winter).

Jack London's Bar & Grill
$$–$$$ Carmel-by-the-Sea AMERICAN

Come here when you tire of Carmel's high prices and pretentious airs. This quarter-century-old bar and restaurant is a completely unpretentious hangout that has nevertheless been lauded by the *New York Times* for its charms. The huge menu ranges from burgers and chicken-breast sandwiches to pizzas, Tex-Mex specialties, and Black Angus steaks. It offers great bathtub-size margaritas, too.

San Carlos St. at Fifth Ave. ☎ *831-624-2336. Main courses: $8.50–$21. AE, DISC, MC, V. Open: Daily 11:30 a.m. to midnight (bar open till 2 a.m.).*

Exploring Carmel-by-the-Sea

At the foot of Ocean Avenue sits **Carmel Beach,** one of the most heavenly beaches in the United States, if not the world. A wide crescent of white sand skirts gorgeous, tidepool-dotted Carmel Bay. A screen of gnarled cypresses separates street from sand, and the emerald-green cliffs of Pebble Beach rise in the distance. Swimming is a no-no, because the waves are too rough (and the water's too cold year-round), but the beach is great for strolling, picnicking, and playing fetch with Fido, who's allowed to run off-leash here (you'll see lots of happy dogs cavorting in the sand). Take time to walk along this stretch of beach no matter what season you're visiting; walk north for the best views.

The small parking lot at the end of Ocean gets crowded year-round, but you can often find additional spots along Scenic Road, from which wooden staircases lead down to the beach at various points along the road. (Note that the only restrooms are in the parking lot on Ocean Avenue.)

If you want a little sand space to yourself, follow Scenic Road south around the promontory to **Carmel River State Beach,** a more remote, white-sand, dune-dotted stretch that's a paradise for birders.

Shopping and strolling

Shopping is tops among Carmel activities. Pricey apparel and home-furnishing boutiques, jewelry stores, and art galleries line the streets of downtown. Don't expect to find anything too funky; still, you can do lots of one-of-a-kind browsing. Gallery hounds should pick up the free **"Carmel Gallery Guide,"** available throughout town. Be sure to peek into Carmel's various courtyards, which often hide some of the best finds. The alfresco **Carmel Plaza,** at Ocean Avenue and Mission Street (☎ 831-624-0137), houses about 50 shops, including familiar names like Saks Fifth Avenue and Banana Republic.

Stepping into the past

Mission San Carlos Borromeo del Rio Carmelo, more commonly known as the **Carmel Mission,** 3080 Rio Rd. (☎ 831-624-3600; www.carmel mission.org), is one of the largest and most beautiful of the 21 Spanish missions established by Father Junípero Serra, Spanish founder of California's mission chain. Built in a baroque style with a towering Moorish bell tower, it has been in continuous operation since 1771. The burnished terra-cotta facade and soaring, romantic curves make it worth strolling by even if you don't go inside. Still, history buffs will want to make the effort.

It's open for self-guided tours daily from 9:30 a.m. to 4:15 p.m. (from
10:30 a.m. on Sunday), with extended hours in summer. Admission is
$2, $1 for kids. To reach the mission, take San Carlos Street south from
town and follow the signs, or take Rio Road west off Highway 1 and
follow it for a half-mile.

If you'd like to learn more about the local history and color, take a
two-hour guided walk with **Carmel Walks** (☎ **831-642-2700**; www.
carmelwalks.com). The walks take place Tuesday through Friday at
10 a.m., Saturday at 10 a.m. and 2 p.m., for $20 per person. Tours leave
from the Pine Inn at Lincoln Street and Ocean Avenue; call ahead to
reserve your spot.

Sampling Big Sur's natural beauty

The spectacular beauty of the Big Sur Coast (see Chapter 17) begins
just 3 miles south of Carmel-by-the-Sea at **Point Lobos State Reserve**
(☎ **831-624-4909**; www.pointlobos.org). A cypress-dotted headland,
the Big Sur Coast has been variously called "the greatest meeting of
land and water in the world" and "the crown jewel of the state parks
system." It's a natural wonderland, all right, with sea lions, otters,
harbor seals, and seabirds populating the ocean coves; spectacular
coastal vistas (perfect for whale-watching in winter); picnic areas; and
miles of hiking trails. The entrance fee is $3 per car, which includes a
trail map. Open from 9 a.m. to dusk. Arrive early, especially on weekends; if the lot is full, you'll have to wait for someone to leave before
you can enter.

Gathering More Information

For peninsula-wide information before you arrive, point your Web
browser to www.monterey.com, or contact the **Monterey Peninsula
Visitors and Convention Bureau** on their 24-hour information hotline
(☎ **831-649-1770**). Another useful source of information is the
Monterey County Convention and Visitors Bureau (☎ **888-221-1010**;
www.gomonterey.org). For Carmel-specific information, you can call
☎ **888-434-3891** to order the "Carmel Sample Packet" ($12.95), or visit
www.carmel-california.com.

In Monterey

Stop in at the well-staffed and well-stocked **Monterey Visitors Center,**
near downtown at Camino El Estero and Franklin St. (one block inland
from Del Monte Avenue). It is open Monday through Saturday from 9 a.m.
to 6 p.m. (to 5 p.m. November through March), Sunday from 9 a.m. to
5 p.m. (to 4 p.m. November through March).

There's also a staffed information desk at the **Maritime Museum** at
Monterey State Historic Park, near the entrance to Fisherman's Wharf.

In Carmel

You can pick up information from the **Carmel Business Association,** upstairs next to the Eastwood Building on San Carlos Street between 5th and 6th avenues in Carmel-by-the-Sea (☎ **831-624-2522**). You can also call ahead to have a visitor's guide sent to you. The office is open Monday through Friday from 9 a.m. to 5 p.m. and Saturday from 11 a.m. to 3 p.m. (check for Sunday hours in summer).

You can also stop by the **Monterey County Visitors Center** at the Crossroads Shopping Center, off Highway 1 at the Rio Road exit, Carmel; open Monday through Friday from 10 a.m. to 5:30 p.m., Saturday from 10 a.m. to 6 p.m., and Sunday from 11:30 a.m. to 5:30 p.m.

Chapter 17

The Spectacular Big Sur Coast

. . . .

In This Chapter

▶ Enjoying the state's most spectacular natural scenery

▶ Choosing the best places to stay and dine

▶ Exploring Julia Pfeiffer Burns State Park and other highlights

▶ Watching sea lions, otters, and seals at Point Lobos State Reserve

. . . .

*F*ew shorelines in the world are as breathtaking as the Big Sur Coast. Skirted by rugged shores and crescent-shaped bays, this pristine wilderness of towering redwoods and rolling hills is tranquil, unspoiled, romantic, dramatic, and overwhelmingly beautiful — and, as you may have guessed by now, perfect for a true getaway. If you really want quiet, this is the place to find it.

Although, technically, a Big Sur Village does exist (about 29 miles south of the Monterey Peninsula on Highway 1), blink and you'll miss it. *Big Sur* actually refers to the gorgeous 90-mile stretch of land between Carmel-by-the-Sea and San Simeon. The main thoroughfare and scenic byway is Highway 1, blessed on one side by the 167,000-acre Ventana Wilderness, with the splendid Santa Lucia mountain range rising just beyond, and on the other by the wild, spectacular coast. The region is at its most woodsy and breathtaking in the northern half, but the entire coastline drive is stunning.

Development is minimal, and you'll find little more to do here than commune with nature — but oh, what nature it is! Make time to enjoy it. Hike the state parks, walk the beaches, stop regularly along the drive to watch windsurfers pirouette among the waves and sea lions sun on the rocks, or just perch yourself atop the cliffs and take in the sea breeze. You won't believe the effect Big Sur can have on your soul: Modern life fades into the background as you become absorbed in Mother Nature's world.

The Big Sur Coast

ACCOMMODATIONS ■

Big Sur Lodge **4**
Deetjen's Big Sur Inn **7**
Glen Oaks **2**
Post Ranch Inn **5**
Ragged Point Inn & Resort **9**
Ventana Inn & Spa **6**

DINING ◆

Big Sur River Inn **3**
Cielo **6**
Deetjen's Big Sur Inn **7**
Glen Oaks Restaurant **2**
Nepenthe/Cafe Kevah **8**
Rocky Point Restaurant & Lounge **1**

The flip side to all this poetic waxing, however, is that Big Sur requires some effort to enjoy. With just one winding, hairpin-plagued lane in each direction, Highway 1 is slow going and can be tummy-turning. Tourist facilities along the route are limited, so don't expect a gas station every few miles, or any chain motels or fast-food joints at all. The region's remoteness has fostered a special breed of local: quiet types who fiercely protect their privacy, their rustic lifestyle, and the unspoiled nature around them. A hippie vibe still prevails — most residents came here to get away from it all, and they mean to keep it that way. Stay off private property and unmarked driveways, and stick to clearly marked pullouts, public areas, and parks. Take a cue from the locals: Appreciate Big Sur for what it is — glorious and unspoiled. Enjoy it, respect it, and leave no mark. Pack out everything you bring in.

Timing Your Visit

Like much of California's central and northern coast, Big Sur is at its clearest, warmest, and sunniest best in Indian summer — September and October. Summer is the busiest season traffic-wise and hotel-wise, so plan ahead and expect to pay top dollar.

What's the tradeoff for cooler weather in winter and spring? Clear skies, little fog, no crowds, lower hotel rates, and fabulous offshore views of the mammoth gray whales that migrate from Alaska to Mexico and back again between November and April. For a month-by-month breakdown of the seasons and events, point your Web browser to www.bigsurcalifornia.org and click on Calendar.

Leave yourself plenty of time to mosey along the Big Sur Coast. Even though the distance is only about 110 miles from Carmel to San Simeon, you can't really drive the twisty-turny road in less than three hours. And trust me — you don't want to.

Allow a whole day for the drive. New and exciting views present themselves at every turn, with plenty of vista points for stopping. An entire day gives you time to go hiking at one of the parks along the way, along with time for a picnic or a leisurely lunch.

If you want to spend more time among the trees, book a place to stay for a night or two. However, be aware that the accommodations in this funky neck of the woods fall into two categories: big-money luxurious, or comfort-challenged rustic. You won't find any affordable country inns or reliable chain motels in between, and TVs are not a common amenity no matter which budget level you choose. If the choices in "Where to Stay in Big Sur," later in this chapter, don't suit you but you still want more than a day to explore Mother Nature's handiwork, base yourself just to the north on the Monterey Peninsula (Carmel is particularly convenient) or near Hearst Castle to the south for easy access.

Getting There

You can access all the main attractions via Highway 1. If you're dedicating a day to the drive, set out early so that you can take full advantage of daylight. The slow, curving drive is not only a drag at night, but you can't see any of the great scenery — so why bother? Leaving early is especially important if you're heading north, as the region's finest parks, Pfeiffer Big Sur and Julia Pfeiffer Burns state parks, are about two-thirds of the way up the coast.

Where to Stay in Big Sur

Expect 10½% in taxes to be tacked on to your hotel bill.

Camping is certainly the truest way to experience this unspoiled region. If camping's your thing, visit www.bigsurcalifornia.org for a complete list of campground options.

Big Sur Lodge
$$ Big Sur

Tucked among the redwoods of Pfeiffer Big Sur State Park are these 61 rustic cabins, many large enough to house families. Well-kept, spacious, and newly remodeled, all have private baths and patios with lovely views, but no TV, telephone, or even an alarm clock to interrupt as you meditate on nature. Spend a bit more for a fireplace and/or kitchenette if you can afford it; nights get cool, and who wants to run out for coffee in the morning? A restaurant, country store, and heated pool, plus all park amenities, are on-site.

In Pfeiffer Big Sur State Park, Hwy. 1, Big Sur (26 miles south of Carmel). ☎ *800-424-4787 or 831-667-3100. Fax: 831-667-3110. Internet:* www.bigsurlodge.com. *Parking: Free! Rack rates: $99–$219 1-bedroom cottage, $129–$229 2-bedroom cottage. Rates include day-use fees for five Big Sur-area parks. AE, MC, V.*

Deetjen's Big Sur Inn
$$–$$$ Big Sur

Built by a Norwegian homesteader and his missus in the 1930s and now a national historic site, Deetjen's is quintessential Big Sur: Lovely, rustic, and funky to a fault. If you don't mind sacrificing creature comforts for rustic-cozy, you'll love the oddball collection of hand-hewn cabins. The cabins do not include phones, TVs, or central heating. Walls are single-board thin, so don't pass on a fire-heated room — even in summer — and don't expect privacy or quiet (families with kids under 12 must book two adjoining rooms). The restaurant is one of the local best. Book well ahead, because the inn fills up two months or more in advance.

Hwy. 1, Big Sur (30 miles south of Carmel). ☎ *831-667-2377. Parking: Free! Rack Rates: $85–$170 double with shared bath, $120–$190 double with private bath. MC, V.*

Glen Oaks
$–$$ Big Sur

This well-run, well-maintained post-adobe-style motel is Big Sur's best standard lodging. The basic rooms are clean and comfortable and, in true Big Sur fashion, have no TVs or phones. Rooms with two queen-size beds can accommodate families. Two cottages feature well-outfitted kitchens and tub/shower combos in lieu of the standard walk-in showers. The dinner-only restaurant is a cozy local favorite, and a cafe next door serves breakfast and lunch.

Hwy. 1, (1 mile north of Pfeiffer Big Sur State Park, 25 miles south of Carmel). ☎ 831-667-2105. Fax: 831-667-1105. Internet: www.glenoaksbigsur.com. *Parking: Free! Rack rates: $69–$104 double, $130–$145 cottage. No credit cards.*

Post Ranch Inn
$$$$$ **Big Sur**

Wide expanses of glass bring the outside in to 30 gorgeous, amenity-filled oceanfront cottages, spread out over 98 unspoiled, four-star acres at this environmentally friendly, ultra-exclusive resort. No TVs, but you'll have CD players and everything else you could want — even your own private slice of Big Sur to explore. A full menu of spa treatments is available in your room or outdoors — you decide. The restaurant is excellent, too. This place is ridiculously expensive (not to mention a tad pretentious), but worth every penny. Under 18s are not invited to stay here.

Hwy. 1 (28 miles south of Carmel). ☎ 800-527-2200 or 831-667-2200. Fax: 831-667-2824. Internet: www.postranchinn.com. *Rack rates: $455–$835 double, $700 for 2–6 people. Rates include continental breakfast. AE, MC, V.*

Ragged Point Inn and Resort
$$–$$$ **Ragged Point**

This rustic motel at the southern gateway to Big Sur isn't perfect — expect worn tiled entryways and dated baths — but the glorious ocean-front setting makes up for any deficiencies. Rooms are clean and feature new furnishings, comfy beds, TVs, and furnished patios for enjoying the views. Upstairs rooms are pricier, but you'll have better coastal vistas. The resort includes a gorgeous stone-pillared restaurant with perfectly decent food and an ocean-facing patio. The grounds are fab, too — stop by for the sightlines even if you don't stay here.

19019 Hwy. 1 (14 miles north of Hearst Castle). ☎ 805-927-4502. Fax: 805-927-8862. Internet: www.raggedpointinn.net. *Parking: Free! Rack rates: $89–$189 double. AE, DISC, MC, V.*

Ventana Inn & Spa
$$$$$ **Big Sur**

Here's another stunning luxury oasis similar to Post Ranch, this one spread over a whopping 243 meadowy, ocean-facing acres. *Travel & Leisure* named much-lauded Ventana the second-best small hotel in the world in 1998, so expect to be wowed. The gorgeous rooms are more country cozy than contemporary, and TVs, VCRs, and CD players are among the in-room luxuries. You can't argue with the fabulousness of the grounds, which include a 2,100-foot spa — with amenities ranging from massages and mud treatments to aromatherapy sessions and astrology readings. Dinner is served in the first-rate **Cielo** (see the following section).

Hwy. 1 (28 miles south of Carmel). ☎ ***800-628-6500*** *or 831-667-2331. Fax: 831-667-2287. Internet:* www.ventanainn.com. *Parking: Free! Rack rates: $340–$850 double or suite. Rates include continental breakfast and afternoon wine and cheese. AE, DC, DISC, MC, V.*

Where to Dine in Big Sur

In addition to the options listed in this section, also consider these excellent choices at Big Sur's top places to stay:

- ✔ Moderately priced, highly regarded **Glen Oaks Restaurant ($$$)**, across the street from the Glen Oaks motel on Highway 1, a mile north of Pfeiffer Big Sur State Park (☎ **831-667-2264**), is a warm and cozy local favorite particularly well known for its homemade pastas. The restaurant is open nightly for dinner except Tuesday; main courses run about $10 to $19.

- ✔ **Cielo ($$$$)**, at the Ventana Inn & Spa, two miles south of Pfeiffer Big Sur State Park (☎ **831-667-2331**), is tops for a sophisticated lunch stop or a special dinner. Grab a midday table on the outdoor patio in nice weather — the views are incredible. The California cuisine doesn't disappoint, either. Main courses run $11 to $17 at lunch, $24 to $30 at dinner.

- ✔ Housed in four wood-polished, candlelit rooms, the lovely restaurant at **Deetjen's Big Sur Inn ($$$$),** 4 miles south of Pfeiffer Big Sur State Park (☎ **831-667-2377**), is regaled for its hearty cooking and intimate ambience. Breakfast ($7–$10) includes all your farmhouse favorites, while dinner ($18–$25) features such sophisticated but unfussy dishes as New York steak with twice-baked potato and herb-crusted New Zealand rack of lamb. A country delight.

Reservations are recommended at all the preceding choices. For further details, see "Where to Stay in Big Sur," earlier in this chapter.

Big Sur River Inn
$$ Big Sur AMERICAN

This popular stop is ideal for taking a break at any time of day. Cozy up to the huge stone fireplace in cold weather, or snag a table on the alfresco deck when the sun shines. Expect American classics ranging from hearty breakfasts to burgers and sandwiches to fresh fish, pastas, and ribs. Service is friendly, and the crowd is a nice mix of locals and visitors. The inn provides live entertainment on Saturday evenings and Sunday afternoons, usually of the foot-stomping variety.

Hwy. 1 (2 miles north of Pfeiffer Big Sur State Park). ☎ *831-667-2700. Internet:* www.bigsurriverinn.com. *Reservations recommended for dinner in season. Main courses: $8–$12 at lunch, $8–$20 at dinner. AE, DC, DISC, MC, V. Open: Breakfast, lunch, and dinner daily.*

Nepenthe

$$$ Big Sur   AMERICAN

Nepenthe's prices are way too high if you consider only the strictly average American fare — steaks, broiled fish, burgers, quiche — but the stupendous views alone are worth the extra cost. The redwood-beamed indoor/outdoor restaurant has a wonderful lodgelike atmosphere, and a casual party vibe prevails. The panoramic views are awe-inspiring, and starlit nights are pure magic. Come by for a drink if you don't want to pay for the food. Or, better yet, on nice days, head a level down to the alfresco **Cafe Kevah ($).** Kevah's amazing patio boasts the same stellar views, and the casual healthy-gourmet daytime fare goes for a fraction of the dough.

Hwy. 1 (2 miles south of Pfeiffer Big Sur State Park, just south of the Ventana Inn). ☎ *831-667-2345. Internet:* www.nepenthebigsur.com. *Reservations accepted for five or more. Main courses: $12–$32 at Nepenthe, $6.50–$12 at Cafe Kevah. AE, MC, V. Open: Lunch and dinner daily at Nepenthe, breakfast and lunch daily at Cafe Kevah March–Jan 5.*

Rocky Point Restaurant

$$$$ Big Sur   STEAKS/SEAFOOD

This pleasing clifftop chophouse at the northern end of Big Sur is one of the area's most spectacularly situated restaurants, second only to Nepenthe — and here you'll get better food for your money. You have an incredible ocean view no matter where you sit, either indoors or out. Sunset views are phenomenal, and floodlights play off the waves after dark. The surf-and-turf menu is traditional and satisfying. Everything is flame-grilled over hardwoods, and all dinners include soup or salad and sides.

Hwy. 1, about 10 miles south of Carmel. ☎ *831-624-2933. Internet:* www.rocky-point.com. *Reservations highly recommended for dinner. Main courses: $12–$18 at lunch, $20–$36 at dinner. AE, DISC, MC, V. Open: Breakfast, lunch, and dinner daily.*

Exploring the Big Sur Coast

The highlights in this section are discussed as you proceed along Highway 1 southbound. This is strictly to match the existing structure of this book; making the drive southbound brings no particular advantage, scenic or otherwise. In addition to these stops, a number of smaller parks and scenic vistas with pullouts exist along the way.

✔ Just 3 miles south of Carmel lies **Point Lobos State Reserve** (☎ **831-624-4909;** www.pointlobos.org), a cypress-dotted headland that has been variously called "the greatest meeting of land and water in the world" and "the crown jewel of the state parks system." It's a natural wonderland, all right, with sea lions, otters, harbor seals, and seabirds populating the sea coves; superb coastal vistas (perfect for whale-watching in winter); picnic areas; and miles of hiking trails. The entrance fee is $3 per car ($2 if you have a senior citizen on board), which includes a trail map.

Arrive early, especially on weekends. If the lot is full, you'll have to wait for someone to leave before you can enter.

✔ About 13 miles south of Carmel is the **Bixby Bridge,** which you'll probably recognize, even if you've never been to Big Sur. Rising 260 feet over **Bixby Creek Canyon,** the much-photographed bridge is one of the world's highest single-span concrete bridges, and one of Big Sur's most iconic images. Park your car in the lot on the north side so that you walk across the span and take in the magnificent views.

✔ South of Bixby Bridge is **Point Sur Lighthouse Station,** in Point Sur State Historic Park (☎ **831-625-4419** or 831-667-2315; www.calparks.ca.gov). Built 361 feet above the surf and first lit in 1889 — and in continuous operation ever since — Point Sur is the only working 19th-century lighthouse on the California coast that's open to the public. Three-hour tours are scheduled on weekends (Sat 10 a.m. and 2 p.m., Sun 10 a.m. only), with some weekday and moonlight tours added in summer. The fee is $5 for adults, $3 for teens 13 to 18, $2 for kids 5 to 13, free for under 5s.

The tour includes a steep half-mile hike each way, including stairs, so wear sturdy shoes and a (preferably waterproof) windbreaker to guard against the elements. Call for exact schedule and meeting-place details.

✔ About 20 miles south of Carmel is **Andrew Molera State Park** (☎ **831-667-2315;** www.calparks.ca.gov), the largest park on the Big Sur Coast, and the least crowded. Miles of trails meander through meadows and along bluffs. The 2½-mile-long beach is accessible via a lovely mile-long path flanked by wildflowers in spring. At low tide, you can walk the entire length of the beach. Otherwise, stick to the bluff trail. No swimming, of course — the water's way too cold. But you can take a horseback ride along the sand with **Molera Horseback Tours** (☎ **800-942-5486** or 831-625-5486; www.molerahorsebacktours.com). Prices are $25 to $59 for 1- to 2½-hour guided rides.

✔ Across from Molera State Park you can pick up the **Old Coast Road,** the original 1880s thoroughfare, when only wagons traversed these parts. If you're heading south, you can follow it as a rough scenic alternative for about 8 miles by turning left before crossing the Bixby Bridge, but if you just backtrack about a mile north from this entrance you get a spectacular view of the Big Sur Valley, Point Sur Lighthouse, and the Pacific beyond.

Don't try the road in wet weather, though; you will get stuck.

✔ Another 5 miles or so down the road (26 miles south of Carmel) is **Big Sur Station** (☎ 831-667-2315), a terrific source for maps, ranger advice, and other Big Sur information.

✔ Big Sur Station is just past the entrance to **Pfeiffer Big Sur State Park,** 800 acres of wildlife-rich parkland that includes excellent hiking opportunities for all levels of ability; pick up a map at the park entrance.

One excellent moderate walk is the 40- to 60-minute route to towering 60-foot-high **Pfeiffer Falls,** which takes you through one of Big Sur's most impressive redwood groves. If you're feeling energetic, add on another hour to follow the trail to the **Valley View Overlook** (a mile from the main trailhead, a half-mile from the falls) for panoramic views.

✔ About a mile south of the Pfeiffer Big Sur park entrance is Sycamore Canyon Road, which leads to beautiful **Pfeiffer Beach.** An arch-shaped rock formation just offshore makes for a distinctive view.

Although the sunsets are spectacular, locals advise that you come to Pfeiffer Beach in the morning hours to avoid windblown sand (the winds can kick up in the later hours). But first you have to find Sycamore Canyon Road: The unmarked route is the only paved, ungated road west of Highway 1 between the Pfeiffer Big Sur State Park and the Big Sur Post Office (you should see a "Narrow Road" sign as an additional clue). Take the sharp turn toward the coast and follow the road slowly for about 2 winding miles to a parking lot; parking is $5. A short path leads to the beach. Skip this trip if you have a trailer or a motor home.

✔ **The Henry Miller Memorial Library** (☎ 831-667-2574; www. henrymiller.org) is on the mountain side of Highway 1, a quarter-mile south of Nepenthe. It is dedicated to the life and work of Miller, who lived in Big Sur from 1944 to 1962 and wrote such classics as *Tropic of Cancer.* First editions of his writings as well as some of his artwork are on display, because this is a rotating exhibit of local art. The library makes a pleasant place for a short stop, especially for Miller fans. Admission is free. Open Wednesday through Monday from 11 a.m. to 6 p.m.

✔ Twelve miles south of Pfeiffer Big Sur is **Julia Pfeiffer Burns State Park,** a gem of a park and our absolute favorite spot for glorious ocean views.

Everyone can follow the **Overlook Waterfall Trail** — it's even wheelchair-accessible. The flat and easy ⅓-mile (each way) trail leads to a cliff top with views of **McWay Falls** plunging into a gorgeous cove where seals and sea otters play in the white-crested blue-green water. Cypress trees stepping down the rocky coast in the background give the view an only-in-Big-Sur mystique. In winter, park yourself on one of the benches to look for migrating whales. The view is particularly magnificent at sunset.

Above the parking lot is a small picnic area and trailheads to two more of the park's hiking trails. The ⅓-mile **Canyon Trail** is steeper and ungraded but still not difficult, and the payoff is a lovely forest waterfall and a bench from which to contemplate it (and rest your weary toes). The day-use fee is $6 per car; ask the park attendant to sell you a trail map for an additional buck.

The big attractions end after Julia Pfeiffer Burns State Park, but the drive is still stunning, and scenic turnoffs abound. About 59 miles south of Carmel, just south of the U.S. Forest Service Station in Pacific Valley, is **Sand Dollar Beach,** which features a very nice picnic area. Take the stairs to reach the beach, which may be devoid of sand if you visit in winter (it usually washes back in summer).

Farther south — just north of **San Simeon,** where the landscape opens up to rolling, golden hills — you'll see elephant seals sunning themselves on rocks and maybe a few colorful windsurfers dancing on the waves beyond. That's when you know you've almost reached the outrageous, infamous, legendary **Hearst Castle,** which is just around the bend. We discuss the Hearst Castle in Chapter 18.

Gathering More Information

Your best source for Big Sur information is the **Big Sur Chamber of Commerce** Web site at www.bigsurcalifornia.org; you can also call the chamber at ☎ 831-677-2100. Additionally, the **Monterey Peninsula Visitors and Convention Bureau** (☎ 888-221-1010; www.gomonterey.org) can provide you with information on Big Sur.

If you'd like more information on Big Sur's state parks, call **California State Parks' Big Sur Station** at ☎ 831-667-2315, or point your Web browser to www.cal-parks.ca.gov, then click on Central Coast, and scroll down to Monterey County. Located 26 miles south of Carmel, a half-mile south of the entrance to Pfeiffer Big Sur State Park, Big Sur Station is your prime information stop for the region after you've arrived.

Chapter 18

Hearst Castle and Cambria

• •

In This Chapter

▶ Visiting the mind-boggling castle that Hearst built

▶ Deciding on the best places to stay and dine nearby

▶ Strolling the village and bumming around the beach

• •

*P*ublishing baron and film mogul William Randolph Hearst was one of the most influential men of the 20th century. His extensive travels throughout Europe as a child fueled a dream to build a house as grand as the castles he admired. In 1919, he inherited 250,000 acres of ranchland from his mother, which had been originally known as "Camp Hill." He instructed his architect to "build a little something" where he could escape the stress of work and public scrutiny. It was to be his country estate, a relaxing and enjoyable environment for family and friends. He renamed his marvelous ranch "La Cuesta Encantada" — The Enchanted Hill. In its heyday, the '30s and '40s — the Golden Age of Hollywood — this real-life Xanadu was the playground for the silver screen's elite, among them Carole Lombard, Clark Gable, Charlie Chaplin, Cary Grant, Harpo Marx, and many others.

The 165-room Mediterranean Revival-style estate — including its three guesthouses, Italian- and Spanish-inspired gardens, and two fabulous oversized swimming pools — has never been completely finished. It houses one of the world's finest collections of priceless antiques and museum-quality art — a collection that millions of people may never have seen if Hearst did not have the vision and money to buy count-less pieces of European art offered for sale by governments after World War II.

From its beautiful gardens and striking architecture to its glorious art and history, Hearst Castle is impressive. Plus, it's a monument to the seemingly limitless powers of money and hubris, and what happens to the American Dream when left unchecked. And, lest we forget, it inspired the greatest movie of all time (wanna fight about it?), *Citizen Kane*. This is a must-see stop in one's exploration of California's central coast, and it has something for everyone. However, children under 6 may find walking and climbing hundreds of steps for almost two hours a bit overwhelming.

Hearst's sprawling compound sits high above San Simeon, which isn't really much of a town. But 6 miles to the south is Cambria (pronounced *Cam*-bree-uh, like "camera," with a short "a" rather than a long one), which makes an excellent base of operations. Not quite northern Californian and not quite southern, not quite coastal and not quite inland, this charming village has a distinct and winning personality and offers terrific opportunities for dining and strolling.

Timing Your Visit

Hearst Castle and Cambria are enjoyable in any season. The biggest considerations are money and crowds.

You'll snare the lowest hotel rates in winter, and the castle is quiet enough that you needn't make advance tour reservations. Spring and fall are pleasant — you'll have the opportunity to take the evening tour (only offered in these seasons), and you'll still beat the crowds if you visit midweek.

You'll pay the highest hotel rates and wrestle with the biggest crowds in summer. You should make weekend hotel reservations, in particular, as far in advance as possible, and we highly recommend purchasing advance tickets for castle tours (more on this subject under "Visiting the Castle," later in this chapter).

Set aside two days to enjoy the castle and the charms of Cambria. If you're just coming to see the castle, one day will do, but expect it to be a longish one and sandwich it between a two-night stay.

Getting There

Cambria is right off Highway 1, smack dab in the middle of the coast. It is located 223 miles south of San Francisco, 105 miles south of Monterey, 130 miles north of Santa Barbara, and 230 miles north of Los Angeles. San Simeon, home to the Hearst Castle Visitor Center, is on Highway 1, 6 miles north of Cambria.

Driving from points north: If you're following the scenic route through Big Sur, just keep going — stay on Highway 1 until you see signs for Hearst Castle, and for Cambria a few minutes beyond.

If you're coming directly from San Francisco or Monterey, take U.S. 101 south to Paso Robles, then Highway 46 west to Highway 1, and Highway 1 north to Cambria and the castle.

Driving from points south: Take U.S. 101 north to San Luis Obispo, where you'll pick up Highway 1 north to Cambria and the castle.

The Cambria and San Simeon Area

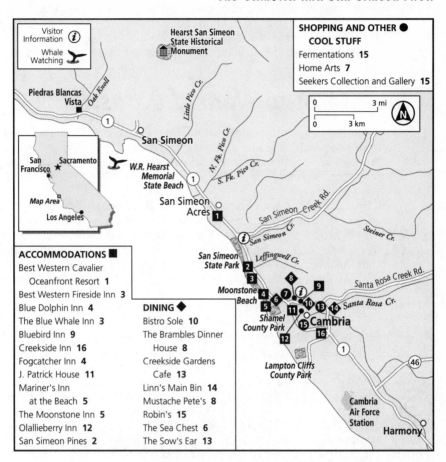

Visitor Information (i)

Whale Watching

SHOPPING AND OTHER ●
COOL STUFF
Fermentations **15**
Home Arts **7**
Seekers Collection and Gallery **15**

Hearst San Simeon
State Historical
Monument

Piedras Blancas
Vista

Oak Knoll

Little Pico Cr.

1

San Simeon

San
Francisco ★   Sacramento

Map Area

Los Angeles

N. Fk. Pico Cr.

W.R. Hearst
Memorial
State Beach

S. Fk. Pico Cr.

1

San Simeon
Acres **1**

0   3 mi
0   3 km

N

San Simeon Creek Rd.

Steiner Cr.

(i) *San Simeon Cr.*

ACCOMMODATIONS ■
Best Western Cavalier
   Oceanfront Resort **1**
Best Western Fireside Inn **3**
Blue Dolphin Inn **4**
The Blue Whale Inn **3**
Bluebird Inn **9**
Creekside Inn **16**
Fogcatcher Inn **4**
J. Patrick House **11**
Mariner's Inn
   at the Beach **5**
The Moonstone Inn **5**
Olallieberry Inn **12**
San Simeon Pines **2**

San Simeon
State Park **2**

Leffingwell Cr.

3

Moonstone
Beach

DINING ◆
Bistro Sole **10**
The Brambles Dinner
   House **8**
Creekside Gardens
   Cafe **13**
Linn's Main Bin **14**
Mustache Pete's **8**
Robin's **15**
The Sea Chest **6**
The Sow's Ear **13**

8
4 7 (i) **9**
5 11 10 13 14 *Santa Rosa Cr.*

Shamel
County Park

Santa Rosa Creek Rd.

15 Cambria
16

12

Lampton Cliffs
County Park

1

46

Cambria
Air Force
Station

Harmony

Orienting Yourself

San Simeon is less a town than a stretch of Highway 1 lined with motels and services catering to castle visitors. The entrance to Hearst Castle rests just north of San Simeon on the inland side of the road.

Cambria lies 6 miles south of the Hearst Castle Visitor Center. The town's Main Street runs roughly parallel to Highway 1 inland, connecting up with the highway at each end of town.

Tiny Cambria actually has three distinct parts. Along Main Street is "the Village," which is divided into two sections: the **West Village** and the **East Village.** The West Village is the newer, somewhat more touristy end of town where you'll find the visitor information center. The more historic East Village is a bit quieter, more locals-oriented, and a tad more sophisticated than the West Village.

If you cross Highway 1 to the coastal side at the far west end of town (or the north end, if you're considering how the freeway runs), you'll reach Cambria's third part, **Moonstone Beach.** Lined with motels, inns, and a few restaurants on the inland side of the street, ocean-facing Moonstone Beach Drive is our favorite place to stay in Cambria.

Where to Stay Near the Castle

If you're planning to explore both Hearst Castle and the Big Sur Coast from one perch, consider staying at the Ragged Point Inn and Resort, just 14 miles north of Hearst Castle near the southern gateway to Big Sur (see Chapter 17).

If Hearst Castle is your only destination, there is only one reason to choose lodging in San Simeon instead of Cambria — money. Standard, run-of-the-mill motels line both sides of Highway 1, which runs through this town. But if you're a little flexible with the time of year you plan to visit the area, you can find some comparable bargains in a couple of the inns in Cambria, such as the Creekside Inn or the Bluebird Inn (see the listings in this section).

In general, hotel rates are usually lowest in the winter season and at their highest during the summer; so plan accordingly. Expect an extra 9% in taxes to be tacked on to your Cambria or San Simeon hotel bill.

You can't go wrong with almost any inn on Moonstone Beach Drive. However, White Water Inn is the only inn that fails to deliver on its promised ambience and charm in comparison to the other comparably priced inns. If atmosphere, charm, and beautiful decor are not necessities, **Mariner's Inn at the Beach ($–$$$),** at 6180 Moonstone Beach Dr., is your best option for price and locale (☎ **805-927-4624;** www.cambrias best.com).

If you want a super-cheap choice, try the **Creekside Inn ($),** 2618 Main St., Cambria (☎ **800-269-5212;** www.cambriacreeksideinn.com). It's more basic than the motels in the following listing and doesn't boast the same oceanfront perch, but the village location is extremely convenient and the rates are considerably lower — $69 to $139 double, year-round.

Best Western Cavalier Oceanfront Resort
$$ San Simeon

This upscale oceanfront motel is freshly renovated and a real gem. It's well situated along the coast, with lots of ocean-view rooms. Every room is very comfortable (cozy bedding!) and outfitted with a VCR, minibar, and hair dryer. Coastal evenings can be chilly year-round, so book a room with a fireplace if you can. On-site extras include two heated pools, a

Jacuzzi, an exercise room, two restaurants, and a coin-op laundry, plus video rentals next door. The motel welcomes kids and pets, too.

9415 Hearst Dr. (3 miles south of Hearst Castle on Hwy. 1). ☎ ***800-826-8168,*** *800-780-7234, or 805-927-4688. Fax: 805-927-6472. Internet:* www.bestwestern. com. *Parking: Free! Rack rates: $89and$184 double, $105–$121 family room (2 queens). AE, DC, DISC, MC, V.*

Best Western Fireside Inn

$$ Cambria

Nicely done in a charming country style with floral prints and warm woods, the spacious rooms are a few steps above motel standard. Each has a coffeemaker and minifridge, most have gas fireplaces, and some have Jacuzzi tubs; VCRs (and movies) are available for rent. Extras include a nice heated pool and spa, and a friendly staff.

6700 Moonstone Beach Dr. ☎ ***888-910-7100,*** *800-780-7234, or 805-927-8661. Fax: 805-927-8584. Internet:* www.bestwesternfiresideinn.com *or* www.best western.com. *Parking: Free! Rack rates: $109–$259 double. Rates include continental breakfast. AE, DC, DISC, MC, V.*

Bluebird Inn

$–$$ Cambria

This simple, modern motel built around a local landmark is centrally located in the East Village. Standard rooms are comfortably furnished, but it's the deluxe rooms that offer the country charm you want, including a fireplace and a private patio or balcony. Family suites and connecting rooms are also available. This is the best bargain around in terms of price, locale, and decor.

1880 Main St. ☎ ***800-552-5434*** *or 805-927-4634. Fax: 805-927-5215. Internet:* www. bluebirdmotel.com. *Parking: Free! Rack rates: $40–$180 double. Children under 12 are free. AE, DC, DISC, MC, V.*

Blue Dolphin Inn

$$–$$$ Cambria

Part country inn, part upscale motel, the Blue Dolphin is an excellent choice if you don't mind paying a bit more for high-quality accommodations. The romantic rooms have nice amenities — gas fireplaces, big TVs with VCRs, hair dryers, and minifridges — and cozy, frilly, chintzy English country decor. The inn also offers a complimentary, expanded continental breakfast and afternoon tea served in a cozy tea room. The best rooms (and most expensive, of course) have private garden patios with ocean views. The inn is very attractive and professionally run, but has no pool.

6470 Moonstone Beach Dr. ☎ ***805-927-3300***. *Fax: 805-927-7311. Internet:* www.blue dolphininn.com *or* www.moonstonehotels.com. *Parking: Free! Rack rates: $85–$220 double. AE, DC, DISC, MC, V.*

The Blue Whale Inn
$$$ Cambria

Near perfect. This is the ultimate seaside getaway — a bed-and-breakfast masquerading as an inn. The incredibly charming white cottage-style building features six ocean-view mini-suites, each with its own outdoor entrance, canopy bed, marble and granite bath (with whirlpool tub), fireplace, TV, and French/English country decor. This is the only bed-and-breakfast between Carmel and Santa Barbara with a AAA Four Diamond rating.

6736 Moonstone Beach Dr. ☎ ***800-753-9000*** *or 805-927-4647. Fax: 805-927-0202. Internet:* www.olallieberry.com. *Parking: Free! Rack rates: $190–$250 single or double. Rates include gourmet breakfast and afternoon tea. Two-night minimum on most holidays and weekends. AE, MC, V.*

Fogcatcher Inn
$$$ Cambria

This is one of our favorite Moonstone Beach inns; it also has an outdoor heated pool and spa. The English Tudor architecture, with thatched roofs and garden pathways, makes it a standout among the seaside inns. Each room features a stone fireplace, a refrigerator, a microwave, a coffee-maker, a TV, and an honor bar. You'll feel as if you're actually in an English seaside village.

6400 Moonstone Beach Dr. ☎ ***800-425-4121*** *or 805-927-1400. Fax: 805-927-0204. Internet:* www.moonstonehotels.com. *Parking: Free! Rack rates: $189–$389 single or double. Rates include a deluxe continental breakfast. Two-night minimum on most holidays and weekends. AE, MC, V.*

J. Patrick House
$$–$$$ Cambria

Tucked away on a woodsy hill just minutes above the East Village is this utterly lovely B&B, Cambria's best. The main house is an elegant log cabin; the nearby carriage house contains seven of the eight impeccable, unfussy rooms. Named for the counties of Ireland and brimming with country warmth, each room boasts beautifully chosen antiques, a wood-burning fireplace, and a private bath. The innkeepers couldn't be more agreeable or attentive.

2990 Burton Dr. ☎ ***800-341-5258*** *or 805-927-3812. Fax: 805-927-6759. Internet:* www.jpatrickhouse.com. *Parking: Free! Rack rates: $125–$180 double. Rates* *include full breakfast, early evening wine and hors d'oeuvres, and bedtime cook-ies and milk. Two-night minimum. AE, DISC, MC, V.*

The Moonstone Inn
$$ Cambria

If you are economically challenged, but still want English-country-style decor and comfort with a personal touch, this is your best bet. The folks at a family-owned and -run operation are committed to giving each guest personal service. Amenities include complimentary breakfast served on china, silver, and crystal in your room, TV and VCR with free video choices, coffeemaker and refrigerator; select rooms offer fireplaces and Jacuzzi tubs. All guests are welcome to indulge in a Jacuzzi on the ocean-front patio. It's not the most attractive inn externally and the rooms had a slight musty odor, but it's a good deal for the locale and price.

*5860 Moonstone Beach Dr. ☎ **800-821-3764** or 805-927-4815. Fax: 805-927-3944. Internet:* www.cambriasbest.com/moonstoneinn.com. *Parking: Free! Rack rates: $85–$150 single or double. Rates include continental breakfast. Two-night minimum on most holidays and weekends. AE, MC, V.*

Olallieberry Inn
$$–$$$ Cambria

Step back in time and indulge yourself in this 19th-century historical house. This bed-and-breakfast has nine guest rooms, six in the main house and three in the Innkeeper's Cottage, and each room is individually named after one of the local towns or a feature unique to the room. Most rooms have fireplaces, and all are charmingly decorated with antiques and floral fabrics. For the same money that you might spend on, say, the White Water on the beachfront (which we tell you to avoid), you could stay here. No contest.

*2476 Main St. ☎ **888-927-3222** or 805-927-3222. Fax: 805-927-0202. Internet:* www.olallieberry.com. *Parking: Free! Rack rates: $105–$200 single or double. Rates include full breakfast, early evening wine and hors d'oeuvres. Two-night min-imum on weekends between Memorial Day and Labor Day. AE, MC, V.*

San Simeon Pines
$$ San Simeon

This camplike resort is nothing fancy, but it's a great alternative to a family motel, and a good choice for anyone looking for a top-notch value. To meet everyone's needs, the resort divides units between family and adult areas. The well-kept grounds feature a solar-heated pool, a play-ground, and a par-3 golf course. The grounds have no view, but they do feature private beach access. Ask for a room away from the highway for total quiet.

7200 Moonstone Beach Dr. (at the north end of Moonstone Beach, just off Hwy. 1).
☎ **805-927-4648**. Internet: www.sspines.com. Parking: Free! Rack rates:
$74–$130 double, $80–$94 family room (2 queens). AE, MC, V.

Where to Dine

Bistro Sole
$$$ Cambria   ECLECTIC/MEDITERRANEAN

This sophisticated but casual indoor/outdoor bistro is one of Cambria's
most contemporary restaurants, and one of its most pleasing. The prepa-
rations are almost decadent, from saffron risotto with rock shrimp and
asparagus to charbroiled rack of lamb in a delectable cabernet sauce.
Don't miss the awesome oysters Rockefeller, finished with a glazed hol-
landaise and better than dessert! If the weather's nice, take a seat on the
leafy garden patio. Service is attentive, plus there's live music at brunch.

1980 Main St. ☎ **805-927-0887**. Reservations recommended. Main courses:
$6–$10.50 at lunch and brunch; $10–$20 at dinner. MC, V. Open: Mon–Sat 5 p.m.–
9:30 p.m.; Sun 10 a.m.–2:30 p.m. and 5 p.m.–9 p.m.

The Brambles Dinner House
$$$$ Cambria   CONTEMPORARY/MEDITERRANEAN

This 130-year-old house has been a restaurant for nearly 50 years, but
it's currently under the proprietorship of a Greek family and features an
eclectic assortment of food, including some Greek specialties. We've tried
the calamari fritti (like buttah!), the saganaki (fried cheese, in this case
feta — not as greasy or as heavy as it sounds), and a Cajun halibut (black-
ened and served with an avocado relish that nicely cut the spiciness).
Desserts are terrific. It's one of the most expensive dinner options in
town, but it also has the most extensive menu, and it's good as well.

4005 Burton Dr. ☎ **805-927-4716**. Internet: www.bramblesdinnerhouse.com.
Reservations recommended. Main courses: $12–$27. AE, MC, V. Open: Sun–Fri
4 p.m.–9:30 p.m, Sat 4–10 p.m. Early-bird dinners: Sun–Fri 4–6 p.m.; Sat 4–5:30 p.m.
Sun champagne brunch: 9:30 a.m.–2 p.m.

Creekside Gardens Cafe
$ Cambria   AMERICAN/MEXICAN

This unpretentious local favorite is the place for breakfast. The pancakes
are to die for. Adventuresome types shouldn't miss the Danish ableskiver,
ball-shaped pancakes served with Solvang sausage. Lunchtime brings
tasty sandwiches, salads, and Tex-Mex specialties, while dinner is strictly
dedicated to the head chef's Jalisco roots. The results are authentic
Mexican specialties accompanied by fresh-from-the-oven corn tortillas.

2114 Main St. ☎ *805-927-8646. Internet:* www.cambria-online.com/ CreeksideGardensCafe. *Reservations not taken. Main courses: $6–$8 break-fast and lunch. No credit cards. Open: Mon–Sat 7 a.m.–2 p.m.; Sun 7 a.m.– 1 p.m.*

Linn's Main Bin Restaurant & Gift Shop
$ Cambria   AMERICAN HOME COOKING

This comfortable and charming farmhouse restaurant/bakery/gift shop is a great place to bring the family and relax over a hearty home-style meal morning, noon, or night or just to enjoy a midday cappuccino and a generous slice of olallieberry pie (a local specialty; the berries taste somewhat like blackberries). Order anything with a crust and you can't go wrong. The homemade pot pies are pure comfort in a pastry dish.

2277 Main St. ☎ *805-927-0371. Internet:* www.linnsfruitbin.com. *Reser-vations not needed. Main courses: $4.50–$7.50 at breakfast, $6–$13 at lunch and dinner. AE, DISC, MC, V. Open: Mon–Sun 7:30 a.m.–9 p.m.*

Mustache Pete's
$–$$ Cambria   CONTEMPORARY ITALIAN

The friendly, casual atmosphere makes this a very good place for fami-lies. The main menu attraction is its gourmet pizzas, a staple that seems indigenous to California/Italian eateries. You won't be disappointed by the variety, however. Also on the menu are traditional pasta dishes that come in big portions and are served with soup or salad.

4090 Burton Dr. ☎ *805-927-8589. Internet:* www.mustachepetes.com. *Main courses: $5.95–$16. AE, DISC, MC, V. Open: Mon–Sun 11 a.m.–10 p.m.; last Sun of each month, Sun brunch 10 a.m.–1 p.m.*

Robin's
$$ Cambria   INTERNATIONAL

Hugely popular Robin's comes through on all counts: It offers cozy ambi-ence, dedicated service, and satisfying cooking from around the globe. Well-prepared with fresh ingredients and a healthy bent, dishes range from house-specialty pastas and bouillabaisse to Indian-spiced lamb and Asian curries. A bit schizophrenic for comfort, perhaps, but you can't argue with success. The menu features lots of good choices for vegetar-ians, too. Don't miss dessert if you respect your sweet tooth.

4095 Burton Dr. ☎ *805-927-5007.* www.robinsrestaurant.com. *Reservations recommended. Main courses: $4.50–$10 at lunch, $9.50–$17 at dinner. DISC, MC, V. Open: Mon–Sun 11a.m.–9 p.m.*

The Sea Chest
$$$ Cambria   SEAFOOD

This place is everything a good seafood house should be: casual, bustling, and dedicated to serving the freshest seafood in preparations that let the quality of the fish shine through. Start with bluepoints on the half shell, follow with a fresh green salad, follow that with one of the day's catches (usually lightly grilled with just a little lemon and butter), and the world is your oyster. You may have to wait for a table, but the wait will be well worth it. Skip the lackluster chowder.

6216 Moonstone Beach Dr. ☎ *805-927-4514. Reservations not accepted. Main courses: $14 and $19. No credit cards. Open: Wed–Mon 5:30 p.m.–10 p.m.*

The Sow's Ear
$$ Cambria   CONTEMPORARY AMERICAN

The kid's menu makes the Sow's Ear good for families, but the relaxing and intimate ambience makes it the place to go for casual romance, as well. You'll know that it's special from the moment you're presented with the addictive signature marbled bread, baked and served in a terra-cotta flowerpot. The beautifully prepared gourmet comfort food includes such favorites as fried brie, shrimp scampi, barbecued baby-back ribs, and chicken and dumplings. Don't miss the Sow's Ear Grilled Chicken Breast with a honey-lemon sauce and served with wild rice and julienned vegetables; or the Warm Cinnamon Bread Pudding with cinnamon frosting oozing down the sides. This restaurant could easily become one of our Cambria favorites.

2248 Main St. ☎ *805-927-4865. Internet:* www.thesowsear.com. *Reservations recommended. Main courses: $14–$22; early-dinner specials (5–6 p.m.) $11–$14. DISC, MC, V. Open: Mon–Sun 5– 9 p.m.*

Visiting the Castle

The only way to see Hearst Castle (which is now run by the California State Parks system and is officially known as **Hearst San Simeon State Historical Monument**) is via guided tour. The castle is open daily except on Thanksgiving, Christmas, and New Year's Day.

Getting on the bus!

Four different 1¾-hour tours depart regularly throughout the day. Each one includes the outdoor Greco-Roman-style Neptune Pool (which you'll likely recognize from photos) and the stunning indoor Roman Pool, decorated from floor to ceiling with clear and colored glass tiles.

Each tour departs from the visitor center by bus and is led by a well-trained guide. Before you board the bus, a mandatory photograph will be taken of you for security purposes (thanks to the 9/11 terrorist attacks). The first tour leaves the visitor center at 8:20 a.m.; the last one leaves at 3:20 p.m. in winter, later at other times of the year. The Evening Tour start times are dictated by the time of sunset.

- ✔ **Tour 1 (The Experience Tour)** is the introductory tour and is recommended for first-time visitors. It is also a less strenuous tour, but a sign at the boarding entrance to the bus warns that there are 150 steps to climb on this tour. It focuses on the opulent ground-floor rooms in **Casa Grande,** as the main house is called, including the **movie theater,** where you'll see a few minutes of Hearst's home movies (starring more than a few famous faces). You'll also see the art-filled **gardens** and some of the luxurious guest quarters in the 18-room **Casa del Sol guesthouse.**

- ✔ **Tour 2** should be called the Kitchens and Baths tour. It concentrates on the private and less formal spaces on **Casa Grande's upper floors.** These rooms include the impressive **library** (one of the most memorable rooms in the house), **Hearst's private suite,** the massive and surprisingly modern **kitchen and pantry,** and **guest rooms** with lots of fabulous bathrooms. The stories are great on this one.

- ✔ **Tour 3** focuses on the construction of Hearst Castle, which never really ended. You'll see a portion of the estate that wasn't completed, all of the 10-room **Casa del Monte guesthouse,** and a **wing of guest suites** in Casa Grande that were completed in Hearst's final years and show the castle's most modern face. Great for anybody interested in the story behind the design and construction of the house.

- ✔ **Tour 4** runs only between April and October, and it's a good one. At the heart of this tour is a detailed overview of the **gardens and grounds,** including a hidden terrace that was never completed and only recovered during restoration. You'll also see more of the **Neptune Pool building; Casa del Mar,** the largest and most eye-popping of the guesthouses; and the **wine cellar.** Be aware that this tour does not visit any of the interiors of the main house.

For each tour, a bus takes you on the 15-minute ride up the hill from the visitor center to the castle and back. You cannot linger at the castle on your own or wait for your next tour there. No matter how many tours you take in a day, you must return to the visitor center each time and ride the bus back to the top of the hill with your tour group, so allow at least two hours between tours when you buy your tickets. All tours involve a good deal of walking, including climbing between 150 and 400 steps, so be sure to wear comfortable shoes.

Specialty tours worth considering

Evening Tours are held most Friday and Saturday nights in spring and fall, and usually nightly around Christmas. This 2¼-hour tour is a real gem, and worth the extra money (see "Getting tour tickets," later in the chapter) and the extra stairs. The illuminated tour offers all the castle highlights from Tours 1, 2, and 4, and features docents in 1930s period costume who wander the grounds and occupy the rooms. These living history players, plus the stories told during the tours about the famous visitors to the castle, provide the closest glimpse of what life may have been like in Hearst's day. In December, when the house is decked out for Christmas, it's pure magic. Don't miss this one if it's offered.

Family Tours are now available in summer, generally between Memorial Day and Labor Day. These are standard tours reconfigured just a bit so that the young ones in your group will understand and enjoy what they're seeing. Ask about these tours when you reserve your tickets (see "Getting tour tickets," later in the chapter).

Accessibly Designed Tours are offered at least three times a day and cover the ground floor of the main house as well as the castle gardens and grounds. Book at least ten days in advance by calling ☎ 800-444-4445.

Focus Tours — where such themes as architecture, textiles, or tilework serve as the topic of discussion — are also offered. For information, call ☎ 805-927-2020.

Selecting the tour that's right for you

We recommend that you take two of the four standard 1¾-hour tours; this way, you can see a few different views of the estate without being overwhelmed. You can easily suffer from museum overload here, however — all the over-the-top excesses can really start looking the same after a while. Taking in two tours and the other castle attractions makes for quite a full day.

Because you'll pay for each tour individually, you may want to spread your castle visit over two half-days, especially if you quickly tire of walking, crowds, or theme park–like bureaucracy. We strongly suggest this approach if you decide to take more than two tours.

Getting tour tickets

Tickets for Tour 1 are $14 for adults, and $7 for kids 6 to 17. Tours 2 through 4 are $10 for adults, and $5 for kids 6 to 17. The Evening Tour is $20 for adults, and $10 for kids. Children under 6 are free.

Booking your tour tickets in advance is always a good idea. You can buy tickets right at the visitor center, but you have no guarantee that they'll be available — a day's slate of tours can easily sell out. You pay no fee for advance reservations, and you can make them from one hour to eight weeks in advance. Call the **California State Parks reservations line** at ☎ **800-444-4445,** where a knowledgeable operator will assist you. Ask about packages that include big-screen movies at the new National Geographic Theater (see the next section). By the time you read this, you may be able to order tickets via the Internet at www. hearstcastle.org. If you're ordering tickets from outside the United States, call ☎ **916-414-8400, ext. 4100.** If you need more information, call ☎ **805-927-2020.**

Keeping busy between trips to the top

You'll find plenty to keep you busy at the visitor center before, after, and in between tours. In addition to an **observation deck** offering a good view of the Enchanted Hill, **two gift shops,** and **food vendors** (think ball-park variety and you'll get the picture), the center also includes a surprisingly good small **museum.** There is also a permanent exhibit — the **William Randolph Hearst Exhibit** — where visitors can learn more about the castle's history, art, and architecture, and even touch examples of the materials used in the construction of the estate.

The center's newest attraction is **Hearst Castle Experience National Geographic Theater** (☎ **805-927-6811;** www.ngtheater.com). In this theater, you can watch larger-than-life films, including the 40-minute *Hearst Castle: Building the Dream* and other films (no other films were featured at press time), in five-story-high iWERKS format (just like IMAX) with seven-channel surround sound. Shows begin every 45 minutes throughout the day. Tickets are $7.50 for adults, $5.50 for kids 6 to 17, or $14 for adults and $7 for kids if you also take the Experience Tour.

Hitting the Central Coast Beaches

Just across Highway 1 from the entrance to the Hearst Castle Visitor Center is **W. R. Hearst Memorial State Beach.** This pleasant day-use beach is generally too cold for swimming, but picnic tables, barbecues, and bathrooms make it perfect for in-between- or after-tour picnicking. You can even do some fishing. Look for whales offshore in winter.

Just north of San Simeon is a wonderful vista point called **Piedras Blancas** where you can watch elephant seals doing their natural thing up close and personal, frolicking and sunning themselves on the rocks year-round. If you have questions about these creatures, don't hesitate to ask the docents on hand. Finding this beach is easy — just stop at the packed parking lot 4½ miles north of the castle and follow the crowds along the short, sandy walk for a good vantage. Keep your distance from these giant mammals, and don't go beyond the marked areas — not only is it unhealthy for them, but it can be dangerous for you.

In Cambria, Moonstone Beach is great for strolling and whale-watching in season. Keep your eye on the sand for the semi-precious jasper stones that give the beach its name.

Exploring Cambria

Strolling the streets of laid-back Cambria is a pleasant change of pace after a day of lines and hectic sightseeing at Hearst Castle. This charming artists' colony has little more than four or five blocks to explore, but they're worth checking out even if you're based up in San Simeon and not here. You'll find the area's best restaurants (see "Where to Dine," earlier in this chapter) and shops, less of the tacky touristy variety and more focused on good-quality crafts.

Before you set out, pick up the Cambria Historical Society's "Welcome to Cambria" brochure at your hotel and take a simple but fun **self-guided tour** of the historical buildings in the East Village. You'll not only get a history lesson about this quaint village, but you'll also discover a few places you may have overlooked otherwise, such as the **blacksmith shop** at 4121 Burton Drive or the **Santa Rosa Chapel and Cemetery** at 2352 Main Street.

The shopping highlight of the West Village is **Home Arts,** 727 Main St. (☎ 805-927-ART1; www.home-arts.com), which boasts an appealingly eclectic mix of country and contemporary home fashions and gifts.

The East Village has lots of worthwhile stops. Tops among them is **Seekers Collection and Gallery,** 4090 Burton Dr. (☎ 800-841-5250 or 805-927-4352; www.seekersglass.com), a museum-quality art-glass gallery. We also love **Fermentations,** 4056 Burton Dr. (☎ 800-446-7505; www.fermentations.com), which serves as a great introduction to the central coast wine country through tastings, wine sales, and wine-themed gifts.

Gathering More Information

For Hearst Castle information, call ☎ 800-444-4445, or visit the comprehensive Web site at www.hearstcastle.org.

For information on Cambria, contact the **Cambria Chamber of Commerce,** which operates a visitor center at 767 Main St. (☎ 805-927-3624), or go online to www.cambriachamber.org. Another terrific source is www.cambria-online.com.

Chapter 19

The Santa Ynez Valley and Solvang, California's Little Denmark

. . . .

In This Chapter

▶ Experiencing the highs and lows of the San Marcos Pass

▶ Picking your pickled food and surviving sugar overload in a fairy-tale village

▶ Exploring artsy outposts and rural recreations

▶ Discovering the coastal dunes of Guadalupe-Nipomo

. . . .

*T*he glowing Santa Ynez Valley, like much of Southern California, was once part of the land-grant *ranchos* of the Spanish settlers. Grapes and apples have flourished in the rolling hills, and herds of cattle now share space with miniature horses, llamas, and ostriches.

The valley is home to some of the finest small vineyards in the state, and from August to October, the apple trees groan with fruit that is sold fresh from roadside stands. There are also luxury spa retreats, art galleries, museums, golf courses, and the peculiar tourist town of **Solvang,** where storybook sweetness is celebrated 365 days of the year.

Located almost equidistant between Hearst Castle and Los Angeles, the Santa Ynez Valley towns of **Los Alamos, Los Olivos, Ballard, Buellton, Santa Ynez,** and the aforementioned Solvang offer a chance to stretch your legs, wallow in art and history, eat an astoundingly varied amount of sugary treats, and generally take a respite from the road for a few hours or even a day or two.

Timing Your Visit

The valley is geared for tourism, and certain times are busier than others. Definitely call in advance if you plan to stay on weekends, which often demand a two-night stay. The towns get very crowded from June to

October, when the **Pacific Conservancy of the Performing Arts** (PCPA)
(☎ 805-922-8313; www.pcpa.org) presents alfresco theater, including
comedies, dramas, and musicals at the **Solvang Festival Theatre.**

The festivities go on year-round, but things really pick up when the
apples are ready for picking from August to October. Come for **Solvang
Danish Days** (late September), the annual **Celebration of Harvest** (mid-
October), **Winterfest Celebration** (month of December), and other
mini-fests that the visitors' bureaus will be happy to tell you about.
Contact the **Santa Ynez Valley Visitors Association** (☎ 800-742-2002;
www.santaynezvalleyvisit.com) or the **Solvang Conference and
Visitors Bureau** (☎ 800-468-6765; www.solvangusa.com) for more festival information.

Getting There

The sunny Santa Ynez Valley lies inland from the coast, and rarely does
a day pass without sunshine. During the summer it can get hot, and
sunblock is recommended year-round.

To reach the Santa Ynez Valley from the north, take Highway 101 to
Highway 154 at the artist colony of Los Olivos. Tiny Ballard lies 3 miles
south off Baseline Road. The turn off for Solvang is just beyond, west
on Highway 246, while a straight jaunt on Highway 154 will take you
through the spectacular **San Marcos Pass** and onto Highway 101
towards Santa Barbara, Los Angeles, and Hollywood.

From the south, take Highway 154 off Highway 101 at Goleta (just north
of Santa Barbara), up through the San Marcos Pass. A turn west on the
246 takes you into Solvang; continuing along Highway 154 takes you
quickly through Los Olivos and onto Highway 101 towards Cambria.

And why do we keep pushing the San Marcos Pass? Because it offers
some of the most stunning vistas in the southern half of the state. Of
course, if a two-lane highway with an arch bridge makes you nervous,
this may not be the route for you, but then you'd miss the **Los Padres
National Forest;** sparkling **Cachuma Lake,** with the chance to see
eagles and hawks soaring overhead; and the **varied views** — the road
changes from 2,200 feet, dropping down to sea level — of sun-dappled
fields, gazing herds, and craggy hills on this 15-minute detour. Plus, in
the spring, **wildflowers,** especially the golden California poppy and
purple lupine, erupt in startling displays of bold, clashing colors (don't
pick them, there's a stiff fine!).

But if you'd prefer a more sedate route, simply bypass the pass from
the north by taking Highway 154 to Highway 246 through Solvang, then
onto Highway 101; and from the south by doing the reverse. But then

you'll have missed some of the most glorious, glowing scenery in the state. Take the pass; you'll be glad you did.

Orienting Yourself

There are six towns that make up the urban side of the Santa Ynez Valley, and they lie within a 10-mile radius.

Buellton, on Highway 246 is the southernmost. Solvang, just 3 miles northeast from Buellton, is the largest tourist draw; Highway 246 becomes Mission Drive, the town's main thoroughfare. To get to Ballard from Solvang, take Highway 246 (Mission Dr.) to Highway 154 and turn west on Baseline; or follow Alisal Road out of town. Alisal Road becomes Alamo Pintado Road; Ballard lies east on Baseline off of Alamo Pintado. Staying on Alamo Pintado takes you past many wineries and drops you in the heart of Los Olivos, on Grand Avenue.

Los Alamos, tied with Ballard for the teensiest-town award, is reached by taking Highway 154 north to Highway 101; you'll pass through the town if you're coming in from the north on Highway 101. Eponymous San Ynez lies east of Solvang on Highway 246, and boasts Indian gaming and entertainment at the **Chumash Casino** (3400 Highway 246; ☎ **805-686-0855, ext. 866**; fax 805-686-8671; www.chumashcasino.com) at the outskirts of town, plus an airport, where **Windhaven Glider Rides** (900 Airport Rd.; ☎ **805-688-2517**) offer bird's-eye views of the valley.

If you have a passion for cemeteries, you may enjoy browsing through **Oak Hill Cemetery** (2560 Baseline Ave., Ballard) where Andy Warhol's troubled muse, Edie Sedgwick, is buried, and vintage tombstones abound.

Where to Stay

Solvang and Buellton offer a good number of reasonably priced rooms. But — and this is a very important point — Solvang hotels often require a two-night stay on weekends. For Friday- or Saturday-night stays, check into **Best Western Pea Soup Andersen's Inn** (☎ **800-PEASOUP** or **805-688-3216**; www.bestwestern.com) in Buellton, where you will pay $76 to $119 per night. Next door, Andersen's Pea Soup Family Restaurant serves their legendary pea soup, along with basic family fare.

If the following are booked or you want more options, contact the **Solvang Conference and Visitors Bureau** (☎ **800-468-6756** or 805-688-6144; fax 805-688-8620; www.solvangusa.com) for additional listings. The **Santa Ynez Valley Visitors Association** (☎ **800-742-2843**; www.santa ynezvalleyvisit.com) also lists lodgings in the valley.

Room tax in the valley is 10%.

Ballard Inn
$$$$ Ballard

Each of the 15 rooms at the Ballard Inn reflects an aspect of the valley's cultural heritage from vineyards to fiestas to wildflowers. Most of the rooms have a Victorian/vintage feel with modern comforts, and the inn itself is elegant, yet casual. The onsite restaurant, Cafe Chardonnay, uses local wines and produce, emphasizing the bounty of the valley. This is a favorite spot for small company retreats and honeymoons.

2436 Baseline Ave. ☎ 800-638-2466 or 805-688-7770. Fax: 805-688-9650. Internet: www.ballardinn.com. Parking: Free! Rack rates: $195–$245 double. Weekday golf and winery packages available through their Web site. AE, MC, V.

Best Western King Fredrick Inn
$–$$ Solvang

This very nice chain motel is located in the heart of Solvang. The rooms have a bit of charm, and some come with refrigerators. The pool is large, the rates are reasonable, so book early; this popular spot often sells out, and always requires a two-night stay on weekends.

1617 Copenhagen Dr., facing Mission Dr. ☎ 800-549-9955 or 805-688-5515. Fax: 805-6888-1500. Parking: Free! Rack rates: $89–$129 doubles; higher on weekends and in the summer. Theater packages available. AE, DISC, MC, V.

Fess Parker's Wine Country Inn and Spa
$$$$ Los Olivos

Owned by TV's Daniel Boone himself, Fess Parker, who also has a winery nearby, this resort hotel/spa has been awarded four diamonds by AAA. It's definitely not cheap, but if you're longing to indulge yourself, you'll find the massages and facials at the adjacent Spa Vigne and the food in the Vintage Room — along with the bucolic environment — worth the stiff tariff. Plus there's a collection of Fredric Remington bronzes on display.

2860 Grand Ave. ☎ 800-446-2455 or 805-688-7788. Fax: 805-688-1942. Internet: www.fessparker.com. Parking: Free! Rack rates: $250 king; $265 double queen; $350 suite. Rack rates $100 more on weekends, which require a two night stay. Discounts for AAA and corporate guests; weekday golf and winery tour packages available. AE, DC, MC, V.

Solvang Gardens Lodge
$–$$ Solvang

Solvang's oldest motel is also one of the best values in the entire Santa Ynez Valley. The rooms are all nonsmoking and comfortably sized, with floral prints and marble bathrooms. Nine rooms have full kitchens and seating areas, and the lodge offers weekly and monthly rates, as well as dinner, golf, and theater packages. Rates vary depending on the season.

293 Alisal Rd. ☎ *805-688-4404. Fax: 805-688-9975. Internet:* www.solvang gardens.com. *Parking: Free! Rack rates: Oct 1–May 31 Sun–Thurs $49–$129, Fri–Sat $65–$149; June 1–Sept 30 Sun–Thurs $59–$139, Fri–Sat $75–$159. DISC, MC, V.*

Solvang Inn & Cottages
$–$$$ Solvang

It's clean, it's convenient, it's inexpensive. Plus you get a complimentary continental breakfast at delicious Olsen's Bakery across the street! It's certainly not the fanciest hotel in town, but it does quite nicely, and the staff is very friendly.

1518 Mission Dr. ☎ *800-848-8484 or 805-688-4702. Fax: 805-688-6907. Parking: Free! Rack rates: $65–$210 double. Deals: AAA discount. AE, DISC, MC, V.*

Storybook Inn
$$–$$$ Solvang

One of the most expensive lodgings in town, this hotel captures the essence of Solvang and distills it for your sleeptime. Each of the nine rooms at the Storybook Inn has a romantic theme based on Hans Christian Andersen's fairy tales, which, after a day spent ogling dirndl skirts and statues of the Little Mermaid, can be a mite overwhelming. It's very, very cute, with antiques and marble fireplaces and that bedtime-story vibe. Some rooms have Jacuzzi tubs; all have queen-size feather beds and down comforters. A full breakfast, plus wine and cheese each evening, are included.

409 First St. ☎ *800-786-7925, 805-688-1703. Fax: 805-688-0953. Internet:* www.solvangstorybook.com. *Parking: Free! Rack rates: $120–$214 double. DISC, MC, V.*

Where to Dine

Paula's Pancake House
$ Solvang   DINER

You can't go wrong here, especially if you love the house speciality: you guessed it, pancakes, of all varieties, along with other breakfast items all day and burgers, sandwiches, and salads for the lunchtime crowd. Kids love it.

1531 Mission Dr. ☎ *805-688-2867. Main courses breakfast: $5–$8, lunch $5–$10. Open: Mon–Sun 6 a.m.–3 p.m.; lunch from 11:30 a.m., Sun from noon. AE, DC, DISC, MC, V.*

Stalking the Solvang smorgasbords

While in Solvang, one can always try the smorgasbords, which are, um, interesting to say the least (who knew ravioli was a Danish specialty?). In their desire to please everyone — read: tourists — the Danish restaurateurs of Solvang have resorted to some odd smorgasbord choices (like ravioli and fried chicken) along with the traditional *frikadeller* (meatballs), *medisterpolse* (sausages), and *rodkaal* (warm pickled red cabbage). And herring. Pickled herring to go with the pickled cabbage and pickled beets. Herring in mustard sauce, herring in a scary, sweetish red sauce. And then more pickled foodstuffs (which are all very traditional, given the long winters in Denmark), sandwich meats, creamed cold peas, pasta salad, green salad, fruit salad, cheese — sort of a potluck that nonplussed us. But if you can't say no to a buffet, then go for it at **Bit O'Denmark** (473 Alisal Rd., ☎ 805-688-5426; smorgasbord lunch: $8.50 Mon–Fri; $9.95 Sat–Sun; smorgasbord dinner: $13 Mon–Sun; open 11:30 a.m.–9 p.m.); the **New Danish Inn** (1547 Mission Dr.; ☎ 805-688-4311; smorgasbord lunch: $8.95; smorgasbord dinner $14; open 11 a.m.–9 p.m.); or the **Red Viking** (1684 Copenhagen Dr.; ☎ 805-688-6610; smorgasbord lunch: $7.50; smorgasbord dinner $9.50; open Mon–Sun 8 a.m.–8 p.m.) owned by the Olsens of bakery fame. All restaurants serve sandwiches and regular food as well as the Danish all-you-can-eat specialty, and most post their menus outside to help with your choice. And ask to look at the smorgasbords; you may just see something you can't resist!

Los Olivos Cafe

$–$$ Los Olivos   CALIFORNIA/MEDITERRANEAN

Mediterranean-style food, including gourmet sandwiches, salads, and pastas — think grilled eggplant and ham on hearth bread, pesto ravioli, raspberry walnut salad. The sunny patio is prefect for lunch, the inside is warm and beckoning, and the place is comfortable enough that locals eat here. Plus, you can sample some amazing wines with your meal, and do pick up their signature olive oil.

2879 Grand Ave. ☎ 805-688-7265. Fax: 805-688-5953. Internet: www.losolivos cafe.com. *Main courses: lunche: $6–$15; dinner $10–$20. AE, DISC, MC, V. Open: Sun–Thurs 11a.m.–9 p.m.; Sat–Sun 11 a.m.– 9:30 p.m.*

Meadows

$–$$$ Solvang   CALIFORNIA

Meadows is located in the Royal Scandinavian Inn. Their menu is ambitious and adult oriented, with most of the food served with wine-based sauces (the exception is the somewhat out of place macadamia crusted Hawaiian escolar filet with coconut curry sauce). But the salmon's nice, and the Pinot Noir risotto successful. There are vegetarian dishes at lunch and dinner; the lunch sandwiches are a bit too fussy for children.

Friday and Saturday night, they present the ubiquitous smorgasbord, and breakfast daily.

420 Alisal Rd. ☎ 805-688-9003. Breakfast: $7–$9. Main courses: lunch: $7–$10; dinner: $13–$18. Smorgaasbord: $15. AE, DC, DISC, MC, V. Open: Mon–Sun 7 a.m.– 9 p.m.

Exploring Solvang and the Valley Environs

There's really not much to do in **Ballard** after you see the old schoolhouse and Edie Sedgwick's grave. Itty-bitty **Los Alamos** — population 1,200 at last count — is notable for the **Depot Mall** (515 Leslie St., ☎ 805-344-3315; www.losalamosdepotmall.com), the largest antique store on the Central Coast, housed in a huge railroad station. With 50 dealers, there's lots to pick through here, including Budweiser collectibles, Victorian glass, wrought iron, Indonesian imports, and, well, stuff.

It's really up to **Los Olivos** (population 3,800) and the quaint town of **Solvang** ("more Danish than Denmark" is the oft-heard local mantra) to provide most of the entertainment during your trip to the valley. And they do make an effort, and for the most part succeed. A good thing, too: Solvang alone sees over a million tourists a year.

Founded in 1911 by Danish immigrants longing for plenty of sunny weather, the tourist town of Solvang boasts plenty of tourist attractions of the most leisurely sort, centered around eating and shopping. Free parking! A bakery on every block! Thatched roofs! Windmills! Cozy shops bursting with needlework, clogs, trolls, and quaint handicrafts! Plus plenty of pickled foods and butter cookies! Flying flags! Hans Christian Andersen! Antiques! Blooming flowers! Wood-carvings of storks! No litter! The whole town looks like a Thomas Kinkade painting, so it's no wonder that America's most populist painter has an outlet located on the main drag (**Thomas Kinkade Places in the Heart Gallery** (1576 Mission Dr.; ☎ 805-693-8337).

One of the biggest attractions in Solvang is the conspicuous abundance of baked goods. Oh yes, delectable pastries abound — not only Danishes (duh) but Sarah Bernhardts, kringles, kransekage, and their equally salubrious cousins beckon from shop windows, making incredibly visitor-friendly Solvang a great place to stop for a leg stretch and a sugar rush between Hearst Castle and Santa Barbara. **Olsen's Danish Village Bakery** (1528 Mission Dr.; ☎ 800-621-8238; www.olsensdanishbakery.com) is our favorite, and justly the most famous. All of Solvang's bakeries offer tubs of butter cookies for sale — an excellent road snack indeed. Go ahead, sample a little from every bakery you can spot, and see if you concur with our suspicions that they all come from the same central oven.

Solvang is also full of Danish import shops stuffed with Royal Copenhagen collectibles, lace, and carvings. **Gerda's Iron Art Gift Shop** (1676 Copenhagen Dr.; ☎ 805-688-3750), the **Royal Copenhagen Shop** (1683 Copenhagen Dr.; Solvang ☎ 805-688-6660), and **Gaveaesken** (433 Alisal Rd.; ☎ 805-686-5699) all offer a large selection of china, cookware, potholders, and cute Danish gift items, while **Lemos Feed and Pet Supply** (1511-C Mission Dr.; ☎ 805-693-8180) has the best-ever selection of gifts for pets and their humans who love them. Antique fiends will find plenty to admire and buy at the **Solvang Antique Center** (486 First St.; ☎ 805-686-2322) where over fifty dealers display their collections.

The mission and museums

If you feel the need to wedge some history and culture between bites of pastries and sips of wine, the valley is the home of the historic, tragic **Mission Santa Ines** (1760 Mission Dr.; ☎ 805-688-4815; winter hours: Mon–Fri. 9 a.m.–5:30 p.m., Sat–Sun 9 a.m.–5 p.m.; summer hours: daily 9 a.m.–7 p.m.), with its interpretive display of Chumash, religious, and Spanish artifacts, paintings, and documents. Built in 1804, the mission fell into disuse and disrepair after a series of natural and manmade disasters, but near-divine intervention — in the form of Capuchin monks — helped resurrect the mission, which now serves Mass and hosts an annual fiesta in midsummer.

Sampling the local wines

Santa Barbara County, and the Santa Ynez Valley in particular, has an excellent reputation for producing estate-bottled wines and for providing tourists — especially first-timers — with a non-intimidating wine-tasting experience. **Los Olivos Cafe and Wine Merchant** (2879 Grand Ave.; ☎ 805-688-7265; www.losolivoscafe.com) offers more than 300 local and international wines, with tastings until 8 p.m., while the smallest winery in Santa Barbara County, **Kahn Winery** (2990 Grand Ave.; ☎ 805-686-2455) showcases its own limited bottlings — including Cab Franc, which features a painting by Frank Sinatra as the label art.

You can also sample your way through the many fine vintages at the **Los Olivos Wine & Spirits Emporium** (2531 Grand Ave.; ☎ 888-SB-WINES or 805-688-4409; www.sbwines.com) or the **Los Olivos Tasting Room & Wine Shop** (2905 Grand Ave.; ☎ 805-688-7406).

If you'd prefer to visit wineries, there are more than 50 vineyards in the area with tasting rooms. Try **Firestone Vineyard** (5000 Zaca Station Rd., Los Olivos ☎ 805-688-3940; www.firestonewine.com), the oldest estate vineyard in Santa Barbara County, with two gold medal wins for their sauvignon blanc wine. The **Vintner's Festival** occurs in late April, and mid-October is the **Celebration of Harvest**. Contact the **Santa Barbara County Vintners' Association** (☎ 800-218-0881; www.sbcountywines.com).

Dedicated to documenting and preserving America's flora and fauna, the small and utterly wonderful **Wilding Museum** (2329 Jonata St., Los Olivos; ☎ 805-688-1082; open Wed–Fri 1–5 p.m., Sat–Sun 11 a.m.–5 p.m.; free admission) is solely supported by donations. Its three rooms offer a changing display of photographs and paintings depicting the history of our vanishing lands and wildlife, and it's truly a labor of love.

Both the **Hans Christian Andersen Museum** (1680 Mission Dr., upstairs; ☎ 805-688-2052; open Mon–Sun 9 a.m.–5 p.m.) and the **Elverhoj Museum** (1624 Elverhoy Way, Solvang; ☎ 805-686-1211; open Wed–Sun 1–4 p.m.) have displays made to delight children, especially the Elverhoj, which is designed to stimulate children to celebrate the life of Denmark's most famous citizen. Downstairs is the Bookloft and Kaffe Hus, with a reading area for children.

Adventures with (really cute) animals

Miniature horses supposedly make great house pets, but you may not want to mention that to your kids until you are far, far away from **Quicksilver Miniature Horse Ranch** (1555 Alamo Pintado Rd.; ☎ 800-370-4002 or 805-686-4002), because the things are so darn cute! No more than 34 inches high, these four-legged Lilliputians can be petted and played with during visiting hours. If you're enthralled with full-sized equines, visit **Day Dream Arabians** (2065 Refugio Rd.; ☎ 805-688-9106) for a presentation, tour, and the opportunity to stroll with and feed the mares and foals. If you'd rather visit more-exotic animals, call in advance and book a tour at the **Flying V Llama Ranch and Llama Memories Gift Shop** (6615 E. Hwy. 246, Lompoc; ☎ 805-735-3577) — 6½ miles west of Buellton, and technically just outside of the Santa Ynez Valley — for a chance to see and pet the gentle, graceful llamas, a South American relative of the camel. If birds are more your bag, **Ostrich Land** (610 E. Hwy. 246, Buellton; ☎ 805-686-9696) lets you view the 8½-feet-tall, 350-pound bipeds from a safe distance, and then buy some low-fat ostrich meat, which surprisingly tastes like — no, not chicken! — beef.

Gathering More Information

For Santa Ynez Valley information, contact the **Santa Ynez Valley Visitors Association** (☎ 800-742-2843; www.santaynezvalleyvisit. com). The local and comprehensive Web site www.solvangca.com also carries information about the entire valley, as well as Santa Barbara, Lompoc, and Santa Maria. The **Solvang Conference and Visitors Bureau** (☎ 800-468-6765 or 805-688-6144; www.solvangusa.com), with two offices (1511 Missions Dr. and 1639 Copenhagen Dr.), can provide maps and brochures; the Copenhagen Drive office is also the town's lost and found. Lost and found — how quaint! For information on wineries, contact the **Santa Barbara County Vintners' Association** (☎ 800-218-0881; www.sbcountywines.com).

Off the beaten track — discovering the dunes

California was once rich in dramatic, windswept sand dunes, replete with sheltered valleys of wildflowers and willows, and lakes full of pond turtles, red-legged frogs, muskrats, and nesting birds. San Francisco's dunes are now covered in part by Golden Gate Park, while Los Angeles's dunes were leveled to create beach towns and the airport. But travelers cruising the coast north of Solvang have a unique opportunity to visit what's now a rare sight, by stopping at the **Guadalupe-Nipomo Dunes Preserve** just north of the tiny agricultural hamlet of Guadalupe.

The preserve comprises 18 miles of the largest, most biodiverse coastal dune-lagoon ecosystem on the planet. They have been the subject of photographers including Ansel Adams and Brett Weston; home to the Dunites, a utopian group of artists founded in 1931; and the setting for Cecil B. DeMille's spectacular 1923 film, *The Ten Commandments.* Designated by the Nature Conservancy as number one in its "Last Great Places on Earth" campaign, these dunes are now permanently protected for wildlife and passive recreation.

The **Dunes Center interpretative facility** (1055 Guadalupe St., Hwy. 1, Guadalupe; ☎ 805-343-2455; www.dunescenter.org), located in a restored 1910 Craftsman-style home, is open for self-guided tours Mondays through Thursdays from 9 a.m. to 4 p.m. Docent tours are available Fridays through Sundays from noon to 4 p.m., and a schedule of walks is available on the Web site.

The Dunes are accessible at the southern end by driving on West Main St. (Highway 166) to a parking lot just below Mussel Rock Dunes, the highest coastal dunes in the world. The middle of the dunes are accessible off Highway 1, 3 miles north of Guadalupe. Turn west onto Oso Flaco Lake Road, pay a $4 parking fee, and walk along a rare riparian corridor to a bridge that crosses Oso Flaco Lake. A 1-mile boardwalk leads you to the ocean through one of the best examples of coastal dune scrub in the country.

Chapter 20

Santa Barbara and the Ojai Valley

*L*ooking for the perfect realization of the Southern California dream? Stop reading now — you've found it. If Carmel is the gold standard of up-coast Golden State beauty (and it is), gorgeous **Santa Barbara** is the Southland version. It's a sleepy, sunny berg, as pretty and sweet as it can be. And it's only miles away from another California archetype, the mystical New Age Shangri-La, **Ojai** (pronounced *oh*-high) **Valley.** Here's how to see both worthy destinations.

The Jewel of the Coast: Santa Barbara

Santa Barbara has natural assets galore. This stretch of coast has a unique situation that makes all the difference: If you look at a map, you'll see that Santa Barbara lies at the foot of the Santa Ynez Mountains on a narrow strip of coastline that has the singular, jaunty confidence to run east-west rather than north-south. So even when it's cool, cloudy, rainy, or smoggy all over the rest of the region, this Spanish-Mediterranean beauty tends to sparkle in the sun like the rare jewel it is. (But forgive us if it's overcast or foggy when you read this!) Offshore islands and tide breaks even keep the Pacific waves calm and under control.

What's more, this picture-perfect beach hamlet remains unspoiled thanks to its distance from Los Angeles. Located about 100 miles to the northwest, it's a smidgen too far outside the city's reach to be absorbed into the megalopolis, even by L.A.'s otherworldly commuting standards.

These idyllic, sun-drenched environs don't exactly inspire a bustling business world or low real estate prices — so don't quit your job to move here just yet. Santa Barbara is the self-proclaimed domain of the "almost wed and almost dead" — mainly college students (at UC Santa Barbara) and rich retirees who can afford to kick back and go with the mellow flow. So come join these well-rehearsed relaxees for a little downtime. You couldn't pick a better place to do it.

Timing your visit

Any time is a good time to visit Santa Barbara. The climate is mild and sunny year-round, with temperatures hovering between the low 60s and mid 70s most of the time. Santa Barbara has little in the way of an off-season, because the strolling and sightseeing are great no matter when you visit. Still, come before mid-October if you want guaranteed beach time and perpetual sunshine. Avoid weekends in summer and fall if you want to miss the capacity crowds.

Attention, moms and dads: Santa Barbara is family-friendly enough, but teens may well be bored, while the little ones would prefer plenty of beach time.

Plan on staying two nights so that you can enjoy Santa Barbara at the pace that it warrants — slow. Definitely give yourself the two days/three nights combo if you're planning to park yourself on the beach for an extended period or venture into the surrounding wine country. Unless you really need some serious relaxation time, the town can get a bit stale after a few days.

Getting there

Santa Barbara is 134 miles southeast of Hearst Castle, 35 miles southeast of Solvang, and 102 miles northwest of Los Angeles. U.S. 101 is the fastest and most direct route to Santa Barbara from points north or south. The highway runs right through town.

Attention, southbound travelers: For a scenic detour that will add no more than a few minutes to your drive, pick up the **San Marcos Pass (Highway 154)** near Los Olivos, about 35 miles northwest of Santa Barbara. Highway 154 offers a gorgeous peek at ranchlands and forests before depositing you back onto U.S. 101 just north of Santa Barbara. See Chapter 19.

Winging it

You can fly into **Santa Barbara Municipal Airport** (☎ **805-683-4011** or 805-967-7111; www.flysba.com), located 8 miles west of downtown in Goleta. Nonstop service is available from San Francisco, San Jose, and L.A. aboard **American Airlines** (☎ **800-433-7300**; www.im.aa.com) and **United Airlines** (☎ **800-241-6522**; www.united.com). **America West**

Express (☎ 800-235-9292; www.americawest.com) serves Santa Barbara from Phoenix and Las Vegas only.

The car-rental companies with airport locations include **Avis** (☎ 800-331-1212; www.avis.com); **Budget** (☎ 800-527-0700; Internet: https://rent.drivebudget.com); **Enterprise** (☎ 800-RENT-A-CAR; www.erac.com); **Hertz** (☎ 800-654-3131; www.hertz.com); and **National** (☎ 800-CAR-RENT; www.nationalcar.com).

You can also catch a ride with **Yellow Cab** (☎ 805-965-5111), **Rose Cab** (☎ 805-564-2600), or **Orange Cab** (☎ 805-964-2800), which usually have cabs lined up outside the terminal. Expect the fare into downtown Santa Barbara to cost $20 to $25, plus tip. If, for some reason, no cab is on hand, call Yellow Cab or Orange Cab and they'll send one right over. Rose Cab will schedule advance pickups with 24 hours' notice.

Before you pay for a taxi, check to see if your hotel offers complimentary shuttle service.

Riding the rails

Amtrak (☎ 800-USA-RAIL; www.amtrak.com) offers daily service to Santa Barbara along its San Diegan and Coast Starlight routes. Trains arrive at the Amtrak station at 209 State St., just two blocks from the beach (☎ 805-963-1015). Taxis are usually available, or you can pick up the electric shuttle; see the following section, "Orienting yourself and getting around."

Orienting yourself and getting around

Downtown Santa Barbara is laid out in a grid and is easily navigable — though keep in mind that the coastline here generally faces south. When you're taking in a romantic ocean view, you're likely gazing in the direction of Santa Monica, not Hawaii as you might think, which can make directions confusing. Restaurant- and boutique-lined State Street is the main drag. It runs perpendicular to the coastline — which means it goes north-south — and serves as the east-west dividing line: Ortega Street, for example, is East Ortega to the east of State Street, West Ortega to the west. Cabrillo Boulevard runs along the ocean and separates the city's beaches from the rest of the town.

Even if you drive into town, you may want to leave your car parked for the duration of your stay, because parking can be tough to find downtown, and weekend traffic can be a nightmare.

Santa Barbara is a joy for strollers, and most attractions are easily reachable on foot. A popular method for exploring the coast is by bike or surrey; see "Hitting the beaches," later in this chapter, for rental information. Taxi companies like Yellow Cab, Rose Cab, or Orange Cab (see "Getting there," earlier in this chapter) can get you from your hotel to dinner and back again, or wherever else you'd like to go.

Santa Barbara

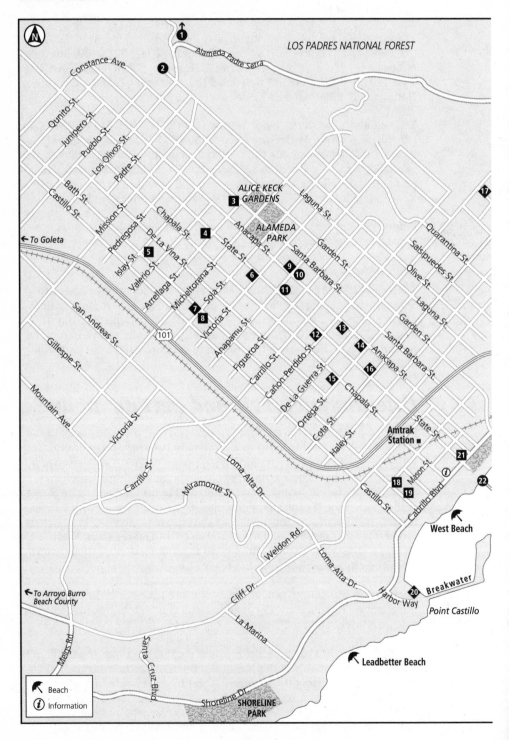

LOS PADRES NATIONAL FOREST

Alameda Padre Serra

Constance Ave.

Qunito St.

Junipero St.

Pueblo St.

Los Olivos St.

Padre St.

Bath St.

Castillo St.

Mission St.

Pedregosa St.

Chapala St.

← To Goleta

Islay St.

De La Vina St.

Valerio St.

Arrellaga St.

Micheltorena St.

Sola St.

Victoria St.

State St.

Anacapa St.

ALICE KECK GARDENS

ALAMEDA PARK

Laguna St.

Garden St.

Santa Barbara St.

Quarantina St.

Salsipuedes St.

Olive St.

Laguna St.

Garden St.

Santa Barbara St.

Anacapa St.

San Andreas St.

101

Gillespie St.

Mountain Ave.

Victoria St.

Anapamu St.

Figueroa St.

Carrillo St.

Cañon Perdido St.

De La Guerra St.

Ortega St.

Cota St.

Haley St.

Chapala St.

Amtrak
Station ■

State St.

Carrillo St.

Miramonte St.

Loma Alta Dr.

Castillo St.

Mason St.

Cabrillo Blvd.

West Beach

Weldon Rd.

Loma Alta Dr.

Cliff Dr.

← To Arroyo Burro
Beach County

Harbor Way

Breakwater

Point Castillo

La Marina

Meigs Rd.

Santa Cruz Blvd.

Leadbetter Beach

Shoreline Dr.

SHORELINE PARK

Beach

Information

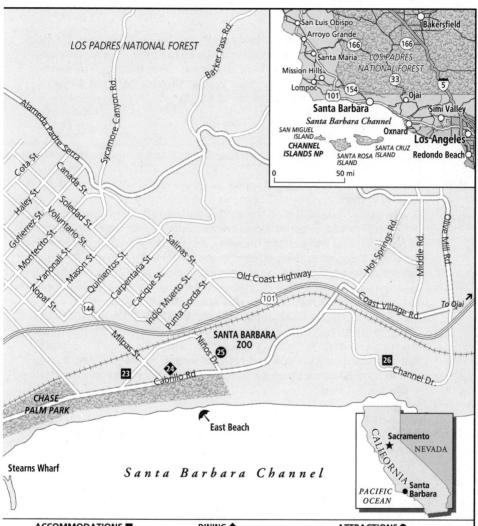

ACCOMMODATIONS ■
Bath Street Inn **5**
El Prado Inn **4**
Four Seasons Biltmore **26**
Franciscan Inn **18**
Glenborough Inn **8**
Harbor View Inn **21**
Marina Beach Motel **19**
Motel 6– Santa Barbara #1 **23**
Simpson House Inn
  Bed & Breakfast **3**

DINING ◆
Arigato **6**
Baccio **12**
Brigitte's **7**
Brophy Bros. Clam Bar
  & Restaurant **20**
Citronelle **24**
Figaro Bakery and Bistro **9**
Four Seasons Biltmore **26**
The Palace Grill **16**
Sage & Onion **14**
La Super-Rica Taqueria **17**
Tupelo Junction **15**
Wine Cask **13**

ATTRACTIONS ●
County Courthouse **10**
Old Mission, Santa Barbara **2**
Santa Barbara Botanic Garden **1**
Santa Barbara Museum
  of Art **11**
Santa Barbara Zoo **25**
Stearns Wharf **22**

Another option is to hop aboard the **Downtown-Waterfront Shuttle.** These electric shuttles run along State Street every ten minutes and Cabrillo Boulevard every half-hour daily from 10:15 a.m. to 6:00 p.m. The visitor-friendly shuttles are foolproof; you can pick them up at designated stops every block or two along each route. The fare is 25¢ (free for kids under 5); if you'd like to transfer to the other line at the junction of State and Cabrillo, ask the driver for a free transfer. For more information, call the **Metropolitan Transit District (MTD)** at ☎ 805-MTD-3702 or the **visitor center** at ☎ 805-965-3021, or go online to www.sbmtd.gov.

Where to stay

Santa Barbara is so hugely popular as a weekend destination that every lodging in town can be fully booked — so make your arrangements well in advance if your visit includes Friday and Saturday. If you're coming between May and October, book even a midweek stay as far in advance as possible. You will pay the highest rates during the summer season (mid-May through mid-September at most hotels). If you can't get a room on short notice, consider nearby Solvang (see Chapter 19).

Two free reservations services, **Hot Spots** (☎ 800-793-7666; www.hotspotsusa.com) and **Coastal Escapes** (☎ 800-292-2222; www.coastalescapes.com), can refer you to other reliable properties in the area if the accommodations listed in this section are full. Hot Spots also maintains a walk-in center at 36 State St., between Cabrillo Boulevard and Mason Street, but we strongly recommend having reservations before you come to town.

Be aware that most places require a two-night minimum stay on weekends. And expect an extra 12% in taxes to be tacked on to your hotel bill at checkout time.

Bath Street Inn

$$ Santa Barbara

Bath Street Inn is a top choice for value-minded B&B lovers. Each of the 12 immaculate and super-charming rooms in this Queen Anne–style Victorian has its own singular appeal, be it a clawfoot tub, a gas Franklin stove, or a sliver of an ocean view in the distance. The inn includes wonderful common and outdoor areas, and the lovely innkeeper serves elegant afternoon and evening munchies as well as breakfast. Frankly, she could charge more and this place would still be a great deal.

1720 Bath St. (just north of Valerio St.). ☎ *800-341-2284, 800-549-2284, or 805-682-9680. Fax: 805-569-1281. Internet: www.bathstreetinn.com. Parking: Free and easy street parking. Rack rates: $125–$240 double, $240 suite. Rates include generous breakfast, afternoon tea, and evening wine and cheese. Deals: Midweek rates 20% off Sept–June. Also ask about AAA, senior, and corporate discounts. MC, V.*

El Prado Inn

$$ Santa Barbara

Full disclosure: Author Herczog is married to the family who owns this hotel, and author Tevis has been friends with that same family since infancy. Nepotism aside, there is much to recommend the El Prado. Start with a basic hotel (one regularly upgraded and renovated for additional guest comfort, earning a AAA two diamond rating), albeit one that is family owned and operated — which translates to friendly and personal service — and add nice touches like a good continental breakfast, afternoon cookies, and even lobby mascots (one cat, one dog). Then there's the location, which is hard to beat for downtown accessibility: three blocks from the Arlington Theater and the start of the main State Street action, eight blocks from the bustling Paseo Nuevo, and 15 blocks from the beach. Rooms are clean and large, and the pool area is most pleasant (we love that the hills loom as a backdrop). *Insider tip:* Ask for manager specials for even lower prices.

1601 State St. ☎ *800-669-8979 or 805-966-0807. Internet:* www.elprado.com. *Rack rates: $85–$180. AE, DC, DISC, MC, V.*

Four Seasons Biltmore

$$$$$ Montecito

Built in 1927 and spread over 19 luxuriant acres, this Spanish Revival resort is the place to stay if you're looking to experience the "American Riviera" in its full, four-star glory. You won't want for anything here. The hotel includes 217 sumptuous rooms (including 12 cottages), amenities galore, and resort dining at its best. On the down side, the beach is not for swimming, and downtown is a ten-minute drive away. But at a resort as fab as this one, who wants to leave? Guests can enjoy the wonderful beachside pool at the Coral Casino Club, and a full-service salon with spa treatments provides nonstop pampering. Kids are pampered, too, with bedtime milk and cookies, video game units, and a Kids for All Seasons program, which offers organized activities, such as swimming, arts and crafts, and a painting jamboree.

1260 Channel Dr. (use Olive Mill Rd. exit off of U.S. 101). ☎ *800-332-3442 or 805-969-2261. Fax: 805-565-8323. Internet:* www.fourseasons.com. *Parking: Free self-parking, $18 to valet. Rack rates: $295–$635 double, $1,125–$2,275, suite. Deals: Ask about midweek rates and package deals, which may include tee times, and other perks. AE, DC, MC, V.*

Franciscan Inn

$–$$ Santa Barbara

Beautifully kept and smartly outfitted, it's way better than you'd expect for the money. All of the cute rooms have VCRs and free HBO. Suites are terrific for families, and most have fully equipped kitchenettes. The grounds have a nice heated pool and Jacuzzi, plus a coin-op laundry.

Movie rentals and morning newspapers are free. The staff is terrific, and West Beach is a block away. A real winner that will even please motel-o-phobes. Book well ahead.

109 Bath St. (at Mason St.). ☎ *805-963-8845. Fax: 805-564-3295. Internet:* www. franciscaninn.com. *Parking: Free! Rack rates: winter (Sept 15–May15): $110–$130 double, $125–$155 suite; summer (May16–Sept14): $140–$155 double, $165–$180 suite. Rates include continental breakfast and afternoon cookies and drinks. AE, DC, MC, V.*

Glenborough Inn
$$–$$$$ Santa Barbara

This is precisely what you want in a B&B (well, maybe you would want lower prices, and we can't blame you): sweet rooms (each with its own personality — and they vary in size), with perhaps a fireplace or Jacuzzi or patio; a full breakfast (brought right to your room for breakfast in bed!); a welcoming atmosphere (including evening snacks like homemade cookies); and a hot tub in the garden, for private use if you wish. It's a real romantic getaway.

1327 Bath St. ☎ *805-966-0589 or 888-966-0589 (resevations). Fax: 805-564-8610. Internet:* www.glenboroughinn.com. *E-mail:* glenboro@silcom.com. *Rack rates: $120–$250 (some suites/cottages higher); rates include breakfast. AE, DC, DISC, MC, V.*

Harbor View Inn
$$$–$$$$ Santa Barbara

It's pricey, but worth the splurge if you're looking for something special by the sea. The hotel is built hacienda-style, like a mini Biltmore in the heart of town (and facing a better beach, no less). The gorgeous, contemporary-styled rooms are big enough to host a cocktail party; and all boast granite baths (some with oversize tubs) and patios or balconies. Ocean views are expensive, but you won't need one to be happy here. On-site is a restaurant, a gym, and a lovely pool.

28 W. Cabrillo Blvd. (at State St.). ☎ *800-755-0222 or 805-963-0780. Fax: 805-963-7967. Parking: Free! Rack rates: $250–$800 double, $350–$800 suite. Deals: Inquire about 10-percent discounts for AAA or AARP members. AE, DC, MC, V.*

Marina Beach Motel
$$ Santa Barbara

It's a mere 37 steps to the beach from this button-cute motel — just ask the friendly owners, who've turned the step-count into their biggest selling point. This is another very good Santa Barbara motel bet. Rooms are spotless, and country/beachy touches save them from the budget doldrums. More than half have full-size kitchens at no extra charge, so ask for one when you book. Amenities include lovely tropical gardens, but no pool. Bicycles are on hand for your use. Children stay free, and cribs are available.

21 Bath St. (at Mason St.). ☎ *877-627-4621 or 805-963-9311. Fax: 805-564-4102. Internet:* www.marinabeachmotel.com. *Parking: Free! Rack rates: $89–$189, queen; $119–$229, double. Rates include continental breakfast. AE, DC, DISC, MC, V.*

Motel 6 — Santa Barbara #1
$ Santa Barbara

The first Motel 6 ever is the best super-cheap sleep in town — and it's less than a block from fab East Beach, no less. The rooms are what you'd expect, but they're well-kept, management is friendly, and there's a petite pool. Book as far ahead as possible, because this place fills up way in advance.

443 Corona del Mar (less than a block from Cabrillo Blvd.). ☎ *800-4-MOTEL-6 or 805-564-1392. Fax: 805-963-4687. Internet:* www.motel6.com. *Parking: Free! Rack rates: $66–$92 double. AE, DC, DISC, MC, V.*

Simpson House Inn
$$$$ Santa Barbara

AAA's only five-diamond B&B (in all of North America!) is simply spectacular. Hidden behind towering hedges on dazzlingly manicured grounds, this Victorian oasis feels like a world unto itself. Rooms are decorated to perfection and overflowing with luxuries. The staff provides concierge-style service, and an evening hors d'oeuvres spread makes dinner redundant. Very expensive, but it's money well spent if you're celebrating. Some may find it too formal, though.

121 E. Arrellaga St. (between Santa Barbara and Anacapa sts.). ☎ *800-676-1280 or 805-963-7067. Fax: 805-564-4811. Internet:* www.simpsonhouseinn.com. *Parking: Free! Rack rates: $215–$550 double, $525–$550 suites and cottages. Rates include full gourmet breakfast, evening hors d'oeuvres, and wine. AE, DISC, MC, V.*

Where to dine

Reservations are *always* a good idea on weekends year-round and weeknights in summer.

If you're in town for the weekend, consider the all-you-can-eat Sunday brunch ($45 per person) at the **Four Seasons Biltmore** (see "Where to stay," earlier in the chapter). This feast is the ultimate in elegant pig-outs — and trust us, you won't have to eat for the rest of the day. Reservations are recommended.

Arigato

$$$ Santa Barbara SUSHI

This chic sushi bar serves top-notch sushi to a hip crowd that appreciates the excellent quality and super-freshness of the fish, much of it flown in daily from Hawaii and Japan. The young servers are friendly and attentive, and the dimly lit room has a dash of romance about it.

In Victoria Court, 11 W. Victoria St. (just west of State St.). ☎ *805-965-6074. Reservations not taken. Sushi: 2-piece orders and rolls $4–$10; other dishes $9.50–$15. AE, MC, V. Open: Mon–Sun 5:30–10 p.m.*

Baccio

$$ Santa Barbara MEDITERRANEAN

Often, after we've tried to find a nice place to eat lunch in Santa Barbara and settled for something less, we recall Baccio and smack our heads. It's a most pleasant, reliable place, with fresh pastas, salads, and seafood dishes, all with a Mediteranean angle (read: predominantly Italian, but feta cheese creeps in, and either way, expect olive oil), all of it tasty, and all of it appearing at least vaguely healthy.

905 State St. ☎ *805-564-8280. Reservations accepted. Main courses: Lunch $7–$8, dinner $11–$15. AE, MC, V. Mon–Sun 11:30 a.m.–2:30 p.m.; lunch Sun–Thurs 5–9:30 p.m., Fri–Sat 5–10 p.m.*

Brigitte's

$$ Santa Barbara CAL-MEDITERRANEAN

A pretty, pretension-free bistro. The kitchen specializes in flavorful, unfussy cuisine that makes the most of such ingredients as fresh mozzarella, sun-dried tomatoes, roasted garlic, and mellow chiles. Look for wood-roasted meats, wood-fired pizzas, and Mediterranean-style fresh seafood preparations. The room is light, airy, and comfortable, and service is casual and friendly.

1325 State St. (at Sola St.). ☎ *805-966-9676. Reservations recommended. Main courses: $10–$16. AE, MC, V. Open: Lunch Mon–Fri 11:30 a.m.– 2:30 p.m., Sat 11 a.m.–3:30 p.m.; dinner Sun–Thurs 5–10 p.m., Fri–Sat 5–11 p.m.*

Brophy Bros. Clam Bar & Restaurant

$$ Santa Barbara SEAFOOD

Serving fresh-off-the-boat seafood in a casual, boisterous maritime setting, Brophy Bros. is everything a good seafood house should be. Belly up to the bar for fresh-shucked clams, oysters on the half shell, or a bowl of killer chowder. Or take a table and choose from the day's catches, which can range from local thresher shark to flown-in Alaskan king salmon. Outdoor seating on two sides, but the bar also boasts great harbor views. The only down side? Everybody loves this place — locals and visitors alike — so the wait can be unbearable on weekend nights.

In the Santa Barbara Marina, 119 Harbor Way (at Cabrillo Blvd.), 2nd floor. ☎ *805-966-4418. Reservations not taken. Main courses: $6.95–$18. AE, MC, V. Open: Sun–Thurs 11 a.m.–10 p.m., Fri–Sat 11 a.m –11 p.m.*

Citronelle
$$$$ Santa Barbara CALIFORNIA

One of L.A.'s finest chefs, Michel Richard, maintains this Santa Barbara outpost, which serves up first-rate Cal-French cuisine and priceless panoramic ocean views from a second-floor perch. The vibe is a just-right blend of California casual and special occasion, and the food is always pleasing. A great local wine list is on hand, too. Book a window table for sunset and the world is yours — for the duration of your meal, at least.

At the Santa Barbara Inn, 901 Cabrillo Blvd. (at Milpas St.). ☎ *805-963-0111. Internet:* www.santabarbarainn.com/citronelle.html. *Reservations recommended. Main courses: $8–$13 at breakfast and lunch, $19–$25 at brunch, $24–$32 at dinner. AE, DC, DISC, MC, V. Open: Mon–Thurs 6:30–10 a.m. breakfast, 11:30 a.m.–2:30 p.m. lunch, 6–9 p.m. dinner; Fri–Sat 6:30–10:30 a.m. breakfast, 11:30 a.m.–2:30 p.m. lunch, 6–10 p.m. dinner; Sun 6:30–10 a.m. breakfast, 10:30 a.m.–2:30 p.m. brunch, 6–9 p.m. dinner.*

Figaro Bakery and Bistro
$$ Santa Barbara FRENCH CAFE

This sweet little cafe (that has gone through several incarnations at this charming sidewalk location) serves French specialities, all of it fresh and fun. Croque Figaro is sliced fresh white-meat chicken with goat-cheese sauce on good bread, topped with bubbling browned Swiss cheese (it's all run under the broiler). There are also fat stuffed crepes, perfect little quiches, and nice omelets at breakfast time. Outdoor seating on nice days is at a premium.

129 E. Anapamu Street. ☎ *805-884-9218. Main courses: breakfast $4.95–$7.95, lunch $7.50–$13, dinner $13–$20. AE, DC, DISC, MC, V. Open: Daily 7:30 a.m.–9 p.m. (call to arrange for later reservations).*

La Super-Rica Taqueria
$ Santa Barbara MEXICAN

A legend that reaches well beyond the confines of this small beach town. People drive just to eat here, which explains why this unassuming taco shack has earned a whopping 25 (out of a possible 30) rating from the restaurant bible Zagat — no mean feat for a place where nothing costs over $6.90. Portions are small, so order generously — but at these prices, you can afford to. The prices also make this a good family-friendly choice.

The soft tacos are divine, and the weekend brings freshly made tamales. A few casual tables allow for instant satisfaction. Expect lines.

622 Milpas St. (just north of Cota St.). ☎ *805-963-4940. Reservations not taken. Main courses: $1.30–$6.90. No credit cards. Open: Mon–Sun 11 a.m.–9 p.m.*

The Palace Grill
$$$ Santa Barbara   CAJUN-CREOLE

This rollicking Creole-Cajun restaurant is a nice antidote to Santa Barbara's wealth of romantic bistros, and one of our perennial favorites in town. Come for big portions of bold and fiery N'awlins favorites like jambalaya, etoufée, house-smoked andouille sausage, our favorite chicken Tchoupitoulas (a cajun hollandise sauce), and even bananas Foster for dessert (though we prefer the pastry swan filled with ice cream, floating on a lake of warm chocolate). Saturdays bring a sax player and a singalong rendition, complete with toasting, of Louis' "What a Wonderful World." Free valet parking is a nice plus, as are their baskets of warm muffins. The lunch menu offers significantly lower prices on some items like the blackened filet.

8 E. Cota St. (between State and Anacapa sts.). ☎ *805-963-5000. Internet:* www. palacegrill.com. *Reservations accepted Sun–Thurs (Fri–Sat for 5:30 p.m. seating only). Main courses: Lunch: $5.50–$25, dinner $12–$25. AE, MC, V. Open: Daily 11:30 a.m.–3 p.m. lunch; Sun–Thurs 5:30–10 p.m. dinner; Fri–Sat 5:50–11 p.m. dinner. Note: They also own the Palace Express, which offers a simpler, cheaper version of the menu, in the Paseo Nuevo.*

Sage & Onion
$$$$ Santa Barbara   CALIFORNIA

A lovely, utterly marvelous establishment, perhaps the best restaurant in town, so good even the most snooty of foodie cities would be glad to have it. The menu changes seasonally (check out past menus on its Web site), but among the entrees from the past that have thrilled us are: an English cheddar souffle, silky Hudson Valley foie gras, venison with maple-glazed garnet yams, and roast pork with potato-apple-onion purée. It's a natty place but not stuffy, and it would be a mistake to miss it.

34 East Ortega St. ☎ *805-963-1012. Internet:* www.sageandonion.com. *Reservations suggested. Main courses: $24–$30. AE, MC, V. Open: Sun–Thurs 5:30–10 p.m., Fri–Sat 5:30–10:30 p.m.*

Tupelo Junction
$$$ Santa Barbara   SOUTHERN

This is a delightful new addition to the Santa Barbara dining scene, with whimsical dishes rooted in the South. This is a place that is not afraid to get silly — which explains the hearty buttermilk biscuit with "chocolate" gravy (essentially warm and liquid chocolate pudding! It's more dessert than entree). Try the messy BBQ pulled pork, with a splash of Jack Daniels in the sauce, and Gouda sloppy Joe; the hush puppies, with shrimp and more Gouda; the fried green tomatos; or the lobster and sweet corn chowder. Or anything, really, as long as you save room for the chocolate, peanut butter, and banana beignets. Breakfast is served at lunchtime, so you can still get the biscuits, even with traditional cream gravy. The place is small, so you may want to book ahead.

739 N. Chapala St. ☎ *805-899-3100. Reservations recommended. Main courses: $9–$14 breakfast and lunch; $17–$25 dinner. MC, V. Open: Tues–Sat breakfast and lunch 8 a.m.–2 p.m., dinner 5–9 p.m.*

Wine Cask
$$$$ Santa Barbara   CAL-ITALIAN

Choose between the gorgeous dining room (request a table by the fire-place for maximum romance) or the wonderful terra-cotta-tiled courtyard, complete with bubbling fountain. The menu features consistently terrific California fare with an Italian flair, and the award-winning wine list is an oenophile's dream come true. And, even with genuine special-occasion appeal, it's not overly pricey.

In El Paseo, 813 Anacapa St. (between Cañon Perdido and de la Guerra St.). ☎ *805-966-9463. Internet:* www.winecask.com. *Reservations recommended. Main courses: $10–$28 at lunch, $16–$34 at dinner. AE, DC, DISC, MC, V. Open: Lunch Mon–Fri 11:30 a.m.–2:30 p.m.; dinner Sun–Thurs 5:30–9 p.m., Fri–Sat 5:30–10 p.m.*

Exploring Santa Barbara

For the best and most efficient overview, catch a ride on the **Santa Barbara Old Town Trolley** (☎ 805-965-0353). These motorized red trolleys offer narrated 90-minute tours of SB's main sightseeing areas, including State Street, the beachfront, and Santa Barbara's mission. It's a particularly good bet if you're short on time and long on curiosity. The fee is $10 for adults, $7 for kids 12 and under. The trolley runs daily, and you can pick it up anywhere along the route. Call for the stop nearest you.

Hitting the beaches

Santa Barbara has a terrific collection of beaches. Most are flat and wide, with calm waters, gorgeous white sands, and lots of blanket space, even on busy summer days.

East Beach/West Beach: These sister beaches run as an unbroken strip along Cabrillo Boulevard for about 2 miles. **Stearns Wharf,** at the end of State Street, serves as the dividing line: The wide white sands to the east of the pier are **East Beach,** and those to the west are (you guessed it) **West Beach.** West Beach is fine, but East Beach is the real beaut. A grassy median and a palm-lined bike path separate it from the busy boulevard. On Sundays, a local artists' mart pops up along here. On the sand you'll find volleyball courts, a picnic area with barbecue grills, good facilities, and a landmark bathhouse from the 1920s. An excellent choice, and the best one for families.

Rent bikes, in-line skates, tandems for couples, and four-wheeled surreys to accommodate the whole family at *Beach Rentals,* just up from the beach at 22 State St. (☎ **805-966-2282**). Rates are $7 to $35 for the first hour ($12 to $60 for three to five hours), depending on the kind of wheels you want. Beach toys are available for rental, too.

Leadbetter Beach: On Cabrillo Boulevard just west of the harbor (turn left past La Playa School), this very pretty beach runs to Santa Barbara Point. Less protected than other local beaches, Leadbetter is popular with the local surfers when the waves kick up; fortunately, the waters generally stay calm for swimmers in summer. This is a great vantage point for watching boats cruise in and out of the harbor. The nice facilities include a sit-down cafe and limited free 90-minute parking. Otherwise, parking is $6 for the day.

You can rent kayaks, paddleboats, boogie boards, and other beach toys from **Kayak Rentals,** on the sand at Leadbetter Beach (☎ **805-266-2282**).

Shoreline Park: Long, grassy Shoreline Park sits atop the cliffs just past Leadbetter Beach. Spectacular panoramic ocean views make it a marvelous spot for a picnic. A lovely, bench-lined strolling path leads to neatly kept facilities and a small playground. Parking is free.

Arroyo Burro Beach County Park (Hendry's Beach): Arroyo Burro Beach County Park is well worth the 2-mile drive from downtown. This narrow but long crescent-shaped beach nestled below the cliffs feels secluded thanks to its distance from the main road — and its status as a wetlands sanctuary for shorebirds adds an appealing natural element. The sands are dark but still lovely, and locals love 'em for sunbathing, shelling, and swimming. This beach makes a great choice for sunset strolling, too. The Brown Pelican restaurant is here, plus restrooms, showers, and free parking. To get there, follow Cabrillo Boulevard west as it turns into Shoreline Drive. Turn right on Meigs Road, then left onto Cliff Drive; go 1.1 miles and turn left into the signed lot.

Seeing the county courthouse and other cultural highlights

The county courthouse serves as a great starting point for the **Red Tile Tour,** a self-guided walk covering a 12-square-block area of historic downtown. Pick up the map and brochure at the visitor center (see "Gathering More Information," at the end of this chapter). Allow 1½ to 3 hours to see everything along the route.

County courthouse

In a city of stunning Spanish Colonial Revival architecture, the courthouse serves as the finest example of the vernacular. Completed in 1929 and taking up an entire downtown block, the building is utterly magnificent, and well worth a look. You can explore on your own. If the clock tower is open, you'll be rewarded for the climb to the observation deck with great views of the surrounding red-tile roofs and the ocean and mountains beyond. Don't miss the courtyard garden. Free guided tours are offered Monday, Tuesday, and Friday at 10:30 a.m. and Monday through Saturday at 2 p.m. — but times can vary, so call ahead.

1100 Anacapa St., between Anapamu and Figueroa sts. (enter mid-block from the Anacapa St. entrance to reach the information desk). ☎ *805-962-6464. Admission: Free! Open: Mon–Fri 8 a.m.–5 p.m., Sat–Sun 10 a.m.–5 p.m.*

Old Mission, Santa Barbara

Founded in 1786, this majestic hilltop complex is considered the queen of the California mission chain. Even if you're not interested in the Spanish Colonial and/or Native American history of California, it's well worth a look. The mission set the architectural tone for the rest of Santa Barbara, and offers spectacular views all the way out to the Channel Islands. The self-guided tour includes a very cool cemetery.

2201 Laguna St. (at Los Olivos St., at the north end of town). ☎ *805-682-4149. Internet:* www.sbmission.org. *Admission: $4, free for kids under 12. Open: Daily 9 a.m.–5 p.m.*

Santa Barbara Botanic Garden

Situated in the foothills above town, this lovely garden is great for walkers, as 5½ miles of trails wind through indigenous California greenery. Guided tours are offered daily at 2 p.m., plus Thursday, Saturday, and Sunday at 10:30 a.m.

1212 Mission Canyon Rd. (1½ miles north of the mission). ☎ *805-682-4726. Internet:* www.sbbg.org. *To get there: From the mission, go north and turn right on Foothill Rd., then left on Mission Canyon; the garden is ½ mile up on the left. Admission: $5 adults; $3 seniors, students, and teens; $1 kids 5–12. Open: Mar–Oct, Mon–Fri 9 a.m.–5 p.m., Sat–Sun 9 a.m.–6.p.m.; Nov–Feb, Mon–Fri 9 a.m.–4 p.m., Sat–Sun 9 a.m.–5 p.m.*

Santa Barbara Museum of Art

This little gem feels like a private gallery — one with works by Monet, Picasso, Braque, Chagall, Rodin, and other masters. It contains some good 20th-century Californian and Asian art, too, and is well worth an hour.

1130 State St. (at Anapamu St.). ☎ *805-963-4364. Internet:* www.sbmuseart.org. *Admission: $6 adults, $3 seniors, $3 students and kids 6–17, free for the under-6 set; free every Thurs and the first Sun of the month. Open: Tues–Thurs and Sat 11 a.m.– 5 p.m., Fri 11 a.m.–9 p.m., Sun noon to 5 p.m.*

Santa Barbara Zoo

This charming, pint-size zoo is ideal for the little ones, and is easy to explore in less than an hour.

500 Niños Dr. (east of Milpas St., turn up Niños from Cabrillo Blvd.). ☎ *805-962-5339. Internet:* www.santabarbarazoo.com. *Admission: $8 adults, $6 seniors and kids 2–12. Parking: $2. Open: Daily 10 a.m.–5 p.m. (arrive before 4 p.m.).*

Experiencing the harbor life

At the end of State Street is **Stearns Wharf,** a 19th-century vintage pier that offers great views but is otherwise pretty touristy. Head instead to **Santa Barbara Harbor** for a genuine look at local maritime life. To get there, follow Cabrillo Boulevard west, past Castillo Street, and turn left on Harbor Way. While you're there, **Brophy Bros. Clam Bar & Restaurant** makes a great place to soak in the atmosphere, not to mention some divine chowder and oysters on the half shell (see "Where to dine," earlier in this chapter).

If you want to hit the water, **Sea Landing** (☎ 805-963-3564) offers half- and full-day sportfishing trips. **The Santa Barbara Sailing Center** (☎ 800-350-9090 or 805-962-2826; www.sbsailctr.com) has a wide array of excursions, including dinner cruises, afternoon sailing, and whale-watching (February through May).

If you'd like to cruise over to **Channel Islands National Park,** check out the offerings from the fleet at **Truth Aquatics** (☎ 805-962-1127; www.truthaquatics.com), which offers hiking, camping, and natural history trips as well as fishing, diving, and whale watching.

Shopping 'til you drop

The main shopping area is the Paseo Nuevo, the new mall that was nicely built to copy the classic State Street Spanish architecture. You won't find many non-chain stores within this meandering landmark, but it's so pretty (splashing fountains, carts with jewelry and such), even usual mall haters don't mind. State Street between Canon Perdido and Ortega Streets.

Boutiques abound along State Street and in the offshoot blocks, where you'll find such local treats as the **Book Den** (11 East Anapamu St.; ☎ 805-962-3321), a used bookstore.

Antiques hounds should seek out **Brinkerhoff Avenue,** a block-long passage 1½ blocks west of State between Cota and Haley streets that brims with vintage goodies. Most shops along Brinkerhoff are closed Monday, and close as early as 5 or 6 p.m. on weekdays.

Also worth seeking out is **El Paseo,** at 814 State St. (between Cañon Perdido and de la Guerra Street), a charming arcade lined with boutiques and galleries that's reminiscent of an old Spanish street. It also happens to be the oldest shopping street in southern California — and is across the street from the Paseo Nuevo (hence the name).

Touring the local wine country

In the past few years, Santa Barbara's wine country has really come into its own, with local labels achieving national prominence and wineries attracting visitors from the far reaches of the globe. If you'd like to explore the local tasting rooms — which include such familiar labels as Cambria, Firestone, Meridian, and Au Bon Climat — stop into the local visitor center here or in nearby Solvang (see Chapter 19) and pick up the brochure and map called **Santa Barbara County Wineries.** You can also order a copy in advance by contacting the Santa Barbara County Vintners Association at ☎ **800-218-0881** or 805-688-0881. You can even download a version online at www.sbcountywines.com.

Gathering more information

The **Santa Barbara Conference and Visitors Bureau** (☎ **800-549-5133** or 805-966-9222) has a wealth of information, much of it in easily printable form, at www.santabarbaraca.com. The **Santa Barbara Tourist Information Center** is just across from the beach at 1 Garden St., at Cabrillo Boulevard (☎ **805-965-3021**). This center offers good maps and other literature, and the friendly staff can answer specific questions. Open Monday through Saturday from 9 a.m. to 5 p.m. and Sunday from 10 a.m. to 5 p.m.

You may also want to pick up a copy of the ***Independent,*** a free weekly paper with comprehensive events listings. It's available from sidewalk racks and in shops and restaurants around town.

Serene Shangri-La: The Ojai Valley

The Ojai Valley has been known as Shangri-La ever since director Frank Capra chose the area as the background for his 1947 movie *Lost Horizon.* To local Native Americans, the valley had long been a sacred holy place, but it was Capra who put it on the international map. One look around this landscape, handsomely tucked into the mountains between Santa Barbara and Los Angeles, and you'll understand why everyone who visits finds it so special. For visitors to Southern California who think the state consists of nothing but bright lights and big cities, Ojai is the perfect soul-soothing antidote.

It was in the late 19th century that settlers from the East Coast began to arrive in Ojai in search of a healthful climate — believed to be beneficial for sufferers of everything from allergies to tuberculosis — and spiritual enlightenment. Just as the Native Americans believed that the area possessed sacred qualities, later visitors found the valley (with its unusual east-west orientation) especially conducive to certain loftier pursuits.

Those lofty pursuits really took off in 1923 with the arrival of J. Krishnamurti, an Indian prophet whose work in combining eastern and western philosophies marks him as the founder of what later would become the **New Age movement.** He was later joined by such luminaries as Aldous Huxley in developing institutions of higher understanding in Ojai. Those institutions are still operating and can be visited today.

With folks like Krishnamurti and Huxley in residence, Ojai became a logical choice for **artists and musicians.** The famed sculptor Beatrice Wood, known as the Mama of Dada, moved to the valley in the 1940s. She was followed by countless other artists. Her studio remains open to the public today, as are those of many other working artists (Wood died in 1998, at age 105).

Music is another legacy that remains strong in Ojai. The annual **Ojai Festival,** in May of every year, brings together performers and scholars from all over the world for a series of concerts and symposia celebrating both classical and modern orchestral music.

If you love the outdoors, Ojai offers an unparalleled set of opportunities for **camping, hiking,** and **mountain biking** in Los Padres National Forest, which borders the northern edge of town. The forest is the largest in the national forest system and presents countless options for recreational fun. And if you prefer a less active outdoor experience, the scenic beauty of the Ojai Valley is alone worth the trip. Rising up to 6,000 feet above sea level at the east end of the valley is the magnificent **Topa Topa Bluff.** Every evening as the sun sets, the bluff takes on a remarkable shade of coral, creating the "pink moment" for which Ojai is famous.

Timing your visit

Ojai is a wonderful place to visit all year long. The summer months of July, August, and September can be on the hot side (but not as hot as Palm Springs). The rest of the year is quite pleasant. The city of Ojai is only 16 miles from the ocean, and sea breezes rising up the valley provide a natural air conditioning and cool things off nicely, especially in the evenings. Weekends are the busiest time, especially in spring and fall.

Getting there

The best way to get to Ojai is by car. Ojai is located 85 miles northeast of Los Angeles and 35 miles southeast of Santa Barbara, about 15 miles inland from the city of Ventura.

From Los Angeles: Take Interstate 5 (I-5) north to Castaic, then go west on Highway 126 to Santa Paula, then north on Highway 150 to Ojai; or go north on U. S. 101 to Ventura, then go east on Highway 33 to Ojai.

From Santa Barbara: Take U. S. 101 south to Highway 150, which leads to Ojai.

Orienting yourself and getting around

Ojai is compact and laid out simply along one main road, Highway 150, also known as **Ojai Avenue.** In the center of town, the principal shopping district is clearly distinguishable by the **Arcade,** a blocklong row of shops with a Spanish Colonial–style colonnade of arches. Ample parking is located behind the shops. Across the street is **Libbey Park,** with a great play area for kids, tennis courts, and the Libbey Bowl, home of concerts and plays. Directions to everything else in the valley are generally given in relationship to the Arcade.

For getting around Ojai, the **Ojai Trolley** makes a circuit around town (the full ride is about an hour) and stops at shops, schools, hotels, and more. The service operates Monday through Friday from 7:15 a.m. to 5:40 p.m. and Saturday and Sunday from 9 a.m. to 5 p.m. Riding the trolley costs a quarter.

Where to stay

Ojai offers a wide range of accommodations, from the most luxurious to the charming and funky to basic and affordable.

Ojai is a very popular destination for weekend visitors from all over Southern California, so you should make reservations before arrival if your visit involves a Friday- or Saturday-night stay. Many of the top establishments have two-night minimums on weekends, and minimums or higher rates during important events or festivals. Many offer lower rates during the week. Ojai is also a popular destination for business travelers, with substantial facilities for conferences and corporate meetings.

Blue Iguana Inn
$$ Ojai

The Southwest-style buildings of the Blue Iguana surround a courtyard filled with beautiful gardens and a pool and Jacuzzi. The small inn features studio and one- and two-bedroom units with fully equipped kitchens. Continental breakfast is included on the weekends. A sister property nearby, the **Emerald Iguana Inn,** offers similar rooms with fireplaces or wood-burning stoves, in California Craftsman–style buildings.

Highway 33, 11794 N. Ventura Rd. ☎ *805-646-5277.* www.blueiguanainn.com. *Rack rates: $95–$179. Weekly rates available. AE, DC, DISC, MC, V. Pets on approval.*

Moon's Nest Inn
$$ Ojai

Located in a historic Victorian house in the heart of town, this charming inn offers seven rooms (five with private bath), most with a private balcony overlooking the exquisite gardens or with a view of the mountains. Breakfast (included) is served on the deck overlooking the landscaped grounds and pond.

210 E. Matilija St. ☎ 805-646-6635. www.moonsnestinn.com. *Rack rates: $95–$140. AE, MC, V. Pets on approval. No smoking.*

The Oaks at Ojai
$$–$$$ Ojai

One of Ojai's highlights, this relatively affordable health-spa experience offers guests three (decent quality) meals totaling a mere 1,000 calories per day (!!) and a slate of daily exercise classes, from pool aerobics to yoga. Spa treatments are available for an additional fee, and it's all served up in a bucolic mountain setting. Morning walks through the sweet town of Ojai and amid surrounding mountains make exercise far more enjoyable than it ought to be. Rooms vary in size and quality; the ones in the main house can be quite tiny, while the cottages are plenty large but have frumpy furnishings. The new suites are smashing — good furniture, lovely tile, private patios, Jacuzzi tubs — well worth it if you want the whole spa pampering experience. Sure, it's less posh than pricier places, but it's also less terrifyingly chic. Real people with real-people thighs are among the loyal clientele.

122 E. Ojai Ave. ☎ 800-753-6257. www.oaksspa.com. *Rack rates: $155–$285 per person, per night. AE, DISC, MC, V. Pets OK.*

Ojai Valley Inn & Spa
$$$–$$$$ Ojai

Consistently ranked by major travel magazines as one of America's top resorts, the Ojai Valley Inn is a destination in itself. Start with stunningly beautiful grounds, add luxury rooms and a staggering array of activities, including a championship 18-hole golf course, swimming pools, horse ranch and stables, tennis courts, banquet and meeting facilities, casual and fine dining, plus the elegant **Spa Ojai,** which offers complete spa services and a state-of-the-art fitness center. The inn also has a variety of children's programs. All this comes at a price, of course.

Country Club Road. ☎ 800-422-6524 or 805-646-5511. Fax: 805-640-0305. www.ojai resort.com. *Rack rates: $279–$349. Suite rates also available upon request. Check Web site for special packages. AE, DISC, MC, V. Pets OK.*

Rose Garden Inn
$$ Ojai

Low-slung ranch-style buildings surround (what else?) an immaculate rose garden, which always seems to be in bloom. Simply decorated rooms have kitchen units. The inn has a pool, a spa, a sauna, and other outdoor amenities.

615 W. Ojai Ave. ☎ *805-646-1434. Fax: 805-640-8455. Rack rates: $99–$119. AE, DC, DISC, MC, V.*

Theodore Woolsey House
$–$$ Ojai

Located in one of Ojai's oldest homes, set on seven lush acres with mountain views, this seven-room inn offers elegant yet casual sophistication in a peaceful, secluded setting. It offers a pool, a hot tub, a croquet court, and a putting green. Rooms are nicely equipped with private baths, balconies, and fireplaces. The inn is adjacent to the **Day Spa of Ojai** (see "Mind-body quests," later in this chapter).

1484 E. Ojai Ave. ☎ *805-646-9779.* www.theodorewoolseyhouse.com. *Rates: $80–$150. MC, V. No pets.*

Where to dine

The dining choices in Ojai are remarkably diverse, from high-end California cuisine to basic American or Mexican fare. There's a general emphasis here on local ingredients and healthy food.

Bonnie Lu's
$ Ojai BREAKFAST/LUNCH

Another Ojai institution, located in the Arcade, Bonnie Lu's is the place to come for traditional American breakfasts and lunch-counter fare. Beware the morning crowds on weekends.

328 E. Ojai Ave. ☎ *805-646-0207. Nothing over $10. MC, V. Open: Daily (except Wed) 7 a.m.–2:30 p.m.*

Deer Lodge
$$$ Ojai HEARTY AMERICAN

An Ojai institution since 1932, the Deer Lodge offers hearty fare in a rustic but comfortable environment. The main feature on the menu is venison, but there are plenty of other choices ranging from coconut shrimp to vegetarian fettucine Provencal. The restaurant features live music and dancing on weekends. Sundays feature an oak barbecue and blues music. The hamburgers at lunch are big and tasty, and breakfasts are hearty.

2261 Maricopa Hwy. ☎ *805-646-4256. Appetizers: $4.50–$8. Main courses: $12–$27. AE, MC, V. Open: Mon–Thurs 10 a.m.–10 p.m., Fri 10 a.m.–2 a.m., Sat 8 a.m.–2 a.m., Sun 8 a.m.–10 p.m.*

Pisacali Grill

$$ Ojai   ITALIAN/CALIFORNIAN

The imaginative chef/owner of this relative newcomer dubs his personal cuisine "Italifornian," combining Italian traditions with California influences and assorted other elements from around the world. The atmosphere is relaxed, in a space reminiscent of an artist's loft. There is an emphasis on pizzas and pasta, with such interesting entrees as cedar-planked salmon.

585 El Roblar. ☎ *805-640-3726. Pizzas and pasta: $7.50–$12. Main courses: $11–$18. MC, V. Open: Tues–Sun 5–9 p.m. Call for lunch hours in summer.*

Rainbow Bridge

$ Ojai   HEALTH-FOOD/DELI

Strictly speaking, Rainbow Bridge is a health-food grocery store. But it also has a full deli serving takeout and extra items presented at lunch and dinner to eat in. It's the perfect place to acquire provisions for a picnic or a hike, and it's the top choice in town for vegetarians and health-conscious diners.

211 E. Matalija St. ☎ *805-646-4017 or 805-646-6623. Nothing over $6. Open: 9 a.m.– 7:30 p.m. daily. AE, MC, V.*

The Ranch House

$$$ Ojai   CALIFORNIA CUISINE

One of the pioneers of California cuisine, this garden restaurant presents creative interpretations of classic dishes using regional produce. The setting is an intimate wooded glen with meandering streams. Service is top-notch, and an on-premises bakery supplies fresh breads. The wine list is nationally recognized.

South Lomita Ave. ☎ *805-646-2360.* www.theranchhouse.com. *Appetizers: $6–$12. Main courses: $14–$28. AE, MC, V. Open: Wed–Fri 5:30–8:30 p.m., Sat seatings 5–6:30 p.m. and 8–8:30 p.m., Sun 11 a.m.–7:30 p.m. Reservations required.*

Ruben's Burritos

$ Ojai   MEXICAN

This is real Mexican food, with a heart-healthy choice of ingredients. There are two locations, a tiny place behind the Arcade and a larger place 2 miles west of the Arcade. Ruben's doesn't have a lot of atmosphere, but it does offer plenty of good choices in the burrito category, ranging from *carne azada* (pan-seared steak) to chicken en mole to vegetarian options, plus daily specials of traditional soups and stews. It also has dinner plates of chile relleno or pollo pico, sturdy breakfasts of huevos rancheros, and a children's menu.

104 N. Signal St. (behind the Arcade). ☎ *805-646-6111. 11420 N. Venture Ave.* ☎ *805-649-5133. Nothing over $8. MC, V. Open daily 8 a.m.–9 p.m.*

Sea Fresh
$$ Ojai   SEAFOOD

A restaurant with its own boat can't help but serve great seafood. Using fresh-caught fish from local waters with the best seafood from other sources, Sea Fresh presents an impressive array of classic dishes, such as fish and chips, fried calamari, and char-broiled red snapper, plus fish tacos and a full-service sushi bar. There's also a market for fresh fish to take home.

533 E. Ojai Ave. ☎ *805-646-7747. Fried combos or tacos: $7.45–$12. Dinners: $9.95–$16. Sushi items: $3.50–$11. Open: Sun–Thurs 11 a.m.–9 p.m., Fri–Sat 11 a.m.– 10 p.m.*

Exploring the Ojai Valley

Ojai is home to a number of annual events that draw visitors from all over the country and the world. Among them are: the **Ojai Tennis Tournament** (every April; featuring the Pacific 10 and National Juniors championships); the **Ojai Music Festival** (the first weekend after Memorial Day; presenting the latest in adventurous classical music); the **Ojai Wine Festival** (every June; presenting wines from 40 Central Coast makers in the Lake Casitas Park); the **Ojai Shakespeare Festival** (every July); **Bowlful of Blues** (every October; blues and jazz on the shores of Lake Casitas); and the **Ojai Studio Artists Tour and the Detour** (every October; for self-guided tours through 70 artists studio).

Detailed information on dates can be obtained from the Ojai Valley Chamber of Commerce (see the "Gathering more information" section at the end of this chapter). Keep in mind that the town will be more crowded when these events are going on, so be sure to make your lodging reservations well in advance if you plan to be here on these dates.

Here are some of the other attractions in and around Ojai to keep you occupied during your stay.

The arts in Ojai

If art is your interest, you'll find plenty of year-round opportunities to appreciate the local talent. The Arcade is filled with interesting galleries and shops offering works from local and other artists. Among the best are **Human Arts Gallery and Home** (310 and 246 E. Ojai Ave; ☎ 805-646-1525 and 805-646-8245; open daily 11 a.m.–5p.m.), featuring art, crafts, and jewelry from more than 206 artists, and **Primavera Gallery** (214 E. Ojai Ave.; ☎ 805-646-7133; www.PrimaveraArt.com; open daily 10 a.m.–5 p.m.), offering contemporary American art.

In the upper valley, the **Beatrice Wood Studio** (8560 Hwy. 150; ☎ 805-646-3381; www.beatricewood.com) presents a permanent collection of the late artist's pottery and artwork, plus visiting exhibits and a wonderful gift shop. Call for an appointment. To see a real artist at work, visit the studio of octogenarian **Otto Heino** in the East End (971 McAndrew Rd.; ☎ 805-646-3393; open Wed–Sun 10 a.m.–4 p.m.). Otto offers wood-fired pottery with unique glazes and decorative porcelains and tiles.

Outdoor adventures

The first stop for the outdoor adventurer is the Ojai Ranger Station of the **Los Padres National Forest** (1190 E. Ojai Ave.; ☎ 805-646-4348; call for hours). The rangers can provide trail maps, parking permits, and information for camping. For campsite reservations, call ☎ 800-280-CAMP.

If you prefer less-strenuous outdoor exercise, try the **Ojai Valley Trail,** a 16½-mile paved track running from Ojai to the beach at Ventura. The trail is perfect for walking, biking, or horseback riding. To rent a bicycle, contact **Bicycles of Ojai** (108 Canada St.; ☎ 805-646-7736). For horses, call the **Ojai Valley Inn Ranch & Stables** (☎ 805-646-5511, ext. 51).

If you'd prefer to see the outdoors without breaking a sweat, contact **Pink Moment Jeep Tours** (☎ 805-646-3227 or 805-653-1321). That company offers guided tours of area sites in open-air Jeeps, including excursions to the best spots to witness the famous "pink moment."

Gathering more information

Contact the **Ojai Valley Chamber of Commerce and Visitors Center** (150 W. Ojai Ave., P.O. Box 1134, Ojai, California 93024-1134; ☎ 805-646-8126; fax 805-646-9762; Internet www.the-ojai.org; e-mail info@the-ojai.org). They publish an excellent visitors guide and other brochures and can answer any questions you have about Ojai.

Part V
The Southland Cities and the Desert

The 5th Wave   By Rich Tennant

In this part . . .

This part focuses on Southern California — Los Angeles,
San Diego, and the Disneyland Resort — along with
California's *real* hot spots: Palm Springs and the desert. In
addition to being rich in glitz and gloriously fun, Los
Angeles is the state's finest museum town — no kidding.
The Disneyland Resort is the original theme park, an
unadulterated blast for kids of all ages. San Diego is a
sunny, laidback city with lots of kid-friendly attractions
and golden beaches galore.

Unlike other destinations in this book — which are generally popular in summer and largely pleasant to visit year-
'round — Southern California is fun to visit in any season
but summer, when the scorching heat can be a bit much to
bear. Still, even on the most simmering days, you can find
respite from the heat. The Palm Springs area is the place
to go for desert cool by a sparkling swimming pool, and if
you're looking for the perfect day at the beach, head to
easy-going Laguna. The fabled mission at San Juan
Capistrano has lush gardens that burst forth with color,
celebrated by a flower and garden festival in June.

And if really hot isn't hot enough for you, head for the
otherworldly beauty of the state's desert parks, Joshua
Tree National Park and Death Valley National Park.

Chapter 21

Los Angeles

● ●

In This Chapter

▶ Knowing when to go and how to get there — and deciding how long to stay

▶ Getting to know the lay of La-La Land

▶ Choosing your neighborhood and deciding on the best places to stay and eat

▶ Seeing the sights, shopping, and living it up after the sun goes down

● ●

*W*e love L.A. — we really, really do, but that's because we know how to best find and experience its admittedly subtle charms. Yeah, it's got smog (though increasingly less), yes, it has traffic (alas, more than ever), and yes, much of the distinctive architecture has been torn down thanks to an utter disinterest in preservation. And yes, it's far-flung and public transportation stinks, so you absolutely have to buck that aforementioned heavy traffic to get anywhere to enjoy anything.

But. Here's a place where you can surf and ski on the same day. Here's a place where your sightseeing will only be enhanced by one of the 350 cloudless days a year. Here's a place where movie-star footprints are enshrined, and Gettys give a great deal of money to amass one of the finest art collections in the world. Here's a place where you can enjoy the L.A. Philharmonic (and other internationally known artists) for just a few dollars (of course, for that price, way up high) out in the fragrant night air, at the gorgeous Hollywood Bowl. Here's a place where just a one-mile stretch of Hollywood Boulevard peacefully holds Thai, Mexican, Romanian, Armenian, Vietnamese, and Persian restaurants, all of them with some of the most wonderful food you've ever tasted, for a bargain price. Here's a place where weirdness and eccentricity are embraced — and of course, if you can turn it into a sitcom, so much the better. Here's a place where you can grocery shop right next to the actors who star in those very sitcoms, just like they were regular folks.

El Pueblo de la Señora, la Reina de Los Angeles ("the city of Our Lady, Queen of the Angels") was founded by the Spanish in 1781, but truth be told, it wasn't really on the map until the movie folks came out here in search of outdoor locations that didn't suffer from snow. By World War I, the movie business had a hold on the town, and in the 1920s and '30s, people came here in droves seeking their fortunes. Very few of them were discovered sipping sodas in malt shops, à la Lana Turner, but that didn't stop anyone from trying.

That crush of people came with cars, and as early as 1940, the Arroyo Seco Parkway, the first freeway, was opened. The automobile business solidified L.A.'s total dependence on cars by crushing the then quite handy public transport (the Little Red Cars trolley system). More freeways followed, and more people came to work in the thriving aerospace industry (lead by McDonnell Douglas) and the new television industry. It didn't help that every year, Pasadena put on the glorious Rose Parade under inevitably clear blue skies, causing snowbound Midwesterners and others to throw everything in the car and go to permanently join the balmy fun. In no time at all, L.A. became an urban sprawl of impossible dimensions.

And they keep on a'comin', although a few events have quenched migration enthusiasm, at least briefly. In 1971, an earthquake measuring 6.2 on the Richter scale rocked nearby Sylmar, but although it loomed in legend for more than 20 years, it was nothing compared with the Biggish One, the Northridge quake (6.8 on the Richter scale) that left nearly 60 people dead and a portion of the freeway collapsed. Riots in the wake of the Rodney King verdict shut the city down for several days, as homes and businesses burned and the National Guard came out to restore order. And then there was O.J.

But thanks to its blessedly short memory, floods, fires, and football players haven't stopped this town. And on one of those clear days — after the Santa Ana winds have blown away the smog — when the sky is a memorable blue, the mountains stand out so sharply they seem cut out of glass, the impossibly blooming bougainvillea flaunts a floozy pink, the air smells of gardenia, and you're in your shirt sleeves, enjoying the sun on your face as you sip some coffee, you think to yourself "It's January?" . . . and, well, you may find yourself loving L.A., too.

Timing Your Visit

People are fond of complaining that Los Angeles has no seasons. Sure, certain flowers bloom all year long, but the seasonal changes are there — they're just subtle, that's all. In the winter, trees are bare (well, not the palm trees), and spring here looks like spring most anywhere.

If it's going to rain — and odds are, it won't, unless another *El Nino* snakes its way out of the tropics — it's most likely going to happen in spring. Even then, heavy rainstorms are unusual. It can get nippy — oh, not Minnesota, 40°F-below nippy — but it can get down in the 20s at night in winter, so bring a coat. Actually, a light wrap is always a good idea, thanks to temperatures that can annoyingly flit from 80°F during the day to 50°F at night. Fall can bring the Santa Anas, the surprisingly strong, warm winds that are a bane to firefighters. Note also that the

Westside neighborhoods (Santa Monica, Brentwood, Pacific Palisades, and even Westwood) always seem to be 20°F (or more) cooler than Hollywood, Pasadena, and the Valley (the latter two are the hottest places in the city area). Go figure. Thank the ocean breezes.

Most people visit in summer, but Los Angeles is pleasant all year long. The daytime temperatures seldom drop below the mid-60s, and night-time lows waffle between the 40s and 50s year-round (bring a jacket anytime you come), except during the height of summer, when it stays more balmy.

Summer comes late to L.A. June is often on the cool side and plagued by *June gloom* — morning fog that doesn't burn off until early after-noon (and can actually last into August). On the up side, low humidity and ocean breezes keep the climate relatively dry and comfortable, even 20 miles inland, in the heat of summer (July, August, and well into September). The valleys can get smoggy and miserable on the hottest days — which means you could end up broiling at Universal Studios — but otherwise you'll likely be comfortable.

Winter provides a great time for avoiding crowds and escaping the bitter cold back home. While the weather will likely be too cool for the beach, the occasional 80°F day will pop up, and hotel bargains are common (except at holiday time). And the rain and winds blow away smog and haze, leaving a landscape of such beauty that you suddenly understand why people live here — and you may even want to join them.

L.A.'s attractions are spread out and traffic can be horrendous, which means one of two things:

✔ You need three full days to get a good overview of the city.

✔ If you're not a city person and you know that L.A. is going to get under your skin quickly (or you just don't have three full days to give), you should zero in on where your interests lie, see those attractions in a day or two, and skedaddle outta town.

Getting There

Los Angeles International Airport, commonly called **LAX** (☎ 310-646-5252; www.lawa.org), is the city's major gateway, and most likely where you'll fly in. LAX is on the ocean south of Marina del Rey at the intersection of the 405 and 105 freeways, 9½ miles from Santa Monica and 16 miles from Hollywood. From the airport, it's approximately a half-hour drive to Downtown, and a 40-minute drive to West Hollywood, depending on the traffic.

Burbank-Glendale-Pasadena Airport (☎ 800-U-FLY-BUR, 818-840-8840; www.burbankairport.com) is usually just referred to as "Burbank." You'll find it 8 miles northeast of Hollywood within a rough square bounded by the 5, 134, and 170 freeways. Burbank is far smaller and more manageable than LAX and is definitely the most convenient gateway if you're basing yourself in Hollywood. Most flights coming into Burbank arrive from other California cities or nearby cities like Phoenix and Vegas. From the airport, it's approximately a 25-minute drive to downtown and a 20-minute drive to West Hollywood, depending on the traffic.

All the major car-rental companies have branches at both airports. Each company provides shuttle service between the terminals and their off-site lot.

Getting to your hotel from LAX

If you're staying in Santa Monica, take Sepulveda Boulevard north and follow the signs to Lincoln Boulevard/Highway 1 (Pacific Coast Highway, or PCH) north. To reach West L.A., Beverly Hills, or Hollywood, take Century Boulevard to I-405 north; Santa Monica Boulevard east is the likeliest exit, but check with your hotel for exact directions.

If you won't be renting a car at the airport, **SuperShuttle** (☎ **800-554-3146,** 310-782-6600; www.supershuttle.com) offers door-to-door shuttle service. Expect to pay between $14 and $30 (plus tip) per person, depending on your drop-off point. Although you don't need reservations for your arrival, you must make them at least a day in advance for your return trip to the airport.

Taxis line up curbside at each terminal. Expect to pay between $31 and $40 (plus tip), depending on your destination. All LAX pickups include a $2.50 surcharge. Taxis can accommodate up to five riders.

Getting to your hotel from Burbank

Follow the signs to U.S. 101 south (the Hollywood Freeway), and exit at Vine Street for Hollywood hotels; continue south on the I-110 to the I-10 west if you're staying on the Westside or at the beach.

SuperShuttle (☎ **818-556-6600;** www.supershuttle.com) offers door-to-door shuttle service from Burbank; expect to pay $15 plus tip to Hollywood. Reserve airport pickups and returns in advance. If you forget, taxis wait outside the terminal. Taxi fare will depend on your final destination, but expect to pay between $20 and $30 to Hollywood.

Arriving by car

If you're driving from Santa Barbara and coastal points north, follow U.S. 101 south to Interstate 405 (I-405):

✔ For **West L.A., Beverly Hills,** or **West Hollywood,** exit at Santa Monica Boulevard.

✔ **For Santa Monica,** pick up I-10 west, which will drop you right at the ocean.

✔ **If you're heading to Hollywood,** stay on U.S. 101 until it becomes the Hollywood Freeway (be sure to take the Hollywood Freeway/U.S. 101 turnoff, or you'll end up in Pasadena before you know it). Exit the Hollywood Freeway at Vine or Gower streets.

If you're arriving directly from San Francisco or Monterey and prefer to bypass the scenic coastal route for a much quicker route, follow Interstate 5 (I-5) through the middle of the state. Heading south on I-5, you'll pass a small town called Grapevine, which marks the start of the Grapevine Pass, a mountain pass that will lead you into the San Fernando Valley and L.A. Take I-405 south to Santa Monica, West L.A., Beverly Hills, and West Hollywood; for Hollywood, follow I-5 past I-405 to Highway 170 south to U.S. 101 south (this route is called the Hollywood Freeway the entire way).

From points east, either Palm Springs or Phoenix farther afield, take Interstate 10 (I-10) west, which dead-ends in Santa Monica. For Hollywood, take I-110 (the Harbor Freeway) to U.S. 101 (the Hollywood Freeway) north; for West L.A. and Beverly Hills, follow I-10 to I-405 north.

From Disneyland or San Diego, head north on I-5 (the Santa Ana Freeway). If you've been following along, you'll know to pick up I-405 north to Santa Monica, West Los Angeles, and Beverly Hills, and continue on to U.S. 101 for Hollywood.

Arriving by train

Amtrak (☎ **800-872-7245;** www.amtrak.com) trains arrive at Union Station, 800 N. Alameda St. (☎ **213-624-0171**), on the northern edge of downtown just north of U.S. 101. From there, you can take one of the taxis that line up outside.

Orienting Yourself and Getting Around

Los Angeles is sandwiched between mountains and ocean, on the flatlands of a huge basin, with downtown L.A. as its midpoint 12 miles east of the Pacific. The huge, sprawling city includes dozens of neighborhoods and independent municipalities that are so complex even a city planner would need some serious time to sort it all out. The web of freeways knits it all together. The major freeways form a rough box around the area you'll concentrate your time in:

Los Angeles' Neighborhoods

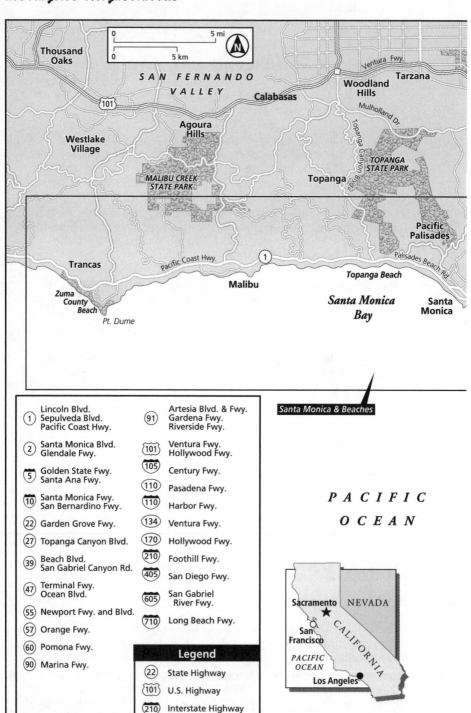

①	Lincoln Blvd. / Sepulveda Blvd. / Pacific Coast Hwy.	⑨①	Artesia Blvd. & Fwy. / Gardena Fwy. / Riverside Fwy.
②	Santa Monica Blvd. / Glendale Fwy.	⑩①	Ventura Fwy. / Hollywood Fwy.
⑤	Golden State Fwy. / Santa Ana Fwy.	⑩⑤	Century Fwy.
⑩	Santa Monica Fwy. / San Bernardino Fwy.	⑪⓪	Pasadena Fwy.
㉒	Garden Grove Fwy.	⑪⓪	Harbor Fwy.
㉗	Topanga Canyon Blvd.	⑬④	Ventura Fwy.
㊴	Beach Blvd. / San Gabriel Canyon Rd.	⑰⓪	Hollywood Fwy.
㊼	Terminal Fwy. / Ocean Blvd.	㉑⓪	Foothill Fwy.
㊵	Newport Fwy. and Blvd.	④⓪⑤	San Diego Fwy.
㊶	Orange Fwy.	⑥⓪⑤	San Gabriel River Fwy.
㊿	Pomona Fwy.	⑦①⓪	Long Beach Fwy.
⑨⓪	Marina Fwy.		

Legend

㉒	State Highway
⑩①	U.S. Highway
㉑⓪	Interstate Highway

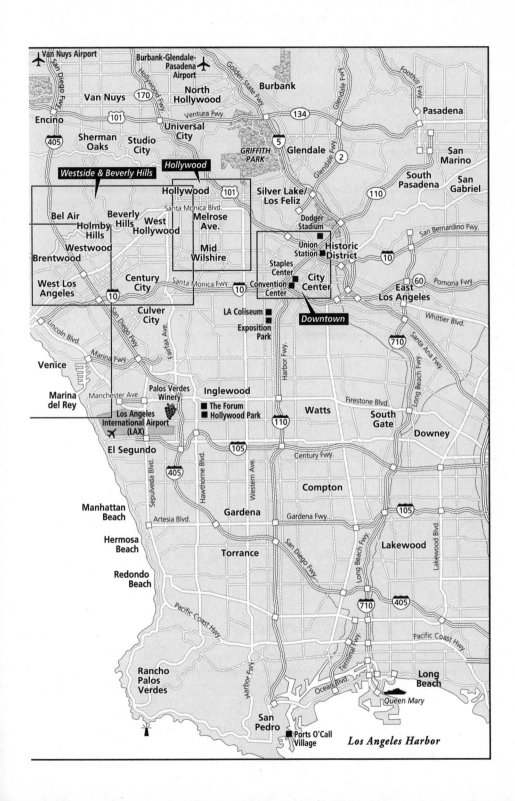

✔ **I-10 (the Santa Monica Freeway)** runs east-west from Palm Springs (actually from Georgia) all the way to within a few miles of the ocean in Santa Monica.

✔ **Highway 1 (the Pacific Coast Highway, or just PCH),** is a standard four-lane avenue called Lincoln Boulevard from just north of the airport to Santa Monica, where it turns into a surface highway and cuts west to hug the coast all the way to Malibu.

✔ **I-405 (the San Diego Freeway)** runs north-south through L.A.'s westside, roughly parallel to PCH and about 3⅓ miles inland from the coast.

✔ **U.S. 101** is the **Ventura Freeway** as it runs east-west through the San Fernando Valley (on the north side of L.A.), becoming the **Hollywood Freeway** after U.S. 101 takes a sharp turn right, running northwest-southeast to connect the Valley with downtown L.A. (The Ventura Freeway continues on directly east along Calif. 134.)

✔ **I-110 (the Harbor Freeway)** starts in Pasadena (as the Pasadena Freeway) and runs directly south. You'll likely use the section that runs along the western edge of downtown, connecting the Hollywood Freeway to I-10.

✔ **I-5 (the Golden State Freeway)** runs along the eastern edge of downtown on its way from San Francisco to San Diego.

An underlying grid of surface streets complements the freeways. The major east-west boulevards connecting downtown to the beaches are, from north to south, Sunset, Santa Monica, Wilshire, Olympic, Pico, and Venice boulevards.

Freeways are variously referred to both by their numbers and their names. You'll hear locals call I-10 both "the 10" and "the Santa Monica Freeway."

A good city map is a must; even born-and-raised Angelenos carry one in their cars. AAA publishes the best maps of L.A., bar none. Members can stop in at one of the local offices (see the "Fast Facts" section at the end of this chapter). If you're not a member, any good foldout map will do, as long as all streets and freeways are clearly marked and the map has address number notations.

L.A.'s neighborhoods

In L.A.'s neighborhoods, the wheat is separated from the chaff in a really big way, boiling down the city to the neighborhoods where most visitors (and most locals) head for sightseeing, entertainment, and general fun in the sun. Who really wants to go to Van Nuys, anyway?

Unlike in most cities, urban life in L.A. doesn't focus on downtown. You'll likely spend the bulk of your time in the beach communities, on the city's Westside, and in Hollywood.

Santa Monica

Santa Monica is L.A.'s premier beach community. It's fun, festive, and pretty, with a deserved left-of-center reputation. It extends for 3 miles along the coast, starting out artsy-funky around Ocean Park Boulevard and getting ritzier as you go north. Ocean Avenue runs blufftop along the coast, meeting Colorado Boulevard at the **Santa Monica Pier,** famous for its amusements. Dining and shopping north of Colorado centers on the **Third Street Promenade** and along Main Street south of Colorado. I-10 drops you into the heart of the action.

Venice and Marina del Rey

South of Santa Monica is Venice, an early-20th-century planned community with its very own canals. But the real draw is wild, wacky, funky boho **Venice Beach,** which just may be the ultimate human carnival. Main Street will lead you into Venice from the north — you'll know you've arrived when it becomes Pacific Avenue — and Venice Boulevard and Washington Avenue serve as the main routes in from points east.

Malibu

Malibu is the ultimate symbol of beachy super-celebrity. Its vast network of rugged canyons leads from Santa Monica north all the way to the northern border of L.A. County. Only the Pacific Coast Highway (and an almost-unbroken row of ocean-facing houses that are *much* larger — and pricier — than they look from PCH) separates Malibu's canyons from its gorgeous wide beaches. Malibu is extremely remote (one of its great appeals for the rich and famous) and without freeway access. Consequently, the drive to Malibu from just about anywhere else in the city takes around an hour.

West Los Angeles

West L.A. is basically an umbrella for the collection of middle- and upper-middle-class communities sandwiched between Santa Monica to the west and Beverly Hills to the east. Some of these communities lack exact labels beyond "West L.A." but they are perfectly nice nonetheless. Among the most notable are:

- ✔ **Brentwood,** the upscale residential area north of Wilshire Boulevard and west of I-405 that O.J. Simpson made famous (to the chagrin of his former neighbors).

- ✔ **Westwood,** home to UCLA and a restaurant- and shop-laden village that caters largely to the college kids. It's the area between I-405 and Beverly Hills, bounded by Santa Monica and Sunset boulevards; the village is just north of Wilshire Boulevard.

- ✔ **Bel Air** is the gated domain of the rich and famous north of UCLA above Sunset Boulevard.

✔ **Century City** is the pocket of high-rises just west of Beverly Hills, between Santa Monica and Pico boulevards. It offers the Westside its only real city skyline, but is otherwise quite sanitized and uninteresting.

Beverly Hills

You know; it's where the swimming pools and the movie stars are. Aren't they? Well, some, for sure. The traditional bastion of L.A.'s ultra-rich and famous is a glitzy but easily enjoyable community. The area south of Wilshire Boulevard is largely upper-middle-class residential, and home to some surprisingly affordable hotels. North of Wilshire is the **Golden Triangle,** Beverly Hills' downtown, where you'll find the ritzy shops. North of Santa Monica Boulevard is the hilly, star-studded residential area.

West Hollywood

Ground zero for L.A.'s gay and rock 'n' roll communities, West Hollywood houses some of L.A.'s best (or liveliest, anyway) hotels, restaurants, bars, and clubs. It's long and narrow, shaped kind of like a house key, and feels either upscale or lowbrow, depending on where you are. The main drags are Santa Monica Boulevard and the stretch of Sunset Boulevard between Doheny Drive and Crescent Heights Boulevard known as the **Sunset Strip** — L.A.'s tattooed-and-pierced party central, packed with trendy bars and rocking clubs.

Hollywood

The original epicenter of Movie City glamour had degenerated into one of the seediest parts of town by the 1980s, but it's a whole different story of late. A major urban revitalization (much like the one that transformed New York's Times Square) was launched in the late '90s and continues apace. **Hollywood Boulevard** isn't ever going to be a bastion of high culture — in fact, L.A. hardly gets more touristy than this, and it never has had anything to do with the actual Movie Business — but it's cleaner, safer, and more attractive than it has been in decades. The boulevard's **Walk of Fame** and the new shopping/entertainment center **Hollywood-Highland Complex** are the main attractions, but the neighborhood actually extends from Beverly Boulevard north into the Hollywood Hills, encompassing the famously funky alterna-shopping strip **Melrose Avenue.**

Mid-Wilshire District/Miracle Mile

This corridor flanks Wilshire Boulevard east from Beverly Hills to (roughly) Western Avenue. The highlight is the stretch of Wilshire between Fairfax and La Brea avenues, which serves as the city's impressive **Museum Row.**

Los Feliz

This hip haven between Hollywood and downtown is further notable as a gateway to **Griffith Park,** the massive urban park that's home to the Griffith Observatory (remember *Rebel Without a Cause?).*

Universal City and Burbank

These San Fernando Valley communities are the joint capitals of TV Land, and all you need to know about the Valley. Universal City, west of Griffith Park between the Hollywood and Ventura freeways (U.S. 101 and Calif. 134), houses **Universal Studios Hollywood** and **Universal CityWalk,** the adjoining shopping-and-dining spread.

Just north of Universal City and Calif. 134, Burbank hosts L.A.'s secondary airport and the **NBC** and **Warner Bros.** studios, open to the masses for TV tapings and tours.

Downtown

Boxed in by U.S. 101, I-110, I-10, and I-5, downtown is the entertainment-industry-free business center of the city. After a scruffy period, it has cleaned up quite nicely in recent years and has even drawn in some hip restaurants. But beyond the main visitor center and **El Pueblo de Los Angeles,** the original Mexican heart of the city, you won't find a whole lot of interest here, unless you hold tickets to an event at one of the spiffy performing arts venues or you love chaotic urban messes.

Pasadena

Pasadena, blissfully free of Hollywood glam, is the premier draw of the San Gabriel Valley (the network of pretty, upscale bedroom communities east of the San Fernando Valley). The biggest day of the year here is January 1, when the **Tournament of Roses Parade** draws national attention to the attractive 'burb. You'll also find a few year-round attractions here, too, such as the **Norton Simon Museum of Art.**

Drive, she said: Getting around

Yes, driving around L.A. is a hassle. Yes, you pretty much have to do it. There may be the brave tourist who will dare to use the public transportation system, and if you are he (or she), we say, Godspeed and drop us a note to tell us how it went.

The complex web of freeways and surface streets may seem intimidating at first. After you get the hang of it, however, it's not bad at all; driving in New York City, or even the daunting hills of San Francisco, is worlds more difficult. Just think of L.A. as one big, bad suburb and you'll do just fine.

Do yourself a favor and keep these tips in mind as you drive — and park — around the city:

- ✔ **Allow more time than you think it will actually take to get where you're going.** You need to make time for traffic and parking. Double your margin in weekday rush hours, from 7 to 9 a.m. and again from 3 to 7 p.m. We've often found the freeways to be much more crowded than we expect all day on Saturdays, too, especially heading towards the ocean on a warm sunny day.

- ✔ **Plan your exact route before you set out.** Know where you'll need to exit the freeway and/or make turns — especially lefts — and merge in plenty of time. Otherwise, you're likely to find yourself waving at your freeway exit from an inside lane or your turnoff from an outside one. Pulling over and whipping out your map if you screw up is never easy, and it's darn near impossible on the freeways.

- ✔ **Those kids you brought with you can come in handy.** Most freeways have a High Occupancy Vehicle (HOV) — a carpool — lane, which will let you speed past some of the congestion if you have three people in the car (sometimes two; read the signs). Don't flout the rules; if you do, expect to shell out close to 300 bucks for the ticket.

- ✔ **Watch turning right on red.** You can turn right on red as long as a posted sign doesn't tell you otherwise. Come to a full stop first — no rolling.

- ✔ **Accept the fact that you will sometimes have to pay for parking.** Your hotel will cover your parking, either for free or a charge. Many other establishments (in some areas, most) don't have their own self-park lots, so free street parking is the holy grail. It's sometimes available, but not always. Side streets are often a good bet, but beware of residential neighborhoods, because an increasing number allow only permit parking — and you will be towed or ticketed. Metered street parking is much easier to find, but can still be tough to locate in the most popular areas of Santa Monica, Beverly Hills, and Hollywood.

  Otherwise, expect to valet or garage it and to pay between $3 and $10 for the privilege. Many restaurants, nightclubs, and even some shopping centers offer curbside valet parking.

- ✔ **Have plenty of quarters on hand.** Angelenos scrounge for parking-meter quarters like New Yorkers do for laundry quarters: They are the equivalent of pure gold. Save yourself some hassle and just buy a roll or two at your bank before you leave home.

- ✔ **Always read the street-parking signs, because they often limit your parking time.** You will be ticketed if you overstay your welcome. Read the meters as well as street signs. On the up side, meter fares are often waived in the evenings.

> ✔ **Don't lose your car in a parking garage.** Take it from a reasonably intelligent, well-educated person who has done it more than once — *it happens.* You know how you feel when you forget where you parked your car at the mall? Multiply that by ten levels. Most garage levels and subsections are letter-, number-, and color-coded. Always make a mental note or a physical one, if need be.

If you must: By bus and metro

Sigh. We really want to encourage visitors to travel by bus or subway, but we can't, not in good conscience. This city is too large, for one, to be covered by a good public transportation system, and what is here is a wildly inefficient one.

But the award-winning **Blue Buses** in Santa Monica do actually work quite well, and a case could be made for getting around via subway if all you plan to do is go around Hollywood, Universal City, and Downtown. Try it if you dare. The Metropolitan Transit Authority (MTA) runs the bus network in addition to the limited three-line **Metro Rail system,** really conceived as a park-and-ride system for suburban commuters. For information, call ☎ **800-COMMUTE** (800-266-6883), 213-626-4455, or go online to www.mta.net, where you'll find a custom online trip planner (have the exact addresses of your start and endpoint on hand).

By taxi

Taxis don't cruise the streets, so call well ahead for pickup. Keep in mind that distances are long, so the meter adds up quickly. If you need a cab, call **L.A. Taxi** (☎ **310-715-1968**) or **Independent Taxi** (☎ **323-666-0045**).

Where to Stay in Los Angeles

In choosing Los Angeles's best hotels, we've concentrated on those neighborhoods that are the most visitor-friendly and offer the easiest access to L.A.'s main attractions. Still, consider what your major sight-seeing goals are before you decide where to stay. That beach hotel that's just right for some of you may be all wrong for others who are avid shoppers or club-hoppers.

Count on an extra 12 to 18% in taxes being tacked on to your hotel bill, depending on where you're staying. Ask what the local percentage is when you book.

For hotels with locations in Westside and Beverly Hills, see the "Westside and Beverly Hills Accommodations, Dining, and Attractions" map. For

Westside and Beverly Hills Accommodations, Dining, and Attractions

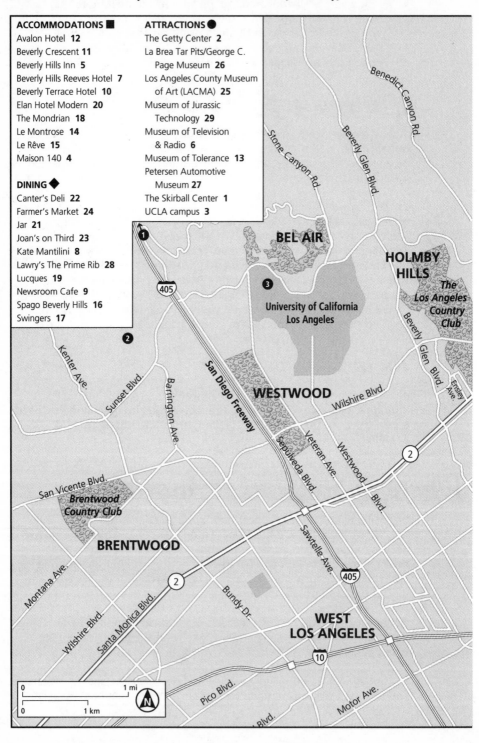

ACCOMMODATIONS ■
Avalon Hotel **12**
Beverly Crescent **11**
Beverly Hills Inn **5**
Beverly Hills Reeves Hotel **7**
Beverly Terrace Hotel **10**
Elan Hotel Modern **20**
The Mondrian **18**
Le Montrose **14**
Le Rêve **15**
Maison 140 **4**

DINING ◆
Canter's Deli **22**
Farmer's Market **24**
Jar **21**
Joan's on Third **23**
Kate Mantilini **8**
Lawry's The Prime Rib **28**
Lucques **19**
Newsroom Cafe **9**
Spago Beverly Hills **16**
Swingers **17**

ATTRACTIONS ●
The Getty Center **2**
La Brea Tar Pits/George C.
    Page Museum **26**
Los Angeles County Museum
    of Art (LACMA) **25**
Museum of Jurassic
    Technology **29**
Museum of Television
    & Radio **6**
Museum of Tolerance **13**
Petersen Automotive
    Museum **27**
The Skirball Center **1**
UCLA campus **3**

BENEDICT CANYON RD.

Stone Canyon Rd.

Beverly Glen Blvd.

BEL AIR

**HOLMBY
HILLS**

*The
Los Angeles
Country
Club*

405

❸

**University of California
Los Angeles**

Beverly Glen Blvd.

Ensley Ave.

❷

Kenter Ave.

Sunset Blvd.

Barrington Ave.

San Diego Freeway

WESTWOOD

Wilshire Blvd.

Veteran Ave.

Sepulveda Blvd.

Westwood Blvd.

2

San Vicente Blvd.

*Brentwood
Country Club*

BRENTWOOD

Montana Ave.

Wilshire Blvd.

Santa Monica Blvd.

2

Bundy Dr.

Sawtelle Ave.

405

**WEST
LOS ANGELES**

10

Pico Blvd.

Motor Ave.

Blvd.

0   1 mi
0   1 km

Ⓝ

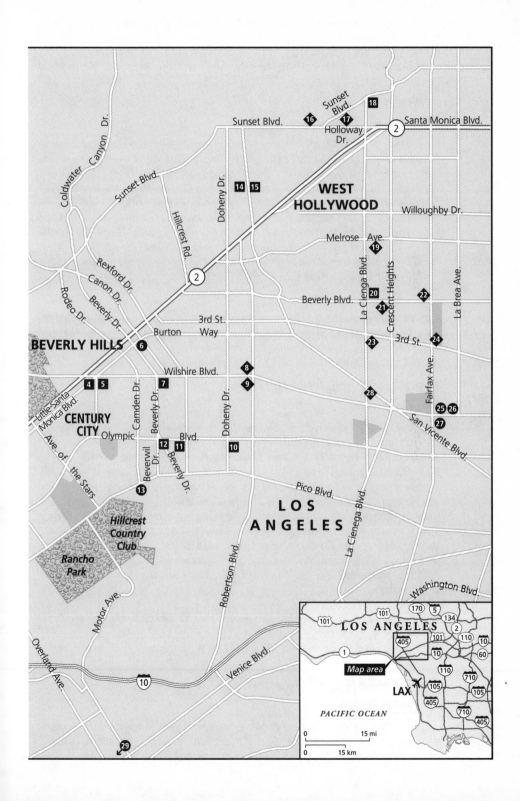

hotels with locations in Hollywood, go to the "Hollywood Accommodations, Dining, and Attractions" map. For hotels with locations in Santa Monica and the beaches, go to the "Santa Monica and the Malibu Beaches" map in the "Hitting the beaches" section, later in this chapter.

Avalon Hotel
$$$ Beverly Hills

Once upon a time, Mae West and Marilyn Monroe lived here, when it was an apartment building, and Lucy and Ricky Ricardo stayed here when they went to Hollywood in *I Love Lucy.* Now, it's a small, chic hotel, aggressively styled and inadvertently harkening back to the 1950s/ Jetsons' futurism — look for all that green polished concrete and atom-age emblems. Rooms are spare but oh so comfortable — Frette linens! Philosophy brand bathroom amenities! CD players and VCRS! The bathrooms are smallish, with inexplicable bamboo poles (for stripper practice?). The pool demands a good bathing suit and a figure to match. Ask about rooms 240 through 244, which include furnished terraces for no extra charge.

9400 W. Olympic Blvd. (at Cañon Dr.). ☎ *800-534-4715, 310-277-5221. Fax: 310-277-4928. Internet:* www.Avalon-hotel.com. *Rack rates: $235–$475 double. AE, DC, DISC, MC, V.*

Best Western Hollywood Hills Hotel
$$ Hollywood

Famous for the huge sign declaring this to be the "LAST CAPPUCCINO BEFORE THE 101" and with a coffee shop (now under new ownership and design, and renamed the **101 Coffee Shop**) that was featured in the movie *Swingers,* this motel is usually crowded with local musicians, actors, and lounge-abouts digging on the hearty, reasonably priced food. The rooms are large, the large pool is tiled and heated, and the location is good for public transportation and excellent for driving. There are star-spotting spots within walking distance (Victor's Deli and Café, Mayfair Market, Bourgeois Pig, and Cosmopolitan Books and Music), Universal Studios is five minutes away on the freeway, and Hollywood is just down the hill. And for the kids, Dodger Stadium and the Los Angeles Zoo are just around the corner.

6141 Franklin Ave. (between Vine and Gower sts.). ☎ *800-528-1234, 323-464-5181. Fax: 323-962-0536. Internet:* www.bestwestern.com/hollywoodhillshotel. *Rack rates: $79–$129 double. AE, DC, DISC, MC, V.*

Best Western Ocean View Hotel
$$ Santa Monica

A Best Western, but a top-of-the-line one, so if you're looking for a standard modern hotel, with a slippery marble foyer/lobby, this is it. Rooms are medium-sized, comfortable, heavy on the pinky-goldy color scheme and instantly forgettable (although some rooms do have ocean views, and more are handicapped accessible, which isn't always the case in the older Santa Monica hotels). Palisades Park is across the street, and the Pier and the Third Street Promenade are but a block or so away.

1447 Ocean Ave. (across the street from Palisades Park). ☎ *800-452-4888, 310-458-4888. Fax: 310-458-0848. Rack rates: $99–$149 (depending on season).*

Beverly Crescent Hotel
$$ Beverly Hills

Originally used as an auxiliary building for Paramount (in the '20s when the studio was located in this area, actors used it for naps between scenes), and currently undergoing a renovation, this delightful, secret little European-style place in the heart of Beverly Hills is quite charming and friendly. Rooms are both elegant and cute, and there are plans to make them appear more spacious (something about a frosted glass wall between the sleeping area and the bathrooms). The baths are showers only but do have Aveda products, plus robes and slippers. Other niceties include down comforters, bottles of water, complimentary continental breakfast, and plans for flat-screen TVs in every room and a lobby restaurant.

403 N. Crescent Dr. (at Brighton Way). ☎ *800-451-1566, 310-247-0505. Fax: 310-247-9053. Internet:* www.beverlycrescenthotel.com. *E-mail:* Beverly crescenthotel.com. *Rack rates: $159–$239 (ask about discounts). AE, DC, DISC, MC, V.*

Beverly Hills Inn
$$$ Beverly Hills

The inn is in the process of tranforming its somewhat chain-hotel looks into that of a more boutique, traditional European-style hotel. This ultimately means a concierge, cartless maid service, 24-hour room service, and a hearty welcome to pets. Budget-minded businesspeople stay here and then take their meetings at the fancier (and considerably more costly) Peninsula Hotel, adjacent. Beds are remarkably comfortable, the amenities are nice, and each room has a little recessed vanity area. The pool is heated to 85°F year-round, and there is an on-site restaurant, with room service from 7 a.m. to 11 p.m. For the area, this is a reasonable alternative to more costly venues.

125 S. Spalding Dr. (south of Wilshire Blvd.). ☎ *800-463-4466, 310-278-0303. Fax: 310-278-2723. Internet:* www.innatbeverlyhills.com. *E-mail:* inn@beverly hillsinn.com. *Rack rates: $189–$429 double. AE, DC, DISC, MC, V.*

Hollywood Accommodations, Dining, and Attractions

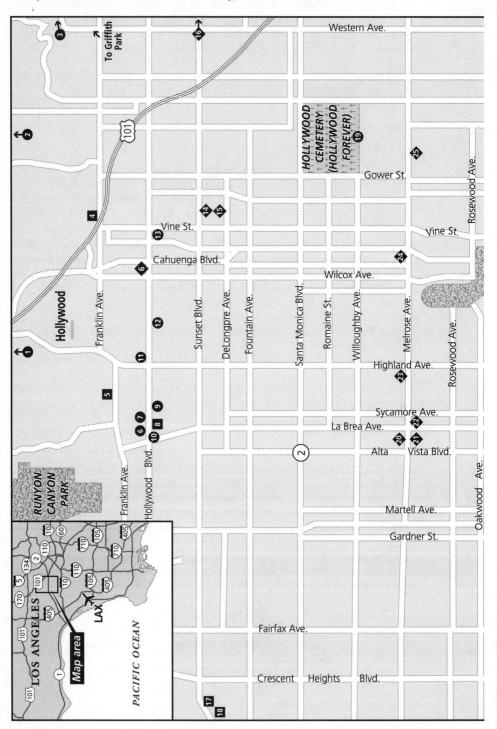

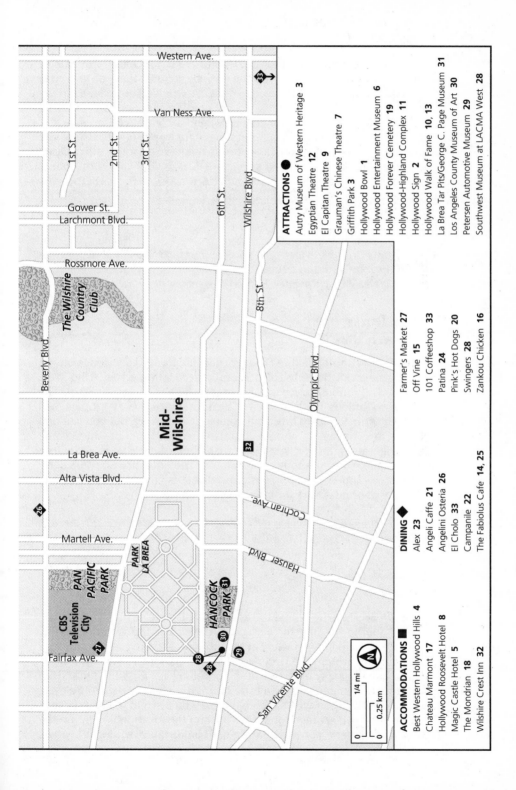

ATTRACTIONS ●
Autry Museum of Western Heritage **3**
Egyptian Theatre **12**
El Capitan Theatre **9**
Grauman's Chinese Theatre **7**
Griffith Park **3**
Hollywood Bowl **1**
Hollywood Entertainment Museum **6**
Hollywood Forever Cemetery **19**
Hollywood-Highland Complex **11**
Hollywood Sign **2**
Hollywood Walk of Fame **10, 13**
La Brea Tar Pits/George C. Page Museum **31**
Los Angeles County Museum of Art **30**
Petersen Automotive Museum **29**
Southwest Museum at LACMA West **28**

DINING ◆
Alex **23**
Angeli Caffe **21**
Angelini Osteria **26**
El Cholo **33**
Campanile **22**
The Fabiolus Cafe **14, 25**
Farmer's Market **27**
Off Vine **15**
101 Coffeeshop **33**
Patina **24**
Pink's Hot Dogs **20**
Swingers **28**
Zankou Chicken **16**

ACCOMMODATIONS ■
Best Western Hollywood Hills **4**
Chateau Marmont **17**
Hollywood Roosevelt Hotel **8**
Magic Castle Hotel **5**
The Mondrian **18**
Wilshire Crest Inn **32**

Beverly Hills Reeves Hotel
$ **Beverly Hills**

This is the cheapest hotel in Beverly Hills, so if you want to maximize your shopping dollar and still tell the folks back home that you stayed in that famous burg, this is the place to do it. We wouldn't go so far as to say this hotel is shabby, but it's definitely not chic. Small rooms with older 13-inch TVs (albeit with satellite channels) and a continental breakfast of canned orange juice and doughnuts make for super-low tariffs. If you want to go ultra econo, you can request one of the rooms with shared bathrooms and biweekly maid service ($45 a night). Weekly discounts are available, and security parking can be arranged. All rooms in this *very* basic hotel have air-conditioning, small electric space heaters, micro-waves, and refrigerators (most of the tiny bathrooms have showers; you can request a tub).

120 S. Reeves Dr. (a half-block from Wilshire Blvd.). ☎ *310-271-3006. Fax: 310-271-2276. Internet:* www.bhreeves.com. *E-mail:* Reservations@bhreeves.com. *Rack rates: $45–$75 per day, $225–$420 per week. AE, DC, DISC MC, V.*

Beverly Terrace Hotel
$$ **Beverly Hills**

This is the best hotel deal in Beverly Hills. It's located six (long) blocks from the heart of Beverly Hills, literally across the street from West Hollywood, and about a steep quarter-mile hike from Sunset Strip. The exterior is fabulous 1950s glamour; the interior has a cozy, tropical feel and a pair of cockatiels. The entire hotel is nonsmoking, but you can puff poolside next to the lush jungle murals. The rooms, all of which come with refrigerators, are not large, and that's being kind, and most feature showers only; you can request a tub room. The hotel has no room service, but complimentary continental breakfast is served daily poolside, and the restaurant **Amici Italian** is located on-site.

469 North Doheny Dr. (at Santa Monica Blvd.). ☎ *310-274-8141. Fax: 310-385-1998. Rack rates: $95–$145. AE, DISC, MC, V.*

Cadillac Hotel
$ **Venice**

Built in 1905 as Charlie Chaplin's residence, this hotel is funky but cheap, a sort of Southern California version of the classic European pensione. Yes, some of the paint is peeling in the lobby, yes, there can be homeless people lurking around the (free, don't forget) parking lot, and yes, services are most basic (check out the Internet access for which you drop quarters into a machine), *but* all the rooms are clean, easy on the eyes, and come with ocean views (though it may be a strain in some cases). Plus, the staff will arrange tours for you, and the location is right on the beach. Rooms vary in size but are quite comfortable, while bathrooms are serviceable. Exercise machines are in the basement next to the laundry, which tells you a lot, but the hotel is also just a couple blocks from the happening part of Main Street — and did we mention that it's right on the beach?

8 Dudley Ave. (at Speedway). ☎ *310-399-8876. Fax: 310-399-4536. Internet:* www.thecadillachotel.com. *Rack rates: $79–$110 (Sept 1–May 31), $89–$130 (June 1–Aug 31). AE, MC, V.*

Chateau Marmont
$$$$ Hollywood/West Hollywood

Although its most notorious fame comes from John Belushi's overdose death (in Bungalow 2 in 1982), this is a fabulously romantic, slightly spooky old hotel much favored by celebs who value naturally acquired style and quirk. The whole thing looks like a setting for a Raymond Chandler–style mystery, to say nothing of discreet assignations, which is probably why the legendary studio boss Harry Cohn famously said "if you must get into trouble, do it at the Chateau Marmont." It was once a residence hotel (and there remain many a long-time occupant), so the rooms can often be ridiculously large, especially the suites (to say nothing of the cottages and bungalows), which were originally intended as apartments. The furnishings and style in said rooms may put you in mind of the slighty faded Art Deco grandeur of the Coen Brothers' movie *Barton Fink* (although beds are modern and comfortable). The tree-rimmed pool area is gorgeous, and, along with the '20s Spanish Mission lobby, is a hot spot for star spotting.

8221 Sunset Blvd. (near Laurel Canyon Blvd.). ☎ *800-CHATEAU (800-242-8328), 323-656-1010. Fax: 323-655-5311. Internet:* www.designhotels.com. *Rack rates: $280 and up (double). AE, DC, MC, V.*

Crowne Plaza Hotel
$$$ Airport

The airport is not the most desirable part of town to stay, but sometimes it's unavoidable. When that happens, we like to stay here. It's clean, modern, a bit stylish for a chain business hotel, and has a nifty service where guests can leave their cars for a week — plus it has a Krispy Kreme doughnuts. The airport is essentially next door, but you get free transportation to and from the airport, and who can forget those Krispy Kreme doughnuts?

5985 W. Century Blvd. (near the airport). ☎ *800-227-6963, 310-642-7500; TTY: 310-348-9061. Fax: 310-417-3608. Internet:* www.crowneplaza.com. *Rack rates: $179–$450. AE, DC, DISC, MC, V.*

Elan Hotel Modern
$$–$$$ West Hollywood

Sleek, chic, and not that cheap, the elegant Elan prides itself on service and discretion. Room furnishings are clean-lined and modern, with touches like Irish linen bathrobes, fresh flowers, and Wolfgang Puck coffee for the coffeemakers. Instead of calling room service, you can order from Jan's Coffee Shop across the street from 6 a.m. to 2 a.m., and they'll jaywalk it over for you (because it's too far to cross at the light). Complimentary continental breakfast is served daily from 6:30 a.m. until 10:30 a.m., and as of this writing, there's a nightly manager's wine and cheese reception for guests. The Beverly Center is two blocks east.

8435 Beverly Blvd. (at La Cienega Blvd.). ☎ *888-661-0398, 323-658-6663. Fax: 323-658-6640. Internet:* www.elanhotel.com. *Rack rates: $165–$215 double (ask about corporate discounts). AE, DC, DISC, MC.*

Hollywood Roosevelt Hotel
$$$ Hollywood

This Tinseltown legend — host to the first Academy Awards, not to mention a few famous ghosts — also happens to be one of the best bargains in town. You'll get pedigree, comforts, and the kinds of services that usually cost twice the price elsewhere. Now under the Clarion banner, the hotel is as spiffy as ever, and the location is ideal, because this stretch of the Walk of Fame has cleaned up beautifully.

7000 Hollywood Blvd. (between La Brea and Highland aves.). ☎ *800-950-7667, 323-466-7000. Fax: 323-469-7006. Internet:* www.hollywoodroosevelt.com. *Rack rates: $159–$299 double. AE, DC, DISC, MC, V.*

Hotel California
$$–$$$ Santa Monica

Cute, clean, and friendly. Only the suites have ocean views, but everybody has direct beach access down a courtyard path, plus loveseats, VCRs, minifridges, pretty florals, and freshly tiled baths. The location is A-1, just a stone's throw from the pier. Pay the extra $20 for a courtyard view, because the cheapest rooms face noisy Ocean Avenue and lack the polished wooden floors in the pricier units.

1670 Ocean Ave. (south of Colorado Ave.), Santa Monica. ☎ *800-537-8483, 310-393-2363. Fax: 310-393-1063. Internet:* www.hotelca.com. *To get there: Lincoln Blvd./ Hwy. 1 to Pico Blvd. west to Ocean Ave. north. Parking: $7. Rack rates: $152 double. AE, DISC, MC, V.*

Hotel Figueroa
$$ Downtown

The Figueroa has, hands-down, the most gorgeous public spaces of any Downtown hotel: decor in a Moorish theme (think Moroccan meets Spanish), all exotic fabrics, wrought-iron and wood furniture, tiles and other decorative bits of fancy, and soaring ceilings — how the heck did this place land here? Rooms are not quite as splashy, but boy, did somebody try, successfully tarting up what was probably an old dumpy hotel by painting the walls with bold faux finish paint, liberally incorporating gaily colored tiles in the (teeny) bathrooms, and adding more of that exotic furniture and fabric. Too bad the acoustical tile ceilings and antiquated TVs remain. Rooms vary in size; 25s and 09s have cunning archways, 30s are the biggest. With its desert succulents and splashing fountains, the pool area is *so* Palm Springs — who would expect to find such a quiet, secluded spot right in the middle of Downtown? The across-the-street location from Staples Center sports and entertainment complex means that this is a favorite meeting spot for sports fans (pop into that lobby for a drink or a bite at one of the two restaurants) as well as a prime record-company party location. Given that you can get similarly priced (at least, on weekends), more up-to-date rooms at the Wyndham Checkers, this may not be the place for you, but we love it!

939 South Figueroa (at Olympic Blvd.). ☎ ***800-421-9092**, 213-627-3971. Fax: 213-689-0305. Internet:* www.figueroahotel.com. *Rack rates: $104–$136 double. AE, MC, V.*

Le Montrose
$$$ West Hollywood

Discreetly tucked onto a residential side street south of the Sunset Strip (which makes one feel a tad safer, especially with kids in tow) and one block from Beverly Hills, Le Montrose offers quiet European-style comfort amid Art Nouveau decor in the lobby and elevators (which are something to see, honest), plus a restaurant, health club, and rooftop tennis court and pool. All rooms are suites with sunken living rooms with fireplaces, fax machines, and twice-daily maid service; most come with kitchenettes. Free bicycles (adult size) and tennis rackets are available for guests. Compared with equivalent places in the area, this is reasonably priced, and if you ask sweetly, discounts can be had. Because they also have bed-and-breakfast packages and children under 14 aren't generally charged, this isn't a bad upscale choice for families.

900 Hammond St. (at Sunset Blvd.). ☎ ***800-766-0666**, 310-855-1115. Fax: 310-657-9192. Internet:* www.lemontrose.com. *Rack rates: $149–$950 per night. AE, DC, DISC, MC, V.*

Le Rêve

$$ West Hollywood

Located in a residential neighborhood and within walking distance of the Sunset Strip, Le Rêve is a small European-style hotel with a rooftop pool and spa, 24-hour room service, a decent fitness room, and best of all, fireplaces in almost every room. All rooms are suite-style, with a separate sitting area, fax machine, HBO, coffeemaker, and minibar; most rooms come with kitchenettes. The room furnishings are cheery, the staff is pleasant, there's underground parking, and our experience is that the rates can be negotiated based on availability. The only (minor) drawback is that the hotel is two blocks from the main fire station for the City of West Hollywood, so sirens may pierce your sleep.

8822 Cynthia St. (off San Vicente Blvd.). ☎ ***800-835-7997**, 310-854-1114. Fax: 310-657-2623. Internet::* www.lerevehotel.com. *Rack rates: $149–$290. AE, DC, DISC, MC, V.*

Magic Castle Hotel

$$ Hollywood

This little hotel at the base of the Hollywood hills is a great L.A. budget deal. You won't see it in *Metropolitan Home* anytime soon, but everything is new and extremely well kept. Situated around a cut courtyard with a heated pool, each apartment-like unit has a big bath and a furnished patio; all but the smallest have a fully outfitted kitchen. A great location, free underground parking, and a self-serve laundry clinch the deal. This place is an excellent value — book now!

7025 Franklin Ave. (between La Brea and Highland aves.). ☎ ***800-741-4915**, 323-851-0800. Fax: 323-581-4926. Internet:* www.magiccastlehotel.com. *Rack rates: $59–$159. AE, DC, DISC, MC, V.*

Maison 140

$$ Beverly Hills

Once upon a time, Maison 140 was a boardinghouse owned by silent-screen star Lillian Gish. Now it's the sexiest, most decadently decorated hotel in the greater Los Angeles area. From the all-black lobby with the most minimal touches of white and red to the smallish but luxe rooms stocked with Frette linens, chinoiserie furnishings, and Philosophy bath products (most rooms have showers only, but you can request one with a tub), this boutique hotel swathes you in glamorous, sybaritic elegance. The hotel's sitting area serves continental breakfast in the morning and then shifts into a full bar at cocktail hour. Twenty-four-hour room service is provided by an off-site kitchen, there's a small fitness center with clean new machines, and you're within walking distance of all Beverly Hills. Oh, this place is gorgeous!

140 S. Lasky Dr. (just south of Wilshire Blvd.). ☎ *800-432-5444 or 310-281-4000. Fax: 310-281-4001. Internet:* www.maison140.com. *Rack rates: $119–$179 (Internet discounts available). AE, DC, MC, V.*

The Mondrian
$$$$ West Hollywood

If you want creature comforts and a high hip factor, skip the equally hip Standard and stay here. It's as pretentious as can be and not quite cozy enough for the price, but celeb-heavy **Skybar** is still L.A.'s hottest watering hole; book a room to guarantee admission. If you're an early-to-bed type, beware — shutting out the din is difficult.

8440 Sunset Blvd., West Hollywood. ☎ *800-525-8029, 323-650-8999. Fax: 323-650-9241. Internet:* www.mondrianhotel.com. *To get there: I-405 to Sunset Blvd. east. Valet parking: $20. Rack rates: $320 double. AE, DC, DISC, MC, V.*

Sea Shore Motel
$$ Santa Monica

Located more or less at the beginning of the interesting bits of Main Street, this family-owned and -operated establishment admittedly looks a little dumpy on the outside, but rooms are better than that, although inexplicably Southwestern in theme (inspired, possibly, by the California Heritage Museum, across the street), some with tile floors, and most with oddly roomy, very clean bathrooms. No room service is offered, but laundry facilities are next door, the beach is just another couple of blocks west, and free parking is provided in an area where spots are otherwise impossible to come by. Unless you absolutely need a posh place to rest your head, this is a fine bargain.

2637 Main St. (just south of Ocean Park Blvd.). ☎ *310-392-2787. Fax: 310-392-5167. Internet:* www.seashoremotel.com. *Rack rates: $75–$130 double; "discounts available, just ask us." AE, DISC, MC, V.*

Shutters on the Beach
$$$$$ Santa Monica

Staying at Shutters is like staying at a really rich friend's L.A. beach house. Facing Santa Monica Beach in all its gray-clapboarded glory, this oceanfront gem is a stunner. Rooms are airy and gorgeous, with such playful touches as rubber duckies in the whirlpool tubs and nighttime storybooks on the Frette-made beds. The food is great, and the casually elegant service is excellent.

1 Pico Blvd. (at the beach!), Santa Monica. ☎ *800-334-9000, 310-458-0030. Fax: 310-458-4589. Internet:* www.shuttersonthebeach.com. *To get there: Lincoln Blvd./Hwy. 1 to Pico Blvd. west. Valet parking: $19. Rack rates: $380–$580 double. AE, DC, DISC, MC, V.*

Wilshire Crest Inn
$ Near Beverly Hills

Wilshire Boulevard is a major artery for Los Angeles, moving from downtown to the beach, past museums and shopping areas with regular, swift public transportation along its busy lanes. And the owner-operated Wilshire Crest Inn (which is actually right off Wilshire on a side street), a reasonably priced, attractive hotel, is perfectly situated to take advantage of all that the boulevard offers. Rooms are good-sized, and the lobby has complimentary pastries, bagels, coffee, and tea in the morning, which draws visiting staff from the nearby consulates and guest speakers and curators from the many museums down the road.

6301 Orange St. (off Wilshire Blvd.). ☎ *800-654-9951, 323-936-5131. Fax: 323-936-2013. Internet::* www.wilshirecrestinn.com. *Rack rates: $82 for one, $92 for two people. Senior citizen discounts available. AE, DC, DISC, MC, V.*

Wyndham Checkers
$$ Downtown

This stylish 1927 hotel has elegant, old-timey public spaces, and rooms that are currently undergoing a total redecoration, from a mock Regency style to something more business-like (at press time, no one at the hotel knew precisely how it would all look). Note that rooms ending in 02 are big enough to swing a cat, but only just, while 07s are the largest. Bathrooms, however, are surprisingly roomy. A tiny rooftop lap pool offers fantastic views of the downtown cityscape, which is visible from rooms on the 8th floor and up — otherwise, guests are treated to views of office-building windows.

535 S. Grand Ave. (between 5th and 6th Streets). ☎ *213-624-0000. Fax: 213-626-9906. Internet:* www.wyndham.com. *$189 weekdays, $99 weekends (double). AE, DISC, MC, V.*

Where to Dine in Los Angeles

You can eat very well in Los Angeles, whether you're feasting at gold-plated institutions, innovative up-and-comers, or one of the innumerable hole-in-the-wall ethnic joints that serve up delicious creations for a pittance. We try to give you a cross section of all that, mostly in the areas of town in which you are most likely to find yourself.

Alex
$$$$ Hollywood   MODERN EUROPEAN

A brand-new restaurant from a chef who made his name at the highly regarded (and highly priced) Saddlepeak Lounge in Malibu. Speaking of pricing, we love the prices here: At dinner, all first courses are $15, all middles $12, all mains $29. No muss, no fuss. But wait! A prix fixe that includes one of everything, plus dessert ($9 normally), is $58 ($29 for three courses at lunch)! Go for it, oh do. Because this may be one of the best meals of your life.

6703 Melrose Ave. (west of Highland Ave.). ☎ *323-6933-5233. Reservations highly recommended. Lunch main courses: $18 ($29 three-course prix fixe). Dinner main courses: $29 ($58 four-course prix fixe). Open: Tues–Fri noon–2 p.m., Tues–Sat 6–10 p.m. AE, DC, DISC, MC, V.*

Angeli Caffe

$$ West Hollywood   RUSTIC REGIONAL ITALIAN

The chef/owner of this much-beloved near-institution is known for her dedication to haunting the local farmers' markets, ensuring that her menu always reflects the seasons. (She also hosts the local public radio station's food show on Saturdays.) Curious experiments with produce aside, you can expect dedicatedly authentic Italian. *Note:* This may seem like a chic café, but it's quite child friendly; kids who come in are given a ball of dough to mash and shape as they please. The dough is then cooked in the oven and presented to them when it's done, a process that can keep even the most wriggly kid entertained long enough for the parents to enjoy a nice meal.

7274 Melrose Ave. (near Alta Vista Blvd.). ☎ *323-936-9086. Internet:* www.angeli caffe.com. *Reservations highly recommended. Main courses: $8–$17. Open: Mon–Thurs noon to 10 p.m., Fri–Sat noon to 11 p.m., Sun 4–10 p.m. AE, DISC, MC, V.*

Angelini Osteria

$$$ West Hollywood   HOME-STYLE ITALIAN

The operators of this instantly likable restaurant (everyone seems so darn pleased you came in) are long-time fixtures on the L.A. dining scene (chef Gino Angelini cooked for the now-defunct Rex in Downtown L.A.); consequently, their new establishment was an almost instant hit. Of course, that success is also due to the quality of the food — genuine Italian cooking, lovingly and thoughtfully prepared. All the pastas are heavenly, but only at lunch will you find Nonna Elvira's (that's Gino's mom) green lasagna, light and airy, topped with flash-fried spinach, a favorite at Rex. A children's menu contains a few simple dishes for the less curious of palate.

7313 Beverly Blvd. (near Martell Ave.). ☎ *323-297-0070. Reservations recommended. Lunch main courses: $7–$17. Dinner main courses: $7–$30. AE, MC, V. Open: Daily 11:30 a.m.–11 p.m.*

Border Grill

$$$ Santa Monica   MEXICAN

This modern cantina from Mary Sue Milliken and Susan Feniger, the Food Network's "Too Hot Tamales" (and the authors of *Mexican Cooking*

For Dummies, published by Wiley Publishing, Inc.), is a brash, bold, colorful space serving up inspired South-of-the-Border cuisine. The ladies' creative cooking is firmly rooted in the traditional Mexican canon, so purists will be pleased as punch.

1445 4th St. (between Broadway and Santa Monica Blvd.). ☎ *310-451-1655 (also in Pasadena: 260 E. Colorado;* ☎ *626-844-8988). Internet:* www.millikenand feniger.com. *Reservations recommended; online reservations (for four people and fewer) require 48-hour notice. Lunch main courses: $8–$14. Dinner main courses: $15–$26. Open: Sun–Thurs 11:30 a.m.–10 p.m., Fri–Sat 11:30 a.m.–11 p.m. AE, DC, MC, V.*

Bread & Porridge
$ Santa Monica AMERICAN

This adorable little café is most notable for breakfast, although lunch is worthwhile, as well. Omelets are huge affairs (the vegetarian: three eggs, spinach, mushroom, tomato, cheddar cheese, and onion, garnished with red potatoes and fruit), and the fluffy, well-constructed pancakes aren't much smaller (we admit to having a great fondness for the kid-pleasing chocolate chip ones, oozing melted chocolatey goodness) — in short, all of it portioned to share. *Note:* It's a popular place, and on the small side, so you may want to time your meal for off-hours.

2315 Wilshire Blvd. (near 26th St.). ☎ *310 453-4941. Breakfast main courses: $3.95–$8.55. Lunch main courses: $6.25–$9.95. Open: Daily 7 a.m.–2 p.m.*

Campanile
$$$$ West Hollywood CALIFORNIA/MEDITERRANEAN

Campanile is one of two restaurants most likely to be the answer to the question "What's the best restaurant in LA?" (the other is Patina). We won't say for sure that Campanile can live up to the hype (but to be fair, what could?), but we will say it's someplace special. Chef/owner Mark Peel is a great talent, and his wife, Nancy Silverton, is the genius behind La Brea Bakery (you may have eaten their bread, which is served all over the city), the original of which is next door. Come for dinner, where you might eat the likes of rosemary-charred baby lamb, cedar-smoked Tasmanian salmon, pulled-pork ravioli, or roasted beets and blood-orange salad; or for brunch, considered the best in town; or for Thursday night, when they try gourmet twists on the humble grilled cheese sandwich. And always save room for dessert; the pastry chef is renowned. If you do come by during the day, remember that La Brea Bakery is still right next door — as if you needed one more incentive.

624 S. La Brea Ave. (north of Wilshire Blvd.). ☎ *323-938-1447. Internet:* www. campanilerestaurant.com. *Reservations recommended. Main courses: $23–$33. Open: Lunch Mon–Fri 11:30 a.m.–2 p.m., Sat–Sun 9:30 a.m.–1:30 p.m.; dinner Mon–Thurs 6–10 p.m., Fri–Sat 6–11 p.m. AE, MC, V.*

Canter's Deli
$$ West Hollywood   DELICATESSEN

We just love Canter's. It's the whole package: classic old deli, open 24 hours, full of both elderly Jewish couples and young hipsters, both drawn to the large menu and solidly good food. (Okay, the musicians come because they can get soup at 3 a.m., and because two good clubs are across the street; plus, Canter's own **Kibbitz Room** still hosts its own music shows — for years, before he was anyone other than his father's son, Jacob Dylan played there regularly.) We've eaten more than our share of Canter's brisket (the Brooklyn: brisket, Russian dressing, slaw, on a roll) when we weren't eating a bagel liberally covered with lox. But that's just us.

419 N. Fairfax Ave. (just north of Beverly Blvd.). ☎ *323-651-2030. Sandwiches: $3.60–$10. Entrees: $8.50–$15. Open: 24 hours. AE, MC, V.*

Cuidad
$$$ Downtown   LATIN

The "Two Hot Tamales," Mary Sue Milliken and Susan Fenniger, the hard-working chefs behind Border Grill, branched out a bit with this Downtown location. Hearty, world-wise dishes like Argentine wild-mushroom empanadas, short ribs glazed with South American barbecue sauce, super-moist chicken bathed in sweet garlic, and traditional Cuban pressed sandwiches are served in a sophisticated space that's a playful blend of contemporary art and Austin Powers mod. Ciudad is perfect for pre-theater dining — or as a special trip on its own.

445 S. Figueroa St., Suite 100 (at 5th St.). ☎ *213-486-5171. Internet:* www.milliken andfeniger.com. *Reservations recommended; online reservations (for four people and fewer) require 48-hour notice. Lunch main courses: $7.75–$19. Dinner main courses: $16–$27. Open: Mon–Thurs 11:30 a.m.–9 p.m., Fri 11:30 a.m.–10 p.m., Sat–Sun 5–10 p.m. AE, DC, DISC, MC, V.*

El Cholo
$$ Hollywood/Santa Monica   MEXICAN

L.A.'s oldest Mexican restaurant — since 1927 — is as popular as ever, thanks to legendary frosty margaritas, marvelous green corn tamales, classic monster combo plates, and fresh, chunky guacamole that sets the standard. Nothing ground-breaking, but that's the whole, satisfying idea. For best results, bypass the newer beach location for the original pink hacienda on Hollywood's outskirts.

1121 S. Western Ave. (south of Olympic Blvd.). ☎ *323-734-2773 (also 1025 Wilshire Blvd:* ☎ *310-899-1106). Reservations recommended at dinner. Main courses: $8–$16. Open: Mon–Thurs 11 a.m.–10 p.m., Fri–Sat 11 a.m.–11 p.m., Sun 11 a.m.– 9 p.m. AE, DC, DISC, MC, V.*

The Fabiolus Cafe

$$ Hollywood ITALIAN

Sure, this often overlooked Italian restaurant may not be as innovative as some, but it ain't just all spaghetti and meatballs. Portions are generous (we've rarely finished one), prices are reasonable, and everything is cooked fresh. In addition, they put bowls of olive oil dipping sauce on the table with the bread, they have three locations, and each one is colorful and pleasant. What more could you want? (Well, avoid the Melrose locations at lunchtime, for both are located near Paramount and tend to fill up with studio folks, so they can get crowded.)

6270 W. Sunset Blvd. ☎ 323-467-2882 (also 5750 Melrose Ave.: ☎ 323-461-1549; and 5255 Melrose Ave.: ☎ 323-464-5857). Reservations always recommended. Main courses: $5.75–$19. Open: Daily 11:30 a.m.–10 p.m. AE, DC, DISC, MC, V.

Farmer's Market

$ Hollywood GLOBAL

Can't agree on what to eat? No problem! Head to this L.A. landmark, the original food court. The 65-year-old indoor-outdoor bazaar is a global bonanza of good eats, from French crepes and Chinese combo plates to home-baked cakes and pies to gumbo and beignets and pizza and panini . . . you get the picture. You can choose from two sit-down diners (one trendy, one traditional), plus an oyster bar and a couple of beer-and-wine bars. The atmosphere is pleasingly festive, especially at weekend brunchtime, and the vendors are budget-friendly across the board.

6333 W. 3rd St. (at Fairfax Ave.), Hollywood. ☎ 323-933-9211. Internet: www. farmersmarketla.com. To get there: I-10 to Fairfax Ave. north. Main courses: Most meals less than $10. Open: Mon–Sat 9 a.m.–6:30 p.m., Sun 10 a.m.–5 p.m. (slightly later in summer).

Grand Central Market

$ Downtown VARIOUS

Operating since 1914, the Grand Central Market is precisely the sort of chaotic market place (open sides, but with a roof overhead) you'd find in, say, Turkey or Asia but not in Los Angeles. Stall after stall offers fresh produce, spices, meats (check out those cow tongues!), and junky toys and kitsch, and in between all that is stall after stall selling some of the best and most affordable Mexican food in town — when they aren't hawking Thai, Chinese, or deli fare.

317 S. Broadway (near 3rd St.). ☎ 213-624-2378. Prices vary (but nothing over $10). Open: Mon–Sat 9 a.m.–6 p.m., Sun 9 a.m.–5 p.m. Cash only.

Jar

$$$$ West Hollywood STEAKHOUSE

A new restaurant from Mark Peel and Suzanne Tracht (he brought us Campanile, considered one of the best restaurants in town; she cooked the line with him there), this instantly likable space (modern, clean, just a step or two above cozy) is meant to be a more modest outing — food more familiar and prices less dear. Hence, a steakhouse, and while hardly burger-stand cheap, it's certainly more affordable than its peers around town. Even so, who could have predicted the single most popular dish would be pot roast? Braised with care and cooked for hours until it falls apart at a touch, it's what Mom would make if she were a gourmet cook. The steaks are just fine, but oh, that pot roast.

8225 Beverly Blvd. (corner of Harper Ave., between La Cienega and Fairfax Blvds.). ☎ 323-655-6566. Internet: www.thejar.com. *Reservations recommended. Main courses: $18–$29. Open: Lunch: Mon–Fri 11:30 a.m.–2:30 p.m. Dinner: Sun–Mon 5:30–10 p.m., Tues–Sat 5:30–10:30 p.m. AE, DC, MC, V.*

Joan's on Third

$ West Hollywood TUSCAN/MEDITERRANEAN

It's just a tiny little cafe, better known for takeout (though they do have a few tables), but it's an absolute treasure. From the lovely sandwiches (ham and brie with mustard caper sauce or turkey meatloaf) on fresh, terrific bread (the baguettes, especially) to daily specials (pesto-crusted salmon or grilled maple-rosemary chicken breast), salads of all sorts, and finally, but most importantly, the desserts, everything is a delight. They also have a small but well-chosen cheese counter. Skip some fancy place for dinner and get Joan's for takeout to eat in your hotel room or in a nearby park.

8350 W. Third St. (near Beverly Blvd.). ☎ 323-655-2285. Everything under $10. Open: Mon–Sat 10 a.m.–8 p.m., Sun 11 a.m.–6 p.m. AE, MC, V.

Kate Mantilini

$$$ Beverly Hills AMERICAN

This perennial favorite is still stylish and popular, especially among the late-night crowd. The mammoth menu offers something for everyone, including upscale takes on traditional American diner fare. The restaurant features a full bar, excellent meatloaf, and valet parking.

9101 Wilshire Blvd. (at Doheny Dr.). ☎ 310-278-3699. Reservations accepted for six or more. $14–$30. Open: Mon–Thurs 7:30 a.m.–1 a.m., Fri–7:30 a.m.–2 a.m., Sat 11 a.m.–2 a.m., Sun 10 a.m. to midnight. AE, MC, V.

Lawry's The Prime Rib
$$$$$ **Beverly Hills   PRIME RIB**

Okay, it has been around a long, long time. But darn it, Lawry's is good —
as long as you like prime rib. Otherwise, it's not so good. Time was when
Lawry's had only one dish — the prime rib — but now they've added
chicken and fish. Don't bother with those. Come instead for a ritual
shared by generations of Angelenos, one unchanged by time. You eat one
heck of a good cut of prime rib, possibly as good as you've ever had. You
might have dessert. That's all. And that's enough.

*100 N. La Cienega Blvd. (just north of Wilshire Blvd.). ☎ 310-652-2827. Reservations
recommended. Main courses: $24–$40. Open: Mon–Thurs 5–10 p.m., Fri 5–11 p.m.,
Sat 4:30–11 p.m., Sun 4–10 p.m. AE, DC, DISC, MC, V.*

The Lobster
$$$$ **Santa Monica   SEAFOOD**

Terrific and ultra-modern, this new version of an old favorite is a deserved
sensation, if a pricey one. The Lobster presides over Santa Monica Pier,
packing in a chic, party-hearty crowd drawn to the drop-dead-gorgeous
indoor/outdoor setting, top-quality seafood menu, stellar cocktail scene,
and the best ocean views in L.A., bar none. Book well ahead.

*1602 Ocean Ave. (at Colorado Blvd.). ☎ 310-458-9294. Reservations recommended.
Main courses: $16–$32 (lobster priced $25–$28 per pound). Open: Sun–Thurs
11:30 a.m.–10 p.m., Fri–Sat 11:30 a.m.–11 p.m. AE, DC, DISC, MC, V.*

Lucques
$$$ **West Hollywood   CALIFORNIA**

A new star in the L.A. foodie firmament, Lucques (say "Luke" — it's a kind
of olive, and one that is placed on your table, along with salt, sweet butter,
and wonderful bread) features California cuisine with French and
Mediterranean influences. The menu changes seasonally; a recent lunch
menu found duck confit with celery root remoulade, and a grilled pork
burger with chipotle aioli. Dinner features items like grilled snapper with
winter vegetables, Portuguese pork and clams with chorizo, and Lucques'
(quickly growing famous) braised short ribs. Desserts may feature bitter-
sweet chocolate pot de crème.

*8474 Melrose Ave. (east of La Cienega Blvd.). ☎ 323-655-6277. Internet: www.
lucques.com. Reservations recommended. Main courses: $18–$25. Sun 3-course
prix fixe dinner: $30. Open: Tues–Sat noon–2:30 p.m., 6–11 p.m.; Sun 5:30–10 p.m.
AE, DC, MC, V.*

Newsroom Cafe
$$ West Hollywood   ECLECTIC

So-called for its bank of TVs set to CNN and the rack of periodicals in the front, the Newsroom is a happening spot, both the West Hollywood location (where we have never yet gone and not seen a celebrity) and the Santa Monica location. It's also heaven-sent for vegetarians and anyone trying to eat a bit healthy. With a focus on low-fat (if not low-carb, too) and meatless dishes (like vegan burgers, vegetarian Caesars, and lots of fun with tofu including tofu scrambles), not to mention an array of juices and smoothies, it attracts the young and healthy crowd who want to stay that way. Fear not, however: There is meat to be found here, and all the portions are generous.

120 N. Robertson Blvd. (near 3rd St.). ☎ 310-652-4444 (also in Santa Monica: 530 Wilshire Blvd., ☎ 310-319-9100). Breakfast main courses: $5–$9. Lunch and dinner main courses: $5–$13. Open: Mon–Thurs 8 a.m.–9 p.m., Fri 8 a.m.–10 p.m., Sat 9 a.m.–10 p.m., Sun 9 a.m.–9 p.m. AE, MC, V.

Off Vine
$$ Hollywood   AMERICAN

A charming restaurant in an old Craftsman house, Off Vine doesn't have the high profile it used to, and that's a shame, for we've never *not* enjoyed a meal here, both for taste and ambience. There's nothing, truth be told, shockingly innovative at Off Vine, but you aren't going to feel cheated, because the food is interesting enough and done well, and the prices are reasonable. The room is pretty, as is the plant-filled courtyard. It's romantic but not intimidating, and nicely situated for the Hollywood area.

6263 Leland Way (off Vine St.). ☎ 323-962-1900. Reservations accepted. Lunch main courses: $8.95–$15. Dinner main courses: $11–$18. Open: Mon–Fri 11:30 a.m.–2:30 p.m., Sat–Sun 10:30 a.m.–2:30 p.m., Mon–Thurs 5:30–10 p.m., Fri 5:30–11:30 p.m., Sat 5–11:30 p.m., Sun 4–10 p.m. AE, DC, DISC, MC, V.

101 Coffee Shop
$$ Hollywood   DINER

A landmark restaurant, kinda, in that it's housed in the Best Western Hollywood Hills Hotel, the side of which carries a large sign informing the freeway-bound that it is the LAST CAPPUCCINO STOP UNTIL THE 101, a sign that has turned up in various movies, including *The Brady Bunch*. However, the coffee shop the sign used to signal has now moved to Vermont and lost considerable gusto; the 101 has taken its place, and nicely. Check out the hours ("Why even close at all?" wonders one loyal patron), check out the patrons in the booth next to you (you've probably seen them in some movie, TV show, or commercial), and check out the menu: thick, hearty soups, honest tuna melts, more-exotic salmon and grilled skirt steak, wonderful banana shakes, and honest-to-gosh breakfasts (served all day). It's an essential, you bet.

6145 Franklin Ave. (in the Best Western Hollywood Hills Hotel). ☎ ***323-467-1175.*** *Main courses: $6.25–$13. Open: Daily 7 a.m.–3 a.m. AE, MC, V.*

Patina
$$$$$ Hollywood   FRENCH-CALIFORNIAN

This supremely elegant Cal-French restaurant (more French than Cal, in our estimation) is one of L.A's finest places to eat, and a favorite place for locals to celebrate. Celeb chef Joachim Splichal keeps the kitchen in top form, and the dining room is as romantic as ever. Go to Spago if you're looking for gourmet glamour — but come here if you're looking for gracious understatement.

5955 Melrose Ave. (near Cahuenga Blvd.). ☎ ***323-467-1108.*** *Internet:* www.patina group.com. *Reservations a must. Lunch main courses: $12–$19. Dinner main courses: $29–$35 (tasting menus higher). Open: Fri noon–2:30 p.m., Sun–Thurs 6–9:30 p.m., Fri 6–10:30 p.m., Sat 5:30 p.m.–10:30 p.m. AE, DC, DISC, MC, V.*

Philippe the Original
$ Downtown   AMERICAN/SANDWICHES

Believe it or not, there are people in L.A. who have never heard of Philippe's, which completely bemuses those who consider it an essential component of life in this city. Founded in 1918 — which, right there, is reason enough to come — Philippe's claims that one day its owner dropped part of a sandwich roll in the juices of a roast beef and gave it to a customer who raved. Voila!, the French dip was invented. Add in a 10¢ cup of coffee and a clientele that ranges from punks to opera goers, and you have a true L.A. experience. And the sandwiches are darn good.

1001 N. Alameda St. (at Ord St.). ☎ ***213-628-3781.*** *Internet:* www.philippes.com. *Everything under $10. Open: Daily 6 a.m.–10 p.m. Cash only.*

Pink's
$ West Hollywood   HOT DOG STAND

A dumpy little hot dog stand, you might think, except there *is* that line of people standing outside at all hours of the day or night. Hmmm. Do they know something you don't? You bet — except, of course, we're letting you in on the secret: Pink's has divine hot dogs, juicy, with a casing that has the right amount of snap, available with chili or Chicago dog style, or just plain.

709 N. La Brea Ave. (at Melrose Ave.). ☎ ***323-931-4223.*** *Everything under $5. Open: Sun–Thurs 9:30 a.m.–2 a.m., Fri–Sat 9:30 a.m.–3 a.m. Cash only.*

Spago Beverly Hills
$$$$$ Beverly Hills   CALIFORNIA

America's first celebrity chef, Wolfgang Puck, has created a fitting temple to California cuisine in his high-style signature restaurant. Is his signature restaurant, the one that started it all, everything it's cracked up to be? No. But it probably never was, except briefly at the very beginning. Still, it's an experience. Expect accents from Puck's native Austria on the Cal-French menu, and a high glam factor in the crowd. Book a table on the twinkle-lit patio if the weather's nice, and be sure to ask for the not-on-the-menu favorite, the Jewish Pizza (smoked salmon and crème fraiche).

176 N. Canon Dr. (just north of Wilshire Blvd.). ☎ 310-385-0880. Reservations a must. Lunch main courses: $15–$28. Dinner main courses: $29–$42. Open: Mon–Fri 11:30 a.m.–2:15 p.m., 5–10 p.m.; Sat noon to 2:15 p.m., 5:30–11 p.m.; Sun 5:30–10 p.m. AE, DC, DISC, MC, V.

Sushi Gen
$$ Downtown   JAPANESE

Although to a certain extent an argument can be made that all sushi places are created equal, that argument is made only by someone who has never experienced truly good sushi. And then there are those who say that you can have that kind of experience only in pricey locales, such as Los Angeles' Matsuhisa, and perhaps they are right — but you can come darn close for considerable less money at Sushi Gen. When you've had Sushi-Gen's lovely, ultra-fresh cuts of yellowtail or toro (fatty tuna), it's hard to go back. Plus, the appetizer menu features "original salted squid guts."

422 E. 2nd St. (near S. Central Ave.). ☎ 213-617-0552. Sushi: $4 and up. Open: Mon–Fri 11:15 a.m.–2 p.m., 5:30–10 p.m., Sat 5:30–10 p.m, Sun closed. AE, JCB, MC, V.

Swingers
$ West Hollywood   COFFEE SHOP

The best way to describe this place is classic-coffee-shop-meets-Kid-Rock, with a dash of "Love, American Style" retro-hip thrown in for good measure. The neo-diner grub is actually terrific, and nobody in town can beat the super-thick milkshakes. The restaurant is hugely popular with L.A.'s tattooed-and-pierced crowd — don't be surprised if you see a rock star roll in for breakfast (around 1 p.m., of course).

In the Beverly Laurel Hotel, 8020 Beverly Blvd. (between Fairfax Ave. and La Cienega Blvd.). ☎ 323-653-5858 (also: 802 Broadway, Santa Monica, ☎ 310-393-9793). Everything under $10. Open: Wed–Mon 6:30 a.m.–4 a.m., Tues 6:30 a.m.–1:45 a.m. AE, DC, DISC, MC, V.

Yang Chow

$$ Downtown CHINESE

Okay, foodies, we admit there are better Chinese restaurants in town, but most of those require a drive to the San Gabriel Valley, and you don't have time for that. This downtown Chinese is awfully good, and nowhere else can you eat Yang Chow's Slippery Shrimp, a dish that inspires devotion in countless customers and that's not at all slippery but rather features shrimp battered and deep-fried and then doused in a sweet, garlicky sauce of indefinite origin (but it came from somewhere good). They make platters and platters of this stuff daily; hardly a table is without one.

819 N. Broadway (at Alpine St., Chinatown). ☎ *213-625-0811 (also: 3777 E. Colorado Blvd., Pasadena,* ☎ *626-432-6868). Internet:* www.yangchow.com. *Main courses: $5–$15. Open: Sun 11:30 a.m.–9:45 p.m., Fri–Sat 11:30 a.m.–10:45 p.m. AE, MC, V.*

Zankou Chicken

$ Los Angeles ARMENIAN/CHICKEN

The day we accidently stepped into this unprepossessing strip-mall hole-in-the-wall joint, with its dull Formica tables and utter lack of decor, is a day that will forever live in our hearts, for it is the day we discovered Zankou chicken. It's not just because when you place an order, you barely have time to read one of the many reviews (nearly every foodie in town ranks this place on their top-10 list) on the wall, praising the place, before the order is ready. It's not just because the roast chicken is, well, perfect — juicy and flavorful, with a crispy seasoned skin that has you forgetting all the health warnings about fat and battling your loved ones for that last piece. It's all that, and then there's the garlic sauce. Trust us when we say that when we die, the food served to us in heaven will have Zankou garlic sauce accompanying it. Trust us also when we say that every time we bring a first-timer here, he or she tries to go back the very next day to do it all over again.

5065 W. Sunset Blvd. (near N. Mariposa Ave.). ☎ *323-665-7842 (also: 5658 Sepulveda Blvd # 103, Van Nuys,* ☎ *818-781-0615; 1296 E Colorado Blvd, Pasadena,* ☎ *626-405-1502). Everything under $7. Open: Daily 11 a.m. to midnight. AE, MC, V.*

Exploring L.A.'s Top Attractions

You won't lack for exciting things to do in the City of Angels, whether it's seeing top museums, taking a back-stage studio tour, visiting an old movie palace, or riding the rides at Universal and Anaheim's Disneyland Resort. Heck, you might just come for the beaches and the year-round welcoming weather. This section gives you the highlights from which you can pick and choose.

You can save a few bucks on admission fees to eight major attractions — including Universal Studios, the Autry Museum of Western Heritage, the Petersen Automotive Museum, Hollywood's Egyptian Theatre, the Museum of Tolerance, and the Museum of Television & Radio — by purchasing the pay-one-price CityPass for $59 ($39 for kids 3 to 11). You may not get to all the covered attractions, but because admission to Universal Studios alone is $49, you'll start saving with CityPass as long as you visit two additional attractions — not bad. You can purchase CityPass at any of the aforementioned attractions, from the CityPass Web site at www.citypass.net, or in advance from **Ticketweb** (☎ **310-641-TWEB;** www.ticketweb.com).

For attractions with locations in Westside and Beverly Hills, see the "Westside and Beverly Hills Accommodations, Dining, and Attractions" map. For attractions with locations in Hollywood, go to the "Hollywood Accommodations, Dining, and Attractions" map. Both are located earlier in this chapter.

Universal Studios Hollywood

Situated on the real Universal lot, the one-time studio tour has grown into a sizable theme park that will likely absorb an entire day. The hour-long **Backlot Tram Tour** is still the heart of the matter. Tours take in such classic movie sites as the **Bates Motel,** plus a few silly-but-fun staged "disasters," including a not-so-secret one starring Jaws the shark. Silliness aside, this is an actual working studio, so you could see filming in action — although it's not likely.

The rest of the fun is tied to more typical theme park–type rides and attractions, albeit with a movie slant. The big ones are impressively high-tech, especially the exciting **Terminator 2: 3D,** a multisensory virtual adventure in Ah-nuld land, and the state-of-the-art, Spielberg-sanctioned **Jurassic Park — The Ride** (pay extra for raincoats, unless you don't mind spending the day in wet togs). The all-new **The Mummy Returns: Chamber of Doom** is an interactive ride through the mummy's tomb, where riders will encounter lots of creepy-crawly things along the way. You may be sick of USA reruns, but don't skip **Back to the Future — The Ride,** a rollicking simulation-style ride that was the first of Universal's mega-budget thrill rides; it has stood the test of time well. You can rest your tootsies at one or two live-action shows; best are the **WaterWorld** stunt show (more fun than watching the Kevin Costner stinker) and **Animal Planet Live!** where furry thespians get to strut their stuff.

Come midweek if you can, preferably not in summer, to avoid long lines. Little ones will be plenty entertained, but the park really targets kids 7 and up. Adjoining the park is Universal's cartoony shopping-and-dining complex **CityWalk** (in case you haven't spent enough dough already), which boasts good after-park dinner options.

At this writing, Universal was offering one of the best tour packages in Los Angeles; for $10 over regular admission, guests receive one-time use tickets (good for 30 days) on **Starline Tours, the Petersen Automotive Museum, the Museum of Radio and Television, American Cinematheque, the Hollywood Entertainment Museum,** and the **Gene Autry Museum of Western Heritage.** At times, special savings coupons are passed out upon admission to the park. Check Universal's Web site, www.universalstudioshollywood.com, for updates, changes, and additional specials, as well as changes in shows and attractions.

Universal Studios Hollywood: 100 Universal City Plaza, Universal City. ☎ *800-864-8377. Internet:* www.universalstudioshollywood.com. *Admission: Adults $49, children 3 to 9 $33, seniors $44. Director's Pass: $69 per person. V.I.P.: $125 per person, no children under 5 permitted on V.I.P. tour. Open: Hours can vary, so call ahead.*

Hooray for Hollywood!

Right off the bat, we must explain that "Hollywood" is both a neighbor-hood in Los Angeles and a catchall term for the motion-picture industry that is not, contrary to popular belief, based in Hollywood. Or anywhere near Hollywood. Nor was it ever. Well, okay, that's not strictly true. Columbia had studios at Sunset and Gower and still shoots TV shows there, and many of the silent-movie studios were in the eastern part of Hollywood (Los Feliz and Silver Lake). But none of the studios was on Hollywood Boulevard, much less at the legendary corner of Hollywood and Vine.

Of course, the reality doesn't explain the mythos that has arisen around that name, term, and locale. And while locals may rarely be caught dead on **Hollywood Boulevard,** sniffing that it's either full of clueless tourists or tourist traps, or that it's rundown (true, but expensive efforts are seeking to change that) or kitschy (ditto), we stand firm that all tourists, especially first-time tourists, need to visit, puzzle over some of the unrecognizable names in the boulevard's **Walk of Fame,** and compare their own footprints with those enshrined in cement outside **Grauman's Chinese Theater.**

Enormous amounts of money are being thrown at the Hollywood area, in the hopes of cleaning up the boulevard and giving it a whole new legitimate personality. Right now, the results are mixed. Sure, there is the fabulous new **Hollywood-Highland Complex,** home to the Kodak Theatre (which, on the fourth Sunday of each March, hosts the Oscars; when it's not hosting the Oscars, plays, concerts, and other live enter-tainment fill the seats), along with many generic shopping-mall stores, not to mention several fine glamorous **old theaters.** But the neighbor-hood still lacks few good, affordable restaurants. Instead, it remains an excess of tacky souvenir and T-shirt stores and a number of shops sell-ing naughty lingerie and high heels clearly meant for strippers. Sparkly glitter in the asphalt only goes so far, you know.

The following are the most obvious and prominent Hollywood locales. Don't be snooty; it's your job as a visitor to see these places at least once (and frankly, we rather delight in having out-of-town guests, because then we have a legitimate opportunity to make return visits ourselves). If you hit each site listed and spend a certain amount of time at each listed site (but don't linger), it will take about half a day to see them all. If you want to tour the *real* Hollywood (studios and scandals), get yourself a copy of Ken Schessler's *This is Hollywood* (Ken Schessler Publishing; $5.95), a comprehensive guide to the history of Hollywood, from landmarks to murders and suicides. Updated regularly, it offers a number of tours of all the significant local sites of renown and infamy.

Grauman's Chinese Theater
Hollywood

Normally, this is when we haul out phrases like "newly restored to its former glory." Although it's true that Sid Grauman's fabulous movie palace, built in 1927 and designed to look like a Chinese temple, has been given a massive facelift, the restoration removed some of the 1950's glitz — usually a good thing, but in this case it turned what was a riot of Oriental stylings into a rather dull gray concrete structure. Authentic is not always best, we note. Heck, even the neon dragons are gone! But at least the Mann chain (which bought the theater some years ago) officially returned the name Grauman (locals never did cave and call it *Mann's* Chinese Theater), and the interior remains a classic example of glorious movie-theater pomp, all deep reds and gilt and fanciful curlicues, along with one giant screen. And of course, there are the footprints immortalized in concrete outside the theater. It began as a publicity stunt — oh, heck, it's *still* a publicity stunt, but thank heavens for it, because how else could we see that Mary Pickford had such itty-bitty feet? How else could there have been one of the best *I Love Lucy* shows of all time, when Lucy "borrowed" John Wayne's bootprints as a souvenir? (The Duke's bootprints are still here.) Yes, the stars of yesteryear, and some of today, have enshrined their shoeprints, hand prints, and in some cases nose prints (Jimmy Durante) and leg prints (Betty Grable) in concrete, to last beyond their ruin. Go ahead, compare your appendages to theirs, you know you want to. And when you're done, see *any* movie at the theater (as long as it's on the big screen), even if it's terrible, because it's what the movie-going experience ought to be.

6925 Hollywood Blvd. ☎ ***323-464-MANN*** *(323-464-6266), 323-461-3331. Showtimes vary.*

Hollywood Entertainment Museum
Hollywood

Even though we're utterly jaded about the dubious value, artistic or otherwise, of the relics of movies or television (taken away from their context, placed into a glass cabinet, they seem even more irrelevant than an archaeological find from some forgotten culture), this museum isn't quite as schlocky as it seems. We recommend this attraction if you promise, solemnly vow, that you'll never visit a Planet Hollywood. See, it's a bunch of Hollywood memorabilia — really good stuff, like an entire *Star Trek* set, to say nothing of the by-gosh *original* bar set from *Cheers* (everybody yell "NORRRRRRRMMMMM!!!"). You can also find all the old fixings from the defunct (and lamented) Max Factor Museum (check out the lipstick testing machine), plus costumes and the like. Not in and of itself an essential sight, but it's right there along Hollywood Boulevard, so why not?

7021 Hollywood Blvd. ☎ *323-465-7900. Internet:* ww.hollywoodmuseum. com. *Admission: $8.75 adults, $5.50 seniors, $4.50 students, $4 children 5–12, children under 5 free. Open: Labor Day–Memorial Day, Thurs–Tues 11 a.m.–6 p.m. Memorial Day–Labor Day, daily 11 a.m.–6 p.m.*

Hollywood-Highland Complex
Hollywood

Actually, the Hollywood-Highland Complex could have been listed in any number of places in the guide — it's a little bit Nightlife, a little bit Attractions, and a whole lot Shopping — but we're sticking it here because it's in Hollywood, right in the middle of everything else you're going to be seeing and doing. Plus, it's the centerpiece of what the city desperately hopes will be a major rejuvenation of Hollywood Boulevard. But basically, when you get right down to it, it's a shopping mall — a grand shopping mall. We glory in the detailing that includes quotes in mosaic from anonymous actors and others about their epic struggles to "make it," the way the staircase entrance is designed to frame the Hollywood sign, the courtyard full of stands and umbrellas and café tables, and, best of all, the **Babylon Court,** which pays homage to D.W. Griffith's fantastic Babylon set for his movie *Intolerance* (in case you were wondering why the heck there are elephants). The complex also features (along with all your basic shops) the **Hollywood Motion Picture Museum** (featuring Debbie Reynold's own extensive memorabilia collection, which includes Dorothy's gingham *Wizard of Oz* dress, Marilyn's breezy *Seven Year Itch* subway grate dress, many more costumes, props, and even some whole sets). The **Kodak Theatre** was built specifically as a permanent home for the annual Academy Awards, and throughout the year it will host concerts and theater road companies. And there are **two nightclubs,** including One Seven, a club designed to give those under 21 and without fake IDs a place to party. There are also **movie theaters, restaurants,** and a chance to take a **self-guided audio tour of the Walk of Fame.** We have to admit that they did a fine job of design — for a shopping mall.

Northwest corner of Hollywood and Highland. Internet: www.hollywoodand highland.com. *Hours: 10 a.m.–10 p.m. (some establishments may be open later).*

The Hollywood Sign
Hollywood

"Icon." We so rarely get to use this word properly, so let's savor the moment. What else would you call those nine 50-foot-tall white letters, perched high up in the Hollywood hills? They constitute one of the most instantly recognizable sights in the world. The sign dates back to 1923, and it originally read "Hollywoodland," the name of the development it was drawing attention to. (The last four letters came down in the '40s.) Struggling actors, despairing of ever getting their big break, were rumored to have made it a favorite suicide spot, but the only person confirmed to have actually done so was actress Peg Entwhistle, who jumped off the letter H in 1932, poor despondent dear. You can't drive up to the sign, nor can you walk right up to it, but you can hike up from Durand Avenue off of Beachwood Canyon. You can get a good picture from Sunset Boulevard at Gower and also Bronson, but otherwise, drive up Beachwood 'til it gets closer and closer, and you get the shot you want.

At the top of Beachwood Canyon.

Hollywood Walk of Fame
Hollywood

Granite stars rimmed in brass are implanted in the sidewalk along Hollywood Boulevard (and down Vine Street toward Sunset Boulevard), with the names of the Greats and the once Greats (and those who had really good publicists and some pocket change) of film, radio, television, and the recording arts. We hate to shatter any illusions, but the stars *pay* for their stars; pretty much anyone, of a rather minimal level of success, can get nominated. The Hollywood Chamber of Commerce, after making sure he or she can cough up the money, gives out a star. But so what? Walk along Hollywood Boulevard and see how many of those names you still recognize (to say nothing of seeing what strange accidental neighbors the juxtaposition of names creates). It's something you should do at least once.

*Hollywood Blvd., between Gower St. and La Brea Ave. and Vine St. between Hollywood Blvd. and Sunset. ☎ **323-469-8311** for information (like who's where and who may be getting a star while you're in town).*

Museum row

Along Wilshire Boulevard in the Miracle Mile area lies L.A.'s greatest concentration of museums, including three standouts. To get there, take I-10 to Fairfax Avenue north.

Los Angeles County Museum of Art
Los Angeles

The Getty Center (see the "More terrific museums" section, later in this chapter) is worth seeing for the house, but this museum complex (itself a wacko marriage of architectural styles) is the place to come if you want to see first-rate art collections. Indeed, this museum contains the finest encyclopedic art collection west of the Mississippi, perhaps second only to the Met in NYC. Most impressive is the Japanese Pavilion (the only building outside of Japan dedicated to Japanese art), which has shoji-like exterior walls that let in soft natural light, allowing you to see the magnificent collection as it was meant to be seen. The museum also excels at modern and contemporary works, and includes a mind-blowing Dada collection as well as a terrific costumes and textiles collection. Because LACMA usually draws in the high-profile traveling collections (Van Gogh, Pharoahs of the Sun, and so forth), the special exhibitions are standouts more often than not.

LACMA can easily occupy you for an entire day, but we suggest not trying to see the whole place. Instead, pick up a map upon arrival, dedicate three hours to those areas that most interest you, and then move on to another museum along Museum Row for something completely different.

5905 Wilshire Blvd. ☎ 323-857-6000 (general information). Internet: www.lacma. org. *Admission: $7 adults, $5 seniors and adult students with ID, $1children 6–17, children under 6 free. Open: Mon, Tues, Thurs noon to 8 p.m., Fri noon–9 p.m., Sat–Sun 11 a.m.–8 p.m., closed Wed.*

La Brea Tar Pits/George C. Page Museum
Los Angeles

It's goopy, it's smelly, it's oozing, and it's wonderful . . . it's the La Brea Tar Pits. It's a gruesome story, so let's repeat it. Millions of years ago (okay, 40,000 — *whatever*), unsuspecting prehistoric critters (wooly mammoths, saber-toothed tigers) would wander over to an attractive pool of water and wade out in it, only to discover that the water was floating on top of tar, in which they would then be permanently stuck. Death would follow (starvation or suffocation), their bodies would sink down into the muck (sometimes thus additionally condemning a predator, who had hopped on thinking it was getting an easy meal by preying on a trapped beastie — sucker!), and there they stayed, until the world discovered archaeologists. The archaeologists found that if you dredge those pits (and a messy business that is), you can find whole, beautifully preserved skeletons. And so they dig, or exhume, or whatever you call it when you have to grope around in tar pits, and they put what they find on display. And amazingly, all this is located right along Wilshire Boulevard, one of the busiest streets in L.A. In fact, all the buildings in this complex (including the Los Angeles County Museum of Art/LACMA next door) are built to float, more or less, on the tar, which remains in full forceful presence. (And it's still sticky, even if you are just picking up a little bit to give to someone as a souvenir — not that we know from personal experience, or anything.) Kids love it. During the late summer, the pits are open to the viewing public, so you can see the scientists at work as they try to excavate more bones.

5801 Wilshire Blvd. ☎ 323-934-7243. Internet: www.tarpits.org. *Admission: $6 adults, $3.50 students and seniors, $2 children 5–10, under 5 free. Open: Mon–Fri 9:30 a.m.– 5 p.m., Sat–Sun 10 a.m.–5 p.m.*

Petersen Automotive Museum
Los Angeles

The quintessential Southern California museum is dedicated to — what else? — car culture. Four floors creatively display more than 200 sets of wheels, from the first Ford Model Ts to groovy hot rods, one-of-a-kind movie rides, and cars of the future. This terrific museum is a real blast — and so mythically, marvelously L.A. It is well worth a couple of hours; put it high on your sightseeing list.

6060 Wilshire Blvd. (at Fairfax Ave.). ☎ *323-930-2277. Internet:* www.petersen. org. *Parking: $4.50. Admission: $7 adults, $5 seniors and students, $3 kids 5–12. Open: Tues–Sun 10 a.m.–6 p.m.*

More terrific museums

Autry Museum of Western Heritage
Los Angeles

The Singing Cowboy, Gene Autry, loved the Wild West and the money it made him. This was his gift to southern California. It's mostly a romanticized view of the Old West, with emphasis on the romance of the cowboy. The uninformed could easily come away from a visit believing that nothing really bad happened during the country's relentless pursuit of Manifest Destiny, it was all for the Good of America. (You know, as in, it's kind of too bad we killed the buffalo, but wasn't it fun to shoot them from trains?) Still, even though the museum is rather Hollywood pop culture, it is most entertaining, and popular with the kids (and, alas, school groups). Seven galleries feature all aspects of the West, including the Gallery of Western Expansion. Combine it with other Griffith Park sightseeing (see "Playing in Griffith Park," later in this chapter) for a solid half-day full of fun.

7400 Western Heritage Way. ☎ *323-667-2000. Internet:* www.Autry-museum. org. *Free parking. Hours: Tues–Sun 10 a.m.–5 p.m.; Thurs 10 a.m.–8 p.m. Admission: $7.50.*

Southwest Museum
Highland Park

Opened in 1907, this was the first museum in Southern California. Exhibits focus on the grim flip side of the Old West myth presented by the Autry Museum (see the preceding listing). This fine, serious museum outlines different aspects of Native American life from clothing to religion, by covering the western tribes. There are three ways to enter this Mission-style building; you can journey through a tunnel lined with very good dioramas of Native Americans; you can walk up the Hopi Trail, which is very steep and landscaped; or you can bypass it all and drive up to the tippy-top. Local educators prefer the Southwest Museum (politically correct, sensitive, and enlightened, not to mention educational) to the Autry (rip-roaring cowboy fun), and we certainly understand and don't disagree. Nonetheless, if you have to pick only one, do you want to learn or do you want to have a really good, goofy time?

234 Museum Dr. ☎ *323-221-2164. Internet:* www.southwestmuseum.org. *Admission: $6 adults, $4 students and seniors, $3 youths 7–18, under 6 free. Open: Tues–Sun 10 a.m.–5 p.m.*

California ScienCenter
Downtown

This highly enjoyable institution, another long-term staple of L.A. childhood, formerly known as the Museum of Science and Industry (and located, more or less, in the same complex as the Natural History Museum), got a complete makeover, which helped bring it as up to date as a museum that focuses on the wonders of science and industry ought to be (it's so hard to keep pace, isn't it?). Learn about the human body thanks to Tess, the 50-foot woman (she's like a giant version of that fabled model toy), build miniature structures and see how earthquake-proof they are (and sample some quake-shaking yourself), learn about physical development (from how a single cell turns into that complex system known as a human being to the timeless fun of watching chicks hatch), or ride a bike on a cable three stories above ground (it's safe, but it costs more). There is plenty of hands-on, interactive fun, again of the sort that probably thrills adults for its cleverness more than kids, who are often more interested in the bright lights and loud noises than learning. But that's okay, you're on vacation, and a little education is bound to sink in anyway, even by accident. Naturally, it's hugely popular with school field trips, so take that that into consideration when you plan your own visit. An IMAX theater generally shows features tied to either permanent or traveling exhibits.

700 State Dr. ☎ *323-724-3623. Internet:* www.casciencectr.org. *Parking: $6 per vehicle at the lot at 39th and Figueroa. Admission: Free. Open: Daily 10 a.m.– 5 p.m.*

Museum of Contemporary Art/MOCA at the Geffen Contemporary
Downtown

See, first they decided to build L.A. a contemporary art museum, but they needed to start the museum up before the real building was in place, so they used a warehouselike building near Little Tokyo. It was dubbed the Temporary Contemporary. Then the real building (a geometric structure that promptly won architectural awards) opened, on Grand Street, near the Music Center, but by then everyone loved the Temporary Contemporary so much (for one thing, it's fun to say!) that it was made permanent. Then David Geffen gave a great deal of money, as he is wont

to do, to the institution and the Temporary became the Geffen Contemporary, except many locals still don't call it that (because it's not as
euphonious). Anyway, the upshot is that L.A. has one museum in two locations. All mediums are represented, from abstract to pop art to emerging
new artists. Both locations offer permanent collections (Lichtenstein,
Kooning, Warhol, Rauschenberg, Rothko, Schnabel, Stella, Pollack, and
Arbus) and special exhibits. The Geffen is more likely to have conceptual
or installation art, simply because the shape of the facility is conducive to
such exhibits. Free gallery tours, offered by most-knowledgeable docents,
are regularly offered several times most days — we highly encourage you
to plan a visit around these, because they are one of the best deals in L.A.
Admission covers both buildings, and a shuttle runs regularly between
the two buildings. Figure on spending at least an hour at each locale, probably a bit more.

250 S. Grand Ave. and 152 N. Central Ave. ☎ *213-626-6222. Internet:* www.moca.
org. *Admission: $8 adults, $5 students with ID and seniors, children under 12 free.
Open: Tues–Wed, Fri–Sun 11 a.m.–5 p.m.; Thurs 11 a.m.–8 p.m.; closed Mon.*

Getty Center
Brentwood

If you're not the Universal Studios type, chances are good that you're visiting L.A. to see this high-profile arts center, which opened to great acclaim
in late 1997 and houses 20th-century millionaire (sounds so quaint now,
doesn't it?) J. Paul Getty's enormous collection of art. The collection
includes not only the antiquities that were at the old Getty Museum, but
also early Renaissance and Impressionist paintings (including van Gogh's
Irises), French decorative arts, illuminated manuscripts, and contemporary photography and graphic arts. The galleries are state of the art and
the collections extensive, but, as a whole, not nearly as impressive as
what you can see at LACMA (which also mounts the best traveling exhibitions) or, even better, the Norton Simon (detailed later in this section).
In fact, if it weren't for fear of art majors everywhere gunning for us, we'd
say it's a bit underwhelming. Ultimately, Richard Meier's ultra-modern
complex is the real draw. It presides over the landscape with appropriate
grandeur, and the views are stunning. The alfresco spaces are as impressive as the interior ones, particularly the circular gardens.

The need for parking reservations is legend when it comes to the Getty.
However, because the community hasn't embraced the new center like it
did the old museum — and there's simply more available parking here —
getting a reservation is much easier than it used to be. Still, book your
reservation before you leave home, both to get your first-choice day and
time and generally to avoid disappointment. Call as much as a month in
advance for weekend and summer visits. You may want to make dining
reservations at the same time, but the restaurant is disappointing and
we suggest skipping it. (The museum offers casual munchies, too.)

Park at the base and take a tram up the hill. And don't bother coming unless you have at least three or four hours to spare.

A great way to avoid the crowds is to visit later in the afternoon, especially on Friday, when the center remains open until 9 p.m. The sunset and after-dark panoramic views are lovely, and the Westside and Santa Monica are convenient for a late dinner.

You may want to pair your visit to the Getty Center with a stop at the new (and also strikingly modern) **Skirball Center,** 2701 N. Sepulveda Blvd., at Mulholland Drive (☎ **310-440-4500;** www.skirball.org), whose galleries focus on the marriage of Jewish life and the American Dream. It's quickly establishing a reputation for top-flight temporary exhibits, too. To get to the Skirball Center, take I-405 one exit north, to Skirball Center Drive, or just follow Sepulveda up the hill. Admission is $8 adults, $6 seniors and students, free for kids under 12. Open Tuesday through Saturday from noon to 5 p.m., Sunday from 11 a.m. to 5 p.m.

1200 Getty Center Dr. ☎ *310-440-7330.* www.Getty.edu. *Admission: Free. Parking: $5. Open: Tues–Thurs and Sun 10 a.m.–6 p.m., Fri–Sat 10 a.m.–9 p.m. Closed major holidays. No parking reservations needed on Sat and Sun or after 4 p.m. on weekdays. College students with current school ID and visitors arriving by public transportation, motorcycle, or bicycle can visit without parking reservations at any time. Reservations are required for weekday parking, event seating, and groups of 15 or more. Parking reservations for RVs and other oversized vehicles required at all times. Parking on surrounding streets is restricted. Visitors to the Getty Center may now use a free parking and shuttle service available during public hours from a nearby lot on Sepulveda Blvd. and Constitution Ave. (located just north of Wilshire Blvd.). This shuttle is offered in addition to on-site parking as a service to Getty visitors and does not require reservations. The bus lines serving the Getty Center are the MTA Bus 561 and the Santa Monica Bus 14. Passenger drop-offs are permitted from vehicles of 15 passengers or less.*

Museum of Television & Radio
Beverly Hills

This museum has a few galleries to see, but the real heart of the matter are the private consoles, which allow you to conjure up your favorite moments of broadcast history, from the Beatles' first appearance on Ed Sullivan to the crumbling of the Berlin Wall. Open screenings can range from "Laurence Olivier: Four Crowning Achievements" to "The World of Hanna-Barbera" — call or check the site for the current calendar. There's a two-hour limit on the consoles — but if no one is waiting, getting a second library pass for a second two hours is easy.

465 N. Beverly Dr. (at Little Santa Monica Blvd.), Beverly Hills. ☎ *310-786-1000. Internet:* www.mtr.org. *To get there: I-405 to Santa Monica Blvd.; go 3 miles east, then right on Beverly Dr. Parking: $1 per hour; first two hours are free. Admission: $6 adults, $4 seniors and students, $3 kids under 13. Open: Wed and Fri–Sun noon to 5 p.m., Thurs noon to 9 p.m.*

Museum of Tolerance
West Los Angeles

One can make the argument that tolerance or, rather, lack thereof, is at the base of many of the most pressing issues of our day. Note that this isn't to say everyone has to like each other; they just have to *tolerate* each other by learning to understand each other and allow for differences in appearance, religious worship, and cultural mores. The Holocaust is the most obvious example of the tragedies and horrors that occur when this sort of understanding and acceptance fails to manifest, and this excellent facility naturally focuses much attention on that horrific event. The exhibits include many interactive and video displays. Located in the Simon Weisenthal Center, the museum covers many more related areas — in other words, this isn't just a Holocaust museum. It's designed to topple many of your preconceived notions from the very beginning, when you have a choice of starting your tour through one of two doors — "prejudiced" and "not prejudiced." Guess which one simply doesn't open at all? Note that the museum is laid out so that you follow a mandatory route, which can take up to three hours to complete.

9786 W. Pico Blvd. ☎ *310-553-8403. Internet:* www.wiesenthal.com/mot/. *Admission: $9 adults, $7 seniors, $5.50 students and children 3–10. Open: Mon–Thurs 11:30 a.m.–6 p.m., Fri (Nov–March) 11:30 a.m.–3 p.m., Fri (Apr–Oct) 11:30 a.m.–5 p.m., Sun 11 a.m.–7:30 p.m., closed Sat.*

Norton Simon Museum of Art
Pasadena

Packaged-foods mogul Norton Simon gathered a mind-blowing art collection, now housed on the Rose Parade route (and under the direction of his widow, actress Jennifer Jones). It's a stunning — and undisputedly excellent — assemblage of European painting and sculpture spanning the 14th through 20th centuries, with the masters extremely well represented. The museum is well worth an afternoon excursion for serious art lovers, although the rest of us may find it a little less than enthralling.

411 W. Colorado Blvd. ☎ *626-449-6840. Internet:* www.nortonsimon.org. *Admission: $6 adults, $3 seniors, children under 17 and students with valid ID free. Open: Wed–Thurs, Sat–Mon noon to 6 p.m., Fri noon to 9 p.m.*

Hitting the beaches

The following sections describe L.A.'s best beaches as they run along PCH (Highway 1) from south to north.

Santa Monica and the Malibu Beaches

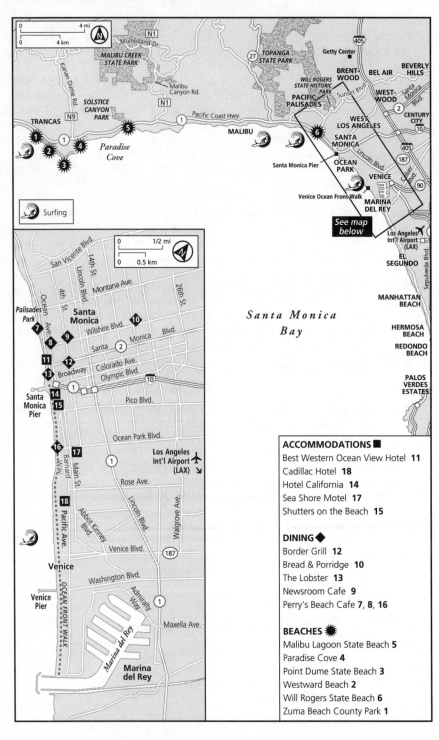

ACCOMMODATIONS ■
Best Western Ocean View Hotel **11**
Cadillac Hotel **18**
Hotel California **14**
Sea Shore Motel **17**
Shutters on the Beach **15**

DINING ◆
Border Grill **12**
Bread & Porridge **10**
The Lobster **13**
Newsroom Cafe **9**
Perry's Beach Cafe **7**, **8**, **16**

BEACHES ☀
Malibu Lagoon State Beach **5**
Paradise Cove **4**
Point Dume State Beach **3**
Westward Beach **2**
Will Rogers State Beach **6**
Zuma Beach County Park **1**

Venice Beach and Ocean Front Walk

Starting at Venice Boulevard and running north to Rose Avenue is L.A.'s beach scene at its wackiest, wildest, and sleaziest. The sand is less the draw than the continuous carnival on the paved promenade known as **Ocean Front Walk** that runs along the beach, where vendors sell dirt-cheap merchandise from sunglasses to silly tchotchkes, and busking entertainers run the gamut from talking-parrot wranglers to chainsaw jugglers. The constant crowd is the city's most eye-popping and includes plenty of muscle-bound pretty boys, buxom beach bunnies on in-line skates, and tattooed biker types and their chicks.

Head elsewhere if you want to relax on the sand; come here for the color. Look in the blocks east of Pacific Avenue for a street parking space or west of Pacific Avenue for a pay lot.

Santa Monica Beach and Pier

As you move north on Ocean Front Walk and cross into Santa Monica, the scene gets appreciably prettier and more subdued. The walk opens up for bikers and skaters, the beach is more suitable for playing and sunbathing, the bay waters are calm, and the food options and facilities improve.

The best beach access is along Bernard Way, which runs parallel to Ocean Avenue (called Neilson Way here) along the ocean from Marine Street (two blocks north of Rose Avenue) to Pico Boulevard. The scene is very relaxed; this is where locals come to kick back. The sands are wide, white, flat, and gorgeous, with grassy areas great for picnicking, good facilities, a playground, and lots of parking.

If you're looking for a livelier scene and more facilities, you may prefer gathering midbeach on either side of the **Santa Monica Pier** (☎ 310-458-8900; www.santamonicapier.org), at the end of Colorado Avenue. After some years of neglect, the landmark wooden amusement pier is back in top form. It boasts a number of snack shacks and attractions, including a turn-of-the-century carousel (☎ 310-458-8867) that had a featured role in the movie *The Sting*. **Pacific Park** (☎ 310-260-8744; www.pacpark.com) is a fun zone with a roller coaster, a dozen other rides, and old-fashioned midway games. You can also stop in **Playland Arcade** (☎ 310-451-5133) for high-tech arcade games. Below the carousel, at beach level, is the **UCLA Ocean Discovery Center,** 1600 Ocean Front Walk (☎ 310-393-6149; www.odc.ucla.edu), where you can learn a thing or two about the Santa Monica Bay marine environment (admission $3).

Weekends and summer daytimes are best for experiencing all that the pier has to offer. If you're visiting at another time, call the specific attractions that catch your interest before you go to avoid disappointment. The pier is about a mile up Ocean Front Walk from Venice; it makes a great round-trip stroll.

North of the pier along Ocean Avenue is **Palisades Park,** a lovely, grassy bluff-top park with benches. Anyplace along here is a good place to stop and take in the stunning ocean views; you'll find lots of metered parking (getting a spot is generally easier as you go north).

Rent bikes, in-line skates, boogie boards, baby joggers, beach chairs, and umbrellas from **Perry's Beach Cafe** (www.perryscafe.com), south of the pier at 2400 and 2600 Ocean Front Walk, at Ocean Park Boulevard (☎ **310-372-3138**); and north of the pier at 930 and 1200 Pacific Coast Hwy. (☎ **310-458-3975,** 310-451-2021). Bike and skate rentals run $6 per hour or $18 per day ($4 and $10 for kids). Call for info on skating lessons if you're a newbie.

The Malibu beaches

An alternative to coming up through Santa Monica to reach these beaches is to head west on Sunset Boulevard for a gorgeous, winding drive. Turn left on Temescal Canyon Road (follow the "to PCH" signs) to reach Will Rogers Beach; continue on Sunset all the way to PCH and turn right to reach the others.

Will Rogers State Beach, which runs from Temescal Canyon Road north to Sunset Boulevard, is where the Malibu vibe begins. The Temescal (south) section of the beach is especially nice — wide, flat, and pretty, with calm, swimmer-friendly surf, lifeguards, a snack bar, restrooms, beach-toy rentals, and easy parking. Surfers hang out at the north end, near Sunset.

Malibu Lagoon State Beach, the curvaceous dark-sand beach and natural wetlands north of the Malibu Pier, is extremely popular with surfers. Swimming is allowed only in a small area near the pier, where the waters are protected by rocky shallows. Come instead to watch the locals hang-ten on the waves; weekends or after-work hours are best. The entrance is just south of Cross Creek Road. Parking is $2; do as the locals do and park along PCH to save the bucks.

If you want to rent a surfboard — smart only if you already know what you're doing — head to **Zuma Jay Surfboards,** about ¼-mile south of Malibu Pier at 22775 PCH (☎ **310-456-8044;** www.zumajay.com). Surfboards are $20 for the day, wetsuits $8. You can also rent body-boards and kayaks.

Paradise Cove is nestled well off the highway at the base of a cliff at 28128 PCH, a mile south of Kanan Dume Road. This lovely private cove beach is pricey to visit but well worth the dough if you're looking for a pretty place to spend the day. The beach is just a narrow curve, but a small parking lot keeps the crowds at bay. Come early (before noon on weekends); the $20 parking charge ($5 for walk-ins) keeps out the riff-raff, but plenty of families are more than happy to shell out for such a private haven. The waters are especially calm and well-protected, and

therefore great for little ones. Claim your blanket space at the south
end if you plan to spend the whole day, because the north end
becomes shaded by mid-afternoon. On-site is **Bob Morris's Paradise
Cove Beach Cafe,** plus picnic tables, restrooms, and nice changing
rooms with showers.

Zuma Beach County Park is L.A.'s largest beach playground. Zuma
starts a mile north of Kanan Dume Road (watch for the turnoff on the
right, which takes you under the highway). Beach-goers pack the more
than 2 miles of sand on warm summer weekends. They're drawn by the
wide sand beach and comprehensive facilities, including lifeguards, volleyball courts, swing sets, snack bars, and beach-toy rentals. Restrooms
are strategically placed along the beach, so you're never far from a bathroom. The wide expanse of sand (and even wider parking lot) means that
street noise isn't a big problem, especially when the revelers kick into
high gear. Come midweek to have plenty of sand for yourself, on the
weekend to catch the scene. Parking is $2; bring exact change in the off-
season, because the fee is collected automatically.

You can separate yourself from the masses and the highway noise by
heading to **Westward Beach,** hidden by sandstone cliffs at the south
end of Zuma. To get there, turn left at Westward Beach Road (at the
Malibu Country Inn), two minutes after the Heathercliff Road light (just
before the right-hand turnoff for Zuma). At the end of Westward Beach
Road is a $6 parking lot for **Point Dume State Beach,** another wonder-
ful stretch of sand below the cliffs.

Playing in Griffith Park

Hilly, 4,000-acre **Griffith Park** (☎ **323-913-4688;** Internet: `www.cityof
la.org/RAP/grifmet/griffith.htm`) is the nation's largest public
municipal park and urban wilderness (five times as large as New York's
Central Park). It was a donation of the double-barreled-named Colonel
Griffith J. Griffith, who was trying to a) get on the city's good side after
a messy courtroom drama involving the attempted murder of his wife,
b) seek tax relief, and c) remove a curse from his first wife (bad luck
with women), a Spanish land-grant heiress from whom he stole much
of this property. It's popular with a strong cross section of Angelenos,
from families at play to picnicking bohos to the healthy and health-
seeking, marching up and down trails that range from easy to challenging. It has a number of attractions worth seeking out, and makes a good
place to unwind or let the kids run off steam if you tire of the urban
madness. The park is open daily from 6 a.m. to 10 p.m.

In addition to the **Autry Museum of Western Heritage** (see "More terrific museums," earlier in this chapter), the park's other biggest attraction is the **Griffith Observatory,** 2800 E. Observatory Rd., at the end
of Vermont Ave. (☎ **323-664-1191;** Internet: `www.griffithobs.org`).
Unfortunately, the Observatory is closed for a major renovation, so the

best you can do right now is admire it as it sits, a gleaming white jewel on the hillside above Griffith Park. When it does reopen, it will feature state-of-the-art sky-watching.

At the **Travel Town Transportation Museum,** 5200 Zoo Dr. (☎ 323-662-5874), kids can climb aboard vintage trains. The adjacent **Los Angeles Live Steamers** (☎ 323-664-9678) can take you choo-chooing on a scale-model steam train. Travel Town also rents bikes for two-wheel exploring (☎ 323-662-6573). Also in the park is the **Los Angeles Zoo** (☎ 323-644-6400; www.lazoo.org), which has experienced ups and downs in its career but is always a hit with kids, and always has some extremely rare animals on display.

Hiking the trails

LA's other favorite outdoor activity — no, it's not that — it's hiking! There are some lovely trails, but figure you'll never be alone, which can be good — look carefully, there are movie stars hiding under those baseball caps. **Will Rogers State Historic Park** (1501 Will Rogers State Park Rd., **310-454-8212**) off of Sunset Boulevard in Pacific Palisades is the former home of the man who never met a man he didn't like. It's a sweet little respite area and has easy trails through the Santa Monica Mountains.

In Los Feliz, **Griffith Park** (see the "Playing in Griffith Park" section, earlier in this chapter) has a 53-mile network of trails, including the Bronson Canyon Trail, on the west side of Griffith Park, which goes past the Bat Cave entrance from the old *Batman* TV series; the canyon itself starred in many a TV western. Trails close at dusk.

Runyon Canyon (Franklin Avenue at Fuller Boulevard in the Hollywood Hills) is part of the old Errol Flynn estate, and the easy trails offer astounding views. But they are crowded, and if you don't like dogs (many of which are off-leash), avoid this place, especially on weekends and after 4 p.m. daily. Though keep in mind that anytime you go you may run into famous faces catching fresh air alone or with their dog or trainers.

Always bring a nice big bottle of water on your hikes and wear sunblock. If you're hiking in the spring and summer, be aware that there are snakes, specifically rattlesnakes, and they can be very cranky when disturbed. Wear light-colored clothes and appropriate shoes, stay on the trails, and don't try to pick up anything that looks like a stick.

Studio tours and TV tapings

This is Tinseltown; of course you want to see Hollywood in action! Note that, as of this writing, in reaction to September 11, many of the studios have cut or at least severely curtailed their tour offerings. That is likely to have changed by the time you read this, but we urge you to call in advance.

Studio tours

NBC Studios
Burbank

This 70-minute, behind-the-scenes walking tour includes sets of *The Tonight Show with Jay Leno;* wardrobe, makeup, and set construction demonstrations; and special effects and sound effects sets. You should call at least two weeks in advance for tickets.

3000 West Alameda, Burbank. The Tonight Show tour: ☎ 818-840-3538. Mon–Fri 9 a.m.–3 p.m. on first-come basis. Admission: $7 adults, $6.25 seniors, $3.75 children 5–12, and children under 5 free.

Paramount Studios
Hollywood

This two-hour narrative walking tour features a historical and informative overview of the renowned movie and television lot. Highlights include a working soundstage (when available), a brief movie clip, an Oscar showcase, and photos taken at the *Forrest Gump* bench.

5555 Melrose Ave. (☎ 323-956-4552). Tours available Mon–Fri; call for hours. Admission: $15 adults and children 10 and over. No one under 10 admitted.

Sony Pictures Studios
Culver City

Home to Columbia Pictures and Columbia TriStar Television, this two-hour walking tour guides visitors through the facets of a real working studio. Visit the archival museum, watch movie clips in a private screening room, sneak a peek at artists painting scenic backdrops, and visit the stage set of current television shows.

10202 West Washington Blvd., Culver City. ☎ 323-520-TOUR. Tours available Mon–Fri; call for hours. Admission: $20 adults and children 12 and over. No one under 12 admitted.

Universal Studios Hollywood
Universal City

Enjoy a behind-the-scenes tour of the world's biggest motion picture and TV studio. Attractions include the new *Mummy Returns: Chamber of Doom,* as well as *Terminator II 3-D, Back to the Future,* and *Jurassic Park The Ride.* Nickelodeon Blast Zone and Animal Planet Live! are geared to families.

100 Universal City Plaza, Universal City. ☎ *818-508-9600. Call for hours. Admission: $39 adults and children 12 and older, $34 seniors, $29 children 3–11, free for children under 3.*

Warner Brothers Studio Tour

Burbank

Visitors to this working movie and TV studio observe filming whenever possible. The two-hour tour includes a film collage (Errol Flynn to Denzel Washington), the Warner Bros. Museum, historic backlots, cavernous soundstages, and the "world's most extensive costume department."

Gate 4, Hollywood Way and Olive Ave., Burbank. ☎ *818-972-TOUR. Mon–Fri 9 a.m.–3 p.m. Admission: $30.*

TV tapings

For tickets to live tapings of TV shows, contact **Audiences Unlimited** at ☎ **818-753-3470** or go to the Web site (www.tvtickets.com). They provide audiences for over two dozen shows, and their schedule is updated daily, listing available shows up to 30 days in advance. Your best chance to ensure getting tickets is to request shows that are new or not big hits. The highest-rated comedies are sold out months in advance, so don't plan a special trip on the off chance that you'll get tickets to your fave show.

Audiences Unlimited also has a booth inside Universal Studios, near the tour departure area that provides tickets for shows taping that day. Often, it provides bus transportation from Universal Studios to the set of the show. For details on show requirements (some talk shows include shots of the audience, for example, and may require a dress code for some tapings), go to Audiences Unlimited's Web site or voice mailbox.

The far side of fame

The former Hollywood Memorial Park, now **Hollywood Forever**, 6000 Santa Monica Blvd. (between Gower and Van Ness streets), Hollywood (☎ 323-469-1181), is the resting place of many of early Hollywood's biggest names, from Rudolph Valentino and Cecil B. DeMille to Alfalfa from *The Little Rascals.* The new owners have spiffed up the place nicely and embrace its status as a bona-fide sightseeing attraction, so they're very friendly to sightseers. Stop in at the office to pick up a free map for a self-guided tour (open 8:30 a.m. to 5 p.m. on weekdays, 10 a.m. to 4 p.m. on weekends), or call for the current schedule of guided tours (offered most days). Remember, this is your only guaranteed way of getting within six feet of a star!

Note: Although **Paramount Studios** have suspended their tours until further notice, they do offer the opportunity to be an audience member at shows taped on the Paramount Lot. Call ☎ **323-956-1777.** Tickets are released five business days prior to a taping; however, you can call and ask what shows have seats available.

Seeing L.A. by Guided Tour

We pretty much sniff at guided tours for Los Angeles; they just load you on a bus or some other vehicle and show you the cheesiest sights. You can easily do that on your own. But one we highly recommend is **Architecture Tours L.A.** (P.O. Box 93134, Los Angeles, CA, 90093; ☎ 323-464-7868; Internet: www.architecturaltoursla.com; e-mail: info@architecturetoursla.com) which offers several two-hour tours, ranging from overviews and highlights of L.A. architecture to specific programs designed around various neighborhoods and their own special look (the Pasadena tour might specialize in Greene and Greene, for example, and the Silver Lake gives you plenty of Neutra and Schindler). Customized tours are also available. The owner has a master's degree in architecture history and she does most of the tours — in a 1962 vintage Caddie, no less.

Shopping 'til You Drop

Ardent shoppers won't lack for diversions in Los Angeles. What follows are L.A.'s finest hunting grounds.

Santa Monica

For the average tourist, this charming beach town offers the best shopping possibilities, with a range from affordable to movie-star wealthy, and all of it in pleasant walkable settings.

Third Street Promenade

This sunny pedestrian-only walk is a real crowd-pleaser, with something for everyone: record shops, bookstores (both independents and chains), and familiar clothing chains and one-off boutiques. It's a browser's delight, and most stores stay open for after-dinner shopping. Take I-10 to 4th Street and park in a structure between 4th and 2nd streets.

Main Street

This hip, casual strip is the place to find the beach vibe in Santa Monica shopping. The nice mix of national favorites, one-of-a-kind boutiques, and sidewalk cafés between Rose Avenue and Strand (north of Ocean Park Boulevard) makes for a lovely stroll. Check out the Web site at www.mainstreetsm.com.

Los Angeles Shopping Neighborhoods

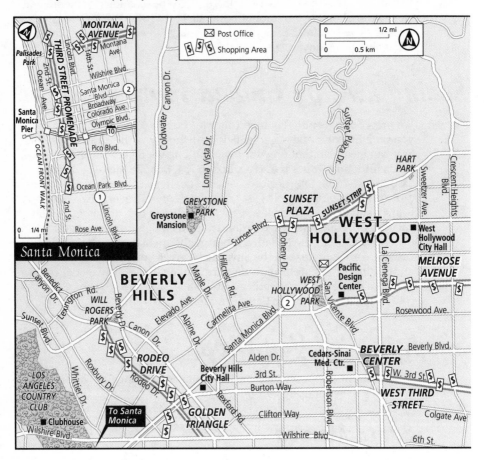

Bergamot Station

Bergamot Station is the city's top stop for contemporary art. Twenty beautifully browsable galleries run the gamut from Japanese paper to jewelry, painting, and sculpture. At 2525 Michigan Ave. (☎ 310-829-5854; www.bergamotstation.com); take I-405 to Cloverfield/26th Street, turn right on Cloverfield Boulevard, and right on Michigan; parking is free and plentiful.

Montana Avenue

This grown-up shopping strip at the upscale north end of town is wonderful for one-of-a-kind browsing. The best boutiquing is just east of 9th Street, where you'll find lots of casually elegant clothing boutiques for women. Visit www.montanaave.com for a rundown.

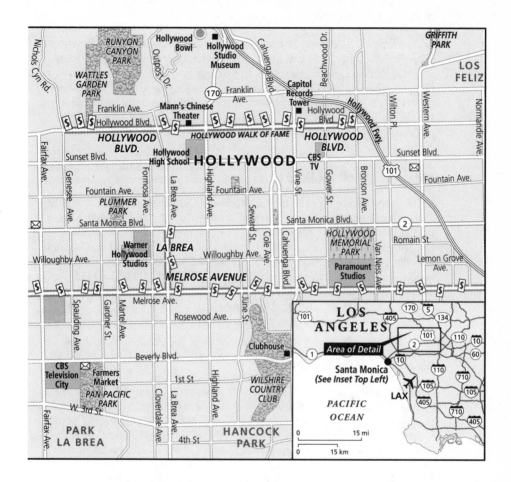

West L.A.

Skip the creatively challenged, teen-targeted shopping in **Westwood Village** and head to **Rhino Records,** 2028 Westwood Blvd., three blocks south of Santa Monica Boulevard (☎ **310-474-8685**). This record collector's dream of a new/used store spawned the wildly successful retro record label.

Beverly Hills's Golden Triangle

This world-famous corner of couture is more accessible than you may think. You may not be able to afford it, but good for you if you can! Anchoring the retail area north of Wilshire Boulevard between Santa Monica Boulevard and Rexford Drive are three high-fashion department stores, NYC's **Barneys New York** and **Saks Fifth Avenue,** plus

Texas couturier **Neiman Marcus,** sitting like ducks in a row between 9500 and 9700 Wilshire.

Rodeo Drive is the most famous — and most exclusive — of the shopping streets, with two Euro-style, piazza-like couture malls (**2 Rodeo** and the **Rodeo Collection**), plus top designer boutiques from Tommy Hilfiger, Chanel, Van Cleef and Arpels, and many more. But you'll find plenty of reasonably priced booty throughout the easily walkable area, too. For a list, see www.bhvb.org/shop1.html. Expect to pay for a parking lot space (bring quarters!) unless you get lucky.

West 3rd Street

Right in the shadow of the famous **Beverly Center** mall — which sits like a prison at Beverly and La Cienega boulevards (☎ 310-854-0070) — is one of the city's most appealing shopping streets. Running east from La Cienega, West 3rd's shops are whimsical, accessible, and just upscale enough, like **ga-ga,** 8362 W. 3rd St. (☎ 323-653-3388), a magical spot for unique kids' gifts; **Traveler's Bookcase,** no. 8375 (☎ 323-655-0575), and **The Cook's Library,** no. 8373 (☎ 323-655-3141), two of the best specialty bookstores around; and **Freehand,** no. 8413 (☎ 323-655-2607), a first-rate crafts gallery. You'll find easy meter parking.

West Hollywood

Sunset Plaza is one of the oldest and poshest shopping districts in Los Angeles. It lines both sides of Sunset Boulevard, from 8720 Sunset to 8589 Sunset, anchored by celebrity dining spot **Le Dome** on the southwest (James Coburn, Elton John) and the celebrity caffeination spot **Coffee Bean & Tea Leaf** on the northeast (Britney Spears, Mark Wahlburg). There you'll find superstar retailer **Tracey Ross** (8595 Sunset Blvd.; ☎ 310-854-1996) whose clients include some of the brightest stars in Hollywood. Jeweler **Philip Press** (8601 Sunset Blvd.; ☎ 310-360-1180) offers fine platinum, colored stones, and diamonds, while **Armani Exchange** (8700 W. Sunset Blvd.; ☎ 310-659-0171) and other boutiques beckon. With over a half-dozen restaurants offering sidewalk brunching, lunching, and dining (expect smokers on the patios), Sunset Plaza provides a wealth of people-watching and a cosmopolitan flair.

Hollywood

The hip, moneyed, and otherwise find the most righteous duds and trends here.

Melrose Avenue

L.A.'s wildest shopping strip starts out sophisticated at La Cienega Boulevard and gets progressively more rock-and-roll as you move east.

This area is great for star sightings, and the first place you should start is the **Fred Segal** boutique mini-mall, at Crescent Heights (☎ 323-651-1800), where the famous faces come and go at a fast and furious pace. East of Fairfax is where the Angelina Jolie/Courtney Love skanky/cool style kicks in. **Retail Slut,** no. 7308 (☎ 323-934-1339; www.retail slut.com), is one of many shops dealing in cutting-edge duds. You'll also find lots of faddish shoes and funky toys.

La Brea Avenue

The unsung stretch between Wilshire and Santa Monica boulevards is terrific for fashionable and retro-fascinated shoppers. Best is mammoth, eternally hip **American Rag, Cie.,** 150 S. La Brea, north of 2nd Street (☎ 323-935-3154), for high-end vintage wearables and vintage-like new wear. Antiques shops and other curious furniture stores are thick along this strip.

Hollywood Boulevard

Come here if you're looking for dusty memorabilia shops full of vintage movie posters, autographed lobby cards, dog-eared scripts, and the like. You'll pay top dollar for top quality at **Hollywood Book & Poster,** 6562 Hollywood Blvd. (☎ 323-465-8764). Ignore all the silly T-shirt and souvenir stores, unless you absolutely promised someone a piece of kitsch.

Universal CityWalk

Adjacent to Universal Studios is a kid's dream of a mall (☎ 818-622-4455; www.mca.com/citywalk). It's a fake version of a real urban setting, but kids love it. CityWalk also offers some good dining and nightlife options — but, at $7, the parking fee is inexcusable. Take U.S. 101 to Universal Center Drive or Lankershim Boulevard.

Living It Up After Dark

To see what's on, get the Sunday *Los Angeles Times* for its "Calendar" section, or the free *L.A. Weekly* and *New Times LA.* Also check "The Guide" at the back of the glossy monthly mag *Los Angeles.* Use the Web resources (see the "Gathering More Information" section, later in this chapter) if you want to plan from home.

The major and the minor: Theater

One of the great surprises about L.A. is the high quality of its live theater scene. All those wannabes have to do something before they get their big break on the WB, right? Actually, movie and TV actors often feel the urge to conquer the stage after their celluloid successes — or to exercise their atrophied live-acting chops.

The Theatre League Alliance of Southern California, a.k.a. Theatre LA (☎ 213-614-0556), offers half-price, same-day Web tix. Here's how it works: Go online to www.theatrela.org before 6 p.m. Choose the show you want, enter your credit card number, and the tickets will be waiting for you at the box office. Full-price tickets for major stagings generally vary from $25 to $75, but smaller productions can be as cheap as $10; you'll pay half, plus a service charge between $2 and $5.

The major

Of course, Los Angeles has theater on a larger level, and that brings us to Downtown's venerable **Music Center** (the Performing Arts Center of Los Angeles County; Internet: www.musiccenter.org). Actually, it's three separate theaters: the **Dorothy Chandler Pavilion,** which usually hosts classical music and opera (135 N. Grand Ave.; ☎ 213-972-8001); the **Ahmanson,** the midsize theater that runs about four plays a year; and the smaller **Mark Taper Forum,** with nearly in-the-round seating (both the Ahmanson and Mark Taper Forum: 135 North Grand Ave.; ☎ 213-628-2772; Internet: www.taperahmanson.com). Together, they are known as the Center Theater Group. Productions at the **Ahmanson** tend toward familiar favorites and Broadway imports, while the more intimate **Mark Taper** focuses on new plays and creative restagings of contemporary works.

Another terrific stage is the **Geffen Playhouse,** 10886 Le Conte Ave., Westwood (☎ 310-208-6500, 310-208-5454; www.geffenplayhouse.com).

The minor

This town contains so many small theaters that your best bet is to start with **Theatre LA** (☎ 213-614-0556; www.theatrela.org), which has all the current listings. Their Web site is particularly useful, but you can call if you don't have access. You can also find ads for plays in the *L.A. Weekly.* Companies worth seeking out include the **Colony Studio Theatre** (☎ 818-558-7000; www.colonytheatre.org), generally considered to be L.A.'s finest small company; the scrappy and irreverent **Actors' Gang Theater** (☎ 323-465-0566; www.actorsgang.com), which counts Tim Robbins among its founders; the **West Coast Ensemble Theater** (☎ 323-525-0022; www.wcensemble.org), known for smart stagings of familiar but well-chosen musicals and dramas; and **L.A. Theatre Works** (☎ 310-827-0889; www.latw.org), more often than not showcasing big-name actors in productions at the new Skirball Center.

A little night music

Hollywood Bowl

If you seek out one special venue before all others, it should be this legendary alfresco bandshell, set in the hills above Hollywood in a natural amphitheater. It's a magical place to see a show under the stars, whether it's the Los Angeles Philharmonic Orchestra (in residence all summer) performing Beethoven's Ninth or Rosemary Clooney and Michael Feinstein pairing up for classic pop songs. The season runs from June through September and always includes a jazz series, summer fireworks galas, and other events.

Box seats are usually sold to season subscription holders, so single-ticket buyers generally end up in the bleacher seats or on the lawn. The bleachers are packed tight for sold-out events, and the set-up is not overly comfortable. The magic of the evening more than compensates, but if you prefer more space, opt for the lawn. (That extra blanket in the closet of your hotel room will finally come in handy.)

One of the great Bowl traditions is picnicking before or during the show. Most concertgoers bring their own gourmet spread and wine. If you'd rather not bother, order a portable feast (with or without wine) from the Bowl's Food Services Department, now under the ownership of Patina, one of L.A.'s best restaurants (see "Where to Dine in Los Angeles," earlier in this chapter). Pricing was not set at press time, but should be reasonable considering the quality of the grub. Order by phone (☎ **323-850-1885**) at least a day prior.

2301 N. Highland Ave. (at Odin St.), Hollywood. ☎ ***323-850-2000***. *Internet:* www. hollywoodbowl.org. *To get there: U.S. 101 to Highland Ave. exit. Parking at the Bowl is extremely limited, so your best bet is to reserve a parking space in advance, or use one of the Bowl Park-and-Ride or shuttle services, for which you can purchase advance tickets. Call the Bowl at* ☎ *323-850-2000, Ticketmaster at* ☎ ***213-480-3232***, *or go online to* www.hollywoodbowl.org *and click on Getting to the Bowl for all the details.*

The symphony in Los Angeles

We won't say there's just one game in town, but that's sort of true (certainly, it's hard to get anyone other than the critics to recall any other options), and its name is the **Los Angeles Philharmonic** (135 N. Grand Ave.; ☎ **213-850-2000**; Internet: www.laphil.com), led by Finnish poster-boy Esa-Pekka Salonen. The 2002–2003 season will be its last at the Dorothy Chandler Pavilion. Then it's off to a new home, the **Walt Disney Concert Hall.** Still being constructed at the time of this writing, designed by Frank Gehry, the building has already received cries ranging from "Genius! Breathtaking!" to "Explosion in a blueprint factory!" Regardless, it is supposed to be state of the art, in terms of the acoustics, and certainly its opening will introduce a new major phase in the L.A. performing-arts world. Expect the Philharmonic to continue its programs, which will include, along with its annual slate of regular performances, celebrity artist recitals, chamber music, and visiting artists-in-residence. Prices vary according to the kind of performance, but can be as cheap as $12 (up in the heavens) and as expensive as $80.

Opera in Los Angeles

It may not be La Scala (but then, what is?), but the **Los Angeles Opera** (the Dorothy Chandler Pavilion, 135 N. Grand Ave.; ☎ **213-972-8001;** Internet: www.losangelesopera.com) regularly stages some extra- ordinary shows, generally earning across-the-board raves. No wonder; besides the depth of musical talent, the company has regular access to superb visual artists, always creating sets and staging that sparks seri- ous talk (even if, as with a recent stark, modern staging of Bach's *Mass in B Minor,* that talk runs to controversy). One complaint may be that the company relies too heavily on tried-and-true classics, but then again, they also stage and perform said classics magnificently. Placido Domingo is the opera's Artistic Director, and has been known to turn up as guest conductor, and none other than Hollywood director Billy Friedkin (yes, *The Exorcist* guy) recently directed Bartok's *Bluebeard's Castle*, so you can see the company does have a curious range.

Play it big and play it loud

For the less sedate, from rock to world and all points between, you'll likely find it playing at the **Universal Amphitheatre** or the **Greek Theatre.** The difference between them, more or less, is that the former is indoors, and the latter outdoors. Given our druthers, we like the Greek; built in the '20s, it's graceful and pretty and set in the middle of Griffith Park, though their parking lot is a nightmare. (We've taken to parking around Los Feliz Boulevard, and walking the .7 mile up to the Greek. You will have company, so it's safe enough.) Bring a sweater, in case it gets chilly. The Universal is fine, but it's located in the middle of Universal Studios, which means you will be parking a considerable dis- tance away — and you may want to forgo high heels. (**Greek Theater:** 2700 N. Vermont Ave.; ☎ **323-665-1927;** Internet: www.greektheatre la.com. **Universal Amphitheatre:** 100 Universal City Plaza; ☎ **818-622- 4440;** Internet: www.hob.com/venues/concerts/universal/.)

For those about to rock

Ah yes, L.A. rocks. The city is thriving with new and veteran rock clubs, and the music scene is hotter than Riverside asphalt (ouch!). The area with the highest concentration of good rock clubs is the Sunset Strip in West Hollywood. It's well lit at night, and most venues have valet parking.

The Roxy
West Hollywood

Since the early '70s, this Sunset Strip club has been part of the celebrated Hollywood rock triumvirate that included the Whisky a Go-Go and the Troubadour. Although its history includes storied superstar shows by

Neil Young, Bruce Springsteen, David Bowie, and many others, these days the Roxy tends to be the home of unknown local acts trying to break into the business.

9009 W. Sunset Blvd. ☎ 310-276-2222. Cover varies.

Key Club
West Hollywood

At the west end of the Sunset Strip is the ultra-snappy Key Club. This postmodern rock club was built at the site of a legendary L.A. rock club called Gazzarri's (think the early Doors but later Van Halen), and in a few short years has become a very popular destination for live music and late-night dancing.

9039 Sunset Blvd., West Hollywood. ☎ 310-274-5800. Cover varies.

The Viper Room
West Hollywood

The music legacy of the Viper Room is unparalleled. Since its '93 debut, this black-hot nightclub owned by that red-hot actor Johnny Depp has featured world-class talent on a weekly basis. You never know who's going to show up on stage.

8852 Sunset Blvd. ☎ 310-358-1881. Cover $10–$15.

The Troubadour
West Hollywood

Just down the hill from the Sunset Strip is this veteran nightclub offering cutting-edge live music. The wood-grain interior is a relic from the days when this cozy Hollywood club showcased the Byrds and Eagles in the '60s and '70s. It was also a key stop for such quintessential L.A. acts as Van Halen in the '70s and Motley Crue in the '80s. In recent years the booking has been something of a hodgepodge, but it's a good bet that some local, national, and international alt-rock acts on their way up will stop here.

9081 Santa Monica Blvd. ☎ 310-276-6168. Internet: www.troubadour.com. Cover varies and is free on Mon for anyone over 21 ($3 for anyone under 21 on Mon).

Spaceland
Silver Lake

The Silver Lake nightclub that started it all still rocks. The live-music venue born out of an old discothèque is permanently art-damaged and not terribly fancy, but that's part of its charm. Surprise guests show up often during the week, and artists such as Beck, Daniel Lanois, and Fiona Apple have performed spontaneous sets.

1717 Silver Lake Blvd. ☎ 323-833-2843. Twenty-one and older only. Cover varies.

Dragonfly
Hollywood

This way-happening rock venue in mid-Hollywood is at the heart of L.A.'s rock 'n' roll hurricane. On Wednesdays, the Pretty Ugly Club takes over, cranking up the volume to 11. Its cohost, Taime Downe, singer for Faster Pussycat and the Newlydeads, brings in stellar rock acts from around the country. On Fridays, it's Rawk House, another hot spot for new music and cute rock 'n' rollers. Ke-*rang*!

6510 Santa Monica Blvd. ☎ 323-466-6111. Twenty-one and older only. Cover varies.

Largo
Hollywood

People are so devoted to this live music supper club that if you duck out of the show early, you may get the stink-eye. It's understandable — musical mad-hatter Jon Brion, who produced the *Magnolia* soundtrack and such artists as Fiona Apple, performs quirky sets each Friday to a star-studded audience. On Saturdays, Grant Lee Buffalo takes over, and a variety of musical and comedy acts fill out the rest of the week.

432 N. Fairfax Ave. ☎ 323-852-1073. All ages. Cover varies.

Snazzy bars

There's nothing like a night on the town at one of Hollywood's gorgeous bars. We handpicked some of our favorites, narrowing the list down from many choices based on style, comfort, and easy access.

One of Hollywood's hottest bars is **Beauty Bar** (1638 Cahuenga Blvd., Hollywood; ☎ 323-464-7676), a luscious pink confection with deejays nightly. The bar, which is designed to look like an old-school beauty parlor (the original in New York *was* an actual beauty parlor), serves real martinis and real manicures (on weekends by appointment). No cover.

If you like the idea of chilling like a genie in a bottle, you'll probably enjoy **Belly** (7929 Santa Monica Blvd., Los Angeles; ☎ 323-692-1068). The artfully designed tapas bar and lounge is a favorite spot for singles on the prowl, and the soulful DJ'd music adds to the mix. Every food item is priced at appetizer rates, but the portions are plentiful — an added bonus. No cover; open nightly.

What if you could shop for shoes while supping on a cocktail? Well, **Star Shoes** (6364 Hollywood Blvd., Hollywood; ☎ 323-462-STAR/7827) can grant you your wish. The beautiful bar doubles as a shoe store, with eye-popping displays of vintage shoes enticing customers in off the street. There's a dance floor for late-night frolicking and an easy breezy attitude-less atmosphere. No cover; open nightly.

During the warm weather months, the **Cat & Fiddle** (6530 Sunset Blvd., Hollywood; ☎ 323-468-9300) is a favorite watering hole for the beer-drinking set. The British pub features a large outdoor patio, with live music on weekends. The staff is particularly nice, and the authentic fish-and-chips lure people back year after year. It's a good place for a large party. Open nightly; no cover; 21 and older at night, all ages during the day.

The legendary **Lava Lounge** (1533 N. La Brea Ave., Hollywood; ☎ 323-876-6612) opened its doors a month before the great quake of January '94, and it's still shaking. The tiki-themed bar, which erupts with live music Wednesday through Saturday nights, once called Quentin Tarantino and Jon Favreau (of *Swingers* fame) regulars, and now it's serving up a whole new breed. The exotic drinks are adorned with plastic monkeys and mermaids, and you can't beat that with a swizzle stick. 21 and older; open nightly.

Don't forget to stop by the **Dresden Lounge** (1760 Vermont Ave., Los Feliz; ☎ 323-665-4294) and give a thumb's up to Marty and Elayne, the jazz combo popularized in the movie *Swingers*. We have known that lovely couple for a long time now, and frankly, they're tired of being asked to play "Stayin' Alive." Do us a favor: Ask Elayne to play "Autumn In New York"; she'll blow you a kiss. Marty and Elayne perform Monday through Saturday. 21 and older in lounge; no cover.

At 10 years old, the **Three Clubs** (1123 N. Vine St., Hollywood; ☎ 324-462-6441) was among the first of the new wave of hipster bars that took Hollywood by storm in the late '80s and '90s. It still has that sizzle, with its dark interior, friendly bartenders, and casual-cool clientele. Some nights you may find a DJ lurking in the back room, where it's *really* fun to lurk. 21 and older; no cover.

Drinks with a view

There are any number of reasons to visit the **Highlands** (6801 Hollywood Blvd., Hollywood; ☎ 323-461-9800), a grand nightclub and restaurant at the new Hollywood-Highland development, home to the Academy Awards and the new Kodak Theatre. First, the bi-level club is located on the fourth floor of Hollywood and Highland and offers a terrific view of Hollywood Boulevard. Second, its Friday- and Saturday-night dance parties are fueled by top local and touring deejays. The club includes three outdoor decks and plentiful parking at the complex. And when you get tired of boogeying, you can window shop at swanky and trendy Hollywood and Highland boutiques. 21 and older; cover varies ($15 to $20 on weekends).

One of the legendary L.A. haunts, **Yamashiro** (1999 Sycamore Ave., Hollywood; ☎ **323-466-5125**) still has our favorite view. The classic Japanese restaurant overlooks Hollywood in all its glory, and if you arrive in time for sunset, you can settle in for the night and watch the colors of the sky fade from pink to ink. It's terribly romantic and worth the long, winding drive up the hill. No cover; open nightly.

Gay faves

Tiger Heat at **7969** on Thursdays (7969 Santa Monica Blvd., West Hollywood; ☎ **323-654-0280**) is a pop lover's paradise. This mostly boy-toy scene revels in all things Britney, Pink, Madonna, and Jacko. Fun, fun, fun. 18 and older. Thursdays only. Cover $5 to $7.

Girl Bar at the **Factory** on Fridays (652 La Peer Dr., West Hollywood; ☎ **310-659-4551**) is L.A.'s hottest lesbian nightclub. The spacious dance party boasts women DJs, go-go dancers, and promoters. It's a weekly girl-power pow-wow. Fridays only. $10 cover.

No matter what year or what day of the week, **Rage** (8911 Santa Monica Blvd., West Hollywood; ☎ **310-652-7055**) rages. The long-running gay dance club in the heart of boy town is a scorcher of a scene. Rage keeps things interesting by booking a wide variety of DJs, who spin everything from progressive house to disco and alternative rock. 21 and older. Cover varies.

Fast Facts

AAA
Multiple Tinseltown offices include 1900 S. Sepulveda Blvd., south of Santa Monica Boulevard in West L.A. (☎ 310-914-8500); 5550 Wilshire Blvd., between Fairfax and La Brea avenues, Hollywood (☎ 323-525-0018); and 2601 S. Figueroa St., at Adams Boulevard, downtown (☎ 213-741-3686).

American Express
You'll find L.A. offices at 8493 W. 3rd St., at La Cienega Blvd., across from the Beverly Center (☎ 310-659-1682); 327 N. Beverly Dr., between Brighton and Dayton ways, Beverly Hills (☎ 310-274-8277); and 1250 4th St., at Arizona St., Santa Monica (☎ 310-395-9588).

Baby-Sitters
Your hotel can usually recommend a reliable baby-sitter. If not, contact the Baby-Sitters Guild (☎ 323-658-8792, 818-552-2229), L.A.'s only bonded baby-sitting agency and recently named best in the city by *Los Angeles* magazine. Book a Saturday-night sit no later than Thursday morning.

Emergencies
For police, fire, or other emergencies, dial **911.**

Hospitals
Cedars Sinai Medical Center, 8700 Beverly Blvd., at San Vicente Blvd., a block west of La Cienega Blvd. (☎ 310-855-5000), has a 24-hour emergency room.

Internet Centers
Kinko's, 7630 Sunset Blvd., between Fairfax and La Brea avenues in Hollywood (☎ 323-845-4501), offers Internet access 24 hours a day for 20¢ per minute.

Newspapers and Magazines
The daily is the *Los Angeles Times;* the "Calendar" section in the Sunday edition is the source for arts-and-entertainment listings. The *L.A. Weekly* is L.A.'s answer to New York's *Village Voice;* this free alternapaper is easily available around town. *Los Angeles* magazine is a glossy monthly with good coverage of L.A.'s dining and arts scenes. *New Times LA* is also free, and while smaller than the Weekly, has fine tips and terrific restaurant reviews and suggestions.

Police
Dial 911 in an emergency. For non-emergency matters, call ☎ 877-ASK-LAPD (800-275-5373) or 213-485-2121.

In Beverly Hills, call ☎ 310-550-4951 for non-emergencies.

Post Office
Call ☎ 800-ASK-USPS (800-275-8777) to find the nearest post office.

Taxes
Sales tax is 8.25%. Hotel taxes range from 12 to 17%, depending on the municipality you're in.

Taxis
Call L.A. Taxi (☎ 310-715-1968) or Independent Taxi (☎ 323-666-0045).

Weather
Call ☎ 212-554-1212 for the daily forecast.

Gathering More Information

Contact the **Los Angeles Convention and Visitors Bureau** (☎ 800-366-6116, 213-689-8822; Internet: www.lacvb.com) to request a free visitor's kit, learn about upcoming events, or ask specific questions.

After you're in town, you'll find an excellent walk-in **Visitor Information Center** downtown at 685 S. Figueroa St., between Wilshire Boulevard and Seventh Street; it's open Monday through Friday from 8 a.m. to 5 p.m. and Saturday from 8:30 a.m. to 5 p.m. You may also want to stop by the staffed **Hollywood Visitor Information Center** at 6541 Hollywood Blvd., just west of Cahuenga Boulevard, which is open Monday through Saturday from 9 a.m. to 5 p.m. You can find Hollywood information at www.hollywoodcoc.org.

Chapter 22

The Happiest Place on Earth: The Disneyland Resort!

In This Chapter

▶ Planning your visit

▶ Getting there

▶ Finding the perfect places to stay and eat

▶ Practicing proven tips for touring the legendary park

▶ Exploring the resort's newest attractions

*1*s it really the "Happiest Place on Earth?" Who can say (there are places in Bali that are very happy indeed), but we have to admit, we get happy just writing the word "Disneyland."

Sure, the one in Florida may be bigger, and the one in France may have Pirates singing in French (*quelle* hoot!), but this is the original. "Walt's Folly," the naysayers called it, because they predicted an embarrassing, costly failure, bless them. It didn't fail, naturally. And decades after its conception, it remains *the* top sight of Southern California. With or without a kid, we recommend going there at least once.

Disneyland is no longer just Disneyland; it is now the **Disneyland Resort,** which encompasses Walt's original amusement park, the ambitious new theme park **California Adventure**, three hotels, and the big dining/entertaining/shopping complex known as **Downtown Disney.** Downtown Disney is actually located outside the park (although it's considered part of it), but you may find yourself walking through it to get to Disneyland (on the left) or California Adventure (on the right), depending on your arrival point. Downtown Disney has no entrance fee and no gate, but you will have to pay for parking if you drive in. Anyone who wants to leave the resort to visit Downtown Disney can have a hand stamped for readmittance to the parks. To lure teens and the college crowd, Downtown Disney offers clubs and other late-night attractions; to lure moms and dads, there are fancy restaurants and shopping.

It would be easy to dismiss the park as commerce over fantasy, because Disneyland has always been about product tie-ins (although really slick about it — a spoonful of sugar helps the medicine go down, don't you know). But in every inch of the place there is still given a tremendous amount of thought, detail, research, and, yes, imagination. No matter how it evolves, Disneyland remains a place of delight, a place where even in the midst of souvenir stands and overpriced snacks, a kid can burst into pure giggles of joy because a mouse waved at him. And every time we go, we still play the game of who can spot the Matterhorn first, and shiver with pleasure when it appears, because that means we're almost there.

Choosing When to Visit

The best time to visit may be when you have vacation and the kids are off from school. If you're flexible with your schedule, though, a number of factors can influence your decision, because the Disneyland Resort has seasons of its very own.

✔ **Busiest times:** Disneyland is busiest in summer (between Memorial Day and Labor Day), but it can also be crowded on holidays (Thanksgiving week, Christmas week, President's Day weekend, Easter week, and Japan's Golden Week in early May) and weekends year 'round. All other times make up the off-season.

During the busy summertime, Tuesday through Thursday is the best time to come; Friday and Saturday are the most crowded days.

✔ **Fireworks, shows, and parades:** If you want to see all the shows and parades, you'll have to come during the high season, because scheduling is sporadic on off-season weekdays. Disneyland's famed fireworks display only happens in summer. Christmas also brings its own special magic to Disneyland, when the park is dressed up for the holidays, complete with giant decorated trees, wreathes everywhere, and visits with Santa and the Candlelight Parade, wherein carolers from all over the Southland lead visitors in a special recital of "The Christmas Story."

✔ **Summr scorchers:** Consider the summer heat when deciding when to go. Scorching days in July, August, and September can make waiting to board a ride feel like a death march, with every-one crowding into available shady spots, and super-long lines to buy cold drinks. Visiting during these months can be fine; just plan to take advantage of the indoor attractions during the midday heat. Your reward later on will be a pleasantly balmy evening, when being outdoors becomes a delight.

✔ **Crowd-free days:** If you want to avoid crowds, visit on a week-day, preferably in November, December, or January (excluding Thanksgiving and Christmas weeks). You run the risk that some rides may be closed for maintenance (never more than three or four at a time), but visiting during this low, low season is the best way to maximize a single day.

✔ **First-quarter rains:** Southern California gets most of its precipitation between January and April, but only a sustained downpour should affect your Disney plans. If the forecast predicts rain, bring both a collapsible umbrella and a waterproof rain poncho (or splurge on the cute Mickey Mouse ponchos that suddenly appear when the first raindrop falls). Even if you get wet, you'll enjoy the lightest crowds of the year! (The locals know the truth: The very best time to visit Disneyland is a drizzly, slightly cold winter day mid-week.)

Deciding How Long to Stay

You'll want to devote at least one (very) full day to the original park. If you're planning to visit during one of the peak periods, crowds and wait times will limit the attractions you're able to enjoy in a single day, so plan to spend the night and re-enter Disneyland fresh the following morning. If California Adventure holds any interest for you, set aside two days to experience both parks.

Park Hopper passes (see the following section) are a great deal for the money, and don't require you to visit on consecutive days (if you want to break up your Disney stay with a day at the beach, for example). Families with small children will especially want the multi-day option, regardless of the season. While surviving a marathon Disney day is a badge of honor for older kids, you all know that naptime crankiness will eventually rear its ugly head with the young ones.

All in all, we suggest allotting two or three full days for the Disney attractions, which gives you enough time to immerse yourself in the fantasy before moving on to the next leg of your California visit. (If you're staying elsewhere in Southern California but would like two days at the park, plan on spending the night at the park rather than driving back again the next day. You'll be glad you did.)

Getting the Lowdown on Admission

At press time, admission to Disneyland or California Adventure — including unlimited rides and all festivities and entertainment — is $45 for adults and kids 10 and over, and $35 for kids 3 to 9 (kids under 3 enter free). These figures are given only as guidelines, because new prices can pop up at any time. This price allows you admission to one park of your choice.

Disney currently offers a multi-day **Park Hopper pass,** which allows the holder unlimited access to both Disneyland and California Adventure. A three-day pass is $114 for adults, and $90 for kids ages 3 to 9. Four days costs $141 and $111, respectively. While the passes must be used within a two-week period, the days spent at the park need not be consecutive, so this is a most practical way to go. There are good reasons to have access to both parks, provided you don't pay full price for California Adventure.

Disney offers regular deals on ticket prices, especially during the slow winter months (when those three-day Park Hopper passes were going for $99 each). At press time, however, those Park Hopper passes, for use during the summer months, were going for $90 each, if purchased online (www.disneyland.com). So it is well worth your time to do some checking around.

Expect to pay a parking charge between $7 and $10, which may be included in some admission packages.

Opening the starting gate

The Disneyland Resort is open every day of the year, but operating hours vary widely. Call for the information that applies to the time frame of your visit (☎ 714-781-4565). You can also find exact open hours, ride closures, and show schedules online at www.disneyland.com.

Generally speaking, the park is open from 9 or 10 a.m. to 6 or 7 p.m. on weekdays, fall to spring; and from 8 or 9 a.m. to midnight or 1 a.m. on weekends, holidays, and during summer vacation periods. If you'd like to receive a copy of the park's Vacation Planner brochure to orient yourself before you go, call ☎ 800-225-2024.

Buying in advance can be an enormous time saver. If you plan to arrive during a busy time (either when the gates open in the morning or between 11 a.m. and 2 p.m.), purchasing your tickets in advance and getting a jump on the crowds at the ticket counters is your best bet. You can buy your tickets through the Web site, at Disney stores throughout the United States, or by calling the mail-order line (☎ 714-781-4043). Many area hotels also sell the tickets at regular cost (including whatever special deal is being offered at the time) through an arrangement with Disney.

Discovering the art of the (package) deal

If you intend to spend two or more nights in Disney territory, investigating the available package options can pay off. Start by contacting your hotel (even those in Los Angeles or San Diego) to see whether they offer Disneyland Resort admission packages. Some of the airline vacation packagers include admission to Disneyland in their inclusive packages (see Chapter 6 for more information).

In addition, check with the official Disney agency, **Walt Disney Travel Co.** (☎ **800-225-2024,** 714-520-5050; Internet: www.disneyland.com), whose packages are value-packed time- and money-savers with lots of built-in flexibility. As this was being written, they were offering a free child's Park Hopper pass with every paid adult Hopper Pass — so you can see that bargains are to be found there. You can request a glossy catalog by mail or log onto the Web site and click on "Book Your Vacation" to peruse package details, take a virtual tour of participating hotel properties, and get online price quotes for customized, date-specific packages.

Hotel choices range from the official Disney hotels to one of 35 neighboring hotels in every price range. A wide range of available extras includes admission to other Southern California attractions and guided tours (such as **Universal Studios** or a Tijuana shopping trip) and behind-the-scenes Disneyland tours, all in limitless combinations. Rates are highly competitive, especially considering that each package includes multi-day admission, early park entry, and free parking (if you choose a Disney hotel), plus keepsake souvenirs and coupon books. If you want to add air transportation or car rental, the Disney Travel Co. can make those arrangements, too.

Getting to the Disneyland Resort

The Disneyland Resort is located in the heart of Anaheim in Orange County, about 30 miles south of Los Angeles and 98 miles north of San Diego. To get there from either city, follow I-5 until you see signs for Disneyland; dedicated off-ramps from both directions lead directly to the park's parking lots and surrounding streets.

From the Palm Springs area, follow I-10 westbound to Highway 60 west. In Riverside, pick up Highway 91 west to Anaheim and then take Highway 57 south. Exit at the Ball Road off ramp and turn right (west), proceeding 2½ miles to Disneyland. The drive totals 110 miles.

If you'd rather wing it, **Los Angeles International Airport (LAX)** serves as the region's major airport, about 30 miles away. You can rent a car at the airport and drive to Anaheim, or you can take advantage of the many public-transportation services at LAX; see Chapter 21 for details.

If you'd rather fly directly into Anaheim from another state or another California city, the nearest airport is **John Wayne International Airport** in Irvine, 15 miles from Disneyland at the intersection of I-405 and Highway 55 (☎ **949-252-5200;** www.ocair.com). Most national airlines and major rental-car agencies serve the airport. To reach Anaheim from the airport, rent a car and take Hwy. 55 east, then follow I-5 north to the Disneyland exit.

An entire family can also catch a ride with **American Taxi** (☎ 888-482-9466), whose cabs queue up at the Ground Transportation Center on the lower level; reservations are not necessary. Expect the fare to Disneyland to run about $26. If only two of you are making the trip, however, consider using Super Shuttle (☎ 800-BLUE-VAN; www.super shuttle.com), which charges $10 per person to the Disneyland area. Advance reservations are recommended.

Before you pay for a taxi or shuttle service, ask if your Anaheim hotel offers airport transportation when you make your reservation.

Deciding Where to Stay

The official Disney hotels are our favorites, both for convenience and ambience. But lots of reasons exist to stay at one of the many other hotels and motels that line the surrounding blocks, not the least of which is that sometimes all 2,200-plus Disney guest rooms are full.

Staying in official Disney digs

Can't decide whether to stay off-campus, or splurge on one of the official Disney hotels? The main advantages of going 100% Disney are:

- ✔ **The Disney monorail:** Circumnavigating the theme park, the monorail also stops at each official hotel (and soon at California Adventure as well). So when you get weary of hoofing it, simply hop aboard and zip straight to your room. Dedicated ticket booths and entry turnstiles at the monorail stations mean you can also avoid the main entrance crush.

- ✔ **Early admission:** All Disney hotel guests qualify for early admission. That's right — you get to enter the park 1½ hours early, which means you can enjoy the major rides before long lines form (be sure to wave to the patient folks roped off along Main Street). This shouldn't be your deciding factor, though, because at press time, there were plans to potentially cancel this long-standing perk.

- ✔ **Just plain fun:** The official properties are just plain fun to stay at. Each gets the patented Disney treatment, with fantasy settings and imagination-stimulating diversions. Rooms, too, bear the Disney touch: bath amenities, for example, are plastered with Disney characters — and simply scream "free souvenir"!

Disneyland Hotel
$$–$$$ Disneyland

The original Disney hotel, bless its heart, and for so long the only one. It was once so very, very grand and so fun to stay at, but now it's looking a little worn around the edges. Rooms are in the process of being

The Disneyland Resort

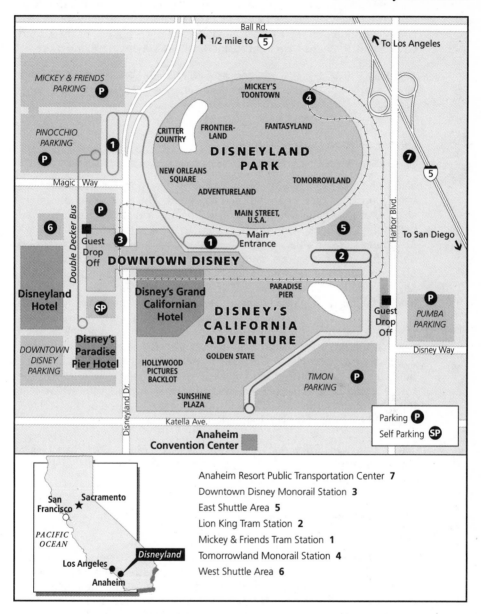

Anaheim Resort Public Transportation Center **7**
Downtown Disney Monorail Station **3**
East Shuttle Area **5**
Lion King Tram Station **2**
Mickey & Friends Tram Station **1**
Tomorrowland Monorail Station **4**
West Shuttle Area **6**

upgraded, thank heavens, because that '70s decor and those tough mattresses just aren't aging well. The new rooms each have a theme, so you get to choose between, say, the Goofy room or the Minnie room or the Donald room. Each will have a different (bright pastel) color scheme, with the character in question painted on the walls of the room's foyer or showing up in prints. Baths are white and unmemorable, but at least the shower is separated from the tub. There are many shops, plus a Peter Pan–themed pool area, complete with water slide and pirate ship. Oh, what the hay; it's what you want in a Disney hotel, especially if you're a family with kids under 10. Still, having seen the wonders of the Grand Californian, it's hard to get enthusiastic about staying here any more.

1150 Magic Way, Anaheim. ☎ *714-956-6400 (714-642-5391). Fax: 714-956-6597. Internet:* www.disney.com. *Parking: free self-serve and valet ($24). Rack rates: $170–$255.*

Disney's Grand Californian
$$$ Disneyland

It's a thing of lavish and loving beauty, a drop-dead gorgeous hotel that has been painstakingly researched and designed. The curmudgeonly might snark that it has the potential to give one an Arts and Crafts–overload headache. To heck with them. Styled to evoke Yosemite's landmark Ahwahnee Hotel (it's the Mock-wahnee, if you will), it has incredible period detail, from the cavernous, multistoried lobby with the giant roaring fireplace right down to the door fixtures and even the trash cans in each room. Several times a day, a storyteller thrills kids with campfire tales geared toward California; it's a charming free service parents must take advantage of. The rooms are Arts and Crafts smashes, with pocket doors, nature themes (branches and leaves), lush amenities, and even a lack of maid carts in the hallways (baskets deliver the fresh linens in the morning). Suites are even better, but all rooms have robes, cribs, irons and boards, duel vanities, and coffee pots. The beds are comfy and firm, although the towels could be a bit softer, tell the truth. Aren't we ungrateful? We just love this place to pieces — Disney should be justly proud of themselves. Come take a look at it even if you don't stay over.

1600 S. Disneyland Drive, Anaheim ☎ *714-956-6400 (714-642-5391). Fax: 714-300-7300. Internet:* www.disney.com. *Parking: free self-serve and valet ($24). Rack rates: $200–$310.*

Disney's Paradise Pier
$$–$$$ Disneyland

The second of the Disneyland hotels and the first to get a facelift, it's styled to evoke sunny California beach culture, with a little Asian mellow to top it off. It's the smallest of the three (500 rooms) and has the lowest profile. But it does have its own entrance into California Adventure (although not, as with the Grand Californian, right from the hotel into the park — it's a few steps away). Basically, the only reason to stay here is, well, because the other Disney hotels are full. There's nothing *wrong* with it; it is, however, the only nonthemed hotel of the three, and as such it remains undistinguished. You could be staying at any high-end chain hotel for all you know. It's pretty, it's more intimate, it's more adult-oriented, which can be nice. But still. Rooms, wearing sunny beach pastel colors (corals, blue-greens), are elegant, modern, and forgettable. The pool is rooftop, which can be kind of cool, but it pales against the ones at its siblings.

1717 S. Disneyland Dr. ☎ ***714-956-6400*** *(714-642-5391). Fax: 714-776-5763. Internet:* www.disney.com. *Parking: free self-serve and valet ($24). Rack rates: $140–$230.*

Bunking beyond the resort

You can usually find more economical rooms at the many hotels lining the streets surrounding the park than at those within the park. Naturally, they're not as lavish and entertaining as the Disney hotels; but if saving money is your prime concern, the off-campus hotels offer such advantages as free shuttles, free parking, and free breakfast.

Disney has a relation with a number of hotels in the area called the "Good Neighbor Package." You can purchase Disneyland tickets from the participating hotel at the regular price, thus saving yourself a stand in a potentially very long line at the parks. If Disney is offering any special ticket discounts at that time, the hotels will offer the same discount.

Candy Cane Inn
$–$$ Anaheim

This is more or less the heir to those fairy-tale-themed motor courts that sprung up outside the Disneyland gates after the park opened in 1955. It's a sweet family-run place just this side of shabby, but in a really good way. (That is not to imply that the hotel is in any way dirty or run down.) There is something to be said for staying in a place that tries to look like an old cartoon village (complete with cobblestones, balconies, flowers, and vines), and certainly it's a fun and friendly place. Excessively floral in decor, with a little pool (and a kiddie wading pool), it does feel more like a retreat than you would expect of a place smack dab on a major boulevard. It offers an expanded continental breakfast buffet served poolside. Because it's independent, you'll have to pay a bit more than its chain-hotel neighbors charge.

1747 S. Harbor Blvd., Anaheim. ☎ ***800-345-7057,*** *714-774-5284. Fax: 714-772-5462. Internet:* www.candycaneinn.net. *Parking: free self-serve. Rack rates: $72–$108.*

Holiday Inn Anaheim at the Park
$$ Anaheim

The most upscale non-Disney hotel on our list. Although it's on Harbor Boulevard, it is a couple of minutes down from the park (but they do offer a shuttle). Rooms are large, with a separate living area, and while it's hotel generic, it feels like better-quality wood (not veneer pasteboard, let's say). Bathrooms are also bigger than those found in the more moderately priced hotels listed. Basically, you're paying for more space and somewhat better amenities. This is more a hotel for grownups visiting the park who want only a certain amount of childhood fun — a resort hotel but without the theme or any kind of Disney stamp. Special deals (senior discounts, lower rates during slow times) pop up all the time, so ask. Dataports and cable are free here, whereas at the other places, they're nonexistent or cost extra.

1221 S. Harbor Blvd., Anaheim. ☎ *800-545-7275, 714-758-0900. Fax: 714-917-0794. Internet:* www.holiday-inn.com. *Parking: free self-serve. Rack rates: $110–$150.*

Howard Johnson Hotel
$–$$ Anaheim

Comfortable, reliable, unsurprising except that it's a bit nicer than you may expect from the orange-roofed conglomerate. It's actually pretty attractive-looking — that orange roof isn't even visible in the courtyard pool area. This hotel is directly across the street from Disneyland and has a regular cable-car-looking-trolley that shuttles guests to and from the park. The recently renovated rooms are spacious, light, and airy. Each has a small fridge. Three garden pools (one especially for kids) top it off. They have a room service with Mimi's Café (open 7 a.m. to 11 p.m.), a French/New Orleans family-style restaurant offering American cuisine. Laundromat on premises.

1380 S. Harbor Blvd. ☎ *800-422-4228, 714-776-6120. Fax: 714-533-3578. Internet:* www.hojoanaheim.com. *Parking: free self-serve. Rack rates: $79–$102.*

Park Inn Anaheim
$ Anaheim

Of all the many hotels on Harbor Boulevard, this is the only one that has any kind of interesting architecture, sort of old-world Tudor (okay, prefab, but still) rather than just a typical concrete block. All the rooms are in the process of being upgraded, and the new color scheme should make them look lighter and fresher. The rooms are adequately sized and come complete with microwaves and a small fridge, which makes this a fine choice for families looking to save some money on dining. There is a terrace-level pool and Jacuzzi on the third story, more or less facing Disneyland. It's an extremely friendly place (winner of the 2002 President's Award for commitment to customer service), with a fireplace going in the lobby and a decent continental breakfast (muffins, juices, fruit, coffee). And it's right at the corner of Disney Way, so you can't beat the location. Millie's, the family coffee shop next door (good home cooking, see the review in the following section), offers 24-hour room service.

1520 S. Harbor Blvd., Anaheim. ☎ *714-635-7275. Fax: 714-635-7276. Internet:* www.parkinn-anaheim.com. *Parking: Free self-serve. Rack rates: $79–$99.*

Dining Out

You'll go broke before you go hungry at the Disneyland Resort. You can find food everywhere: a dozen sit-down restaurants and cafeterias inside the park, and seven more full-service restaurants between the **Disneyland** and **Paradise Pier** hotels (with two more in the works at the **Grand Californian Hotel**). And that doesn't count snack carts, casual walk-up stands, and packaged food shops. As you would expect, you can also find a number of good restaurants conveniently located outside the park and near your hotel.

Dining at the resort

Most dining facilities inside Disneyland are overrated, overcrowded, and overpriced, redeeming themselves only by convenience. The exceptions are the offerings at **California Adventure,** described in this section, and the dining/entertainment complex known as **Downtown Disney,** described in the following section. It's not as bad as the day when Twinkies and space punch (and not much else) were served in Tomorrowland, but hamburgers and carbs still rule the day, and while it all works as fuel, it hardly works as *haute cuisine* (and don't get us started on those fake beignets offered in New Orleans Square). On the other hand, it tickles us that those giant dill pickles are still inexplicably offered as snacks at stands in Adventureland and in the Bountiful Valley Farm section of California Adventure. Here are some exceptions worth seeking out:

- ✔ Scattered throughout Disneyland — but (thank goodness!) plotted on the official park map — are **churro carts,** which dispense these absolutely addictive cylindrical Mexican donuts (rolled in sugar) beginning at 11 a.m.

- ✔ The food itself may be unremarkable (although there are great fans of their authentic Monte Cristo sandwich), but don't miss a chance to eat at New Orleans Square's **Blue Bayou Restaurant,** the only restaurant in the park that requires reservations (stop by early in the day to make yours). It meticulously re-creates a classic New Orleans veranda, complete with lush, vine-wrapped ironwork, lazily chirping crickets, and (nonalcoholic) mint juleps. Its misty, sunless atmosphere comes from being literally inside the Pirates of the Caribbean ride, so boatloads of pirate-seeking parkgoers drift by during your meal.

- ✔ For healthy snack options, head to Adventureland for refreshments at the **Tiki Juice Bar** and **Indy Fruit Cart,** which offer tropical juices and unembellished fresh fruit for a natural sugar boost and healthier options.

- ✔ The **Royal Street Veranda** in New Orleans Square offers those same faux-beignets, but also some decent (if hardly authentic) gumbo in a sourdough bowl.

Breakfast places fill up as soon as the park opens. Because these are expensive and uninspired, we say skip it; have some cereal before you arrive and get right to the rides. In fact, try to avoid prime eating hours as much as you can, because everyone else will be noshing at that time as well.

California Adventure

But do the bulk of your eating, if possible, at **California Adventure,** where the options are better in terms of quality and crowds. If you have the Hopper Pass, head on over to California Adventure, especially if you're an adult who doesn't want hot dogs. Even the fast food seems a bit more inventive and interesting over there. Among the highlights is **Golden Vine Winery,** which offers two dining options: a more casual, delicious little trattoria downstairs, and a formal dining room upstairs that offers prix fixe tasting menus. Both are surprising entries in an amusement park (actual mature dining options), and both serve excellent, grownup food. Patronize them, please, so there's a chance that more such ventures will be in the future. **Pacific Wharf Café** is modeled after restaurants found in San Francisco — tourist traps of course, but at Disneyland, what the hay. It sits on the edge of the mock harbor (full of hungry ducks), and you can get real sourdough bread (made on park premises; after, you can go over to the Boudin Bakery and watch loaves bake) and clam chowder, maybe in a sourdough bowl. **Cocina Mexican Grill** offers decent Mexican food made with fresh tortillas on the premises. A visit to the tortilla press is riveting fun for small children.

Downtown Disney

The big dining/entertaining/shopping complex known as **Downtown Disney** is another part of the Disneyland Resort, but it has no entrance fee and no gate, so it's considered to be "outside the park." If you want to leave the resort to visit Downtown Disney, you can have your hand stamped for readmittance to the parks. You really can't go wrong dining at one of the restaurants in Downtown Disney, unless, of course, you're on a strict budget. In that case, you may want to resort to the fast food or chain restaurants.

In addition to the restaurants listed in this section, you can try the theme restaurants (**ESPN Zone, House of Blues, Rainforest Café**), or better still, the **La Brea Bakery Café,** where you can nibble on the best bread southern California has to offer. All the restaurants have outdoor balcony or patio seating facing the Downtown Disney traffic, so the people-watching potential is very high.

Catal

$$–$$$ MEDITERRANEAN RIM

One of two Pinot group restaurants (the Pinot Group was founded by the creator of L.A.'s Patina, considered one of the best restaurants in town) in Downtown Disney, this one specializes in more coastal Mediterranean dishes, such as bouillabaisse, cassoulet, braised lamb, lots of rotisserie items, and light pastas. It's set in a lovely two-story space, with a Deco facade and a strong wood decor throughout that emphasizes a wine and harvest theme. Casual dining is on the first floor, more formal on the second.

1510 Disneyland Dr. ☎ 714-774-4442. Main courses: $8.50–$25. AE, MC, V. Open: Daily 5–10 p.m.

Napa Rose
$$$$ CALIFORNIA CUISINE

It's elegant, but not stuffy (the architect MacIntosh designed it); all you want to do is sit and look at the detailing, the floor-to-ceiling stained glass, the storytelling mural that lines the ceiling, the fireplace, and on it goes. This is Very Important Dining, with a price tag to match, but what a treat. Clearly, you're meant to think you're in the heart of California wine country, where they take dining (to say nothing of wine) very seriously indeed. Menus change seasonally, but here are some highlights from the most recent winter list: scallops with a sauce of lemon, lobster, and vanilla; pheasant with merlot-date essence; truffled risotto cake stuffed with fontina with rock shrimp Bolognese. Wasted on children, you say? Perhaps, but note that they have a child's menu, with things like simple buttered noodles, quesadillas, and pizzas — so Mom and Dad can have gourmet fun and won't have to fret about Junior's finicky food habits. Oh, and they have 22 sommeliers, so, naturally, you can guess what that wine list looks like.

1600 S. Disneyland Dr. ☎ 714-MICKEY-1 (reservations). Open: 5:30–10 p.m. daily. Sunday brunch 11 a.m.–2 p.m.

Naples Ristorante E Pizzeria
$$ ITALIAN

The other of the two Pinot Group eateries here lands squarely in fancy pasta land in a space with a decidedly California decor. It has a large outdoor patio, a bright, colorful ambience, and a very fun atmosphere.

1510 Disneyland Dr. ☎ 714-776-6200. Main Courses: $11–$15. AE, MC, V. Open: Sun–Thurs 11 a.m.–10:30 p.m., Fri–Sat 11 a.m.–12 a.m. (note that closing hours are often based on how busy they are that particular night).

Ralph Brennan's Jazz Kitchen
$$$ CREOLE/CAJUN

New Orleans comes to Disney — well, it already did, over at the park in the New Orleans square — in the form of a building that looks as if it were lifted straight off Royal Street in the French Quarter (in fact, they copied the iron grillwork on the outside from the Royal Street Café). The "Brennan" in the name is that of the finest New Orleans restaurant family — the same ones who bring you Commander's Palace (perhaps the best restaurant in that food-mad city). Get the *couchon de lait* (Cajun roast pork) po boy, or better still, the BBQ shrimp, which is actually done in a peppery butter sauce that demands to be soaked up with French bread. A shrimp napoleon has remoulade sauce layered between fried green tomatoes. Jambalaya, gumbo, seafood. Heavenly. Fattening. Who cares, you're on vacation. And they have live music nightly. If we were to eat at one place in Downtown Disney, it would be here.

1590 S. Disneyland Dr. ☎ 714-776-5200. AE, MC, V. Open: Sun–Thurs 10 a.m.–10 p.m., Fri–Sat 10 a.m.–11 p.m.

Dining outside the parks

Casa Garcia
$–$$ Anaheim   MEXICAN

Mexican food, family-style and family-friendly — and authentic (well, in that southern California Mexican way). Located about ½ mile from Disneyland (in a strip mall), it has nothing on the menu over $14, and that's for the paella (rice with all kinds of meats and seafood in it). The award-winning menu (with the occasional charming mistake: "Barbacoa — oven cooked in a red chile sauce"; doesn't that sound like the oven itself is cooked in red chile sauce?) covers the ground from shrimps *al mojo de ajo* (in garlic sauce) to taco combo platters to Texas BBQ pork ribs. It's a local favorite (always a good sign), with a casual cafe style. Come early, because there will be a line for dinner. But they are also open for breakfast!

531 W. Chapman Ave., Anaheim. ☎ 714-740-1108. Main courses $5.95–$15. AE, DC, MC, V. Open: Daily 8 a.m.–11 p.m.

Chu's Wok Inn
$–$$ Anaheim   CHINESE

A slightly more upscale restaurant than you may think from the name, with a very attractive Chinese decor. It's not daring Chinese food, more like Chinese food for timid tourists, but it's tasty, well prepared, and generously portioned.

13053 Chapman Ave., Anaheim. ☎ 714-750-3511. AE, MC, V. Open: Daily 11:30 a.m.–10 p.m.

Millie's
$–$$ Anaheim   HOME COOKING

Miss home cooking? Sure you do. We won't say this is like your mom used to make (or your grandma, more likely, because moms don't often cook like this anymore) because we don't know her, but we hope it is, because it's that good. For breakfast, we seriously recommend the "world-famous" cinnamon rolls. Omelets are fresh and fluffy and come with fresh biscuits and buttermilk gravy, the sort we just don't get often enough here in southern California. For dinner try the pot roast — at $10, you get a huge portion of falling-apart meat (no knives required!) served over carrots and potatoes (both mashed and otherwise) with soup or salad and corn-bread. That one portion may serve an entire family, unless you're with a lot of teenagers. Force yourself to eat dessert; they have an Oreo fudge berry sundae. Skip the nearby Denny's and IHOP and come here.

1480 S. Harbor Blvd. (next to the Park Vu Inn, which uses the restaurant for room service). ☎ 714-535-6892. Main courses: breakfast $4.30–$7.50, lunch and dinner $7–$13. AE, DC, DISC, MC, V. Open: 24 hours.

Exploring the Resort

You've done your homework, you've packed the right park-going clothes, and you've got a game plan in order. Now it's time to hit the parks.

Plan to get to the gates of either park a few minutes, at least, before opening. This means, if you are driving down, getting an early start, because you need to take into account early-morning rush-hour traffic, plus the drive itself, and the parking, and the getting to the gate from the parking lot, all before 9 a.m. That alone may be reason enough to stay in the Anaheim area.

The **ticket booths** are located precisely between the entrances to Disneyland and California Adventure (one on the left, the other on the right).

If you have limited time, here is a suggested game plan. **If you have only one day:** Get to the park early and start by riding the most popular rides (described in the following sections) first — or obtaining FastPasses early (see the following paragraph) — so that you don't waste precious time in line. **If you have two or more days:** You have the luxury of enjoying some Disney extras not essential enough to pack into a single day. Avoid the midday-rides crush by strolling along **Main Street U.S.A.,** shopping for **Disney souvenirs,** and ducking into **Great Moments with Mr. Lincoln,** the patriotic look at America's 16th president, Walt Disney's first foray into audio-animatronics.

One of the finer innovations in recent Disney history, the automated **FastPass** system allows visitors to buy advance tickets to certain rides, permitting them to return in, say, 45 to 90 minutes (having gone on some other rides or had a snack in the mean time), bypass the regular line, and more or less hop right on. Not all rides have this option, but the most popular ones in both Disneyland and California Adventure do, and while it doesn't eliminate lines entirely — after all, other people have the same return time as you — it does help you do the park more efficiently; Disney allows only a limited number of people to be in the

FastPass queue at the same time. Get your FastPass tickets at the FastPass machines located at or near the entrances to the attractions where the pass is offered. You will be assigned a one-hour window of time during which you can board the attraction. Look for the signs directing you to the FastPass queue (not the Standby queue); it can be a bit confusing, so read the signs carefully or just ask. There is absolutely no reason not to take advantage of this option as often as you can. And by the way — it's *free*.

Tips from the pros

Avoid common pitfalls by learning from the mistakes of others:

- ✔ **Wear your most comfortable walking shoes.** You'll spend many hours walking, standing, and putting lots of strain on your legs and feet. Running or tennis shoes are best. Open-toed shoes are fine, especially on hot days; just make sure they have impact-cushioning soles and support your feet.

- ✔ **Expect a dramatic temperature drop after dark, even in summer.** Bring a sweatshirt or jacket, perhaps even long pants; you can store them in a locker, leave them in the car, or tote them in a backpack. Too many visitors have shown up in shorts and tank tops, only to discover that by 10 p.m. they're freezing their buns off!

- ✔ **Don't forget such bare necessities** as sunscreen (the park gets a lot of direct sun); camera film (more than you think you'll want; film costs more in the park) and spare batteries; extra baby supplies; bottled water or a sports bottle you can refill at drinking fountains; and snacks (if the kids get hungry in line, or you just balk at the concession prices). Although anything you may forget is available for purchase inside Disneyland, you'll cringe at the marked-up prices.

- ✔ **Purchase tickets in advance** (over the Internet or phone, or through your hotel): Not only do Disney Resort hotels sell tickets, so do many area hotels, through an arrangement with Disney, as a service to their guests. This saves you from standing in what can be slow and long ticket lines. Visit the Web site at www.disneyland.com.

- ✔ **Make sure your child is ready to play.** It is certainly not a given that all children love, or will love, Disneyland. Some rides may simply be too intense (fast, dark, subtle) for certain ages or personalities. We strongly urge you to seriously consider your own child's tolerance level and individual tastes, phobias, and neuroses before bringing him or her to this fabulous, but pricey, destination.

- ✔ **Ask about ride restrictions before you come.** Some rides have age and height restrictions, so check in advance so that your kids won't be crestfallen to find that they can't ride a particular ride when they get to the park. For most attractions, you have to be 7 years or older to ride alone, for example. For the more active, high-speed rides, like Space Mountain, Splash Mountain, and **Big Thunder Mountain Railroad,** kids are required to be at least 40 inches high and 3 years old. Forty-inch-handstamps are issued at certain locations, to last throughout the day.

Disneyland

As the clock strikes 9 a.m., the gates open, and the crowd floods in. You start on **Main Street,** the famous ⅔ replica of an ideal American small town — Mark Twain's mid-19th-century with a little Beaver Cleaver thrown in. (Actually, all buildings in the park are ⅔ size, the better to make kids feel at ease, and adults sentimental.) We urge you, even if you have never been here before, not to linger — everyone else is bolting to their favorite rides, and every minute you dally, the lines are getting longer.

Main Street feeds into the central area of Disneyland, from which several main "lands" branch off, rather like the fingers on a hand: **Fantasyland, Tomorrowland, Frontierland, Adventure Land, New Orleans Square, Critter Country,** and **Mickey's Toon Town.** Where you go at this point depends on your preferences. We detail each area in this section, highlighting the most popular rides, to help you decide which you should target first. From experience, however, we can say that among the most perennially popular rides, park-wide, are the **Pirates of the Caribbean, Haunted Mansion, Indiana Jones, Space Mountain,** and **Roger Rabbit.**

Although many visitors tackle Disneyland systematically, beginning at the entrance and working their way clockwise around the park, the most effective method historically has been to arrive early and run to the most popular rides first, where midday lines can last an hour or more.

Adventures with kids

If you have small kids with you, concentrate on **Fantasyland** (behind Sleeping Beauty's Castle), a kids' paradise with fairy-tale-derived rides like **King Arthur Carousel, Dumbo the Flying Elephant, Mr. Toad's Wild Ride, Peter Pan's Flight, Alice in Wonderland, Pinocchio's Daring Journey,** and the Disney signature ride **It's A Small World.**

Elsewhere in the park, little ones will enjoy clambering through **Tarzan's Treehouse,** singing along with the audio-animatronic **Country Bear Jamboree,** and doing space wheelies on **Rocket Rods,** which is tamer than the name implies (not worth a long wait for grown-ups). **Mickey's Toontown** is a wacky, gag-filled world inspired by the *Roger Rabbit* films, featuring endless amusement for young imaginations.

Adventures for thrill-seekers

If high-speed thrills are your style, follow the **Indiana Jones Adventure** into the Temple of the Forbidden Eye, with hair-raising perils that include the familiar cinematic tumbling boulder — very realistic in the front seats!

Most of Disneyland's best action roller coasters are "mountain" themed. Perennial favorite **Space Mountain** is a pitch-black indoor roller coaster that assaults your ears and equilibrium. **Splash Mountain** is a water flume with a big, wet splash at the end (be prepared!). The **Matterhorn Bobsleds** offer a zippy coaster ride through faux-alpine caverns and fog banks, while runaway train cars careen through a deserted 1870s gold mine on **Big Thunder Mountain Railroad.**

Diverging from the mountain theme, stationary **Star Tours** encounters a space-load of misadventures on the way to the Moon of Endor. This **Star Wars**–inspired Tomorrowland virtual ride manages to achieve realistic queasiness with motion seats and video effects.

Longtime faves

Some of Disneyland's highlights are long-time favorites that have stood the test of time. Two all-time best bets are in New Orleans Square: The intriguingly spooky **Haunted Mansion** showcases the brilliance of Disney "imagineers" and boggles your mind with too many details to absorb in just one visit. **Pirates of the Caribbean** presents an enchanted world of swashbuckling and rum-running that you glide through via a realistic southern bayou.

Parade and show-going tips

The park's parades and shows draw huge crowds into relatively small areas. Parades usually run twice a day, in the late afternoon and mid-evening. If a parade doesn't interest you, make a point to steer clear of these areas during and immediately after the parade; use this time to take advantage of shorter ride lines in Frontierland (**Big Thunder Mountain Railroad**), Tomorrowland (**Space Mountain**), and New Orleans Square (**Haunted Mansion** and **Pirates of the Caribbean**).

California Adventure

Ah, now you come to the "new" park, which opened to great fanfare in 2001. The first major new development at Disneyland since, hmm, maybe Toontown — except this is so much bigger. Toontown was just a new land; this is a whole new park.

After we have been going on — and on and on and on — about the general overall perfection of Disney, we now have to say California Adventure may have been a major misstep. And unless you get one of those multiday Hopper Passes, you can safely save your money and skip the new park altogether.

Don't get us wrong; it's gorgeous. Disney design would produce no less. Every detail, as always, is extensively researched and exquisite. But did you notice the name? Do you know what the theme is? That's right; California. It's a mini version of California in (need we point out?) *California*. It boasts a mock version of Yosemite, a highly stylized version of San Francisco, and a wishful-thinking version of Hollywood Boulevard.

Look ma — no lines!

That's what *you* think. Nearly every Disney ride is fiendishly designed to look as if there's no line in front of it — either by having the line snake in such a way that its true length is obscured, or by having most of it hidden inside the ride structure itself. You walk up and think "Hey, there's no line, let's try this ride!" only to get inside and find out there are quite a few people and a lengthy wait ahead of you. It's a clever psychological trick we fall for *each and every time*. The upside is that many of the newer rides have some kind of visual device, little sights, details, or other amusements (talking cars before Autopia, say, or a "set" that makes you think you are "backstage" at Roger Rabbit) that can help while away the time. It's a good idea to bring a book or a magazine, though, and if you have kids in tow, make sure they have a book or comic to keep themselves occupied during the wait.

But never mind that. A more egregious sin (one that could easily be a by-product of the overall failure to meld design and place) is that the entire park lacks the same magic of Disneyland — which is, after all, based on mythologies or faraway lands and times, rather than a re-creation of something that lies right outside the gates. Consequently, it's artificial in a Vegas way, not a Disney dazzle way. Plus, it's a much more generic amusement park; there aren't many rides for the space, and those that are here often disappoint or are completely ordinary, lacking the special Disney touch.

Which is not to say that there isn't plenty to enjoy, but California Adventure is much more a stroll-around-and-admire park than an amusement park, much better for adults weary of lines or rides in general. And if the place didn't cost a whole separate expensive admission, we would probably think more kindly of it than we do. Which is where that Hopper Pass comes in; it pays for itself in just a couple days of Disneyland admission alone. With it, families can readily take advantage of the admittedly better food options in CA (get the initials?) and the smaller crowds.

California Adventure for kids

Grizzly River Run is a thoroughly enjoyable water ride; expect to get either somewhat damp or soaked through. **The Redwood Creek Challenge Trail** is part of a kid's playground area, allowing them to run around, climb on ropes or on rock-climbing walls, and just generally get their ya-yas out in an area designed to look like Yosemite ("oh, it's *faux-semite*," observed one attendee). Also featured is the **Soarin' Over California** ride; riders pile into rows of seats that are then lifted up so that they may sway and tilt, hang-glider style, while watching an IMAX-type film. It's one of the better rides, although prone to long lines, and a tad disappointing if you thought you were going to do more actual hang-gliding-type activity. If, when you read this, the **Bug's Life Theater** is still showing its 3-D attraction (there are plans to convert it to something else), by all means, go — it is one of the best attractions in the park — but note that it is (honestly) too dark and intense for young kids.

Paradise Pier is essentially Disney's version of a traditional amusement park. It's Carnie Central, with the sort of rides that fly around on chains or whiz into the air and generally make you sick to your stomach. It's nothing you haven't ridden before and, as such, hardly a must-do, but then again, how lovely that in this manic, high-tech, short-attention-span world there are still kids who get thrilled riding a merry-go-round or Ferris wheel.

California Adventure for adults

For adults, there is honest-to-gosh wine tasting at the **Golden Vine Winery,** where you can learn about wine-making (right out of Napa Valley) and even taste the juice of the grape. There is also a replica of the **rotunda of San Francisco's Palace of Fine Arts** (it serves the same purpose as Cinderella's Castle: It's a good meeting spot), and a copy of the **Pacific Wharf,** where you can watch bread being made or, better still, a tortilla-making machine in action (and you get a free tortilla, fresh off the machine, just for coming in).

California Adventure for superstar wannabes

The **Hollywood Pictures Backlot** is possibly the most dubious portion of the park. We've already mentioned how very odd it is to see this highly stylized, cartoon version of Hollywood Boulevard (which, as we mention in Chapter 21, has no real association with Hollywood the motion-picture industry), but that pales in comparison to the sensations experienced when riding the **Superstar Limo,** wherein you enjoy the whole panoply of stardom, from your agent bossing you around, to paparazzi flashing their bulbs, to seeing your visage on a billboard (and you get waved at by cardboard representations — what, animatronics are too expensive? — of such ABC and Disney stars as Tim Allen and Whoopi Goldberg), all touting a value system even more gross than those telling little girls that someday their prince will come. Otherwise, there isn't much to do on this side, although the **Muppet 3D Adventure** is sweetly enjoyable.

Gathering More Information

For the latest **Disneyland** and **California Adventure** developments, call the park's information line at ☎ **714-781-4565** or 714-781-4560 to talk to a real person. You can find online information at www.disneyland.com.

To get more information on the surrounding area, check with the **Anaheim/Orange County Visitor and Convention Bureau,** 800 W. Katella Ave. (☎ **714-765-8888;** www.anaheimoc.org). The bureau is located just inside the Convention Center (across the street from Disneyland) and welcomes visitors Monday through Friday from 8 a.m. to 5 p.m.

Chapter 23

San Juan Capistrano and Laguna Beach

In This Chapter

▶ Seeing the sights at San Juan Capistrano

▶ Enjoying the sun, sand, and special events at Laguna Beach

T wo favorite getaway destinations for Los Angelenos are San Juan Capistrano and Laguna Beach, both close to the city in distance but far away in feel. San Juan Capistrano is located 15 minutes southwest of Laguna Beach, so you can hit both in the course of a short trip. We suggest that you visit the historic sights of San Juan Capistrano during the day, have lunch at one of the restaurants described in this chapter, and stay in one of Laguna's fine lodgings at night. You can spend a most enjoyable few hours getting to know the area.

San Juan Capistrano

It's easy to understand why San Juan Capistrano's famed swallows return to the town's ten-acre mission every March 19, but the real question is why would they ever want to leave in the first place? Although spectacular unto itself, this "Jewel of the Missions," as it has become known, with its botanical courtyards and narrative displays, was founded November 1, 1776, and is only a tiny portion of what makes San Juan Capistrano special.

Getting there by car

San Juan Capistrano marks the halfway point between Los Angeles and San Diego, about an hour and ten minutes from the heart of each city. Exit I-5 at Camino Capistrano and head due west about three blocks to break up the monotony of the San Diego–to–Los Angeles (or vice versa) drive.

What to see and do

This diverse community offers glimpses into the past, present, and future, with architecture ranging from the 18th-century **Montanez Adobe** (31781 Los Rios St.), to renowned architect Michael Graves' postmodern **Regional Library** (31495 El Camino Real).

The **Mission San Juan Capistrano** (Ortega Hwy./Calif. 74; ☎ 949-234-1300; Internet: www.missionsjc.com; admission: $6 adults, $5 seniors, $4 children 3 to 11, free for children 3 and under; open daily 8:30 a.m.–5 p.m.) is the seventh of the 21 California coastal missions. Centuries-old adobe walls shelter gardens and fountains. The ruins of the Great Stone Church (begun in 1796, completed in 1806, collapsed by an earthquake in 1812), with its 125-foot native-stone bell tower, are undergoing preservation to stem the structure's decay. The mission is best known for its swallows, which, according to legend, return to nest here each year on March 19, St. Joseph's Day. Legend aside, swallows can be seen here year 'round.

Adjacent to the Mission, just across the railroad tracks, is **Los Rios Street**, the oldest remaining residential street in all of California. Nestled between a couple of distinctive gift stores lies the **Ramos House Cafe** (31752 Los Rios St.; ☎ 949-443-1342; open Tues–Sat 8:30 a.m.–3 p.m.; Sun brunch; closed Mon), undoubtedly one of the yummiest breakfast and lunch spots in Southern California. The owner lives in the 1881 house with a converted commercial kitchen and treats his guests to contemporary American cuisine (with Southern influence) on the open patio.

Former President Richard Nixon so loved the local flavor served up in the Mexican kitchen of the National Historical Landmark **El Adobe** (31891 Camino Capistrano; ☎ 949-493-1163; open daily 11 a.m.–9 p.m.), they actually named a combination dinner after him. If you simply don't have time for a leisurely meal, **Pedro's Tacos** (31721 Camino Capistrano; ☎ 949-489-7752; open daily 10 a.m.–8 p.m.), across the street from the mission, serves delicious, authentic, not to mention wonderfully inexpensive, Mexican fare.

Gathering more information

For a complete listing of shops, events, restaurants, and accommodations, contact the **San Juan Capistrano Chamber of Commerce** at ☎ 949-493-4700 or simply log onto www.sanjuancapistrano.org.

Laguna Beach

Laguna Beach has long been a favorite getaway for Southern Californians, and for many a good reason. Number one, with its clean beaches, beautiful homes, and terrific landscape, it is simply gorgeous. Number two, while it could be considered a sleepy little town, the artists' community here ensures that you're never at a loss for things to do. And finally, it's just a short road trip from most SoCal metropolises.

When to go

The height of tourist season is between Memorial Day Weekend and Labor Day weekend, because everyone yearns to engage in Laguna's magnificent summer events as well as frolic on the sand in the warm sun. Room rates go up (not tremendously, but enough to notice should your stay be for more than a night or two), and the village becomes a wee bit more congested than in the winter.

Keep in mind, however, that Southern California usually gets hit with what we call June Gloom — overcast mornings that tend to burn off by mid to late afternoon. Does this detract from the town's beauty? Heck no! And tanning fiends can still get good color because UV rays are intensified through the clouds. On the other hand, while California's mild winter may not be necessarily conducive to bathing trunks and bikinis, it can be inviting to beachcombers who enjoy taking in long walks in cool, fresh air.

Getting there by car

From John Wayne Airport (SNA-Orange County): Laguna Beach is about 20 minutes from John Wayne Airport. Simply exit the airport (take the soft left) and merge (right) onto the 405 (San Diego) Freeway South. Continue down the 405. Veer onto the 133 South toward Laguna Beach. This highway will become Laguna Canyon, which will then become Broadway and take you directly to Coast Highway.

From Los Angeles: The directions remain the same, except you'll spend about 40 minutes longer on the 405 South.

From San Diego: Take I-5 North until you reach the CA-1 exit toward Beach Cities. This exit takes you under the freeway and onto Coast Highway (CA-1). Continue North on CA-1 through Dana Point. Within a scenic 15-minute drive, you will be in South Laguna Beach.

Getting around

As is true in much of California, relying solely on your feet may not be in your best interest. If you're staying in the village, you'll be fine, but if you like to explore, you'll want to rent a car. Be forewarned: Although most hotels are kind enough to provide complimentary parking, should you park at a meter, be sure to pay attention to the signs and feed the meters as posted, usually one quarter for 15 minutes.

Where to stay

Casa Laguna Inn
$$–$$$$ Laguna Beach

Incorporating the enchanting spirit of Laguna Beach, this former artists' colony turned bed-and-breakfast features 20 romantic rooms laden with luxurious linens and antiques. Most of the rooms boast incredible ocean views amid traditional early-20th-century Spanish-California architecture. The warm and friendly staff prepares an extended continental breakfast and provides afternoon refreshments.

2510 South Coast Hwy. ☎ *800-233-0449 or (949) 494-2996. Fax: 949-494-5009. Internet:* www.CasaLaguna.com. *Rack rates: $99–$395. AE, DISC, MC, V.*

Hotel Laguna
$$–$$$ Laguna Beach

Slightly south of Main Beach, in the heart of the village, this Laguna Beach classic boasts the best rates for an oceanfront hotel. The view and food from the Terrace and Claes restaurants attract diners from all over, while Le Bar is a great spot to enjoy a cocktail or two.

425 South Coast Hwy. ☎ *800-524-2927, 949-494-1151. Fax: 949-497-2163. Internet:* www.hotellaguna.com. *Rack rates: $85–$250. AE, DC, DISC, MC, V.*

Inn at Laguna Beach
$$–$$$$$ Laguna Beach

On the ocean side of Coast Highway stands this family-friendly, comfortably appointed hotel. Adjacent to Main Beach and overlooking the town's infamous volleyball and basketball courts (where, if you're lucky, you may very well see a Clipper or Laker on his day off), it features a heated pool, a spa, and a sun terrace. Complimentary continental breakfast is served in your room.

211 North Pacific Coast Hwy. ☎ *800-544-4479 or (949) 497-9722. Fax: 949-497-9972. Internet:* www.innatlagunabeach.com. *Rack rates: $99–$599. AE, DC, DISC, MC, V.*

If you're in the mood for a more secluded territory, you needn't head more than a few miles south. Offering both a luxury resort and the charming bed-and-breakfast, the quaint beach town of Dana Point may suit you perfectly.

The Blue Lantern Inn
$$–$$$$$ Dana Point

Located atop a bluff overlooking Dana Point Harbor, this is one of the Four Sisters Inns' elegant collection of California and Pacific Northwest properties, and it easily lives up to their standard of service, beauty, and comfort. Each of the 29 romantic rooms features a fireplace, Jacuzzi tub, coffeemaker, and a refrigerator stocked with soft drinks. A gourmet breakfast is available free of charge every morning, and wine and hors d'oeuvres are offered each afternoon. Other features include a fitness room and bicycles for sightseeing. As you take in the surroundings, stop by **J.C. Beans** (34114 Pacific Coast Hwy.) for the best latte in Orange County in a friendly, non-franchise environment.

34343 St. off the Blue Lantern, Dana Point. ☎ *800-950-1236, 949-661-1304. Fax: 949-496-1483. Internet:* www.foursisters.com. *Rack rates: $155–$500. Check the Web site for specials. AE, DC, MC, V.*

The St. Regis Monarch Beach Resort & Spa
$$$$–$$$$$ Dana Point

Oh, the excitement in Southern California when this new ultimate luxury resort (or so they bill themselves) opened! The celebs came out in droves, and everyone else cooed over photo spreads. The results: sumptuous rooms, a breathtaking location, a world-class spa, a private beach club, and a championship golf course all in one spectacular location. This personification of elegance and luxury is further defined by a staff that's dedicated to providing impeccable service. Feel free to specify a canine-friendly room should Fido be joining you in your travels; that is, if your travels can bear the cost to stay here at all.

One Monarch Beach Resort, Dana Point. ☎ *800-722-1543, 949-234-3200. Fax: 949-234-3201. Internet:* www.stregismb.com. *Basic rates begin at $355 for the off-season (after Labor Day through the beginning of June) and escalate from there. Package deals are subject to availability. AE, DC, DISC, MC, V.*

Where to dine

Dizz's As Is
$$–$$$ Laguna Beach   INTERNATIONAL

Located a few miles south of the village, this local favorite since 1977 serves up an eclectic mix of mouth-watering international cuisine with a French-Belgian flair. Upon being seated at one of their cozy tables, you and your party will be given a stack of pages describing the special entrees of the evening. Their generous portions will leave you wondering how you can possibly fit in a bite of one of their delectable desserts, but you'll find a way.

2794 South Coast Hwy. at Nyes Place. ☎ *949-494-5250. Reservations accepted only for large parties. Dinners (including appetizers and soup or salad: $19–$29. AE, MC, V. Open: Tues–Sat 6 p.m.–1 a.m.*

La Sirena Grill
$ Laguna Beach MEXICAN

This order-at-the-counter-and-try-to-find-yourself-a-seat spot has the freshest Mexican tasties in Laguna. Whether you try a *carne asade* burrito, an avocado-lime salad with chicken, or any one of their vegetarian specialties, your taste buds will dance with glee. Perfect to take with you on a picnic.

Downtown Laguna: 347 Mermaid St.; ☎ *949-497-8226. South Laguna: 30862 South Coast Hwy.;* ☎ *949-499-2301. Everything less than $10. Cash only. Open: Mon–Sat 11 a.m.–9 p.m.*

The Sundried Tomato
$–$$ Laguna Beach CALIFORNIA CUISINE

The truly delicious California cuisine is reason enough to embrace this new lunch and dinner spot. Lunch features an array of creative salads, pastas, and sandwiches; dinner incorporates more entrees and specials. The cream of sundried tomato soup is a must! The dog-friendly patio allows you and your pooch to dine in tandem amidst the sun-drenched courtyard complete with waterfall.

361 Forest Ave., two blocks east of Coast Hwy. ☎ *949-494-3312. Reservations recommended for dinner and can be handy for lunch. Main courses: lunch $6.95–$9.95; dinner $9.95–$24. AE, MC, V. Open: Daily 11:30 a.m.–3:30 p.m., 5–9:30 p.m.*

Ti Amo
$$ Laguna Beach ITALIAN

This is south Laguna Beach's quintessential restaurant of romance. Modeled after an Italian villa, it offers a cozy, charming atmosphere with a fireplace and ocean views. The extensive wine list and divine Italian-Mediterranean menu embrace Ti Amo's philosophy that the marriage of food and wine is the key to good health and living. Who are we to argue with that kind of logic? And their Chocolate Sin is even more wonderfully wicked than it sounds.

31327 South Coast Hwy. ☎ *949-499-5350. Fax: 949-499-9760. Reservations recommended. Main courses: $13–$19. AE, DC, DISC, MC, V. Open: 5:30–10:30 p.m.*

Laguna events

Laguna Beach Art Walk

On the first Thursday of every month, locals and visitors alike converge upon the eclectic group of galleries that line Laguna's Pacific Coast Highway for the **Laguna Beach Art Walk.** While some proprietorships rely solely on the merit of the artists' work to bring in a crowd, others resort to bribery in the form a light snack and beverages ranging from Evian to chardonnay. Adding to the festival feel is music, sometimes live and sometimes canned. With all the inviting restaurants, a beautiful stretch of beach, and a dose of culture in such close proximity, your vacation should start on a Thursday night. Admission is free. Free trolley service from approximately 6 p.m. to 9:00 p.m. starts at the Laguna Art Museum. For more information, call ☎ **949-497-0716** or go to www.firstthursdaysartwalk.com.

The Festival of Arts and Pageant of the Masters

Presented in July and August since 1932, California's oldest annual art show, **The Festival of Arts,** is held in a scenic six-acre Laguna Canyon park, at 650 Laguna Canyon Road. For a nominal entrance fee, this celebration of the area's most esteemed artists offers an introduction to their work, as well as the opportunity to purchase original artworks to add to your personal collection.

Running concurrently with the festival since 1935 is the renowned **Pageant of the Masters.** Set in an outdoor amphitheater accompanied by live narration and a professional orchestra, this nightly show features real people in elaborate costumes and settings re-creating classical and contemporary works of art. It sounds hokey, we know, but it's not — it's pretty incredible, and we bet it elicits a wow from you even if you're jaded. (And we've seen how they do it — they assemble one piece right from scratch, and you still can't believe it.) Nearly 500 volunteers are selected every year to serve as cast members; headpiece, costume, and backstage assistants; makeup artists; and as refreshment servers, in a triumph of speed, organization, and, yes, art.

The highly coveted tickets to these events go on sale in December, many months prior to the July opening. They range in price from $15 to $65, should you be able to get them from the box office (☎ **949-497-6582**), and believe the nice people when they tell you that there are no bad seats. You may want to skip the first two rows, however — you lose some of the grand scope. Binoculars are a must regardless of where you're seated, because they are the only way to hone in on the fine details. If you're unable to get tickets the old-fashioned way, fret not — you have a few alternatives. The box office generally releases a limited number of tickets each show date, so plan to line up early and cross your fingers. Of course that leaves you with no guarantee. A reliable way is to try a hotel concierge desk. The most foolproof — although not exactly inexpensive — way to get tickets is to contact a ticket broker: **Titonium** (☎ **949-248-8555**) or **Good Time** (☎ **714-432-7383**) may be able to help you out.

To confirm dates and times for both the pageant and the festival — they change annually — go the Web site at www.foapom.com or call ☎ **949-494-1145.** You can reach the box office at ☎ **800-487-3378** or 949-497-6582.

Sawdust Art Festival

Over 150 local artists, artisans, and craftspeople exhibit and sell their wares at the annual summer **Sawdust Art Festival.** Each booth or display has a personality of its own — and it's a fine way to dispense with the year's Christmas shopping as you wander across, yes, the sawdust (you were expecting gold dust?) from wooden booth to wooden booth, checking out pottery, jewelry, painting, and sculpture. Be sure to seek out the entertainment, craft displays, and cafés. The festival also returns for a brief stint for four winter weekends — perfect for more holiday shopping! The Sawdust Art Festival is located at 935 Laguna Canyon Road. For information, call ☎ **949-494-3030** or go to www. sawdustartfestival.org.

Vistas, views, and adventure

Whether you're a mountain biker, a couple in search of the perfect sunset, a walking enthusiast trying to burn off what you've been indulging in, or a family with children, the **Alta Laguna Park** will intrigue you. Begin by heading east on Park Avenue (the first light south of Forest at Coast Highway). You'll drive up a steep hill and pass many architectural delights until you can no longer drive forward at Alta Laguna; at that point, make a left. Continue over two speed bumps, and then pull into the parking lot on your right-hand side. After parking, exit the lot the way you came, only this time by foot, and make a right. On a clear day, as you reach the picnic tables, you'll be able to see the coastline extending all the way from Palos Verdes to the north down to southernmost San Diego. Offshore, Catalina Island will seem much, much closer than 26 miles across the sea. If you're yearning for exercise, head in the other direction through the toddler-friendly playground to the miles of trails overlooking the expansive canyons and parks of South Orange County. The park closes at dusk.

Theater

Founded in 1920 by some of Hollywood's most prestigious elite, including Bette Davis, Charlie Chaplin, and Mary Pickford, the **Laguna Playhouse,** at 606 Laguna Canyon Road, is the oldest continuously operating theater on the West Cast. Offering a year-round performance schedule, this renowned venue always has something wonderful to be seen. It's adjacent to the Festival of Arts. Call ☎ **800-946-5556** or go to www.lagunaplayhouse.com for detailed program information and ticketing.

Gathering more information

For more information about Laguna Beach, contact the **Laguna Beach Visitors Bureau** (252 Broadway, just east of Coast Highway; ☎ **800-877-1115,** 949-497-9229; Internet: www.LagunaBeachinfo.org).

Chapter 24

Ring-a-Ding-Ding: Palm Springs

● ●

● ●

*V*isitors have a love-hate relationship with Palm Springs. If you love desert landscapes, bikinis, bronzed complexions, and an easy-going vibe, you'll likely fall into the former category. If you want more culture and less hot sun, you'll probably fall in the latter.

Long a place for the rich and the elderly to while away their time, Palm Springs has a new ring-a-ding-ding hipness for Gen X, lured by the spa-and-sun lifestyle, while golfers have always loved it. The majesty of the surrounding landscape is undeniable: the soaring palms and flowering cacti, the surprising natural lushness and vivid hues of the landscape, the brilliant blue of the daytime sky and the pink-purple glow that dusk ushers in, and the jagged mountains that rise from the flat desert floor not too far in the distance. The scale alone is enough to impress.

But the main drag of Palm Springs is frozen in time in a '50s-meets-modern-day-strip-mall boredom. And while there are plenty of ways to sit back and relax, if you're looking for more stimulation than can be found by a pool with a frothy drink, look elsewhere.

On the other hand, in this fast paced, hectic world, what could be better than a little peace and quiet? Palm Springs is the place to experience the kind of renewal that only comes from getting away from it all. Whether you draw inner peace from communing with spectacular nature or renewing your acquaintance with a gleaming set of nine-irons, Palm Springs has the answer for you. And bring the kids: Virtually all the big resorts, and a few of the smaller ones, welcome them with open arms — and who's happier than a kid allowed to frolic the day away in a sun-splashed pool?

Timing Your Visit

Unlike most of the rest of California, Palm Springs' off-season is summer. From mid- or late May through September, daytime highs soar into the 100s. We're talking 110°F or more during July and August. And one memorable, apocalyptic day, it was 135°F. Those kinds of numbers can keep away all but the most salamander types, or those looking for serious hotel deals.

"In-season" is everything else: From October through April, average highs range between 69°F and 92°F. Keep in mind, however, that you can't always count on pool weather during these months; anyone who knows the desert will tell you that 70°F doesn't really feel like summer with virtually no humidity in the air and a sprinkling of clouds in the sky. The coolest months are usually December through February, when highs seldom get past the low 70s and nighttime temps dip into the 40s (perfect weather if you're a golfer who probably doesn't relish the notion of a broiling midday sun). Fall and spring are best — that's when it feels like a regular summer, with highs generally in the 80s and nights in the 50s or 60s. Spring and early summer can bring serious winds, gusting about like nobody's business.

With the "season" comes the crowd, especially urban-escaping week-enders and "snowbirds" (annual refugees from colder climes, often retirees, who head back home — just like their feathered friends — 'round about April). Luckily, the area seldom feels overcrowded. Still, if you have your heart set on staying in a certain hotel, or you want prime tee times, plan ahead, especially if your visit falls over a week-end. Spring Break — usually sometime before or around Easter — is worth avoiding if you can help it.

If you're not averse to packing an economy-size bottle of sunscreen and dealing with a little sizzling heat, off-season — summer — can be a bargain-hunter's bonanza. Nothing is very crowded, and hotel rooms go for a song: You can get terrific accommodations for as little as $49, and luxury resorts sell $300-a-night rooms for less than $150. Of course, it's not a great time to take full-day hikes in the desert, but if your plan is to lie under the umbrella poolside, taking a cooling dip every once in a while, summer is just fine. Even as a golfer, you can enjoy yourself in summers, as long as you book 6 or 7 a.m. tee times. After the sun goes down, summer evenings are lovely. Still, know what you're in for if you plan a July or August stay: The weather is going to be hot, hot, hot.

If you're treating this as a vacation from your vacation, a chance to unwind, you will probably need at least three days — it takes a couple of days alone to really relax! But don't plan on staying more than two nights if you're easily bored.

If you want to work in a side trip to **Joshua Tree National Park** or **Death Valley National Park** (see "Joshua Tree and Death Valley: A Trip to the Dry, Hot Desert Parks," later in this chapter), you should set aside enough time in your schedule for it.

Getting There

The Palm Springs resorts are about 108 miles east of Los Angeles and 141 miles north of San Diego.

✔ **From L.A.,** it's a straight shot east on Interstate 10. Take the Highway 111 turnoff into Palm Springs, which will drop you directly onto North Palm Canyon Drive, the main thoroughfare. The drive takes about two hours.

If you're heading to Palm Desert, stay on I-10 past the Highway 111 junction. Exit at Monterey Avenue and turn right. The distance is 122 miles from L.A. to Palm Desert.

✔ **From San Diego,** take Interstate 15 north to I-215, then head east on Highway 60 until you connect to I-10 in Banning. From I-10, take the Highway 111 turnoff into Palm Springs, which will drop you directly onto North Palm Canyon Drive, the main thoroughfare. The 141-mile drive takes about 2½ hours.

If you're heading from San Diego to Palm Desert, the route changes a bit. Take I-15 north to Temecula, where you'll pick up Highway 79 to Highway 371 to Highway 74, which will lead you into Palm Desert from the south. This nice 122-mile drive takes about 2½ hours. If you'd rather stick to the interstate, follow the directions to Palm Springs and allow three hours.

Flying right into Palm Springs is also easy. Pleasant Palm Springs International Airport is just a mile from the heart of downtown at 3400 E. Tahquitz Canyon Way, at El Cielo Road (☎ **760-318-3800;** www.ci.palm-springs.ca.us/Airport). The following airlines fly in:

✔ Alaska Airlines: ☎ **800-426-0333;** www.alaskaair.com

✔ American Airlines: ☎ **800-433-7300;** www.aa.com

✔ America West: ☎ **800-235-9292;** www.americawest.com

✔ Continental: ☎ **800-525-0280;** www.continental.com

✔ Delta/Skywest: ☎ **800-453-9417;** www.delta-air.com

✔ Horizon: ☎ **800-547-9308;** www.horizonair.com

✔ Northwest Airlines: ☎ 800-225-2525; www.nwa.com

✔ United Express: ☎ 800-241-6522; www.united.com

All the national car-rental companies have airport locations. You can also set up a ride with one of the desert's many taxi companies, such as **Airport Taxi** (☎ 760-321-4470) or **Yellow Cab of the Desert** (☎ 760-345-8398). However, we strongly suggest renting a car, unless you plan on parking yourself at a destination resort or at one of the inns a walk away from Palm Springs' Palm Canyon Drive, and intend to do zero exploring.

Orienting Yourself

The desert resorts are a breeze to navigate after you get a handle on what's where. They cover a roughly 25-mile-long stretch of desert running parallel to I-10, from Desert Hot Springs in the northwest to Indio in the southeast. With the exception of Desert Hot Springs (only worth a visit if you're visiting Two Bunch Palms; see "Ahhh — The spa" later in the chapter), all the big resort communities lie on the south side of I-10, laid out in an angled grid pattern far enough away from the interstate that through traffic doesn't interfere.

Palm Springs, the oldest community, serves as the heart of the desert resort action. North Palm Canyon Drive is downtown Palm Springs' main drag, where many — but not all — of the restaurants and mall and boutique shopping are. Tahquitz Canyon Way meets North Palm Canyon at the town's primary intersection, tracking a straight line from the airport into the heart of town.

You find most of the luxury resorts and championship golf courses in newer communities to the east of Palm Springs, notably Rancho Mirage, Palm Desert, and La Quinta. The main connecting road between them is East Palm Canyon Drive, known as Highway 111 as soon as you leave Palm Springs. **Palm Desert** is the desert communities' other tourism-oriented commercial hub. Its central intersection is Highway 111 and Monterey Avenue, with El Paseo (often likened to Beverly Hills' Rodeo Drive), one block to the south, serving as the main dining-and-shopping drive.

Where to Stay in Palm Springs

We can't stress it enough: The off-season and other slow times can bring tremendously discounted rates, so if you can plan your trip accordingly, you can get some great bargains. Be sure to check hotels' Web sites, when applicable, where some of these said bargains may be lurking.

The Palm Springs Desert Resorts

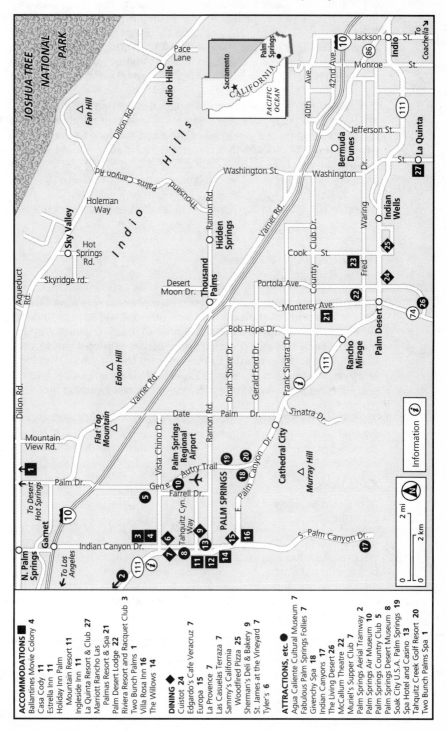

If the following are full, you can book a room at one of the gazillion other places to stay in the area through the free reservation services offered by the **Palm Springs Visitor Information Center** (☎ 800-347-7746; www.palm-springs.org) and the **Palm Springs Desert Resorts Convention and Visitors Bureau** (☎ 800-41-RELAX [417-3529]; www.desertresorts.com). The Palm Springs Visitor Information Center is particularly helpful if you're looking for gay-oriented accommodations.

Palm Springs is a major gay and lesbian destination, with more than 40 hotels catering to a gay clientele alone — and vast numbers of lesbians filling the town on the weekend of the **Kraft Nabisco Championship golf tournament** (☎ 760-324-4546; Internet: www.nabiscodinahshore.com) in March. If a gay- or lesbian-only resort is something you would like to explore, you can review the choices and reviews at www.psgay.com.

An extra 10 to 11% in taxes will be tacked on to your hotel bill at check-out time.

Ballantines Movie Colony
$$ Palm Springs

This fab resort hotel is set in a renovated '50s motel, where the original style is chockfull of the sort of kitsch fun that will appeal to retro-lovin' Gen-X types, or anyone with a sense of humor (unless midcentury modern, even served up with a wink, makes you break out into hives). Each room (and suite and villa) has its own theme, from Tiki Madness to Marilyn, '50s modern to Jackson Pollack. It's a complete hoot, and a likely place to find self-aware young Hollywood types lounging by the pool.

726 North Indian Canyon Dr. ☎ *800-780-3464, 760-320-1178 . Fax: 760-320-5308. Internet:* www.ballantineshotels.com. *Rack rates: $99–$209 (suites and villas higher). AE, MC, V.*

Casa Cody
$$ Palm Springs

Founded by Buffalo Bill's cousin back in the '20s, Casa Cody is a charming and surprisingly modern place to stay. Two dozen lovely rooms, all decorated with Southwestern panache, are set hacienda-style around two pools and a Jacuzzi. Studios and suites have equipped kitchens, and some have fireplaces and/or private patios. This is a terrific value — and a great location, too, with Palm Canyon shopping and dining a mere stone's throw away.

175 S. Cahuilla Rd. (between Tahquitz Canyon Way and Arenas Rd.), Palm Springs. ☎ *800-231-2639, 760-320-9346. Fax: 760-325-8610. Internet:* www.palmsprings.com/hotels/casacody. *Parking: Free. Rack rates: $79 –$149 room or studio; $149–$189 one-bedroom suite; $239–$349 two-bedroom suite. Rates as low as $59 in the summer. AE, DC, DISC, MC, V.*

Estrella Inn
$$–$$$ Palm Springs

This stylish and romantic inn is undergoing a major renovation (to be completed by fall 2002) in Modern Hollywood Regency design with Greek accents. Look for a black-and-white color scheme, sleek marble-like statues, and landscaped gardens. The upscale amenities included in all 77 rooms are top-end Frette linens and bathrobes, down comforters and pillows, a complete entertainment center, high-speed Internet service, 27-inch flat-screen TVs, CD/DVD players, and refrigerators. An on-site restaurant/bar and spa should also be finished by fall 2002. Although the inn welcomes children and pets, you may prefer to leave the kids at home and treat yourself (and a companion) to its contemporary elegance and lush environment.

415 S. Belardo Rd. (between Ramon and Baristo rds.), Palm Springs. ☎ 800-237-3687, 760-320-4117. Fax: 760-320-7887. Internet: www.estrellapalmsprings. com. *Parking: Free. Rack rates: $119–$175 room or single, $260–$375 one- or two-bedroom suite or villa. AE, DC, MC, V.*

Holiday Inn Palm Mountain Resort
$$ Palm Springs

Built around an excellent pool area with a Jacuzzi and poolside bar, this casual resort is comfortable for families. The nice rooms are done in a regionally appropriate Southwest style; each has a microwave, minifridge, coffeemaker, and patio furniture. Go for a ground-floor poolside room, with only a sliding-glass door separating you from the drink. The location is A-1, a two-minute walk from the heart of the Palm Canyon action. On site is a midpriced Continental restaurant with a happy hour and early-bird specials. Nice!

155 S. Belardo Rd. (at Tahquitz Canyon Way), Palm Springs. ☎ 800-HOLIDAY, (800-465-4329), 760-325-1301. Fax: 760-323-8937. Internet: www.palmmountain resort.com *or* www.holiday-inn.com. *Parking: Free. Rack rates: $89–$155 double. AE, DC, DISC, MC, V.*

Ingleside Inn
$$–$$$ Palm Springs

If these walls could talk, you would know a lot more about your favorite movie star (the host-owner has rubbed shoulders with everyone from Sinatra to Travolta over the past 25 years). Old Hollywood is preserved in the heart of the desert — with rich fabrics, dark woods, antiques, art, and fireplaces. In a word, elegant. No two rooms are alike in this historic full-service inn, which has welcomed celebrities for more than 60 years. Enjoy cocktails by the pool (oddly located across the driveway) or watch the sun set on the wooden porch swing. Dine on Continental cuisine at **Melvyn's,** the hotel's sophisticated restaurant.

200 W. Ramon Rd. (at Belardo Rd.), Palm Springs. ☎ ***800-772-6655,*** *760-325-0046. Fax: 760-325-0710. Internet:* www.inglesideinn.com. *Valet parking: Free. Rack rates: $95–$165 room; $250–$300 mini-suite; $160–$265 villa; $375–$600 one- or two-bedroom suite. AE, DC, DISC, MC, V.*

La Quinta Resort & Club
$$$$$ **La Quinta**

If you want to hit the links or courts — or simply surrender to the lap of luxury — come to La Quinta. Destination resorts don't come much finer than this Spanish-style spread. Set in single-story *casitas* (freestanding houses) on lush, oasis-like grounds, each room has an air of intimacy and privacy. Championship golf and tennis, first-rate dining and spa facilities, kids' programs — the works. A bit far removed from the rest of the Palm Springs area, but who cares? You won't want to leave.

49499 Eisenhower Dr., La Quinta. ☎ ***800-598-3828,*** *760-564-4111. Fax: 760-564-5758. Internet:* www.laquintaresort.com. *Valet parking: Free. Rack rates: $355–$575 double, $575–$3,745 suite or villa. Rates from $175 double in summer. AE, DC, DISC, MC, V.*

Marriott Rancho Las Palmas Resort & Spa
$$$$ **Rancho Mirage**

This relaxing and attractive faux-hacienda-style resort is not quite as luxurious as La Quinta, but it's also far more down to earth. You'll find 27 terrific holes on a Ted Robinson–designed golf course, 25 tennis courts, a slate of restaurants to choose from, an excellent full-service spa, and a whopping 100-foot waterslide at the pool complex that the kids will just love. Guest rooms and public spaces are comfortable, attractive, and neatly suit the desert mood.

41000 Bob Hope Dr., Rancho Mirage. ☎ ***800-I-LUV-SUN*** *(800-458-8786), 760-568-2727. Fax: 760-568-5845. Internet:* www.marriotthotels.com. *Valet parking: Free. Rack rates: $285–$325 double. Rates can go as low as $79–$195 in summer. AE, DC, DISC, MC, V.*

Palm Desert Lodge
$$ **Palm Desert**

This family-run motel is a great bet if you want to be near world-class golf or El Paseo shopping without paying resort prices. The rooms are clean, fresh, and attractive. Each has a minifridge, and most are double-doubles big enough to sleep four; some of the poolside units are even bigger and boast VCRs and/or fully equipped kitchens. A very nice pool and Jacuzzi area is simply but pleasingly landscaped.

74-527 Hwy. 111 (at Deep Canyon Rd.), Palm Desert. ☎ ***760-346-3875.*** *Fax: 760-773-0084. Internet:* www.palmdesertlodge.com. *Parking: Free. Rack rates:*

$79–$179 double. Deals: Rates as low as $59 in summer; ask about autumn and senior discounts. AE, DC, DISC, MC, V.

Riveria Resort and Raquet Club

$$–$$$ Palm Springs

This is perhaps the largest centrally located Palm Springs resort (just a hop from the main drag), with nearly 500 rooms (including a number of suites) set on 24 acres with two swimming pools (one of them featured in the Troy Donohue vehicle *Palm Springs Weekend*!) and nine tennis courts. Sunny (if Palm Springs bland) rooms have large beds; some have patios or pool access. Traditional, for sure.

1600 N. Indian Canyon Dr. ☎ 800-444-8311, 760-327-8311. Fax: 760-778-2560. Internet: www.palmsprings.com.riviera/index.html. *Rack rates: $119–$249 (but a substantial discount available — that low end room as low as $83 — if you mention palmsprings.com when making reservations). AE, DC, MC, V.*

Two Bunch Palms

$$$$ Desert Hot Springs

If you're coming to the desert to do the spa thing, here's your heaven. Push thoughts of bouffanted ladies in designer sweatsuits out of your mind — Two Bunch is intimate, easygoing, and understated, the kind of low-key oasis where multimillionaire movie execs and splurging suburban housewives are at one in their quest to de-stress. Spread over 56 lush acres, this eclectic low-rise complex has been here since the 1930s (Al Capone used it as a hideout). Accommodations range from simple but comfortable guest rooms to full-on villas. Frankly, they're nothing special; the real draw is the phenomenal menu of spa treatments, the oh-so-soothing natural mineral grotto, and the unparalleled service. More than divine — sublime.

67425 Two Bunch Palms Trail (off Palm Drive/Gene Autry Trail), Desert Hot Springs. ☎ 800-472-4334, 760-329-8791. Fax: 760-329-1317. Internet: www.twobunch palms.com. *Parking: Free. Rack rates: $175–$305 double, $405–$675 suite or villa. Rates include continental breakfast buffet. Money-saving spa packages are almost always on offer. AE, MC, V.*

Villa Rosa Inn

$–$$ Palm Springs

This hidden and charming gem is under new management, has undergone renovation, and is a terrific bargain. Built hacienda style around a lovely courtyard pool landscaped with colorful potted flowers and plants, each of the six individually decorated units reflects a Southwestern theme. Amenities include a television, refrigerator, pool towels, morning paper, and continental breakfast with fruit plucked from the inn's fruit trees.

1577 S. Indian Trail (off E. Palm Canyon Dr., between S. Palm Canyon and Sunrise Way), Palm Springs. ☎ 800-457-7605, 760-327-5915. Fax: 760-416-9962. Internet: www.villarosainn.com. Parking: Free and easy street parking. Rack rates: $59–$109 king room; $79–$119 studio; $109–$155 suite w/full kitchen. Two-night minimum. AE, MC, V.

The Willows
$$$$$ Palm Springs

Hideaways don't get more romantic than this restored 1930s Mediterranean villa, which once played host to names like Gable, Lombard, and Einstein. Set against the mountains just a stone's throw from Palm Canyon Drive, it's both conveniently located and deliciously private. Eight luxurious rooms overflow with antiques, sumptuous textiles, and other impeccable appointments, plus modern comforts like TVs. Gorgeous gardens and a fine pool complete the perfect picture. A stay here makes a worthy special-occasion splurge.

412 W. Tahquitz Canyon Way (just west of Palm Canyon Dr.), Palm Springs. ☎ 800-966-9597, 760-320-0771. Fax: 760-320-0780. Internet: www.thewillowspalm springs.com. Parking: Free. Rack rates: $295–$575 in season; $225–$425 in summer (two-night minimum for weekends). Rates include three-course breakfast and afternoon hors d'oeuvres. AE, DISC, MC, V.

Where to Dine in Palm Springs

The Palm Springs area boasts lots of excellent restaurants, but don't expect much in the way of innovation. Strangely, the trend is toward traditional styles of cuisine, which may strike some as too formal or heavy for the desert. But desert dwellers really *love* classic French food served by tuxedoed waiters on white linen and bone china. That said, diversity abounds — it's just a matter of knowing where to look.

Cuistot
$$$$ Palm Desert CAL-FRENCH

Here's the desert's best restaurant — no small claim in an area that invites so much disposable income. Expect dazzling French cuisine with enough innovation and lightness of touch to give it a distinct California flair, with unpretentious, welcoming service, and the kind of perfectly calibrated lighting that makes diamonds sparkle just that much more. Inside seating is preferable to the patio thanks to the winning ambience of the contemporary room. A real star — perfect for celebrating.

73-040 El Paseo (at Ocotillo Ave.), Palm Desert. ☎ 760-340-1000. Reservations highly recommended. Main courses: $21–$33. AE, MC, V. Open: Tues–Sat: Lunch 11:30 a.m., closing based on reservations. Tues–Sun: Dinner 6 p.m., closing based on reservations.

Europa
$$$$ Palm Springs   CALIFORNIA-CONTINENTAL

This longtime favorite is one of the desert's most romantic restaurants. Housed in what was once ice skater and B-movie actress Sonja Henie's house, the dining room shines with candlelight and old-world charm. Expect lots of modern accents on the Continental menu; the succulent rack of lamb is a standout. Everything is prepared with care and beautifully presented, including the divine desserts. The patio is pure magic on a lovely desert evening.

At the Villa Royale, 1620 Indian Trail (off E. Palm Canyon Dr., between S. Palm Canyon and Sunrise Way), Palm Springs. ☎ *800-245-2314, 760-327-2314. Reservations recommended. Main courses lunch: $19; dinner $18–$38. AE, DC, DISC, MC, V. Open: Dinner Tues–Sun 6–10 p.m.*

La Provence
$$$ Palm Springs   FRENCH

This authentic slice of the south of France is a refreshing change from the mostly classic, fairly snooty French restaurants that dot the desert. It's charming, affordable, and unpretentious. You'll find Mediterranean touches in the French comfort food, which is hearty without being heavy. Highlights include phyllo-wrapped escargot on mushroom caps in shallot-garlic butter — delicious! — and monster-size tiger prawns served atop mushroom risotto in a not-too-rich red-wine demi-glace. A winner.

254 N. Palm Canyon Dr. (between Andreas and Amado rds.), 2nd floor, Palm Springs. ☎ *760-416-4418. Reservations recommended. Main courses: $18–$28. AE, DC, DISC, MC, V. Open: Tues–Sat 11 a.m.–2 p.m., Sun–Thurs 5:30–10:30 p.m., Fri–Sat 5:30–11 p.m.*

Las Casuelas Terraza
$$ Palm Springs   MEXICAN

You'll enjoy the terrific Mexican cuisine, but it's the sidewalk patio — good for people-watching — that makes this place the choice for locals and tourists. Live music and an even livelier happy hour set the tone for the festivities.

222 S. Palm Canyon Dr. (between Baristo and Arenas rds.), Palm Springs. ☎ *760-325-2794. Internet:* www.lascasuelas.com. *Reservations recommended for dinner. Main courses lunch: $7.25–$14; dinner $7.25–$19. AE, DC, DISC, MC, V. Open: Mon–Thurs 11 a.m.–11 p.m., Fri 11 a.m. to "when the last person leaves"; Sat–Sun 10 a.m. to "when the last person leaves."*

Sammy's California Woodfired Pizza
$–$$ Palm Desert   PIZZA

The menu at this bright, airy gourmet pizzeria also features entree-size salads, wraps, and pastas, but come for the pizza. Sammy's specializes in single-serving-size traditional pies as well as more innovative versions with toppings like smoked duck sausage and artichokes. The restaurant is friendly, well-priced, and satisfying.

At the Gardens of El Paseo (at Larkspur Dr.), 2nd floor, Palm Desert. ☎ *760-836-0500. Internet:* www.sammyspizza.com. *Main courses: $8–$17 (most less than $13). AE, DISC, MC, V. Open: Mon–Thurs 11 a.m.–9 p.m.; Fri–Sat 11 a.m.–10 p.m.*

Sherman's Deli & Bakery
$ Palm Springs   DELI

A kosher-style family restaurant that serves healthy portions of typical deli food in a casual and friendly atmosphere. Leave room for desserts like the sugar-free chocolate cake (moist and tasty) or the coconut cream cake (light and sweet), which are baked daily on the premises.

401 Tahquitz Canyon Way (1 block east of Indian Canyon Dr.), Palm Springs. ☎ *760-325-1199. Breakfast: $3.25–$16. Sandwiches: $6.25–$13. Early-bird dinners (4 p.m.–6 p.m.): $9.95. AE, DC, MC, V. Open: Mon–Sun 7 a.m.–9 p.m.*

St. James at the Vineyard
$$$$$ Palm Springs   ECLECTIC

A candlelit hacienda in the heart of the Palm Canyon action houses one of the desert's most thrilling restaurants. The kitchen excels at preparing innovative, globe-hopping cuisine, from coriander-steamed New Zealand mussels to rich curries with chutney and papadum to tequila-fired shrimp to homemade wild mushroom ravioli. The bold flavors, sophisticated ambience, gracious service, and top-flight wine list make for an exciting night on the town. The bar plays host to a lively weekend scene.

265 S. Palm Canyon Dr. (between Baristo and Arenas rds.), Palm Springs. ☎ *760-320-8041. Internet:* www.palmsprings.com/dine/stjames. *Reservations recommended. Main courses: $10–$36. AE, DC, DISC, MC, V. Open: Sun–Thurs 5–10 p.m., Fri–Sat 5–11 p.m.*

Tyler's
$ Palm Springs   BURGERS

This cute and utterly casual indoor/outdoor burger shack serves up juicy burgers, crispy fries, and on-tap brew, plus hot dogs, turkey and egg-salad sandwiches, and yummy root-beer floats and malts. The burgers come piled high with traditional fixin's, and portions are generous. The Fridays-only clam chowder is a must for chowderheads.

149 S. Indian Canyon Dr. (at La Plaza), Palm Springs. ☎ *760-325-2990. Burgers and sandwiches: $5–$6. Cash only. Open: Mon–Fri 11 a.m.–4 p.m., Sat 11 a.m.–5 p.m.*

Exploring Palm Springs and the Resorts

There are a surprisingly number of activities out here, but if you just want to hang around the pool or pamper yourself with a spa treatment, we won't blame you at all.

Touring the top attractions

Palm Springs Aerial Tramway

Probably Palm Springs' best-known traditional sightseeing attraction is this cool funicular, which takes you on a 14-minute ascent 2½ miles to the top of Mt. San Jacinto, the second highest point in Southern California. It's quite a remarkable ride, straight up the side of the mountain through five different climate zones — somewhat akin to moving from Mexico to Alaska inside of 15 minutes. The ride is perfectly stable, and sleek new Swiss funicular cars rotate to give you 360-degree views along the way. Still, it's not for anyone who's afraid of heights, because the car ascends at a very steep angle — that cable looks mighty small, even to bravehearts, after you're far enough off the ground to notice. Otherwise, the entire family will love it.

At the top is the 13,000-acre Mt. San Jacinto State Park and Wilderness Area, an alpine setting, complete with 54 miles of hiking trails, plus a '60s ski-lodge-style building housing a mini museum and the less-than-stellar cafeteria-style Alpine Restaurant (skip the Ride 'n' Dine package unless you're planning on spending the day). You can spend the whole day here or just come up for the panoramic views and head back down on the next tram out. Temperatures are typically 40 degrees cooler than down on the desert floor, so bring a sweater in summer, a full-fledged coat in winter. Snow covers the ground in the cold months; locals bring the kids up for sledding and other snowy fun. An **adventure center** (☎ 760-325-1449) rents snow tubes, snowshoes, and cross-country skis. Bring your AAA card or check for an online coupon to soften the blow.

*At the end of Tramway Rd. (turn toward the mountains off Hwy. 111/N. Palm Canyon Dr.), Palm Springs. ☎ **888-515-TRAM** (888-515-8726), 760-325-1449. Internet:* www. pstramway.com. *Open: Cars depart every half-hour Mon–Fri 10 a.m.–8 p.m., Sat–Sun 8 a.m.–8 p.m. (daily to 9 p.m. Memorial Day–Labor Day). Admission: $20.80 adults, $18.80 seniors, $13.80 kids ages 3–12. Ride 'n' Dine combo (available after 2:30 p.m., dinner served after 4 p.m.) $27.80 adults, $18.80 kids Tues–Thurs.*

Palm Springs Desert Museum

This small but well-endowed museum is Palm Springs' secret weapon in the culture wars, standing brave and tall against the schmaltz that tends to dominate the desert. Highlights include terrific Western and Native American art collections, as well as natural science and history exhibits focusing on the local Coachella Valley desert and its first people, the Cahuilla tribe. The well-curated special exhibits stick to similar themes.

101 Museum Dr. (at Tahquitz Canyon Way, just west of N. Palm Canyon Dr.), Palm Springs. ☎ *760-325-7186. Internet:* www.psmuseum.org. *Open: Tues–Sat 10 a.m.–5 p.m., Sun noon to 5 p.m. Admission: $7.50 adults, $6.50 seniors, $3.50 kids 6–17, free to all first Fri of the month.*

The Living Desert

Part museum, part zoo, and all learning center, this wildlife and botanical park is dedicated to introducing the wonders of the local ecosystem to those who consider the desert a flat, colorless, inhospitable wasteland. You can walk or take a tram ride through re-creations of several distinct desert zones, seeing and learning about the local geology, plants, insects, and wildlife as you go. Critters run the gamut from tarantulas to mountain lions, with bighorn sheep, roadrunners, and golden eagles in the mix. While you can't beat seeing the real desert with the help of an outfitter (see "Desert excursions," later in the chapter), this is a great alternative if you're not so inclined or if you have a family with little ones.

47-900 Portola Ave. (off Hwy. 111, between Monterey Ave. and Cook St.), Palm Desert. ☎ *760-346-5694. Internet:* www.livingdesert.org. *Open: Sept–mid-June, daily 9 a.m.–5 p.m. (last entrance 4 p.m.); mid-June–Aug, daily 8 a.m.–10 p.m. Admission: $8.50 adults, $7.50 seniors, $4.25 kids 3–12.*

Soak City

Your kids will be in waterhog heaven at this 21-acre playground, which boasts 13 thrilling water slides (five dedicated to tots), the state's largest wave-action pool, an inner-tube ride, and lots more wet 'n' wild fun. Landlocked facilities include private beach cabanas, a video arcade, a 20,000-square-foot health club, and dressing rooms and lockers. You'll find height restrictions on some rides.

1500 S. Gene Autry Trail (between Ramon Rd. and E. Palm Canyon Dr.), Palm Springs. ☎ *760-327-0499. Internet:* www.soakcityusa.com. *Open: Daily 10 a.m.–5 p.m.; Admission: $21.95 adults, $14.95 kids 3–11, free 2 and under.*

Palm Springs Air Museum

This museum holds one of the world's largest collections of WWII flyers. It's adjacent to the airport, so flying demonstrations are a regular part of the program. Many of the tour guides are veterans, so expect lots of good real-life stories, too.

745 N. Gene Autry Trail (between Ramon and Vista Chino rds.), Palm Springs. ☎ *760-778-6262. Internet:* www.palmspringsairmuseum.org. *Admission: $8 adults, $6.50 seniors and military, $3.50 kids 6–12. Open: Daily 10 a.m.–5 p.m.*

Hitting the links

If fairways and five-irons draw you to the desert, your best bet is to stay at one of the area golf resorts, such as **La Quinta** or **Marriott Rancho Las Palmas,** where you can play on some of the country's best champion-ship golf courses without ever leaving the grounds (see "Where to Stay in Palm Springs," earlier in the chapter). La Quinta, in particular, is home to some of the finest fairways around; in fact, three of the four are ranked in *Golf* magazine's "Top 100 courses you can play."

Other resorts you may want to consider include **Hyatt Grand Champions** (☎ **800-633-7313,** 760-341-1000; Internet: www.hyatt.com) and **Westin Mission Hills** (☎ **888-625-5144,** 760-328-5955; Internet: www.westin.com). Westin's Resort Course is a stellar Pete Dye design that's more forgiving than most of his legendary greens. Expect greens fees to be between $135 and $175; twilight rates cut the fees nearly in half.

If you want to experience desert golf but you're not up to splurging on one of the big boys, consider **Tahquitz Creek,** 1885 Golf Club Dr., off East Palm Canyon Drive between Gene Autry Trail and Cathedral Canyon Drive, Palm Springs (☎ **800-743-2211,** 760-328-1005; Internet: www.tahquitzcreek.com), whose two diverse courses run by the Arnold Palmer Group appeal to mid-handicappers. Greens fees range from $45 to $70, and discounted twilight rates are available.

Another good bet is **Palm Springs Country Club,** 2500 Whitewater Club Dr., off Vista Chino Road (☎ **760-323-2626;** Internet: www.palm springs.com/golf/pscc.html), home to the oldest public course in Palm Springs, and especially popular with golfers on a budget. Greens fees are just $40 before 1 p.m., $25 after 1:30 p.m.

Tee times at many courses can't be booked more than a few days in advance (a problem for non-hotel guests who want to play at the big resorts), but several companies can make advance arrangements for you, the best of which is **Golf à la Carte** (☎ **877-887-6900;** www.palm springsgolf.com). Go online to www.desertgolfguide.com and click on Book Tee Times for other visitor center-sanctioned agents, many of whom can arrange a complete golf vacation for you. **Palm Springs Tee Times** (☎ **760-324-5012;** www.palmspringsteetimes. com) may be able to book you in at a discount as much as 60 days in advance.

Always ask about golf packages when you're making hotel reserva-tions, because many area properties — even the most unassuming motels — offer packages that include tee times.

If you arrive in the desert without prebooked tee times, **Stand-By Golf** (☎ **760-321-2665**) specializes in same-day and next-day tee times. Ditto for **Next Day Golf** (☎ **760-345-8463**).

The visitors bureau is dedicated to making golfers happy and can provide you with tons of additional golf information (see "Gathering More Information," later in this chapter). Their great *Desert Golf & Tennis Guide* is online at www.desertgolfguide.com, which also offers a complete list of the many tournaments held in the area (mainly from November to April), including celebrity Pro-Ams, if you're more the spectating type than a hands-on golfer. Other excellent sources include the online version of the free *Palm Springs Golfer* magazine (www.great golfing.com) and Golfer's Guide.com (www.golfersguide.com).

Ahhhh — the spa

The desert is the perfect place to indulge in some serious pampering. Without a doubt, our top place to relax is at **Two Bunch Palms** in Desert Hot Springs (☎ **800-472-4334,** 760-329-8791; Internet: www.two bunchpalms.com). You can enjoy this place even if you don't stay over. Book one of the little-advertised Day Spa packages, which include two one-hour treatments, lunch or dinner, and full access to the grounds for six to nine hours (ditto), plus taxes and gratuities for (at press time, at least) $235 to $275. You can even get a super-decadent 12-hour version that includes four treatments and two meals for $495 — plus the cost of a taxi back to your hotel when it's all over, because human gelatin just can't drive. Call seven days in advance to make your reservations. For further information, see "Where to Stay in Palm Springs," earlier in the chapter.

If you don't want to dedicate the majority of a day — or a few hundred bucks — to a spa, other resorts provide excellent full-service spas that offer more flexibility. If you're looking for chic, try the **Givenchy Spa** at Merv Griffin's Resort Hotel, 4200 E. Palm Canyon Dr., between Farrell Drive and Gene Autry Trail, Palm Springs (☎ **800-276-5000,** 760-770-5000; Internet: www.merv.com).

For something a little more down to earth, book a treatment or two at the **Spa Hotel and Casino,** 100 N. Indian Canyon Dr., Palm Springs (☎ **888-293-0180,** 760-778-1772; Internet: www.sparesortcasino.com), run by the Aqua Caliente tribe on a square block of reservation land in the heart of town. The natural therapeutic hot-spring waters are the same that the local Native Americans have been taking for hundreds of years, but now they've built a sleekly modern, full-service spa around 'em.

Desert excursions

In addition to the following options, you may also consider a day trip to **Joshua Tree National Park** (see "Joshua Tree and Death Valley: A Trip to the Dry, Hot Desert Parks," later in this chapter).

OI' Blue Eyes slept here

In the mood for some sanctioned gawking? Then hitch a ride on a nice air-conditioned bus on one of the **Palm Springs Celebrity Tours**, in the RimRock Plaza Center, at Gene Autry Trail and Highway 111 (☎ **760-770-2700**; Internet: www. celebritytour.qpg.com). Some actual history is thrown into the mix, but most of the tour is dedicated to seeing the stars' homes. The company also offers a streamlined one-hour version for $17 adults, $15 seniors, and $8 kids 16 and under. But if you're gonna do it, go for the whole enchilada: The 2½-hour tour heads into Rancho Mirage and Palm Desert to take in the grandest estates of the biggest celebs — yep, including Sinatra — at a cost of $23 adults, $20 seniors, $10 kids. Make advance reservations.

Taking a guided tour

To the untrained eye, the desert can look like a lot of nothing. Put yourself in the hands of a knowledgeable and enthusiastic guide, however, and it's a whole different story — an entire, fascinating world you never knew existed will open up to you like a rare flower.

Hands down, the area's best tour operator is **Desert Adventures Jeep Eco-Tours** (☎ **888-440-JEEP** (888-440-5337), 760-324-JEEP; Internet: www.red-jeep.com), whose off-road ecotours, offered in signature seven-seater red jeeps, are led by naturalist guides. The company is extremely reliable, and the experienced guides are great at communicating their vast knowledge of desert ecology, geology, history, and lore as well as earthquake science in a manner that's both smart and enjoyable. They're expert at giving meaning to what you see around you.

Still, the experience isn't for everyone. For one thing, the open jeep is bouncy and dusty, and the weather can get really hot in summer. (Springtime, in particular, is a great time to go, because the weather is ideal and the wildflowers are in bloom.) If you have mobility issues, ask whether the tour can comfortably accommodate you. Kids, on the other hand, will love the rough-and-ready "on safari" feeling, although the tours don't accept children under six.

Offerings change periodically, so call or check the Web site to see what's on while you're in town. Most tours include a visit to the legendary **San Andreas Fault,** with detailed explanations of how tectonic forces work and a look at evidence of recent and ongoing fault activity. If you have cultural interests, you can choose to tour an authentically re-created ancient Cahuilla village to find out how Native Americans carved a life out of the barren land. Tours that include desert walks are also offered for hikers. Tours last three or four hours and vary in price from $79 to $129 ($5 off for seniors and kids under 12). Reservations are required; call at least a day in advance.

Hiking

The reservation land that comprises **Indian Canyons** (☎ 800-790-3398, 760-325-5673; Internet: www.palmsprings.com/points/canyon), at the end of South Palm Canyon Drive (3 miles south of the turnoff for East Palm Canyon/Highway 111), is terrific hiking territory. At press time, three stunning canyons were open to hikers of all levels; stop at the **Trading Post** for detailed trail maps.

Admission is $6 for adults, $4 for seniors and students, $1 kids 6 to 12. Open daily from 8 a.m. to 5 p.m.; tours are offered Monday through Thursday at 10 a.m. and 1 p.m., Friday through Sunday at 9 a.m., 11 a.m., 1 p.m., and 3 p.m. for $3 per person, $2 for children. Call ahead in summer, because the canyons have been known to close from late June through Labor Day.

A visit to the **Agua Caliente Cultural Museum,** in the Village Green Heritage Center, 219 S. Palm Canyon Dr., at Arenas Road (☎ 760-778-1079, 760-323-0151; Internet: www.prinet.com/accmuseum), pairs up well with a visit to Indian Canyons. Of particular note is the beautiful collection of basketry. Admission is free; call for hours.

Shopping

If you're looking to spend money, you'll have no trouble in Palm Springs. Boutiques are abundant along Palm Canyon Drive and the side streets in the heart of Palm Springs. If you're an antique and collectibles hunter — especially if you have groovy midcentury-modern tastes — you'll enjoy the many '50s finds along North Palm Canyon, north of the downtown action.

Over in Palm Desert, you'll find Beverly Hills-style boutiquing along El Paseo, which curves south off Highway 111 between Fred Waring Drive and Cook Street and is lined with about 200 upper-end shops. For a complete directory of what's available, visit www.elpaseo.com.

The Gardens at El Paseo is a lovely open-air mall at El Paseo and Larkspur Drive (☎ 760-862-1990), with offerings that run the gamut from Ann Taylor to terrific one-of-a-kind shops and galleries. One of our favorites is the **Tommy Bahama's Emporium** (☎ 760-836-0288), a terrific source for island and desert resort wear.

Living It Up After Dark

For the latest bar and club happenings, pick up the free weekly *Desert Sun Weekend,* easily available around town. Also check out the *Desert Guide,* available at the visitor centers (see the next section).

Nightlife revolves largely around North Palm Canyon Drive, at the heart of downtown Palm Springs. Restaurants and bars spill out onto the street until late, so your best bet is to just wander down the street and pop into whichever establishment pleases you. Among the lively spots is **Muriel's Supper Club,** 210 S. Palm Canyon Dr., at Arenas Road (☎ 760-325-8839; www.muriels.com), a chic dinner-and-dancing joint with an abundance of live music, from swing and mambo parties to concerts by funky New Orleans pianist Dr. John.

The rollicking street festival known as **VillageFest** takes over Palm Canyon Drive, between Amado and Baristo roads, on Thursdays from 7 to 10 p.m. (6 to 10 p.m. October through April). The all-ages fun offers arts-and-crafts vendors, food booths, and street entertainers.

The **Fabulous Palm Springs Follies,** 128 S. Palm Canyon Dr. (☎ 760-327-0225; www.palmspringsfollies.com), is a Vegas-style extravaganza filled with show tunes from the 1930s and '40s and lively production numbers complete with leggy showgirls. This silly show is so popular that it has run for over a decade; reserve in advance. Tickets run $37.50 to $70 for the 2½-hour show; matinees are slightly lower.

For more highbrow entertainment, see what's on at the **McCallum Theatre,** at the **Bob Hope Cultural Center,** 73000 Fred Waring Dr., Palm Desert (☎ 760-340-ARTS; www.mccallum-theatre.org).

Gathering More Information

Palm Springs Desert Resorts Convention and Visitors Bureau (☎ 800-96-RESORTS [967-3767] or 760-770-9000) can send you information and offer assistance with accommodations (call ☎ 800-41-RELAX [417-3529] for accommodations information). It also operates a **24-hour activity hotline** (☎ 760-770-1992) and an extensive Web site at www.desertresorts.com.

You can get excellent assistance at the **Palm Springs Visitors Information Center** (☎ 800-34-SPRINGS [347-7746] or 760-778-8418), which concentrates on Palm Springs proper and has a great site at www.palmsprings.org. The well-stocked and -staffed visitor center is at 2781 N. Palm Canyon Drive, just south of Tramway Road, an easy stop on your way into town.

If you're interested in Palm Desert, call the **Palm Desert Visitors Information Center** at ☎ 760-568-1441 or visit them online at www.palm-desert.com. The walk-in center is at Hwy. 111 and Monterey Avenue (pull into the Denny's parking lot).

Free publications with good maps are available at hotels, restaurants, shops, and visitor centers throughout the area. The best of the bunch is *Palm Springs Life* magazine's free monthly *Desert Guide.* Gay visitors will want to pick up the free *Palm Springs Gay Guide,* which is also easy to find. Other useful Web sites include www.palmsprings.com and www.inpalmsprings.com; the latter is excellent for arts and entertainment coverage.

To check the local weather, dial ☎ 760-345-3711.

American Express has an official travel office in Palm Springs at Andersen Travel Service, 700 E. Tahquitz Canyon Way (☎ 760-325-2001).

Joshua Tree and Death Valley: A Trip to the Dry, Hot Desert Parks

Sure, Palm Springs is hot and dry. But it's just steps away from a wet martini, served poolside under shady palms, and within crawling distance of a frosty air-conditioned hotel suite. If it's *really* dry and *really* hot you crave, however, you're in the right neighborhood. California's desert parks are great places to experience the wonders of the desert outside the carefully pruned environs of Palm Springs resort living. As national parks, they preserve refuges of rare beauty, where living things thrive in a seemingly hostile environment. Here are two wilderness areas where you can fully experience the desert's rough-edged grandeur:

Joshua Tree National Park

Joshua Tree National Park got its name from the oddball tree that's actually a yucca. The park encompasses two quite different desert environments: In the northwestern section — where you'll enter the park — is the **Mojave Desert,** the cragged, hilly land where rugged boulders set the tone and the Joshua tree lives. Head southeast through the park, and the elevation drops and the landscape morphs into the hotter, drier, **Colorado Desert,** which looks more like the desert you expect, dotted with cactus and creosote. Oases here point to natural water sources and serve as gathering spots for the park's wildlife — a range of critters, from roadrunners to golden eagles to bighorn sheep.

> ✔ **When to come:** Spring or fall.
>
> ✔ **How much time to set aside:** A full day's trip from Palm Springs. Leave early in the morning; the park entrance is a good hour from the resorts.

✔ **Getting there:** None of the three access points is close to Palm Springs. The **South (Cottonwood Spring) Entrance** is off I-10, about 53 miles east of Palm Springs, but we don't suggest you use it. Instead, use either the **West Entrance,** at the village of Joshua Tree, or the **North (Oasis of Mara) Entrance** in Twentynine Palms. To reach both entrances from Palm Springs, take Gene Autry Trail to I-10 west; after 6 miles, take the turnoff for Hwy. 62 (the Twentynine Palms Highway), which curves around the west and north sides of the park. The distance is about 44 miles to the West Entrance, 55 miles to Twentynine Palms and the main gate.

At the corner of National Park Drive and Utah Trail, a half-mile south of Hwy. 62 in the funky desert town of Twentynine Palms, is the **Oasis Visitor Center,** the park's official main visitor center, open daily from 8 a.m. to 5 p.m. The park has no restaurants or stores, so pick up any supplies you'll need in Twentynine Palms.

✔ **Where to stay:** The park offers no lodgings, but Twentynine Palms has a few basic options within 5 miles of the North Entrance. Or choose from nine very basic campgrounds scattered throughout the park. Find further details, including fee information, online at www.nps.gov/jotr.

✔ **What to see:** The best bet if you're a day-tripper looking for the full Joshua Tree experience is to enter the park at either the West or North entrance and explore the northern loop (Park Boulevard) first. Then follow the **Pinto Basin Road** to the lush southeast Cottonwood section of the park where you can exit the park, go south to I-10, and be back in Palm Springs for dinner. This drive will take you past all the major highlights and through both desert climate zones. (The distance through the park from the North Entrance to the Cottonwood gate is 41 miles.)

✔ **For more information:** Contact the **Park Superintendent** at ☎ 760-367-5500; www.nps.gov/jotr. The **Joshua Tree National Park Association**'s site at www.joshuatree.org is even more useful.

Death Valley National Park

Death Valley National Park may not be on your agenda on your first trip to California. No easy way exists to get there, it's not close to anything, and services are minimal. Still, plenty of people manage to work Death Valley in to their vacation plans. You can't deny the draw of such extremes: The hottest, the highest, the largest, the lowest, the driest — you want it, Death Valley's got it. The landscape is both savage and spectacular.

✔ **When to come:** Most people prefer to visit the park in the temperate months, from October through April. Heat-seeking desert lovers come in the summer when the crowds thin out and daytime temperatures soar well past 100°F.

✔ **How much time to set aside:** Death Valley is the largest national park in the lower 48 states. Because you need to set aside two days for driving alone, a visit to Death Valley requires a minimum of three days. Four is smarter.

✔ **Getting there:** Even though Death Valley is basically due east of the Central Coast, some pesky mountains and a couple of national forests conspire to make you go south — way south — to get there. **From Southern California:** Go via I-15 (which connects with I-10 midway between L.A. and Palm Springs) to Baker, where you connect with Hwy. 127 north to Hwy. 190 east. The drive is 300 miles or 6½ hours. Or you can take I-14 north from the L.A. area (it connects with I-5) to Hwy. 178 to Hwy. 190, which takes roughly the same amount of time.

✔ **What to see:** Death Valley has been called a "windshield wilderness" because the best way to see the park is by car. Two-lane roads wind through a remote landscape devoid of commercial activity. Note that you should only tackle many of the park's back-country roads in a four-wheel-drive vehicle or a light truck.

The place to start is **Death Valley Visitor Center,** in the middle of the park at **Furnace Creek,** 15 miles inside the eastern boundary at the junction of highways 190 and 178, open daily from 8 a.m. to 6 p.m. If you're traveling out of the Furnace Creek Visitor Center, take the 24-mile drive through Furnace Creek Walsh badlands to **Dantes View,** a scenic overlook with a park basin panorama amid enveloping mountain ranges. Or take **Artists Drive,** which coils through colorful canyon terrain. In the northwest section of the park is **Scotty's Castle,** a 1920s mansion built in the desert as a vacation retreat. It's got a pool fit for a desert — all 270 feet of it. Reserve ahead for tours of the house and grounds.

✔ **Where to stay:** The valley holds four places to stay. Among them, the elegant **Furnace Creek Inn ($$$$)** is a beautifully restored 1930s desert oasis with a formal dining room (☎ **760-786-2361**). For camping information and reservations, call ☎ **800-365-CAMP** (365-2267; reservations.nps.gov).

✔ **For more information:** Contact the **Death Valley National Park Service** at ☎ **760-786-2331**; www.nps.gov/deva. Admission to the park is $10 per car, and it's good for seven days; keep your stub.

Chapter 25

San Diego

● ●

In This Chapter

▶ Determining the perfect time to visit

▶ Getting there and orienting yourself, neighborhood by neighborhood

▶ Sleeping and dining in the city

▶ Exploring the city's sights, on your own or by guided tour

▶ Discovering San Diego's top shopping sites

▶ Enjoying a night on the town

● ●

San Diego is California's grown-up beach town. Year-round sunshine, postcard-perfect beaches, vibrant Spanish-Mexican heritage, and three fantastic family-oriented attractions (four, if you count LEGOLAND in nearby Carlsbad) make an appealing combination, especially for families — and anyone with a kid-like sensibility and a need to kick back.

Little more than an overgrown Navy base just a few decades ago, San Diego still feels more provincial than one would like, but that's a good part of its appeal. An influx of new residents has forced San Diego to start keeping up with culinary styles and cultural trends. It's still not bright lights/big city — "Buffalo by the Beach" sniffs one visitor — but an astonishing growth rate does threaten to bring Los Angeles–style ills (traffic, noise, pollution) into the oasis best known for squeaky-clean fun. Still, the easygoing pace and sunny beach-town optimism you'll find here remains worlds apart from L.A.'s congestion and commitment to trends and appearance.

Count on one or more of the city's animal-themed fun spots — the San Diego Zoo, SeaWorld, and the Wild Animal Park — to be at the top of your sightseeing agenda.

San Diego's Neighborhoods

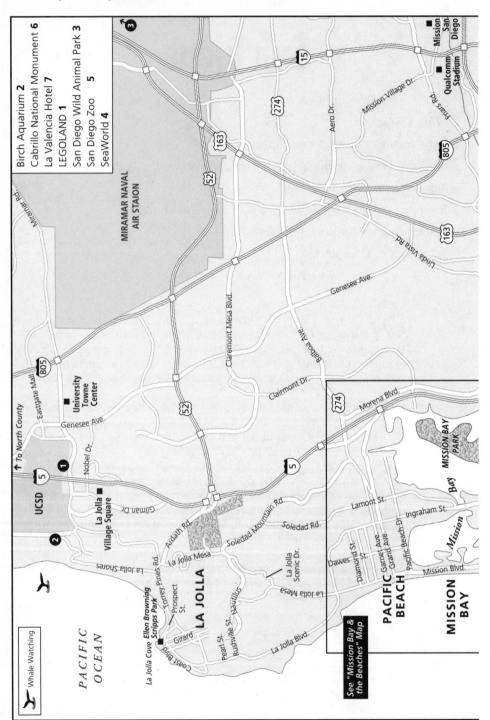

Birch Aquarium **2**
Cabrillo National Monument **6**
La Valencia Hotel **7**
LEGOLAND **1**
San Diego Wild Animal Park **3**
San Diego Zoo **5**
SeaWorld **4**

MIRAMAR NAVAL
AIR STAION

Aero Dr.

Mission Village Dr.

Friars Rd.

Qualcomm
Stadium

Linda Vista Rd.

Genesee Ave.

Claremont Mesa Blvd.

Balboa Ave.

Clairmont Dr.

Morena Blvd.

MISSION BAY
PARK

Lamont St.

Ingraham St.

Soledad Rd.

La Jolla
Scenic Dr.

Pacific Beach Dr.

Mission Bay

Genesee Ave.

University
Towne
Center

Eastgate Mall

To North County

Nobel Dr.

UCSD

La Jolla
Village Square

Gilman Dr.

Ardath Rd.

La Jolla Mesa

Soledad Mountain Rd.

La Jolla Mesa

Dawes St.

Diamond St.

Garnet Ave.

Grant Ave.

PACIFIC
BEACH

MISSION
BAY

Mission Blvd.

La Jolla Shores

Torrey Pines Rd.

La Jolla Cove Ellen Browning
Scripps Park

Prospect
St.

Pearl St.

Rushville St.

Nautilus

Girard

Coast Blvd.

La Jolla Blvd.

LA JOLLA

PACIFIC
OCEAN

Whale Watching

See "Mission Bay &
the Beaches" Map

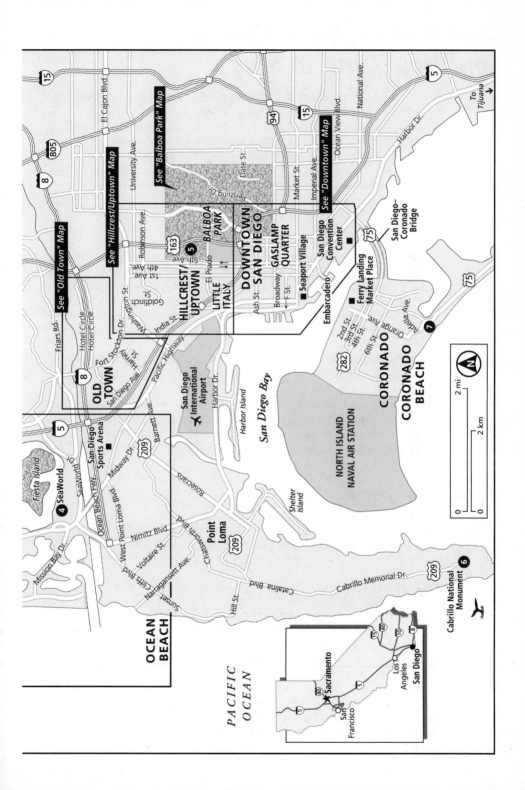

Deciding When to Visit — and How Long to Stay

San Diego has a reputation for reliably mild weather. Is it deserved? You bet. Average daytime highs range seasonally from 65° to 78°F, with nighttime lows between 46° and 66°F. The sun shines all year-round, except (believe it or not) in June and July, when ocean fog rolls in during the wee morning hours and burns off slowly, sometimes not until midafternoon. A puny 9½ inches of rain falls annually, primarily between mid-December and mid-April.

Summer — between Memorial Day and Labor Day — means crowds of people on the sand, in the restaurants, at the major attractions, and occupying hotel rooms reserved months before. The best time to visit is in the fall — September through early December — when the crowds have vanished, winter snowbirds are still months away, and the possibility of rain is nearly nil. You can still comfortably bare it all at the beach through October. No matter when you visit, though, pack a swimsuit because "freak" warm weather (often in November or January) is common.

The few weeks between Thanksgiving and mid-January constitute the city's only bona-fide low season, just in time for lucky holiday travelers.

You'll likely want to spend two to four nights in town, depending on your sightseeing goals (which is governed, mainly, by how many animal parks you want to visit). You can get acquainted with the rest of the city in just a couple of days.

Getting There

As a top destination, San Diego is accessible by plane and train, as well as by automobile. So take your pick.

By plane

San Diego International Airport (☎ 619-231-7361; www.portofsan diego.org), locally known as Lindbergh Field, is right on the water on Harbor Drive, just 3 miles from downtown. Most of the major domestic carriers fly into the airport, and all the major car-rental agencies maintain offices at the airport.

Chances are very good you'll want to have a rental car (for more on this subject, see "Getting Around," later in the chapter). If not, taxis line up outside the airport and charge around $8 (plus tip) to take you downtown.

- ✔ **To reach downtown** from the airport, take Harbor Drive south to Broadway, the main east-west thoroughfare, and turn left.

- ✔ **To reach Hillcrest or Balboa Park,** exit the airport toward I-5 and follow the signs for Laurel Street.

- ✔ **To reach Mission Bay** (home of SeaWorld), take I-5 north to I-8 west.

- ✔ **To reach La Jolla,** take I-5 north to the Ardath Road exit, turning onto Torrey Pines Road.

If you're the plan-ahead type and would prefer to arrange for shuttle service, contact **Cloud 9** (☎ **800-9-SHUTTLE** (800-974-8885), 858-9-SHUTTLE; Internet: www.cloud9shuttle.com). Expect to pay $6 to $9 for downtown and Hillcrest and $19 to La Jolla (quoted rates are for the first person; additional members of your party pay less).

San Diego hotels commonly offer airport shuttle service — usually free, sometimes for a nominal charge — so ask before you make other arrangements. Make sure the hotel knows when you're arriving and get precise directions on where they'll pick you up.

By car

Interstate 5 (I-5) is the route from Los Angeles, Anaheim, and coastal points north. The drive is about 120 miles, or two hours flat, from L.A., and 97 miles from Disneyland.

Interstate 15 (I-15) leads from inland destinations and the deserts to the north. As you enter San Diego, take I-8 west to reach the main parts of the city. From Palm Springs, take I-10 west to Highway 60, then I-215 south to I-15 south. The distance is 141 miles, or about 2½ hours.

I-8 cuts across California from points east like Phoenix, crossing I-5 and ending at Mission Bay.

By train

Amtrak (☎ **800-872-7245;** www.amtrak.com) trains arrive at Santa Fe Station, 1850 Kettner Blvd. (at Broadway), within walking distance of many downtown hotels and 1½ blocks from the Embarcadero (waterfront). Taxis line up out front, the trolley station is across the street, and a dozen local bus routes stop on Broadway or Pacific Highway, a block away.

Orienting Yourself

Thinking of San Diego without envisioning the water is impossible. You'll probably never be more than 5 miles from the bay while in San Diego, and you may never even lose sight of the blue Pacific.

The bay is San Diego Bay — not to be confused with Mission Bay, which is a protected body of water, fed by the sea but isolated from it by thin strips of land. Mission Bay is directly north of San Diego Bay. The airport rests between the bays, merely a stone's throw from most city neighborhoods.

The neighborhoods are well-defined by the undulating geography of foothills, shallow canyons, and coastline: Downtown grew up on the waterfront, wrapping around San Diego's huge natural bay, which brought in crucial shipping commerce and, later, the influential U.S. Navy presence. Downtown, the historic Gaslamp Quarter sits several blocks inland from the bayfront Embarcadero, and the uptown neighborhood of Hillcrest has prime bay views from about a mile away.

Almost — but not quite — an island, Coronado lies smack-dab in the middle of San Diego Bay. The communities of Ocean Beach, Mission Beach, and Pacific Beach — as their names imply — sit directly on the water, upcoast from the city proper, with La Jolla (pronounced la-HOY-ya) occupying its own hilly peninsula at the northernmost edge.

You'll probably spend freeway drive time on I-5, which runs through San Diego north-south, jogging a bit around downtown before it leads straight to the border. East-west I-8 passes above Hillcrest and Old Town on its way to Mission Bay.

Here's a quick rundown of what you can expect in San Diego's main neighborhoods.

Downtown

You'll probably be directed, early on, to the original downtown, especially the commercial **Gaslamp Quarter.** Once known as a raunchy red-light district, the Quarter — loosely bounded by Broadway, Island Avenue, and 1st and 5th avenues — now boasts splendid late-19th- and early-20th-century buildings housing trendy restaurants and upscale nightspots — and frankly, we think it's a bit overrated. It really vibrates on weekend nights, when folks come to hang out in the bars and cafés, and most of the appeal, honestly, is during that time. Otherwise, there aren't enough shops or sights to keep you interested. (And, by the way, the gas lamps have been converted to electricity.)

Situated along Harbor Drive between Ash and Market streets, the **Embarcadero** is San Diego's waterfront, with hotels, attractions, and plenty of activity, from commercial fishing to a busy cruise-ship terminal.

North of the downtown core (between downtown and the airport), **Little Italy** is quickly gaining a reputation as an art and interior-design district. It stretches along India and Columbia streets and Kettner Boulevard between Cedar and Kalmia streets. And yes, it still boasts the best pizza and cannoli in town!

Downtown San Diego

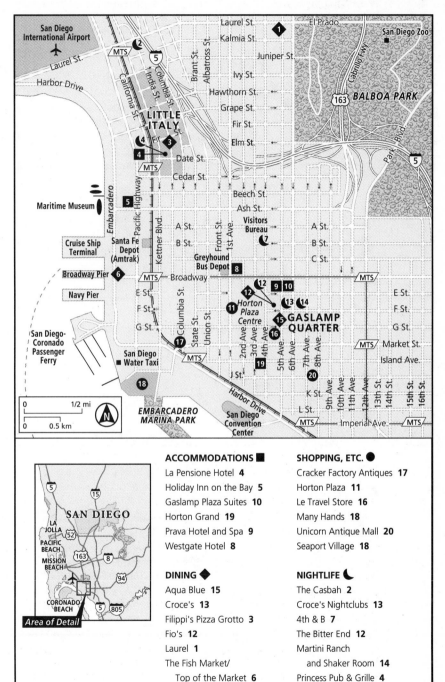

ACCOMMODATIONS ■
La Pensione Hotel **4**
Holiday Inn on the Bay **5**
Gaslamp Plaza Suites **10**
Horton Grand **19**
Prava Hotel and Spa **9**
Westgate Hotel **8**

DINING ◆
Aqua Blue **15**
Croce's **13**
Filippi's Pizza Grotto **3**
Fio's **12**
Laurel **1**
The Fish Market/
   Top of the Market **6**

SHOPPING, ETC. ●
Cracker Factory Antiques **17**
Horton Plaza **11**
Le Travel Store **16**
Many Hands **18**
Unicorn Antique Mall **20**
Seaport Village **18**

NIGHTLIFE ☾
The Casbah **2**
Croce's Nightclubs **13**
4th & B **7**
The Bitter End **12**
Martini Ranch
   and Shaker Room **14**
Princess Pub & Grille **4**

Hillcrest/Uptown

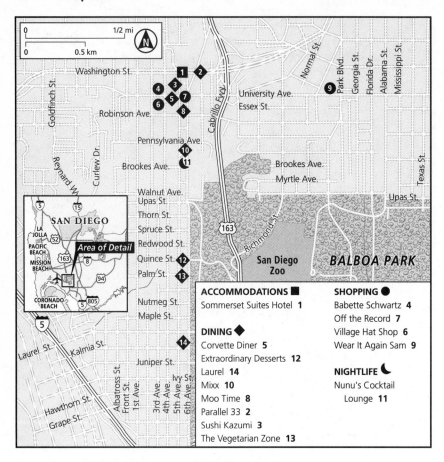

ACCOMMODATIONS ■
Sommerset Suites Hotel **1**

DINING ◆
Corvette Diner **5**
Extraordinary Desserts **12**
Laurel **14**
Mixx **10**
Moo Time **8**
Parallel 33 **2**
Sushi Kazumi **3**
The Vegetarian Zone **13**

SHOPPING ●
Babette Schwartz **4**
Off the Record **7**
Village Hat Shop **6**
Wear It Again Sam **9**

NIGHTLIFE ☾
Nunu's Cocktail
Lounge **11**

Hillcrest

San Diego's early elite rode home in horse-drawn carriages to uptown neighborhoods with nicknames like "Banker's Hill" and "Pill Hill" (the doctors' 'hood). Preservation-minded residents, including a very active and fashionable gay community, have restored Hillcrest's charms after years of neglect. It's now our favorite part of the basic city of San Diego. Think of Hillcrest as the local equivalent of L.A.'s West Hollywood or New York's SoHo. Loosely bounded by Washington and Hawthorn streets to the north and south, deep, hilly ravines to the west, and 6th Avenue at the east, Hillcrest stretches along the edge of San Diego's green jewel, Balboa Park (see "Balboa Park," later in the chapter).

Old Town

Its official name is **Old Town State Historic Park,** and this "Williamsburg of the West" is closed to vehicular traffic. Nestled into a wedge north of the airport where the I-5 and I-8 freeways intersect, the compact, Spanish-era core of San Diego is a genuine historic area that has been bastardized by commercialism. It's the equivalent of L.A.'s Olvera Street, so you may appreciate the opportunity to experience the vestige of history that remains. The interactive and educational aspects have been steadily improving (making it a decent place to bring kids), and you may enjoy the history lesson and the notable 19th-century buildings. The shopping is generally avoidable unless you're prowling for souvenirs, but even locals come here for Mexican food.

Coronado

Located in the middle of San Diego Bay west of downtown, the "island" of Coronado is actually a peninsula, best known for the landmark **Hotel Del Coronado,** the Victorian grand dame most famous for its costarring role — alongside Marilyn Monroe, Jack Lemmon, and Tony Curtis — in *Some Like It Hot.* Coronado is home to the U.S. Naval Air Station, a village of pretty cottages, charming shops along Orange Avenue, and a lovely duned beach. It's sleepy and completely adorable, and walking the gold-glitter beaches (it must be pyrite) is a pleasure. You can reach it from the "mainland" via the soaring Coronado Bay Bridge, a thrilling span to drive.

The duchess from Coronado

From 1917 to 1921, a woman named Wallis Spencer lived in San Diego, primarily on the peninsula of Coronado, and was a well-known social figure about town. Eventually, Wallis divorced her husband, married a man named Simpson, and moved to England, where she once more became a well-known social figure around town and, eventually, the girlfriend of the then Prince of Wales. The prince later became King Edward VIII, but gave up his throne to marry her. Yes, the eventual Duchess of Windsor was a local, for a time (her friends placed a $75 transatlantic call to her when the royal scandal hit), and you can stay in her former house, which is now part of the Hotel Del Coronado property. Just imagine, if she had stayed put on Coronado, how different things may have been: no Diana, no Fergie, and, when the Queen Mum died, just a simple paragraph about the death of a long-lived, minor royal.

Old Town

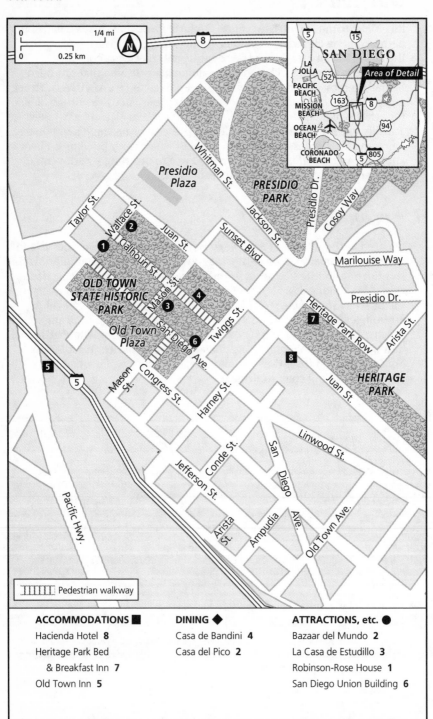

ACCOMMODATIONS ■

Hacienda Hotel **8**

Heritage Park Bed
  & Breakfast Inn **7**

Old Town Inn **5**

DINING ◆

Casa de Bandini **4**

Casa del Pico **2**

ATTRACTIONS, etc. ●

Bazaar del Mundo **2**

La Casa de Estudillo **3**

Robinson-Rose House **1**

San Diego Union Building **6**

Mission Bay

This labyrinth of protected waterways may look artificial, but Mission Bay is really a natural saltwater bay that selective dredging has enhanced for use as an aquatic playground. Condos, cottages, and a few choice hotels line the shore, along with paved paths for joggers, in-line skaters, and bicyclists. **SeaWorld** is located on prime bayfront property.

The bay, bounded on the south and east by the San Diego River and I-5, is separated from the ocean by a narrow strip of land known as **Mission Beach,** a funky community of artists, free spirits, and surfers. This is a great place to base yourself if you want to be close to both the beach and downtown's attractions.

Pacific Beach

Looking for superlative dining or sophisticated culture? Then don't come to Pacific Beach. This water-hugging neighborhood north of Mission Bay is laid-back to the extreme, featuring acres of family-friendly beach and dozens of casual pub-style restaurants where the cuisine takes a back seat to the sunset view (and happy-hour discounts). **Ocean Front Walk** is a paved promenade featuring an eye-popping human parade akin to L.A.'s Venice Ocean Front Walk. This is another great place to stay for easy access to both the beach and downtown.

La Jolla

Both chic and conservative, this wealthy Rodeo-Drive-meets-the-Mediterranean community is surrounded by beach and boasts out-standing restaurants and pricey shopping in "the village." The scenic spot that appears on most postcards is stunning **La Jolla Cove.** The cliffs above the cove hold grassy **Ellen Browning Scripps Park,** a perfect spot for picnicking.

On the down side, La Jolla is insulated from most of San Diego, because it's at the northernmost edge of the city with no convenient freeway access. In rush hour, getting from the village to I-5 can take half an hour, plus a ten-minute drive to downtown. This makes La Jolla a poor base if you're planning to hop in the car every morning for far-flung sightseeing, but ideal for experiencing the "California Riviera" vibe that this jewel is known for. If you choose to stay elsewhere, La Jolla is worth an after-noon and evening for window-shopping and excellent dining. To reach Torrey Pines Road, La Jolla's main artery, take I-5 north to Ardath Road, or I-5 south to La Jolla Village Drive.

Mission Bay and the Beaches

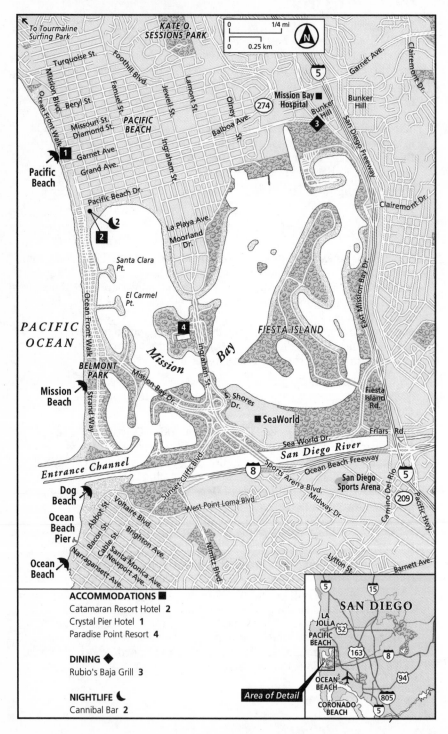

To Tourmaline
Surfing Park

KATE O.
SESSIONS PARK

0   1/4 mi
0   0.25 km

N

Turquoise St.

Foothill Blvd.

Garnet Ave.

Clairemont Dr.

5

Mission Bay ■
Hospital

Bunker
Hill

Beryl St.

Fanuel St.

274

Bunker
Hill

3

San Diego Freeway

PACIFIC
BEACH

Missouri St.
Diamond St.

Jewel St.

Lamont St.

Olney Ave.

Balboa St.

1

Garnet Ave.

Pacific
Beach

Grand Ave.

Ingraham St.

Clairemont Dr.

Pacific Beach Dr.

2

2

La Playa Ave.

Moorland
Dr.

Santa Clara
Pt.

El Carmel
Pt.

4

Ingraham St.

FIESTA ISLAND

East Mission Bay Dr.

PACIFIC
OCEAN

Mission   Bay

BELMONT
PARK

Mission Bay Dr.

Mission
Beach

Strand Way

Ocean Front Walk

S. Shores
Dr.

Fiesta
Island
Rd.

■ SeaWorld

Friars   Rd.

Entrance Channel

Sea World Dr.

San Diego River

8

Sports Arena Blvd.

Ocean Beach Freeway

San Diego
Sports Arena

5

Dog
Beach

Sunset Cliffs Blvd.

West Point Loma Blvd.

Midway Dr.

Camino Del Rio

209

Pacific HWY.

Ocean
Beach
Pier

Abbot St.

Voltaire Blvd.

Bacon St.

Brighton Ave.

Nimitz Blvd.

Ocean
Beach

Narragansett Ave.

Cable St.

Santa Monica Ave.

Newport Ave.

Lytton St.

Barnett Ave.

ACCOMMODATIONS ■
Catamaran Resort Hotel **2**
Crystal Pier Hotel **1**
Paradise Point Resort **4**

DINING ◆
Rubio's Baja Grill **3**

NIGHTLIFE ☾
Cannibal Bar **2**

5   15

SAN DIEGO

LA
JOLLA   52

PACIFIC
BEACH

163   8

OCEAN
BEACH

94

Area of Detail

CORONADO
BEACH   5

805

Getting Around

Chances are very good that you'll want to have a car in San Diego. The city is pretty spread out, but the it's one of California's easiest cities to drive around. Streets are clearly marked (and often in grids, but beware the many one way streets), and traffic is relatively light except for brief morning and evening rush hours. Although the public transit system isn't as worthless as L.A.'s, it's certainly not as comprehensive as San Francisco's.

Driving is a nuisance in certain areas, most notably the **Gaslamp Quarter,** Pacific Beach, and La Jolla. When you visit these spots, park your car on the street or in a parking garage and walk, instead. If you stay in one of these neighborhoods and don't plan to venture much beyond it other than where public transportation can take you efficiently, you can easily make do without a car. But if you want to explore more of the city or visit the **Wild Animal Park** or **LEGOLAND,** mass transit will leave you in the lurch.

If you're planning to do without wheels, consult a map and pick your hotel carefully so you won't feel stranded.

Tips for driving and parking

Pay careful attention to freeway exits, because the names can differ from one direction to the other. For example, to reach La Jolla, you take Ardath Road from I-5 north, but La Jolla Village Drive from I-5 south.

Finding a place to stow a car is pretty easy in San Diego, but it may strain your supply of small change. Parking meters are plentiful in most areas: Posted signs indicate operating hours — generally between 8 a.m. and 6 p.m., even on weekends — and most meters accept only quarters.

In the **Gaslamp Quarter,** consider parking in Horton Plaza's garage (G Street and 4th Avenue), which is free to shoppers for the first three hours and costs only $1 for every additional hour; it's also free daily after 5 p.m.

Spaces are elusive in downtown La Jolla, because street parking is free and public lots are scarce.

By bus and by trolley

The **San Diego Metropolitan Transit System** or **MTS** (☎ **619-685-4900,** 619-233-3004; Internet: www.sdcommute.com/sdmts) operates city buses and trolleys.

The terrific **San Diego Trolley** system runs bright-red trains south to the **Mexican border** (a 40-minute trip) and north to **Old Town** and **Mission Valley,** a sprawling slice of suburbia with mega shopping centers. Within the city, trolleys stop at many popular locations, and the fare is $1; the fare to the Mexican border is $2. Children under 5 ride free; seniors and riders with disabilities pay 75¢.

Trolleys operate on a self-service fare-collection system; purchase your ticket from machines in the station before boarding. Trains run every 15 minutes during the day, every half-hour at night. Trolleys generally operate daily from 5 a.m. to about 12:30 a.m., although the Blue Line, which goes to the border, runs around the clock on Saturday.

Unfortunately, the trolleys don't come close to covering the entire city. If they go where you're going, *hooray*. If not, take the bus.

Rectangular blue signs mark bus stops at every other block or so on local routes. Most fares range from $1.75 to $3, depending on the distance and type of service (local or express). Exact change is required ($1 bills are accepted). Get a transfer from the driver when boarding.

For recorded MTS information, call ☎ **619-685-4900.** To talk to a real person, call ☎ **619-233-3004** daily between 5:30 a.m. and 8:30 p.m. Because the MTS controls both the buses and trolleys, they do a pretty good job of providing you with information on using them in conjunction. The **Transit Store,** 102 Broadway, at 1st Avenue (☎ **619-234-1060**), is a complete information center, supplying passes, tokens, timetables, and maps. The store is open weekdays from 8:30 a.m. to 5:30 p.m., Saturday and Sunday from noon to 4 p.m.

The **Day Tripper pass** allows unlimited rides on the public transit system (buses and trolleys). Passes are good for one, two, three, and four consecutive days, and cost $5, $8, $10, and $12, respectively. You can get Day Trippers from the Transit Store and at all Trolley Station ticket vending machines.

Some hotels offer complimentary shuttles to popular shopping and/or dining areas around town. Check to see whether yours does.

By taxi

Taxis don't cruise the streets, so call ahead for quick pickup. If you're at a hotel or restaurant, the front-desk attendant or maitre d' will call for you.

Among the local companies are Orange Cab (☎ **619-291-3333**), San Diego Cab (☎ **619-226-TAXI**), and Yellow Cab (☎ **619-234-6161**). In La Jolla, use La Jolla Cab (☎ **858-453-4222**).

Ferry on over to Coronado

The pedestrian-only **Coronado Ferry** (☎ 619-234-4111) is a charming way to get a quickie harbor cruise, and a boon if you're concerned about fighting street traffic on crowded summer weekends. It leaves from the Broadway Pier on the **Embarcadero** (at the foot of Broadway) every hour; the one-way fare is $2 per person.

After the 15-minute ride across San Diego Bay, the ferry docks at **Coronado's Ferry Landing Marketplace,** which is a stop along the Coronado Shuttle route (☎ 619-233-3004). Run by the MTS (and officially known as bus route no. 904), the Coronado Shuttle runs between Coronado's bay side and its ocean side primarily along Orange Avenue (Coronado's main drag) daily from 9:30 a.m. to 5:30 p.m. Stops include the **Hotel Del, Loews,** and the **visitor center.** The fare is $1.

Where to Stay in San Diego

The San Diego lodging scene has multiple personalities. Downtown hotels cater to conventions, so they tend to have reduced weekend rates. Seaside hotels, on the other hand, sometimes offer deals midweek, and always have lower prices after summer ends. We have noticed that many of the hotels in older buildings seem to have the sorts of problems you would encounter in similar places in Europe — they're often dark and creaky, and the plumbing can be unreliable. This holds true even for some very high-end hotels in older buildings, so if you require brand-spanking-new, stay at a newer facility.

If you're planning to visit between Memorial Day and Labor Day, make your reservations several months in advance, especially if you want a hotel on the beach.

Some people worry about air-conditioning in hotels, but San Diego's cooling ocean breezes make that a minor concern. Still, if you're visiting between July and September and are particularly sensitive, ask about air conditioning when booking.

Count on an extra 10½% in taxes being tacked on to your hotel bill.

Catamaran Resort Hotel
$$$ Pacific Beach

Lush palm groves and night-lit tiki torches amplify the Polynesian theme at this large, activity-oriented bay-front resort — imagine Gilligan's Island with in-room coffeemakers and poolside cocktails. Tower rooms offer the best views, while the low-rise rooms feel the most resort-like. After dark, the Cannibal Bar pumps up the volume, and the Pacific Beach party scene is just a couple of blocks away.

3999 Mission Blvd., Pacific Beach. ☎ 800-422-8386, 858-488-1081. Fax: 858-488-1387. Internet: www.catamaranresort.com. *To get there: Take I-5 to Grand/Garnet exit; go west on Grand Ave., then four blocks south on Mission Blvd. Parking: $8 to self-park, $10 to valet. Rack rates: $265–$355 double. Rates often drop based on occupancy; packages are also available, like the B&B deal, which includes breakfast and room tax for as little as $139 per night. AE, DC, DISC, MC, V.*

Crystal Pier Hotel
$$–$$$$ Pacific Beach

Built on an ocean pier, these 26 wooden cottages (circa 1936, but recently renovated) are San Diego's most unusual lodgings. Like tiny vacation homes, they're as darling as can be and book up fast for summer. Each has a private patio, living room, bedroom, full kitchen, and breathtaking sunset views. Beach gear is available for rent, but BYO beach towels.

4500 Ocean Blvd., Pacific Beach. ☎ 800-748-5894, 858-483-6983. Fax: 858-483-6811. To get there: Take I-5 to Grand/Garnet exit; follow Garnet Ave. to the pier. Parking: Free. Rack rates: Mid-June–mid-Sept, $235–$265 cottage, 3-night minimum; late Sept–mid-June, $195–$220, two-night minimum. DISC, MC, V.

Gaslamp Plaza Suites
$$ Gaslamp Quarter

Once an office building, this 64-room boutique hotel can be a frustrating experience because the well-intentioned management does everything so close to right, yet often just misses. It's impeccably restored, complete with exquisite period detail (wood, marble, etched glass, brass) in the public areas, but the rooms are puzzlingly done in a mock Regency style with Asian art prints — and to make things even more confusing, each is named after a prominent literary figure. Standard rooms are better lit, oddly, than the one-bedroom suites, although the higher-priced suites are better yet again. The cheapest rooms are too tiny for anyone with personal-space issues to consider. Management is friendly yet distracted, the complimentary breakfast is surprisingly generous, and the rooftop has a Jacuzzi. All in all, if this were a Euro-pension-type hotel, we might cut it more slack.

520 E. St. (at 5th Ave.), Gaslamp Quarter. ☎ 800-874-8770, 619-232-9500. Fax: 619-238-9945. Valet parking: $11. Rack rates: $93–$139 double. Rates include a very basic continental breakfast. AE, DC, DISC, MC, V.

Hacienda Hotel
$$ Old Town

At this Best Western all-suite hotel perched above Old Town, walkways thread through attractive courtyards bearing a rustic Mexican Colonial ambience. This hotel is tops in its price range, with extensive in-room amenities, tons of on-site services, and plenty of fun 'n' food within easy walking distance.

4041 Harney St., Old Town. ☎ 800-888-1991, 619-298-4707. Fax: 619-298-4771. Internet: www.haciendahotel-oldtown.com. *To get there: Take I-5 to Old Town Ave. exit, turn left onto San Diego Ave. and right onto Harney St. Parking: Free. Rack rates: $145–$155 double. AE, DC, DISC, MC, V.*

Heritage Park Bed & Breakfast Inn
$$–$$$ Old Town

Surrender to the romance of utterly charming bedrooms, polished and pampering service from a friendly staff, and attention to every conceivable detail in this exquisite 1889 Queen Anne mansion, set on a hillside a short walk from Old Town dining and shopping.

2470 Heritage Park Row (off Harney St.), Old Town. ☎ 800-995-2470, 619-299-6832. Fax: 619-299-9465. Internet: www.heritageparkinn.com. *To get there: I-5 to Old Town Ave. exit; turn left onto San Diego Ave., then right on Harney St. Parking: Free. Rack rates: $135–$250 double. Rates include an extravagant breakfast, abundant tea sandwiches, and in-room goodies. AE, DC, DISC, MC, V.*

Holiday Inn on the Bay
$$–$$$ Downtown

Sprawling along the Embarcadero, this predictable but appealing and well-maintained chain hotel offers 600 rooms in a variety of buildings; choose the tower for cool bay or city views. Airport-convenient, the hotel boasts a bevy of on-site dining options and swimming pools, plus the restaurants and recreation of the bay boardwalk across the street, making families happy as clams.

1355 N. Harbor Dr. (at Ash St.). ☎ 800-HOLIDAY (800-465-4329), 619-232-3861. Fax: 619-232-4924. Internet: www.holiday-inn.com. *To get there: From the airport, follow Harbor Dr. south. Parking: $15 to self-park. Rack rates: $189–$249 double. AE, DC, DISC, MC, V.*

Horton Grand
$$–$$$ Gaslamp Quarter

Two historic hotels (one a former brothel) were linked to form this likable facility just steps from hot nightlife. Rooms tend toward frilly and a tad precious, complete with gas fireplaces and pull-chain toilets. Ask for one with lighter decor, because the dark ones can be dark indeed, although all are of good size, and some king rooms have balconies.

311 Island Ave. (at 4th Ave.), Gaslamp Quarter. ☎ 800-542-1886, 619-544-1886. Fax: 619-544-0058. Internet: www.hortongrand.com. *To get there: From the airport,* take Harbor Dr. south to Market St. east; turn right on 4th Ave. Bus 1 or 4; Convention Center trolley stop. Valet parking: $10. Rack rates: $139–$169, single $20 extra for double. Deals: Packages prices start at $165, including parking, tax, and tips, plus extras like breakfast and/or champagne. AE, DC, MC, V.

Hotel del Coronado
$$$–$$$$$ **Coronado**

This grand old seaside Victorian is our favorite place to stay in San Diego. Opened in 1888, it's loaded with personality and storybook architecture. You can see the landmarked red turrets from miles away — and you may recognize them when you do, because the hotel had a supporting role in the classic movie *Some Like It Hot* (it stood in for the Miami resort where most of the shennanigans took place). Rooms range from compact to extravagant. Those in the original building overflow with antique charm and perfectly modern appointments (we prefer those), while Ocean Towers rooms sport a contemporary look. Views vary; ocean views go for more money, but *parking lot views* are actually of a stretch of the island and not half bad. A pristine white-sand beach (glittering with pyrite gold dust) awaits, along with swimming pools, tennis, day-spa facilities, nice dining facilities, and a worthwhile guided tour. Service is superb, with staff fretting if there is a spot on the carpet and catering to any need or whim. At Christmas time, the hotel is festooned with thousands of tiny white lights that can be seen from miles around. We love it and would stay here forever.

1500 Orange Ave., Coronado. ☎ **800-468-3533**, 935-435-8000. Fax: 935-522-8238. Internet: www.hoteldel.com. To get there: From Coronado Bridge, turn left onto Orange Ave. Parking: $14 to self-park, $19 to valet. Rack rates: $250–$350 double (garden or city view, called by the hotel "no view rooms"), $305–$480 double (ocean view). AE, DC, DISC, MC, V.

La Pensione Hotel
$ **Little Italy**

This remarkable value is conveniently located near Downtown attractions and draws folks who seek out economy without compromise (that is, no youth hostels). While not large, guest rooms make the most of their space and feature minimalist modern furniture that's durable without looking cheap. Extras include fridges and microwaves, plus Little Italy shopping and dining just outside. Ask for a city or bay view; the nearby train tracks may bother you if you're an extra-light sleeper, but most guests never even notice the noise.

1700 India St. (at Date St.), Little Italy. ☎ **800-232-4683**, 619-236-8000. Fax: 619-236-8088. Internet: www.lapensionehotel.com. To get there: From the airport, follow Harbor Dr. south to A St. east; turn left on India. Bus 5. Parking: Free. Rack rates: $65–$75 double. AE, DC, DISC, MC, V.

La Valencia Hotel
$$$$$ La Jolla

Within its bougainvillea-draped walls and wrought-iron garden gates, this clifftop bastion of gentility has been La Jolla's crown jewel since it opened in 1926. Though the bathrooms can be smallish, every fabric and furnishing is of the finest quality, and the service is exceptional. The hotel overlooks La Jolla Cove and features the clubby **Whaling Bar,** heady with expensive Scotch. It has long been a hideaway for Hollywood celebs, and its colorful dome was used as a civil defense lookout during World War II.

1132 Prospect St. (at Herschel Ave.), La Jolla. ☎ *800-451-0772, 858-454-0771. Fax: 858-456-3921. Internet:* www.lavalencia.com. *To get there: From Torrey Pines Rd., turn right on Prospect Place, which becomes Prospect St. Valet parking: $15. Rack rates: $275–$750 double. AE, DC, DISC, MC, V.*

Old Town Inn
$–$$ Old Town

This is a basic motel, but a sweet one, so don't expect much from the rooms, although they are clean. The Spanish-style public areas are unexpectedly nice, however, and the pool will only get better as the landscaping matures. Grounds are well kept up, a continental breakfast is offered, TVs have HBO, and it's conveniently located across the street from access to the Old Town Historical District and the trolley to the rest of the city. Yes, it sits on a very busy highway, surrounded by industrial blech, but with the low rack rates, plus AAA discounts galore, you'll be hard-pressed to do better if you're on a budget.

4444 Pacific Hwy. ☎ *619-260-8024, 619-296-0524. Fax: 800-643-3025. Internet:* www.oldtown-inn.com. *Rack rates: $60–$130. AE, DC, DISC, MC, V.*

Paradise Point Resort
$$$–$$$$$ Mission Bay

Situated on its own island in Mission Bay, this complex is as much a theme park as is its closest neighbor, SeaWorld (a three-minute drive). You can have so much fun at this resort that you may never want to leave. Single-story duplex bungalows dot 44 acres of tropical gardens and swim-friendly beaches. All have private patios (many facing duck-filled lagoons) and plenty of thoughtful conveniences. Recent renovations kept the low-tech '60s charm but lost the tacky holdovers; rooms now sport refreshingly colorful beach-cottage decor.

1404 W. Vacation Rd., Mission Bay. ☎ *800-344-2626, 858-274-4630. Fax: 858-581-5977. Internet:* www.paradisepoint.com. *To get there: I-8 west to Mission Bay Dr. exit; take Ingraham St. north to Vacation Rd. Parking: self-parking only: $12. Rack rates: Memorial Day–Labor Day, $315–$459 double; mid-Sept–mid-May, $189–$295 double. AE, DC, DISC, MC, V.*

Prava Hotel and Spa
$$$ Gaslamp Quarter

Here is a potentially creative budget solution; while the rack rates on this hotel are none too low, rooms are *studio suites,* which means they are large, with king and queen beds. Each has a full-size fridge, a microwave, and all sorts of cooking devices. And they don't charge extra for additional guests or kids. It may be a smart cost-cutting way to go for a family (or even a small group of friends), especially if you factor in having a meal or two in your room. As a bonus, the hotel has a good fitness room, and beds (down comforter, blanket, and pillows, plus feather bed and fancy sheets) are the nicest in the area. Rates subject to increase; at press time, the hotel was undergoing renovations.

911 Fifth Ave. ☎ *619-233-3300. Fax: 619-233-0340. Internet:* www.pravahotel. com. *Rack rates: $249. AE, DC, DISC, MC, V.*

Sommerset Suites Hotel
$$–$$$ Hillcrest

This all-suite hotel on a busy street has an apartment-like ambience and unexpected amenities like huge closets, medicine cabinets, and fully equipped kitchens in all rooms; executive suites even have dishwashers. Other terrific touches include a basket of welcome snacks, a courtesy van to shopping and attractions, and an afternoon wine reception. Several blocks of chic Hillcrest lie within easy walking distance.

606 Washington St. (at 5th Ave.), Hillcrest. ☎ *800-962-9665, 619-692-5200. Fax: 619-692-5299. Internet:* www.sommersetsuites.com. *To get there: I-5 to Washington St. exit. Parking: Free. Rack rates: $135–$195 double. AE, DC, DISC, MC, V.*

Westgate Hotel
$$$–$$$$ Gaslamp Quarter

A venerable history accompanies this grand hotel (San Diego's only *Leading Hotel of the World* member) in the heart of the Gaslamp district, because dignitaries, celebrities, and the briefly famous have stayed here throughout the decades (from princesses to presidents to pop stars). It's elegant and frilly, gracious and dignified, all marble and chandeliers and antiques. Rooms are generously sized, with down comforters and robes, and decorated in a mock Regency style that is veering towards rococo, and fast. (At press time, they were planning to update the already new furnishings.) It has a small, nice gym, an even smaller business center, and a restaurant that serves rich food at prices to match. The staff could not be more well-mannered or well-trained. Rack rates are a bit high, but hidden discounts are there for the asking, so do so.

1055 Second Ave. ☎ *619-238-1818. Fax: 619-557-3737 Internet:* www.westgate hotel.com. *Parking: Valet only, $18. Rack rates: $159–$339. AE, DC, MC, V.*

Where to Dine in San Diego

So far, San Diego doesn't compete with New York or San Francisco on the culinary playing field, but its growing sophistication has sparked a new spirit of experimentation and style. There are many little cafés in the Gaslamp and especially in the Hillcrest districts, and you may well consider taking a chance on any one of them.

Aqua Blu
$$ Gaslamp Quarter   ASIAN FUSION

We get a little bit manic about wanting fresh fish when we come to a sea-side town like San Diego, and that's why we were drawn to this menu, which includes entrees like miso herb-crusted halibut, seafood wontons with an orange ginger plum sauce, and lemongrass *beurre blanc*. You may also dig their trendy drinks, all of which seem to be the color blue.

735 Fifth Ave. ☎ *619-544-6456. Main courses: $15–$22. AE, DC, DISC, MC, V. Open: Sun–Thurs 11:30 a.m.–11 p.m., Fri–Sat 11:30 a.m. to midnight.*

Clayton's Coffee Shop
$ Coronado   COFFEE SHOP

A dying breed, your basic neighborhood coffee shop/diner — you know the sort, with the curved sit-down counter, soda fountain, and booths, plus righteous hamburgers, shakes (which taste so good after a day spent roaming the Coronado beach), hearty breakfasts (marvelous omelets) made to order, and daily specials like meatloaf. Adorable local kids work here during the summer, and you should come all year 'round.

979 Orange Ave., Coronado. ☎ *619-435-5425. Nothing over $10. Cash only. Open: Mon–Sat 6 a.m.–8 p.m., Sun 6 a.m.–2 p.m.*

Corvette Diner
$ Hillcrest   DINER

A faux-'50's diner, complete with loud sassy waitresses who sport hair-sprayed wigs and poodle skirts, yucking it up with the many customers who fill the place, while DJs add to the party. Okay, we're a tad cynical, because, too often, real old diners, without the embellished frills, get overlooked in favor of commercially created places like this. Then again, we are also the last to deny the pleasures of a great burger and shake, both of which are to be had here (along with vegetarian specials). Besides, it's a hoot for the kids.

3946 Fifth Ave. ☎ *619-542-1001. Nothing over $10. AE, MC, V. Open: Sun–Thurs 11a.m.–10 p.m., Fri–Sat 11a.m.–11p.m.*

There's Mexican, Mexican, and also Mexican

Yep, those are pretty much your dining choices when you come to Old Town. What's more, we have to point out that it's all largely predictable and generic Southern California Mexican. Which is fine — many a homesick expat Californian dreams of exactly the sort of meals offered here. You'll find several (to our minds) inter-changeable restaurants within the Bazaar del Mundo and just outside it; locals will have the favorites they swear by. We think you can pretty much just pick the one with the shortest line or the nicest courtyard. Most are open daily for lunch and dinner from 10 a.m. or so until closing. Among your options are **Casa Del Pico** (in the Bazaar del Mundo; ☎ **619-296-3267**), which, if the lines are any indication, is the most popular right now, and **Casa de Bandini** (2754 Calhoun St.; ☎ **619-297-8211**).

Croce's

$$$–$$$$ **Gaslamp Quarter**   AMERICAN/ECLECTIC

This restaurant was founded by Ingrid Croce, widow of singer-songwriter Jim, and she has turned this large (and beautifully restored) 1890 building into a semi-shrine to her late husband. Her efforts on one hand should be applauded, because it helped spark the resurgence of the Gaslamp area. But the food is disappointing and overpriced, and that Croce sound-track during lunch gets repetitive and almost a litte creepy. But at night, it's a jumping spot, thanks to live jazz and R&B, so consider stopping by for a drink then.

802 5th Ave. (at F St.). ☎ *619-233-4355. Internet:* www.croces.com. *Call for same-day priority seating (before walk-ins). To get there: Bus lines 1, 3, 5, 15, or 16; 5th Ave. trolley stop. Main courses: $14–$23. AE, DC, DISC, MC, V. Open: Mon–Thurs noon to 2:30 p.m. and 5:30 p.m. to midnight; Fri noon to 1:30 a.m.; Sat and Sun 8:30 a.m.–1:30 a.m.*

Extraordinary Desserts

$ **Hillcrest**   PASTRIES/CAKES

If you're a dessert-lover, don't miss chef Karen Krasne's shrine to all things sweet, which serves only the favorite course (plus gourmet cof-fees and teas). Among the dozens of divine creations that blend Parisian style with exotic ingredients and homespun favorites are raspberry linzer torte layered with white-chocolate buttercream and Grand Marnier chocolate cheesecake on a brownie crust and sealed with bittersweet ganache. Definitely extraordinary!

2929 5th Ave. (between Palm and Quince sts.), Hillcrest. ☎ *619-294-7001. Internet:* www.extaordinarydesserts.com. *Reservations not accepted. To get there:*

Bus 1, 3, or 25. Desserts: $2–$6. MC, V. Open: Sun–Thurs 8:30 a.m.–11 p.m.; Fri. 8:30 a.m. to midnight.; Sat. 11 a.m. to midnight.

Filippi's Pizza Grotto
$–$$ Little Italy   ITALIAN

Several reasons explain why Filippi's has been a Little Italy anchor since 1950 — the food is molto bueno, the portions enormous, and the staff welcomes everyone like family. Just follow the intoxicating aroma of traditional Sicilian pizza, lasagne, spaghetti, and antipasto through the Italian grocery/deli to the back dining room, traditionally outfitted with Chianti bottles and red-checkered tablecloths.

1747 India St. (between Fir and Date Sts.), Little Italy. ☎ 619-232-5095. Reservations not taken. To get there: Little Italy trolley stop or bus 5. Main courses: $4.75–$13. AE, DC, DISC, MC, V. Open: Sun–Mon 11 a.m.–10 p.m.; Tues–Thurs 11 a.m.– 10:30 p.m.; Fri and Sat 11 a.m.–11:30 p.m.

Fio's
$$$ Gaslamp Quarter   NORTHERN ITALIAN

The granddaddy of San Diego's trendy trattorias has a sophisticated ambience and a constant crowd. While the Northern Italian cuisine is no longer cutting edge, practice has made the kitchen consistently good at delivering delicately sauced pastas, crispy gourmet pizzas, and impressive meats like veal shank on saffron risotto. Come without a reservation, and you can still get the full menu at the elegant bar.

801 5th Ave. (at F St.), Gaslamp Quarter. ☎ 619-234-3467. Internet: www.fios italian.com. *Reservations recommended. To get there: Bus 1, 3, 5, 15, or 16; 5th Ave. trolley stop. Main courses: $15–$26. AE, DC, DISC, MC, V. Open: Sun–Thurs 5 p.m.–10 p.m.; Fri–Sat 5 p.m.–11:30 p.m.*

The Fish Market/Top of the Market
$$$/$$$$ The Embarcadero   SEAFOOD

Ask San Diegans where to go for the freshest fish, and they'll send you to the bustling Fish Market. Chalkboards announce the day's catches, available in a number of simple, classic preparations. Upstairs, Top of the Market offers similar fare at jacked-up prices; we recommend having a cocktail in the posh, clubby **Top** — which has stupendous bay views — then heading downstairs to the more cheery, casual restaurant for affordable eats, including treats from the sushi and oyster bars.

On the Embarcadero, 750 N. Harbor Dr. ☎ 619-232-3474 downstairs, 619-234-4867 upstairs. Internet: www.thefishmarket.com. *Reservations not taken downstairs, recommended upstairs. To get there: Seaport Village trolley stop or bus 7/7B. Main courses lunch: $7–$33 downstairs, $9–$38 upstairs; dinner: $11–$38. AE, DC, DISC, MC, V. Open: Daily 11 a.m.–10 p.m.*

George's at the Cove/George's Ocean Terrace
$$$$/$$–$$$ La Jolla   CALIFORNIA

These sibling restaurants — a fancy downstairs dining room and a breezy upstairs cafe — share an ahh-inspiring ocean view, attentive service, and tasty smoked chicken/broccoli/black bean soup. George's downstairs kitchen turns up the finesse factor for inventive and formal California cuisine, while the Ocean Terrace cafe offers crowd-pleasing versions. Both are great, so choose based on your mood and budget.

1250 Prospect St., La Jolla. ☎ *858-454-4244. Internet:* www.georgesatthecove. com. *Reservations recommended at George's, not accepted at Ocean Terrace. To get there: From Torrey Pines Rd., right on Prospect Place, which becomes Prospect St. Main courses: George's, $10–$15 at lunch, $24–$31 at dinner; Ocean Terrace, lunch $8–$10, dinner $14–$18. AE, DC, DISC, MC, V. Open: Daily 11 a.m.–10 p.m.*

Laurel
$$$$ Downtown/Hillcrest   FRENCH/MEDITERRANEAN

Here's a restaurant that takes itself seriously. It offers a swank room, formal service, and classic French cuisine tempered with some refreshingly rustic Mediterranean elements. This restaurant is pleasant evidence that the San Diego restaurant scene has gotten with it.

Laurel is the best choice for pre-theater dining, thanks to the shuttle service they offer to and from the Old Globe Theatre, which allows you to leave your car at the restaurant and not bother with Balboa Park parking. The ride is pleasant, efficient, and absolutely free (for the price of dinner, of course).

505 Laurel St. (at 5th Ave.), on the border between downtown and Hillcrest. ☎ *619-239-2222. Internet:* www.winesellar.com. *Reservations recommended. To get there: Bus 1, 3, or 25. Main courses: $19–$34. AE, DC, DISC, MC, V. Open: Sun–Thurs 5–10 p.m.; Fri–Sat 5–11 p.m.; lunch Fri only 11:30 a.m.–1:30 p.m.*

Mixx
$$$ Hillcrest   CALIFORNIA/ECLECTIC

Aptly named for its subtle global fusion fare, Mixx embodies everything good about Hillcrest dining: an attractive and relaxing room, a sophisticated crowd, thoughtfully composed meals, and polished, friendly service. Hip locals gravitate toward this comfy, jovial place to see what the inventive chef will think up next. Allow time to search for that elusive Hillcrest parking space!

3671 5th Ave. (at Pennsylvania Ave.). ☎ *619-299-6499. Reservations recommended, especially on weekends. To get there: Bus 1, 3, or 25. Main courses: $14–$24. AE, DC, DISC, MC, V. Open: Sun–Thurs 5–9:30 p.m.; Fri–Sat 5–10:30 p.m.*

Pacific Coast Grill
$$–$$$ Solana Beach   ECLECTIC

An easy jump off the freeway on your way to or from San Diego, and probably worth the short drive from the city, this modern, gaily decorated establishment has a number of curious, clever dishes, but our favorite is the shrimp dumplings, served in a port-wine butter sauce that will have you calling for more of the good house bread to soak it up. Fresh fish dishes dominate the menu, from lobster tacos to grilled mahimahi, but carnivores will be happy to discover that the burger comes on a fluffy roll and is stuffed with herb butter. Note that lunchtime sandwiches can be ordered at dinner even though they aren't on the menu.

437 S. Hwy. 101. ☎ *858-794-4632. Main courses: Lunch $7.75–$12; dinner $13–$22. AE, DC, DISC, MC, V. Open: Sun–Thurs 11:30 a.m.–9:30 p.m., Fri–Sat 11:30 a.m.– 10:30 p.m.*

Parallel 33
$$$ Mission District   ECLECTIC

Named for the mythical line on which, geographically, you can find Morocco, Japan, India, and yes, San Diego, this is a delightfully sophisticated but not intimidating little place just a few blocks away from the Hillcrest district. On a recent trip, we started with *b'stilla* (the chicken, phyllo, sugar, and cinnamon Moroccan dish) plus a wonderful salad dressed with a preserved lemon vinaigrette. From there, we went on to pan-seared halibut with a yellow tomato coulis (perfect), salmon with a roasted sesame crust on braised veggies (even better), and an Asian duck breast and five-spice sauce (the best of all). Desserts are made with style and care (do try the vanilla-rose ice cream, a special Middle Eastern treat). This is a most promising entry in the San Diego dining scene and well worth your time.

741 W. Washington St. ☎ *619-260-0033. Main courses: $18–$25. AE, DISC, MC, V. Open: Mon–Thurs 5:30–11 p.m., Fri–Sat 5:30–11 p.m.*

Primavera Ristorante
$$–$$$ Coronado   ITALIAN

This is one of a number of cute little cafés and restaurants on Coronado, especially along the main drag heading to and from the Hotel Del. It's a popular place for dinner, a cheaper nice-night-out option than some of the hotel dining rooms, with fresh fish and pasta entrees (we prefer the latter; simpler seems to be more successful here). It's classy, but not overwhelmingly so, and most friendly. Next door is its pastry cafe, which, despite the Italian name, emphasizes French pastries — come here to get your eclair fix.

932 Orange Ave., Coronado. ☎ *619-435-0454. Main courses: $14–$28. AE, DC, DISC, MC, V. Open: Daily 5–10 p.m.*

Rubio's Baja Grill

$ Pacific Beach   TACOS

Local-surfer-made-good Ralph Rubio brought home the simple recipe common to Mexican fishing villages — batter-dipped, deep-fried fish fillets folded in corn tortillas and garnished with shredded cabbage, salsa, and tangy white sauce — and launched the you-can't-eat-just-one Baja fish tacos craze. Wash 'em down with an ice-cold something. Locations are all over San Diego, but the original is the most fun.

4504 Mission Bay Dr., Pacific Beach. ☎ *858-272-2801. Internet:* www.rubios.com. *Main courses: Most under $5. MC, V. Open: Sun–Thurs 10 a.m.–9 p.m.; Fri–Sat 10 a.m.–10 p.m.*

Sushi Kazumi

$$–$$$ Hillcrest   JAPANESE

If you don't come early to this tiny cafe, you may have to battle locals for a seat. The owner and his son oversee the sushi bar; the former is so dedicated that he gets visibly pained when asked to make some silly roll. Why put him through that when you can have this master sushi chef (who will serve only fish that meets his exacting standards) or his lovely, knowledgable son choose your fish for you? You may end up trying Japanese snapper, sea urchin, or giant clam. If raw fish isn't your game, try one of their regular meals, reminiscent of what you might find in corner diners all over Japan.

3974 Fifth Ave. ☎ *619-682-4054. Main courses: Sushi around $3, entrees $5–$12. AE, MC, V. Open: Tues–Thurs 4:30–10 p.m., Fri–Sat 4:30–11 p.m., Sun 4:30–9 p.m.*

Trattoria Acqua

$$$ La Jolla   ITALIAN/MEDITERRANEAN

Enjoy the Italian Mediterranean ambience of this romantic restaurant, where diners are encouraged to relax and linger over rich pastas like veal-and-mortadella tortellini in fennel cream sauce. The menu always has plenty of *secondi* (second courses) of meat and fish, as well, and every pasta is available in an appetizer portion (how considerate!). The wine list is a perennial *Wine Spectator* award-winner.

1298 Prospect St. (on Coast Walk), La Jolla. ☎ *858-454-0709. Internet:* www.trattoriaacqua.com. *Reservations recommended for dinner. To get there: From Torrey Pines Rd., right on Prospect Pl., which becomes Prospect St. Main courses lunch: $7.95–$18; dinner $14–$30. AE, DC, MC, V. Open: Daily 11:30 a.m.–2:30 p.m. and 5–9:30 p.m.*

Gimme some of that sweet stuff

Moo Time is a local chain with branches throughout San Diego (we like the one in Hillcrest at 3803 Fifth Ave., open Sun–Thurs 11 a.m.–10 p.m., Fri and Sat 11 a.m.–11 p.m.) serving creamery ice cream, with your choice of *mixers* (you know, Oreos, candy, nuts). We think ice cream is essential on hot summer days, and our first choice to rescue our poor wilting selves is this place.

The Vegetarian Zone
$–$$ Hillcrest   INTERNATIONAL VEGETARIAN

Even if you're wary of tofu and tempeh, you'll like this ethnically accented food, which is so mainstream — and good — you'll forget that it just happens to be vegetarian. Menu standouts include Greek spinach-and-feta pie, daily soups and stews, and homemade salad dressings that taste too good to be this healthy. San Diegans from all walks of life quickly fill the casual indoor/outdoor seating at mealtimes.

2949 5th Ave. (between Palm and Quince sts.), Hillcrest. ☎ **619-298-7302.** *Reservations not taken. To get there: Bus 1, 3, or 25. Main courses: $6–$20. AE, DISC, MC, V. Open: Tues–Fri lunch 10 a.m.–3 p.m, dinner 5–9 p.m.; Sat and Sun 10 a.m.–10 p.m. Deli open: Tues–Sun 9 a.m.–7 p.m.*

Exploring San Diego

What do San Diego and central Florida have in common? They both feature big-name family attractions, the spend-all-day kinds of places around which you're probably planning your stay. This section contains everything you need to know about them, plus suggestions for filling any free time after you're done.

The "Big Four" — the animal and theme parks

Each of these parks can eat up at least half a day — a lot more if you have kids.

San Diego's three main family attractions have joined forces, offering **combo ticket deals** that reward you with big savings for taking on what we like to call the Vacation Endurance Challenge. Here's how it works: You get to visit both the **San Diego Zoo** and **Wild Animal Park** (deluxe zoo package, Wild Animal Park admission) for $38.35 adults and $23.15 for kids 3 to 11. The two-park ticket includes one visit to each attraction, which you must use within five days of purchase.

What's that? You say you want more? Add **SeaWorld** to your plans with a three-park ticket (deluxe zoo package, Wild Animal Park admission, SeaWorld admission) for $73.95 adults, $50.95 kids 3 to 11. With this one, you get unlimited use at all three parks for five days from date of purchase — wow! Deals often change, so check with the parks.

Note also that many hotels in the area offer advance tickets for all the parks at a discount.

SeaWorld

One of the best-promoted attractions in California, this 165-acre aquatic playground is a showplace for marine life, made politically correct with an only nominally "educational" atmosphere that we wish the park took further. At its heart, it's a (genuinely) fun-filled family entertainment center with performing dolphins, otters, sea lions, walruses, and seals. Several successive four-ton black-and-white killer whales have functioned as the park's mascot, Shamu.

The hands-on area called **Shamu's Happy Harbor** encourages kids to play and get wet. The newest attraction is **Shipwreck Rapids,** a wet adventure ride on raftlike inner tubes that float through caverns, water-falls, and wild rivers. Shows for short attention spans run continuously throughout the day, and you can rotate through the various theaters; best is the silly, plot-driven sea lions-go-to-Gilligan's Island show. Other draws include **Wild Arctic,** an extremely cool virtual-reality trip to the frozen North, complete with polar bears, beluga whales, walruses, and harbor seals, that's well worth making time for; and **Shamu Close Up,** where you can watch the whales in their off hours through underwater windows while keepers explain what you're seeing.

500 Sea World Dr., Mission Bay. ☎ *858-226-3901. Internet:* www.seaworld.com. *To get there: From I-5, take the Sea World Dr. exit; from I-8, take W. Mission Bay Dr. exit to Sea World Dr. Bus 9. Admission: $39 adults, $35 seniors, $30 kids 3–11. Open: Memorial Day–Labor Day, daily 9 a.m.–11 p.m. (sometimes midnight); Sept–May, daily 10 a.m.–5 p.m.*

San Diego Zoo

More than 4,000 animals reside at this world-famous zoo, founded in 1916. Even if other zoos have caught up to it in terms of animal awareness in the intervening century, this granddaddy is still highly respected in the field. Every new exhibit features an even more high-tech method for simulating the climate, flora, and other conditions of the residents' natural habitat, and the preservation of endangered species is a primary concern. It also happens to be a whole lot of fun.

The 1996 loan of two magnificent giant pandas from the People's Republic of China brought the zoo more attention than ever, and in 1999, Bai Yun and Shi Shi became the parents of Hua Mei, an adorable baby panda who's quite an achievement of reproductive research (pandas rarely conceive in captivity). The pandas are the big attention-getters — and deservedly so — but the zoo contains many other rare and exotic species, with the cuddly koalas drawing the next biggest crowds.

The zoo offers two types of **bus tours,** a 35-minute guided tour, and an on/off bus ticket you can use throughout the day. Both provide a narrated overview and allow you to see 75% of the park. We strongly encourage first-timers, especially parents with young kids, to spend the extra few bucks on the bus, because the zoo covers a lot of acreage, much of it terraced and extremely hilly. You can then use your energy to revisit the creatures that you like best, and to see those not covered on the tour, like the pandas. Even by starting with the bus tour, you'll have a hard time visiting everything in the course of a long day, so wear your most comfortable sneakers. Come extra-early or later in the afternoon and plan on spending the evening in summer, because the animals tend to hibernate in the heat of day. And don't miss the hippos — if you get lucky, you'll see them frolicking, which is a sight to behold.

2920 Zoo Dr. (off Park Blvd.), Balboa Park. ☎ *619-234-3153. Internet:* www.san diegozoo.org. *To get there: Bus 7/7B. Admission: $19.50 adults, $11.75 kids 3–11. Deluxe package (admission, guided bus tour, round-trip Skyfari aerial tram) $32 adults, $28.80 seniors 60 and over, $19.75 children. Open: Daily 9 a.m.–4 p.m. (grounds close at 6 p.m.); summer 9 a.m.–9 p.m. (grounds close at 10 p.m.).*

San Diego Wild Animal Park

Originally begun as a breeding facility for the **San Diego Zoo,** the **San Diego Wild Animal Park (WAP)** now holds around 3,200 animals — many endangered species — all roaming freely over the park's 1,800 acres. Approximately 650 baby animals are born every year in the park.

The real beauty of the park is that you, not the animals, are the caged ones. The park has recently added a network of paths (with catchy but meaningless names like "Kilimanjaro Safari Walk" and "Heart of Africa") that skirt many of the enclosures. The best way to see the animals, however, is by riding the monorail, which is included in the admission price; for the best views, sit on the right-hand side. During the 50-minute ride, you'll pass through vast landscapes resembling Africa and Asia. Trains leave every 20 minutes from the station in **Nairobi Village,** the commercial hub of the park, with souvenir stores and refreshment vendors. (The food is mediocre and overpriced, so think about smuggling in your own snacks.) Otherwise, Nairobi Village is not much more than a small, traditional zoo whose best feature is the nursery area, where you can watch irresistible young-uns frolicking, being bottle-fed, and sleeping.

If you really want to experience the vast landscape and large animals that make the WAP so special, take a **photo caravan tour** ($98.95 to $145 per person, park admission included). The photo-taking is secondary — for us, anyway — to the enjoyment of crossing the fence to meet rhinos,

The Zoo versus the Wild Animal Park: How do you choose?

Do both if time allows: Both parks are so different that you won't regret it. If you can't, convenience may be enough of a deciding factor; the zoo is in the heart of San Diego, while the Wild Animal Park is a hefty 45-minute drive from San Diego. Additionally, consider the following factors when making your choice:

✔ The safari-like **Wild Animal Park** gives you the chance to see greater numbers of bigger animals living in a vastly larger territory. The animals don't even know people are spying on them, which means that you have a much better opportunity to see them exhibit natural behavior. They're free (and have space enough) to display herd behavior, and are comfortable enough to do almost anything.

✔ The **San Diego Zoo,** on the other hand, is home to a much more diverse population of animals from around the globe, thanks to the zookeepers' intense effort to reproduce authentic habitats. What's more, shows and attractions lend the zoo more of a colorful amusement park atmosphere, which makes it a better choice if you have little ones in tow. And if you have a passion for pandas, the zoo's for you, no question!

ostriches, zebras, deer, and giraffes on their home turf. You can even feed the giraffes along the way — an amazing experience. Advance reservations are recommended.

15500 San Pasqual Valley Rd., Escondido (30 miles northeast of San Diego). ☎ *760-747-8702. Internet:* www.sandiegozoo.org. *To get there: I-15 north to Via Rancho Pkwy.; follow signs for about 3 miles. Admission: $26.50 adults 12 and over, $23.85 seniors, $19.50 kids 3–11, free for kids under 3. Open: Daily 9 a.m.–4 p.m. (grounds close at 5 p.m.); extended hours in summer and December.*

LEGOLAND

New in 1999, this theme park is the ultimate monument to the world's most famous plastic building blocks. Two other enormously successful LEGOLANDs exist, in Denmark and Britain, but this is the only one in America. Boy, do we want to like this place, but boy, does it make it hard for us. Although there are quite a few giant displays made of LEGOS, there aren't as many as you would wish for. The rides are strictly for kiddies (short in duration and on thrills; height and age restrictions vary on each ride), while the single best part, scale models of international landmarks (the Eiffel Tower, Sydney Opera House, and so on, all constructed out of real LEGO bricks), will appeal only to grownups, who don't mind just looking at stuff. Although the official guidelines imply that the park is geared toward children of all ages, the average MTV- and PlayStation-seasoned kid over 10 will find it a snooze.

1 Lego Dr., Carlsbad (30 miles north of San Diego). ☎ *877-534-6526, 760-438-5346. Internet:* www.legolandca.com. *To get there: I-5 north to Cannon Rd. exit east, following signs for Lego Dr. Admission: $39.95 adults, $33.95 kids 3–16, ask at gate about senior discounts. Open: Daily 10 a.m. to dusk; extended summer and holiday hours.*

Balboa Park

Balboa Park is one of San Diego's must-see attractions. Not only does it house the world-famous **San Diego Zoo** (see the preceding section), but this 1,200-acre verdant wonderland — which bills itself as the largest urban cultural park in the country — serves as the cultural and recreational heart of the city. Spanish-Moorish buildings originally built for the 1915 Panama-California Exposition house most of the city's museums, surrounded by a series of cultivated gardens, small forests, tropical oases, and shaded groves coaxed from a formerly scruffy brown canyon. Lest it all sound too refined for you, the park boasts plenty of places to play, as well.

Balboa Park lies at the northern edge of downtown, bordered on the west by 6th Avenue. From downtown, 12th Avenue leads directly in, becoming Park Boulevard and passing the entrance to the zoo. From 6th Avenue, Laurel Street becomes El Prado, the park's main thorough-fare; many of the park's major museums, along with the Visitor Center, are lined up along this avenue. The park contains plenty of parking lots, although you may not have your first choice on busy days. That's all right, though, because walking from place to place is part of the fun. Distances are easily manageable, but if the hills start to dog you, hop aboard the free park trams that run regularly through the park. (The one exception to the distance rule is the zoo. It sits far enough away that you'll want to use its own lot.)

Sure, San Diego has other museums in town, but because you have limited time (not to mention limited patience), make sightseeing easy on everyone by choosing from among the park's 14-plus museums, which offer more museum fix than you'll need in the course of your visit. The best of the bunch are described in this section; for a complete list of park attractions, go online to www.balboapark.org or, after you arrive, pick up a map at the well-staffed **Balboa Park Visitors Center,** 1549 El Prado (☎ 619-239-0512). To get there, take either bus 7/7B, 16, or 25.

In the courtyard behind the center you'll find the brand-new **Prado** (☎ 619-557-9441), an upscale Nuevo Latino restaurant set within the historic walls of the House of Hospitality. If you'd prefer something lower on the food chain price-wise, snack bars and casual cafes are scattered throughout the park.

Balboa Park Attractions

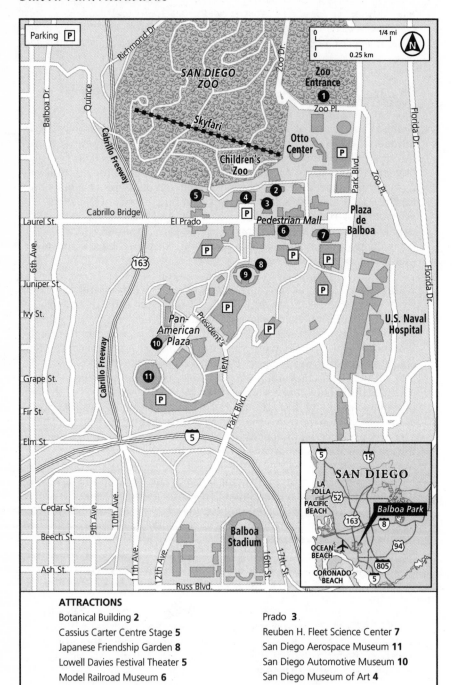

ATTRACTIONS

Botanical Building **2**	Prado **3**
Cassius Carter Centre Stage **5**	Reuben H. Fleet Science Center **7**
Japanese Friendship Garden **8**	San Diego Aerospace Museum **11**
Lowell Davies Festival Theater **5**	San Diego Automotive Museum **10**
Model Railroad Museum **6**	San Diego Museum of Art **4**
Museum of Photographic Arts **6**	San Diego Zoo **1**
Old Globe Theatre **5**	Spreckels Organ Pavilion **9**

All the park's museums are free one Tuesday each month. The museums participate on a rotating schedule so that three or more waive their entrance fees every Tuesday. If you plan to visit more than three of the park's museums, buy the **Passport to Balboa Park,** a coupon booklet that allows one entrance to each of 11 museums that charge an entry fee (the others are always free) and is valid for one week. You can purchase the $21 passport at any participating museum or the visitor center.

Note that many park attractions are closed on Mondays.

San Diego Aerospace Museum

The number-two kid-pleaser in town (after the Fleet Science Center — see the following entry), this enormously popular museum provides an overview of national and local aviation history, from hot-air balloons to the space age, with plenty of biplanes and fighters in between. The Ford Motor Company built the stunning cylindrical hall, which houses an imaginative gift shop with goodies like freeze-dried astronaut ice cream, in 1935. Plan on spending 1½ to 2½ hours.

2001 Pan American Plaza. ☎ **619-234-8291.** *Internet:* www.aerospacemuseum. org. *Admission: $8 adults, $6 seniors, $3 kids 6–17, free for those under 6 or an active duty member of the military. Open: Daily 10 a.m.–4:30 p.m., 5:30 in the summer.*

Reuben H. Fleet Science Center

A must-see for kids of any age — yep, including grown-up kids. This tantalizing collection of hands-on exhibits is designed to provoke the imagination while teaching scientific principles. The newest feature is **SciTours,** a virtual-space simulator ride that resembles Disneyland's Star Tours ride. Although it doesn't seem to have any educational element, it's fun nonetheless. The Fleet also houses a 76-foot domed OMNIMAX theater, an excellent place to experience larger-than-life IMAX films. You'll need 1½ to 3 hours to explore all the exhibits, not counting IMAX movie time.

1875 El Prado. ☎ **619-238-1233.** *Internet:* www.rhfleet.org. *Admission (includes IMAX film, SciTours ride, and exhibit galleries): $11.50 adults, $9.50 seniors, $8.50 kids 3–12. Free first Tues of the month. Student and AAA discounts. Open: 365 days a year, at 9:30 a.m.; closing varies by day and season.*

San Diego Museum of Art

With one of the grandest entrances along El Prado, this museum also boasts outstanding collections of Italian Renaissance and Dutch and Spanish baroque art, along with an impressive collection of Toulouse-Lautrec's works. The museum often shows prestigious traveling exhibits, and the interactive computer image system allows you to locate highlights and custom-design a tour. Plan on spending one to three hours here.

1450 El Prado. ☎ *619-232-7931. Internet:* www.sdmart.com. *Admission: $8 adults, $6 seniors and young adults 18–24 and military with ID, $3 kids 6–17. Free third Tues of the month. Open: Tues–Wed, Fri, and Sat 10 a.m.–4:30 p.m.; Thurs 10 a.m.–9 p.m.*

San Diego Automotive Museum

Even if you don't know a distributor from a dipstick, you'll ooh and aah over the classic, antique, and exotic cars here. Every one is in such pristine condition you'd swear it just rolled off the line, from the 1886 Benz to the 1981 DeLorean. You can easily see the collection in a little over an hour.

2080 Pan American Plaza. ☎ *619-231-2886. Internet:* www.sdautomuseum.org. *Admission: $7 adults, $6 active military and seniors, $3 kids 6–15. Free fourth Tues of the month. Open: Daily 10 a.m.–5 p.m. (later in summer).*

Museum of Photographic Arts

If names like Ansel Adams, Margaret Bourke-White, Imogen Cunningham, Edward Weston, and Henri Cartier-Bresson pique your interest, don't miss this 3,600-plus image collection, one of few in the United States devoted exclusively to photography. Set aside one to two hours.

1649 El Prado. ☎ *619-238-7559. Internet:* www.mopa.org. *Admission: $6 adults; $4 students, seniors, active military; free for kids under 12 (with adult). Free second Tues of the month. Open: Sun–Wed 10 a.m.–5 p.m., Thurs 10 a.m.–9 p.m.*

Model Railroad Museum

It may not be high culture as we know it, but this museum is cool and cute, and well worth 30 to 60 minutes of your time, even if you don't consider yourself a train buff. Six permanent, scale-model railroads depict Southern California's transportation history and terrain with an astounding attention to detail. Kids will love the hands-on Lionel trains, and train buffs of all ages will appreciate the interactive multimedia element.

1649 El Prado. ☎ *619-696-0199. Internet:* www.sdmodelrailroadm.com. *Admission: $4 adults; $3 seniors; $2.50 students and active military; free for kids under 15 (with adult). Free first Tues of the month. Open: Tues–Fri 11 a.m.–4 p.m., Sat–Sun 11 a.m.–5 p.m.*

Along El Prado, just beyond the Lily Pond, is the **Botanical Building,** a 250-foot-long wooden lath conservatory from the 1915 Exposition that looks like something out of a Victorian costume drama and houses about 1,200 tropical and flowering plants. Admission is free.

The largest outdoor pipe organ in the world is at **Spreckels Organ Pavilion,** south of El Prado (☎ 619-702-8138), an ornate, curved amphitheater offering free Sunday concerts at 2 p.m. year 'round and free evening concerts in July and August. The sound is stupendous, and the whole experience serves to amplify (pun intended) the old-fashioned Sunday-in-the-park quality of your visit.

Scanning the winter seas for whales

Whale-watching is a hugely popular pastime between mid-December and mid-March. California gray whales hug the shore on their annual migration from Alaskan feeding grounds to breeding lagoons in Mexico — and back again, with calves in tow. If you've ever been lucky enough to spot one of these gentle behemoths, you'll understand the thrill.

Grab binoculars and head to Cabrillo National Monument (☎ 619-557-5450; Internet: www.nps.gov/cabr), on Point Loma, where an elevated, glassed-in observatory offers a prime vantage point. Take I-5 or I-8 to Highway 209/Rosecrans Street and follow signs to the monument; admission is $5 per car.

On the UCSD campus in La Jolla, the outdoor plaza at the Birch Aquarium at Scripps Institution of Oceanography (☎ 858-534-3474; www.aquarium.ucsd.edu) offers another excellent whale-watching perch. Take I-5 to La Jolla Village Drive, go west for a mile (past Torrey Pines Road), and turn left at Expedition Way.

If you want to get a closer look, head out to sea with Classic Sailing Adventures (☎ 800-659-0141 or 619-224-0800).

The **Japanese Friendship Garden** (☎ 619-232-2721), adjacent to the organ pavilion, is a serene, meticulous oasis. From the elaborately carved gate, a crooked path (to confound evil spirits, who move only in a straight line) threads its way past nearly 100 carefully arranged plantings, a stream with colorful koi, and a traditional zen garden. Admission is $2, $1 for seniors and juniors, free to kids under 7.

Old Town State Historic Park

Whether you're a history buff looking for an authentic slice of early California or a hungry theme-park refugee in search of a Mexican combo plate and a cheesy souvenir, chances are very good that you'll end up in **Old Town** — and you should.

The birthplace of San Diego — indeed, of California — Old Town was founded by Spanish friars in 1769, along with Mission San Diego. The town of San Diego grew up around the mission and its military presidio, which thrived here until the early 1870s. After San Diego's commercial core moved closer to the harbor (to "New Town," now the **Gaslamp Quarter**), Old Town was abandoned. In 1968, the park was established to preserve the structures that remained and rebuild several atop their original foundations. As the years have gone by, sensitivity to historical accuracy has improved greatly, making the park a combination of Disneyesque attractions and eerily authentic sites.

If you can get past the touristy veneer and into the true spirit of this pedestrians-only six-block historic district, you'll step back to a time of one-room schoolhouses and village greens, when the people who lived, worked, and played here spoke Spanish. Depending on your interest level — whether you want only to cover the main points of interest or see everything *and* have lunch — you can spend anywhere from one to five hours here.

Old Town is bounded by Congress, Juan, Wallace, and Twiggs Streets. To get there: Take I-5 to Old Town Avenue exit; parking is free in the many lots scattered around the park's perimeter, and the large lot for Old Town's trolley station (another option) holds more spaces, at the northwest end. Admission: Free, although donations are encouraged. Open: Daily from 10 a.m. to 5 p.m.

Stop first at the **Robinson Rose Visitor Center,** the visitor center for Old Town State Park, on San Diego Ave. (☎ **619-220-5422**), to get your bearings, join up with a walking tour (daily at 10:30 a.m. and 2 p.m.), or simply check out the old wagons, carriages, and stagecoaches. Other notable stops include:

- ✔ **La Casa de Estudillo,** the 1827 adobe home of a wealthy family, furnished with typical upper-class furniture of the period.

- ✔ **Robinson-Rose House,** built in 1853 and containing a scale model of Old Town the way it looked in 1872, before a fire destroyed much of the district.

- ✔ The **San Diego Union Building,** where a forerunner to today's *Union-Tribune* began publishing in 1868.

- ✔ The reproduction **Silvas-McCoy House,** currently under construction as an interpretive visitor center for Old Town.

One of Old Town's top draws is its Mexican restaurants. See the "There's Mexican, Mexican, and also Mexican" sidebar, earlier in the chapter, for our top recommendations. See "Shopping at the Top," later in the chapter, for the lowdown on Old Town shopping.

Hitting the beaches

San Diego's justifiably famous beaches are its second-biggest visitor draw (after the animal parks). "Beach weather" lasts virtually all year. Any sunny day is perfect for a walk, a little in-line skating, or a picnic.

Coronado Beach

If you're spending any time on Coronado, don't miss this wide, sparkling-sand paradise of a beach, framed by the fabulous Hotel Del Coronado and extending along Ocean Avenue up to grassy Sunset Park. It's a flat, benign beach (that can glitter with gold pyrite flakes) perfect for sunbathing, strolling, and wading. Street parking (some metered) is plentiful even in summer, and the beach includes lifeguards, restrooms, and a picnic area with a few fire rings. The islands visible from here — "Los Coronados" — are 18 miles away and belong to Mexico.

Ocean Beach

This beach sits just across the channel from Mission Bay. To reach it, take West Point Loma Boulevard all the way to the end. The northern end of **Ocean Beach Park** is known as **Dog Beach** after the pooches that frolic on the sand. Surfers generally congregate around **Ocean Beach Pier,** mostly in the water but often at the snack shack on the end. *Riptides* (dangerous currents) are strong here, so venturing in beyond waist depth is not a good idea. Facilities include restrooms, showers, picnic tables, and plenty of metered parking lots; the funky shops and food stands of Newport Avenue are a couple blocks away.

Mission Beach and Pacific Beach

These neighbors along Mission Boulevard share a popular boardwalk: **Ocean Front Walk,** a fun, free-for-all human parade. To the south, **Mission Beach** features several dozen blocks of narrow but popular sandy beach known for a youthful surf culture and beginner-friendly waves. Grassy **Belmont Park** sits at midpoint (at West Mission Bay Drive), offering rides and carnival-style entertainment.

Pacific Beach begins around Pacific Beach Drive, where the scene is only slightly more sophisticated, and the surfers a little more experienced. Waves break pretty far out, making this one of San Diego's best swimming beaches. One exception is **Tourmaline Surfing Park,** at the northernmost end of Pacific Beach, where the sport's old guard gathers to ride the waves. Swimming is prohibited, but come to watch the masters in action.

You can find metered lots spaced along Mission Boulevard's side streets, and maybe even a few curbside spaces, if you're lucky. Both beaches have lifeguards and well-spaced restroom facilities.

Just east of Mission Beach is **Mission Bay,** whose labyrinth of calm waters and pretty peninsulas are ideal for exploring. Check with **Seaforth Boat Rental,** 1641 Quivera Rd. (☎ **888-834-2628,** 619-223-1681; Internet: www.seaforth-boat-rental.com/seaforth), which offers half- and full-day rentals on powerboats, sailboats, personal watercraft (PWCs), motorized skiffs, kayaks, or paddleboats. If you don't want to get your feet wet, **bikes are available for rent** at the **Marriott Hotel** (☎ 619-234-1500 x6535) for $12 an hour, $30 a day. They also rent surreys for $30 a day. You do not have to be a guest to rent. **Bike Tours San Diego** (☎ 619-238-2444) offers guided tours that vary in price depending on area covered; they also just rent bikes (about $18–$35 per day). For inline skates or traditional quads, **Mission Beach Club,** 704 Ventura Pl., at Ocean Front Walk (☎ 858-488-8889), can set you up with skates and all necessary safety gear.

La Jolla Cove

This scenic jewel appears regularly on La Jolla postcards and is worth the drive even if you're staying closer to downtown. Framed by grass-carpeted bluffs and sheltering a snorkel-friendly marine preserve just below the surface, the cove is also a terrific spot for swimmers of all abilities. It's on the small side, so avoid peak summer weekends if you can; the free parking spaces along Coast Boulevard tend to fill quickly, as well, but it's an easy walk from anywhere in the village.

Many visitors never know about the seals who hang out about four blocks south of La Jolla Cove at **Children's Pool Beach,** a tiny cove originally named for the toddlers who could safely frolic behind a manmade seawall. These days, the sand is mostly off-limits to humans, who congregate along the seawall railing or onshore to admire the protected seals who sun themselves on the beach or on semi-submerged rocks. You can get surprisingly close — truly a mesmerizing sight.

Taking a Guided Tour by Trolley (and Other Means)

Not to be confused with the public transit trolley trains, the fully narrated **Old Town Trolley** (☎ 619-298-TOUR [619-298-8687]) is a constant favorite. You can get a comprehensive look at the city — or just the parts that interest you — aboard the old-fashioned motorized trolley car as it follows a 30-mile circular route. Hop off at any one of a dozen stops (ticket sales reps are on hand at each), explore at leisure, and reboard when you please (the motorized trolley runs every half-hour). Stops include the Embarcadero, Horton Plaza, Gaslamp Quarter, Coronado, San Diego Zoo, Balboa Park, and Heritage Park. The trolleys run daily from 9 a.m., with final pickup at each stop between 4 and 6 p.m. The tour costs $20 for adults and $8 for kids 6 to 12 (free for under 5) for one complete loop, no matter how many times you hop on and off; if you get on and stay on, the ride takes about two hours.

The old soft shoe (s)

Many parts of San Diego are quite walkable. The following are places that offer good walking tours:

✔ **The Gaslamp Quarter Historical Foundation** (☎ 619-233-4692; www.gaslampquarter.org) offers two-hour tours of San Diego's liveliest neighborhood. Tours depart of the Gaslamp neighborhood on Saturdays at 1 a.m. from the **William Heath Davis House Museum,** 410 Island Ave., at 4th Avenue. An $8 donation is requested ($6 for seniors, military personnel, and students). Private group tours of six or more can be arranged.

✔ **La Jolla Walking Tours** (☎ 719-260-8787; www.lajollawalking tours.com) offer a 1½ hour walking tour of lovely La Jolla. The tours depart from the **Grande Colonial Hotel,** 910 Prospect St. (between Fay and Gerard avenues), Friday and Saturday at 10 a.m. Tours are $9. Reservations are required.

✔ **Coronado Touring** (☎ 935-435-5993 or 935-435-5444) is a great way to learn a ton about charming Coronado. The 90-minute tour is upbeat and informative, including a delicious dose of local scandal and gossip. Tours leave at 11 a.m. on Tuesday, Thursday, and Saturday from the **Glorietta Bay Inn,** across the street from Hotel Del Coronado; the price is $8. Reservations are suggested, because walk-ins are subject to availability.

Bay cruises

When the weather's fine — which is most of the time — nothing says "San Diego" like a little waterborne sightseeing. **Hornblower Cruises** (☎ **800-ON-THE-BAY** [800-668-4323], 619-686-8715; Internet: www. hornblower.com) is the local big cheese. In addition to one- and two-hour narrated tours of San Diego Bay, the company offers evening dinner/dance cruises, Sunday brunch cruises, and whale-watching trips in winter. Prices start at $13 for harbor cruises, $36 for meal cruises; kids are half-price.

Shopping at the Top

If you like to do your shopping in a mall, head to **Horton Plaza** in the **Gaslamp Quarter,** bounded by Broadway, 1st and 4th avenues and G Street (☎ **619-238-1596;** www.hortonplaza.shoppingtown.com). It's multilevel and rather whimsical, but the stores are rather conventional. The quarter is also known for its excellent art galleries, including **Many Hands,** 302 Island Ave. (☎ **619-557-8303**), a cooperative with 35 artists working in a variety of crafts. **Le Travel Store,** 745 4th Ave., between F and G streets (☎ **619-544-0005;** www.letravelstore.com), offers a good selection of luggage, travel books and maps, and groovy travel accessories.

Aunt Teek's guide to vintage treasures

If you're a collectibles hound, two enormous antique malls are guaranteed to leave you with dusty hands and a lighter wallet: Cracker Factory Antiques, 448 W. Market St. (at Columbia Street), downtown (☎ 619-233-1669), and Unicorn Antique Mall, 704 J St. (at 7th Ave.), just south of the Gaslamp Quarter (☎ 619-232-1696). Merchandise ranges from kitschy collectibles to "real" antiques (you know, Louis the Whichever stuff).

Depending on your tastes, you may think the Embarcadero's **Seaport Village,** 849 W. Harbor Dr. (☎ 619-235-4014), is quaintly appealing or completely contrived. This faux New England–style village is big for souvenir shopping and dining with a view. It's worth the trip, though, for a ride on the 1890 Looff carousel imported from Coney Island, New York.

Hillcrest

Compact Hillcrest is an ideal shopping destination. You can browse a unique and sometimes wacky mix of independent boutiques, bookstores, vintage clothing stores, memorabilia shops, chain stores, bakeries, and cafés. Start at the neighborhood's hub — the intersection of University and 5th avenues — and prepare yourself to drop a few dollars on parking (either meters or lots). Shops here tend to stay open later than in other parts of the city, and Tuesday nights, many local merchants offer 15% off all purchases.

Highlights include **Babette Schwartz,** 421 University Ave. (☎ 619-220-7048; www.babette.com), a provocative pop-culture emporium named for a local drag queen. The **Village Hat Shop,** 3821 4th Ave. (☎ 619-683-5533; Internet: www.villagehatshop.com), features head gear from straw hats to knit caps to classy fedoras, plus a mini-museum of vintage headwear.

If you love used and rare books, you'll want to poke around on 5th Avenue between University and Robinson. This block is also home to **Off the Record,** 3849 University Ave. (☎ 619-298-4755), a new and used record store with an alternative bent and the city's best vinyl selection. If vintage clothing is your passion, don't miss **Wear It Again Sam,** 3823 Fifth Ave., (☎ 619-299-0185), a classy step back in time.

Old Town

Yes, it's touristy (the local shopkeeper's motto is "ka-ching!"), but when you're looking for a classic souvenir of the cheesy variety — you know, San Diego-labeled T-shirts, baseball caps, snow domes, or those movable pens — this is the place to go. Milking the "old" even further, many of these shops boast a quasi-historic general-store theme. Keep your eyes open for artist's workshops and bona-fide galleries tucked away amidst the commercialism, where higher quality commands higher prices.

With mariachi music and Mexican archways setting the stage for import shops with wares from Central and South America, colorful **Bazaar del Mundo,** 2754 Calhoun St. (☎ 619-296-3161; Internet: www.bazaardel mundo.com), is a magnet. You won't find anything rare (or bargain-priced), but browsing can be fun.

La Jolla

Shopping is a major pastime here. Women's clothing boutiques tend to be conservative and costly, especially those lining Girard and Prospect streets. The many home-decor stores make for great window shopping, as do the ubiquitous jewelers — where Swiss watches, tennis bracelets, precious gems, and pearl necklaces sparkle in windows along every street.

No visit to La Jolla is complete without seeing **John Cole's Bookshop,** 780 Prospect St., at Eads Avenue (☎ **858-454-4766**), a local legend housed in a turn-of-the-century, wisteria-covered cottage. Look for cookbooks in the old kitchen, paperbacks in a former classroom, and CDs and harmonicas in the music corner. Sitting and reading in the patio garden is accepted, even encouraged.

Nightlife

For a rundown of the latest performances and evening events, check the "Night and Day" section of Thursday's *Union-Tribune* (www.uniontrib.com). You can easily find copies of the free weekly *Reader* (www.sdreader.com) and *What's Playing?,* the San Diego Performing Arts League's bimonthly guide (www.sandiegoonline.com/sdpal), around town.

You can save a bundle on theater and musical events at the half-price **Arts Tix** kiosk in Horton Plaza Park, at Broadway and 3rd Avenue. It's open Tuesday through Thursday from 11 a.m. to 6 p.m., Friday and Saturday from 10 a.m. to 6 p.m.; tickets are available day-of-show only (except for Sunday and Monday shows, sold on Saturday). Cash only. Call ☎ **619-497-5000** for more information and the daily offerings, or go online to www.sandiegoperforms.com and click on "Arts Tix." *Parking tip:* The Horton Plaza garage is most convenient, and Arts Tix will validate.

The play's the thing

It's well worth making the effort to catch a show at the Shakespearean-style **Old Globe Theatre** or its adjacent theaters, the open-air Lowell Davies Festival Theater and the intimate in-the-round **Cassius Carter Centre Stage.** Not only do these venues occupy a magical setting within lovely **Balboa Park,** but they attract expertly casted classics along with thought-provoking regional and experimental offerings. The season runs from January through October, with two to four plays going at any one time. Ticket prices range from around $23 to $39, with discounts for students and seniors. Call ☎ **619-239-2255** or the 24-hour hotline at ☎ **619-23-GLOBE** (619-234-5623), or go online at www.oldglobe.org.

The **La Jolla Playhouse,** on the University of California–San Diego (UCSD) campus at 2910 La Jolla Village Dr., at Torrey Pines Rd. (☎ **858-550-1010;**

Internet: www.lajollaplayhouse.com), stages six productions each year, usually from April or May through November. Each one has something outstanding to recommend it, whether a nationally acclaimed director or a highly touted revival. Tickets range from $21 to $52.

Any unsold tickets are available for $10 in a "public rush" sale ten minutes before the curtain goes up.

Play it loud: Live music

The Casbah

It may be a total dive, but this blaring downtown club has a well-earned rep for showcasing alternative and rock bands that either are, were, or will be famous. Consider buying advance tickets to avoid disappointment.

2501 Kettner Blvd., near the airport. ☎ **619-232-4355**. *Internet:* www.casbah music.com.

Belly Up

Another reason to head north to Solana Beach is the still-going-strong-after-nearly-30-years Belly Up, perhaps San Diego's best live venue, with acts ranging from locals to terrific out-of-towners, from rock to roots to regular Sunday-night salsa.

143 S. Cedros Ave., Solana Beach. ☎ **858-481-9022** *(recorded schedule), 858-481-8140 (information and tickets). Internet:* www.bellyup.com.*CA 92075*

Croce's Nightclubs

This loud, crowded gathering place is the cornerstone of Gaslamp Quarter nightlife. Two separate clubs a couple doors apart offer traditional jazz (Croce's Jazz Bar) and rhythm and blues (Croce's Top Hat) nightly. The music blares onto the street, making it easy to decide whether to go in or not. The cover charge is waived if you eat at the restaurant (see "Where to Dine in San Diego," earlier in this chapter).

802 5th Ave. (at F St.). ☎ **619-233-4355**. *Internet:* www.croces.com.

4th & B

Haphazard seating (balcony theater seats, cabaret tables) and a handful of bar/lounge niches make this no-frills venue, housed in a former bank, comfortable. The genre is no genre; everyone from B.B. King to Dokken to local-girl-made-good Jewel has performed here (recently, Pete Yorn and Lucinda Williams), in between regular bookings of the San Diego Chamber Orchestra.

345 B St. (at 4th Ave.). ☎ **619-231-4343**. *Internet:* www.4thandB.com.

Come here often? Bars and lounges

The Bitter End

With three floors, this self-important Gaslamp Quarter hot spot manages to be a sophisticated martini bar, after-hours dance club, and relaxing cocktail lounge all in one. Weekends are subject to velvet rope/dress code nonsense.

770 5th Ave. (at F St.). ☎ *619-338-9300. Internet:* www.thebitterend.com.

Cannibal Bar

Attached to the lobby of the Polynesian-themed Catamaran hotel, this loud bar is the place to go for a mean Mai Tai. Party central at the beach for thundering DJ-driven music, the Cannibal also books some very admirable bands now and then.

3999 Mission Blvd., Pacific Beach. ☎ *858-539-8650.*

Martini Ranch and Shaker Room

This Gaslamp Quarter's crowd pleaser boasts a 30-martini menu that may stretch the definition of "martini" a bit, but nevertheless features an impressive selection of vodkas and gins. Downstairs resembles an upscale sports bar, while upstairs is dotted with love seats and conversation pits. Dance Tuesday through Saturday in the Shaker Room.

528 F St. (between 5th and 6th aves.). ☎ *619-235-6100.*

Nunu's Cocktail Lounge

This is a perfect neighborhood place, provided you and your neighbors are more the cocktail-lounge hipster types. (We mean all this as a positive thing.) While neither snooty nor tony — though someone sure paid attention to the details here — it's both increasingly fashionable (in terms of popularity; in terms of decor, it's over the top in its efforts to please all tastes) and just the right place to stick $5 in the jukebox and drink through your selections. Noted for their Razzmatazz: raspberry Smirnoff mixed with cranberry juice.

3537 Fifth Ave. (in the Hillcrest area). ☎ *619-295-5878.*

Princess Pub & Grille

A local Anglophiles' haunt that's the place for a pint o' Bass, Fuller's, Watney's, or Guinness. This slice of Britain (in Little Italy, go figure) also serves up hearty pub grub.

1665 India St. (at Date St.). ☎ *619-702-3021. Internet:* www.princesspub.com.

Fast Facts

AAA

Downtown at 815 Date St., between 8th and 9th avenues (☎ 619-233-1000; www.aaa calif.com).

American Express

Travel services are available at the Hazard Center office (☎ 619-297-8101, 7610 Hazard Center Dr. #515).

Baby-Sitters

Marion's Childcare (☎ 619-582-5029) has bonded baby-sitters available to come to your hotel room.

Emergencies

For police, fire, highway patrol, or life-threatening medical emergencies, dial ☎ **911.**

Hotel Docs (☎ 800-468-3537) is a 24-hour network of physicians, dentists, and chiro-practors who claim they'll come to your hotel room within an hour to an hour and a half of your call.

Hospitals

The most conveniently located emergency room is at **UCSD Medical Center–Hillcrest,** 200 W. Arbor Dr. (☎ 619-543-6400); to get there, take 1st Avenue north, past Washington, and turn left on Arbor.

Internet Centers

Kinkos Copy Centers have ten outlets in San Diego with Internet access. Call 800-254-6575 for nearest location. Hours vary by location.

In Northside, the coffeehouse/study hall **Other Side,** 4096 30th St. (☎ 619-521-0533),

has one Internet terminal. Open daily from 6:30 a.m. to 12:30 a.m.

Newspapers and Magazines

The city's daily is the *San Diego Union-Tribune,* available from newsstands and vending machines around town. The free alternative weekly *Reader* is available at shops, restaurants, and public hot spots.

Police

Dial 911 in an emergency. For non-emergencies, contact the downtown precinct, 1401 Broadway (☎ 619-531-2000).

Post Office

Post offices are located downtown, at 815 E St. (at 8th Avenue), and at 51 Horton Plaza (beside the Westin Hotel). Call ☎ 800-ASK-USPS or log on to www.usps.gov to find the branch nearest you.

Taxes

Sales tax in shops and restaurants is 7%. Hotel tax is 10.5%.

Taxis

Orange Cab (☎ 619-291-3333), **San Diego Cab** (☎ 619-226-TAXI), and **Yellow Cab** (☎ 619-234-6161). In La Jolla, use **La Jolla Cab** (☎ 858-453-4222).

Transit Info

☎ 619-685-4900 for 24-hour recorded info, ☎ 619-233-3004 daily from 5:30 a.m. to 8:30 p.m. to speak with a real live person.

Weather

For local weather and surf reports, call ☎ 619-289-1212.

A side trip to Tijuana

Tijuana (tee-*wah*-nah), the fourth largest city in Mexico, lies just half an hour south of San Diego. If you asked us, of course, we wouldn't go there on a bet. And yet, we would tell you to go. Why? Well, for starters, you've never been, and at all times, we're in favor of new experiences, to say nothing of any opportunity to cross any border. It's just that Tijuana is hardly the best Mexico has to offer, and it's hardly the most authentic Mexican experience. It's a tourist trap of mass-produced crafts, knock-offs, and other dubious goods, and in between, there is mucho drinking going on (it's a sacred destination for rowdy frat boys). But it's an experience, to be sure, and easy to be had.

Getting to Tijuana from San Diego is simple and inexpensive, but beware; the crossing at the border is taking longer and longer. Driving yourself is also a bad idea because of the following:

✔ U.S. insurance (and many rental-car agreements) isn't valid across the border.

✔ Traffic is terrible in Tijuana.

✔ Getting through customs and back across the border can be more difficult if you're on your own.

✔ Having an accident in Mexico, major or minor, is a bad idea.

Note: Although a passport isn't required of U.S. citizens, carrying yours will speed up your return across the border. Be sure to at least have your driver's license handy.

Leave your car behind instead and hop aboard the **San Diego Trolley** (☎ **619-685-4900**, 619-233-3004; Internet: www.sdcommute.com/sdmts), nicknamed the "Tijuana Trolley" for good reason. Get off at the last stop in San Ysidro. From there, just follow the signs to walk across the border. The one-way fare for the 40-minute trip is $2, and the trolleys run constantly, with the last return from San Ysidro after midnight. On Saturdays, the trolley runs 24 hours. Or leave your car at one of many **border parking lots,** which cost $8 to $10 for the day. Most lots are just a block or two away from the pedestrian walkway into Tijuana. Exercise caution, especially after dark, and don't be one of the last cars left.

After you're in Tijuana, getting around by walking or taxi is easy. Cabs line up around most of the visitor hot spots. Tijuana's main event is bustling **Avenida Revolucion,** the city's original bawdy center for illicit fun. Changing times and civic improvement have toned it down a bit; shopping and drinking are now the main order of business. If a marketplace atmosphere and spirited bargaining are what you're looking for, head to **Mercado de Artesanias (Crafts Market),** located at Calle 2 and Avenida Negrete, where vendors with pottery, clayware, clothing, and other crafts fill an entire city block.

Before you go, get information and maps from **Baja California Tourism Information,** 7860 Mission Center Court, no. 202, in Mission Valley (☎ **800-522-1516**, 800-225-2786, 619-299-8518; Internet: www.travelfile.com/get/bajaca).

Gathering More Information

The **San Diego Convention and Visitors Bureau's International Visitor Information Center** (☎ 619-236-1212) is downtown on 1st Avenue at F Street, street level at Horton Plaza. They can provide you with the slick, glossy *San Diego Visitors Planning Guide,* as well as a money-saving coupon book. Open Monday through Saturday from 8:30 a.m. to 5 p.m., plus Sunday from 11 a.m. to 5 p.m. June through August.

The **Mission Bay Visitor Information Center** (☎ 619-276-8200) is on Mission Bay Drive at the end of Clairemont Drive. Near the San Diego Zoo is the **Balboa Park Visitors Center** (☎ 619-239-0512), in the House of Hospitality on El Prado.

Information on La Jolla is distributed by the **La Jolla Town Council,** 7734 Herschel Ave., between Silverado and Kline streets (☎ 858-454-1444). You'll find all you need to know about Coronado at the Coronado Visitors Bureau, 1047 B Ave., near Orange Avenue (☎ 619-437-8788 Internet: www. coronadohistory.org).

You can find San Diego's official Web site at www.sandiego.org. A guide to Gaslamp Quarter dining and shopping is at www.gaslamp.org. Official Coronado information is available at www.coronado.ca.us.

A great source for club and show listings is the *San Diego Reader* site at www.sdreader.com. *San Diego* magazine's www.sandiego-online. com features listings for dining and events. CitySearch's www.signon sandiego.com, is run by the *Union-Tribune* and offers a mix of current news, entertainment listings, and visitor information. *Digital City San Diego,* at www.digitalcity.com/sandiego, targets locals, making it great for off-the-beaten-tourist-path recommendations.

Part VI

The Part of Tens

The 5th Wave   By Rich Tennant

In this part . . .

Every *For Dummies* book contains a Part of Tens. If Parts III through V are the main course of your meal, think of these fun chapters as dessert. If you feel like watching California-specific movies to get you in the mood before your trip, check out Chapter 26. Or if you want to catch a whiff of West Coast craziness, go to Chapter 27, where you discover where you can get down and wacky the way real Californians do.

Chapter 26

Ten Quintessentially Californian Movies to Watch Before You Leave Home

In This Chapter

▶ Seeing California through Hollywood's eyes

▶ Going on location through film

The Golden State is synonymous with the silver screen, of course. So what better way to bone up for your vacation than to pop a few flicks into the VCR? Here are our picks, in no particular order, for the movies that best capture the spirit of the most dramatically diverse and phenomenally photogenic state in the Union.

What's Up, Doc? (1972)

This Peter Bogdanovich–directed, Buck Henry–scribed gem starring Barbra Streisand and Ryan O'Neal shows off the hilly streets of San Francisco — especially Chinatown — at their most colorful and romantic.

Vertigo (1958)

Possibly the greatest movie director of all time, Alfred Hitchcock always used locations well — remember Mount Rushmore in *North by Northwest?* In *Vertigo,* the suspense master uses San Francisco to dizzying effect (pun intended).

 Watch for a few key locations. The Empire Hotel (where James Stewart eventually finds Kim Novak) is now the York Hotel, home to the sexy Plush Room cabaret showroom (see Chapter 9). Also, if you visit the Spanish mission of San Juan Bautista, featured in the film (it's a short drive from Monterey, near the junction of U.S. 101 and Highway 156), you'll find that it doesn't actually have a bell tower. Hitchcock's minions added the movie's bell tower with editing-room smoke and mirrors.

The Big Picture (1989)

Director Christopher Guest's first feature is a dead-on and deadly satire of the movie industry, filmed presumably on a shoestring around Hollywood and just outside in the desert. Hilarious — we watch it once a year just to laugh ourselves silly, and wince over how recognizable it all is — and we don't just mean the locations.

Monterey Pop (1969)

Monterey Pop, D.A. Pennebaker's first-rate rockumentary, chronicles the glorious three-day music festival that was actually a better realization of the Summer of Love dream than Woodstock ever hoped to be. The film wonderfully captures '60s' San Francisco's Haight-Ashbury vibe and the California sound, including groups such as the Mamas and the Papas (whose leader, the late John Phillips, was the brains behind the event), Jefferson Airplane, Janis Joplin with Big Brother and the Holding Company, Jimi Hendrix, Canned Heat, The Who, and others, plus a stunning performance by Otis Redding.

Star Trek IV: The Voyage Home (1986)

The Leonard Nimoy–directed movie — the fourth full-length feature in the *Star Trek* canon, and maybe the best — draws Kirk and crew to 20th-century San Francisco with the call of the humpback whale. The movie includes wonderful and hugely entertaining fish-out-of-water city scenes, great footage shot at the Monterey Bay Aquarium and the Golden Gate Bridge, and a terrifically eco-minded save-the-whale storyline.

Play Misty for Me (1971)

Clint Eastwood made his directorial debut with *Play Misty for Me,* the winningly creepy thriller co-starring Jessica Walter (and Donna Mills, of quintessentially Californian *Knots Landing* fame). Young, studly Clint looks mighty fine, but the real star of the show is stunning Carmel, which Clint films with a genuine hometown love and a master's eye.

(You may remember that Eastwood was elected mayor of Carmel-by-the-Sea in 1986; he still owns the Mission Ranch, an elegant country inn, and resides in town.) Watch for the great footage of Big Sur's Bixby Bridge, too.

The Grapes of Wrath (1940)

The John Ford–directed, Academy Award–winning film of dispossessed "Okie" dustbowl farmers who migrate west to the promised land — California — wins a spot on this list not for its tremendous footage of the Golden State, but because it beautifully evokes California's agrarian story. An ideal moving-picture rendition of one of the many classic California novels written by Monterey's favorite son, John Steinbeck, *The Grapes of Wrath* also serves to curry excitement for a visit to the new National Steinbeck Center, a stone's throw from Monterey in Steinbeck's hometown of Salinas (often called the breadbasket of California).

Gidget (1965)

Perky Sally Field is the ultimate California beach girl in the ultimate California beach movie, *Gidget*. This innocent romp is really a joy to watch — far superior to the Frankie Avalon/Annette Funicello beach movies — with excellent footage of Malibu Beach and Pacific Coast Highway (cruisin' with the top down, of course). Dave Grusin is responsible for the super-groovy soundtrack.

Chinatown (1974)

Possibly the finest noir ever committed to film, *Chinatown* uses L.A. in the '70s to re-create L.A. in the '30s impeccably. Not only did director Roman Polanski (pre-exile) capture the City of Angels masterfully, but writer Robert Towne works in an essential slice of city history: the dirty dealing and power-grabbing of water rights that allowed — for better or worse — the infant desert city to blossom into the sprawling metropolis you see today. And, of course, this true classic features Jack Nicholson as the hard-boiled detective embroiled with femme fatale Faye Dunaway, plus legendary Hollywood heavyweight John Huston as the evil genius behind the Chandleresque web of intrigue.

The Player (1992)

One of Robert Altman's many "comeback" films, *The Player* realistically captures the seedy underbelly and soul-selling seductive power of Hollywood influence and celebrity. Everybody who's anybody in the movie industry knows how scarily close to home Tim Robbins' portrayal of beleaguered studio exec Griffin Mill hits. The film features great studio backlot shots and city footage throughout, plus some terrific scenes at the Palm Springs spa resort Two Bunch Palms.

The restaurant where Griffin runs into Angelica Huston and John Cusack is the **Ivy,** still a hotter-than-hot power lunch spot at 133 N. Robertson Blvd. in West Hollywood (☎ **310-274-8303**).

Runners-up: The Second-Best California Flicks

Try these films for more California cool:

- ✔ *Some Like It Hot* (1959), stars Marilyn Monroe, Tony Curtis, Jack Lemmon, and San Diego's legendary **Hotel del Coronado.**

- ✔ In the original *Dirty Harry* (1971), gruff Clint Eastwood takes on the scum of the earth on the streets of San Francisco.

- ✔ *East of Eden* (1955), another classic John Steinbeck–scribed California story translated to film, features James Dean.

- ✔ In *Same Time, Next Year* (1978), Alan Alda and Ellen Burstyn rendezvous on the glorious Mendocino coast for 26 consecutive years.

- ✔ *Palm Springs Weekend* (1963), stars Troy Donahue, an apple-cheeked Connie Stevens, and America's coolest desert town in its full Atomic Age finery.

- ✔ Steve Martin's *L.A. Story* (1991) a romantic look at everything that's wonderfully silly about life in contemporary Tinseltown.

- ✔ *Valley Girl* (1983), starring a teenage Nicolas Cage, is an underdog in a teen genre that includes *Fast Times at Ridgemont High* and *Clueless,* but it comes out a winner because of its New-Wave-Boy-meets-mall-lovin'-Valley-Girl love story at the height of Valley Girl mania.

- ✔ *L.A. Confidential* (1997) is *Chinatown's* finest successor in the L.A.-as-noir-landscape category.

- ✔ *Pretty Woman* (1990) is appropriate for the Sunset Strip and Rodeo Drive locations.

- ✔ Finally, check out any movie with "Beverly Hills" in the title (*Slums of Beverly Hills, Down and Out in Beverly Hills, Beverly Hills Cop . . .*).

Chapter 27

The Ten Wackiest Annual Events

● ●

In This Chapter

▶ Having a one-of-a-kind California experience

▶ Jumping frogs, racing worms, telling tales, and performing artistically

▶ Celebrating garlic, building sandcastles, showing weeds — all the doo-dah-day

● ●

California, in case you haven't heard, can be a kooky place. After all, strangeness is one of the Left Coast's most appealing qualities.

The yearly proceedings listed in this chapter — which hold their own on the annual statewide calendar next to such respected traditions as the Tournament of Roses Parade and cultured celebrations like the Monterey Jazz Festival — offer you the chance to throw your reserve to the wind and join in the nutty fun. Or you're welcome to just point and hoot from the sidelines, if you prefer.

Peg Leg Smith's Liars Contest

Where: Borrego Springs, San Diego County

When: Saturday nearest to April Fool's Day (natch)

This tall-tale-telling competition is the legacy of wooden-limbed yarn-spinner Thomas Long "Peg Leg" Smith, who, in 1829 or thereabouts (dates tended to be somewhat fluid in Peg Leg's world), found a few gold-specked rocks in the desert. Rather than actually bothering to look for more, Peg Leg spent the next 35 years weaving an increasingly Bunyanlike tale about his lost Borrego Springs gold mine into Old West legend.

Storytellers and listeners gather annually at the Peg Leg Monument in Anza Borrego Desert State Park to honor Peg Leg's chutzpah and have a little fun. You're welcome to gather around the campfire and just listen or do some spinning yourself, as long as your tale

✔ Has something to do with gold mining in the Southwest

✔ Doesn't last longer than five minutes

✔ Contains nothing that any reasonable listener might actually mistake for the truth

Call the **Borrego Springs Chamber of Commerce** at ☎ **800-559-5524** or 760-767-5555 for details.

Calaveras County Fair and Jumping Frog Jubilee

Where: Angels Camp, Gold Country

When: Third weekend in May

Inspired by Mark Twain's joyful short story "The Celebrated Jumping Frog of Calaveras County," this yearly competition is the Olympics of frog jumping. Really. Frog jockeys (yep, that's what they're called) arrive from all over the globe with their lean 'n' mean amphibians in tow, which compete for cash prizes as large as 5,000 smackeroos. The races are a hoot to watch, and the accompanying three days of festivities — which include the crowning of this year's Miss Calaveras (a human teenage beauty, not a frog) — are festive and fun. If you and your leaper dream of riches and glory, however, start training now: The current world frog-jumping record is 21 feet, 5¾ inches, set in 1986 by Rosie the Ribiter of Santa Clara, CA. Call the **Calaveras County Fairgrounds** at ☎ **209-736-2561** or visit www.frogtown.org.

Ferndale Cross-Country Kinetic Sculpture Race

Where: Humboldt County, Redwood Country

When: Memorial Day weekend

One of the country's coolest annual events is this ingenious race, in which wild and crazy people in wild and crazy people-powered sculptures race for three days and 38 miles across land, sand, and sea, from Arcata to the Victorian-cute town of Ferndale.

The mobile art must be entirely people powered, must measure no more than 8 × 14 feet, and cannot be inherently dangerous to driver or spectator. Otherwise, anything goes and usually does; in the 30-plus-year history of the race, contraptions have ranged from giant watermelons to amphibious armadillos, and pilots have run the gamut from lone souls to teams of 12.

Just reading the rules is great fun; witness no. 201a, which includes the following provision: "Since mothers are discouraged from running alongside, racers must carry a comforting item of Psychological Luxury no smaller than a restaurant coffee cup at all times. An old security blanket (i.e., your 'binkie'), a soft teddy bear or sock doll will suffice. Teddy bears are highly recommended." Needless to say, it's about the race, not the winner. For more information on participating and spectating, call ☎ **707-786-9259** or visit www.humguide.com/kinetic.

International Worm Races

Where: Clearlake, Lake County (north of Napa Valley)

When: Independence Day

Launched in 1966 by a descendant of Mark Twain, this hugely popular event wins first prize for sheer ridiculousness. The "race" track is a four-foot-square board with a two-foot target painted on it. Two to five worms — either night crawlers or reds — are placed on the bull's-eye, and the first to inch its way across the edge of the outer circle wins. The day's grand champion wins a $100 cash prize (which begs the question, what do worms do with money, anyway?).

The ultimate worm-on-worm challenge takes place at Clearlake's Redbud Park immediately following the annual Lions Club Fourth of July Parade. Entry is $2; sign up early, because the first 200 entrants receive official Worm Race Pins. Don't have your own red worm or night crawler to enter? No problem! You can rent fully trained worms from the worm "stable" (whatever that is) just prior to race time. Call ☎ **707-994-3600** for details and entry forms, or visit www.clearlake.ca.us.

Gilroy Garlic Festival

Where: Gilroy (east of Santa Cruz, south of San Jose)

When: Last full weekend in July

The Garlic Capital of the World celebrates its cash crop with this ultra-stinky food fest. This is one of the biggest, best, and most well-attended food festivals in the entire Golden State, ideal for garlic addicts (and you know if you are). In addition to garlicky eats from all over the culinary map — garlic ice cream, yum! — the festival features arts and crafts vendors, live bands, the Tour de Garlique bike ride, the Miss Gilroy Garlic pageant (a dubious honor if ever there was one), and a Listerine table (just kidding). Attention, cooks: Enter the Great Garlic Cook-off, and you could go home a thousand bucks richer. Call ☎ **408-842-1625** or visit `www.gilroygarlicfestival.com` for further details.

Pageant of the Masters

Where: Laguna Beach, Orange County

When: July–August

Ever think *The Last Supper* was too flat, the *Mona Lisa* too stiff, *The Blue Boy* a tad too, well, two-dimensional? Then this is the event for you. Watch master artworks spring to life in this truly bizarre yet awe-inspiring performance-art gala, first launched in artsy Laguna in 1932 and going strong ever since. This very serious affair features trained actors working on intricate artist-designed sets to create living, breathing tableaux that remain remarkably faithful to the original, with dramatic narration and full orchestral accompaniment in a lovely alfresco setting. This pageant is fantastic, in the truest sense of the word.

You can, and should, order your pageant tickets in advance by calling ☎ **800-487-3378** or 949-497-6582. Come early in the day so you can also enjoy the **Festival of the Arts,** an outdoor art show featuring first-rate artists working in all media. You can find additional details on the excellent Web site (`www.foapom.com`).

U.S. Open Sandcastle Competition

Where: Imperial Beach (just south of San Diego)

When: A three-day weekend in late July or August

What's more fun than sandcastles? Nothing — especially when they're astoundingly complex, larger-than-life sand sculptures of everything from Noah's Ark to lobsters (complete with melted butter- and lemon-shaped sand on the side) to scenes from the San Diego skyline. This world-class competition may be the best of California's many beach events — the huge crowds think so. The throng comes out in full force not only for the main competition but also for the pancake breakfasts, food and music vendors, parade, and kids' sandcastle-building competition. Even if you don't make it for the actual event, you may be able to view the leftovers in the weeks that follow — as long as rain doesn't wash 'em away, that is. Call ☎ **619-424-6663** or 629-424-3151, or point your Web browser to www.ci.imperial-beach.ca.us/sand-hm.htm.

Underwater Pumpkin-Carving Contest

Where: La Jolla

When: Weekend before Halloween

Underwater pumpkin carving seems even a couple of notches less practical than underwater basketweaving, yet plenty of sporting divers have turned out for this Halloween event each year since 1981. Nobody takes it very seriously — one year the panel of judges was the staff of a local dive shop, the next year five kids off the beach — but it's always a fun party, and the surfacing jack-o'-lanterns are mighty impressive. Even though the bulk of the action takes place below sea level, the event is still fun to watch. For details, call **Ocean Enterprises** at ☎ **858-565-6054.**

Weed Show

Where: Twentynine Palms (gateway to Joshua Tree National Park)

When: Usually the first weekend of November

No, this festival doesn't focus on *that* kind of weed. Still, you'll think the locals have been smokin' it, what with the mind-boggling sculptures they create in the name of art using found objects and, yes, weeds. Lest you think this desert event, sponsored by the Twentynine Palms Historical Society, is small potatoes, think again: More than 250 entries are usually up for critique in multiple-judged categories during this weekend-long event. Call ☎ **760-367-3926** or 760-367-3445 for the exact date and additional details (including entry forms), or point your Web browser to www.twentynine.com.

Doo Dah Parade

Where: Pasadena

When: Thanksgiving weekend

This outrageous annual event — referred to in town as the "other" parade — was born way back in 1978 as a zany spoof of New Year's Day's annual Tournament of Roses promenade. Doo Dah has since grown into a left-of-center institution all its own, but age hasn't cost it an ounce of silliness.

Parading participants usually include the Synchronized Precision Briefcase Drill Team (whose twirling skills are unparalleled), drag queen cheerleaders (representing West Hollywood, of course), the BBQ and Hibachi Marching Grill Team, a kazoo-tooting marching band, and many more — plenty to make the Ministry of Silly Walks mighty proud. Radio personality Dr. Demento often serves as Master of Ceremonies.

New surprises pop up every year, so even if you've been before, joining the wild, weird party is worth the effort. Call ☎ **626-449-3689** or the **Pasadena Convention and Visitors Bureau** at ☎ **626-795-9311** for this year's date.

Appendix

Quick Concierge

• •

Fast Facts

American Automobile Association (AAA)

Call ☎ 800-564-6222 or visit www.aaa.com for national information. The **California State AAA** serves Northern California; call ☎ 800-922-8228 or visit www.csaa.com to locate the office nearest your current Northern California location (on the Web, click on Member Services for the office locator). The **Automobile Club of Southern California** is AAA's Southern California arm; call ☎ 800-222-8794 or point your Web browser to www.aaa-calif.com for more information or to locate an office.

For roadside assistance, members can call AAA at ☎ 800-400-4AAA in California, ☎ 800-AAA-HELP anywhere else in the United States.

American Express

The San Francisco walk-in office is located at 455 Market St., at First Street (☎ 415-536-2600), open Monday through Friday from 9 a.m. to 5:30 p.m., Saturday from 10 a.m. to 2 p.m.

On the Central Coast, you'll find an official Amex travel office in Cambria at Traveltime, 4210 Bridge St. Unit 6 (☎ 805-927-7799) and at two Santa Barbara Travel Bureau locations: 1028 State St., Santa Barbara (☎ 805-683-1666) and in neighboring Montecito at 1127 Coast Village Rd. (☎ 805-969-7746).

Los Angeles area locations include 8493 W. 3rd St., at La Cienega Blvd., across from the Beverly Center (☎ 310-659-1682) and 327 N. Beverly Dr., between Brighton and Dayton ways, Beverly Hills (☎ 310-274-8277).

San Diego has an office at the Hazard Center office (☎ 619-297-8101, 7610 Hazard Center Dr. #515).

In Palm Springs, Andersen Travel Service, 700 E. Tahquitz Canyon Way (☎ 760-325-2001), serves as an official travel office.

To make inquiries or to locate other branch offices, call ☎ 800-AXP-TRIP or visit www.americanexpress.com.

ATM

Unless you need dough in the backwoods of Big Sur, you'll have no trouble finding an ATM in California. Branches of the Golden State's most popular banks are everywhere, with virtually all connected to the global ATM networks that your home bank is affiliated with. **Cirrus** (☎ 800-424-7787) and **Plus** (☎ 800-843-7587) are the two most popular networks; call or check online for ATM locations at your destination. Most supermarkets also contain ATMs.

One of California's most popular banks, with branches throughout the state, is **Wells Fargo Bank,** which is linked to all the major worldwide networks. To find the one nearest you, point your Web browser to www.wellsfargo.com/findus.

Emergencies

No matter where you are in California, dial ☎ **911** in any emergency, whether it requires police, the fire department, or an ambulance.

Highway Conditions

Call **Cal-Trans** at ☎ **800-427-ROAD** (800-427-7623) or 916-445-1534, or point your Web browser to www.dot.gove/hq/ roadinfo for complete California highway information. Whether you call or go online, keep the highway numbers you're interested in handy at all times.

Information

The **California Division of Tourism** (☎ **800-862-2543**) can send you a free vacation planner that serves as a good introduction to the Golden State. Their extensive Web site, at www.gocalif.com, is an equally useful source that can link you to local visitor bureaus throughout the state.

The state also runs convenient welcome centers in San Francisco at Fisherman's Wharf, Pier 39, at Beach and Embarcadero streets (☎ **415-956-3493**), and in Los Angeles at 8500 Beverly Blvd. (☎ **310-854-7616**).

See the "Gathering More Information" section in each destination chapter for the best local information sources for individual destinations.

Liquor Laws

The legal drinking age of 21 is strictly enforced throughout the state, so have your ID handy even if your college days were a decade or two ago. Liquor and grocery stores, as well as some drugstores, can legally sell packaged alcoholic beverages between 6 a.m. and 2 a.m., although in some communities the hours of sales may be less at certain outlets, such as grocery stores.

Maps

AAA supplies good maps of California to members only, and they're free if you're a card carrier. You can obtain a terrific freeway map covering the entire state and pick and choose city and regional maps to suit your needs. For more information on becoming a member or locating the nearest office in California, see the American Automobile Association listing at the beginning of this appendix (also check out Chapter 4).

If you're not going the AAA way or you just want other sources, a comprehensive road guide is the Thomas Bros. California Road Atlas. You can get this and other maps from major online booksellers and bookstores. We highly recommend acquiring a good state map before you come, but keep in mind that you'll often get the best local maps after you arrive, especially in smaller towns.

Safety

For **general safety issues,** use your common sense, just like you would at home or anywhere else. Avoid deserted and poorly lit areas, especially at night. Always lock the doors of your rental car and don't keep anything valuable inside; any thief worth his or her salt can get into your locked car quicker without a key than you can get in with one.

Be alert in **hotels** and don't let strange folks into your hotel room unless they are clearly personnel that you expect or have summoned. Don't hesitate to call the front desk to verify an employee's identity; nothing's too silly where your safety's concerned. And be sure to store your valuables and cash in the in-room or behind-the-desk safe; don't just leave them in your hotel room.

If you have a **cellphone,** bring it with you, or rent a phone after you're in California to avoid paying high roaming charges. You'll likely be doing a lot of driving, and having a cellphone with you can make all the difference in the world if your car breaks down or you get lost.

In the unlikely event of an **earthquake,** keep these basics in mind: Don't run outside;

instead, move away from windows and toward the building's center. Crouch under a desk or table or other sturdy piece of furniture or stand in a doorway. If you must leave the building, use the stairs, not the elevator. If you're in the car, pull over to the side of the road and stay in your car — but don't pull over until you're away from bridges, overpasses, telephone poles, and power lines. If you're out walking, stay in the open, away from trees, power lines, and buildings.

Smoking

California has the best and worst smoking laws in the United States, depending on your point of view. Basically, the rule is this: If you're indoors, you're not allowed to light up.

Smoking is prohibited in virtually all indoor public spaces — yes, including restaurants (hence the proliferation of patio dining, where smoking is usually allowed). Many bars and clubs openly defy the law, however.

A good number of hotels, especially smaller places, also prohibit in-room smoking, so be sure to ask, if it matters to you.

You must be 18 or older to buy cigarettes in California.

Taxes

California's statewide sales tax is 7.25%. Some cities tack on an additional percentage up to 1.25%. The base hotel tax is 10%, with some municipalities adding an additional surcharge (which is noted in the hotel section of each chapter of this book).

Time Zone

California lies in the Pacific time zone, which is eight hours behind Greenwich mean time, and three hours behind the east coast. The entire state practices daylight saving time from April to October.

Weather

To check the weather forecasts online, log onto www.weather.com or www.cnn.com/weather. Also note that many local visitors bureaus have weather links, so you may want to check each city or region's official site (listed in the "Gathering More Information" section of each destination chapter) to get a local link.

Useful Toll-Free Numbers & Web Sites

Airlines

Air Canada
☎ 800-776-3000
www.aircanada.ca

Alaska Airlines
☎ 800-426-0333
www.alaskaair.com

Aloha Airlines
☎ 800-367-5250 or 877-879-2564
www.alohaairlines.com

American Airlines
☎ 800-433-7300
www.aa.com

American Trans Air
☎ 800-225-2995
www.ata.com

America West Airlines
☎ 800-235-9292
www.americawest.com

British Airways
☎ 800-247-9297
☎ 0845-77-333-77 in Britain
www.britishairways.com

Continental Airlines
☎ 800-525-0280
www.continental.com

Delta Air Lines
☎ 800-221-1212
www.delta.com

Hawaiian Airlines
☎ 800-367-5320
www.hawaiianair.com

Horizon Air
☎ 800-547-9308
www.horizonair.com

Northwest Airlines
☎ 800-225-2525
www.nwa.com

Southwest Airlines
☎ 800-435-9792
www.southwest.com

United Airlines
☎ 800-241-6522
www.united.com

US Airways
☎ 800-428-4322
www.usairways.com

Virgin Atlantic Airways
☎ 800-862-8621 in Continental U.S.
☎ 01293 450 150 in Britain
www.fly.virgin.com

Car-Rental Agencies

Advantage
☎ 800-777-5500
www.advantagerent.com

Alamo
☎ 800-327-9633
www.goalamo.com

Avis
☎ 800-230-4898 in U.S.
☎ 800-272-5871 in Canada
www.avis.com

Budget
☎ 800-527-0700
☎ 800-826-5510 TTY
https://rent.drivebudget.com

Dollar
☎ 800-800-4000
www.dollar.com

Enterprise
☎ 800-325-8007
www.enterprise.com

Hertz
☎ 800-654-3131
www.hertz.com

National
☎ 800-CAR-RENT
www.nationalcar.com

Payless
☎ 800-PAYLESS
www.paylesscarrental.com

Rent-A-Wreck
☎ 800-944-7501
rent-a-wreck.com

Thrifty
☎ 800-367-2277
www.thrifty.com

Major Hotel & Motel Chains

Best Western International
☎ 800-528-1234
www.bestwestern.com

Clarion Hotels
☎ 800-CLARION
www.hotelchoice.com

Comfort Inns & Suites
☎ 800-228-5150
www.hotelchoice.com

Courtyard by Marriott
☎ 800-321-2211
www.courtyard.com

Days Inn
☎ 800-325-2525
www.daysinn.com

Doubletree Hotels
☎ 800-222-TREE
www.doubletree.com

Econo Lodges
☎ 800-55-ECONO
www.hotelchoice.com

Fairfield Inn by Marriott
☎ 800-228-2800
www.marriott.com

Four Seasons Hotels & Resorts
☎ 800-819-5053
☎ 800-268-6282 in Canada
☎ 00800-6488-6488 in Britain
www.fshr.com

Hampton Inn
☎ 800-HAMPTON (800-426-7666)
www.hampton-inn.com

Hilton Hotels
☎ 800-HILTONS (800-445-8667)
www.hilton.com

Holiday Inn
☎ 800-HOLIDAY (800-465-4329)
www.basshotels.com

Howard Johnson
☎ 800-654-2000
www.hojo.com

Hyatt Hotels
☎ 800-228-9000
www.hyatt.com

La Quinta Motor Inns
☎ 800-531-5900
www.laquinta.com

Marriott Hotels
☎ 800-228-9290
www.marriott.com

Motel 6
☎ 800-4-MOTEL6 (800-466-8536)
www.motel6.com

Quality Inns
☎ 800-228-5151
www.hotelchoice.com

Radisson Hotels International
☎ 800-333-3333
www.radisson.com

Ramada Inns
☎ 800-2-RAMADA (800-272-6232)
www.ramada.com

Red Carpet Inns
☎ 800-251-1962
www.reservahost.com

Red Lion Inns
☎ 800-RED-LION (800-733-5466)
www.redlion.com

Red Roof Inns
☎ 800-RED-ROOF (800-733-7663)
www.redroof.com

Residence Inn by Marriott
☎ 800-331-3131
www.marriott.com

Rodeway Inns
☎ 800-228-2000

Sheraton Hotels & Resorts
☎ 800-325-3535
www.sheraton.com

Super 8 Motels
☎ 800-800-8000
www.super8.com

Travelodge
☎ 800-255-3050
www.travelodge.com

Vagabond Inns
☎ 800-522-1555
www.vagabondinns.com

W Hotels
☎ 877-946-8357
www.whotels.com

Wyndham Hotels & Resorts
☎ 800-822-4200 in Continental U.S. and Canada
www.wyndham.com

Where to Get More Information

For information on the state as a whole, contact the **California Office of Tourism** (801 K. St., Suite 1600, Sacramento, CA 95812; ☎ **800-862-2543**; www.gocalif.ca.gov) and ask for a free information packet. For information on specific California cities or towns, contact that town's tourism bureau or chamber of commerce (see the appropriate chapter in this book for listed contact information). For information on California's national parks, contact the **Western Region Information Center** (National Park Service, Fort Mason, Building 201, San Francisco, CA 94123; ☎ **415-556-0560;** www.nps.gov). For information on California state parks, contact the **Department of Parks and Recreation** (P.O. Box 94296-0001; ☎ **916-653-6995;** http://cal-parks.ca.gov).

Making Dollars and Sense of It

Expense	Daily cost	x	Number of days	=	Total
Airfare					
Local transportation					
Car rental					
Lodging (with tax)					
Parking					
Breakfast					
Lunch					
Dinner					
Snacks					
Entertainment					
Babysitting					
Attractions					
Gifts & souvenirs					
Tips					
Other					
Grand Total					

Fare Game: Choosing an Airline

When looking for the best airfare, you should cover all your bases — 1) consult a trusted travel agent; 2) contact the airline directly, via the airline's toll-free number and/or Web site; 3) check out one of the travel-planning Web sites, such as www.frommers.com.

Travel Agency_____ Phone_____

    Agent's Name_____ Quoted fare_____

Airline 1_____ Quoted fare_____

    Toll-free number/Internet_____

Airline 2_____ Quoted fare_____

    Toll-free number/Internet_____

Web site 1_____ Quoted fare_____

Web site 2_____ Quoted fare_____

Departure Schedule & Flight Information

Airline_____ Flight #_____ Confirmation #_____

Departs_____ Date _____ Time _____ a.m./p.m.

Arrives_____ Date _____ Time _____ a.m./p.m.

Connecting Flight (if any)

Amount of time between flights_____ hours/mins

Airline_____ Flight #_____ Confirmation #_____

Departs_____ Date _____ Time _____ a.m./p.m.

Arrives_____ Date _____ Time _____ a.m./p.m.

Return Trip Schedule & Flight Information

Airline_____ Flight #_____ Confirmation #_____

Departs_____ Date _____ Time _____ a.m./p.m.

Arrives_____ Date _____ Time _____ a.m./p.m.

Connecting Flight (if any)

Amount of time between flights_____ hours/mins

Airline_____ Flight #_____ Confirmation #_____

Departs_____ Date _____ Time _____ a.m./p.m.

Arrives_____ Date _____ Time _____ a.m./p.m.

Sweet Dreams: Choosing Your Hotel

Make a list of all the hotels where you'd like to stay and then check online and call the local and toll-free numbers to get the best price. You should also check with a travel agent, who may be able to get you a better rate.

Hotel & page	Location	Internet	Tel. (local)	Tel. (Toll-free)	Quoted rate

Hotel Checklist

Here's a checklist of things to inquire about when booking your room, depending on your needs and preferences.

- ❏ Smoking/smoke-free room
- ❏ Noise (if you prefer a quiet room, ask about proximity to elevator, bar/restaurant, pool, meeting facilities, renovations, and street)
- ❏ View
- ❏ Facilities for children (crib, roll-away cot, babysitting services)
- ❏ Facilities for travelers with disabilities
- ❏ Number and size of bed(s) (king, queen, double/full-size)
- ❏ Is breakfast included? (buffet, continental, or sit-down?)
- ❏ In-room amenities (hair dryer, iron/board, minibar, etc.)
- ❏ Other_____

Places to Go, People to See, Things to Do

Enter the attractions you would most like to see and decide how they'll fit into your schedule. Next, use the "Going My Way" worksheets that follow to sketch out your itinerary.

Attraction/activity	Page	Amount of time you expect to spend there	Best day and time to go

Going "My" Way

Day 1

Hotel_____ Tel._____

Morning_____

_____

Lunch_____ Tel._____

Afternoon_____

_____

Dinner_____ Tel._____

Evening_____

_____

Day 2

Hotel_____ Tel._____

Morning_____

_____

Lunch_____ Tel._____

Afternoon_____

_____

Dinner_____ Tel._____

Evening_____

_____

Day 3

Hotel_____ Tel._____

Morning_____

_____

Lunch_____ Tel._____

Afternoon_____

_____

Dinner_____ Tel._____

Evening_____

_____

Going "My" Way

Day 4

Hotel _____ Tel. _____

Morning _____

_____

Lunch _____ Tel. _____

Afternoon _____

_____

Dinner _____ Tel. _____

Evening _____

_____

Day 5

Hotel _____ Tel. _____

Morning _____

_____

Lunch _____ Tel. _____

Afternoon _____

_____

Dinner _____ Tel. _____

Evening _____

_____

Day 6

Hotel _____ Tel. _____

Morning _____

_____

Lunch _____ Tel. _____

Afternoon _____

_____

Dinner _____ Tel. _____

Evening _____

_____

Going "My" Way

Day 7

Hotel_____ Tel._____

Morning_____

_____

Lunch_____ Tel._____

Afternoon_____

_____

Dinner_____ Tel._____

Evening_____

_____

Day 8

Hotel_____ Tel._____

Morning_____

_____

Lunch_____ Tel._____

Afternoon_____

_____

Dinner_____ Tel._____

Evening_____

_____

Day 9

Hotel_____ Tel._____

Morning_____

_____

Lunch_____ Tel._____

Afternoon_____

_____

Dinner_____ Tel._____

Evening_____

_____

Notes

Notes

Notes

Index

• Z •